Constructing Economic Science

Constructing Economic Science

The Invention of a Discipline 1850–1950

KEITH TRIBE

OXFORD
UNIVERSITY PRESS

OXFORD
UNIVERSITY PRESS

Oxford University Press is a department of the University of Oxford. It furthers the University's objective of excellence in research, scholarship, and education by publishing worldwide. Oxford is a registered trade mark of Oxford University Press in the UK and certain other countries.

Published in the United States of America by Oxford University Press
198 Madison Avenue, New York, NY 10016, United States of America.

Library of Congress Control Number: Available
ISBN 978–0–19–049174–1

DOI: 10.1093/oso/9780190491741.001.0001

3 5 7 9 8 6 4

Printed by Integrated Books International, United States of America

Contents

Acknowledgements

During the very long time that I have worked on this book I have benefited from many sources of financial support that made possible the initiation of the project, and eventually its completion. I began serious work with the aid of an Economic and Social Research Council (ESRC) grant for the academic year 1988–1989, at the end of which the project had expanded considerably and I was very much further from finishing it than I had been when I started. I subsequently received assistance from the Nuffield Foundation that enabled me to continue travelling to libraries and accumulating material, while the ESRC also financed study visits to Germany and France. A Hallsworth Fellowship from Manchester University meant that I was able to devote the entire academic year 1992–1993 to research, during which I extended the period of study up to the 1960s and planned a series of interviews with academics who would be able to throw light on the development of departments and careers during the postwar period.[1] The British Academy provided funds for the initial batch of 25 interviews, subsequent interviews being supported by my own department at Keele. The Leverhulme Foundation gave me a Research Fellowship for half of the academic year 1997–1998, which together with leave from Keele University enabled me to spend the academic year 1997–1998 completing a number of papers, only one of which, on the Cambridge Tripos, was directly related to this project. Many years later, the project has been terminated with the writing of this book, for which I have been supported since March 2019 by an Estonian Research Council Grant [PRG 318].

While I had from the beginning thought in terms of a major monograph on the development of economics as an institutional creation, it proved difficult to find a publisher that could see much merit in the idea. Added to this, the progressive restructuring of British higher education during the 1990s brought with it a very particular frustration: the more that I learned about the history of British universities, the more I realised that those who were currently arguing for reform and change had very little understanding, historical or otherwise, of the institutions they were actively reorganising. This remains true today. Disenchanted and dismayed with what was being done to British universities, I left the system in my early fifties, abandoned the ambition of pulling all the material I had written into a coherent story, and the book project was shelved. I eventually formulated a new project related to work on the language of political economy, spending two months at the Swedish Collegium for Advanced Study (SCAS), Uppsala, in the autumn of 2012 as guest of the Principal, Björn Wittrock. I wrote up more material for this book during 2013 and 2014, completing a manuscript that Scott Parris at Oxford University Press in New York took up, and which was published in 2015 as *Economy of the Word*. The efficiency and engagement with which Scott and his assistant editor Cathryn Vaulman oversaw final

[1] A total of 35 interviews was completed, and an edited selection published under the title *Economic Careers* in 1997.

revision and production of this book, coupled with the encouragement of the series editor, Steve Medema, revived my interest in writing books, and so once *Economy of the Word* was published, my thoughts turned back to the project I had abandoned. Both Steve and Scott were very supportive, and in the spring of 2016 Oxford University Press gave me a contract for this book. Since the retirement of Scott and Cathryn Vaulman's departure, James Cook and Macey Fairchild have been as helpful and responsive as were Scott and Cathryn.

My next problem was organising the mass of material that I had collected over 30 years. I began working on a Toshiba laptop in 1988 and so the great majority of the notes and data connected with this project is digital. Digital cameras and smartphones, on the other hand, postdate my archival and library research, from which I had accumulated very many boxes and files of photocopies. My organisational problem was not only conceptual, but also very physical. However, shortly after Oxford University Press gave me a contract, the referendum on British membership of the European Union was held. The narrow majority in favour of departure immediately set me thinking of ways to mitigate the damage that Britain's secession from the European Union would do to my future work and the lives of my family; the morning after the referendum I decided to apply for a fellowship at SCAS. This would not only give me the focus I needed to complete the book; it would also give me the physical space and library resources that completion demanded. I was fortunate to be granted a Professorial Fellowship for 2017–2018, enabling me to begin concluding a project initiated 35 years before, in joint work with Istvan Hont.

At SCAS I had once again an ideal environment for thinking and writing. Besides the challenge represented by the mass of material that I had collected, I had never entirely resolved the problem of writing a coherent historical monograph that accounted for the emergence of the discipline of economics, and for the shape that it subsequently took. There were so many overlapping chronologies in different institutions, careers, and countries that it was difficult to convey the *Gleichzeitigkeit des Ungleichzeitigen*. Presenting an account of the Cambridge Moral Sciences Tripos to a SCAS seminar in September 2017 gave me the thread that I needed for the book; and then in March 2018, presenting the work of William Ashley to the economic historians at the University of Uppsala helped me shape two of its central chapters. Needless to say, over the years I have also presented material from this book in very many different contexts, and I am grateful for all the help and criticism that I have received.

More chastening during my time at SCAS was the realisation of just how much time I had devoted to collecting material that I would never be able to use; and how the clarity with which, over 20 years ago, I had mastered details of careers and institutions has now faded. On the other hand, historical understanding of the path taken by modern economics seems barely to have shifted from a very rudimentary story in 40 years; I encounter many of the same generalisations and misunderstandings in recent commentary on institutions and ideas that set me off on my work in the first place all those years ago. While this does illustrate the stubborn resilience of received ideas, it has a personal compensation: the arguments made in the following are still worth making.

Besides the staff and fellows of SCAS, many individuals have helped me conceive and complete this work. In Göttingen during the early 1980s, Pasquale Pasquino reoriented my scholarly sensibilities: besides introducing me to Wilhelm Hennis's new work on Max Weber, whose social and economic analysis suffuses this book, Pasquale also introduced me to the work of Reinhart Koselleck. While many of my underlying ideas were formed in Cambridge during the 1970s, it was my time in Germany during the 1980s that enabled me to reconfigure and develop them, also greatly helped by the friendship of Istvan Hont in Cambridge, in New York and Princeton, and then back in Cambridge. In 2005 Roger Backhouse gave me the opportunity to teach his University of Birmingham course on the history of economic thought while he took study leave to work on his biography of Paul Samuelson. This was my first opportunity to convert my dispersed understanding of the history of economics into something like a coherent narrative; and the account that I present here would never have gained the form it has without the generous support of Roger through the years. His meticulous reading of the final draft was of major help in cleaning up a long and dense argument. More recently, the work and criticism of Ryan Walter has been a constant source of inspiration and support, and any coherence my concluding chapter has is owed to his comments upon earlier drafts. Finally, I was fortunate to have the enthusiastic support of Chris Stray, whose main interest is in the teaching of Classics and who is the leading authority on nineteenth-century Oxford and Cambridge. He was especially helpful in reviewing and commenting on several draft chapters, besides having for many years encouraged my interest in teaching and textbooks. I would also particularly like to thank:

Nafsika Alexiadou, Salma Ahmad, Paul Bew, Jeff Brider, Upal Chakrabarti, Ramesh Chandra, Simon Cook, Helen Curry, Maxime Desmarais-Tremblay, Mike Devereux, Colin Divall, Rebecca Earle, Alison Gaukroger, Geoff Harcourt, Jon Harwood, Akira Hayashima, Christine Heward, Anna Hont, Pat Hudson, Greta Jones, Béla Kapossy, Alon Kadish, Sharmin Khodaiji, Jürgen Kocka, Tony Lane, Gauthier Lanot, Roger Middleton, Robert Milward, Mike Savage, Stephen Savage, Marten Seppel, Nadim Shehadi, Jim Thomas, Grahame Thompson, David Vincent, Mike White, Richard Whitley, and Robbie Wokler.

I would also like to thank those who agreed to be interviewed about their careers, providing me with a perspective upon the development of economics in Britain I would not otherwise have gained:

Tibor Barna, Wilfred Beckerman, Michael Beesley, Bob Black, A. J. Brown, Charles Carter, Dennis Coppock, Bernard Corry, Alec Cairncross, Barrie Davies, Walter Eltis, Jack Gilbert, Sam Goldman, Douglas Hague, Henry Hardman, Bryan Hopkin, Terence Hutchison, Michael Kaser, Charlotte Lythe, Edgar Lythe, Sarah Orr, Henry Phelps Brown, Glyn Picton, Sigbert Prais, Brian Reddaway, Richard Lipsey, Eric Roll, Christopher Saunders, Albert Sloman, Marjorie Tivey, Ronald Tress, Bruce Williams, Tom Wilson, and G. D. N. Worswick.

Apart from the usual felicitations and apologies to family, I am also indebted to my wife Lin Jönsberg for the forthright way in which she challenged what I thought I was doing and helped me clarify my ideas.

I would like to thank the staff of the following libraries, archives, and institutions for their help in locating material:

Barclays Record Services (Jesse Campbell)
Institute of Bankers Library
Queen's University Library, Belfast
University of Birmingham Library
University of Birmingham Archives (Christine Penny)
Marshall Library, University of Cambridge (Rhona Watson)
University Library, Cambridge (Dr. E. S. Leedham-Green)
Trinity College Library, Cambridge (Jonathan Smith)
University of Dundee Archives
University of Edinburgh Library, Special Collections
University of Exeter Library Archives
Glasgow University Library
Keele University Library (Martin Phillips and ILL staff)
Brotherton Library, University of Leeds, Special Collections
University of Liverpool Archives
The London Library
The British Library
University of London Library Archives (Carole Ibrahim)
British Library of Political and Economic Science Archives (Sue Donnelly)
King's College, London Archives
University College, London, Special Collections
John Rylands University Library Archives, Manchester (Peter Nockels)
Centre for the History of Science and Technology, UMIST (Joe Marsh)
Manchester Central Library
Nuffield College Library, Oxford
Bodleian Library, Oxford
University of St. Andrews Special Collections
County Library, Worcester
Trinity College Library, Dublin
Universitätsbibliothek, Gießen
Niedersächsische Staats- und Universitätsbibliothek, Göttingen
Max Planck Institut für Geschichte, Göttingen
Universitätsbibliothek, Mannheim
Bayerische Staatsbibliothek, Munich
Bibliotheque Nationale, Paris
University of Toronto Library Archives
Uppsala University Library.

Note to Readers

This is a book with a clear objective and a conclusion that, like any good *Krimi*, is not fully revealed until the last moment. There are many pages between here and there, and some readers could well be deterred by the structure and/or the institutional detail. The sequence of argument and evidence is, however, intended first of all to reorient the reader, and then lead that reader towards a denouement that follows on from the argument and evidence that has gone before.

That is the way I read the argument of this book, as grounded both empirically and analytically. Nonetheless, writers are in no position to dictate how their work is read; true, I think of this as a printed book with a beginning, middle, and end, but I have no idea in what conditions, for what purposes, or on what kind of devices it will be read. Nor am I in any position to insist that it be read in a particular way. This is a monograph that develops an argument about how, and why, the discipline of economics emerged in the early twentieth century as a university science, but along the way it demonstrates that this was no logical, determinate path with a pregiven outcome. Much of the detail documents the existence of alternatives that were either never adopted, or eventually rejected. There were also alternatives of which few contemporaries seemed aware at all. For example, while the teaching of commerce at the London School of Economics in interwar Britain never developed into an autonomous business curriculum, this was not for want of an available model. By the early 1920s German institutions had, in the space of about 20 years, invented not only a business curriculum, but also a unique form of managerial accounting. At the time few outside Germany, none in Britain, seem to have been aware of this.[2]

This one example demonstrates why the idea of any "rational reconstruction" of disciplinary development is flawed, is essentially teleological. I offer here instead a "historical reconstruction" in which false turns, individual ignorance, and institutional failure are fully documented. There is therefore a lot of detail. A reader is of course free to skip over this; indeed, many will read sections of the book as individual chapters on Oxford Scholar, using only the initial abstract as orientation. Readers of the print book can do likewise, but they would always have the option of leafing back to clarify points, skimming again through sections whose relevance has become more obvious to them as they work further through the text.

While this is indeed a book with a beginning, middle, and end, there is some signposting that will help readers who choose to read it differently; references backwards and forwards, of course, but the introductions to each part, and some repetition of relevant points within each chapter. While making the same point repeatedly is

[2] Jack Gilbert attended Berlin's Handelshochschule on a Cassel Travelling Scholarship in 1927–1928, but when asked for details of this in my 1994 interview with him he could recall nothing about why he went, nor could say how the teaching of the *Handelshochschule* differed from the London School of Economics, from which he graduated with a BCom (Honours) in 1929.

wearisome, the opposite extreme of expecting the reader to pick up on a point made perhaps several thousand words before is unhelpful. I have here sought to strike a balance.

Keith Tribe
Malvern, December 2020

PART I
FROM PUBLIC KNOWLEDGE TO INSTITUTIONAL DISCOURSE

1
Discourse and Discipline

This is a book about the transformation of economic discourse into a specialised form of knowledge acquired through university training, validated not through public discussion and debate, but through the procedural framework of the academy. Economic discourse became a form of knowledge with a career structure: legitimacy is now conferred on those advancing economic arguments by placement in this structure, not by reason alone. And so to understand the reproduction and legitimation of economic knowledge, we must look first to institutions and their functions, not to 'ideas' and 'theories'.

It was the emergence of the modern university in late nineteenth-century America that facilitated this transformation in forms of knowledge that had existed since the seventeenth century. In the modern university, specialised academics were employed to teach students, submit them to competitive written examinations, and confer graded qualifications upon them. Those who were most successful in these examinations became qualified to teach the students who succeeded them; this process quickly standardised what was taught, and so what counted as modern economic reasoning. The career structure of the teachers became a function of the skill with which they elaborated the principles that were taught; the brightest students identified themselves by their facility in the increasingly refined and arcane knowledge to which they were exposed. By the 1930s there was a clear convergence between British, American, German, Austrian, Swedish, Dutch, French, and Italian specialised journals around a common core for the discipline of economics. In the course of 50 years, a new academic discipline had emerged and established itself.[1] Then, during the second half of the twentieth century, the language of economics permeated the formulation and presentation of public policy. The national accounting framework that was developed in the 1940s, and the new macroeconomics into which it could be fitted, transformed the work of economic government into the pursuit of economic growth measured as Gross Domestic Product (GDP), the maintenance of a low rate of inflation, and a sustained low rate of unemployment. Economics had become a specialised form of knowledge whose principles and instruments suffused debate on public policy.

This two-stage process—first the formation of a discipline, and then the framing of public policy in the language of this discipline—was initiated in Britain, where the first honours degree in economics was created, in Cambridge in 1903. However, before demonstrating how and why this happened, we need to form a clear understanding of the social and educational context within which this took place: not only what a

[1] A discipline is a body of knowledge secured by its place within academic institutions. It can be characterised by a common mainstream core discourse supported by the career structures of teachers and students, journals, departments, training programmes, awards, reputations, textbooks, and specialist associations.

Constructing Economic Science. Keith Tribe, Oxford University Press. © Oxford University Press 2022.
DOI: 10.1093/oso/9780190491741.003.0001

university was in the later nineteenth century, but the broader educational structure of which Cambridge University was a part. As I will demonstrate, the course of events in Cambridge leading to the creation in 1903 of the first three-year undergraduate economics degree could not have been replicated in Oxford; while what Alfred Marshall achieved in Cambridge depended upon a number of factors not directly linked to the existence of Cambridge University. We need to identify the relevant context in which Marshall was working; and this context was primarily shaped by social institutions and economic constraints, not by the existing understanding of political economy. While 'ideas in context' has become the watchword of modern intellectual history, here 'context' means not 'other ideas', but primarily the institutional framework that determines hierarchies of knowledge and their legitimation.

The following chapter will show that, while the main features of the modern university[2] were created in the United States, a number of factors there initially hindered the rapid disciplinary development of economic knowledge that was possible in Britain around 1900. For a time, yet other circumstances constrained disciplinary development in Germany, France, and Italy, in all of which there were, however, many academics teaching and writing economics. Nonetheless, while Cambridge and its Professor of Political Economy, Alfred Marshall, did play a vital role as first mover in creating a new discipline, the rapid development of the London School of Economics (LSE) during the 1920s quickly challenged this pre-eminence. Maynard Keynes retained a base in Cambridge after resigning his lectureship in 1920, and in the 1930s was prominent in organising student discussion and steering talented Cambridge economics graduates into employment. However, by this time the LSE was becoming the national hub for graduate and undergraduate economic training, and so critical to the reproduction of what counted as economic knowledge.

At the LSE, Lionel Robbins set out explicitly to shape economics as a 'science', although he did not possess the technical skills of Marshall, Maynard Keynes, or Pigou. His appointment in 1929 as head of economics at the LSE coincided with the expansion of American departments and, critically, from 1933 onwards, a significant transatlantic movement of young German and Austrian refugees whose mathematical abilities were generally superior to those of their American peers. The increasingly technical development of economics in American universities during the 1930s and 1940s was linked to their developing graduate programmes, massively augmented by veterans' programmes after the Second World War and substantial government funding. In the course of the 1940s, accelerated by the demands of war, there was a transition to the second stage of development, in which the technical economic reasoning that originated in universities found a public role. While this transition also occurred in Britain, it remained on a much more limited scale than in the United States, and it was not until the 1960s that taught Master's programmes were introduced—at

[2] Where disciplines are aligned with departments in which specialised academics who are both teachers and researchers cover the disciplinary core at different levels of teaching. This internal division of labour is doubled by a career hierarchy, replacing a university structure in which individual professors represented an entire subject of study—such as, for instance, Adam Smith as Professor of Moral Philosophy at the University of Glasgow from 1752 to 1764, or Henry Sidgwick with the same title at Cambridge from 1883 to 1900.

the University of Essex, and at the LSE. As English became the new world language, the language of economics became American.

This account of the formation of the discipline of economics is focussed upon the first of these two stages, the 'British' phase. Why did this process originate in Cambridge, and how did the form it was given shape international understanding of the nature of economic reasoning? Why did the form of reasoning developed in Cambridge soon lose ground to the alternative conception of 'economic science' associated with the LSE? As we shall see, rapid disciplinary advancement in Britain was hampered by the fact that relatively few students wished to study the new economics, at least in part because there was little that one could do with a university qualification in the subject, other than teach economics in school, college, or university. Outside school, college, and university, British employers in both the private and public sector generally remained indifferent to university-trained economists up until the 1970s at least. Hence Robbins was faced with an uphill struggle at the LSE in persuading students that the study of economics, as he conceived it, was a more worthwhile activity than the study of commerce, social administration, government, or even economic history.

This is not an institutional history; but institutions made 'economics' what it is today, and so schools, colleges, and universities are central to my story. However, understanding of even the recent history of formal education is today at a discount; personal experience and prejudice still shape educational debate and educational policy. As will become apparent, arguments made more than a century ago are still today confidently advanced as though they were new. In part, this is a recurrent property of the educational process. Formal education is the first direct experience of the social world that most children have beyond their family or household; but while in every case this experience is novel for each child, this does not mean that what that child experiences is new. Everyone grows up with their own experiences of the educational system. There is, however, little academic curiosity about the social institutions that have formed these life experiences, or their history.[3]

The discipline of economics was long in the making, but the reason it eventually became a discipline was owed to international changes in schooling and university towards the end of the nineteenth century. Cambridge was here a laggard; despite this, innovation became possible. To understand the circumstances conditioning both laggardliness and innovation, a broader context than Cambridge University has first to be laid out; this is done in the following two chapters. Running through this broader context are arguments about economic education and vocational training—the perennial issue of the suitability of the education provided by school and university to the demands of employment and the labour market. Since the mid-nineteenth century at the latest, the distinction of vocational training from the training of minds has been a constant. Economics has been variously presented both as a vocational subject suited to the demands of the modern economy, and/or as an intellectually

[3] And the low status of 'history of education' among academic historians was the first point that Peter Mandler made in a series of lectures reviewing secondary and tertiary education in Britain during the twentieth century: 'Educating the Nation I: Schools', *Transactions of the Royal Historical Society* Vol. 24 (2014), p. 5.

demanding subject whose apparent detachment from immediate everyday circumstances is a mark of its scientific status. As we shall see, in arguing for the Economics Tripos, Alfred Marshall used both lines of argument simultaneously.

Part II then provides an explanation of why it was that Cambridge became the first mover in disciplinary development, even though it was in the early 1900s still adapting to the new disciplinary dynamics unleashed by the modern university. Marshall occupied the chair of political economy for some 20 years before he was successful in establishing a three-year honours degree in economics as the Economics Tripos.[4] But in order to understand what he sought to achieve, and why he found existing teaching unsuitable as a vehicle for this, we need to understand the nature of the Mathematical Tripos that gave him his model for training. He considered the Moral Sciences Tripos, the framework in which economics was taught in later nineteenth-century Cambridge, more hindrance than help in training young economists. This is the context out of which Marshall constructed his conception of a modern economics, embodied in the Economics Tripos inaugurated in 1903. Nonetheless, this was only a new beginning, not a final destination; and it was a new beginning that proved less successful than has usually been assumed. The second chapter of Part II presents the work of the Tripos over its first 50 years through an analysis of degree results, turning our attention away from the recollections of the select few for whom success in the Tripos was the foundation of a career as an economist, and towards the more modest achievements of the mass of students who passed through it. Part II is then concluded with a consideration of what kind of economics Marshall and his colleagues sought to promote: What was 'Marshallianism'? Clarity is needed on this question since it is central to explaining the waning of what at first appeared to be the international hegemony of Cambridge economics.

However, before dealing with the waning influence of Cambridge, Part III examines two important 'paths not taken'. Firstly, before his appointment to the Cambridge chair Alfred Marshall had been teaching political economy to Indian Civil Service students in Oxford. Furthermore, from the later 1880s onwards, many Oxford graduates moved into important positions—E. C. K. Gonner to the new chair of economics in Liverpool, W. J. Ashley to the chair of commerce in Birmingham, Edwin Cannan to teach at LSE in 1895, then becoming professor in 1907. The first Director of the LSE, W. A. S. Hewins, was also an Oxford man; Francis Edgeworth, appointed Professor of Political Economy in Oxford in 1891, was another. It would, therefore, be natural to conclude that Oxford would have been a suitable base for what Marshall sought to achieve in Cambridge. However, as Chapter 7 demonstrates, had Marshall remained in Oxford it would have been unlikely that he could have achieved there what he did achieve in Cambridge. There were differences between Oxford and Cambridge with regard to teaching and learning that made it easier to innovate in Cambridge at the level of university rather than college, even though 'Oxford economists' were nationally prominent in the later nineteenth century.

[4] A Cambridge Honours undergraduate programme is called a Tripos, possibly after the three-legged stool on which students are said to have sat during oral examinations, during the years before the development of written examinations towards the end of the eighteenth century.

Related to this 'path not taken' by the newly-emerging discipline is a second idea that has gained common acceptance: that the emergence of Marshall's form of analytical economics contributed to the sidelining of an alternative, historical vision of what the discipline of economics could be. Chapter 8 outlines a story in which Oxford plays a prominent part, given the influence of Arnold Toynbee at Balliol in the 1880s and the more general pedagogic importance of Modern History in Oxford. I demonstrate that the apparent alternative supplied by 'Historical Economics' as a model for disciplinary development was chimerical; the critique of contemporary developments in economics made by Ashley and Cunningham remained a critique, and was never translated into a viable alternative disciplinary programme.

Part IV then turns to examine the way in which the teaching of economics did actually develop outside Cambridge in the early twentieth century: through the medium of the teaching of commerce, a more broadly vocational enterprise. When Alfred Marshall in his 1885 Cambridge Inaugural lecture made the case for economics as a modern university subject with important vocational implications, he was in fact repeating an argument already rehearsed in the United States, France, and Germany concerning the importance of commercial education. Marshall's argument was significant not because of its general content, but because his vision of vocationally-oriented university education involved the teaching of economics, not commerce. In fact, outside Oxford and Cambridge all advanced teaching of economics in Britain until mid-century would for the most part be done in university departments or faculties oriented to commercial education that to a greater or lesser extent modelled themselves upon the American, French, or German experience. Chapter 9 provides an overview of the international development of higher commercial education in the later nineteenth and early twentieth centuries to lend perspective to British developments that often invoked these foreign models. British developments are then outlined in Chapters 10 and 11, in the latter dealing with the LSE separately, given the significance of its place as part of the University of London in the organisation of higher learning in Britain and its Empire. Common to Chapters 10 and 11 is, however, a single theme: that there was a consistent, if limited, demand for advanced commercial education from both students and employers, but that in a university context the vocational focus of commercial education had little academic support. The LSE was until at least the mid-1950s an institution the bulk of whose graduates had pursued strictly vocational courses of study in social administration, commerce, and government within the framework of a new bachelor of science degree—the BSc (Econ). However, staff appointments made from the later 1920s increasingly emphasised academic rather than vocational capacities, and it was in this context that Lionel Robbins sought to develop economics as a 'science'. Chapter 12 examines quite what this science was, and how it established itself in opposition to the 'Marshallian tradition' of economic analysis outlined in Chapter 6. The transition in Britain towards the science of economics coincided with parallel developments in the United States that would during the 1940s become established as the new mainstream for economics on an international scale.

The Initial Framework

My interest in these matters dates from the mid-1980s, when I was a contributor to an international project, led by Istvan Hont, studying the institutionalisation of political economy.[5] Initially conceived as a review of the founding chairs of political economy in Europe, its scope was extended to include the United States and Japan, and was broadened into a history of the national origins of regular university teaching in economics. Working groups assembled their own regional histories, often enough starting from a presumption that economics as an institutionalised discourse had diffused from Britain, Adam Smith's *Wealth of Nations* being generally accepted as the founding text of modern economic thought. Robert Malthus and David Ricardo were at that time seen as building upon Smith, shaping a 'classical economics' that was later displaced by a 'neoclassical economics' linked to an academic turn heralding the emergence of modern economic science.[6] The broad international acceptance of this essentially canonical history of theory owed much to an anglophone prejudice centred on the emergence of modern economics as the work of 'great thinkers' from Smith to Jevons, whose 'ideas' flowed forth irrespective of awkward issues such as the fact that if there was a global language in the nineteenth century it was French; or that Jean-Baptiste Say was the primary influence on early American teaching of political economy, and that his work provided a crucial bridge in Germany and Britain to the emergence of 'neoclassicism'.[7]

As the project developed, this starting point was superseded by the growing realisation that the institutionalisation of economics—the first step in creating the discipline of economics—seemed in fact to have been a more or less simultaneous occurrence, across Continental Europe, North America, Japan, and also, importantly, in Britain. From a project initially concerned simply with charting the 'first national chairs' in political economy, there developed a broader view of international developments; one focussed more upon political economy as public knowledge than upon the history of economic 'thought' as such. The national histories that were written and published[8]

[5] From 1982 to 1986 the project was organised from the Research Centre of King's College, Cambridge—see, for a brief account, Gregory Claeys, Istvan Hont, Alon Kadish and Keith Tribe, 'Editorial Preface: The Institutionalization of Political Economy in Europe, the United States and Japan', in Alon Kadish, Keith Tribe (eds.) *The Market for Political Economy. The Advent of Economics in British University Culture, 1850–1905*, Routledge, London 1995, pp. viii–xi.

[6] For a survey of the 'history of economic thought' in the twentieth century, see Roger E. Backhouse, Philippe Fontaine, 'Contested Identities: The History of Economics since 1945', in Backhouse and Fontaine (eds.) *A Historiography of the Modern Social Sciences*, Cambridge University Press, Cambridge 2014, pp. 183–210.

[7] I have sketched this argument in *The History of Economics. A Course for Students and Teachers* (with Roger E. Backhouse), Agenda, Newcastle upon Tyne 2018 Lectures 6 & 7.

[8] The French contributions were published under the editorship of Lucette LeVan-Lemesle as *Les problèmes de l'institutionnalisation de l'économie politique en France au XIXe siècle*, Oeconomia, Paris 1986. Further national volumes that have appeared are C. Sugiyama, H. Mizuta (eds.) *Enlightenment and Beyond. Political Economy Comes to Japan*, University of Tokyo Press, Tokyo 1988; M. Augello, M. Bianchini, G. Gioli, P. Roggi (eds.) *La cattedre politica in Italia. La diffusione di una disciplina <sospetta> (1750–1900)*, Franco Angeli, Milan 1988; N. Waszek (ed.) *Die Institutionalisierung der Nationalökonomie an den deutschen Universitäten*, Scripta Mercurae Verlag, St. Katherinen 1988; W. J. Barber (ed.) *Breaking the Academic Mould. Economists and American Higher Learning in the Nineteenth Century*, Wesleyan University Press, Middletown Conn. 1988. Lucette LeVan-Lemesle has more recently published *Le juste et la riche. L'enseignement de l'économie politique 1815–1950*, Comité pour l'histoire économique et financière

remained, however, so many strands in a process whose own dynamics were obscure; why did so many of these strands interlink and overlap in the last two decades of the nineteenth century? This was implicitly the question of how the uniformity of a new discipline emerged and propagated, a process upon which conventional historiographic models in the history of the sciences shed little light. Considering this problem in the later 1980s, a rather different perspective began to emerge: working not from the question of how 'modern economic thinking' became embedded in institutional sites, but instead from the way in which the creation of the modern university shaped and validated what counted as 'modern economic thinking'.

As already noted, the history of formal and informal education in Britain is poorly understood; there is little in the way of informed public debate about the evolution of schooling and universities, and little readily-available literature to which one can refer for illumination. Alison Wolf's *Does Education Matter?*[9] confronts many of the misconceptions about the relationship of education to economy still repeated in current debate, and Stefan Collini has charted the development of the 'postmodern' university in Britain;[10] but there is an absence of an integrated, historical analysis of education, schooling, training, further and higher education that places British developments in an international context. The elements from which such an understanding could be built do, however, exist in three key texts: Fritz Ringer's *Education and Society in Modern Europe* (1979), Michael Sanderson's *Universities and British Industry 1850–1970* (1972), and Robert Locke's *End of Practical Man* (1984). No comparable synthetic overview drawing on original research has since been published.

Not only did Ringer keep the vocational connection of education and employment clearly in view; he treated secondary-level schooling and university education together in considering the social basis of admission to advanced education and recruitment to professional occupations and public employment. The advance of European universities, both in number of students and range of study, presupposed the existence of schooling that would prepare middle- and lower-class students; no modern university system could develop on the basis of highly selective, elite schooling, since such selection was primarily social, not by ability, and hence was limited. Correspondingly, a broadly-based schooling system screened and certified its pupils in relation to the labour market, and he made three systematic distinctions relevant to this:

1. An inclusive system is one that schools a relatively large proportion of the population of the relevant age group.
2. A progressive education system is one that draws a large proportion of its advanced students from the lower middle and lower classes.

de la France, Paris 2004; and Augello and Guidi have also considerably extended their original work into *Economisti e scienza economica nell'Italia liberale (1848–1922)*, 2 vols., Franco Angeli, Milan 2019.

[9] Alison Wolf, *Does Education Matter? Myths about Education and Economic Growth*, Penguin Books, London 2002.

[10] Stefan Collini, *Speaking of Universities*, Verso, London 2017.

3. A segmented or tracked system is one in which parallel courses of study are separated by institutional or curricular barriers, as well as differences in the social origins of their students.[11]

The core of his book deals with a comparison of nineteenth-century German and French educational systems, using the insights gleaned from this to shed light on English and American systems. His approach was elaborated in later collaborative work that adopted his focus upon university and secondary education in the context of occupational structure and labour market demands. One point relevant here was the argument that proposals for more practical training were aimed chiefly at students from middle or lower social classes, while the retention of more elevated pathways preserved the social standing of children of an elite. He argued, therefore, that it would be more appropriate to consider educational transformation more in terms of *social effects* than *economic needs*. Hence his conclusion that '[t]he old assumption that educational expansion has meant "democratisation" in the sense of increased individual socio-occupational mobility has thus lost most of its credibility.'[12]

Whereas Ringer injected a rare analytical perspective into the history of schooling and education, Michael Sanderson's *Universities and British Industry*[13] provided a path-breaking account of the way in which British universities had contributed to technological change and industrial innovation from the later nineteenth century. Broadly a story of 'education, research and economy', this study is notable for the detailed treatment of university institutions on the basis of archival records. Although Sanderson's main focus is on the way in which university physics, chemistry, and engineering interacted with industrial development, the fact that he devoted twice as many pages to the civic universities (Chs. 2 and 3) as he did to Oxford and Cambridge (Ch. 1) was at the time very unusual, while he also devoted a separate chapter to the development of the teaching of commerce as an early form of business education. While his treatment of early economic and commercial education is now superseded by the following chapters, Sanderson did provide a valuable baseline from which research could develop.

Sanderson's book was an early inspiration for my own work in this area, and was the model for an earlier version of the present book that would have presented a comprehensive account of the development of commerce and economics in British universities up to the 1960s. However, this ambition soon foundered on the realisation that British university records from the 1940s to the early 2000s were sparse. While the *Cambridge University Reporter* has provided a consistent record of teaching, degree results, and university organisation from the later nineteenth century to the present, from the later 1940s most university publications ceased even listing current members of departments and courses of study; and departmental records were not archived.

[11] Fritz Ringer, *Education and Society in Modern Europe*, Indiana University Press, Bloomington 1979, pp. 22–29.

[12] Fritz Ringer, 'Introduction', in Detlef K. Müller, Fritz Ringer, Brian Simon (eds.) *The Rise of the Modern Educational System: Structural Change and Social Reproduction 1870–1920*, Cambridge University Press, Cambridge 1987, p. 3.

[13] Michael Sanderson, *The Universities and British Industry 1850–1950*, Routledge and Kegan Paul, London 1972.

For the second half of the twentieth century we will never be able to reconstruct with any degree of accuracy the composition of departments, courses taught, student numbers, and degrees, let alone the future employment of graduates.[14] What can be done with properly maintained archives is shown by Jan-Otmar Hesse's exemplary history of academic economics in postwar West Germany.[15] The core of his work is constructed from the ground up, tracking appointments, the formation of professional associations, the funding of research, the flows of students, and the training of future teachers of the subject. When I turned in the 1990s to interviewing some of those who had built teaching and departments in British universities during the 1950s, seeking a substitute for the absence of records outside Cambridge and the LSE, it transpired that most of my subjects no longer had a clear memory of this phase of their careers, although their memory of their own education remained clear, and verifiable from contemporary records. I am, however, fortunate that archival records became scarce only at the point that here forms a natural conclusion, in the 1940s.

The merit of Robert Locke's *End of Practical Man* was to bring together the systematisation of Ringer and the subject matter of Sanderson. He noted that arguments by economic historians concerning the presence or absence of entrepreneurial failure in later nineteenth-century France and England paid no attention to the role of education. Ringer, by contrast, emphasised the manner in which higher education in France and Germany was used as a vehicle for social mobility, neglecting the impact of commercial education on economy and labour market. Locke noted that

> [a]n investigation into the curricula of competing national systems of higher education may not be essential to the writing of the social history of education but it is crucial for an analysis of higher education *and* entrepreneurial performance. Ringer's emphasis on social history has, therefore, led him to follow analytical procedures which, in my opinion, have ended in erroneous revisionist conclusions about the relative efficaciousness of French and German higher technical and commercial education. His work suffers from the defect of most education histories. It makes observations about the impact that education had on economic activities without adequately studying the relationship between the two.[16]

Locke sought to marry the economic historian's focus upon industrial development to the curricular organisation of the educational institutions established to further vocational ends linked to economic development. Engineering, in general, and factory organisation, in particular, were in this way brought into contact with what it meant

[14] And investigating contemporary higher education policy in the late 1980s, I was surprised to find that the official annual UK data on university graduates by subject and first destinations was available only as duplicated pages of A4; my own university department could have done better. By contrast, the data I obtained on US Higher Education for 1988 was a model of presentation and detail. See my 'The "US Model" for Higher Education: Structure and Finance', in Peter W. G. Wright (ed.) *Industry and Higher Education. Collaboration to Improve Students' Learning and Training*, Society for Research into Higher Education & Open University Press, Buckingham 1990, pp. 43–58.

[15] Jan-Otmar Hesse, *Wirtschaft als Wissenschaft. Die Volkswirtschaftlehre in der frühen Bundesrepublik*, Campus Verlag, Frankfurt am Main 2010; and my review in *German History* Vol. 31 (2013), pp. 443–44.

[16] Robert R. Locke, *The End of the Practical Man. Entrepreneurship and Higher Education in Germany, France, and Great Britain 1880–1940*, JAI Press, Greenwich, Conn. 1984, p. 5.

to be an engineer. Locke noted, for example, that in late nineteenth-century Britain engineers were almost without exception recruited from the shopfloor. As with the law, professional associations and their examinations provided the qualifications, not universities.

In France, on other hand, there was an early formal commitment to the education of engineers. The *École des Ponts et Chaussées* (founded 1715) was followed by an artillery school in 1720 and an academy for military engineering in 1748. The School of Mines was founded in 1783, and the *École Polytechnique* in 1794. By 1900 graduates of the *École Polytechnique* dominated the upper reaches of technical services in several sectors of private industry, in railways for example. In Germany the emphasis was on *Bildung* and the role of the *Gymnasien*—but it was the *Realschulen*, funded by municipalities and not the state, that provided a modern curriculum. Out of this there developed a number of colleges for higher engineering education, and the creation in 1856 of the *Verein Deutscher Ingenieure* lent focus to efforts in raising the status of schools and of the profession.[17]

The Institutionalisation of Political Economy

These three books provided a broad framework for approaching the social and economic factors at work in reshaping political economy as public discourse into a new academic economics. Some more specialised studies of political economy upon which I could draw also existed. In the early 1950s Sydney Checkland published a number of articles that were for the time very unusual for the emphasis that they placed upon social and political networks in the development of political economy. However, when in the 1970s new approaches to the history of the sciences took up these and related ideas, Checkland's own contribution had been largely forgotten; and so we need here to recall (what turned out to be) his premature start. The key article was published in 1951, and provided for the first time a clear and detailed account of the foundation of chairs in Oxford and Cambridge in the early nineteenth century, together with the disputes to which they gave rise. Here the early history of political economy in Britain was firmly linked to academic politics in Oxford and Cambridge, beginning with the Townshend Prize in Cambridge.[18] Checkland records how in Cambridge, George Pryme began lecturing on political economy in 1816, while the following year there were indications of an interest in the subject in Oriel College, Oxford.[19] He does not fail to recognise the somewhat patchy nature of teaching in the two universities of the time, but presumes that this initial course of lectures was part of a university teaching programme, and so marks the point of entry of political economy into the university. However, he construed the content of Pryme's lectures in terms of the wider significance of contemporary political economy, rather than the immediate pedagogical

[17] Locke, *The End of the Practical Man*, pp. 30–33.

[18] In 1987 Istvan Hont drafted a lengthy paper on the brief history of the Prize: 'The Townshend Prize in the Theory of Trade at the University of Cambridge, 1755–56'.

[19] S. G. Checkland, 'The Advent of Academic Economics in England', *Manchester School* Vol. 19 (1951), p. 46.

tasks of the university. He therefore presents political economy as a set of ideas deducible from contemporary writings, not as a discourse whose nature and purposes need to be demonstrated from its practice. Consequently, although university institutions provide the backdrop to Checkland's account, in the foreground are the 'ideas' that it is assumed these institutions (automatically) transmitted. No consideration is given to what in fact a university professor of the time actually did, how he related (if at all) to any students, where this teaching took place (college or university), who was 'taught', why they might wish to be 'taught', and so ultimately whether these were anything more than general lectures that happened to have been given in an Oxford or Cambridge college.

Checkland had begun publishing on the history of economics three years before by linking the ideas of Thomas Attwood, a Birmingham banker, to a dispute on the banking system and the general principle of underconsumption.[20] This was followed by an article on the diffusion of Ricardian economics in Britain which recognised the degree to which this 'new economics' was embattled, but which sought to situate the Ricardian 'victory' with respect to '... the propaganda weapons of the day, the character of the parties to the debate, the ground on which they fought, and the manner in which they were deployed and used.'[21] Checkland therefore treated early English political economy as a set of discursive moves in political argument, placing these moves within a broader policy framework of the kind that, by the 1960s, was being increasingly lost to view in commentary that favoured a modern theoretician's perspective upon economic argument in early nineteenth-century Britain. This latter approach, seeking to identify the theoretical 'origins' and 'anticipations' of modern ideas in past ideas, if not entirely rewriting the latter in the terms of the former, became a common approach in commentary on the history of economic thought at about the same time that it was becoming discredited in the history of the sciences. Checkland had not assumed that what were once new ideas had become accepted because they were, by later theoretical standards, 'better arguments'; he placed emphasis on the way in which ideas were contested, and related this contestation to contemporary issues in the wider economy.

Checkland's interest shifted away from the history of political economy and into social and economic policy at about the same time that Bob Coats, who took a more explicitly sociological approach to the history of political economy, began publishing what became a long series of essays on the institutionalisation of economic argument. As his work proceeded, he framed institutional developments in terms of the current sociological literature on 'professionalisation', using this to highlight the regularity concealed by apparent diversity. During the 1950s Coats had pursued research on the early history of the American Economic Association (AEA), and in 1960 he published a summary report on its early years.[22] Twenty-five years later he presented a broader account, this time 'focused on certain problems arising in the professionalization

[20] S. G. Checkland, 'The Birmingham Economists, 1815–1850', *Economic History Review* 2nd series Vol. I (1948), pp. 1–19.

[21] S. G. Checkland, 'The Propagation of Ricardian Economics in England', *Economica* New Series Vol. 16 (1949), p. 41.

[22] A. W. Coats, 'The First Two Decades of the American Economic Association', *American Economic Review* Vol. 50 (1960), pp. 555–574.

process.'[23] While recognising that economists are not members of a profession in the sense of lawyers and physicians, who must be registered with and approved by an official body in order to be able to practice, he invoked 'current convention' in treating the AEA as a 'professional organization.'[24] This enabled him to treat the AEA as a group of individuals whose identity derives from shared knowledge and skills, and who have succeeded in gaining public recognition of this shared status by their possession of academic degrees or other qualifications requiring formal, specialised training. While Coats himself never pulled his many articles and papers into a unified narrative, his student John Maloney did write a coherent and informative account of Marshall and Cambridge that drew on this historiographical model.[25]

Nonetheless, while 'professionalisation' directs attention to the way in which social orders create a sense of communal purpose, the term fails to discriminate between the kinds of knowledge and practice associated with this purpose. The AEA or the Royal Economic Society (RES) cannot explicitly restrict admission, and so cannot directly confer membership of a profession on individuals. These are not associations that validate, regulate, and police the activities of their membership, but more an interest group of like-minded people. My former colleague at Keele University who was Professor of Signal Processing was a professional not by virtue of his being a professor, but by virtue of being a member of the Institution of Electrical Engineers.[26] Much the same would have been true of a colleague in the Law Department, or one in the Medical School.

For Coats, a 'professional' economist is a university-trained economist, and so it appears natural that the history of 'professionalisation' of economics should centre upon the formation of the national bodies capable of representing the discipline independently of any one department or institution. In his related history of the RES, Coats does note the fact that for much of its early life (as the British Economics Association) it was dominated by members who had neither a university qualification in economics, nor indeed any specific academic links, but this is not treated as something that requires any special explanation.[27] In fact, it was not until about the 1930s that in Britain 'economist' became an occupational description for a person with a university qualification in the subject and employed to teach it; hitherto it had denoted a person interested in, and with opinions upon, economic affairs, whatever their qualification or employment—a self-description which reaches back to the original members of the Political Economy Club in 1821. And while university qualification has today become the mark of an economist, neither the AEA nor the RES could or would deny membership to any candidate simply on the grounds that they did not hold a university degree in the subject.

[23] A. W. Coats, 'The American Economic Association and the Economics Profession', *Journal of Economic Literature* Vol. 23 (1985), p. 1697.

[24] Ibid., p. 1698 fn. 1.

[25] John Maloney, *Marshall, Orthodoxy and the Professionalisation of Economics*, Cambridge University Press, Cambridge 1985.

[26] Since 2006 part of the Institution of Engineering and Technology. The British habit of referring to mechanics and technicians as 'engineers' blurs this point, as does American usage referring to drivers of steam locomotives; but it is a point that has global validity.

[27] A. W. Coats, 'The Origins and Early Development of the Royal Economic Society', *Economic Journal* Vol. 68 (1968), pp. 349–71.

However, 'professionalisation' is not so much a singular trend in the forging of the modern world, but instead the *effect of* other forces and contingencies. The term implies a legitimate identity; but we should focus on the social processes that legitimate this identity, not on the fact of the identity itself. In the labour market, recognition as a 'profession' is something to which occupational groups seeking legitimacy and exclusivity of practice aspire. To adopt the label 'profession' signifies a claim for legitimacy.[28] 'Professions' are therefore socially-constructed; emergent occupational groups will naturally employ the language of 'professionalism' as part of their public rhetoric, overlooking the awkward fact that there remain ineradicable differences in the practical significance of skills, the ease with which competences are acquired and tested, and, once certified, practitioners regulated. The study of 'professionalisation' fails to take account of the fact that while the status-claims that are related to the possession of certain skills are indeed socially constructed, some skills are more difficult to acquire than others; their safe practise requires constant regulation by peers competent in those practices, and this work of regulation can therefore only be reliably exercised by a professional association—of lawyers, of general practitioners, of electrical engineers, or surgeons.[29] We need to distinguish *claims* to be a profession from the *recognition* and *legitimacy* enjoyed by genuine, self-regulating professional associations. When Coats links the formation and growth of the RES to the 'professionalisation' of economics in Britain, the process to which he is pointing would be better conceived in terms of the emergence of the modern university and the transformation of practical knowledges into academic disciplines—what has been termed *Verwisse nschaftlichung*,[30] or as rendered in the title of Chapter 12, 'scientisation'.

Coats later moved on from his work on the early history of the economics discipline to its development in the course of the second half of the twentieth century—the second stage identified previously, in which public policy becomes suffused with the language of economics. An initial step was the systematic study of the relationship of economists and government, linked to a related study of the place of economists in international organisations.[31] The internationalisation of economics in this period was entwined with what was perceived as the 'Americanisation' of the discipline, conceived 'not merely as an aspect of the sociology of a particular profession but also as an integral component of the culture of modernization'.[32] The British part of this story

[28] Harold Perkin's history of the Association of University Teachers is entitled *Key Profession* (London 1969); the title employs the aspirational language criticised here.

[29] See W. J. Reader, *Professional Men: The Rise of the Professional Classes in Nineteenth-Century England*, Weidenfeld and Nicolson, London 1966, p. 164, for a list of the principal chartered professional bodies which set examinations controlling qualification and entry to an occupation.

[30] Lutz Raphael, 'Die Verwissenschaftlichung des Sozialen als methodische und konzeptionelle Herausforderung für eine Sozialgeschichte des 20.Jahrhunderts', *Geschichte und Gesellschaft* Jg. 22 H. 2 (1996), pp. 165–93.

[31] A. W. Coats (ed.), *Economists in Government: An International Comparative Study*, Duke University Press, Durham N.C. 1981; A. W. Coats (ed.), *Economists in International Agencies: An Exploratory Study*, Praeger Scientific, New York 1986.

[32] A. W. Coats, 'Introduction' to *The Post-1945 Internationalization of Economics*, Duke University Press, Durham N.C. 1996, p. 3.

is tracked in this volume by Roger Backhouse, while William Barber focuses upon the main driver of American expansion in the 1950s and 1960s, graduate education.[33]

This second main phase of the history of the discipline of economics defies easy generalisation at the national level, requiring specialised knowledge and collaborative work. While Coats provided the leadership required for this much more diffuse part of the history of economics he did not, as already noted, seek a synthetic overview.[34] Marion Fourcade's *Economists and Societies*[35] could well be seen as standing in for this absence with regard to professional associations and to issues related to internationalisation, while extending Coats's transatlantic emphasis through the inclusion of France. Where Coats approached the discipline of economics as a social historian, Fourcade's background is as a sociologist, and she seeks explicitly to develop a comparative sociological framework for her study. But while she does begin from a historical problem—loosely, how did modern economics come to be the way it is?—her study depends heavily upon a synthesis of modern commentary, reinforced by the views of modern economists gleaned in interviews and quoted anonymously throughout the book. For someone more deeply embedded in the historical literature of economics it would, however, be obvious that today's economists are perhaps the last people to credit with any direct insight into the history of economics, whether over the last two centuries or the last two decades; this is a story common to all those working in the history of the sciences today.

Her book identifies three distinct 'national styles' of economics that persisted throughout the twentieth century, creating a typology of three 'political logics', sociopolitical frameworks that shaped national disciplinary systems: American federal constitutionalism, British public-minded elitism, and French statism. She describes these typologies as heuristic tools that 'make sense only when understood as patterns that are *produced, and reproduced* through the particular institutional relations, processes and purposes . . . that constitute the grammar of social life in each particular society.'[36] Five main chapters develop this argument: a review of the role of economics in modern public life, an exposition of the three national institutional 'logics', and then a chapter each on the United States, Britain, and France. This is certainly the most comprehensive account available of the broad international development of economics from the later nineteenth century to the present day.

However, the problem with this kind of comparative sociology is that the need to establish clearly differentiated typologies can lead into national caricatures that then furnish an explanatory framework where national disciplinary development becomes a reflection of the chosen typology. There is an essential circularity in the procedure. What economists write about and teach, how public policy relates to

[33] Roger E. Backhouse, 'The Changing Character of British Economics', in A. W. Coats (ed.) *The Post-1945 Internationalization of Economics*, Duke University Press, Durham N.C. 1996, pp. 33–60; William J. Barber, 'Postwar Changes in American Graduate Education in Economics', in ibid., pp. 12–30.

[34] For a survey of his lifetime's work and a select bibliography see R. E. Backhouse, Bruce Caldwell, Craufurd Goodwin and Malcolm Rutherford, 'A. W. (Bob) Coats, 1924–2007', *History of Political Economy* Vol. 40 (2008), pp. 421–46.

[35] Marion Fourcade, *Economists and Societies. Discipline and Profession in the United States, Britain, and France, 1890s to 1990s*, Princeton University Press, Princeton N.J. 2009.

[36] Ibid., p. 59.

economic argument, these are *fitted into* pre-given sociopolitical typologies, rather than regularities being developed *out of* thick description of institutions, teaching, and career structures. As with some older disciplinary histories on which she draws—Mary Furner's *Advocacy and Objectivity*, Voss and Oleson's *The Organization of Knowledge in Modern America, 1860–1920*, and Reba Soffer's *Ethics and Society in England*[37]—there is a lack of engagement between acting individuals and social institutions. National economic styles are related not to the actual practices of economists working in specific frameworks under particular conditions, but to national social, political, and cultural structures. A lack of direct engagement with institutional organisation and daily practice—the transmission of teaching through syllabus and textbook, the recruitment and training of students, the formation of career structures for students and teachers, the creation of specialised journals, the financing of educational institutions, the role of labour markets—leaves Fourcade hostage to the received opinion regularly recycled in commentary and in the views of contemporary economists. Having taught the history of economics to third-year British economics undergraduates since 2005, I am very clear that the principal objective of the course is to persuade my students that more or less everything they might have picked up from their previous courses bearing on the history of economics, even regarding very recent economic debate, is very likely at best partial or misleading; and that what they might learn from the course is to practice a greater degree of scepticism regarding what they are told, what they hear, and what they read—to think about why they think they know what they think they know.

Roger Middleton's *Charlatans or Saviours?*[38] has a more limited scope than Fourcade's book, dealing with the relation of economists in Britain to public policy from the later nineteenth century to the early 1990s. Here his extensive knowledge of twentieth-century government economic policy is brought to bear on the Marshallian aspiration that those working in economic administration, whether in central or local government, or in private industry, have at their command an understanding of contemporary economic principles and instruments. By adopting a public policy perspective on the development of the discipline, Middleton is able to sidestep the tendency to treat the advance of economic knowledge as a purely theoretical process, while also keeping a focus upon the degree to which the government of a modern economy might be informed by economic principles other than those that are the received opinions of the day. Moreover, his sure grasp of the history of public policy and of the relevant economic literature ensures that the one is not simply seen as the effect of the other—that 'good or bad' economic performance is not the simple outcome of 'good or bad' policy, and that 'policy' is not in turn simply the outcome of 'good or bad' economics. This public policy perspective is not one that is developed here, since my focus is on the emergence and development of the institutions and structures that

[37] Mary O. Furner, *Advocacy and Objectivity: A Crisis in the Professionalisation of American Social Science 1865–1905*, University Press of Kentucky, Lexington 1975; A. Voss, J. Oleson (eds.) *The Organization of Knowledge in Modern America, 1860–1920*, Johns Hopkins University Press, Baltimore Md. 1979; Reba N. Soffer, *Ethics and Society in England: The Revolution in the Social Sciences 1870–1914*, University of California Press, Berkeley 1978.

[38] Roger Middleton, *Charlatans or Saviours? Economists and the British Economy from Marshall to Meade*, Edward Elgar, Cheltenham UK 1998.

mould conceptions of 'what economics is' and facilitate the formation of a relatively homogeneous 'science'. Middleton's book, with its emphasis on the use to which economics is put, does, however, provide a valuable complement to my account of disciplinary development and the labour market conditions that stimulate the demand for particular kinds of university education, or vitiate the employment prospects of those acquiring qualifications for which there is little real demand.

My own account of this 'discipline' treats it as an increasingly arcane body of knowledge whose adepts required years of university training in order to be able to speak with any authority on whatever was deemed to fall within their field of expertise. Specialised economic knowledge quickly assumed the form of a mainstream whose increasing complexity provided it with conceptual legitimacy—it became a 'science' whose 'advances' marked a progress that was thought to make it like other sciences, its past being subsumed by its present. This contradictory quality of economic knowledge—as a special kind of knowledge requiring no legitimation other than a mastery of its techniques, hence self-validating and solipsistic—is a product of the institutional structures within which it is deployed. The creation of mainstream, or neoclassical,[39] economics is a function of the conditions under which it is taught and studied.

This book could therefore be described as providing a 'genealogy of neoclassical economics', demonstrating how something 'new' can emerge from something that already seems to exist: which is different, but in some ways the same. One of the paradoxes of neoclassicism as mainstream economics is that the term 'neoclassicism' presupposes its own novelty while at the same time proclaiming a continuity with what it displaced. What is 'classicism'? And what is 'neo' about this 'neoclassicism'? The term itself implies a selective rejection of existing principles and concepts, while at the same time lending the gloss of novelty to those that it retains or reinvents. What becomes 'science' in this selection process is endowed with a reputation of making epistemological progress, a Whig history written by the new incumbent practitioners. By here treating this genealogy as essentially the product of an institutional process, it is possible to track the diverse forces that have moulded the development of a science whose practitioners subscribe to the illusion that their own ideas are, by virtue of being products of a progressive science, superior to the ideas of their predecessors. We need to step away from this epistemological perspective, and consider the non-cognitive conditions of the existence of scientific knowledge. By creating an

[39] 'Neo-classical' was first used by Veblen, principally of Marshall, in his 'The Preconceptions of Economic Science III', *Quarterly Journal of Economics* Vol. 14 (1900), pp. 261, 265, 268. Shortly afterwards Flux's *Economic Principles* was described in a review by H. J. Davenport as 'neo-classical upon the very highest level of thoroughness, accuracy, and modernity' (*Journal of Political Economy* Vol. 13 (1904), p. 114), this usage being contrasted with the 'classical point of view' represented by Marshall. If we take the *American Economic Review*, founded in 1911, the first use of 'neoclassical' is in 1928 by Jacob Viner, recurring only in the later 1930s and not really taking hold until the later 1950s and 1960s. See his contribution to the roundtable discussion, 'The Present Status and Future Prospects of Quantitative Economics', *American Economic Review* (Papers and Proceedings of the Fortieth Annual Meeting of the American Economic Association) Vol. 28 No. 1 (1928), pp. 31, 34. 36. Coincidentally, the first unhyphenated use of the term in the *Quarterly Journal of Economics* is also in 1928, in Frank Knight's review of Paul T. Homan, *Contemporary Economic Thought* Vol. 43, p. 139.

institutional chronology, we are able to see how particular sets of ideas are either furthered or suppressed.

In the following I demonstrate how this process of discipline formation was initiated; and why, once in motion, it took the direction that it did—the twin processes of *Disziplinierung* and *Verwissenschaftlichung*. It seeks to explain how diverse beginnings turned by the mid-twentieth century into a more or less homogenous body of knowledge with which every 'economist' was assumed to be conversant. This fact of homogeneity was not a property of the knowledge itself—there always were, and still are, different ways of conceptualising economic activity and organisation. What needs explaining is how uniformity was created and sustained, and this is not in the first place an epistemological issue—the rough unity of mainstream economics derives not from its quality as scientific knowledge; the social construction of this knowledge as a modern university discipline is the chief force in lending it plausibility and uniformity. I pay little attention here to emergent 'heterodox' approaches to economic knowledge, since their exclusion from a 'mainstream' is itself a function of the social, political, and economic contingencies and imperatives of university institutions that are my chief focus. While I do deal with some early 'paths not taken', this is only in order to emphasise why resistance to the movement for homogeneity proved ineffective. I show how the modern 'science' of economics was shaped not so much by the advancing frontier of economic thinking, but by the more mundane institutional pressures of teaching, funding, publication, and career structures that made such 'thinking' possible.

2

Reconstructing the University

The German Model, the American Version of That Model, and the University of London

By the later nineteenth century, formal elementary education had become compulsory for the populations of most industrialising economies—in the United States this was a rather longer process, beginning in Massachusetts in 1852 and only being complete in 1930. College and university education expanded in step, elective entry to higher institutions being conditional on graduation and certification from lower institutions. In this way a stratified system of formal education developed, involving four principal levels: primary, secondary, further, and higher education. The ages at which children entered and left elementary education varied from country to country, and still does; there is also still some degree of diversity in the points of transition and levels of teaching. By the mid-twentieth century, however, it was usual for a student entering university to have been in continuous formal education since childhood—at that time, around a dozen years. Since then, of course, the proportion of any cohort attending higher education institutions, and the age at which they finally graduate, has risen. I did not leave university for my first permanent full-time job until I was 26, more than 10 years after the great majority of my cohort had already entered full-time employment or apprenticeships.[1]

Formal education—full-time or part-time, in-service training, 'life-long learning', evening classes, day-release, apprenticeships—is something that today everyone experiences for a significant proportion of their life. But this very familiarity has fostered academic neglect. The 'history of education' is a minor sub-discipline, and there is in Britain a dearth of modern and reliable accounts of the history of primary, secondary, or tertiary education, not to speak of various forms of adult education. Things are done better in the United States, as we shall see; but even so, there is no recent English-language appraisal of the history and function of formal education at all levels and on an international scale upon which we can here rely.

This book aims to shed light on how economics became a university discipline, and how in the process what economics became was shaped by the institutions in which it was taught and learned. However, what a 'university' has been understood to be has altered over time, while this understanding has not necessarily coincided with the

[1] I began school in 1954, in a British two-classroom pre-secondary school in Wilhelmshaven, Germany. I left grammar school at 19 for university, took a year out before graduate work, and completed that in three years, from 1972 to 1975. The school-leaving age in Britain was 15 until 1972; my own parents had left school at 14, after eight or nine years of schooling. Spending some 20 years of one's life in full-time education is not now unusual; it was very unusual in Britain even in the 1970s.

Constructing Economic Science. Keith Tribe, Oxford University Press. © Oxford University Press 2022.
DOI: 10.1093/oso/9780190491741.003.0002

actual nature and function of contemporary university institutions. The ideal of the Humboldtian university combining research and teaching, symbolised by the foundation of the University of Berlin in 1810, has often been advanced as the founding moment of the modern university, but it could be argued that the inauguration of the University of Göttingen in 1737 was a far more significant event in the development of the research-based university.[2] Clarifying these issues, and treating university institutions as just one part of a system of formal education linked to personal development and careers, will make clear why it was that as economics became 'academic', it could be presented either as a new form of vocational education, or as an abstract science, or as both at the same time.

Following some general discussion of these issues, this chapter will outline the emergence of the 'modern university' in the United States towards the end of the nineteenth century, an institution which looked to the existing German model, but where funding and student demand created a dynamic and competitive variant. In fact, the general structure and function of the late nineteenth-century 'German university' was more or less typical of all Continental European institutions, from Uppsala to Bologna. But the contemporary international pre-eminence of 'German science'—in physics, mathematics, chemistry, philology, jurisprudence, and history—combined with the openness of the system at the graduate level, made it the model to be followed by Americans and Japanese alike.

Britain was different, and so by extension the early history of American institutions, for the United States had once been a British colony. Before the 1820s there were only two universities in England: Oxford and Cambridge, which well into the nineteenth century were primarily engaged in the production of clergy and teachers,[3] and which many students left before being examined for a degree. They were, moreover, Anglican institutions, their exclusively male students required to declare allegiance to the established church either on entry or graduation, and college fellows barred from marriage until 1882.[4] The four universities in Scotland (Glasgow, Edinburgh, St. Andrews, and Aberdeen) were in structure and function more like their Continental European counterparts, admitting a socially-broader section of the population for training in law and medicine. The same was true of Trinity College, Dublin. It was, however, in Cambridge that economics first assumed a clear academic shape, with the

[2] As noted by R. D. Anderson: he makes clear that the 'Humboldtian model' was first formulated retrospectively around 1900, characterising a number of largely unrelated changes that had occurred some one hundred years before—see his *European Universities from the Enlightenment to 1914*, Oxford University Press, Oxford 2004, p. 51.

[3] Around two-thirds of graduates became clergymen before 1850, and more than one-third from then until 1900—Hester Jenkins and D. Caradog Jones, 'Social Class of Cambridge University Alumni of the 18th and 19th Centuries', *British Journal of Sociology* Vol. 1 (1950), p. 101. See also A. G. L. Haig, 'The Church, the Universities and Learning in Later Victorian England', *Historical Journal* Vol. 29 (1986), pp. 187–201 for consideration of the balance between law and the Church as a career.

[4] Besides Jews and Roman Catholics, until the 1850s Oxford and Cambridge excluded those Protestant dissenters who were from the later eighteenth century central to the intellectual and cultural life of Britain. Not until 1871 could dissenters become college fellows. Malthus might have been an Anglican, but he was in a distinct minority—Ricardo and Jevons were Unitarians, as also was Wicksteed. The sorry early history of King's College, London, bears testimony to the very real limitations of Tory Anglicanism, both financially and intellectually—see F. J. C. Hearnshaw, *The Centenary History of King's College London 1828–1928*, George C. Harrap, London 1929, Ch. 5.

creation in 1903 of the Tripos in Economic and Political Science, a three-year undergraduate degree devoted chiefly to the study of economics. I demonstrate in the following that this initiative was possible due to a number of institutional and personal circumstances not replicated in Oxford, nor was the path taken in Cambridge closely followed anywhere else.

As university institutions Cambridge and Oxford were, nationally and internationally, followers, not leaders. The major institutional force in British university education throughout the nineteenth century was the University of London. This was the original name for what is now University College, London; opening in 1828, and inspired by Scottish and German models of learning, it applied no religious tests, taught modern subjects, and was open to men and women alike. The University of London as a federal body eventually emerged following the creation in 1829 of King's College, London, as an Establishment (Tory, Anglican) riposte to the 'Godless College'; but it remained a marginal institution for decades. London University, a federal examining body for the remainder of the century, had a major impact on the provinces, and on British university education in general, once students of its degrees were able to sit its examinations in regional locations, and institutions were founded offering tuition for its degrees alongside other forms of training.

To clarify what a 'discipline' is, we first need to understand something of the institutional development of the modern university, for this was based upon, presupposed, disciplinary development. Chapter 3 then turns to the path that the institutionalisation of economic discourse took: from economic societies, periodical literature, popular lectures, and popular education to the formal precepts taught in increasingly elaborated form to young people, who were then examined on their knowledge and certified as a preliminary to their employment; how it came about that a discourse articulated in various formal and informal social situations became something that was taught and learned in a university setting. The institutional destination of this pathway was, however, formed by a distinct set of forces, and was not a simple outcome of the transformation of public discourse.

The 'Idea of a University'

Much has been made since the mid-nineteenth century of the 'idea of a university', a phrase associated especially with Newman's 1852 Dublin lectures,[5] in which he set out his conception of a university as

> [a]n assemblage of learned men, zealous for their own sciences, and rivals of each other, are brought, by familiar intercourse and for the sake of intellectual peace, to adjust together the claims and relations of their respective subjects of investigation. They learn to respect, to consult, to aid each other. Thus is created a pure and clear atmosphere of thought, which the student also breathes, though in his own case he

[5] Newman (1801–1890) was from 1822 a fellow of Oriel College Oxford, was ordained in 1825, and became a leading representative of the Anglo-Catholic revival and the Oxford Movement. In 1845 he renounced his Anglican faith and converted to Catholicism.

> only pursues a few sciences out of the multitude. He profits by an intellectual tradition, which is independent of particular teachers, which guides him in his choice of subjects, and duly interprets for him those which he chooses. He apprehends the great outlines of knowledge, the principles on which it rests, the scale of its parts, its light and its shades, its great points and its little, as he otherwise cannot apprehend them. Hence it is that his education is called 'Liberal'.[6]

In his preface Newman had denied that the role of universities was the 'advancement of learning', arguing that their real concern should be the diffusion and extension of knowledge within a closed community of scholars and students; a distinction, however, that was already being undermined by contemporary developments in the natural sciences, mathematics, jurisprudence, history, and even classics. Newman conceived 'knowledge' to be a fixed stock, accumulated over a lifetime by a scholar and then dispensed to successive generations of students; but by the time he was giving his lectures it was increasingly obvious that a 'scholar' was not an accumulator of past knowledge, but a creator of new knowledge. In the British context, Mark Pattison was another prominent contributor to the idea of a liberal education, arguing, 'It is no part of the proper business of a University to be a professional school. Universities are not to fit men for some special mode of gaining a livelihood; their object is not to teach law or divinity, banking or engineering, but to cultivate the mind and form the intelligence.'[7] Here again, given that the Cambridge chair of Mechanism and Applied Mechanics had been founded two years previously and James Stuart, a leading figure in the University Extension movement, appointed to it, Pattison was already talking of the past, and not of his present.

Nonetheless, in the Oxford lectures that Abraham Flexner gave in 1928 he still took Newman as his point of departure; while now conceding that critical inquiry played a greater role in the modern university than the conservation of knowledge, he denied that technical and vocational education was properly part of a university.[8] He illustrated his point by noting that Columbia University had announced an enrolment of 48,722 students for 1928–1929. However, if summer session, university extension, and home study students were excluded, this number reduced to 16,123; of these, 3,730 were undergraduates, of whom half were at secondary school level; of the 12,393 registered graduate students, almost 8,000 were in business, oral hygiene, journalism, pharmacy, library service, and so on. Hence, he calculated, the real size of Columbia University's student body was about 4,000.[9] Indeed, parsing student body and type of institution had long been recognised as a problem in the United States; while the diversity of the evolving educational system was arguably a strength, enabling wider

[6] J. H. Newman, *The Idea of a University Defined and Illustrated* (1873 ed.), Routledge, London 1994, p. 101. Anderson shows that the phrase was in fact put into circulation by Henrik Steffens in a set of lectures at Halle, 1808–1809; Anderson, *European Universities*, p. 54.

[7] Mark Pattison, 'Address on Education', *Transactions of the National Association for the Promotion of Social Science. Liverpool Meeting 1876*, Longmans, Green and Co., London 1877, p. 61. See A. H. Halsey, *The Decline of Donnish Dominion. The British Academic Professions in the Twentieth Century*, Oxford University Press, Oxford 1992, pp. 28–29.

[8] A. Flexner, *Universities: American, English, German*, Oxford University Press, New York 1930, pp. 8, 28.

[9] Ibid., p. 189.

social access, it continues up to the present day to create problems in comparing educational structures and their levels internationally. In this way, arguments that were already superseded by contemporary developments in the mid-nineteenth century were from time to time revived in the twentieth and twenty-first, wielded to either defend or attack the increasingly diverse field of contemporary higher education. One early and prominent example of this was Thorstein Veblen's *Higher Learning in America*, whose arguments resonate today because of the way in which he predicted the malign consequences of running universities as businesses. Whatever the merits of his arguments, and despite his recognition of the vocational roots of the European university, his conception of the university as dedicated to science and scholarship also presumed that undergraduate education was not a proper part of any university institution.[10]

German Universities in the Nineteenth Century

Whereas in Britain the universities of Oxford and Cambridge were a loose federation of independent colleges whose roots and practices clearly lay in pre-Reformation England, the ancient German universities were state institutions, with some early modern additions, such as Halle in Prussia and Göttingen in the state of Hanover. All these institutions had been based upon the four faculties of theology, medicine, law, and philosophy, the last being more of the nature of general studies suitable for the training of schoolteachers. Although the number of students in each faculty varied from university to university, so that the relative importance of each faculty differed, it was expected that a flourishing university would maintain capable professors in each of the four faculties. By contrast, when Matthew Arnold reported on Italian universities in the 1860s, he found that the vast majority of students were studying medicine and law only. Of 1,200 students attending the University of Padua, for example, he found only 8 were registered in the Faculty of Letters.[11] The classical function of the Continental European university was the training of lawyers, doctors, and priests, the primary professions of early modern Europe. The visions of Newman and Pattison reflected contemporary Victorian values, not any real perspective on the actual history of university institutions.

The German university had developed as a state institution financed directly out of an educational budget, with only a small contribution from student fees. By 1882–1883 there were 24,187 students matriculated in German universities, 42% of them in the three largest universities of Berlin, Leipzig, and Munich.[12] Students registered

[10] See Thorstein Veblen, *The Higher Learning in America: A Memorandum on the Conduct of Universities by Business Men*, ed. Richard F. Teichgraeber III, Johns Hopkins University Press, Baltimore Md. 2015, pp. 47ff.

[11] Matthew Arnold, *Schools and Universities on the Continent*, Complete Prose Works of Matthew Arnold Vol. 4, University of Michigan Press, Ann Arbor 1964, p. 163. This had been published as a book in 1868, based on his report to the Schools Inquiry Commission of 1865–1867.

[12] J. Conrad, *The German Universities for the Last Fifty Years*, David Bryce, Glasgow 1885, p. 17. In his preface James Bryce pointed out that in 1882–1883 Britain had 5,500 students enrolled in a university institution (p. xvii).

by the semester on payment of a tuition fee and followed specific lecture courses, sitting their final examination where and when they chose. This final examination qualified them for entry into their chosen profession. Full 'ordinary' professors constituted an academic core of fully-paid state employees who, once appointed to a post, were expected to teach the full range of material associated with that post. They had an interest in attracting students to their lectures since their salary was only a base income, supplemented by the fees paid by students who registered for a course of lectures. 'Ordinary' professors were assisted by 'extraordinary' professors aspiring to a chair, and who were in some cases paid a salary, but in all cases had gained a higher degree qualifying them for appointment to an ordinary professorship.[13] The lowest level of teaching staff was that of the *Privat-Dozent*, the unpaid assistant possessing the right to teach conferred by the *Habilitation*, but who lived on tutoring fees and acted as assistants to their seniors.

Teaching in German universities was by lecture, complemented by the private study of the student. There was therefore little direct contact between students and teachers. This was, however, altered in the early nineteenth century by the addition of the Seminar—an organisation with its own rooms in which professors and advanced students met on a regular basis, and which provided a forum for the training of doctoral students.[14] The development of the Seminar was prompted by the need on the part of the professoriate to build research teams, and the complementary need on the part of the students to gain doctoral supervision and patronage from professors who would then, once their work was completed and they had gained the status of *Privat-Dozent*, possibly assist them in the development of their careers. This introduced a clear distinction between the *Brotstudenten*,[15] those students concerned only with completing the minimum work necessary to pass the examinations needed for a professional career, and students who sought an academic training and thus embraced the research ethos embodied in the Seminar. In the humanities and the natural sciences, the development of the Seminar and the research laboratory was perceived internationally to be the chief merit of the German university, although as far as the Germans themselves were concerned the primary function of the university as a whole remained that of professional training. The great majority of students were *Brotstudenten*.

In this system, it was usual for the more academically-oriented students to move from university to university, studying under different professors until they were ready to sit their final examinations, in the process taking advantage of studying with the most eminent names in the field. It was therefore important that universities appointed full professors of reputation—for this was one of the factors that attracted numbers of good students, and a flourishing university was thought to be an

[13] During the 1870s the doctorate, which had since the later seventeenth century been the qualification for the post of ordinary professor, was supplemented with a second postgraduate degree, referred to as the *Habilitation*. Max Weber (1864–1920), for example, was awarded his Berlin doctorate in 1889 for a dissertation on medieval trading companies, and then qualified to teach with a *Habilitation* dissertation on Roman agrarian history in early 1892. Gustav Schmoller (1838–1917), by contrast, gained his doctorate in 1861 and was appointed to a full chair in 1865 at Halle without being required to submit a second dissertation, having served there for a year as an extraordinary professor.

[14] Details of the development of Economic Seminars and associated work on *Statistik* can be found in S. M. Wickett, 'Political Economy at German Universities', *Economic Journal* Vol. 8 (1898), pp. 147–51.

[15] Lit. 'bread students', so 'bread and butter students'.

important asset for a state. This reputational factor, and the fluidity that the possibility of mobility implied, would be a key factor in attracting large numbers of American graduate students in the later nineteenth century. For Germans, however, entry into a professional occupation was exclusively via university qualification, and so any prospective lawyer or doctor or teacher had to possess the relevant university qualification; and this vocational path did not require that students move between universities in the course of their studies. In general, the importance of the linkage between qualification and professional grouping meant that the university structure as a whole had to move in step with the dynamics of the labour market, producing enough students of the right kind and with an appropriate academic education. From the later 1890s a steadily increasing proportion of qualified school-leavers went on to attend university, creating pressures within the university system and raising questions about the likely long-term effects on the labour market. One response to an increased demand for vocational qualifications was the foundation of the Business Colleges, beginning with a joint venture between Leipzig University and the Leipzig Commercial College in 1898. This was quickly followed by new, independent colleges in Cologne, Frankfurt, and Berlin, all of which conferred a diploma on their graduates after two years' study. Initially, the intake to these new colleges was a mixture of *Abiturienten* (qualified school-leavers) and qualified apprentices; by 1920, however, they were recruiting almost entirely from the pool of qualified school-leavers, and the introduction of an Economics Diploma into universities in 1923 was part of a convergence between the new, independent colleges and the existing university system.

The requirement that professors qualify to teach by first gaining a doctorate stimulated scholarly activity and publication—the last being a thriving industry in the second half of the nineteenth century. In post-bellum America, students who sought advanced tuition could find nothing suitable domestically in the existing colleges, and began to travel abroad in search of it. There were parallels to the German doctoral qualification and the Seminar in Scandinavia or the Netherlands, but it was Germany that also had a thriving and unique academic culture.[16] While the London School of Economics (LSE) would be the first institution in Britain to offer regular supervision to doctoral candidates, this would not happen until the 1920s; in the later nineteenth century there was no advanced university tuition available in Britain. France, on the other hand, had a complex educational landscape made up of specialised institutes and faculties for engineers, lawyers, and schoolteachers, impenetrable to outsiders; regional universities were only established after 1890.[17] In Germany, not only was there a thriving and internationally-renowned university system, it was open to foreign students and offered them the prospect of doctoral qualification. Conrad records

[16] A listing of lectures during the Winter Semester of 1889–1890 in the Faculties of Law and of Philosophy, organised by university, was published in L. S. Rowe, 'Instruction in Public Law and Political Economy in German Universities', *Annals of the American Academy of Political and Social Science* Vol. I (1890), pp. 83–102. This listing was not of 'universities in Germany', but rather German-speaking universities, so included Strasbourg, Czernowitz, Graz, Innsbruck, Prague, Vienna, Basel, Bern, Zürich, and Dorpat [Tartu], providing a comprehensive overview of the teaching of political economy and who its teachers were at this time.

[17] G. Weisz, *The Emergence of Modern Universities in France, 1863–1914*, Princeton University Press, Princeton N.J. 1983, pp. 149–51.

that in 1880 there were 235 foreign students at the University of Berlin, and 49 in Göttingen.[18] Some of these—the Austrians and the Swiss—could have been regular students, but the 173 American students recorded in the same year[19] were more than likely all studying at postgraduate level, having already gained a qualification in the United States and now attending lectures or being supervised for PhDs.

Key figures in the development of economics in the United States followed this path. John Bates Clark (1847–1938) enrolled for two years in Heidelberg in the early 1870s, where he attended Knies's lectures; Edwin R. Seligman (1861–1939) studied in Berlin and Heidelberg in the early 1880s, taking detailed notes on Knies's lectures that are now among his papers at Columbia University. Frank Taussig (1859–1940) attended lectures in Berlin around the same time. During the summer semester of 1892, Henry Seager (1870–1930) attended Adolf Wagner's Berlin seminar, and reported that

> Professor Wagner's conception of a Seminar is that of a course in which the professor takes for the time the minor role of director and the students themselves become the lecturers. Upon the occasion of our second meeting, the director submitted to each one of us in turn a series of questions in regard to our former work in economics, our preferences in the science and the motives which had led us to enter his course. The answers to these questions were designed more for our own instruction than anything else and accomplished their purpose remarkably well. From them I learned, in a short hour, more about the character and acquirements of my fellow students, about the extent of their work in economics and their intellectual sympathies than I would have learned during the whole semester, if left to myself. I was particularly surprised to observe the advanced age of most of the members. The majority were already doctors of philosophy, many public officials, some advocates. Only the foreigners seemed to be what we would call 'specialists' in political economy, and only a few of them were looking forward to teaching as a profession.[20]

Over the course of the semester, 12 students made 30-minute presentations of papers that had first been read by Wagner, who opened each session with a critical analysis of the paper to be read out, aiming to direct the subsequent course of discussion. Seager noted that this procedure would have worked better with no more than 10 students, and that it was the presenter who learned most from the session, not the auditors.[21] He also attended Schmoller's lectures at this time, and commented that

[18] Conrad, *German Universities*, p. 40.

[19] Ibid., p. 41. In the Prussian universities during 1880–1881 there were 16 American students registered in Faculties of Philosophy, 18 in the sciences, 1 in agriculture and political economy, and 3 in pharmacy (p. 43). Conrad later notes that at this time the Faculty of Philosophy included the study of political economy (p. 154). See also Roger L. Geiger, *The History of American Higher Education: Learning and Culture from the Founding to World War II*, Princeton University Press, Princeton N.J. 2015, pp. 328–29.

[20] H. R. Seager, 'Economics at Berlin and Vienna', *Journal of Political Economy* Vol. 1 (1893), p. 245. His fellow students included 3 other Americans, 13 Germans, 2 Austrians, 3 Hungarians, 3 Russians, and 1 Japanese.

[21] And in fact this was the practice for all my university classes from 1968 to 1971, apart from maths, statistics, or computer science; each of my three principal first-year lectures had a weekly one-hour class attached, in which between 10 and 12 students took turns to open discussion by presenting an essay whose topic had been allocated at the first meeting of term. While it might be said that this was a watered-down version of the Oxbridge supervision/tutorial, I had three one-hour sessions a week, not one. In my second

> [i]n his treatment of value and price he showed his acquaintance with the work of the Austrians by freely borrowing their results, not, however, as consequences of a long and difficult chain of deductive reasoning, but simply as the obvious inferences from his own description of market phenomena. In this part of his lectures the student meets only confusion, loose definitions, description instead of careful analysis, and conclusions arrived at, no one knows exactly how.[22]

During the winter semester of 1892–1893 he went to Vienna, where he attended Menger's series of 80 lectures on general economics, and the seminar run by Böhm-Bawerk. This was held in a lecture room and included around 60 students—at the smaller first meeting he noted that almost all students seemed to be Austrian, and in this context it was not the papers presented that were important, but the sometimes active debate that ensued.[23]

By this time, American universities were increasingly offering advanced tuition, and in the course of the 1890s the number of students travelling to Europe sharply declined: John Bates Clark's son, John Maurice Clark (1884–1963), did not follow in his father's footsteps, and studied at Amherst before completing a PhD at Columbia in 1910. But the impact that the German university system had had on American institutions during their headlong expansion in the final decades of the nineteenth century was considerable. Richard T. Ely (1854–1943) had graduated from Columbia in 1876 and then spent three years studying with Karl Knies in Heidelberg, being awarded his doctorate in 1879. On his return to the United States he published an article summarising his recent experience, warning against a blind adoption of German practice in the United States. He was clear-eyed about the nature of the German university system:

> A German university is, from beginning to end, through and through, a professional school. It is a place where young men prepare to earn their 'bread and butter', as the Germans say, in practical life. It is *not* a school which pretends or strives to develop in a general way the intellectual powers, and give its students universal culture.[24]

He emphasised that, in principle, students could attend whatever lectures they liked, but the overwhelming majority concentrated upon the minimum necessary to pass the examinations that would admit them to their chosen career. While Ely was quite right about the basic function of German universities, the 'German model' served more as talisman than template for the transformation of American higher education in the later nineteenth century.

and third years, this was the model for all courses: weekly lecture + class, or by small weekly class only. This routine ceased to be the norm in British universities in the course of the 1990s, where a 'class' became 25+ students, and teaching reverted to a lecture format.

22 Seager, 'Economics at Berlin and Vienna', p. 250.

23 Ibid., pp. 258–59.

24 R. T. Ely, 'American Colleges and German Universities', *Harpers' New Monthly Magazine* Vol. 61 (1880), p. 254.

The American University

As already noted, since the United States had been a British colony until 1783 it is unsurprising that existing institutions resembled Oxbridge colleges, the curriculum focussed upon classics and maths, with some moral philosophy, history, and natural science. Harvard College had been founded in 1636, Yale in 1701. Typically, colleges had around one hundred students and five teachers,[25] but in any case there were other institutions in which scholarly study was done—museums, observatories, and state geological surveys were important centres for study and training, and the Smithsonian Institute had been founded in 1846 to both develop and diffuse knowledge. Kohler notes that in the mid-nineteenth century there were various schemes to foster advanced study and research in a college or university context, but there was no established market for this and all proposals soon failed.[26] Practical sciences fared better: at Yale, for example, the first proposal to develop graduate instruction was made in 1843, linked to the offer of a chair for agricultural chemistry and animal and vegetable physiology. This led to the development of a School of Applied Chemistry, which in 1854 was combined with the School of Engineering to form the Yale Scientific School. The marriage in 1855 of the incumbent of the chair of agricultural chemistry to Josephine Sheffield brought an endowment that led in 1861 to the renaming of the Yale Scientific School as the Sheffield Scientific School.[27] Chance endowments of this kind would prove vital to the development of American universities in the last third of the nineteenth century.[28]

But, as Kelley also notes, in 1870 there were only 44 graduate students in the entire United States: 24 in Yale, 8 at Harvard, 6 at Michigan, and 3 at Princeton.[29] This reflected the shortcomings of the existing opportunities for advanced study, and demonstrates why so many American students studied in Germany in post-bellum America. Unlike at mid-century, when efforts to develop advanced study had foundered on a lack of demand, students returning from Europe now found ready employment. The older colleges were expanding, and a number of state universities had been created that were bolstered by the Morrill Land Grant Act of 1862,[30] which directed that any grant of land be tied to the promotion of the agricultural and mechanic arts—hence Texas A & M, founded in 1876. The University of Wisconsin, the eleventh

[25] R. L. Geiger, *To Advance Knowledge: The Growth of American Research Universities, 1900–1940*, Oxford University Press, New York 1986, p. 3.

[26] Robert E. Kohler, 'The Ph.D. Machine: Building on the Collegiate Base', *Isis* Vol. 81 (1990), p. 641.

[27] B. M. Kelley, *Yale: A History*, Yale University Press, New Haven Conn. 1974, pp. 181–85.

[28] Between 1872 and 1891 the Colgate family put $320,000 into Colgate University; Clark University was founded by Jonas G. Clark in 1887 with an endowment of $1 million; Leonard Case gave $2 million to Case Western Reserve in 1880–1881; Leland Stanford endowed Stanford University in 1885 with $20 million of railway stock; Anthony G. Drexel gave $3 million to Drexel University in 1891; by 1900 John D. Rockefeller had given $20 million to Chicago; see the complete listing in D. A. Wren, 'American Business Philanthropy and Higher Education in the Nineteenth Century', *Business History Review* Vol. 57 (1983), pp. 326–34.

[29] Kelley, *Yale*, p. 257.

[30] The Land Grant Act gave to each state 30,000 acres of land for each senator or representative in Congress for the purpose of establishing a college—the land could be auctioned off and the proceeds employed in the approved way. In 1890 a second Morrill Act extended the uses to which the grant could be put; W. C. DeVane, *Higher Education in Twentieth-Century America*, Harvard University Press, Cambridge Mass. 1965, pp. 122–23.

American state university to be founded, had for example been established in 1848 along with the state of Wisconsin; in 1866 it became a land grant institution. New institutions were also founded by philanthropic donations, the most prominent early example of this being the opening of Johns Hopkins in 1876.

A corporation to promote education in Maryland had been formed in 1867 at the request of Johns Hopkins, who had made his fortune in the railroad industry. After he died in 1873, his trustees acquired a collection of books for their own instruction: top of the list was Matthew Arnold's *Higher Schools and Universities in Germany* (1874).[31] With an endowment of $7 million to be divided equally between a university and a hospital, at this point it was the largest benefaction ever given for higher education in the United States. The initial vision of its new President was of an institution limited to graduate education and advanced scholarship; only after local criticism did the trustees include undergraduates in what they had conceived as a graduate institution. Opening in 1876 with 54 graduate students and 12 undergraduates, few senior figures could be induced to join; instead, the faculty was filled with enthusiastic young scholars. A fellowship programme originally including 10 appointments was quickly extended to 20, since more than a hundred qualified candidates had applied; some other universities offered fellowships, but none to outsiders. By 1889 Johns Hopkins had conferred 151 PhDs, more than Harvard and Yale combined.[32]

In parallel, the classical curriculum of American colleges was broken up by the introduction of the elective system of study, in which students were permitted to select those courses that would be best suited to their future needs. Cornell, when it opened in 1868, offered instruction to any person in any subject; and in 1869 Harvard also adopted the elective system. The propagation of this student-led form of instruction involved a renunciation of the traditional function of the college as a medium for the transmission of established knowledge, and the adoption of a culture directed towards the dissemination of specialised knowledge. This naturally had repercussions for the training and selection of teaching staff, since generalists were incapable of effectively developing specialised knowledge. Moreover, the elective system made necessary a broad range of staff as student numbers increased, moving responsibility for any one subject away from one senior professor, as was the norm in Germany. As Kohler emphasises, 'The elective movement gave the higher learning its economic base, its machinery of change, and its rhetoric and values.'[33]

American universities adopted the PhD from Germany, but transformed it into a certification of specialisation directed towards the reformed college teaching system, which was the primary market for graduates with higher qualifications. In the German context the doctorate was as much a qualification within a staged career structure as it was a mark of academic achievement. This career culminated in the post of full professor, who would then be formally obliged to cover in his teaching whatever was laid down for the post which he represented. The German 'ordinary' professor was in a sense the personification of the field assigned to him, and was surrounded

[31] J. C. French, *A History of the University Founded by Johns Hopkins*, Johns Hopkins University Press, Baltimore Md. 1946, p. 24.

[32] Geiger, *History*, pp. 323–25.

[33] Kohler, 'The Ph.D. Machine', p. 648.

by apprentices and assistants to whom he could delegate specific areas of work. The American professor, on the other hand, emerged by the later nineteenth century as a member of a department that covered a discipline through the combination of the specialities of its staff; junior members became senior members by the elaboration of their specialism.[34] By contrast, advancement in the German system presupposed that such specialisation was at a severe discount. Hence the discrepancy between Germany, where 'professor' remains a title reserved for senior academics, and the United States, where all are professors of one sort or another, which reflects a genuine difference in the organisation of knowledge, and not simply a dilution of academic rank.

The emergence of the department as the basic element of university organisation for teaching and research is therefore directly related to the development of specialisation as the typical form for training new researchers and for the advancement of knowledge. By the 1890s this organisational form had become established in the United States, most notably in the systematic foundation of whole departments in Rockefeller's University of Chicago. The academic vitality of the new Chicago departments is evident from the fact that many of them established journals that were immediately recognised at an international level.[35] This process was coupled with the formation of scientific societies and the rapid development of academic journals as a form of communication within a developing research field.

The rapid pace of innovation in the United States towards the end of the nineteenth century was not without its problems, however. For one thing, the proliferation of degrees had led to wide variations in quality, which began to cause concern during the 1890s. As a consequence of debate on these and other related issues, the Association of American Universities was founded in 1900 with the objective of introducing greater uniformity among PhD requirements, achieving foreign recognition of the American doctorate, and a general raising of standards among the weaker institutions. This organisation quickly assumed the role of a national co-ordinating council for academic standards, establishing a framework within which institutions and the qualifications that they issued could be compared.[36]

Added to this, by the turn of the century organised benefaction on the part of philanthropic foundations began to displace individual generosity. Chief among these were the General Education Board founded in 1902 with $1 million from Rockefeller, and the Carnegie Foundation for the Advancement of Teaching, established in 1903 with an endowment of $10 million in United States Steel Corporation bonds.[37] One of the first acts of the General Education Board was to survey the provision of higher education in the United States; unsurprisingly, it discovered an abundance of poorly staffed and financed colleges. Ohio, it noted, had over 40 colleges and universities, which was approximately twice as many as the German Empire had at that time.

34 J. Higham, 'The Matrix of Specialization', in A. Oleson, J. Voss, *The Organization of Knowledge in Modern America, 1860–1920*, Johns Hopkins University Press, Baltimore Md. 1979, pp. 11–12.

35 *Journal of Political Economy* (1893), *Journal of Geology* (1893), *American Journal of Sociology* (1896), *American Journal of Theology* (1897), *Classical Philology* (1903); see Geiger, *To Advance Knowledge*, p. 32.

36 Geiger, *To Advance Knowledge*, pp. 18–20.

37 M. Curti, R. Nash, *Philanthropy in the Shaping of American Higher Education*, Rutgers University Press, New Brunswick N.J. 1965, pp. 212–20. Rockefeller allocated $118 million to the General Education Board between 1902 and 1920.

None of them, however, bore comparison in academic stature. The Board instituted a programme aimed at improving the standard of American university education by selective aid; only those which were already well-funded received significant assistance, such that in 1920 a mere 20 select institutions accounted for 75% of disbursements. During the 1920s the same principle was followed in disbursing $100 million for medical education.

The Carnegie Foundation pursued a different line of support, but which likewise exerted a standardising pressure on colleges and universities. The manifest purpose of the Foundation was to provide retirement pensions for academic staff. Quite specific conditions, however, were attached to its grants. First of all, colleges were only admitted to the scheme if they required four years of secondary education for entrants. This was later elaborated into a system of 'Carnegie units', 15 of which had to be required for entrance into a bona fide college. Secondly, recipients of funds had to have at least six (later eight) full professors on the staff. This translated directly into a minimum number of functioning departments. Thirdly, they were to be free of debt and possess an endowment of $200,000. Taken together, these were stringent criteria for the accreditation of educational establishments, ensuring that funds flowed to the strongest, but at the same time clearly establishing guidelines for the admission of excluded institutions.

Then as now, wide variations in standards characterised the American university system. Nonetheless, at the turn of the century there was an increasingly clear hierarchy, at the top of which were to be found institutions of international eminence. Tradition was no guarantee of supremacy; the leading institutions were those which had adopted the features of the modern university, whether newly-founded (such as Chicago) or the long-established (such as Harvard). Nor did the distinction between private and state universities indicate the standing of an institution, since state universities were by definition newly-founded, whereas among the private institutions were both recent and long-established colleges. The benefactions of the General Education Board and of the Carnegie Foundation were blind to the state/private distinction, funds being directed to any qualifying institution, no matter what its status.

Direct funding of research was promoted during the 1920s by the Carnegie Corporation. Specific programmes of research made available to scholars and scientists the means with which to pursue work in their speciality. In this manner a structure of funding for university research was established in which support for research derived from external sources directed to particular projects. During the interwar period, corporations themselves developed substantial research divisions, while state and federal government departments faced new problems that required the establishment of research organisations. Research-related activity remained, however, at the heart of university activities, although technological advance and the sheer scale of higher education eventually took the requirements of universities beyond even the resources of private foundations. After the Second World War, federal funding came to replace much of the private philanthropic support for basic research, but in so doing it assumed a role initially developed by the deliberate activities of philanthropic foundations.

Some of the consequences of these developments were discussed by Thorstein Veblen in a work which, like Max Weber's 1917 lecture 'Science as a Vocation', analyses the university as a capitalist enterprise.[38] Originally drafted in 1904 as a response to developments in the University of Chicago, *The Higher Learning in America* finally appeared in 1918 and presented an indictment of the subversion of learning by business ethics, based upon a firm belief in the centrality of research as the raison d'être of the modern university. As already noted, Veblen defined the objective of the university as the quest for knowledge—in fact a very modern definition and not one that coincided with the established features of contemporary German and English universities. Veblen considered that the primary, central purpose of a university was the advancement of knowledge; such instruction as was given should be compatible with this objective, and not interfere in any way with its realisation:

> The lower schools (including the professional schools) are, in the ideal scheme, designed to fit the incoming generation for civil life; they are therefore occupied with instilling such knowledge and habits as will make their pupils fit citizens of the world in whatever position in the fabric of workday life they may fall. The university on the other hand is specialized to fit men for a life of science and scholarship; and it is accordingly concerned with such discipline only as will give efficiency in the pursuit of knowledge and fit its students for the increase and diffusion of knowledge.[39]

The management of American universities had recently shifted from the clergy to a laity composed chiefly of politicians and business, argued Veblen; and the latter naturally viewed the university as a form of business in which investment had to be made and turnover assessed. The 'Captains of Erudition', the new heads of these institutions, were increasingly obliged to exercise a capacity for business in their management of the institutions in their charge, treating faculty members as paid employees hired to produce the business's product.[40]

The general prestige of an institution governed by such principles meant prestige with the laiety, not with the scholarly classes. This makes it easier to pass off as erudition that which would not pass the scrutiny of scholars. Veblen goes on:

> Competitive business concerns that find it needful to commend themselves to a large and credulous body of customers, as, e.g., newspapers or department stores, also find it expedient somewhat to overstate their facilities for meeting all needs, as also to overstate the measure of success which they actually enjoy.[41]

When combined with the sound business principle that it is bad policy to offer better quality than that which is demanded, 'particularly to customers who do not know the difference . . .',[42] departments are prevented from confining their activities to what they do best. The business ethos, with the application of business principles to the modern university, results, according to Veblen, in a diversion of university activity away from

[38] See my 'Max Weber's "Science as a Vocation": Context, Genesis, Structure', *Sociologica* V. 12 No. 1 (2018), pp. 125–36 [online].
[39] Veblen, *Higher Learning*, p. 50.
[40] Ibid., p. 94.
[41] Ibid., p. 110.
[42] Ibid., p. 116.

its central purpose—the promotion of learning and scholarship—and towards a diffuse involvement in recreational activities of uncertain quality.

Veblen's acerbic critique of the modern university certainly resonates today, but like the views expressed by Newman and Pattison, it presupposes a vanished world that reflects present values, not past reality. As we have seen earlier, the United States quickly gained a global pre-eminence both in building new institutions and developing older ones. Initially, a breathtaking amount of individual philanthropy was supplemented by federal land grants for state universities; if anything, established colleges like Princeton were at a distinct disadvantage in this environment. Then, in the early twentieth century, a series of foundations played a major part in developing institutional standards, the most prominent being those associated with the fortunes of John D. Rockefeller and Andrew Carnegie. But this new funding was not, like the earlier phase of philanthropic giving, channelled exclusively to American universities. The Rockefeller Foundation had been established in 1913 to seek solutions to social problems, especially those related to health. The Laura Spelman Rockefeller Memorial established in 1918 was particularly concerned with the welfare of women and children. By the early 1920s this was extended internationally to include programmes in the social sciences and applied social research.[43] The appointment of Allyn Young as successor to Edwin Cannan at the LSE was made possible by Rockefeller money; by the 1930s large amounts of Rockefeller money were flowing into British projects. Half the cost of building the new Cambridge University Library was financed by Rockefeller money; virtually all the interwar building programme of the LSE came from the same source—during the period 1923–1939 a total of £400,000 was granted to the School by the Foundation, at a time when the total annual income of the School averaged about £50,000.[44]

The University of London

During the 1930s the LSE was central to the establishment of the discipline of economics. However, this role was owed less to its own achievements and rather more to its being part of the University of London. The School thereby gained institutional leverage over the future course of economics in Britain and the Empire, enabling its own teaching to become the template for what happened elsewhere. As already noted, Oxford and Cambridge were followers in the national context; very broadly speaking, they were following the University of London, and so we need to understand what this might mean.

Originally, the University of London was what we today know as University College, London. This had opened in October 1828 with 300 students as a new secular institution teaching a range of modern subjects, rather than the classical curriculum then followed in Oxford, Cambridge, and the American colleges.

[43] Robert O. Kohler, 'A Policy for the Advancement of Science: The Rockefeller Foundation, 1924–29', *Minerva* Vol. 16 (1978), p. 482.

[44] Salma Ahmad, 'Institutions and the Growth of Knowledge: The Rockefeller Foundation's Influence on the Social Sciences between the Wars', University of Manchester PhD dissertation 1987, p. 39.

A coalition of English dissenters led by Henry Brougham (1778–1868), advocates of popular education including George Birkbeck (1776–1841), and the Scottish poet Thomas Campbell (1777–1844) had come together in 1825 to further the vision of a new university in London. Beginning with a joint letter published in *The Times* on 9 February 1825, by July sufficient momentum had been achieved for the Lord Mayor of London to take the chair at a meeting held at the City of London Tavern.[45] Despite the broad support the project enjoyed, disagreements over the place of religion in education persisted, so that in the course of 1827 moves were already being made to establish a rival, Anglican institution. By 1828 this rival project had gained the support of the Archbishop of Canterbury, the Duke of Wellington, and seven Anglican bishops, representing a coalition uniting anti-Catholicism with those who opposed secularism. While the patronage of the King led to its naming as King's College, the coalition soon fell apart and much of the promised financial support was withdrawn. A new building in The Strand was formally opened in 1831, with teaching beginning in the autumn. The college was not a runaway success to begin with; the daytime boys' school run on the same premises was for many years the most successful element financially, because it taught not only classics and mathematics, but modern languages and natural science.[46]

The two rival institutions entered into a federal arrangement in the mid-1830s, agreeing to adopt the name University of London, as well as a common curriculum and system of examinations. Although women were not generally admitted to degrees until 1877, this was also the year that Alfred Marshall left Cambridge to become Principal of University College, Bristol, because his marriage to Mary Paley debarred him from retaining his college fellowship; and degrees were not formally awarded to female Cambridge graduates until 1948. As other colleges opened they were added to the London federation—Westfield College opened in 1882, Royal Holloway College in 1886, both institutions for women and the latter with the single largest endowment made during the nineteenth century.[47] Birkbeck College, founded in 1823 as the London Mechanics' Institution, its name changed in 1866 to the Birkbeck Literary and Scientific Institution, was likewise eventually incorporated into the University of London in 1920, although its students had been sitting London examinations since 1858. In much the same way, the London School of Economics and Political Science began as an independent foundation that was quickly incorporated into the University of London.

In 1838 the first detailed syllabuses were issued for arts, law, and medicine. The Bachelor of Arts degree was in two parts, the first covering mathematics, chemistry, and natural history, and classics; the second, which could not be sat within two

[45] H. H. Bellot, *University College London 1826–1926*, University of London Press, London 1929, pp. 21ff. Bellot lists the diverse membership of the first council appointed in 1826 on p. 29, comprising Whigs, a Catholic, Dissenters, Utilitarians, and Evangelicals, as well as George Birkbeck, Isaac Lyon Goldsmid, Henry Brougham, and Joseph Hume. More general background can be found in Hearnshaw, *Centenary History*, pp. 28ff. See also John Maloney, 'The Teaching of Political Economy in the University of London', in Alon Kadish, Keith Tribe (eds.), *The Market for Political Economy: The Advent of Economics in British University Culture, 1850–1905*, Routledge, London 1993, pp. 20–24.

[46] Hearnshaw, *Centenary History*, p. 101.

[47] Royal Holloway was to a large extent modelled on Vassar College; C. Bingham, *The History of Royal Holloway College 1886–1986*, Constable, London 1987, pp. 44–45.

years of passing the first, in four main subjects: mathematics and natural philosophy; chemistry, physiology, and botany; Latin, Greek, history, and French or German; and logic and moral philosophy.[48] This last was the vehicle through which degree-level teaching in political economy first developed, hence the full title of the Manchester chair awarded to Stanley Jevons in 1866 being 'Professor of Logic, Mental and Moral Philosophy'. Students who passed this examination could proceed to honours in either classics or mathematics, and one year later students could also proceed to a Masters degree by further examination in classics, mathematics, or moral philosophy.

The first London BA examinations were held in May 1839, with 17 candidates passing.[49] By 1858 there were 299 matriculation candidates and difficulties in accommodating them; a solution was found by permitting students to sit the examinations in provincial centres. The first institutions to be approved for this were Owens College, Manchester, and Queen's College, Liverpool. By 1865 the matriculation and BA examinations were being sat in Mauritius; and this was extended to Canada in 1867.[50] As with the gradual incorporation of new institutions in London to a common curriculum and degree qualification, the new institutions of further instruction founded in the provinces were able to offer London degrees, providing a path to the foundation of distinct university colleges (such as Bristol) that, eventually, were chartered as universities in their own right, able to award their own degrees. A select overview runs as follows:

1851	Owens College, Manchester
1862	Hartley College, Southampton
1871	College of Physical Science, Newcastle upon Tyne
1872	University College Aberystwyth
1874	Yorkshire College, Leeds
1876	University College, Bristol
1879	Firth College, Sheffield
1880	Mason College, Birmingham
1880	Victoria University (Manchester, incl. Liverpool 1884, Leeds 1887)
1881	University College, Nottingham
1883	University College, Cardiff
1892	University Extension College, Reading
1893	Technical and University Extension College, Exeter
1895	London School of Economics
1897	University College of Sheffield
1900	University of Birmingham
1902	University College, Reading
1902	Hartley University College, Southampton
1903	University of Manchester
1904	University of Leeds

48 Hearnshaw, *Centenary History*, p. 136.
49 Negley Harte, *The University of London 1836–1986*, Athlone Press, London 1986, p. 93.
50 Ibid., p. 106.

1905	University of Sheffield
1909	University of Bristol
1922	University College, Exeter

On another dimension, the London model itself was copied elsewhere. In 1850, Queen's University was formed in Ireland to include the constituent colleges of Belfast, Cork, and Galway; in 1853 the University of Toronto was founded explicitly on the London model; the first three Indian universities, in Madras, Kolkata, and Mumbai, also followed the London model. In 1874 the University of New Zealand followed suit.[51]

Criticism was raised in the 1870s of a university institution devoted solely to examining, not teaching; and the formation in Manchester of the Victoria University during 1880 gave a further impetus to these arguments.[52] While Victoria University was federal in design, its degrees were in more specific, differentiated subjects. The examining structure of the University of London had facilitated the extension of university-level study and certification to the provinces, but its limitation of qualification to degrees in either arts, or sciences, or medicine ran counter to the specialisation emerging in the United States, as also in Cambridge. By the 1890s plans for the reform of the University of London on a Faculty basis were being drafted, and in 1898 an act of Parliament re-established London teaching. An economics curriculum was drawn up for a new Faculty of Economics, with a new BSc (Econ); and although there was a small department of economics at University College, the LSE quickly became identified with the Faculty of Economics, with its annual *Calendar* as the authoritative guide to teaching and reading. Continuous with London's previous degree-level qualifications, the BSc (Econ) provided a study programme that could be followed through full-time study at the LSE or University College London, at any participating college outside London and across the Empire, or even through private study. Through its role as a core institution of the University of London, the LSE came to define what the study of undergraduate economics meant in twentieth-century Britain.

At the same time, the internal organisation of the American university, based as it is on a transformation of a German model, became the model for the development of British universities during the twentieth century. The faculty and departmental structure of British universities, for example, emerged first in the London colleges and civic universities, and was only later adopted by Oxford and Cambridge. The modern university developed in this way as an institution conducting teaching and research across a broad spectrum of disciplines. The demand for their teaching came from the populations of the new industrial cities—they were both strictly secular, and open to women students. As the Charter of University College, Liverpool stated:

> The object of the College shall be to provide such instruction in all the branches of a liberal education as may enable residents in the city of Liverpool and the

[51] Bellot, *University College London*, p. 138.

[52] For an account of the Victoria University, see my 'Political Economy in the Northern Civic Universities', in Kadish, Tribe (eds.), *The Market for Political Economy*, pp. 188–93, 196–97.

> neighbourhood thereof to qualify for degrees in Arts, Science, and other subjects at any of the Universities granting degrees to non-resident students, and at the same time to give such technical instruction as may be of immediate service in professional and commercial life.[53]

The autonomy of these institutions was also underwritten by the creation of the familiar hierarchy of a University Court composed of representatives of the local business and administrative community, a Senate composed of all professors, with executive power in the hands of a Principal or Vice-Chancellor appointed by the Court. Professors were defined by the fact that they were required to devote themselves to the work associated with their chair and its development, besides concerning themselves with the general work of the college.

So long as these civic colleges were preparing students for a range of examinations, from Cambridge Highers[54] to University of London degrees, part-time students attending evening classes predominated in many subjects and there was no clear impulse to develop teaching in any one subject in a systematic manner. After 1900, many of these colleges won the right to award their own degrees, and with the emergence of more specific student demand the rapid shift to three-year courses with a definite sequence of subjects to be studied meant that a clear differentiation both within and between departments occurred. As student numbers rose, appointments had to be made in such a way that a given syllabus was adequately covered; and the annual appointment of external examiners, another innovation by the civic colleges, meant that there was an approximate equalisation of standards between institutions for any given subject of study. This combined with internal and external imperatives in the elaboration of disciplines to promote specific research traditions. Recruitment of permanent teachers to the modern university was henceforth on the basis of research potential, rather than teaching ability, and promotion became heavily weighted towards research-based criteria. All of these basic structural features of the British system were generated by the new civic foundations, and by the reformed University of London.

However, where British university education would continue to diverge from the American model for almost the remainder of the twentieth century was in its focus on undergraduate education. This focus would provide an early boost in student numbers for the development of the discipline in Britain, but would by mid-century have become a real limitation on disciplinary development. As will be shown in Chapter 5, Cambridge economists during the 1930s spent the greater part of their teaching time in supervising students who would go no further than Part I, and who would in any case achieve a poor classification. By contrast, in 1950 Dennis Coppock took a graduate semester at MIT with perhaps 30 graduate students on his course:

> I never experienced the undergraduate [course] at MIT and for all I know they had one thousand students in the first year course. But Samuelson's would be a good illustration. There would be a lecture room, perhaps twice the size of this [living room]

53 *Calendar of University College, Liverpool, 1882–83*, p. xl.

54 The first national school examinations were administered by Oxford and Cambridge examination boards established in 1857 and 1858 respectively; see Chapter 3, pp. 55–56.

with a sort of horseshoe table, Samuelson at the top; and we all sat round, and it was just a sort of Socratic discussion with Samuelson so far as I know never using a single note, writing his equations on the blackboard and forcing us to do the analysis.[55]

American undergraduate education is generalist, and relatively unspecialised; but the greater degree of specialisation in a British undergraduate degree by no means implies any equivalence with American graduate training. Coppock's comparison of numbers and his account of the teaching style is telling. By the early twentieth century, graduate-level tuition well beyond anything on offer in Britain had become established in the United States, and by the 1930s graduate numbers in economics there were already in excess of the number of undergraduate students of economics in Britain. The LSE was unusual in having a significant number of graduate students, and during the 1930s they played some role in the construction of the School's profile as anti-Keynesian. But these were doctoral students completing theses by independent study, not graduate students completing a number of taught courses.

The stalling of British twentieth-century university development at the level of undergraduate education, and the associated difficulty of building a departmental research culture, has many sources. While it was never recognised to be a problem until the 1960s at the earliest, this does not mean that the issue had not been anticipated. In 1902 Sidney Webb published an essay that identified London as the ideal location for a stratified programme of education, with mass undergraduate education provided locally, and high-level graduate education at the centre—an anticipation of the Californian system. He supposed that London undergraduates would overwhelmingly be London residents, and from its poorer families. This placed clear constraints on the organisation of the University as regards curriculum and geography; but not on its size. The University could certainly not be exclusive in the manner of Oxford and Cambridge; but it should therefore be prepared to enrol not hundreds of undergraduates, but thousands. Comparisons with Paris and Berlin suggested that 20,000 might be the upper limit. For these students a directly vocational appeal was necessary, with three or four years of enrolment terminating at the age of 22. But he envisaged a '... new aristocracy of advanced students, intent on pursuing their chosen subjects above and beyond the first, or 'bread-and-butter' degree.'[56] He already considered that for the highest grades of employment the undergraduate degree was inadequate: London provided the ideal location, so long as faculty-based, not collegiate, organisation became the norm.

The old conception of distinct colleges, each covering the whole range of the university curriculum, and able therefore to afford and employ only a single professor for each of the numerous subjects dealt with, is, as we have seen, for many reasons unsuited to London. The newer conception of university organisation, embodied in the creation of faculties each composed of coequal professors of identical type, teaching the same subject at different institutions, is only one step in the right direction.[57]

[55] Interview with Dennis Coppock, 29 April 1994, Stockport.

[56] Sidney Webb, 'London University: A Policy and a Forecast', *The Nineteenth Century and After* Vol. 51 (June 1902), p. 916.

[57] Ibid., p. 923.

A far more differentiated structure was needed—a 'natural division of labour within each faculty' leading to specialisation, and a stratification between principal professors who will lead research, and enjoy life tenure, high salaries, and abundant leisure, while the bulk of teaching staff on short-term contracts at modest salaries would work at times and seasons convenient to the students that they serve.

> And we cannot afford to waste the most distinguished scientific talent on the drudgery of lecturing day by day to the mere undergraduate.... No university policy can be successful unless it keeps in mind constantly that the duty of the principal professors is not the mere teaching of what is known, but the discovery of new truth. Thus, instead of the teacher's life being subordinated to the needs of the student, as in undergraduate centres it must and should be, every other task imposed upon the professor should, in the post-graduate centres, give way to the professor's own researches.[58]

Although this vision is formally similar to that of Veblen, Webb makes a clear distinction between the importance of undergraduate education for the broad masses, and the relevance of specialised training for the select few.

In 1910 he elaborated his arguments before a Royal Commission, presenting a memorandum on 'The Nature of the University Problem in the Metropolis'. By 1941, he estimated, the London catchment area would have risen to some 15 million people, or three times the contemporary population of The Netherlands. Given the limited means of undergraduates, residential education was not a possibility for most; and the cost of commuting from suburbs to the centre would exceed the fees charged for a degree course at Glasgow or Edinburgh. Hence undergraduate instruction should be dispersed, and take place in the evening as well as the day. It could be attached to polytechnics and technical colleges, with a strictly vocational curriculum. The most imperative task for a great London University is that it become '... the foremost post-graduate centre of the intellectual world'.

> Those who shrink appalled from the vision of 10 or 20 thousand undergraduates, dispersed among 40 or 50 teaching centres, at such unacademic places as Tottenham and West Ham, Farnham and Chatham, Barnet and Brighton, may find comfort in the arrangements for the post-graduate students, whom we might expect to see numbered at least by thousands.... Here the policy ought, in my opinion, to be one of extreme concentration.[59]

The seminars and specialist lectures of the central colleges should be geared principally to postgraduates, undergraduates being only a secondary consideration. Furthermore, it was desirable that students move between universities, as in Germany and Austria. As this became an international process, with students from the United States, Continental Europe, and the Far East, London had special advantages. Younger

[58] Ibid., p. 924.

[59] Royal Commission on University Education in London, *Appendix to First Report of the Commissioners. Minutes of Evidence, July 1909–April 1910*, Cd.5166 HMSO, London 1910, p. 23.

residents could also pursue postgraduate study alongside employment, in day or evening courses. In this way, those trained in overseas universities would be mingled with poorer Londoners with experience of commerce and employment.

> The new centres of University instruction that will gradually develop at such centres of population as Brighton and Colchester and Croydon and West Ham will almost certainly grow out of the 'mixed' institutions that the municipal authorities are slowly building up.
>
> It will be seen that, in my judgement, the only way by which the vast population that London University has to serve can possibly be provided with university education is by a great amount of differentiation—geographical differentiation, differentiation in the kind of education given, differentiation in the hours and seasons of study, differentiation in subjects, differentiation in the professoriate, differentiation in the institutions, differentiation in motives and differentiation even in the spirit of the work. We have so far failed to build up an adequate University for London because we have been too much under the dominion of the ideals and methods of other Universities, which have to deal with a much simpler and essentially different problem.[60]

While not necessarily a mirage, Webb was certainly too many steps ahead of anyone at that time, or since.

[60] Ibid., p. 27.

3

The Social Mediation of Economic Discourse

In the course of the nineteenth century, existing universities underwent a transformation, from 'classical'—both the Continental European four-faculty model, and also the English model focussed upon classics and mathematics—to 'modern', a more broadly-based institution teaching a range of new subjects, from the natural sciences through languages to engineering and commerce. These subjects were works in progress, constructed by the academics whose contribution to disciplinary development was tempered by the need to train their successors. The chief public function of a university remained nonetheless the same: to prepare young people for their future employment.[1] Besides the curricular modernisation, this transition involved a progressive expansion in the number of institutions and students, and the development of specialised qualifications matching student to employment. In the process, new disciplines were created from bodies of knowledge that had been cultivated for other purposes and in different contexts. While this might be viewed as but one part of a process of rationalisation—if not 'modernisation', then a transition to 'modernity'—this narrative implies a degree of teleology: that there is, from the perspective of any given discipline, an implicit movement towards a given end-point that is in turn a starting point, a *longue durée* of institutionalisation.

The story presented here is rather different: that the advance of further and higher formal education fed off existing institutions and practices, constructing for itself bodies of knowledge legitimated by its own academic standing and in the process displacing the more diverse public forms of knowledge on which it had built. This self-constructing, self-validating process is 'scientisation', or *Verwissenschaftlichung*. While often legitimated in terms of its epistemological virtues, at its core lies not the elaboration of theory, but the training of students; for without a body of students possessing the skills and techniques associated with a particular discipline, that discipline cannot advance. That is why the account of the construction of an economics discipline given here focusses upon the question of how it came to be taught the way it is, and what was taught, rather than the more conventional focus on the examination and validation of theories and principles according to a modern sensibility. This chapter develops a response to that question by examining how the media through which knowledge is transmitted shape, define, and legitimate that knowledge.

The first 'economists' were mid-eighteenth-century French writers who developed a particular way of thinking about economic activity in *ancien régime* France—*les Économistes*, who later adopted the title 'Physiocrat' because of their belief that economic policy should conform to the 'laws of nature'. While their particular approach

[1] This is not to deny that enhancing a capacity for personal development is a very important feature of university attendance; but in the absence of modern universities, only the rich would enjoy access to this pathway to cultural capital.

Constructing Economic Science. Keith Tribe, Oxford University Press. © Oxford University Press 2022.
DOI: 10.1093/oso/9780190491741.003.0003

was idiosyncratic, their interest was not—right across eighteenth-century Europe and North America, societies and associations formed to discuss issues chiefly related to agriculture,[2] periodicals were founded, essay prizes announced, libraries established, pamphlets and books composed. Participation in economic discourse required only interest, and the leisure to pursue this interest. An enormous amount of writing was generated, as testified for instance by the 6,741 entries in Henry Higgs's *Bibliography of Economics 1751–1775*.[3] In 1734 Melon published his 'essay on commerce', arguing for the importance of luxury consumption in the promotion of national wealth.[4] Cantillon wrote his *Essai sur la nature du commerce en général* around the same time.[5] By mid-century, treatises were beginning to be published—Justi's *Staatswirthschaft* in 1755, James Steuart's *Inquiry into the Principles of Political Oeconomy* in 1767, Genovesi's *Lezioni di economia civile* in 1768. After Smith's *Wealth of Nations* was published in 1776 there was something of a lull in this progression, resuming with Say's *Traité* in 1803 and a flurry of German academic treatises that culminated in the publication of the first volume of Rau's *Lehrbuch* in 1826. These German, French, and Italian publications reflected a new linkage to systematic teaching, whereas the texts of Smith and Steuart had been contributions to public discussion. An associated subtle alteration in the identification of an 'economist' is also implied in this publishing history. Whereas in the eighteenth century this term would have been applied to any who talked about economic issues, by the early nineteenth century this was coming to mean those who read about them, who were informed rather than merely interested.

In the course of the nineteenth century, popular interest in economic issues broadened, and the media disseminating economic discourse grew more diverse. The formalisation of education at all levels first drew on these processes, then began to systematise them. While the 'principles of political economy' as presented by Malthus and Ricardo went little further than analyses of value, wages, rents, and profits, by the last third of the century a work on the 'principles of political economy' was a textbook delineating a much-enlarged field of knowledge. The earlier literature now became a backstory of early initiatives and proposals. In some cases, such as the teaching of the *Cameralwissenschaften* in eighteenth-century German universities, or the teaching of political economy at East India College,[6] there were clear vocational objectives that made an understanding of economic principles an important element of student education. Likewise, various French initiatives during the first half of the nineteenth century demonstrated the existence of a broader public interest in the acquisition of knowledge of the principles of political economy.[7] Everywhere, however,

[2] For an overview of the extent of this, see Koen Stapelbroek and Jani Marjanen, 'Political Economy, Patriotism and the Rise of Societies', pp. 13–17, the introduction to Stapelbroek and Marjanan (eds.) *The Rise of Economic Societies in the Eighteenth Century: Patriotic Reform in Europe and North America*, Palgrave, Houndmills UK 2012.

[3] Henry Higgs, *Bibliography of Economics 1751–1775*, Cambridge University Press, London 1935.

[4] Jean-François Melon, *Essai politique sur la commerce*, Presses universitaires de Caen, Caen 2014.

[5] For the difficulty in identifying the compositional history of this text, eventually published in 1755, see *Richard Cantillon's Essay on the Nature of Trade in General: A Variorum Edition*, ed. Richard van den Berg, Routledge, Abingdon UK 2015.

[6] Discussed briefly later in this chapter.

[7] Lucette Le Van-Lemesle, *Le juste et la riche. L'enseignement de l'économie politique 1815–1950*, Comité pour l'histoire économique et financière de la France, Paris 2004, pp. 60–77.

these principles were thought to be limited in number, and accessible as much by private study of a few books as from public lectures, not from a dedicated programme of study. Since the emergence of vocational educational provision is so often treated as merely a routine and functional by-product of modernity, the history of educational systems can too easily become written as the emergence of whatever the received wisdom of today might be; a story of the toils of past reformers who, in overcoming the various 'impediments' that were presented to their 'reforms', succeeded in creating the institutions with which we are today familiar. But to see why the discipline of economics took the form that it did, we need to disengage ourselves from such ideas.

By making an elementary distinction between a demand for the systematic teaching of economics and the provision of such teaching in regular educational establishments, we can locate an important element in the forces that made economics part of the curricular menu offered by the modern university: that the origins of the discipline of economics are to be found not in a growing public demand for it, but instead in a concerted but diverse effort to provide training in economics by individuals who believed this was needed, and who worked in institutions that might supply it. Systematic economic instruction creating trained 'economists' was not demand-led, but instead resulted from a supply-push anticipating changes in labour markets and qualifications. What the student of economics got was determined not necessarily by what that student was seeking, but by what academics thought that student should have. In any case, programmes of study had first to be established before students could sign up for them. Furthermore, insofar as student demand for such teaching can be treated as a derived demand, originating in students' perceptions of the kind of skills and qualifications that a changing labour market called for, it is also possible to demonstrate that everywhere the real demand for qualified economists was in fact limited. As Ashley would discover in Birmingham, few employers were interested in students with a degree in commerce. Indeed, during the 1920s there are indications that the primary specialised destination of those with degrees in commerce was as teachers of commerce in colleges. This pattern also seems to have fitted Britain during the expansion of school education in economics during the 1950s—that the primary occupation for which economics graduates were fitted was that of teaching economics in schools and colleges, not in administration and commercial employment as in the United States.

Calls for the development of regular teaching in economic subjects at an advanced level date back to the early eighteenth century in Germany,[8] and the second half of that century in Britain. In the latter case, repeated calls for the teaching of commercial subjects within Dissenting Academies testify not to any demand, but rather to the *absence* of provision and a *lack* of any will to remedy it.[9] This suggests that expressions

[8] See my *Governing Economy: The Reformation of German Economic Discourse, 1750–1850*, 2nd edition, Threshold Press, Newbury 2017, pp. 48ff.

[9] In 1765 Joseph Priestley advocated instruction in '... civil history, and more especially, the more important elements of civil policy; such as the theory of laws, government, manufactures, commerce, naval force &c. with whatever may be demonstrated from history to have contributed to the flourishing state of nations, to rendering a people happy and populous at home, and formidable abroad; together with those articles of previous information without which it is impossible to understand the nature, connections and mutual influences of those great objects.' *An Essay on a Course of Liberal Education for Civil and Active Life*, London 1765, p. 10. Twenty years later, Thomas Barnes spoke of 'the benefits of a liberal education to

of the need for this or that subject to be taught in a university context are not the same thing as a demand on the part of students positively willing to sign up for courses in these subjects. And readiness to 'meet a need' does not of itself constitute any proof that such a need exists. Apart from anything else, we should also pay attention to who is making the argument that such a need exists. For university teaching in any subject to be sustained, an annually-renewed stream of students is required, and there are many factors that enter into the creation of this steady stream. To fully understand the way in which the programmes discussed in the following chapters were eventually designed, and the subject shaped, we first have to understand the shifting and variable public interest in matters economic, in response to which university economics eventually developed and could be represented as meeting that interest.

Societies and Associations

In June 1723 the 'Honourable the Society of Improvers in the Knowledge of Agriculture in Scotland' was founded as the very first of a considerable number of European economic and patriotic societies. A listing of its membership from 1843 shows that of 301 members, most were from the Scottish aristocracy and landed gentry, together with lawyers, administrators, physicians, professors, and six army officers; but only three merchants, three 'gardeners', and no clergy at all. The broad aims of the society were to collect information on best practice in husbandry, and disseminate this among the membership and the wider public through written materials and by the example of the members' own farms. In itself, this was part of the re-establishment of Edinburgh as Scotland's cultural and political centre, combining the diffusion of polite sociability with the patriotic goal of national improvement. Besides the activity it fostered, it also served as a model for later Scottish societies, such as the Select Society (founded 1754), the Edinburgh Society for Encouraging Art, Science, Manufactures and Agriculture (founded 1755), and the Royal Society of Edinburgh (founded 1783), leading to the establishment of a chair in agriculture at the University of Edinburgh in 1790.[10] The Scottish society was quickly followed by the Dublin Society for Improving Husbandry, Manufactures and other Useful Arts, originating in 1731, and which likewise served as a model for many similar societies.[11] As with the Scottish society, its objects were practical, descriptions of good technique being disseminated in discussion and publication.[12]

those destined for the Ministry, together with the purpose of "preparatory instruction for the other learned professions—as well as for civil and commercial life". *Discourse Delivered at the Commencement of the Manchester Academy September XIV MDCCLXXXVI*, Warrington 1786, p. 9. This repetition indicates that the idea remained an aspiration.

[10] Brian Bonneyman, 'Agrarian Patriotism and the Landed Interest: The Scottish "Society of Improvers in the Knowledge of Agriculture," 1723–1746', in Stapelbroek and Marjanan (eds.) *The Rise of Economic Societies in the Eighteenth Century*, pp. 34, 37–38, 28, 50.

[11] See, for example, John Shovlin, 'The Society of Brittany and the Irish Economic Model: International Competition and the Politics of Provincial Development', in Stapelbroek and Marjanan (eds.) *The Rise of Economic Societies in the Eighteenth Century*, pp. 73–95.

[12] During the 1750s the Dublin Society had established an exhibition centre for agricultural machinery and implements, and premiums were awarded for tree-planting, land reclamation and drainage, liming,

The most enduring and successful of these early foundations was, however, the 'Society for the Encouragement of Arts, Manufactures and Commerce', founded with an inaugural meeting in a Covent Garden coffee house in 1754 and soon referred to as the 'Society of Arts'.[13] Those present at its first meeting noted, for example, that cobalt and madder, basic to the dyeing of textiles, were currently imported at great expense, and a prize was offered to anyone discovering a source of cobalt in Britain, and successfully cultivating madder.[14] During the first one hundred years of its existence the Society offered many such prizes and reported on their outcome. Based in London, membership quickly reached 2,500, the *Museum Rusticum et Commerciale* and then later *Memoirs of Agriculture and other Oeconomical Arts* summarising its activities. In the 1840s the Society sponsored exhibitions of manufactured goods, culminating in the Great Exhibition of 1851; and then from 1856 set the first national examinations in modern and commercial subjects, written examinations being sat in 40 centres in 1858.[15] The provision of these national examinations, together with the later Cambridge Local examinations, formed an important bridge in provincial Britain to the new London University BA.

Besides the Society of Arts, dedicated to improvements in technique and practice, societies devoted to public debate flourished in Britain during the latter part of the eighteenth century, such as the Robin Hood Society in London, the Manchester Conversation Society, and the Amicable Debating Society in Birmingham.[16] The broad purpose of these and many similar societies was to bring together men who, on the basis of their reading, could exercise their understanding of what they had read through public discussion. As William Godwin later noted, the ideal society was composed of

> ... a number of individuals who, having stored their minds with reading and reflection, are accustomed, in candid and unreserved conversation, to compare their ideas, suggest their doubts, examine their mutual difficulties and cultivate a perspicuous and animated manner of delivering their sentiments.[17]

These societies were vehicles not only for mutual education, but also for training in argument and persuasion; the Edinburgh Speculative Society was a noteworthy example of this, with a purpose-built debating chamber and a membership limited at first to 25. Here Francis Horner and his contemporaries[18] self-consciously honed their rhetorical skills before making their transition to London in the early 1800s.[19]

and the cultivation of flax, cereals, and hops. K. Hudson, *Patriotism with Profit: British Agricultural Societies in the Eighteenth and Nineteenth Centuries*, Hugh Evelyn, London 1972, p. 7.

[13] In 1908 this became the Royal Society of Arts.

[14] Prizes were also to be given to young people for drawing; D. Hudson, K. W. Luckhurst, *The Royal Society of Arts 1754–1954*, John Murray, London 1954, p. 8.

[15] Ibid., p. 251.

[16] T. Fawcett, 'Eighteenth-Century Debating Societies', *British Journal of Eighteenth Century Studies* Vol. 3 (1986), pp. 216–19.

[17] William Godwin, *Enquiry Concerning Political Justice*, Penguin Books, Harmondsworth 1976, p. 289.

[18] Horner (1778–1817) attended Dugald Stewart's Edinburgh lectures on political economy before, in 1802, contributing to the foundation of the *Edinburgh Review*. He became an MP in 1806.

[19] Fawcett, 'Eighteenth-Century Debating Societies', p. 223, quoting from Horner's journal for 1799.

But during the 1790s public discussion of social and political issues came to be thought potentially seditious. The gagging acts of 1795, prompted among other things by the activities of London Jacobin clubs,[20] put paid to discussion of politics, and by extension political economy, in most provincial clubs and societies—and this proscription survived, self-imposed, into the 1820s and 1830s, when Mechanics' Institutes explicitly excluded discussion of political issues from their proceedings.[21] Seen in this context, it is perhaps more understandable that the public dissemination of political economy in the nineteenth century developed along two broad paths: as a subject of theoretical discussion among the members of closed dining clubs; and as a form of didactic public enlightenment. When, for example, John Barrington discovered that workmen at his Dublin firm had combined together with the intent of raising wages, his response was to endow a series of public lectures on political economy for the purpose of informing workers and others of their true interests. Established in 1834, responsibility for organising lectures was transferred to the Dublin Statistical Society in 1849, lecturers being required to give annually eight lectures in Dublin and not less than 24 in four or more other Irish towns and villages. The venues at which these lectures were delivered were provided by a broad range of mechanics' institutes, literary and philosophical societies, and other mutual improvement societies.[22] The 'diffusion of useful knowledge' in the first half of the nineteenth century was facilitated by a dense network of societies and associations of this kind in both principal cities and the provinces.[23] The Dublin Society—its full title was 'The Statistical and Social Inquiry Society of Ireland'—was itself formed in 1847 to further social reform, and in this case there was a strong connection with political economy in the form of the first President, Richard Whately, while Mountifort Longfield was among the Vice Presidents.[24]

Such open discussion was thought inadvisable in the 1820s. The creation of the Political Economy Club in 1821, limited to 30 members who met monthly to dine and debate in private, highlights the political sensitivity of political economy at this time, something to which George Birkbeck alluded in his 1823 opening address to the London Mechanics' Institution. Thomas Tooke had taken the initiative in forming a

[20] Günther Lottes draws attention to some of the more prosaic difficulties in organising moderate and disciplined public debate at this time—the only indoor space where public discussion could be organised was typically a tavern, and as the evening wore on meetings became increasingly unruly, especially since many of the participants were unpractised in public speaking, and the basic rules of speaking in turn were not consistently observed: Lottes, *Politische Aufklärung und plebijisches Publikum. Zur Theorie und Praxis des englischen Radikalismus im späten 18.Jahrhundert*, Oldenbourg, Munich 1979, pp. 45ff.

[21] George Birkbeck, opening the London Mechanics Institution in 1823, stated, 'All intention of interference with political questions we do therefore disclaim.... If indirectly we shall be supposed to exercise any influence, - and education may extend the views of the Mechanic, - I am persuaded we shall invigorate the attachment which must ever exist to every wise and well-constructed system of legislation.' Cited in T. Kelly, *A History of Adult Education in Britain*, 2nd ed., Liverpool University Press, Liverpool 1970, p. 122.

[22] T. A. Boylan, T. P. Foley, *Political Economy and Colonial Ireland*, Routledge, London 1992, pp. 100–4.

[23] See I. Inkster, 'The Public Lecture as an Instrument of Science Education for Adults: The Case of Great Britain, c. 1750–1850', *Paedogogica Historica* Vol. 20 (1981), pp. 80–107.

[24] M. E. Daly, *The Spirit of Earnest Inquiry: The Statistical and Social Inquiry Society of Ireland 1847–1997*, The Statistical and Social Inquiry Society of Ireland, Dublin 1997, p. 12. Richard Whately (1787–1863) had been Drummond Professor of Political Economy during 1829–1831, before his appointment as Archbishop of Dublin, and he played a prominent part in Irish national education. Mountifort Longfield (1802–1884) was appointed first Professor of Political Economy at Trinity College, Dublin, in 1832.

dining club following his attendance at a dinner party to discuss matters relating to free trade, held in January 1820 at the house of S. C. Holland, a Baring & Co. partner. He had found it disconcerting that, while all present professed allegiance to the principles of free trade, some of his fellow diners had a very rudimentary grasp of political economy, and the more they talked, the greater the number of exemptions from the principles of free trade for this or that good they proposed.[25] He concluded that a means was required through which men of affairs could become better acquainted with the principles of free trade. The following year a small group met and determined to form a society for the promotion of political economy, James Mill being delegated to draft a constitution. Of the 17 men present at the first meeting on 30 April 1821, only five names are today recognisable as political economists: Torrens, Malthus, Ricardo, Mill, and Tooke. The remainder were City men, bankers, MPs, and merchants.[26] Those present agreed to James Mill's proposal that

> [t]he members of this Society will regard their own mutual instruction, and the diffusion among others of just principles of Political Economy as a real and important obligation.
>
> ... It shall be considered the duty of the Society to study the means of obtaining access to the public mind through as many as possible of the periodical publications of the day, and to influence as far as possible the tone of such publications in favour of just principles of Political Economy.[27]

However, Mill's proposal that each member should report orally on their reading since the last meeting was not well-received, nor was his proposal that a standing committee should propagate their discussions to the press; and he later ceased attending.[28] This reticence marked the privacy of the Club's proceedings: that it was not intended as a vehicle for the broader dissemination of political economy.

The chief function of the Club, besides dining, was to discuss questions proposed by members, any member being able to table as many questions as he wished, the existing list being then read out at the conclusion of each meeting, and questions selected from that list in any order that members chose. The minutes record the list of questions, but not the related discussion, and so no direct assessment can be made of the tenor or quality of argument. It is clear, however, that questions were initially tabled faster than they could be discussed, and the fact that by the mid-1830s the minutes record only one or two questions suggests that these represent those actually discussed. It is also from about this time that the great majority of those responsible for tabling questions can consistently be identified as 'economists' rather than MPs or bankers; from which date the pattern is set that the minority of 'economists' proposed the questions and,

[25] Henry Higgs, 'Introduction' to Political Economy Club, *Minutes of Proceedings, 1899–1920*, Macmillan, London 1921, p. x.

[26] See my 'Founders of the Political Economy Club', *Oxford Dictionary of National Biography* (online) for details of membership.

[27] Meeting of 30 April 1821, Freemason's Tavern, Political Economy Club, *Minutes of Proceedings, 1899–1920*, pp. 3, 5.

[28] As noted by Mallet in his diary for 15 April 1831, Political Economy Club, *Minutes of Proceedings, 1899–1920*, p. 224.

we might suppose, guided discussion, notwithstanding the constant predominance of members from the world of commerce and politics.[29]

Popular Pedagogy and Self-Education

The Political Economy Club had baulked at James Mill's proposals for public dissemination of its discussions, but general popular instruction was already developing through the medium of Mechanics' Institutes. This movement began in Scotland, with the appointment of George Birkbeck to the chair of Natural Philosophy at Glasgow's Anderson Institute in 1799. When Birkbeck left Glasgow in 1804 he was replaced by Andrew Ure, whose teaching inspired Leonard Horner[30] to promote the creation in 1821 of the Edinburgh School of Arts. This was the first 'Mechanics' Institute', whose purpose

> ... was to provide for working men systematic courses of lectures, 'in such branches of physical science as are of practical advantage in their several trades'—notably chemistry, mechanics and mathematics—but the other characteristic features of a mechanics' institute quickly developed: classes for more elementary instruction; a library, and a collection of models and apparatus for experiments.[31]

Then, in July 1823, the mechanics' class at the Anderson Institute broke away to form the Glasgow Mechanics' Institution, whose lecture room was a disused chapel, and which had a paid lecturer who organised courses in natural philosophy, chemistry, mechanics, and mathematics. When news of this reached London, the editors of the newly-founded *Mechanics' Magazine* proposed that a London institution be established. This proposal quickly gathered support from George Birkbeck, Francis Place, Henry Brougham, Sir Francis Burdett, Jeremy Bentham, James Mill, and George Grote, among others—basically the same network that would move on to create the University of London.

The movement quickly gathered pace: 13 new institutions were founded in 1824, and 70 in 1825. By 1826 there were well over 100, but in England this was a temporary peak. The outcome of the subsequent consolidation was a shift in the composition of the membership: skilled workers remained, and those who had left were replaced by clerks and shopworkers. Then the numbers headed upwards again, with some 300 institutions in 1841; and, after another brief decline in the early 1840s, there were by 1851 around 700 institutions nationwide, hardly any town without an

[29] The first meeting of the Club in 1900, on 2 February, was attended by 15 members, only four of whom (Llewellyn Smith, Hewins, Foxwell, and Higgs) could be described as 'economists' in the modern sense. (Llewellyn Smith was at this time First Commissioner for Labour in the Board of Trade). Political Economy Club, *Minutes of Proceedings, 1899–1920*, p. 127.

[30] Leonard Horner (1785–1864) was the brother of Francis, also studying political economy at Edinburgh with Dugald Stewart and contributing to the creation of the *Edinburgh Review*. In 1833 he was appointed a factory inspector, from 1837 responsible for Manchester, Yorkshire, and Northern England, retiring in 1859.

[31] Kelly, *History of Adult Education*, p. 119.

institution, and some sited in villages. With the shifts in numbers, the curriculum also altered; the systematic courses on science that had been provided initially gave way to single lectures and short courses, and courses of lectures were displaced by classes. In Huddersfield during 1851, for example, there were classes in reading, writing, and arithmetic, music, elocution, composition, shorthand, geography, history, drawing, French, German, grammar, geometry, book-keeping, literature, chemistry, and natural philosophy.[32] Nationally the social composition of institutions also changed in mid-century. In Scotland and Northern England the membership was still formed primarily of craftsmen, clerks, operatives, and shop assistants; and these institutions began to move towards formal technical education. In the south, however, middle-class members predominated and the institutions became more like Literary and Philosophical Societies, in which there was an emphasis upon the library, general lectures, and social activities, rather than classes.[33]

'Lit and Phil' societies had existed since the later eighteenth century, the Manchester Society being founded in 1781 and the Newcastle Society in 1793. While their functions were formally similar to that of the later Mechanics' Institutes—lectures on the natural sciences and literature, the establishment of a library—they served a more cultural than pedagogic function and were, importantly, more socially exclusive. Until 1799 the Manchester Society met in the Cross Street Chapel, underlining the connection not only to Dissent, but also to the commercial class of Manchester. During the 1820s Lit and Phil societies were formed in many major towns and cities, and their importance for us here is that this network was the basis on which the British Association for the Advancement of Science developed. The Yorkshire Philosophical Society hosted in York the first annual meeting of this organisation in 1831, and inaugurated a pattern that continues to the present day: a peripatetic organisation for the dissemination of scientific knowledge whose annual conferences are organised by a local committee elected at the previous year's meeting. Its programmatic commitment to the diffusion of scientific knowledge was reinforced by its peripatetic character, meeting in a succession of provincial cities whose populations were therefore exposed in turn to national debates and issues.[34] The third 1833 meeting of the British Association was in Cambridge, and this brought together Adolphe Quetelet, Robert Malthus, Richard Jones, and William Whewell, who after discussion in Jones's college rooms proposed that the Association create a new grouping, 'Section F: Statistics'. That year Adam Sedgwick was President, and in announcing the formation of a new, sixth section, he insisted

> ... that it should limit itself to 'matters of fact', 'mere abstractions', and 'numerical results', constituting what might be called 'the raw material to political economy and

[32] Ibid., p. 128.

[33] Ibid., p. 198.

[34] J. Morrell, A. Thackray, *Gentlemen of Science: Early Years of the British Association for the Advancement of Science*, Oxford University Press, Oxford 1981, pp. 92–93. Subsequent meetings were held in Oxford, Cambridge, Edinburgh, Dublin, Bristol, Liverpool, Newcastle, Birmingham, Glasgow, Plymouth, Manchester, Cork, and back to York in 1844: Appendix III Table A3, Morrell and Thackray, p. 548.

> political philosophy', by which perhaps 'the lasting foundations of those sciences may be ultimately laid'.[35]

Guy makes clear that the term 'statistics' derived from the German *Statistik*, a branch of learning originating with Gottfried Achenwall in 1749 and which concerned the description of the advantages, history, and origin of states:

> But it is not everything that can be truly said of a State that properly finds a place in statistics, but only what contributes to political knowledge, and the more any matter concerns the general well-being of a State the more necessary is it that it should find its illustration in statistics.[36]

Within the year the London Statistical Society had been formed to 'illustrate the condition and prospects of society', and committed to excluding carefully 'all opinions from its transactions and publications—to confine its attention rigorously to facts—and, as far as it may be found possible, to facts which can be "stated numerically, and arranged in tables"'.[37]

The renaming of Section F in 1856 as a 'Section for Economic Science and Statistics' made the linkage between political economy and practical social policy more explicit. This was in conformity with Richard Jones's project for an empirically-founded political economy, recalling an earlier understanding of the subject as the 'anatomy of nations'. The broad range of topics that this involved was outlined in a paper presented to Section F in 1838; the categories to be used by local societies in collecting data were grouped according to the following heads:

I. Physical Statistics; relating to Topography, etc.
II. Vital Statistics; relating to the Physical Being of Man.
III. Mental Statistics; relating to the Intellectual and Moral being of Man.
IV. Economic Statistics; relating to the Social Condition of Man.
V. Miscellaneous.[38]

The resulting diversity of papers presented at the annual meetings was ensured by the absence of any formal control over who might attend, present, and join in discussion; in the early years many sections simply accepted offers of papers in the order they were made until their timetable was full. For Section F the outcome was decidedly mixed, most of the papers being extremely descriptive, prompted by no discernible

[35] Quoted by W. A. Guy, 'On the Original and Acquired Meaning of the term "Statistics," and on the Proper Functions of a Statistical Society: also on the Question Whether There be a Science of Statistics; and if so, what are its Nature and Objects, and what is its Relation to Political Economy and "Social Science"', *Journal of the Statistical Society of London* Vol. 28 (December 1865), p. 482.

[36] Ibid., p. 479.

[37] Ibid., p. 482.

[38] S. Hare, 'Abstract of Outline of Subjects for Statistical Enquiries', *Journal of the Statistical Society of London* Vol. 1 (November 1838), p. 427. Hare was President of the Leeds Statistical Society. See also 'Proceedings of Statistical Societies', *Journal of the Statistical Society of London* Vol. 1 No. 9 (January 1839), pp. 546–54, which provides summaries of the proceedings of the London, Manchester, Bristol, Liverpool, and Ulster societies.

agenda. Those attending the annual meetings of Section F were drawn from diverse backgrounds, although contemporary specialists in the literature of political economy were always present, if not as presenters of papers. In 1877 Francis Galton tabled a proposal to dissolve Section F, on the grounds that it represented interests not properly part of an organisation devoted to the advancement of science. His chief complaint concerned the entirely heterogeneous nature of the statistical papers presented to the sessions of Section F, not the inclusion of political economy. But his criticism was motivated by his very modern understanding of 'statistics':

> The principles on which Statistics are founded are derived from the theory of probabilities, and have exercised, and will still exercise, the ingenuity of many generations of the ablest mathematicians.[39]

Few, if any, of his contemporaries shared this understanding of 'statistics'.[40] Galton listed, in just under two pages, the titles of papers read before Section F in 1873–1875, a mélange of topics loosely related to economic matters but which simply reflects the prevailing diffuse interest in matters of social and economic reform.[41] He further argued that the subjects 'commonly brought before Section F cannot be considered scientific in the sense of the word that is sanctioned by the usages of the British Association'. If the Section were suppressed, he suggested that discussion would readily find a forum at the congresses of the Social Science Association, where there 'will always be a larger gathering of experts in these subjects. . . .'[42]

The other paper submitted to the Council on this issue pointed out that the papers listed by Galton belonged in the long line of 'vital statistics', named as such first by Laplace. A letter from Robert Giffen and Hammond Chubb, secretaries of the Section, underlined this objection, also noting that Section F was, more than the other sections, exposed to the attentions of non-specialists:

> Its subjects are also those of practical politics and philanthropy, and this brings to the discussion people who are politicians and philanthropists, but who are not men of science. For the same reason, the discussions on such subjects, whether scientific or not, are likely to be better reported than purely scientific discussions.[43]

[39] F. Galton, 'Economic Science and the British Association', *Journal of the Statistical Society of London* Vol. 40 (September 1877), p. 469.

[40] See Stephen M. Stigler, *The History of Statistics: The Measurement of Uncertainty before 1900*, Harvard University Press, Cambridge Mass. 1986, Chs. 7 and 8, for a discussion of the probabilistic transformation of statistics; also Lorraine Daston, 'How Probabilities Came to Be Objective and Subjective', *Historia Mathematica* Vol. 21 (1994), pp. 330–44.

[41] E.g. 'Industrial Schools', 'Education Statistics of Bradford', 'Prevailing Mode of Preparation for Competitive Examinations', 'Economical Aspects of Endowments of Education and Original Research', to select four successive titles at random.

[42] Galton, 'Economic Science', p. 472.

[43] Robert Giffen, Hammond Chubb, letter of 13 July, included in 'Considerations, in the form of a Draft Report, submitted to Committee, favourable to the maintenance of Section F. By Dr. W. Farr', in *Journal of the Statistical Society of London* Vol. 40 (September 1877), p. 475.

A further defence of Section F was published in *The Economist* for 8 September 1877. The important point was made here that, while the next incumbent President of the British Association was nominated one year in advance, this was not the case for the individual sections, where the individual Section Heads were sometimes appointed just a few weeks before the annual meeting. They were not therefore in a position to choose their speakers, let alone a common theme for discussion, and as a consequence papers were presented by those who happened to turn up on the day. In the case of Section F, this writer also made the entirely sensible suggestion that the London Statistical Society should establish a standing committee charged with providing assistance to the President-elect of the Section, enabling a programme of papers to be determined in advance and to arrange that each session was attended by those capable of sustaining scientific discussion.[44]

The proposal to exclude Section F from the meetings of the British Association turns therefore not upon the lack of development of political economy, but rather on an organisational problem that reveals something rather different about the condition of political economy in the later nineteenth century. There was indeed widespread interest in the subject matter with which it dealt; but popular understanding linked it firmly to social reform, and did not regard it primarily as a theoretical enterprise whose principles required extensive public debate. Galton's listing of the papers presented over a three-year period unintentionally lends insight into the contemporary vitality of interest in political economy. As the University Extension movement of the later nineteenth century demonstrated, there was indeed a wide interest in economic issues; but this interest was informed by only the most rudimentary knowledge of economic principles. The early economic societies reflected both this interest and the generally low level of economic debate; the papers presented at the Social Science Association provide a clearer idea of these practical concerns associated with political economy in the latter half of the nineteenth century.

This organisation had originated as the 'National Association for the Moral and Social Improvement of the People' in a meeting at Henry Brougham's London house in July 1857; the term 'social science' was only introduced shortly before the first meeting in Birmingham later that year.[45] This initiated a series of annual, peripatetic week-long meetings modelled on the practice of the British Association, the organisation dissolving in 1886. Its deliberations were divided among five sections: 'Jurisprudence and the Amendment of the Law', 'Education', 'Punishment and Reformation', 'Public Health', and 'Social Economy' (later the 'Economy and Trade' Department).[46] Whereas the purpose of the British Association was to diffuse an understanding of science, the emphasis in the Social Science Association was to provide a forum through which pressure could be brought to bear upon central and local government for reform. The inaugural General Committee, for example, included 18 peers, 28 MPs, Edwin

[44] F. R. S., 'The Proposed Discontinuance of Section F, Economic Science and Statistics, at the British Association', *Journal of the Statistical Society of London* Vol. 40 (December 1877), pp. 631–32, reprinting the article from *The Economist*.

[45] L. Goldman, 'A Peculiarity of the English? The Social Science Association and the Absence of Sociology in Nineteenth-Century Britain', *Past and Present* No. 114 (1987), p. 139.

[46] L. Goldman, 'The Social Sciences Association, 1857–1886: A Context for Mid-Victorian Liberalism', *English Historical Review* Vol. 101 (1986), p. 97.

Chadwick, Kay-Shuttleworth, John Stuart Mill, John Ruskin, Charles Kingsley, and F. D. Maurice. Its formation resulted from the convergence of three areas of interest: in penal reform, in the legal emancipation of women, and in the reform of legal procedure. It attracted perhaps a less disparate range of speakers than Section F, presumably because of its orientation to social science rather than to statistics.[47] Papers presented to the Social Economy' section at the 1862 meeting in London, for example, were arranged in groups such as 'Employers and Employed', 'Co-operation', 'Condition of the Working Classes', 'The Poor Laws', and 'Taxation', an altogether narrower range than that typical of a contemporary meeting of Section F.[48]

That Jevons chose Section F that year as the appropriate forum for the presentation of his paper on mathematical economics, and not the meeting of the Social Science Association, confirms, however, that the latter was not a forum open to general discussion of political economy. Issues of theoretical principle would at most appear in the addresses given by the President of each section, as for example did Bonamy Price in 1882 in Nottingham, where he contrasted the respective merits of 'free' and 'fair' trade, rehearsing principles that would have probably been entirely familiar to Tooke some 60 years earlier.[49] The existence of the association does, however, underline the presence of a substantial constituency for the discussion of social improvement in later nineteenth-century Britain, a constituency which in all likelihood accepted Brougham's contention in his inaugural address that 'social economy' is the section 'most of all connected with the sister departments'.[50] While drawing attention to the breadth of interest in political economy at this time, this interest was practical, not theoretical. The existing broad constituency for social and economic knowledge would need to be transformed by the perception that knowledge of political economy required acquaintance with the principles of political economy, and a major part here was played by the University Extension Movement, which grew directly out of these provincial social networks and relied on them for its subsequent expansion.

The University Extension Movement

The annual progression of the British Association around British provincial cities was one of several factors in lending focus to diverse proposals for social reform, fostering initiatives that were both local and regional. A prominent example was the formation

[47] See, for example, 'Address by William Newmarch, Esq., F. R. S., as President of the Economy and Trade Department, Social Science Association, at Leeds, 10th October, 1871', *Journal of the Statistical Society of London* Vol. 34 No. 4 (December 1871), pp. 476–98; and W. B. Hodgson, 'The Instruction of the Community, especially the Wage-receiving Classes, in Economic Science', *Transactions of the National Association for the Promotion of Social Science. Aberdeen Meeting, 1877*, Longmans, Green and Co., London 1878, pp. 468–83.

[48] *Transactions of the National Association for the Promotion of Social Science. London Meeting, 1862*, Longmans, Green and Co., London 1863, pp. xii–xiii.

[49] Bonamy Price, 'Address on Economy and Trade', *Transactions of the National Association for the Promotion of Social Science. Nottingham Meeting, 1882*, Longmans, Green and Co., London 1883, pp. 90–110.

[50] 'Inaugural Address by the Right Honourable Lord Brougham and Vaux, President of the Association', *Transactions of the National Association for the Promotion of Social Science, 1857*, John W. Parker and Sons, London 1858, p. 14.

in Liverpool during 1867 of the Council for Promoting the Higher Education of Women.[51] In part this was a reflection of the establishment of regional centres for London University examinations from the later 1850s, creating for the first time in England the prospect of studying at the university level outside Oxford, Cambridge, and London. Calls for the regionalisation of higher education became linked to the movement for female emancipation; during the 1870s both Henry Sidgwick and Alfred Marshall were closely connected with the initiatives for women's education in Cambridge that led to the foundation of Girton and Newnham colleges. An early initiative of the Council for Promoting the Higher Education of Women was to invite James Stuart (1843–1913) to give a series of lectures to women in Manchester, Liverpool, Sheffield, and Leeds on the theory and methods of education, for the benefit of those women intending to becomes governesses and schoolteachers. Stuart had recently been appointed a fellow of Trinity College, Cambridge, after graduating as Third Wrangler in 1866; accepting the invitation, he suggested that it might be better if he were to teach something specific and in this way demonstrate pedagogic technique. He proposed that he present in each city a course of eight weekly lectures on the history of astronomy, choosing the subject because 'as Comte has pointed out, [it is] the only really complete science.'[52] At his first lecture he advised those attending to make notes after every lecture in the form of a syllabus or series of points; and he distributed a printed copy of a syllabus for the first lecture as a model. He quickly realised that an outline of this kind should be distributed in advance of the lecture, and this then became the practice for Extension lectures. Stuart had expected an attendance of 20–30: the total number of pupils attending in all four centres turned out to be around 600.[53]

Following this success, Stuart was asked by a friend to lecture to workmen in the Crewe Mechanics' Institute established by the London and North Western Railway Company. Expecting about 20 for a lecture on meteors, an audience of about 1,500 attended on the night of a great meteoric shower in November 1867. In the summer of 1868 he returned to Crewe for eight weekly lectures, and that winter he lectured for the North of England Council again. Before that he had given a set of lectures in Rochdale for the Equitable Pioneers' Society, which dedicated a percentage of the society's net profit to educational purposes. Stuart suggested that co-operative societies could take the lead and 'engage a group of teachers of the highest class, and to utilise these as peripatetic professors of a Co-operative university.'[54]

The universities of Oxford and Cambridge had already established school examination boards in 1857 and 1858, respectively, creating for the first time national standards of qualification. Stuart's idea was that members of these two universities could in addition provide lecturers for local occasional courses, and in 1871 he presented a memorial to the Vice Chancellor of Cambridge University that included statements from the North of England Council, the Crewe Mechanics' Institute, the

[51] See Chapter 10, p. 280, for how this related to developments in Liverpool.
[52] James Stuart, *Reminiscences*, Cassell, London 1912, p. 155.
[53] Ibid., p. 159.
[54] Ibid., p. 164. Hence the title of Welch's history of the Cambridge Extension Movement, *The Peripatetic University*, Cambridge University Press, London 1973. Stuart was not quite the lone pioneer that he made out in his autobiography, but he gives a good sense of the chronology and background.

Rochdale Pioneers' Society, and the mayor of Leeds. Stuart was made secretary of a syndicate to review proposals; the syndicate reported in favour of an experiment, and courses were then planned for Nottingham, Derby, and Leicester. In Derby three sets of lectures, advertised in local papers, began in October: V. H. Stanton (1846–1924)[55] lectured on political economy 'adapted to Working Men'; Edward Bickersteth Birks, also of Trinity College,[56] lectured on English literature 'mainly for ladies'; and T. O. Harding of Trinity lectured on force and motion 'Mainly for Young Men engaged in commercial and professional pursuits'. The fee for morning lectures and classes was 10s. 6d. per term; for evening lectures and classes 5s.; and for artisans 2s. 6d.[57] Despite an organising committee of 38, including clergymen, members of the City Council, magistrates, and the local MP, there was a rather uncertain beginning; in Nottingham, where the Mechanics' Institute was engaged, the inauguration was much more positive, while the lack of any Mechanics Institution in Leicester initially made organisation more difficult.[58]

The experiment was made permanent before it had even ended, and with this Cambridge became a centre for Extension teaching—sending its college fellows to English towns and cities to give weekly lectures, hold classes, and mark essays. A fixed routine was quickly established. A contemporary source outlines how at the commencement of a course of lectures a printed syllabus of some 20–50 pages, also containing weekly exercises, was sold for a few pence; classes related to these exercises might be arranged to meet either directly before or after each lecture. At the end of each course there was a final written examination set and marked by an independent examiner, and on this basis certificates—either Pass or Distinction—were awarded to those whose performance in class and examination were judged to be satisfactory.[59] For those without any formal school certification—only available at this time via the Oxford and Cambridge local examinations—the Extension certificates provided access to the University of London BA and BSc courses, as well as providing a network through which isolated individuals could find advice and support in considering their educational progression.

By 1875–1876, Cambridge was running some one hundred courses, with a total average attendance of 10,000, but this proved to be a burst of initial enthusiasm, followed by a temporary decline in the number of courses and centres.[60] However, in 1876 a London Society was formed with G. J. Goschen, at the time MP for the City of London, as its President.[61] Alon Kadish's account of the London Society makes clear

[55] Vincent Henry Stanton was appointed Fellow of Trinity College Cambridge in 1872; he was Twentieth Wrangler in 1870, Junior then Senior Dean of Trinity College from 1874 to 1884, Cambridge Professor of Divinity from 1884 to 1916, and then Regius Professor of Divinity from 1916 to 1922. In 1884 he was one of the Electors that appointed Alfred Marshall as Professor of Political Economy.

[56] Vicar of Trumpington, 1880–1885, and eldest son of Thomas Birks, who was succeeded as Knightbridge Professor of Moral Philosophy in 1883 by Henry Sidgwick.

[57] (12 pence to a shilling, and 20s. to a £) In 1871 a teacher might earn around £120 per annum; and a printer £80. See B. R. Mitchell, *British Historical Statistics*, Cambridge University Press, Cambridge 1988, p. 153.

[58] Welch, *Peripatetic University*, pp. 47–49.

[59] R. G. Moulton, *The University Extension Movement*, Bemrose and Sons, London 1887, pp. 7–9.

[60] Kelly, *History of Adult Education*, op. cit. p. 222.

[61] The London Society was formed as a limited company, and its first Annual General Meeting was held in Mansion House on 13 March 1876.

that a great deal of its work was in co-ordinating existing lecturing activity, and also raising money from subscribers that could be used to subsidise its teaching. Cambridge extension centres had to be self-supporting; the London Society supplemented receipts from tickets, making it possible to widen the social constituency to which its work appealed.[62] Oxford was quick to follow: in 1878 the Oxford delegacy for local examinations made Arthur Acland (1847–1926) secretary of a new committee, formed under the chairmanship of T. H. Green, to provide lectures and teaching in the large towns of England and Wales. Acland had graduated in 1870 with an Oxford BA in history, had been ordained and spent some time as a curate in Northumberland; in 1875 he made a tour of northern England and was especially impressed by the working men's club in Rochdale. He became a popular lecturer, and his dedication to northern and working-class students is evident from a map of England and Wales for 1889–1890, showing a dense northern cluster representing about half of all the Oxford centres, with Stoke on Trent in the south and Skipton in the north. The accompanying map of Cambridge centres for the same session shows its centres to be more evenly scattered through the Midlands and the north.[63]

There was a large pool of talented and available young lecturers, many of them beginning what would become distinguished careers in public and academic life. Henry Sidgwick examined in Putney and Wimbledon during 1877–1878 and his report compared the quality of students favourably with those he had recently examined at Oxford;[64] H. H. Asquith, a future Prime Minister, taught the London Society's first course in political economy during the Michaelmas term of 1876.[65] Henry Cunynghame, with a first in Moral Sciences from Cambridge, had like Asquith read for the bar, and also needed to supplement his income by lecturing. Many turned their hand to Extension lecturing as a welcome source of occasional income, given the lack of regular academic appointments in political economy and other modern subjects. Edwin Cannan, future London Professor of Political Economy, was an exception in the 1880s only by virtue of the fact that he had a substantial private income, and did not need to travel the country during the autumn and winter months giving courses of 6 or 12 lectures. During the early 1880s in London, interest in lectures on political economy declined, but in 1886 there was a revival. Early that year Herbert Foxwell delivered a course of lectures on political economy at the City of London College: meeting at 8 p.m., there was an average lecture attendance of 23, with 23 also at each class, 11 of whom submitted themselves to the examiner Neville Keynes, who gave three Firsts and seven Seconds. During the same session George Armitage

[62] Kadish, 'The Teaching of Political Economy in the Extension Movement', pp. 90–92. Lecturers were paid £30 per course, and if local receipts were not sufficient to meet this the Society undertook to subsidise each course by up to two-thirds of this fee. The hire of rooms and the costs of printing and advertising were borne by the local committee; London Society for the Extension of University Teaching, 'Report of the Council 1877 (February 1877)', p. 7; University of London Library Archives EM/1/3/1.

[63] H. J. Mackinder, M. E. Sadler, *University Extension. Has it a Future?*, Henry Frowde, London 1890, maps appended unpaginated. For the 1889–1890 session Oxford is recorded as delivering 148 lecture courses attended by 17,904 students; Cambridge 125 courses attended by 11,301 students; and London 107 courses attended by 10,982 students (pp. 17–18). For Acland's later career as an educationist, see Anne Ockwell's *Oxford Dictionary of National Biography* entry.

[64] London Society, 'Report of the Council 1878', p. 5.

[65] Kadish, 'The Teaching of Political Economy in the Extension Movement', p. 92.

Smith[66] lectured on political economy at the Birkbeck Institute; 62 students enrolled, with an average of 35 at each class, and 15 candidates sat the examination, leading to the award of three Firsts and seven Seconds.[67] That autumn Armitage Smith enrolled 155 students to a course of lectures on political economy in Poplar, where he had 60 in each class. But here only nine students sat for the examination:

> The audience, as in the case of other East-End Centres, was drawn largely from the working classes, and included workmen engaged in shipbuilding, boiler-makers, coopers, sawyers, and dock-labourers. The class following the Lecture was so thoroughly appreciated by the audience, as often to be protracted to a late hour.[68]

Examination presumed reading and revision, and the contrast of the students at Poplar and Birkbeck was between workers seeking enlightenment and clerks seeking to improve their employment prospects. What kind of economic literature might address such different constituencies?

Elementary Textbooks

James Stuart had visited the houses of Northumberland miners in connection with his extension teaching, noting that they possessed '... very remarkably good though small libraries, with such books as Mill's 'Logic', Carlyle's 'Hero Worship', Fawcett's 'Political Economy' and others of that kind.'[69] Fawcett's text had been published in 1863 and was a simplified and condensed form of John Stuart Mill's *Principles of Political Economy*, a long and bulky book that from its first publication remained a standard point of reference in English political economy for the remainder of the century, a new edition being prepared by W. J. Ashley and published in 1909. Mill prepared a 'People's Edition' himself, which after its first publication in 1865 was reprinted once that year, three times in 1866, and six times in the 1870s.[70] Fawcett's *Manual of Political Economy* took a different approach, and then his wife continued the line with her *Political Economy for Beginners* in 1870, which sought to carry political economy into schools.

Fawcett had graduated from the Mathematical Tripos in Cambridge and in 1856 became a Fellow of Trinity Hall. He had already entered Lincoln's Inn, and prepared himself for a political career, taking his philosophy and political economy from John Stuart Mill and keeping abreast of contemporary politics. But then in 1858 he was blinded in a shooting accident, at the age of 25. A career in law being effectively closed to him, he turned to his academic and political prospects.

[66] Armitage Smith (fl. 1844–1923) was a civil servant who had completed a London BA and an MA, was a friend of Stanley Jevons, and from 1898 was Principal of Birkbeck College.

[67] London Society, 'Report of the Council for 1886', Appendix II. 1. January to April 1886.

[68] Ibid., p. 11.

[69] Stuart, *Reminiscences*, p. 174. See my 'Economic Manuals and Textbooks in Great Britain and the British Empire 1797–1938', in Marco Augello, Marco Guidi (eds.) *The Economic Reader*, Routledge, London 2012, pp. 43–75, for a broader review of manuals and textbooks.

[70] Publisher's details in Ashley's 1909 edition. The publisher's details here indicate that the two-volume Library Edition of the text sold at the time for 30s., while Ashley's Student's Edition cost 5s.

Henceforth he had to be read to, and as Phyllis Deane notes, he 'went on to develop his talents within relatively narrow confines'.[71] He consolidated his understanding on what he already knew at the time of the accident: Ricardo, Malthus, Mill, and Buckle. Darwin's *Origin of Species* was published the year following his accident, but with this he rounded off his core knowledge. When the Cambridge Chair in Political Economy fell vacant in 1863, Mill's view that contemporary political economy was as good as complete still reflected contemporary understanding; Fawcett exemplified that contemporary understanding.

Fawcett's *Manual of Political Economy* served as an abridgement of Mill's *Principles* until Marshall published an abridgement of his own *Principles of Economics*, *Elements of Economics of Industry* (1892). The *Manual* went into six editions before his death in 1884, there being two further posthumous editions, the last in 1907.[72] As Phyllis Deane suggests,

> Fawcett's *Manual* is Mill's *Principles* summarised in deliberately unambiguous terms, with most of the subtle qualifications and elaborations of the argument left out, and shorn of its philosophical discussions and speculations.... In short, for the student approaching the subject for the first time, with little or no interest in philosophy or abstract theory, Fawcett's *Manual* must have seemed a more relevant, clear and straightforward introduction to the current state of knowledge in political economy than Mill's discursive treatise.[73]

Fawcett cleaved so strongly to his orthodoxy that he refused to follow Mill in recanting the Wage Fund doctrine. This reappears even in the last, 1907 edition, summarised thus:

> This law affirms that wages cannot generally rise or fall, unless the capital or population of the country is either increased or diminished.[74]

From this we might gain a sense of the clarity, and certainty, of Fawcett's understanding of the principles of political economy.

His ability to express these nonetheless depended entirely on others who were prepared to read and write for him. He met Millicent Garrett in May 1865, and married her in April 1867. Not only did this provide him with a reader and writer, it provided her with an education in political economy, which helped her develop arguments for the emancipation of women upon grounds of rationality, rather than morality. And in 1870 she published her own *Political Economy for Beginners*, which over 10 English editions sold 106,500 copies.[75] The text was aimed not only at beginners, but also at schoolchildren:

[71] Phyllis Deane, 'Henry Fawcett: The Plain Man's Political Economist', in Lawrence Goldman (ed.) *The Blind Victorian: Henry Fawcett and British Liberalism*, Cambridge University Press, Cambridge 1989, p. 94.

[72] Ibid., p. 96. By 1884 it had sold over 22,000 copies.

[73] Ibid., pp. 96–97.

[74] Fawcett, *Manual* (1907) p. 137, cited by Deane, 'Henry Fawcett', p. 99.

[75] Willie Henderson, 'Millicent Garrett Fawcett's *Political Economy for Beginners*: An Evaluation', *Paedagogica Historica* Vol. 40 (2004), p. 435.

> When I was helping my husband to prepare a third edition of his *Manual of Political Economy*, it occurred to us both that a small book, explaining as briefly as possible the most important principles of the science, would be useful to beginners, and would perhaps be an assistance to those who are desirous of introducing the study of Political Economy into schools. It is mainly with the hope that a short and elementary book might help to make Political Economy a more popular study in boys' and girls' schools that the following pages have been written.[76]

Despite the evident popularity of the work, it is hard to escape the conclusion that Alfred Marshall, lecturing to women students studying for the Cambridge Higher Local examinations in the same year as its first publication,[77] would not have viewed it as an introduction to political economy suited for his women students. At least part of his motivation for contributing to what became *Economics of Industry* lay in a desire to displace the confusions brought about by Mill's *Principles* condensed into dogmatic truth at two removes, via Henry Fawcett's own reduction and Millicent's synopsis of that condensation.

Mary Paley had studied for the Cambridge Moral Sciences Tripos informally in the early 1870s, and had been encouraged by Alfred Marshall to pursue the study of political economy. In 1874 she sat the Tripos examination in the drawing room of Dr. Kennedy's house in Bateman Street, the papers being brought by runners from Senate House. Marshall had lectured on political economy for the women, Mary commenting that

> [i]n those days books were few. There were no blue books[78] or Economic magazines and very few text-books. Mill was the mainstay, with Adam Smith and Ricardo and Malthus in the background. Hearn's *Plutology* was thought well of for beginners. Later on we read Jevons' *Principles*, Cairnes' *Leading Principles* and Walker on *Wages*.[79] Mixed up with the lectures on theory were some on the History of Economics, Hegel's Philosophy of History, and Economic History from 1350 onwards, on the lines of the Historical Appendices to the *Principles*.[80]

She was then commissioned by the Cambridge University Extension lecturers to write a suitable textbook; written in collaboration with Alfred Marshall, to whom she became engaged in 1876, *Economics of Industry* was published in 1879. The preface described the book as 'an attempt to construct on the lines laid down in Mill's Political

[76] Millicent Garrett Fawcett, 'Preface', *Political Economy for Beginners*, Macmillan, London 1870, n.p.

[77] Marshall had become examiner for Political Economy for the Cambridge Higher Local Examinations in May 1869, and in Lent term 1870 began his lectures to women students at this level; see Rita McWilliams Tullberg, 'Marshall's Contribution to the Women's Higher Education Movement', in Tiziano Raffaelli, Eugenio Biagini, Rita McWlliams Tullberg (eds.) *Alfred Marshall's Lectures to Women*, Edward Elgar, Aldershot UK 1995, pp. 52, 54.

[78] I.e. collections of official statistics.

[79] This book was not in fact published until 1876.

[80] Mary Paley Marshall, *What I Remember*, Cambridge University Press, London 1947, pp. 19–20. Women were first admitted formally to University of Cambridge examinations in 1881.

Economy a theory of Value, Wages and Profits, which shall include the chief results of the work of the present generation of Economists.'[81]

But before their book was published, Jevons's own textbook, *Political Economy*, was published as part of a 'Science Primers' series. Heavily Millian in substance, the book presented in simplified form the lectures that Jevons had given in Manchester to pupil-teachers—students who would become teachers in elementary schools. This reached a ninth printing in 1905, which is remarkable given the very real limitations of the work. Opening with a definition of political economy, Jevons immediately digresses in the first paragraph into a discussion of the sciences in general; and such deviations are a major feature of the book, seriously obscuring the points he wishes to make. The second chapter is devoted to utility, which turns out to simply be a discussion of wants and use values, displaying one of the key features of the work: instead of seeking to present succinct and clear definitions and explanations, Jevons piles example upon example, obscuring instead of clarifying. The division of labour is introduced as follows:

> There is a popular couplet which says –
>
> 'When Adam delved and Eve span,
> Who was then the gentleman?'
>
> It seems to express the fact that this division of labour existed in very early times, before there were any gentlemen.[82]

In his primer Jevons advanced principles that would have been quite familiar some 70 years previously, containing nothing of the economics for which Jevons was already well-known. However flawed it may have been, it inadvertently demonstrated that a clear exposition of the elementary principles of economics as conceived in the last third of the nineteenth century was well overdue. While the Marshalls's *Economics of Industry* shared some of the defects of Jevons's primer, it quickly became established as the leading general textbook for the study of political economy in extension classes and courses directed to the London BA in the new provincial colleges. In the Manchester classes which Jevons had previously taught, it was adopted as the main textbook in 1880, the year in which Owens College was transformed into the Victoria University of Manchester.

The following year a translation of Cossa's *Guide to the Study of Political Economy* (1880) was added to the list.[83] The opening 'General Part' of the book provided for the first time in English a comprehensive survey of economic method that would only be displaced in 1891 by Neville Keynes's *Scope and Method of Political Economy*. The work had been translated by a female student of a Cambridge extension class who dedicated the work to 'Mrs. Fawcett', and a preface by Jevons forcefully stated the virtues of the book:

[81] Alfred Marshall, Mary Paley Marshall, 'Preface' to *The Economics of Industry*, Macmillan, London 1879, p. v.

[82] William Stanley Jevons, *Political Economy*, Macmillan, London 1878, p. 22.

[83] *The Calendar of Owens College, Manchester*, Session 1881–1882, p. 63.

> This work presents, in a compendious form, not only a general view of the bounds, divisions and relations of the science, marked by great impartiality and breadth of treatment, but it also furnishes us with an historical sketch of the science, such as must be wholly new to English readers.[84]

Jevons is here alluding to the fact that Cossa's 'historical sketch' of the science presents an account of the development of the economic sciences in France, Italy, Spain, and Holland that gives a chapter to 'Adam Smith and his Successors', but more or less excludes Malthus, Ricardo, and MacCulloch from the following 'Political Economy in the Nineteenth Century': English political economy is represented solely by John Stuart Mill. Indeed, this Continental perspective is also evident when Cossa reviews the contemporary state of political economy in the first part of his book, reminding a modern reader that it is only the anglicisation of economics in the twentieth century that has given us an anglicised history of political economy in the nineteenth century. More importantly, if we consider Cossa's book from the perspective of its English readers in the 1880s, we might begin to appreciate that they took for granted an international domain of economic literature with which we have since become unfamiliar.

The appearance of the texts by Jevons, the Marshalls, and Cossa in rapid succession is further evidence that there was now an established demand for elementary teaching in political economy. It should also be recalled that an important element of Mechanics Institutions and Lit and Phil societies had been the establishment of libraries, and so besides the relative cheapness of these works, they were increasingly available to readers in local reading rooms, along with related economic literature. In this way an expanding field of material was accessible to readers, and this in turn made it possible for them to enter for public examinations that required more than the simple rote learning of elementary principles.

Curriculum, Examinations, Employment

A key prerequisite for the creation of vocational pathways from schooling to employment was the creation of nationally-recognised qualifications enabling those so certified to directly enter relevant employment, or move on to a higher level of training and qualification. As already noted, the Society of Arts had begun this process in the 1850s about the same time that the University of London had made its examinations accessible to those living outside the capital. Then, during the 1850s, Oxford and Cambridge inaugurated a system of school certificates, and a number of other bodies began to develop their own requirements for training and examination. In 1853 The Government of India Act had ended the use of patronage by the East India Company to select its administrators, and the following year the Northcote-Trevelyan report on 'The Organisation of the Permanent Civil Service' recommended the generalisation of this measure. Studies of public administration conducted since the later 1840s[85] had

[84] William Stanley Jevons, 'Preface to the English Translation', in Luigi Cossa, *Guide to the Study of Political Economy*, Macmillan, London 1880, p. vii.

[85] E. Hughes, 'Sir Charles Trevelyan and Civil Service Reform, 1853–5', *English Historical Review* Vol. 64 (1949), pp. 53–61; and A. P. Donajgrodski, 'New Roles for Old: The Northcote-Trevelyan Report and the

identified the power of patronage as a major impediment to public administration, an appropriately modern aim that tended to overlook the fact that most departments did have some form of formal entrance procedure,[86] while many specialist skills limited the scope of patronage.[87] The issue was sharpened by the Indian Rebellion of 1857 and the subsequent nationalisation of the East India Company, leading to the closure in 1858 of East India College, where political economy had been taught to cadets ever since Robert Malthus was appointed 'Professor of General History, Politics, Commerce, and Finance in the College of Hertford' in July 1805.

Candidates for Company service in India during the first half of the nineteenth century spent two years at this establishment taking courses in history, law, political economy, and languages. However, since they had been pre-selected at the age of 15 for Company service through a system of patronage exercised by the Directors of the Company, they could not in the ordinary course of affairs fail to progress onwards after two years, however poorly they fared in the written examinations. The Principal had powers neither to select nor expel students, leading to occasional disciplinary problems. The insertion of any kind of educational tests between nomination and appointment to a writership intruded upon the power of patronage wielded by Directors, and hence problems and criticisms arising out of the patronage system stamped the entire history of East India College as an institution qualifying nominees for appointment to the Indian Civil Service. By the end of the eighteenth century the appointment system was already beginning to be exploited for financial gain, with writerships being advertised for as much as £3,000.[88] In 1798 a Committee of Patronage was established to investigate the matter, and it was confirmed that writerships had indeed been sold. The measures adopted to counter this proved ineffectual, however, and it took a parliamentary investigation in 1809 to itemize names and sums paid before these abuses of the patronage system were ended. While the College addressed the Company's need for training, it had no powers over the associated function of qualification.

Opponents of the patronage system cast themselves as reformers of a corrupt and outdated system which failed to draw into the Company the talents that it needed. Later historians have tended to accept this pose, treating the introduction of an examination-based system of selection as part of the gradual shift away from an older order of privilege towards that modern democratic world which we now inhabit. Today, one should adopt a more sceptical attitude toward reform, and look beyond aspirations, reformist rhetoric, and policy measures to the actual functioning of the 'traditional' and the 'modern' regimes. In the case of the East India College, the system of patronage worked quite well as a means of recruiting trustworthy servants for the

Clerks of the Home Office 1822–48', in Gillian Sutherland (ed.) *Studies in the Growth of Nineteenth-Century Government*, Routledge and Kegan Paul, London 1972, pp. 82–109.

86 Whereas the later reputation of competitive Civil Service examinations has centred upon appointment to the higher reaches, the numbers involved were very small for many years, and were far outweighed by more basic examinations for literacy and numeracy, and handwriting—it is said that Karl Marx failed an examination for the post of railway clerk because of his poor handwriting.

87 E. Hughes, 'Civil Service Reform 1853–5', *History* Vol. 27 (1942), pp. 54–55.

88 A. Farrington, 'Introduction' to *The Records of the East India College Haileybury and other Institutions*, HMSO, London 1976, p. 5; and A. T. Embree, *Charles Grant and British Rule in India*, George Allen and Unwin, London 1962, pp. 179ff.

Company, in the absence of any other means of assessing the suitability of recruits. The close social networks from which recruits were drawn provided some kind of assurance that administrators, working perhaps on their own far from colleagues, would bear in mind the dishonour they would bring not only upon themselves, but upon their families, if they were to abuse the position entrusted to them. As was to be pointed out by critics of the Civil Service reforms in the 1850s, it was not evident that an ability to pass examinations indicated good character; nor was proficiency in classical literature and mathematics necessarily an appropriate or advantageous preparation for the life of a public administrator. Although the East India College admitted candidates whose qualifications were social, rather than academic, the curriculum was distinctively vocational; it could not therefore be represented by self-styled reformers as an unambiguous symbol of the old order. Moreover, with the dissolution of the College it became necessary to establish university courses in the subjects that it had taught. Many assumed that the new examination system would draw primarily upon the 'gentlemen' graduates of Oxbridge; but these were always in a minority as compared with the products of Irish universities, commercial schools, and crammers, a development viewed with some distaste by senior members of the Indian Civil Service. Nonetheless, the need to make some provision for the training of candidates for the Indian Civil Service at Oxford and Cambridge itself lent additional impulse to reforms at these established universities, the new Haileybury curriculum thus resonating long after the demise of the institution founded to provide it.[89]

The curriculum of the East India College—including languages, literature, law, mathematics, history, and political economy—was designed to train the future administrators of the Company's Indian territories. Hence the focus of criticism upon the selection of recruits, rather than argument over the suitability of their training, otherwise a perennial issue with any kind of vocational education. The timing of the college's closure coincided, however, with the rapid extension of formal examination as a control on entry to employment of many kinds; and here the question of the relevance of what was examined to the skills required of any one form of employment became a significant issue. A developed system of competitive examination presumed the existence of a broad, modern curriculum. Examination and certification played an increasingly prominent role mediating between education and employment, a process in which employers had little direct leverage. The rise of formal, written examinations stimulated a demand for a range of subjects beyond the standard classical curriculum that, for example, Alfred Marshall had endured at Merchant Taylors' School during the later 1850s. Stafford Northcote dimly perceived the problem, but came to the wrong conclusion:

> There would be a manifest absurdity in inviting the flower of our youth to enter into an exciting struggle, involving the necessity of long and expensive training in the highest branches of human knowledge, and in then rewarding the best mathematician, classical scholar, linguist, historian, and philosopher, not with a wreath of ivy

[89] See, for a detailed account of the College and its teaching, my 'Professors Malthus and Jones: Political Economy at the East India College 1806–1858', *European Journal of the History of Economic Thought* Vol. 2 (1995), pp. 327–54.

> or a crown of laurel, but with a clerkship of 80l. a-year, with the prospect of copying, folding, and sealing up despatches, and registering official documents, for an indefinite length of time, the duration of which, as well as the gradual increase of his salary, must depend, not upon his own exertions, or the fitness he might show for higher duties, but upon the slow wearing out of the body of seniors who stand above him. By such a process the best man would probably be turned into a dull plodder, or a careless and discontented grumbler. It is indeed far more hopeful, as well as far more satisfactory, to make a man of ordinary attainments into a good public servant by employing him wisely, than to seek out men of the highest attainments and to spoil them by employing them unwisely.[90]

Northcote thought that the examination system could not come into full effect until '... some measures for the right division of employment have been taken', that the Civil Service could not therefore be regenerated by the use of examinations alone. But this was primarily because the knowledge that could be subjected to written examination was at the time so limited in range: in the 1850s, there was a binary choice between examining either basic numeracy (the four rules of arithmetic) or facility in Latin and Greek composition and exercises.

In any case, it was not as though the principle of open competition had been, or could be, adopted immediately with any consistency. The previous year another speaker at the annual meeting of the Social Science Association had pointed out that the *Third Report of Civil Service Commissioners* showed that out of 500 permanent clerkships made vacant in 1857, only 82 had been filled by competition. Part of the problems was that the Home Civil Service was already a large and differentiated institution employing some 80,000 persons, directly or indirectly. There were the higher political administrators, the clerks, salaried officers below the level of clerks, artisans and labourers, and the police.[91] Devising relevant tests for recruits and for promotion that were open and equal to all (men) presupposed a differentiation of educational provision that did not yet exist. Hence the ready constituency that university extension found, moving on from the occasional lectures of Mechanics' Institutions or the British Association to a more structured pedagogy.

In some cases the vocational skills required were evident enough for employers to form associations promoting training and examination. The Institute of Bankers, for example, was formed in 1879 and among its aims was to

> ... recognise and arrange for the delivery of Lectures on Banking, Mercantile Law, Political Economy, and other kindred subjects; shall issue Certificates to those who may pass examinations approved of from time to time by the Council of the Institute ...[92]

[90] Sir Stafford Northcote, 'On Competitive Examinations for the Civil Service', *Transactions of the National Association for the Promotion of Social Science 1859*, John W. Parker and Son, London 1860, p. 281.

[91] H. Mann, 'On the Best Mode of Practically Working the Plan of Competition for Civil Appointments', *Transactions of the National Association for the Promotion of Social Science 1858*, John W. Parker and Son, London 1859, p. 203.

[92] 'Constitution of the Institute of Bankers' para. 3, as printed in *Journal of the Institute of Bankers* Vol. 23 (1902), p. 3.

In 1888 the first two papers were on political economy, following by two on practical banking, two on commercial law, two on arithmetic and algebra, and two on bookkeeping.[93] There were 362 candidates for these examinations in 1894, and 452 in 1895; and it was noted that the City of London College, King's College, and the YMCA were in the process of establishing courses of lectures oriented to the requirements of these examinations.[94] In April 1908, 716 students sat the Institute's examinations in London, 202 in Manchester, 169 in Liverpool, and 93 in Birmingham, a total of 3,180 entering, and of these 276 passing the final examination.[95] Graduate entry to banking was, however, long at a severe discount: Barclays Bank's own records show that even in the mid-1930s a graduate entrant would be paid £150 per annum instead of the £100 per annum paid to the non-graduate recruit who, however, after being placed on the permanent staff six months later, received the same salary as a university graduate several years older. Consequently the three years spent gaining a university degree was, as far as Barclays Bank was concerned, worth precisely £25.[96]

This reflected a more general problem about the relation of a university education in Britain to employment, where professional associations, for example in law, accountancy, and medicine, continued until late in the twentieth century to play a major role in accreditation, while most private and state employers preferred to recruit directly from school. While this would remain as a check on the rapid expansion of general university education, below this level open competition at all levels of the Civil Service had been established by 1870, building on the Indian Civil Service examinations at the higher level.[97] The First Report of the Civil Service Commissioners in 1856 makes clear how minimal the basic requirements had to be in the absence of any established school certification:

> There are some qualifications, however, which appear to us to be indispensably necessary to a junior clerk in every Government office, and, with very few exceptions, to all persons appointed to any junior situation; viz. –
>
> To write a good hand.
> To be able to spell correctly.
> To be able to write a simple letter grammatically.
> To be conversant with the elementary portions of arithmetic.[98]

Starting from these elementary principles, the scope for examination and certification was very great, and would in turn play a major role in the development of a modern school curriculum in the second half of the nineteenth century. Quite how slowly this

[93] *Journal of the Institute of Bankers* Vol. 9 (1888), pp. 440–49.
[94] *Journal of the Institute of Bankers* Vol. 16 (1895), p. 547.
[95] *Journal of the Institute of Bankers* Vol. 28 (1907), p. 403.
[96] 'Report to the Board on 8 April 1937', Barclays Bank, Staff Committee Minute Book f. 138. My thanks to Jesse Campbell, Barclays Bank archivist, for providing me with a copy of this minute.
[97] See John Roach, *Public Examinations in England 1850–1900*, Cambridge University Press, London 1971, pp. 195ff, for details of this process.
[98] *First Report of Her Majesty's Civil Service Commissioners*, British Parliamentary Papers 1856 Vol. XXII, p. xix.

developed, however, is made clear by the retention of university matriculation examinations well into the twentieth century; Cambridge did not abandon a general university entrance examination until the 1980s.

From Magazines and Periodicals to Academic Journals

As the readership for political economy and related material extended and became more diverse, the number of periodicals in which there were contributions on political economy also expanded. Early in the nineteenth century there was a gradual shift from the publication of pamphlets to the contribution of articles to new quarterly journals. Malthus wrote essays, pamphlets, and one treatise, but also contributed to reviews. John Stuart Mill wrote books and contributed his essays to periodicals. The first of these new periodicals was the *Edinburgh Review*, founded in 1802, its association with Whig politics countered in 1809 with the appearance of the Tory *Quarterly Review*. In turn Jeremy Bentham founded the *Westminster Review*[99] in 1823 as a forum for the writings of the Philosophic Radicals and both Mills, father and son, were associated with it. These were all publications for an emergent intelligentsia, widely read but whose contents did not demand of the reader specialist capacities beyond the general educational standards of the day. There were also many weekly publications, the first that was explicitly dedicated to economic matters being *The Economist: or The Political, Commercial, Agricultural, and Free-Trade Journal*, founded in 1843.[100] Its founder, James Wilson, was an enthusiastic publisher of facts, and this made it a major source of financial and related information. During the railway mania, for instance, it established a separate section, 'The Railway Monitor', which assembled data relating to railway speculation and construction. R. H. Hutton's[101] brief spell as editor in the late 1850s ran counter to this, since he tended to couch the line of the journal in rather high-flown prose, not immediately accessible to the readership of bankers and financiers, a deficiency that was put right by the appointment of Walter Bagehot as editor in 1861. But besides the London Statistical Society there was no public organisation that brought together those interested in the social and economic issues of the day, and which published a journal for its members on a regular basis.

In France, by contrast, the foundation of the Société des Économistes in 1841 brought together liberal journalists, academics, and businessmen who that same year initiated a monthly, the *Journal des Économistes*, and which had among its members the publisher Gilbert Guillaumin, whose firm became the principal source of French texts on political economy. The *Journal* primarily carried material related to banking, trade, the colonies, commerce, and legislation, but as a monthly it was less news-oriented than the *Economist*. In Germany, of course, there were more academic publications

[99] Later the *London and Westminster Review*, in which John Stuart Mill's seminal article 'On the Definition of Political Economy; and on the Method of Investigation Proper to It' was first published in 1836, and reprinted in *Essays on some Unsettled Questions of Political Economy*, Parker, London 1844.

[100] The title was altered in 1844 to *The Economist, Weekly Commercial Times, and Bankers' Gazette. A Political, Literary and General Newspaper*. See, for an account of its early orientation, Ruth D. Edwards, *The Pursuit of Reason: The Economist 1843–1993*, Hamish Hamilton, London 1993, Ch. 2.

[101] Editor of *The Spectator*, 1861–1897.

that included issues related to political economy and economic legislation, beginning in 1844 with the *Zeitschrift für die gesammte Staatswissenschaft*, followed in 1863 by Conrad's *Jahrbücher für Nationalökonomie und Statistik*. German unification was marked in 1871 with the appearance of the *Jahrbuch für Gesetzgebung, Verwaltung und Rechtspflege im Deutschen Reich* edited by von Holtzendorff, the first item in the first issue being the German Constitution of 16 April 1871. In 1877 Holtzendorff was joined as editor by Lujo Brentano and the name was changed to *Jahrbuch für Gesetzgebung, Verwaltung und Volkswirthschaft im Deutschen Reich*; in 1881 Gustav Schmoller assumed control of the journal. In 1892 the Society of Austrian Economists also began publishing a journal, the *Zeitschrift für Volkswirtschaft, Socialpolitik und Verwaltung*, whose opening editorial statement emphasised that social and economic problems could only be properly dealt with by the efforts of practical men, historians, and theoreticians.[102] The initial article in the first issue was devoted to social reform in Austria, in much the same way that in March 1891 the first main article in the *Economic Journal* was about the eight-hour day in Australia.

In Britain those with an interest in political economy could only publish their shorter essays in the new wave of monthly journals that began appearing in the 1860s, linked to the development of London clubs and a clubland culture.[103] Among the first was *Macmillan's Magazine*, founded in 1859 and including mainly light literary material, the *Cornhill Magazine* appearing the following year and likewise appealing to a broad readership. But with the foundation of the *Fortnightly Review* in 1865, a forum for the occasional article on political economy was created—Thornton's rebuttal of the Wage Fund doctrine appeared here;[104] and John Elliot Cairnes reviewed Stanley Jevons's *Theory of Political Economy* in the same publication.[105] Other contributors included Cliffe Leslie, Robert Giffen, Stanley Jevons, Henry Sidgwick, and Henry Fawcett. In 1877 the *Nineteenth Century* began publication, and this dealt with more directly political topics and numbered MPs among its contributors. Gregory Moore links the sudden appearance of so many similar reviews to the development of a 'clubland culture' in London in which Leslie Stephen was closely involved, both as multiple club-member and editor of the *Cornhill Magazine* from 1871. The new forms of sociability that the clubs made possible might seem to confirm Jürgen Habermas's influential argument linking the development of a 'public sphere' to the Enlightenment and modernity. However, as Moore makes clear, this is to some extent because Habermas, in his account of coffee-house culture in early eighteenth-century London,[106] drew

[102] Eugen von Böhm Bawerk, 'Unsere Aufgaben', *Zeitschrift für Volkswirtschaft, Socialpolitik und Verwaltung* Bd. 1 (1892), p. 6.

[103] In his invaluable guide to London clubland, Gregory C. G. Moore traces 'how the institutional features of these clubbable spaces buffeted the written product in economics at the very time in which the English variant of marginalism was born, the English "Battle of Methods" broke out, and positive liberalism (of the New Liberals) began to displace negative liberalism (of the old Radical Philosophers) as the dominant frame for economic policy.' *Leslie Stephen and the Clubbable Men of Radical London: An Essay in Honour of John King's Retirement*, https://roundedglobe.com/tags/leslie stephen/, p. 61.

[104] W. T. Thornton, 'What Determines the Price of Labour or Rate of Wages?', *Fortnightly Review* Vol. I (New Series) (1867), pp. 551–66.

[105] J. E. Cairnes, 'New Theories in Political Economy', *Fortnightly Review* Vol. XI (New Series) (1872), pp. 71–76.

[106] Jürgen Habermas, *Strukturwandel der Öffentlichkeit. Untersuchungen zu einer Kategorie der bürgerlichen Gesellschaft*, Suhrkamp, Frankfurt a.M. 1990, pp. 92ff. The book was originally published in 1962.

heavily on the analysis of Leslie Stephen, who in writing about the eighteenth century had drawn on his own nineteenth-century experience. Stephen saw parallels between the cultures of coffee house and London clubs; Habermas took up this idea and placed it at the centre of his own account of the public sphere; and so to invoke Habermasian ideas in respect of nineteenth-century London clubland would simply complete the circle that Stephen had originally traced.

The first recognisably academic British publication in the humanities was *Mind*, which began publishing in 1876 and covered a range of topics beyond what would today be thought of as philosophy, including philology and psychology. English-language academic economic journals were first published in the United States: the *Political Science Quarterly*, edited from 1886 by the Faculty of Political Science of Columbia College; followed by Harvard's *Quarterly Journal of Economics* in 1887. The aims of this journal were printed inside the front cover of the first issue:

> The *Quarterly Journal of Economics* is established as an aid to investigators and students. It will supply a medium of publication for studies in Economic History, Criticism and Speculation, and for the Discussion of the important Questions of the Day.
>
> It will cordially welcome any real contribution to Economic study, leaving to the writer the sole responsibility for matters of opinion.
>
> It will present an accurate Record of Current Publications upon Economics, in all of the principal languages, and will reprint important Articles, Documents and Statistical Matter, as its space will permit, for the use of those interested in this and other branches of political science.

With these aims and purposes, the *Quarterly Journal of Economics* became the first recognisably modern academic economic journal in English; the same year the *Revue d'Économie Politique* began publishing as a bimonthly,[107] with broadly the same aims and carrying a number of anonymous reviews. In this and subsequent publications—the *Annals of the American Academy of Political and Social Science* founded in 1890, and Chicago's *Journal of Political Economy* in 1892—the international development of an economics discipline becomes visible for the first time, since all of these new journals not only served to co-ordinate their national readership, but also to keep them abreast of developments in other countries, reviewing foreign-language works, publishing original articles by foreign economists, and reporting on significant academic events elsewhere in the world.

There had been plans in Britain for creating a journal devoted to academic topics, and Foxwell had roughed out a plan for a new association. But he lacked the institutional weight to carry the scheme through; and it was not until Marshall was President of Section F in 1890 that it first gained decisive support. Early proposals had invoked the model of *Mind* and the *English Historical Review* (founded in 1886), but the

[107] The first issue of the *Revue* carried a statement by the editorial committee, 'Notre Programme', which emphasised that, while uniting collaborators of different schools, they shared a common dedication to 'neutrality', the new journal being 'neither the organ of a personality nor of a school' (pp. 1–2). See also Charles Gide, 'Comment est née la Revue d'Économie Politique', *Revue d'Économie Politique* t.45 (1931), pp. 134–57

Quarterly Journal of Economics had already begun publication by the time Marshall circulated a paper to the Committee of Section F in April 1890, seeking support for the establishment of an economic society and a journal. He therefore asked whether there was agreement that 'the time had come for founding an English Economic Journal somewhat similar in character to the American Quarterly?'[108] Some months later, when a formal invitation to the inaugural meeting of the British Economic Association (BEA) was issued, this proposal to found a journal was elaborated in terms of the need for an 'easy means of communication' among British economists, and it was suggested that a future journal might be made up of a long article, two or three shorter articles, reports from foreign correspondents, and a bibliography of new economic literature. Marshall's flysheet argued for a new journal in the following terms:

> The need of an economic journal has long been felt in England. Every other country in which economic studies are pursued with great activity, offers facilities for the publication of thorough scientific work by persons who have not the time, or are unwilling, to write a formal treatise. Since isolated pamphlets, however able, seldom obtain any considerable circulation, Englishmen who have something to say that is too technical for the ordinary magazines, and too short for a book, are sometimes compelled to give their views to the world in the columns of a foreign periodical, or as a publication of the American Economic Association; but more frequently they put it aside till an opportunity should offer for working it out more fully and publishing it as a book; and that opportunity too often does not come. A strong and widespread feeling that English economists, and especially the younger men among them, are thus placed at a great disadvantage through the want of any easy means of communication with one another, has led to the holding of many private meetings and discussions on the subject in Oxford, Cambridge, London, and possibly elsewhere; and lately the matter has come under consideration of the Committee of Section F (Economics and Statistics) of the British Association.[109]

An inaugural meeting of around 200 people, chaired by Goschen, at the time Chancellor of the Exchequer, was then held in London on 20 November 1890. A detailed report and a leading article appeared in *The Times* the following day.[110]

The meeting first established that membership of the BEA was open to anyone who cared to pay the appropriate fee, subject to formal approval by a Council whose first task would be to draft the association's rules. Nominees for membership of the Council were, however, unrepresentative of the meeting as a whole, being drawn chiefly from the minority of members who were academics and teachers of economics, setting a persistent pattern in the relationship between the structure of the membership of the

[108] Marshall to Committee of Section F, 10 April 1890, reprinted in *The Collected Writings of John Maynard Keynes* Vol. XII, Macmillan, London 1983, p. 847.

[109] Alfred Marshall, 'Proposal to Form an English Economic Association' (24 October 1890), flysheet reprinted in Keynes, *Collected Writings* Vol. XII, p. 848.

[110] A full report of the meeting differing in certain details from the *Times* report was published as 'Report of the Proceedings at the Meeting which Inaugurated the British Economic Association' in the *Economic Journal* Vol. 1 (1891), pp. 2–14.

Association and that of its officers.[111] A printed list of members from later in 1891 underlines this discrepancy; including some 470 names, it includes only 11 women, few foreigners,[112] and 31 MPs who outnumbered those who could be plausibly described as academic economists.

The Committee immediately held a brief meeting at which Goschen was elected President, Edgeworth provisionally nominated as editor of the new journal, and an executive committee formed.[113] This new, smaller, committee then convened a few days later in Giffen's Whitehall offices and began a series of meetings devoted to drafting rules, soliciting members, determining levels of subscription and, interestingly, deciding upon the level of payment for contributors to the *Economic Journal*.[114] Bob Coats estimated that by the time the new journal appeared in late March 1891, membership was around 500, rising by the end of 1891 to 710. Broken down into broad occupational categories, the structure of the membership for late March 1891 looks remarkably similar to that of the constituency for political economy that we have noted previously—diverse, unspecialised, with teachers of economics at any level in a distinct minority:[115]

Table 3.1 Early Membership of the British Economic Association by Occupation

Business	113
University teachers[116]	86
Law	51
Bankers	48
Civil Service	44
Administration	29
Landowners, etc.	22

[111] *The Times* report listed the nominees for Council as: A. H. D. Acland, James Bonar, Charles Booth, John Burnett, John Burt, Prof. Edward Caird, Leonard Courtney, Rev. Dr. Cunningham, Prof. Edgeworth, T. H. Elliott, Sir Thomas Farrer, Prof. Foxwell, Robert Giffen, Mr. E. C. K. Gonner, G. J. Goschen, George Howell, Prof. Ingram, J. N. Keynes, Sir John Lubbock, Prof. Marshall, J. B. Martin, Prof. Munro, Prof. Nicholson, Mr. Inglis Palgrave, Mr. L. L. Price, Rev. L. R. Phelps, Sir Rawson Rawson, Frederick Seebohm, Prof. Sedgwick [*sic*], H. Llewellyn Smith, Rev. Philip Wicksteed—*The Times*, 21 November 1890.

[112] The list includes the names of Emile Cheysson, Lujo Brentano, Gustav von Schmoller, Frank Taussig, and Léon Walras—'List of Members of the British Economic Association 1891', BLPES RES Archive 1/1/1.

[113] Meeting of Committee, 20 November 1890, Royal Economic Society Minute Book 1890–1921 BLPES RES Archive 2/1/1 f.3; the Executive Committee was composed of Foxwell, Marshall, Munro, Sidgwick, Bonar, Cunningham, Elliott, Giffen, Martin, Palgrave, and Price.

[114] These were fixed at 10s. a page for an article, and 5s. for reviewers and translators; meeting of 10 April 1891, RES Minute Book 1890–1921 f. 4. A balance sheet dated 10 May 1891 records that £53 19s. 6d. had been paid to contributors, compared with printing costs of £148 10s. 7d; Minute Book 1890–1921 ff. 18–19.

[115] A. W. Coats, 'The Origins and Early Development of the Royal Economic Society', *Economic Journal* Vol. 78 (1968) Appendix I, p. 370. See also A. W. and S. E. Coats, 'The Social Composition of the Royal Economic Society and the Beginnings of the British Economics "Profession," 1890–1915', *British Journal of Sociology* Vol. 21 (1970), pp. 75–85.

[116] Note that at this time in England there were only three academic economists who were employed full-time by a single institution—Marshall, Flux, and Gonner. This category should not therefore be read as representative of 'university teachers of economics', but includes all members who were associated with university institutions in one way or another.

Table 3.1 *Continued*

Accounting	16
Church	16
Journalism	16
Misc.	14
School and college teachers	13
Government	12
Army	8
Insurance	7
Medicine	6
Total	501

The primary purpose of this broad-based association was to provide an organisational structure that would prevent monopoly of its new journal by any one school or tendency.[117] An additional function was to perform the role of a reprint society for economic treatises, a function that the Royal Economic Society has continued. The editor of the *Economic Journal* was to be responsible to an editorial committee answering to a national association, not to a publisher, nor to an independent editorial board, as was the case with other new journals of the time. Moreover, the BEA was, in turn, as the opening lines of the first issue of its journal stated,

> ... open to all schools and parties; no person is excluded because of his opinions. The *Economic Journal*, issued under the authority of the Association, will be conducted in a similar spirit of toleration. It will be open to writers of different schools. The most opposite doctrines may meet here as on a fair field.[118]

Chartered as the Royal Economic Society (RES) in 1902, not until much later in the twentieth century did the RES assume responsibility for co-ordinating academic economists.

Consequently, in the 1920s a separate, largely informal, British organisation was created, the Association of Teachers of Economics, which held annual meetings where university teachers presented current work. First meeting in 1924, attendance over the following years appears to have averaged 60, while in 1926 it was estimated that the 110 members at that time made up around 90% of those eligible.[119] Oxford, Cambridge, and the LSE would have accounted on their own for more than half this estimate, indicating the small scale of British university economics at this time as compared with Germany or the United States. British organisations were not only smaller than their international peers, but also much younger and more informal.

[117] See, for an analysis of the contents of the *Economic Journal* over the first 50 years of its existence, my 'The *Economic Journal* and British Economics, 1891–1940', *History of the Human Sciences* Vol. 5 (1992), pp. 33–58.

[118] 'The British Economic Association', *Economic Journal* Vol. 1 (1891), p. 1.

[119] 'Association of Teachers of Economics', *Economic Journal* Vol. 36 (1926), p. 130. For want of any archival records, the reports in the *Economic Journal* remain the only indication of the association's activity: Vol. 35 (1925), pp. 153–55; Vol. 37 (1927), pp. 151–53; Vol. 40 (1930), pp. 158–59; Vol. 41 (1931), pp. 149–50; Vol. 42 (1932) p. 163. In 1932 the name was changed from the "Association of Teachers of Economics" to the "Association of University Teachers of Economics."

The *Verein für Socialpolitik* had been founded in 1872 as an academic response to the Social Question, and its annual conferences with their published proceedings quickly became an important component of a German network of economists, lawyers and civil servants. By the 1890s it was commissioning its own research for thematic conferences, and represented the international model for active associations of academic economists. In the United States the founding of the American Economics Association in 1885 created a powerful framework for national communication and appointments to positions in the rapidly expanding number of universities and colleges. Like the *Verein*, its annual conference was a major event, and when the Association began publication of the *American Economic Review* in 1911, the proceedings of these conferences formed a separate supplement.[120]

The foregoing can be no more than a sketch, based upon Britain, of what had become by the later 1880s an international movement towards the formal teaching of political economy at university level, even though it would not be until 1903 that such a thing as an undergraduate degree in economics existed. As already noted, the wave of specialised economic periodicals that began publication in the later 1880s gave concrete form to the newly-emerging discipline; if their contents were sometimes diverse, their management was in the hands of university economists who steered them into representing the substance and boundaries of a discipline. In 1890 Simon Patten confidently asserted the superiority of political economy to mathematics and physics:

> It trains the intellect as well as they do and gives that confidence in reasoning needed to properly handle complex subjects. It is also of advantage that the chains of reasoning are not as long and that the return to elementary principles is so frequent.... It is also worthy of mention that political economy trains a student in reasoning similar to that which he has to do in everyday life ... and if the student has had the advantage of a thorough training in economic reasoning, he will be much better prepared for active life than if he were drilled in the dogmatic reasoning from simple premises such as one finds in mathematics or physics.[121]

Charles Dunbar backed him up the following year. For the instructor in the moral sciences, the aim was to train students in scientific reasoning; 'That the student should learn to reason truly is of far more consequence than that he should perceive and accept any particular truth'.[122] That political economy was no longer a dogma, but a means of mental exploration, was a view shared across countries. Responding to Ely's charge that in France political economy had 'degenerated into a mere tool of the powerful class', Charles Gide fell back on the history of the teaching of political economy in France, before listing 15 diverse journals that testified to the representation of different schools, and so to the vibrancy of political economy in contemporary France.[123]

[120] See A. W. Coats, 'The American Economics Association and the Economics Profession', *Journal of Economic Literature* Vol. 23 (1985), pp. 1700–1707.

[121] Simon N. Patten, *The Educational Value of Political Economy*, Publications of the American Economic Association Vol. V No. 6, November 1890, p. 11.

[122] Charles F. Dunbar, 'The Academic Study of Political Economy', *Quarterly Journal of Economics* Vol. 5 No. 4 (1891), p. 413.

[123] Charles Gide, 'The Economic Schools and the Teaching of Political Economy in France', *Political Science Quarterly* Vol. 5 Issue 4 (1890), p. 634.

The first article in the first issue of the *Journal of Political Economy* presents a stocktaking of the condition of study and teaching in the United States, concluding that 'new means of communication between the investigator and the public should be created.'[124]

The new *Economic Journal* embarked on an international *tour d'horizon*, printing reports from corresponding members on associations, courses, teachers, and publications. First came Japan,[125] then Switzerland,[126] Belgium,[127] Italy,[128]and then the United States.[129] Besides this, many journals of the time carried listings of the contents of international periodicals, reviewed books in foreign languages, and reported on meetings and events across the world. A rough consensus on a new discipline in the making was thus reflected internationally in the new specialised journals—apart from in Germany, which was now increasingly detached from these international developments. There was a sense, however, that in all of this activity Britain was being left behind. Shortly after the launch of the *Economic Journal*, Section F formed a committee to assess the situation.[130] The presumption was that British provision for the teaching of economics was inferior to that elsewhere, and two main factors were identified: the tendency of teachers to neglect empirical study, and 'the practical exclusion of Economics from the curricula and examinations preliminary to those professions in connection with which its study would appear particularly suitable.'[131] The following year the Committee reported, confirming that Britain 'had no regular system' compared to Continental Europe and the United States, and advocating the introduction of 'thorough and systematic study' of economics in the honours programmes of British universities.[132] In particular, it was proposed that economics should be more prominent in the Civil Service examinations, and compulsory for those entering the higher branches.

This then was the context in which Alfred Marshall was advocating the development of a separate honours course in economics at Cambridge, to which we can now at last turn.

124 J. Laurence Laughlin, 'The Study of Political Economy in the United States', *Journal of Political Economy* Vol. 1 No. 1 (1891), p. 19.

125 'Jiuchi Soyeda, 'The Study of Political Economy in Japan', *Economic Journal* Vol. 3 (1893), pp. 335–39.

126 August Oncken, 'Political Economy in Switzerland', *Economic Journal* Vol. 5 (1895), pp. 133–37.

127 Ernest Mahaim, 'Economic and Social Science in Belgium', *Economic Journal* Vol. 5 (1895), pp. 462–71.

128 Achille Loria, 'Political Economy in Italy', *Economic Journal* Vol. 7 (1897), pp. 450–59.

129 V. Branford, 'The Organisation of Economic and Political Studies in American Universities', *Economic Journal* Vol. 12 (1902), pp. 535–47.

130 Chaired by William Cunningham, it included E. C. K. Gonner as its secretary, together with Edgeworth, Foxwell, Henry Higgs, and Neville Keynes.

131 E. C. K. Gonner, 'The Methods of Economic Training Adopted in This and Other Countries', *Report of the Sixty-Third Meeting of the British Association for the Advancement of Science (September 1893)*, John Murray, London 1894, p. 571.

132 E. C. K. Gonner, 'Methods of Economic Training Adopted in This and Other Countries', *Report of the Sixty-Fourth Meeting of the British Association for the Advancement of Science (August 1894)*, John Murray, London 1894, p. 365.

PART II
THE CAMBRIDGE MOMENT

Shortly after Alfred Marshall was appointed to the Cambridge chair in political economy, he inserted a notice in the *Cambridge University Reporter*[1] inviting students to call on him at his home for advice on matters relating to political economy. This was his own initiative, and not usual practice for University professors, who at the time played a small part in the education of Cambridge students. This active interest in promoting economic understanding among students indicates his commitment to the subject within Cambridge during the 23 years that he held the chair of political economy. Cambridge was not, however, a modern university of the kind outlined in Chapter 2, and to understand how in Cambridge Marshall succeeded in his ambition to create a three-year degree in economics we first need to understand the framework as he found it when taking up his appointment. Then, having understood this framework, we will be in a position to understand why Marshall became convinced that a separate Economics Tripos was required, the original three-year undergraduate programme of economic education.

Marshall had graduated in 1865 as Second Wrangler in the Mathematics Tripos—the second-highest place in a degree whose students were not only classified, but placed in rank order. As we shall see in the following chapter, at the beginning of the nineteenth century the Mathematics Tripos was the only honours degree offered by the University of Cambridge,[2] and the kind of mathematics it represented and the demands that it placed upon students are essential to an understanding of what kind of economics Marshall wished to further, and how it should be taught.

It was the mental training that the Mathematics Tripos required of its students that shaped Marshall's conception of how economics should be taught. Correspondingly, he considered that the Moral Sciences Tripos was unsuited to the kind of mental training he had in mind. The Moral Sciences Tripos only became a free-standing honours degree in the early 1860s, coinciding with Marshall entering St. Johns College as a student. By the end of the decade it had assumed a form that would last until 1903, when Marshall detached the teaching of economics and politics, and by default the Moral Sciences Tripos subsequently became the Philosophy Tripos. Modern accounts of Marshall's agitation for disciplinary autonomy pass over the question of exactly what Marshall wanted, and why, since there is an underlying assumption that Marshall was "progressing" economics towards its eventual future, what it has since

[1] The *Cambridge University Reporter* is a substantial internal university publication that prints all committee reports, reports of Senate discussion, and examination results.

[2] Those who wished to graduate in Classics had to first pass the Mathematics Tripos, which qualified them to sit the examinations for Classics.

become. As we shall see, this not only obscures quite what it was that Marshall was seeking to achieve,[3] but also that "Marshallian economics" did not in fact become the future of the discipline of economics. To effect the necessary reorientation of perspective, I will first of all outline the institutional and biographical elements that came together in the second half of the nineteenth century and which made it possible to develop the teaching of economics in Cambridge. I will show how Marshall taught within this framework, how he evaluated the students he taught, and the arguments he advanced for the general development of economic education.

The story does not end once the Tripos was established in 1903, although it is often enough assumed that Marshall's success in establishing the Tripos can be read across to the success of the Tripos itself. I show that this assumption is unjustified. No consideration has been given to how the Tripos did in fact function to train young economists, nor whether it can be deemed a success or failure in terms of Marshall's own aspirations for it. Only in the 1930s did it begin to attract a significant number of students who had some prospect, eventually, of putting Marshall's aspirations for economic education into practice—using their degree in economics as a qualification for particular kinds of employment. It did not help that Pigou became Professor of Political Economy in 1908; like Edgeworth in Oxford, he showed little of the drive that had characterised Marshall in his pursuit of economic training, and played little part in the teaching of the Faculty until his retirement in 1943. An examination of the medium-term outcome of the Economic Tripos significantly qualifies the heroic story of its creation.

Nonetheless, independently of these institutional matters, Marshall's version of economics as represented by *Principles* did quickly became hegemonic in Britain and the United States, becoming a prime point of reference for economic argument. But this hegemony was short-lived. Despite the routine invocation of the Marshallian heritage by Cambridge economists through to the 1950s, "Marshallianism" was to all intents and purposes sidelined by the later 1920s, and did not really outlive Alfred Marshall himself. And so following on from the account of the Tripos, I will outline what "Marshallianism" originally represented, and why it was a waning force by the early 1930s.

Later, Part III will take a diversion into why it was that alternative paths of development were not in fact taken: given how institutionally prominent Oxford economists were during the 1890s and early 1900s in positions linked to the emergent discipline, why was it that Marshall returned from Oxford to Cambridge in order to realise his vision? Secondly, Oxford economists have been associated with an "English historical economics" that for a time challenged the elaboration of a more abstract, theoretical approach to economic reasoning, but whose appeal quickly faded in the early twentieth century, transmuting into "economic history" by the mid-1920s. Why was this? I will demonstrate that this was not because new economists progressively sidelined colleagues with historical interests, but because this historical interest never took on a form sufficiently coherent to support disciplinary development.

[3] And I should add that I do not mean that we need to intuit Marshall's 'intentions', 'what he meant to do', but rather identify what the implications were of what he did. Marshall was a contrary character, and there is no point in trying to parse his own understanding and behaviour, or to reconcile these with his actions.

4

The Moral Sciences Tripos and Cambridge Political Economy

In the early nineteenth century the University of Cambridge was, as the historian of the University put it, 'practically a preserve of the Church of England'.[1] College fellows and tutors were not only obliged to conform to the liturgy of the Church of England; they were not permitted to marry, reinforcing the sense of seminary life. To graduate, students had to swear allegiance to the Thirty-Nine Articles of Anglican faith printed in the *Book of Common Prayer*;[2] but a significant proportion of students never got as far as this and left college without formally graduating from the University, suggesting both the centrality of college life and a greater emphasis on sociability than education. Broadly speaking, as the century progressed, emphasis shifted from college society to more systematic university teaching and learning; although students left the university without graduating even in the early 1900s.[3]

When it did come to teaching and examination, the curriculum was dominated by mathematics. This formed the main part, along with some Paley and Locke, of the Senate House Examination, which in time became known as the Mathematical Tripos. While this four- or five-day written examination was taken by a majority of students, this also meant that very many did not, and left Cambridge without a degree. The Tripos results were presented as a rank ordering of individual candidates, a distinction also emerging between 'pass' or 'poll' men[4] and those competing for honours. Reforms in 1822 introduced a Classical Tripos open only to those who had already gained honours in mathematics; and in 1824 an intermediate examination called the 'Previous Examination' was introduced in the fifth term of residence, for which the Gospels or Acts of the Apostles, Paley's *Evidences of Christianity*, a Greek or Latin prescribed author formed the subject matter. By mid-century, with divinity, mechanics, and hydrostatics added in 1837, this had become the ordinary degree, for which attendance and examination at one course of professorial lectures was also required. It had not been that usual in the early part of the century for professors to lecture: in 1809

[1] D. A. Winstanley, *Early Victorian Cambridge*, Cambridge University Press, London 1940, p. 82. For an authoritative modern account of Classics and Mathematics at Cambridge during the early nineteenth century, see Chris Stray, 'The Slaughter of 1841: Mathematics and Classics in Early Victorian Cambridge', *History of Universities* Vol. XXXV No. 2 (2022) (forthcoming).

[2] For a summary of these and their significance, see my 'Henry Sidgwick, Moral Order, and Utilitarianism', *European Journal of the History of Economic Thought* Vol. 24 (2017), pp. 911–13.

[3] During the period 1855–1914 nearly 3,000 students were admitted to Trinity Hall, of whom only 700 were classed in Tripos (Honours) examinations. Of the around 250 students who entered Trinity Hall in October 1918–April 1920, some 25% left without graduating. Of the remainder, 43% took Ordinary BA degrees; C. Crawley, *Trinity Hall: The History of a Cambridge College 1350–1975*, Trinity Hall, Cambridge 1976, pp. 181, 184.

[4] 'Non-reading' students not aiming for distinction; 'poll men' from the Greek *hoi polloi*, the many.

Constructing Economic Science. Keith Tribe, Oxford University Press. © Oxford University Press 2022.
DOI: 10.1093/oso/9780190491741.003.0004

the Professor of Divinity 'broke a well-established tradition of his chair by delivering a course of lectures', and when Whewell became Knightbridge Professor in 1838, he ended the chair's status as a sinecure by delivering at least 12 lectures annually, apart from the year in which he was Vice Chancellor.[5]

Teaching students was a college matter; as is evident from the description of teaching in the 1893 edition of the *Student's Guide*, this was still the case at the end of the century.[6] College 'lectures' were more like schoolroom classes, students being called upon to construe a passage or prove orally a mathematical proposition. However, given the broad scope of the ordinary degree, colleges sometimes lacked appropriate or sufficient tutors, and a system of private coaching developed, which in turn contributed to a low academic standard, since more rigorous examination would only increase the demand for private tutoring, and encourage cramming for the ordinary degree.[7]

The appointment of Prince Albert as Chancellor of the University in 1847 lent a focus to existing arguments in Cambridge for reform. Albert had studied law, philosophy, and the history of art during 1837 and 1838 at the University of Bonn,[8] just like Karl Marx, who had followed the same lectures at Bonn the previous academic year. Having been given a list of Cambridge teaching by the Vice Chancellor, Albert concluded that teaching was very incomplete, and he advocated an extensive broadening of subjects that already had some support among Cambridge fellows. However, since teaching was a college matter and the colleges were already beholden to an extra-college network of private coaches, something other than a simple intensification of college teaching was required. The result was a proposal in February 1848 that all students for the ordinary degree be required to attend for at least one term lectures given by one or more University professors, and be certified by the appropriate professor as having passed an examination in the subject of the lectures. Implicit was therefore a requirement that professors provide regular courses of lectures. Additionally, two new Triposes were added, in Natural Sciences and in Moral Sciences. Corresponding to the new function of professorial lectures, the component subjects for the new Moral Sciences Tripos were simply derived from existing professorial chairs: moral philosophy, history, political economy,[9] English law, and general jurisprudence. Admission to the Tripos no longer required that a Senate

[5] Winstanley, *Early Victorian Cambridge*, pp. 175, 80–81.

[6] *The Student's Guide to the University of Cambridge*, 5th edition, rewritten, Deighton, Bell and Co., Cambridge 1893, pp. 70–71. College lecturing was generally between the hours of 9 a.m. and midday; first-year students would attend for perhaps two hours through a five-day week. 'If the subject be classical, and the class not an advanced one, an author is read, the students translating in turns, while the lecturer interposes his comments as he sees fit. If it be mathematical, the students are often occupied during the whole hour in writing answers to various questions, or in solving problems' (p. 71).

[7] Winstanley, *Early Victorian Cambridge*, p. 179. Winstanley goes on to emphasise that Whewell was not an advocate of University lectures in themselves, but wished to improve the standing of professorial lectures so that they might be linked to subjects for examination, and also reduce the reliance on private tutors. The role of coaching for the Mathematical Tripos was different; here it was the private coaches who supplied the specialised teaching needed for a first-class degree that the colleges could not provide. See the discussion of the role of coaches in the following.

[8] Albert had studied in Brussels before attending Bonn, and he later corresponded with Quetelet about the latter's *On the Social System and the Laws Which Regulate It* (1848); David Palfrey, 'The Moral Sciences Tripos at Cambridge University, 1848–1860', PhD dissertation, University of Cambridge 2002, p. 106 fn. 44.

[9] The formal creation of the Chair for Political Economy in 1863 is discussed later; but until Marshall was appointed to the post in 1884, incumbents had played no role at all in the teaching of political economy

House Examination (the Mathematical Tripos) be sat first, as had been the case when the Classics Tripos was introduced in 1822. Instead, students were admitted only if they had already gained an ordinary degree: so when it was established, the Moral Sciences Tripos was a supplementary one-year graduate degree following on from a general degree, and not from the Mathematical Tripos like Classics. Only in 1860 did the Moral Sciences Tripos become an independent three-year honours undergraduate course, when the content was altered, professorial control loosened, and a Moral Sciences Board appointed to oversee it.

The Mathematical Tripos continued as the flagship course in Cambridge until later in the century, when the Natural Sciences Tripos displaced it as the foundation for the advanced work in theoretical physics initiated with the opening of the Cavendish Laboratory in 1874.[10] Alfred Marshall was himself a product of the Mathematical Tripos, as Second Wrangler to John Strutt in 1865. Strutt inherited the title of Lord Rayleigh in 1873 and is, among other things, notable for being awarded the Nobel Prize for Physics in 1904 for his work on the densities of gases, pointing up the connection between mathematics and physical science in the teaching of Cambridge mathematics.[11] The experience of studying mathematics in Cambridge shaped Marshall's later ideas about the way in which economics should be taught, while at the same time placing mathematical reasoning at the centre of his understanding of how economic analysis should be conducted. To understand both of these factors, we need first of all to examine more closely quite *how* mathematics was taught in Cambridge; but we also need to understand *what kind of mathematics* was taught in Cambridge in the mid-nineteenth century. As we shall see in Chapter 6, Stanley Jevons was taught a rather different kind of mathematics at University College London during the 1850s, while the fact that Francis Edgeworth taught himself the mathematics of Lagrange and Laplace[12] also meant that his understanding of mathematical reasoning was distinct from that which had been conveyed to Marshall by the Cambridge Tripos.[13]

The Mathematical Tripos

In the course of the eighteenth century, mathematical knowledge became more systematic but also more complex, opening a gap between the presentation of finished

in the Moral Sciences Tripos. Hence the story of this chair has only a marginal relevance to my discussion of the teaching of political economy in Cambridge.

[10] Andrew Warwick, 'Cambridge Mathematics and Cambridge Physics: Cunningham, Campbell and Einstein's Relativity 1905–1911. Part II: Comparing Traditions in Cambridge Physics', *Studies in the History and Philosophy of Science* Vol. 24 (1993), pp. 2–3.

[11] Rayleigh had married Evelyn Balfour in 1871, a sister of A. J. Balfour, a student of Moral Sciences who was taught by Marshall; another of Balfour's sisters was Eleanor, who married Henry Sidgwick.

[12] Via Hamilton; see Peter Newman, 'Francis Ysidro Edgeworth (1845–1926)', in his edition *F. Y. Edgeworth's Mathematical Psychics and Further Papers on Political Economy*, Oxford University Press, Oxford 2003, p. xxiv.

[13] See, for a discussion of these differences, Joan L. Richards, 'The Art and the Science of British Algebra: A Study in the Perception of Mathematical Truth', *Historia Mathematica* Vol. 7 (1980), pp. 343–65; and her 'Augustus De Morgan, the History of Mathematics, and the Foundations of Algebra,' *Isis* Vol. 78 (1987), pp. 6–30.

proofs and theorems, on the one hand, and the skills that had to be acquired in order to understand, replicate, or develop them, on the other. Andrew Warwick notes that we do not really know how Newton or Laplace gained their mathematical knowledge, while Wilhelm Weber and Georg Ohm owed their knowledge to family connections, not university training.[14] By the second half of the eighteenth century, the study of mathematics in Cambridge had nonetheless displaced the role hitherto played by moral philosophy or theology, while at the same time competitive written examinations replaced oral disputations. Competitive success in extended written examinations could not be achieved through attending lectures, or by private reading; students had to be drilled in principles and examples by a tutor. Warwick's study focusses on the way in which mathematical knowledge was acquired, highlighting the centrality of a 'progressive syllabus, lectures, tutorials, textbooks, graded examples, written examinations', features that are now so commonplace in elite technical education that they seem 'barely to warrant comment'.[15] But these devices and instruments had once been invented, along with the institutional forms within which they were practised.

The transition from oral disputations between examiners and students to written examinations began in the 1760s, while the examinations themselves became increasingly competitive.[16] The growing complexity of problems and solutions made possible by written examinations, and competition among students for a high rank, created an opening for the use of private tutors, since the colleges could not provide the intensive tuition that was required for success. The teaching supplied by the colleges was limited to routine lectures in which a college fellow took the students through a section of Euclid or Newton, ensuring that all those attending had a basic grasp of geometry, arithmetic, algebra, mechanics, hydrostatics, optics, and astronomy. While this provision might be supplemented in one way or another, the intensive drills required by ambitious students were not something that colleges fellows were able to provide, constrained either by time or by competence. In the early nineteenth century new topics were being added, and during the 1820s Continental notation became more widely used; in 1828 the number of examination days was extended to four, the first two being devoted to simpler problems that required no calculus, with more demanding questions on the last two days. Questions were now also printed, rather than read out to candidates, making it possible for future students to study past papers.[17]

[14] Andrew Warwick, *Masters of Theory: Cambridge and the Rise of Mathematical Physics*, Chicago University Press, Chicago 2003, p. 33. The following account of the Tripos relies heavily on Warwick's detailed presentation. Gregory Moore's review of Warwick, '*Masters of Theory* and Its Relevance to the History of Economic Thought', *History of Economics Review* Vol. 42 (Summer 2005), pp. 77–99, provides an excellent summary of Warwick that is more comprehensive than that given here. Alex D. D. Craik, *Mr Hopkins' Men: Cambridge Reform and British Mathematics in the 19th Century*, Springer, London 2008, covers much of the same ground as Warwick, but deals in more detail with the work of one of the leading coaches in mid-century and his students' biographies.

[15] Warwick, *Masters of Theory*, p. 26.

[16] Warwick, *Masters of Theory*, pp. 55ff., details the evolution of the Senate House examination.

[17] Chris Stray quotes from the account of the 1802 Senate House Examination given in the University Calendar, where examiners would read out a question for the candidates at their desks, but that as soon as one person had completed the answer, the examiner moved on to the next question; 'The Slaughter of 1841'.

These and other changes made private tuition all the more necessary for students seeking high honours; they sought out the services of tutors who had themselves distinguished themselves in the Tripos a few years previously. William Hopkins, Seventh Wrangler in 1827, went on to a lifetime of private tutoring, teaching in small classes of between 10 and 15 students of roughly equal ability who, in competing with each other, learned from each other. Despite the rigours of the class, Warwick notes that there was generally a more personal relationship between student and private tutor than that prevailing in college between students and fellows. This was in part because of a mutual dependence: the student had engaged the private tutor on the strength of his reputation; the tutor needed to maintain that reputation through driving his 'teams' in much the same way that a coachman would. The practice of designating the private tutor as a 'coach' appears to have taken hold in the 1830s, by analogy with the stage and mail coaches that plied between London and Cambridge in, by the mid-1830s, four and a half hours. Although this average speed of just over 13 miles an hour might seem modest enough—it would be faster by bike, although not until the later 1880s[18]—the railway did not reach Cambridge until 1845, and that form of transport never had the cachet of coach travel on good roads.[19] George Pryme (Sixth Wrangler 1803) later wrote that in the early 1800s the idea that a coach could travel between London and Cambridge in only seven and a half hours was greeted with disbelief.

The growing technicality of mathematical training in the second third of nineteenth-century Cambridge did not go unchallenged. William Whewell had himself begun as a private mathematics tutor before rising to the Mastership of Trinity in 1841. He had fostered the introduction of French analysis as a young tutor, and had written textbooks introducing students to the new notation in calculus. He did, however, retain geometric methods where he could, and retained an allegiance to the idea that mathematics was the basis of a liberal education, whose purpose

> ... was to 'develop the whole mental system of man' such that his 'speculative inferences coincide with his practical convictions,' a coincidence best nurtured through practical examples which taught students how to 'proceed with certainty and facility from fundamental principles to their consequences.'[20]

This understanding of the purpose of mathematical training lay behind his hostility to the general introduction of Continental analysis into undergraduate teaching. 'Analytical methods encouraged students to circumvent the intuitive geometrical or

[18] The one-hour record for a high-wheeler was set in Cambridge during 1876 at 15.8 miles, a speed barely above that which today's average cyclist could easily sustain on level ground without a headwind; see David Gordon Wilson, *Bicycling Science*, 3rd edition, MIT Press, Cambridge Mass. 2004, p. 160.

[19] Warwick describes the origin and use of the term, and its entry into fiction during the 1850s. The 'rowing coach' was named by analogy with this usage, and as Warwick also demonstrates there was a symbiotic relationship between the mental gymnastics prescribed by the private tutor and the physical demands of the new sport of college rowing—*Masters of Theory*, pp. 89ff., and pp. 176–200. It might also be pointed out here that the reason that a railway carriage is in Britain referred to as a 'coach' is because in the early days of the railways the best passenger accommodation was created by attaching three horse-drawn coach bodies to an underframe. See Simon Bradley, *The Railways: Nation, Network and People*, Profile Books, London 2015, pp. 26ff.

[20] Warwick, *Masters of Theory*, p. 95.

mechanical steps which ought properly to be followed in solving difficult problems.'[21] In arguing this, he also made use of an analogy with horse-drawn coaches and the railways, forms of transport that rapidly carried their charges from one point to another without calling for any effort of their own.[22] The trend towards longer and more competitive examination and the coaching on which it depended would, he thought, undermine the purpose of a liberal education, which was to nurture the nation's finest intellects. Seeking to preserve the priority of college teaching, he saw the existence of private tuition more in terms of an aid to the slower students. He failed to anticipate that the symbiotic relationship between coaches, students, and examiners would lead into a form of bidding war where students engaged the service of coaches in order to achieve a high ranking, coaches competed among themselves for the best students, and examiners found themselves faced with a rising level of technical competence that required ever-more stringent examinations in order to create a clear rank order of graduates. This was a process driven along not only by the best students; an alternative path emerged in which less talented students could afford to do little work for a year or two, then cram carefully selected theorems and proofs with a private tutor for a few months.[23] Opinions also differed in mid-century about the efficacy of systematic teaching; whether such intensive tuition saved students from the trouble of thinking for themselves, or imbued students with the instruments necessary to conquer diverse problems. The same arguments were advanced in the later twentieth century about calculators and mental arithmetic. They continue today with smartphones.

In 1846 disquiet over the direction that mathematical education was taking led to a review of the examination process that in 1848 resulted in significant reforms. A Board of Mathematical Studies was created to oversee the syllabus and examinations; and the examination period was extended from six[24] to eight days, the first three days being devoted to elementary mathematics, with only those students who had achieved honours in the first three days being allowed to proceed to five days of continuous examinations after one week's interval.[25] The existing tension between private and college teaching remained, however, and earlier arguments over the aims and effects of teaching were rehearsed once more before the Parliamentary Commission appointed in 1850 to investigate undergraduate teaching in Cambridge. After hearing these arguments, the Commission declined to undermine the function of the coaching system and endorsed the importance of a rigorous competitive examination. They proposed, however, that the functions of coaches should be transferred to a body of new 'Public Lecturers'[26] who would

[21] Ibid.

[22] Warwick, *Masters of Theory*, pp. 104–5.

[23] Ibid., p. 97. This resembles what happened to the relationship between Parts I and II of the Economics Tripos in the 1930s; see Chapter 5.

[24] In 1833 four days had become five, and then in 1839 six; Warwick, *Masters of Theory*, p. 84.

[25] This was the sequence that Marshall went through in 1865; see Robert John Strutt, *John William Strutt Third Baron Rayleigh O.M., F.R.S.*, Edward Arnold, London 1924, p. 33.

[26] As Warwick notes (p. 104 fn. 152), the designation 'Public Lecturer' was selected to distinguish their didactic function from the monologic teaching of professors. Hopkins's suggestion that their stipend would have to be the £800–£900 earned by a good coach can be compared with Alfred Marshall's salary of £700 in 1885. This new function was realised in the position of College Lecturer, both Marshall and Sidgwick being appointed to their colleges as Lecturers in the Moral Sciences.

teach students of all colleges according to the best methods employed by private tutors.[27]

Warwick counters the Anglican Toryism of Whewell to Hopkins's more middle-class, aspirational Toryism:

> In his address as President of the British Association in 1853, Hopkins explicitly linked Britain's continued industrial and commercial success to the proper application of both experimental and mathematical science. The 'great duty' owed to the public by the British Association was, he urged, to 'encourage the application of abstract science to the practical purposes of life—to bring, as it were, the study and the laboratory into juxtaposition with the workshop.'

This opposed the view that

> ... coaching undermined the moral and spiritual authority of college and public teachers, [and] subverted the ideals of a liberal education, ... [leaving] ... no leisure for able undergraduates to pursue their own intellectual interests. William Hopkins, by contrast, not only espoused a highly competitive, research oriented, and utilitarian vision of higher mathematics, but helped to develop the training techniques through which his vision could be realized.[28]

When these arguments were recapitulated in the 1870s, they were inflected into another level of familiar dispute: that of teaching to the test. With the proliferation of examinations in the latter part of the century—besides written examinations for the Civil Service and banking, the Cambridge Local Examinations Syndicate was established in 1858, as also the possibility of sitting for London degrees in provincial centres—the argument was made that the importance of examinations reduced the skills of the teacher to predicting what would be the content of an impending examination, and preparing his students accordingly. Competitive examination, in this story, corrupted both students and teachers.[29]

This did, however, presume that the Mathematical Tripos still functioned, as hitherto, to educate the nation's cultural and political elite. In arguing against this view, Isaac Todhunter (Senior Wrangler 1848) pointed out that the Tripos, now one of four,[30] had become primarily a training in mathematics for

[27] Warwick, *Masters of Theory*, pp. 103–4.

[28] Ibid., pp. 107, 109. Warwick continues on to write that 'variations on these training methods ... have remained throughout the twentieth century at the heart of mathematical pedagogy in elite secondary and tertiary education in Britain.' It would also be true to say that this disjunction lies at the heart of all argument about pedagogy in the modern university.

[29] Ibid., p. 111.

[30] Joan Richards is mistaken in writing that Part I of the Mathematical Tripos 'remained the solid core of any Cambridge graduate' after 1848; *Mathematical Visions: The Pursuit of Geometry in Victorian England*, Academic Press, Boston 1988, p. 40. As noted previously, after 1848 the linkage that had existed between the Mathematical Tripos and the Classical Tripos was no longer the model according to which new Triposes were introduced. Initially Moral Sciences was studied for one year after successful completion of the Ordinary degree, rather than sitting the Mathematical Tripos; then after 1860 the Moral Sciences Tripos became a three-year course with its own Board.

mathematicians;[31] an argument that also anticipated the eclipse of the Mathematical Tripos by the Natural Sciences Tripos in the training of Cambridge scientists.[32] In the shift of oral to written examination, the Mathematical Tripos had played a key role; as it became more demanding and complex, oral responses to questions necessarily gave way to written responses to printed questions. A clear ranking of capable students was only possible through scrutiny of a candidate's written working.[33] The path followed by the examinations of the Mathematical Tripos in the first half of the nineteenth century prepared the way for the parallel development of the Natural Sciences Tripos in the second half. Economics itself took more than another century to follow suit; well into the later twentieth century, students of economics in Cambridge and Oxford would primarily write essays, rather than solve problems—this itself being a reflection of the oral culture of the supervision/tutorial, rather than classwork. I will come back to this point in the following chapter.

The mathematical education that Marshall experienced in the 1860s required the rapid solution of problems using theorems and models learned in advance. These theorems and models had been conveyed to the student by the coach through the use of chalk and talk; textbooks were published that were more suited to experienced mathematicians than to students, and so the role of the coach also involved training his teams in mastering the material in the most recently published textbooks.[34] The pressure of classroom and examination was also a mental test of the student; in 1856 Henry Fawcett became so wrought up during his finals that he could not sleep, resorting to running around the college quadrangle in a vain attempt to tire himself into a state of physical exhaustion. As the examination days proceeded, his marks slipped, and he ended up Seventh Wrangler that year. Nonetheless, he was elected to a college fellowship because of the determination he had shown:

> Fawcett was wanting in technical skill and the manipulation of mathematical analysis. He overcame his deficiency by sheer mental force and his power of directly

[31] Warwick, *Masters of Theory*, p. 112. Roy Weintraub's account of mathematical teaching in Cambridge misses this transition, because he treats the Mathematical Tripos throughout the nineteenth century as a (defective) way of training mathematicians. The rise of the Natural Science Tripos appropriated a pathway to the physical sciences that had hitherto been a central function of the Mathematical Tripos, as the example of Rayleigh shows; while Weintraub also discounts the pedagogical function of the Tripos. See E. Roy Weintraub, *How Economics became a Mathematical Science*, Duke University Press, Durham NC 2002, pp. 9–25.

[32] Warwick, 'Cambridge Mathematics and Cambridge Physics', p. 2.

[33] And also the position of the candidate at the end of the Honours ranking, whose position was celebrated with an outsize 'wooden spoon' (initially a malting shovel). The practice of ranking candidates in the Mathematical Tripos was ended in 1909, when the last wooden spoon was awarded (in this case, a rowing blade); see Christopher Stray, 'The Wooden Spoon: Rank (Dis)order in Cambridge 1753–1909', *History of Universities* Vol. XXVI No. 1 (2012), pp. 163–94. Stray notes that the term 'Senior Wrangler' and 'Wooden Spoon' emerged simultaneously sometime after 1753, occurring in the title of a 1793 play (p. 167).

[34] There is a more complex history here, since the function of textbooks altered around 1800; see Warwick, *Masters of Theory*, pp. 140ff. See also Warwick's discussion of why textbooks written by Cambridge authors for Cambridge students were opaque to those trained elsewhere—the role of bookwork questions for which Cambridge students had memorised proofs, theorems, and principles consequently not included in these textbooks; and the Cambridge emphasis on problem-solving; '... even when Tripos questions became widely available in popular textbooks, they remained insoluble to non-Cambridge readers because the techniques by which they were tackled were known only to Cambridge tutors' (p. 153).

> applying mechanical principles. He used plain English where most candidates would apply mathematical machinery.[35]

Rayleigh, on the other hand, Senior Wrangler in 1865 ahead of Alfred Marshall, sought to remain relaxed, and developed the knack of taking a short nap before the afternoon's examination—Warwick contrasts 'Fawcett's failure of nerve and Rayleigh's cool head under pressure', exactly the kind of temperament that Marshall would extol in the peroration to his Inaugural lecture.[36]

The intensive training required to excel in the Mathematical Tripos endowed the student with an engine of reasoning to be applied to any other problem; solutions that fitted one problem could involve principles that could be used by an enterprising candidate in approaching another. The Tripos sought to inculcate a systematic and inventive approach to problem-solving, making use of theorems and examples that had been learned previously. Hitherto the role of mathematics in the intellectual formation of Alfred Marshall has been considered in regard to his use of mathematical techniques in the development of economic analysis.[37] But from the foregoing it should have become clear that the kind of student formed by studying mathematics in mid-century Cambridge was in fact the model for the kind of economist he sought to mould after he became Professor of Political Economy. One sign of this is the way that he encouraged students to visit him at home for advice on their studies, echoing the more familiar relationship of private coach and student. Likewise, the presentation of economic principles as a toolbox to be explored for appropriate instruments of analysis in any one case echoes the way that candidates for the Mathematical Tripos were trained to adapt material learned in advance to the problems with which they were presented in the examination room.[38]

If, therefore, we seek an explanation for why Marshall was so insistent that the Moral Sciences Tripos was an unsuitable vehicle for the training of economists, it is to these features of the Mathematical Tripos that we should look. This does, I think, explain the tenacity with which he pursued his goal, although he never articulated his aim in this way.[39] The material with which he worked—the economic principles and techniques, his students, his colleagues, the future employers he envisaged—all in one way or another resisted being moulded according to the pattern of a Cambridge mathematical education, and this was a continuing source of frustration to him. His project for economics remained largely an aspiration. That in the mid-twentieth century the

[35] Leslie Stephen, *Life of Henry Fawcett*, Smith, Elder & Co., London 1885, p. 32.

[36] Warwick, *Masters of Theory*, p. 188. James Wilson, Senior Wrangler in 1859, suffered a nervous breakdown after his final paper so severe that three months later he accepted that all the higher mathematics he had learned had vanished: 'I could not differentiate or integrate; I had forgotten utterly all lunar theory and Dynamics; nearly the whole of trigonometry and conic sections was a blank.'

[37] See, for example, Weintraub's discussion of Groenewegen's account of Marshall in his biography, *How Economics Became a Mathematical Science*, pp. 22–24.

[38] For a vivid account of the pressures of the examination, see Noel Annan, *Leslie Stephen: His Thought and Character in Relation to His Time*, MacGibbon and Kee, London 1951, pp. 23–25.

[39] In a letter to Gonner, then Professor of Economics in Liverpool, Marshall did outline in some detail his approach to teaching, and expressed his regret that so many of those for whom he had hopes had become schoolteachers—Marshall to Gonner, Letter 448 3 May 1894 in Whitaker, *Correspondence* Vol. 2, pp. 110–12. See the discussion of this in Chapter 6.

teaching of economics would begin to assume the guise of a science that superficially resembled Marshall's aspiration, but that this 'science' would involve a rejection of Marshall's legacy, is an irony that will become more evident in later chapters. Here we need to address Marshall's own project of creating an independent Economics Tripos; and for this we need to consider next exactly what the Moral Sciences Tripos was, so that we might understand why, for him, it was an inadequate vehicle for the training of economists.[40] In this way we can open up an approach to the creation of the Economics Tripos that does not already assume that we know why this came about, and what it was intended to do.

The Organisation of the Moral Sciences Tripos

As already noted, the syllabus for the 'Moral Sciences Tripos' as originally constituted in 1848 was formed simply by combining a number of existing professorial domains; but what were the 'Moral Sciences'? The idea of a moral science can be dated back at least to Adam Ferguson's *Principles of Moral and Political Science* (1792), in which he describes his aim as:

> [i]n treating of him [man] as a subject of moral science, we endeavour to understand what he ought to be; without being limited, in our conception, to the measurement of attainment or failure, exhibited in the case of any particular person or society of men.[41]

The human person is first of all a being distinct from other animals, possessed of mental faculties enabling that person to reason, able to discern the difference between pleasure and pain, beauty and deformity, prosperity and adversity, subject to rules of morality regarding external actions and also to legal statutes, characterised by definite virtues, and living in society with other human persons. And when the *Institut national des sciences et des arts* was established by the Directory in 1795, it was divided into three classes: 'Physical and Mathematical Sciences'; 'Moral and Political Sciences'; and 'Literature and the Fine Arts'. The second class was divided into several sections: for 'The Analysis of Sensations and Ideas'; 'Morals'; 'Social Science and Legislation'; 'Political Economy'; 'History'; and 'Geography and Statistics'.[42] In addition, David Palfrey draws attention to the fact that when John Stuart Mill's *System of Logic* (1843) was translated into German, the 'moral sciences' discussed in Book VI

[40] When Marshall began to make plans for the creation of the Economics Tripos in 1901–1902, he took a route through the History Board, thus tactically by-passing the Moral Sciences Board. Nevertheless, the aim was to detach the teaching of economics from the Moral Sciences, not from History. For an account of the teaching of political economy in the History Tripos, see Alon Kadish, 'Marshall and the Cambridge Economics Tripos', in Kadish, Tribe (eds.) *The Market for Political Economy: The Advent of Economics in British University Culture, 1850–1905*, Routledge, London 1993, pp. 143ff.

[41] Adam Ferguson, *Principles of Moral and Political Science* Vol. I, A. Strahan & T. Cadell, London 1792, p. 2.

[42] Richard Whatmore, *Republicanism and the French Revolution: An Intellectual History of Jean-Baptiste Say's Political Economy*, Oxford University Press, Oxford 2000, p. 112.

were translated as *Geisteswissenschaften*, emphasising the mental rather than the social (political) aspect.[43] Mill doubted whether

> [t]he phenomena with which this science [of human nature] is conversant being the thoughts, feelings and actions of human beings, it would have attained the ideal perfection of a science if it enabled us to foretell how an individual would think, feel, or act, throughout life, with the same certainty with which astronomy enables us to predict the places and the occultations of the heavenly bodies. It needs scarcely be stated that nothing approaching this can be done. The actions of individuals could not be predicted with scientific accuracy, were it only because we cannot foresee the whole of the circumstances in which those individuals will be placed.

No precise and universally true statement can be made regarding human action, he argued; but this was not because an individual's modes of thinking and acting do not depend on causes, rather that causal factors were varied in their combination, such that in the aggregate no two actions were quite alike.[44] We might conclude that, by the later 1840s, the 'moral sciences' were understood to include all phenomena related to human society and sociability, from the philosophical (moral philosophy) through language to the more strictly social, including an understanding of social actions and the formation of enduring human society.

Whewell's version of this sought to integrate law, history, and political economy through a Christian moral philosophy, and within a fortnight of the new Tripos being approved he announced a course of 24 lectures on the history of moral philosophy from Plato to Paley, Dugald Stewart, Bentham, and Mackintosh.[45] James Stephen presented his first lecture course on History three times a week in Trinity Hall during the Easter term of 1850, running from Roman Gaul to the establishment of absolute monarchy under Louis XIV, although he did digress into a critique of Comte as discussed by Mill and John Grote. Pryme had of course begun lecturing on political economy in March 1816, and in 1828 he had been given the title Professor of Political Economy, albeit unpaid and only lecturing for one term every other year.[46] While the

[43] Palfrey, 'The Moral Sciences Tripos at Cambridge University', p. 124.

[44] John Stuart Mill, *A System of Logic Ratiocinative and Inductive*, Collected Works of John Stuart Mill Vol. 7 in 2 pts. Routledge and Kegan Paul, London 1973, pp. 846–47.

[45] He later published *Lectures on the History of Moral Philosophy in England*, John W. Parker, London 1852, which ran roughly from Hobbes to Bentham in 18 lectures.

[46] See Shin Kubo, 'George Pryme, Dugald Stewart and Political Economy at Cambridge', *History of Political Economy* Vol. 45 (2013), pp. 61–97; although no attention is paid here to the context in which Pryme gave his lectures, which rendered them entirely marginal to any teaching at Cambridge. His early lectures were at best a paraphrase of the opening discourse of Jean-Baptiste Say's *Traité*; while he readily admitted his reliance on Say when he eventually yielded to pressure and published his introductory lecture in 1823, the fact that the 1821 English translation of Say omitted its opening discourse remained a matter of great irritation to Say. It was restored in the 1832 American translation. I draw here on Istvan Hont, 'The "Introductory Lecture"', typescript, New York 1986, who summarises Pryme's political economy as follows: 'Pryme's leading idea was that political economy, properly taught, was genuinely politically neutral. The politics of the political economist did not matter in itself. If one thought that political economy was inevitably Whig or radical, the history of its 18th century origins, he claimed, could demonstrate the opposite. The Physiocrats were friends of the absolute power of the sovereign. Looking at British authors such as Sir James Steuart and Adam Smith, one had to notice that one of them was an "exiled Jacobite" the other an "extreme Tory".'

subject of political economy was recognised as broadly belonging to the moral sciences (as also later with the University of London BA degree), until 1848 the subject did not form any part of undergraduate education in Cambridge, and then only contributed to the elementary parts of the Moral Sciences Tripos. Fawcett, who succeeded Pryme as Professor of Political Economy in 1863, lectured mainly to pass men.[47]

Perhaps of more immediate significance in mid-century was the very small number of students who actually attempted the Moral Sciences Tripos from 1851 to 1860: there were only 66 in total. In 1860 no students at all sat for the Tripos.[48] This did not, however, mean that no students attended the professorial lectures related to the Moral Sciences that year; there were also undergraduates studying for the ordinary degree and seeking professorial certificates, such that from 1851 to 1860 political economy averaged 20.8 students per year, civil law 27.8—but moral philosophy 4.7. In 1858–1859 there were 62 students attending political economy lectures, 22 for civil law, and 9 for moral philosophy; the following year 46, 6, and 2, respectively.[49] During the 1850s external pressure on the University to reform both curriculum and the organisation of teaching continued, followed in the 1860s by a number of private members' bills in Parliament aimed at the removal of all religious tests. When John Grote was appointed Knightbridge Professor in 1855, he allied himself with this pressure for reform, seeking to remedy the limitations of the Moral Sciences Tripos as a one-year course that could only admit students who had already graduated with an ordinary degree. He began giving comprehensive courses of lectures, rather than the annual dozen lectures of Whewell.

John Grote had entered Trinity College in 1831, taking the Mathematics and Classics Triposes in 1835 and being elected a Fellow of Trinity College in 1837. In 1842 he was ordained, and in 1847 was given a college living as Vicar of Trumpington, then a village on the outskirts of Cambridge. Here he took the opportunity of founding a dining club in his vicarage, 'The Grote Club'; papers were read after dinner, and by all accounts Grote and Henry Sidgwick were its leading lights. One of the members, J. R. Mozley, wrote a long letter to Joseph Mayor[50] after Sidgwick's death, recalling discussions between Grote, Sidgwick, Venn, Pearson, and Mayor.[51] The club was continued

[47] In November 1879, when attendance at Fawcett's lectures was no longer compulsory for the 'poll men', he was reported in the *Cambridge Review* to have delivered his lecture one Saturday before 'two undergraduates, two gentlemen apparently not members of the University, and a lady'; quoted in Michael V. White, 'Thirsting for the Fray: The Cambridge Dunning of Mr. Macleod', *Journal of the History of Economic Thought* Vol. 12 (2010), p. 324.

[48] Palfrey, 'The Moral Sciences Tripos at Cambridge University', p. 364 Table 9.1.

[49] Ibid., pp. 366–67.

[50] In December 1863, Mayor married Grote's ward and niece, Alexandrina Jessie Grote, and so had to surrender his college living. He taught first at Kensington School in London, then being appointed Professor at King's College, London, initially in classical literature and then, from 1879 to 1883, in moral philosophy. John R. Gibbins, 'Mayor, Joseph Bickersteth (1828–1916)', *Oxford Dictionary of National Biography.* See generally Gibbins, *John Grote, Cambridge University and the Development of Victorian Thought*, Imprint Academic, Exeter 2007.

[51] J. R. Mozley to J. B. Mayor, 21 April 1904, Holly Bank, Headingley, Leeds; Trinity College Library Add. Ms.c 104/66: 'There was no doubt of Sidgwick preferring ethics to metaphysics, as he always did; the practical side in him was always very strong (I remember Alfred Marshall emphasising his admiration of this side of him, very soon after he made his acquaintance) and he distrusted metaphysics as much as Mill did—I remember his saying to me once, that he thought Kant was like a difficult mathematical book; you might hope to understand him if you gave trouble enough to the work; whereas he did not think Hegel was intelligible at all . . .'

after Grote's death in 1866 as the Grote Society, presided over by F. D. Maurice, Grote's successor as Knightbridge Professor.[52] For a short time in the 1860s, Grote's dining club provided an important forum for discussion in the moral sciences, bringing first Grote together with Sidgwick and then, after Grote's death, Sidgwick with Marshall.

In 1860 both Grote and Mayor wrote Senate flysheets outlining the purpose of the Moral Sciences Tripos and its need of reform; Mayor's is considerably more detailed and better organised than that of Grote, while arguing to the same ends. He did not deny, for example, that there was a whispering campaign against the Tripos as it stood: that distinction could be gained with just a small amount of cramming. Mayor denied that this was a general problem, but did concede that '[i]t is possible also that there may be some slight foundation in fact for the stories told of distinction gained by a single night's reading.'[53] He attributed this to the breadth of the course, students having to cover so many different subjects that their knowledge of any one was necessarily shallow. His solution was to purge the Tripos of English Law, and add Logic and Mental Philosophy, making the Tripos more homogeneous; and he would also have preferred to see the removal of Jurisprudence and the conversion of Modern History into Political Philosophy. This would indeed soon come to pass, but we can point up here what is happening. While originally the content of the new Moral Sciences Tripos had been defined purely by the professors who were available to teach on it, and who lectured only because of changes to the ordinary BA, consideration was now being given to what properly belonged to a syllabus for the Moral Sciences. This implied an understanding of the Moral Sciences increasingly distanced from Whewell's Christian theology; even though both Mayor and Grote were, like Whewell, ordained clergymen.

Having conceded that there were some grounds for the criticisms made of the Moral Sciences Tripos, Mayor moved to defend it. If one took a Senior Wrangler or a Senior Classicist unacquainted with these matters, and got them to study Plato's *Republic*, or Aristotle's *Ethics*, or J. S. Mill's *Logic* or *Political Economy*, Mayor thought that even if they studied it for a year it was still conceivable they would fail to produce a good paper on it.

> For in truth such a paper as I allude to, involving the reproduction, illustration, application, and criticism of arguments, as opposed to a mere repetition of opinions, could only be floored by one who had a complete mastery of the principles of the sciences of which they treat.[54]

Mayor therefore identified the substance of the Tripos as the study of canonical texts not in order to mechanically reproduce their content, but to gain an understanding of the arguments to which they contributed. Here again we can see an echo of the argument that the Mathematical Tripos encouraged a more mechanical form of reasoning;

[52] See Alfred Marshall, 'Notes Taken during Discussions at the Grote Club Meetings, February–November 1867', introduced and edited by Tiziano Raffaelli, *Marshall Studies Bulletin* 6 (1996), pp. 49–64.

[53] Joseph B. Mayor, 'Remarks on the Proposal to Grant the Degree of BA to Persons Who Have Obtained Honours in the Moral Sciences Course', Cambridge 1860, pp. 2–3.

[54] Ibid., p. 8.

and the argument that Mayor advances does capture the central pedagogic feature of the Moral Sciences Tripos, and its difference from the class-based learning needed for distinction in the Mathematical Tripos.

Mayor was able to articulate this in a way that Grote could not. Grote and Mayor were clearly in agreement, but Grote's own flysheet was scrappy and brief, failing to counter coherently criticism of the Moral Sciences Tripos, nor presenting arguments in its favour, as Mayor had done. He did generally argue that the University was falling short if all it had to offer was Mathematics and two ancient languages;[55] but while he followed the main lines of Mayor's arguments, he did so with much less clarity. His recommendations were, however, plain enough: that a Pass with Honours would qualify for a BA; that a Moral Sciences Board be established to oversee the Tripos; and that the Laws of England be dropped in favour of Mental Philosophy. These recommendations were all approved in February 1860. Then, in 1867, the Moral Sciences Board proposed that History and Jurisprudence should be excluded, and political philosophy, previously grouped with History, be grouped with Moral Philosophy in the Moral Sciences Tripos. This now became four subjects: Moral and Political Philosophy; Mental Philosophy; Logic; and Political Economy. A further change in regulations in 1883 divided the degree into two parts. This was now the Moral Sciences Tripos of which Sidgwick was the titular head, and on which he and Marshall had been teaching since the later 1860s—Marshall was appointed St. John's College Lecturer in Moral Sciences in 1868, and Henry Sidgwick Trinity College Lecturer in Moral Sciences in 1869.[56]

In 1860 the Moral Sciences Tripos had become a three-year honours degree course, with its own governing Board of Studies. As is plain from the way that Mayor defended the intellectual demands of the Moral Sciences Tripos, the course was defined primarily by the study of key texts, many of them written by its teachers: Sidgwick wrote his *Methods of Ethics* (1874), then a *Principles of Political Economy* in 1883 because Fawcett's own *Manual of Political Economy* was unsuitable for honours teaching. When Alfred Marshall was appointed Fawcett's successor in 1884,[57] he went on to publish his own *Principles of Economics* (1890), together with its catechism, *Elements of Economics of Industry* (1892). Neville Keynes published his *Formal Logic* (1884);[58]

[55] John Grote, 'To Members of the Senate', 22 February 1860, p. 3.

[56] For a discussion of how Sidgwick came to be appointed to this post, see my essay 'Henry Sidgwick, Moral Order and Utilitarianism', pp. 914–16.

[57] Henry Fawcett was appointed Professor of Political Economy in 1863 when its remuneration was for the first time fixed at £300 per annum. The three other candidates were J. B. Mayor, Leonard Courtney, and Henry Dunning Macleod. His chief advantage over Mayor (who gained 80 votes to Fawcett's 90) was that he had published his *Manual of Political Economy* earlier the same year. As already noted, he lectured almost entirely to poll men; and with the repeal of compulsory attendance in 1876 the number of students attending was much reduced; Stephen, *Life*, pp. 122, 123. Stephen summarises Fawcett's presentation of his subject as follows: 'According to him, in fact, the leading principles of political economy, and those which were really valuable, were few, simple, and therefore capable of an exposition on the level of average intelligence. Refined and subtle reasonings were not required to set forth the great truths which had really been established, and which alone possessed much importance or bore directly upon the really interesting questions.' *Life*, p. 124. Stephen provides an outline of Fawcett's essentially Millian political economy in his *Life*, pp. 134–181.

[58] See the discussion of this in Phyllis Deane, *The Life and Times of J. Neville Keynes: A Beacon in the Tempest*, Edward Elgar, Cheltenham UK 2001, pp. 115–19.

Sidgwick his *Elements of Politics* (1891). The Moral Sciences Tripos had, by the last quarter of the nineteenth century, shifted from the somewhat accidental concatenation of subjects it had been in the 1850s to an honours degree defined in terms of central texts, many of which were written by those who taught on it.

The Historical Tripos dates from 1873, the History Board not being created until 1876, making it possible for arguments to be made about the nature of the teaching of history that could be translated into a curriculum.[59] Eventually the History Board would provide the base from which Marshall launched his campaign for a new Tripos, so we need to have some sense of the relationship of the teaching of history and political economy in Cambridge. While the Regius Chair in History had been established in 1724, lecturing on the subject was desultory until the appointment of Sir James Stephen in 1849, when the incumbent of the Regius chair was linked to teaching on the new Moral Sciences Tripos. Stephen was sceptical of lectures and examinations for historical instruction, but applied himself to the task. His successor, Charles Kingsley, drew large audiences attracted by his eloquence and conviction that '[h]istory is the history of men and women, and of nothing else', and that the teaching of history was a moral task.[60] In 1867 the subject of history transferred from the moral sciences to law, consequent upon the final reorganisation of the Moral Sciences Tripos; and then, with the resignation of Kingsley in 1869, John Seeley was appointed, who had very different ideas about the role of historical studies—famous for his dictum that 'history is past politics, and politics present history'.[61]

The first lecture list published by the History Board in 1877 included lectures on political economy, to be given by V. H. Stanton of Trinity College, an extension lecturer in the 1870s and Regius Professor of Divinity from 1916–1922. Discussion of reform to the Tripos began in 1879, with political economy being linked to lectures on economic history in the first year; and then in 1885 being separated from economic history. However, at this time economic history became a compulsory subject for examination, while political economy became an option alongside international law. Further changes during 1895–1897 made a clear distinction between Parts I and II, including in Part I an option between economic history and political economy. At the same time, the possibility of a new Political Tripos was mooted, including comparative politics, deductive politics, international law, and political economy.[62] Evident from McLachlan's careful account of the early years of Cambridge History are two things: that political economy was peripheral to those seeking to lend substance to the new university subject of History, and that the division of economic history from political economy was one effected by historians, not economists.

In 1862 Mayor provided in the new *Student's Guide* an overview of the Moral Sciences Tripos as it then stood. He began with the organisation of the final examinations—who might sit for them, how they would be graded, and the subjects of study. The questions, in 12 papers over six days, were 'in part of a special kind, having

[59] I draw here on the informative account of Jean O. McLachlan, 'The Origin and Early Development of the Cambridge Historical Tripos', *Cambridge Historical Journal* Vol. 9 No. 1 (1947), pp. 78–105.

[60] Ibid., p. 80.

[61] On Seeley, see his *Oxford Dictionary of National Biography* entry by R. T. Shannon.

[62] McLachlan, 'The Origin and Early Development', p. 95.

reference to *books* upon the subject; and in part of a general kind, having reference to the subjects themselves.'[63] This section was followed by a listing of books under each of the main parts of the course, political economy being the fifth and including Smith's *Wealth of Nations*, Malthus's *Essay on Population*, *The Principles of Political Economy* by Ricardo, Mill, and McCulloch, plus Jones on rent, Carey's *Political Economy*, and Michel Chevalier's *Cours d'Économie Politique*. Notes were also supplied on the order in which the books were to be read, the suggestions for political economy being very brief:

> J. S. Mill should be carefully analyzed, and the student should also have a book like McCulloch's by his side as a safeguard against the occasional eccentricities, if I many call them that, of the former writer.[64]

Presumably this limited rubric originated with Pryme, as Professor of Political Economy, although he was non-resident and visiting only every other year. In 1863 he would be replaced by Fawcett, who was resident for 18 weeks of each year but who likewise had little or no connection with the Moral Sciences Tripos. Mary Paley, for example, sat the papers for the Moral Sciences Tripos in 1874, her principal teachers having been Sidgwick and Marshall; she had attended Marshall's lectures on political economy, not those of Fawcett;[65] in the following year Neville Keynes sat his finals, likewise without having attended Fawcett's lectures.[66] Then, from 1877, Foxwell took over responsibility from Marshall for teaching political economy on the Moral Sciences Tripos, following Marshall's appointment as Principal of University College Bristol.[67]

Under Foxwell the rubric for Political Economy was extended, and by 1881 the examinations in the Tripos had been divided into two schedules, the first of which was sat in the first three days of the examination:

I. Moral and Political Philosophy
II. Psychology
III. Metaphysics

[63] J. B. Mayor, 'Moral Sciences Tripos' in J. R. Seeley (ed.) *The Student's Guide to the University of Cambridge*, Cambridge 1862, p. 143.

[64] Mayor, 'Moral Sciences Tripos' [1862], pp. 146, 149. In the 1866 edition of the *Guide* there was an additional sentence: 'Professor Fawcett's *Political Economy*, which has appeared since the list was published, forms an excellent introduction to the subject' (p. 171).

[65] Mary Paley Marshall, *What I Remember*, Cambridge University Press, Cambridge 1947, p. 18.

[66] Deane, *Life and Times*, pp. 14ff. She provides a detailed account of Neville Keynes's undergraduate education in which Fawcett does figure as someone that he consults; but he attended Marshall's lectures on political economy, not Fawcett's.

[67] Also of note in this first edition is an explanation of the role of the Moral Sciences Tripos as compared with that of the Mathematical and Classical Triposes: 'Mathematics cultivate the attention, and develop[e] the power of forming clear conceptions and following out the steps of a long and intricate argument: but they do not tend to awaken the mind to varied interest, they do not teach observation or speculation, they altogether leave untouched the field of probable reasoning which is the most generally useful for the purposes of life.... Logic may be viewed as the abstract form of mathematical reasonings, from which its best examples are borrowed, and a student who has undergone the severe discipline of mathematics has a great advantage in dealing with the more complex questions of Political Economy afterwards.' Mayor, 'Moral Sciences Tripos' [1862], pp. 150–51.

IV. Logic
V. Political Economy

Here political economy covered production, exchange, and the work of government and taxation: 'Governmental interference in its economic aspects. Communism and Socialism'. A list of six books was headed by Mill, with the Marshalls's *Economics of Industry* in second place. The second schedule of examinations was divided into Advanced Psychology and Psychophysics, Logic, and Advanced Political Economy; for the last of these a candidate was expected to show 'fuller and more critical knowledge of the subjects included in the preceding schedule of Political Economy'. This examination also included 'the diagrammatic expression of problems in pure theory with the general principles of the mathematical treatment applicable to such problems: the statistical verification and suggestion of economic uniformities; and a general historical knowledge' of the development of forms of property, contract, competition, and credit, and also of industrial organisation and economic policy. The list of reading was headed by Smith, Malthus, and Ricardo, but included Cournot's *Principes de la Théorie des richesses*[68] and Jevons's *Theory of Political Economy*.[69] A subsequent lecture list shows that Foxwell taught the elementary political course in Lent and Easter terms, the advanced course in Michaelmas and Lent,[70] with Neville Keynes adding an advanced course during Easter term that included 'diagrammatic methods'.[71] Notable here by his absence was any mention of the Professor of Political Economy, Henry Fawcett.

A fourth edition of the *Student's Guide* relating to the Moral Sciences was also published in 1881, presenting the two-phase division of examination to be initiated in 1883 that would then in 1889 underlie the division of the Tripos itself into Parts I and II. The more elementary part of the examination covered the five main subjects listed earlier, plus a more general essay; students were here only permitted to sit five of these six papers. For days four to six of the examination, six papers were timetabled, three historical and three theoretical. Only two of the six subjects could be sat by any one student, with two of the four remaining slots be filled by the writing of an essay—hence a total of six or seven examination papers, plus two or three essays, taken over six days.[72] The more advanced part of the Tripos thus became more

[68] As given in the *Reporter*—presumably *Recherches sur les principes mathématiques de la théorie des richesses* (1838).

[69] 'Schedules of Examination Subjects in the Moral Sciences Tripos', *Cambridge University Reporter* 15 February 1881, pp. 362, 363–64.

[70] 'Michaelmas' = autumn term, 'Lent' = spring term, and 'Easter' = summer term.

[71] 'Open Lectures in Moral Sciences, 1884–85', *Cambridge University Reporter* 15 October 1884, p. 79.

[72] Henry Sidgwick (ed.), *The Student's Guide to the University of Cambridge. Part VIII Moral Sciences Tripos*, 4th edition, revised, Deighton Bell and Co., Cambridge 1881, pp. 3–4. By the later 1880s this had altered again to a Part I with three topics and six papers: Psychology, Logic, and Political Economy, plus an essay; and Part II abandoned the historical/theoretical division in favour of A. Metaphysics, Political Philosophy, and Ethics (one paper each); and B. special subjects of which the student might take one, and no more than two subjects: the History of Philosophy, Advanced Logic and Methodology, Advanced Psychology and Psychophysics, and Advanced Political Economy. Students taking Advanced Political Economy had to take the paper on Political Philosophy, all other students the papers on Metaphysics and Ethics. See *The Student's Guide to the University of Cambridge*, 5th edition, rewritten, Deighton Bell and Co., Cambridge 1893, pp. 1–2.

specialised. Nonetheless, compared with the unrelenting three plus five days of the Mathematical Tripos examinations, this was already a less demanding experience for candidates, although much would depend in Part II on the subject choices made and their timing. A more expansive account of the nominated reading for political economy was supplied by Foxwell; this did begin with Mill's *Principles of Political Economy* as 'still the best systematic treatise on the subject in English, covering the whole ground as defined by the schedule', but recommending for the Elementary Examination the Marshalls' *Economics of Industry* as the key text.[73] Foxwell concluded here by recommending Cournot's *Recherches* as a book 'which no one should neglect who studies the application of mathematics to pure economic theory'.[74]

This edition of the *Guide* also included guidance to students on study: '1. Method of reading' recommended quickly reading through a book before then going back over it a second time, making careful notes, but summarising, not writing out extracts. It is also recommended that students create tables or diagrams of the classifications they might encounter, committing them to memory so that they might be reproduced on paper. Constant practice of writing answers to questions on earlier papers is highly recommended: '... such exercises are naturally the most effective preparation for an examination, which consists of twenty-seven hours of writing.'[75]

While the examinations for the Moral Sciences Tripos now lasted six days, they did not involve the cumulating order of difficulty built into the Mathematical Tripos examination, and the guidance in the *Guide* offered to Moral Sciences students on preparation for examination was, for all subjects, organised in terms of the reading that should be done. In this respect the Moral Sciences in the 1880s were much as Mayor had described in his 1860 flysheet: not the study of problems and principles, but instead the study of canonical texts exemplifying these problems and principles. Phyllis Deane in her biography of Neville Keynes alludes to the problems of intellectual rigour arising from this, quoting Henry Sidgwick's complaint that it was possible to obtain the highest honours in the Tripos 'on less than a year's reading'.[76] Also evident from the preceding outline of the examination is that while Foxwell had lent greater definition to the teaching, the place of political economy in the Moral Sciences Tripos was limited to one elementary paper, with no more than the possibility of sitting an advanced paper. Within this framework any advanced work in political economy would be problematic. Nor did the fact that Sidgwick had published his own *Principles of Political Economy* in 1883 have an impact upon the reading lists for the Moral Sciences Tripos. Although it went into a second edition in 1887, and its preface name-checks several of the works on the Tripos reading list—Mill, Jevons, the Marshalls, Walker—it was never listed in the *Guides* (but see later discussion). It could be speculated that as a Jevonian revision of Mill that owes not a little to Sidgwick's own *Methods of Ethics* (1874) it was too sophisticated a work for use in the existing

[73] Sidgwick (ed.), *The Student's Guide* [1881], pp. 21, 22.
[74] Ibid., p. 24.
[75] Ibid., p. 39.
[76] Deane, *Life and Times*, p. 16, quoting from a statement by Henry Sidgwick printed in the *Cambridge University Reporter* in October 1870.

teaching scheme;[77] and in any case the arrival of Marshall in 1885 would redirect the development of the teaching of political economy in Cambridge around Marshall's own *Principles*, which eventually appeared in 1890.

Marshall's Lectures on Political Economy

When Marshall was elected to the chair in December 1884 he wrote at once to Foxwell, noting that besides his Inaugural he would not lecture until May, but would set aside time for informal instruction twice a week. He was thinking of lecturing in May on 'Rent profits & wages'.[78] As it transpired, he would lecture from Friday 24 April on Wednesdays and Fridays on the 'Distribution of Wealth, with special reference to the causes that determine the incomes of different classes in England now, and to the inquiry how far the existing inequalities are unavoidable'; and also on 'Some Difficult Points in the Theory of the Distribution of Wealth' on Mondays.[79] For the following year he offered 'Money, Foreign Trade, Competition, Crises: - General Course' twice a week in the first term, while also repeating the previous year's Monday lecture on Saturdays. Foxwell was now to lecture on Adam Smith and the political economy of the eighteenth century twice a week in the first term, and elementary political economy in the second and third. Neville Keynes was down for 'Papers in Political Economy' in the second term, and 'Advanced Political Economy' in the third.[80] Two things stand out here: the Professor of Political Economy's lectures are for the first time announced within the framework of the Moral Sciences Tripos, and Foxwell teaches elementary courses only. By 1890 a new division of labour has emerged: Marshall lectures on both the General and the Advanced course in Political Economy; Neville Keynes lectures on 'Political Economy (Papers)'; Arthur Berry teaches 'Diagrammatic and Mathematical Treatment of Economic Theory'; and Foxwell teaches the history of economic thought and elementary political economy.[81]

We can form an impression of how Marshall presented his 'General Course', since Edwin Cannan attended from October 1891 to March 1892 and made notes.[82] For

[77] See, for my account of Sidgwick's *Principles*, 'Henry Sidgwick, Moral Order, and Utilitarianism', pp. 920–25; and for the connection of Mill to Jevons and Sidgwick, my 'Utilitarianism, The Moral Sciences, and Political Economy: Mill-Grote-Sidgwick', in Katia Caldari, Marco Dardi, Steven Medema (eds.) *Marshall and the Marshallian Heritage: Essays in Honour of Tiziano Raffaelli*, Palgrave, Cham 2021, pp. 149–84.

[78] Marshall to Foxwell, 13 December 1884, Letter 145 in John K. Whitaker (ed.) *The Correspondence of Alfred Marshall, Economist. Vol. I Climbing 1868–1890*, Cambridge University Press, Cambridge 1996, p. 179.

[79] *Cambridge University Reporter* No. 582, 21 April 1885, p. 601.

[80] *Cambridge University Reporter* No. 602, 9 October 1885, p. 30.

[81] With Levin of St. Catherine's also lecturing on Credit and Commerce twice a week throughout the year; 'List of Lectures Proposed by the Special Board for Moral Science, 1890–91', *Cambridge University Reporter* No. 880, 20 April 1891, p. 728.

[82] Cannan used a lined quarto notebook for the purpose: 'Notebook of notes on Alfred Marshall's lectures on political economy, 1891 to 1892', BLPES Archive, Cannan Collection 909. He first attended on Wednesday, 14 October, the second lecture of the year, the lectures being scheduled for Mondays and Wednesdays. The 'Advanced' lecture was delivered once a week on Fridays. Steven Medema has brought to my attention a typescript of notes from the same course of lectures in Ronald Coase's papers (University of Chicago Library, Special Collections Research Center Box 104 Folder 13). Comparison of the copies of handwritten notes in Chicago with Cannan's notes for his edition of Adam Smith's lectures (Cannan

this introductory course, Marshall began with a review of the literature, mentioning neither the *Economics of Industry* nor his own *Principles*;[83] but noting that Books II and III of Sidgwick's *Principles* were '[t]o be consulted', while his account of taxation was 'to be used'.[84] Cairnes's *Logical Method of Political Economy* was 'Good'. He maintained that Mill and his generation had been, 'when generously interpreted, accurate on most points. There has been a great change in Polit. Econ. recently; but the New is a development of the old, not in opposition to it. The change is not on the intellectual side; but on the way of regarding the science.'

In the next lecture Marshall began the kind of historical survey familiar from the opening pages of *Principles*,[85] relating climate to civilisation; considering the Greeks, the Romans, and the decline of both, referring his hearers to Hegel's philosophy of history. Cannan recorded that in the third lecture Marshall declared that

> [t]he leadership in industrial affairs belongs exclusively to the Anglo-Saxons, & England is by far the most interesting country for the study of economic questions. In Germany, however, purely governmental work is done well.[86]

He then diverted into a disquisition on racial characteristics involving a comparison of the United States, Australia, and England.

> The resolute, unimaginative English adopted early the doctrines of the Reformation, which was an unmixed blessing politically & economically: thus skilled Protestant workmen from all Europe were brought to England, & the English slow to learn, & supreme in organisation when they had learnt, laid the foundation of all our manufactories.
>
> We are not a nation of shopkeepers, we can organise & make, but cannot bargain; to buy on the continent without bargaining is called the 'English method'.

The lecture of 26 October continued on with an account of early economic development and economic thought; but a question paper had been set for 20 October:

1. Give a classification of the motives by which men are actuated in their economic activities, & enquire how the operation of these motives wd. be affected by the substitution of a socialistic for an individualistic regime.
2. Discuss the definition of wealth. What available statistical data would you select in order to determine (a) whether a country was increasing in wealth, (b) whether the rate of increase was being maintained?

Collection 920) confirms that the transcript in Chicago was made from Cannan's notes. My thanks to Anna Towlson, British Library of Political and Economic Science Archives, for providing copies that confirm this.

[83] His synopsis of the *Principles*, *Elements of the Economics of Industry*, was not published until 1892.

[84] 14 October 1891, Notebook f. 1—although the references given here garble the organisation of Sidgwick's single volume work, divided into an Introduction and three 'Books'.

[85] Later demoted to an appendix—see the discussion of the reorganisation of *Principles* through successive editions in Chapter 6, pp. 161–66.

[86] 21 October 1891, Notebook f. 5.

3. In what relations do individual & national wealth stand to one another. How is each affected by a fire which destroys among others the business papers of a firm, & some bank-notes? Suppose that it causes the firm completely to disappear, & that its sensational character causes insurance shares to rise, how is national wealth affected by these causes?
4. Account for & examine the common statement that traders are not producers.[87]

Then, at the end of the month, Marshall discusses the correct method of study: 'Writers of theoretical school knew any quantity of facts. Ordinary historical writer knows very few. General student of history should pay most attention to the period before 1840, since facts of modern times not yet known. But economical student should pay most attention to recent events.'[88] Two days later, on the Friday, Cannan was back in Cambridge for Marshall's 'Advanced Class', which dealt with income distribution.

In November the General Course moved into demand and consumption, contrasting the demand for water and for diamonds, using diagrams to illustrate the difference between elastic and inelastic demand curves, Cannan noting that

> Jevons statement that 'Theory of consumption is the scientific basis of economics' is wrong. Wants & activities are equally important, & each produce the other.[89]

By the end of November, Marshall was presenting supply and demand curves, and discussing increasing returns.

Cannan continued attending twice a week during the first term—there was at the time a direct rail link between Oxford and Cambridge—missing only the final week.[90] He returned at the beginning of the second term, attending 10 out of 16 lectures. Marshall was now talking about money, trade cycles, credit, and concluding with tariffs and foreign trade, Cannan copying into his notebook statistics of imports and exports by value from 1700–1890. From his notes we can establish three important points about the way that Marshall introduced students to political economy in the early 1890s. First of all, the overall structure resembles that of *Principles of Economics*, moving from general evolutionary arguments to the graphical presentation of supply and demand, also adding economic statistics that students would copy down. Second, Marshall breaks with the Millian framework devised for the same purposes by Foxwell in the 1870s, organised around production, exchange, and government. Third, while the Tripos syllabus was organised in terms of canonical texts, Marshall's presentation only reviews them initially, then makes occasional passing reference. To the novelty of the Professor of Political Economy presenting the introductory course on the Moral

[87] Notebook, verso of f. 8.

[88] 28 October 1891, Notebook, f. 11,

[89] 9 November 1891, Notebook f. 17. He missed the lecture on 5 November, but attended three times the following week, Monday, Wednesday and the Friday Advanced Class, where he again includes in his notebook a tabulation of statistics—the first table related to income, this one to wealth (f. 20).

[90] From 1895 Cannan taught at the London School of Economics, becoming Professor of Political Economy in 1907, but his appointment was part-time only; he lived in Oxford and commuted to London, as he had to Cambridge.

Sciences Tripos, Marshall added a move onward from textual pedagogy, expounding principles.

Marshall's Inaugural Lecture

Marshall had stated his credo in the Inaugural Lecture delivered in Senate House on 24 February 1885. He opened by mourning the recent death of many British economists—some premature, like Jevons, Toynbee, and Fawcett—that had severely depleted the ranks of his contemporaries. He spoke during a time of generational transition, but rejected characterisation of this in terms of theory to empiricism, of inductivism to deductivism. Instead,

> [i]t is due to the discovery that man himself is in a great measure a creature of circumstances and changes with them; and the importance of this discovery has been accentuated bý the fact that the growth of knowledge and earnestness have recently made and are making deep and rapid changes in human nature.... The chief fault then in English economists at the beginning of the century was not that they ignored history and statistics, but that Ricardo and his followers neglected a large group of facts and a method of studying facts which we now see to be of primary importance. They regarded man as so to speak a constant quantity, and gave themselves little trouble to study his variations.[91]

It was for this reason that labour was treated as a simple commodity, ignoring human 'instincts and habits', and consequently treating the forces of supply and demand mechanistically.

> But their most vital fault was that they did not see how liable to change are the habits and institutions of industry. In particular they did not see that the poverty of the poor is the chief cause of that weakness and which are the cause of their poverty: they had not the faith, that modern economists have, in the possibility of a vast improvement in the condition of the working classes.[92]

And he added to this that, while Owen and others had asserted the perfectibility of man, their advocacy was weak. Nonetheless, this basic idea had gradually won acceptance; and so the work of economists could be conceived as contributing to that end.

He then came to his main point: that Ricardo and others failed to appreciate that they were not creating a universal truth to be mechanically applied, but 'machinery of universal application in the discovery of a certain class of truths.'[93] Marshall did not use methodological or philosophical reasoning to support this argument, but historical argument—referring back to Adam Smith's interest in the tension between

[91] A. Marshall, *The Present Position of Economics: An Inaugural Lecture*, Macmillan, London 1885, pp. 13, 14.
[92] Ibid.
[93] *Inaugural Lecture*, p. 19.

acquisitive desire and the effort required to acquire a desired object. Economics, he suggested, 'is not a body of concrete truth, but an engine for the discovery of concrete truth; similar to, say, the theory of mechanics.'[94] His term of choice for this engine of discovery was the *organon*, the means of reasoning instilled in the student economist that would enable that student to select appropriate instruments for the resolution of the problem in hand—a mode of working that was, as we have seen, instilled in the Cambridge student of mathematics aspiring for high honours.

> This organon deals with the play of measurable motives for and against one another, balancing one another and being substituted for one another, though the persons concerned may be in classes or even in countries that have little direct intercourse. And it sets out that most complex play of human motives that changes the purchasing power of money, and thus alters the measure of all motives.[95]

Hence the training of the economist involved the inculcation of powers of judgement, where the various principles and techniques were aids to the forming of judgement, not mechanical means for the generation of a truth. Those who advocated a more intensive study of history missed this point; the interaction of human motivations with changing circumstance meant that no two situations were exactly alike; facts by themselves were also silent, and so the accumulation of historical knowledge could not provide a basis for any training in the exercise of judgement.

> Greedy as the economist must be for facts, he must not be content with mere facts. Boundless as must be his gratitude to the great thinkers of the historic school, he must be suspicious of any direct light that the past is said to throw on problems of the present. He must stand fast by the more laborious plan of interrogating facts in order to learn the manner of action of causes singly or in combination; applying this knowledge to build up the organon of economic theory, and then making use of the aid of the organon in dealing with the economic side of social problems.[96]

Cambridge, he went on, had more persons trained in economics than anywhere else; but some of the metaphysical material associated with the preliminary work of the Moral Sciences Tripos did, he thought, deter some who might otherwise embrace the study of economics. Graduates of the University had an important part to play in the world of the future:

> It will be my most cherished ambition, my highest endeavour to do what with my poor ability and my limited strength I may, to raise the numbers of those, whom Cambridge, the great mother of strong men, sends out into the world with cool heads but warm hearts, willing to give some at least of their best powers to grappling with the social suffering around them; resolved not to rest content till they have done what

[94] Ibid., p. 25.
[95] Ibid., p. 31.
[96] Ibid., p. 48.

> in them lies to discover how far it is possible to open up to all the material means of a refined and noble life.[97]

Cambridge as the 'great mother of strong men' is a phrase that has not attracted attention in the commentary, but it is a reference to the athleticism linked to the Mathematical Tripos that we might misread today, mistakenly contrasting sporting to intellectual prowess. Simon Cook has noted that not only did Alfred Marshall row for his college during his first year at Cambridge, but that he subsequently drew attention to what rowing and other field sports contributed to learning and the formation of character.[98] Karl Pearson (Third Wrangler 1879) travelled to Germany shortly after graduating, studying physics and metaphysics in Heidelberg, and law and evolutionary theory in Berlin. Writing to his mother in May 1879,[99] he admitted that he had thought athleticism to be overestimated at Cambridge, but that he had since changed his mind:

> The Germans here are surprised at my knowing an Englishman always by sight and want to know what it is, but I can hardly tell them it is a compactness, a look of strength which they never possess. I set out with one over the hills, I almost kill him before half-an-hour is over and this is the case where he has served his time as a soldier and one would think ought to be enured to fatigue.[100]

Quite apart then from the 'cool heads but warm hearts', which we can construe as a reference to the rigours of examination on the Mathematical Tripos, this image of Cambridge men setting out into the world with a rigorous training in mind and body captures Marshall's conception of the work that he would do as professor. The Inaugural sets out an argument for the role of economics in the modern world, and from this point onwards Marshall would seek relentlessly to raise the profile of the teaching of economics in Cambridge.

Reorganising the Teaching of Political Economy

As we have seen, the Moral Sciences Tripos as Marshall found it in 1885 had only a limited placed for specialised work in political economy; but an issue that might easily be overlooked in tracing the subsequent rise of specialisation is: how many students took an interest in advanced political economy anyway? Here again, a focus upon Marshall's eventual success in creating a separate Economics Tripos can foster the assumption that there was an underlying unsatisfied demand for the teaching of political economy that Marshall channelled into the new Tripos. This was what Marshall on occasion suggested; but his correspondence also records that he complained more about the absence of any such regular demand from promising students. While it

97 Ibid., p. 57.
98 Simon J. Cook, 'A Wrangling Machine', *History of Political Economy* Vol. 37 (2005), pp. 693–95.
99 He had sat his examinations in the preceding winter.
100 Quoted in Warwick, *Masters of Theory*, pp. 177–78.

might reasonably be objected that, for any new product, supply must anticipate demand, consumers not knowing what they want until they see it, political economy was not a new product. For one thing, John Stuart Mill's *Principles of Political Economy* sold well for decades after its first publication in 1848, as noted earlier (p. 58). As also demonstrated in Chapter 3, there was a broad interest in political economy in later nineteenth-century Britain, reflected in public lectures, extension teaching, even in the popularity of Henry George. But whether there was anything more than this broad interest, an extensive unsatisfied demand for the rigours of advanced political economy in the style, for example, of Edgeworth's *Mathematical Psychics* (1881),[101] or even Wicksteed's *Alphabet of Economic Science* (1888),[102] is debatable.

Marshall's struggle to raise the profile of the teaching of economics from 1885 to 1903 should therefore be seen in less heroic terms: not so much the pioneer winning through despite the hostility of doubters, more a lost prophet without much of a following whose cantankerousness prompted his colleagues to give him what he wanted so that he might leave them alone. True, his *Principles of Economics* was an immediate success, selling out the first printing within a year, a second printing of 3,000 being agreed, plus 500 for the United States.[103] But this was a book to be read, not at this time a textbook suited to any course of study; and it never did become a textbook of this kind, more a lodestar for the elaboration of economic thinking.

On his appointment Marshall had immediately raised the profile of the Professor of Political Economy from that of a teacher of pass men without any connection to the Moral Sciences Tripos. In March 1886 he proposed that a special prize by examination in political economy be inaugurated since 'our present examinations do not allow scope for all the interests that are connected with economic studies.' He went on:

> The events of our own age are leading all thoughtful men constantly to read and talk on economic problems, especially if they intend to become ministers of religion or are looking forward to a political career. Thus Economics holds a singular position. It is, I think, the only subject of which the unsystematic study in the University exceeds the systematic: the only one which finds a great portion of its ablest and most diligent students among those who are preparing for, or have graduated in, Triposes in which it is not represented. I want to supply an Examination which, by offering public recognition of thorough work, will help to steady and systematise this unsystematic study. To do this effectively its standard must be high: but it must be confined to the Science itself, so that it may not repel men who can spare but a limited time from their own pursuits. Those who enter for it will, I trust, often be led on to the philosophical and historical studies which are intimately connected with Economic Science.

[101] Subtitled 'An Essay on the Application of Mathematics to the Moral Sciences'.

[102] Philip H. Wicksteed, *The Alphabet of Economic Science*, Macmillan, London 1888. By p. 3 Wicksteed is deep into the mathematics of the velocity of a falling body, on p. 4 we have the rate of cooling of an iron bar in a stream, on p. 8 there begins a discussion of 'the body projected vertically upwards at a given velocity' (i.e. a ball thrown in the air).

[103] Macmiillan & Co. to Marshall, 9 January 1891, Letter 333 in Whitaker, *Correspondence Vol. II*, p. 1. See, for detail on sales, p. 162.

After some discussion the proposal was accepted, to run for five years from 1887, although it at first had limited success in fostering a lasting interest in economics.[104]

The reorganisation of the Moral Sciences Tripos into a Parts I and II also raised questions about the profile of political economy. Early in 1889 the Moral Sciences Board had expressed the view that, with the shift of metaphysics into Part II, political philosophy could be sat by those taking advanced political economy as an alternative, linking therefore the teaching of economics to that of politics. This was a suggestion from which Cunningham dissented.[105] During Senate discussions of the report, he argued strongly against this uncoupling of metaphysics from political economy in Part II and its replacement by political philosophy, arguing that contemporary political economy was founded upon metaphysics:

> There was a large part of Political Economy which must deal with socialistic difficulties, and behind all these lay the question, What is meant by an individual? How far an individual was to be considered as a sort of monad, or as itself formed by social surroundings, were most important problems in relation to the whole controversy of socialism. Thus in order to take a sound view with regard to socialism, there ought to be preparation in the study of Metaphysics.[106]

As would become evident from his subsequent disputes with Marshall, Cunningham did believe that Marshall considered the individual 'as a sort of monad', an accusation that Marshall firmly denied.[107] But in the Senate discussion, Marshall made the argument for such an uncoupling not in terms of the demands of political economy, but rather in relation to the prospects for political science:

> There was a great deal to be said for separating to some extent these two branches of moral science, the mental and metaphysical side, and the social side; though they had long been united in the Moral Sciences Tripos. Ere long a time might come when

[104] *Cambridge University Reporter* No. 640, 8 June 1886, p. 719. The prize was won in 1887 by Stanley Leathes (1861–1938), a fellow of Trinity College who became a Lecturer in Modern History at Cambridge from 1892 to 1903, after which he was Secretary of the Civil Service Commission. In 1888 it was awarded to J. M. E. McTaggart (1866–1925), who became a fellow of Trinity in 1891 on the basis of a dissertation on Hegel's *Logic*. In 1889 it was won by Alfred Flux, at last the kind of student whom Marshall had had in view with the prize. But then in 1891 it was awarded to James Welton (1854–1942), who had got a first in Moral Sciences, specialising in political economy, but who went on to a career in teacher training.

[105] 'Report of the Special Board for Moral Science', *Cambridge University Reporter* No. 771, 26 February 1889, pp. 481–83.

[106] *Cambridge University Reporter* No. 777, 19 March 1889, p. 593.

[107] Responding to a paper Cunningham had read before the Royal Historical Society in March 1892, Marshall later stated: 'The whole volume [*Principles*] is indeed occupied mainly in showing how similar causes acting on people under dissimilar conditions produce more or less divergent effects. The leading motive of its argument is the opposite of that which Dr. Cunningham ascribes to it.' Alfred Marshall, 'A Reply', *Economic Journal* Vol. 2 (1892), p. 508; replying to Cunningham, 'The Perversions of Economic History', *Economic Journal* Vol. 2 (1892), pp. 491–506. Later that year Benjamin Jowett wrote to Mary Paley Marshall, counselling her husband against further engagement in controversy with Cunningham, whom he described in another letter as a 'troublesome & unscrupulous fellow . . .—Never let Alfred get into controversy: it is bad for him in every way.' Jowett to Mary Paley Marshall 16 October 1892 and 2 January 1893, Letters 422 and 423 in Whitaker, *Correspondence* Vol. 2, pp. 83, 84. For an account of Cunningham's differences with Marshall, see my 'The Historicisation of Political Economy?', in B. Stuchtey, P. Wende (eds.) *British and German Historiography 1750–1950*, Oxford University Press, Oxford 2000, pp. 211–28.

Table 4.1 Numbers of Successful MST Graduates, by Year (*Cambridge University Reporter*, various years)

	Part I	Part II
1888	0	3
1891	10	4
1892	4	3
1893	11	1
1894	10	5
1895	11	4
1896	5	8
1897	17	6
1898	7	6
1899	8	5
1900	9	6
1901	10	7
1902	7	6
1903	6	7

> they would be ready to have a political sciences school. Schools of this kind were already thriving in America. America had two economic journals, and the recent intellectual activity in America in Economics had been very wonderful; he thought the growth of political sciences schools was partly the cause and partly the result of this movement. They might soon have such a school here, and it would very likely be connected with, but not identical with, the Historical Tripos.[108]

In this position Marshall had the support of Sidgwick, and the proposed change was adopted. In 1897 this separation was reinforced, by formally dividing Part II into two groups: Group A, comprising six papers in all—two on Metaphysical and Moral Philosophy, one on the General History of Modern Philosophy, one on Advanced Psychology and Psychophysics, one on Advanced Logic and Methodology, and one on a special subject from the history of modern philosophy; and Group B, a total of five papers including an essay, one paper on Political Philosophy, and three on 'Advanced Political Economy, including English Economic History and the History of Economic Science, especially in their later stages'.[109]

[108] *Cambridge University Reporter* No. 777, 19 March 1889, p. 594.

[109] 'Report of the Special Board for Moral Science on the Regulations for the Moral Sciences Tripos', *Cambridge University Reporter* Vol. XXVII No. 37, 18 May 1897, p. 942. The rubric and reading list for Part I Political Economy (pp. 946–47) is more expansive than before, and includes the outline of a course on Ethics.

Nonetheless, one should not overlook the awkward fact that, as Table 4.1 shows, few students sat for Part II of the Tripos. Of these, only a subset took political economy and politics. Groenewegen's biography of Marshall includes a table of Marshall's students that indicates that in 1886–1889, 16% of them were from the Moral Sciences, nearly 25% from History, and less than 5% pass students for the Special Examination. Graduate students alone accounted for 15%.[110]

More students did take the political economy paper on the ordinary degree, but large numbers failed and the examiners were sometimes scathing about the quality of the work done. In 1897 seven students sat Part I of the Political Economy Special Examination, of whom four failed. One sat for Part II, and failed. The examiners reported that

> The work of the rejected Candidates was of very poor quality. On the subjects of Foreign Trade and Money they appeared to be absolutely ignorant.[111]

In other years, successful candidates were damned with faint praise. For 1893:

> Part II: The work in June was on the whole satisfactory, none of the Candidates showing ignorance of the main outlines of the subject; and the answers were for the most part sensible and to the point. The chief defect was the superficial treatment of the harder questions, especially on finance, taxation and socialism; this was owing in great measure to the general neglect of the books recommended for consultation.[112]

This general lack of interest in political economy among pass men and the small numbers of students succeeding in Part II of the Moral Sciences Tripos provide some perspective upon Marshall's arguments, including of course his efforts to create mechanisms that might attract students to the study of political economy.

In 1891 Marshall had proposed a new prize competition, a triennial Adam Smith Prize, extending the function of the annual Marshall Prize competition. Here his argument was that such a competition might encourage students to take political economy in the new Part II of the Moral Sciences Tripos:

> I desire thus to work by a new route towards my old aim of attracting to the study of Economics men who are able to bring to it highly trained minds, and who may have gradually acquired, by intelligent observation of what goes on around them, a sound knowledge of contemporary economic conditions; but who, for the present at all events, cannot give their whole time to economic studies.[113]

Nonetheless, while he did acknowledge the work of 'the more industrious Newnham girls' when writing to Neville Keynes in 1895, he admitted:

110 Groenewegen, *Soaring Eagle* Table 10.1, p. 325.
111 *Cambridge University Reporter* Vol. XXVIII No. 24, 22 February 1898, p. 525.
112 *Cambridge University Reporter* No. 1020, 6 March 1894, p. 535.
113 *Cambridge University Reporter* No. 869, 17 February 1891, p. 514.

> Were it not for such men as Berry Flux & Bowley who do not take the Tripos at all, & who learn what they do from me chiefly in private conversation, it would [be] little better than hack work to teach Pol Econ here. Sanger is the only student (man or woman) who has taken up economics for Part II & was really worth teaching. But one Sanger, or even one Bowley is a good recompense for 5 years work; & I am content.[114]

There were indeed a few who would take the subject up and establish their reputations as students of Marshall. Nonetheless, the path to the establishment of the Tripos was hardly driven by a clear and consistent unmet demand for teaching in political economy.[115] As the preceding student numbers attest, the Moral Sciences Tripos was itself a very small-scale enterprise, and while successive revisions to examination did lend political economy a clearer profile, it also made it an option students could avoid. Both factors told against the prospect of developing, within its framework, a demanding and rigorous course of economic training that in any way replicated the skills that the Mathematical Tripos fostered.

All the same, the existence of the Moral Sciences Tripos and its Board made it possible to have arguments about the teaching of political economy, logic, and metaphysics that the organisation of Oxford precluded. Simply the existence of the *Cambridge University Reporter*, founded in 1870, demonstrates the importance in Cambridge of a central university administration, something that Oxford lacked;[116] and so arguments for innovation could in Cambridge be made before the University Senate, and then simply imposed upon the colleges in which teaching actually took place, and whose fellows and lecturers did most of the teaching. It was this feature that made it possible for Marshall, after the death of Sidgwick in 1900, to push for the separation of economics and politics from the Moral Sciences Tripos, and in 1903 to inaugurate the first three-year undergraduate degree in economics. The following chapter begins with the arguments made in the early 1900s for and against the separation of economics from the Moral Sciences Tripos, and then considers the performance of the Tripos as an undergraduate programme.

Appendix
Selected Graduates in Mathematics and in Moral Sciences

Graduates from the Mathematics Tripos

Year	Name	College	Result
1803	George Pryme	Trinity	Sixth Wrangler
1855	Leonard Courtney	St Johns	Second Wrangler
1856	Henry Fawcett	Trinity Hall	Seventh Wrangler

114 Marshall to Neville Keynes, 2 November 1895 Letter 471 in Whitaker, *Correspondence* Vol. 2, p. 133.

115 For a summary of this path, see Ch. 15 of Peter Groenewegen, *A Soaring Eagle: Alfred Marshall 1842–1924*, Edward Elgar, Cheltenham UK 1995.

116 The organisation of teaching in Oxford University is discussed in Chapter 7.

Year	Name	College	Result
1859	Henry Sidgwick	Trinity	Thirty-third Wrangler
1866	Alfred Marshall	St. Johns	Second Wrangler
1882	W. E. Johnson		Eleventh Wrangler
1885	Arthur Berry	Kings	Senior Wrangler
1887	Alfred Flux	St Johns	= Senior Wrangler
1891	Arthur Bowley	Trinity	= Tenth Wrangler
1893	C. P. Sanger	Trinity	Second Wrangler
1901	Ralph Hawtrey	Trinity	Nineteenth Wrangler
1905	John Maynard Keynes	King's	Twelfth Wrangler

Graduates from the Moral Sciences Tripos

Year	Name	College	Result
1869	A J Balfour	Trinity	Second
1870	Herbert Somerton Foxwell	St Johns	Senior Moralist
1872	William Cunningham	Trinity	= Senior Moralist
1872	F. W. Maitland	Trinity	= Senior Moralist
1874	James Ward	Trinity	Senior Moralist
1875	John Neville Keynes	Pembroke	Senior Moralist
1877	Joseph Shield Nicholson	Trinity	First Class
1883	W. E. Johnson		First Class
1888	John McTaggart	Trinity	First Class
1891	James Welton	Caius	First Class
1894	Bertrand Russell	Trinity	First Class
1894	C. P. Sanger	Trinity	First Class
1898	Sydney Chapman	Trinity	First Class
1900	A. C. Pigou	King's	First Class
1901	D. H. Macgregor	Trinity	First Class

5

The Cambridge Tripos in Economic and Political Science

Structure and Outcome

When I first approached the reconstruction of the Cambridge Moral Sciences Tripos presented in Chapter 4, my intention had been to establish what was lost when Marshall succeeded in removing the teaching of economics from its connection with logic, psychology, politics, and moral philosophy. This would of course be the context lent economics in Oxford when the PPE (Philosophy, Politics, and Economics) degree was inaugurated in 1920. But Edgeworth, Professor of Political Economy at Oxford from 1891 to 1922, had never shown any great interest in developing undergraduate teaching of economics. Unlike Marshall, who believed that at least three years was needed to acquire a foundation in the subject, Edgeworth thought six months more than sufficient. For better or worse, the Oxford PPE degree has become the qualification of choice for those aspiring to careers in the media and politics; while an increasingly specialised and technical three-year undergraduate economics degree today provides distinctly less in the way of a foundation for future public and private employment than Marshall had in mind.

My initial approach was a reaction to the assumptions of existing accounts of the Economics Tripos, mapped in detail by Peter Groenewegen, and also forming the *telos* of John Maloney's study of 'professionalisation'.[1] Written from the perspective of the existing modern discipline, the emphasis in these and other accounts was on the 'freeing' of economics from a broader framework—the emergence of what we today know as economics through a process of divestment and detachment. It is true that Marshall sometimes expressed himself in this way, in 1902 at least—'this weary & oppressive work for the liberation of economics from the incubus by which I believe it to be oppressed'[2]—but we should not assume that 'economics' as he conceived it then is equivalent to what economics later became. To understand what he meant by this, we have to understand what he thought 'economics' was—a point that will be addressed in the following chapter. There is a variant to this story about the genesis of modern economics, the idea that around the turn of the century a coterie of theoretical economists deliberately detached the study of economics from its historical roots; but as I show in Chapter 8, this is a story that does not withstand close examination.

[1] Peter Groenewegen, *A Soaring Eagle: Alfred Marshall 1842–1924*, Edward Elgar, Cheltenham UK 1995, Ch. 15; John Maloney, *Marshall, Orthodoxy and the Professionalisation of Economics*, Cambridge University Press, Cambridge 1985.

[2] Marshall to Neville Keynes, 30 January 1902, Letter 675 in John K. Whitaker (ed.) *The Correspondence of Alfred Marshall, Economist*, Vol. 2: *At the Summit, 1891–1902*, Cambridge University Press, Cambridge 1996, p. 350.

Constructing Economic Science. Keith Tribe, Oxford University Press. © Oxford University Press 2022.
DOI: 10.1093/oso/9780190491741.003.0005

In any of these versions, the discipline of economics is conceived as an essential, already-existing core discourse that can only develop once it has gained autonomous existence. Here I seek to do without such teleologies; I do not presume that the way things have turned out, the world in which we live today, provides much in the way of a key to understanding how this world came to be. Adoption of a presentist perspective erases historical contingency and imposes current, transient contingencies as if they were fixed rational outcomes; hence my interest in exploring what the teaching of economics within the Moral Sciences Tripos could have amounted to if this process of separation had not been initiated, and what was lost with the severance of this relationship.

However, I began to see matters in a different light once I moved on to explore the Mathematical Tripos. As argued in the previous chapter, while Marshall's efforts after his return to Cambridge in 1885 did centre on the expansion of the teaching of economics within an existing framework, what he had in mind was not only space for the substantive material to be conveyed, but also the kind of training that he believed economics required. Forming and shaping economists involved more than just having more hours to expose students to the subject matter of contemporary economics. Marshall wanted time to train minds, to inculcate judgement and a style of work that was an inherent part of preparation for the Mathematical Tripos that he had sat for in the 1860s. As is evident from Cannan's reports of the lectures in the early 1890s, Marshall not only lectured; he also ran an advanced class and set problems for those students who attended.[3] Likewise, the standing invitation extended to students to visit him informally for advice and discussion was a novel departure in a Cambridge where college teaching meant routine classroom work.[4] As it happened, reforms in the 1920s introduced the system of college supervision built upon a weekly meeting between a

[3] A long-standing disagreement with Foxwell, dating from the 1880s, also involved the latter's refusal to set 'papers' for students, arguing that he was busy in London and, in any case, did not see why he should prepare students for Marshall's advanced lectures. Marshall had, therefore, '... for many years to do *the whole* of the drudgery side of economic teaching.' Marshall to Foxwell, 14 May 1901; Letter 645 in Whitaker *Correspondence Vol. 2*, p. 319. See also Carlo Cristiano, *The Political and Economic Thought of the Young Keynes: Liberalism, Markets and Empire*, Routledge, London 2014, pp. 100ff, for an account of Maynard Keynes's economic studies under the direction of Marshall after his graduation from the Mathematical Tripos, drawing upon Tiziano Raffaelli, 'Keynes's Apprenticeship with Marshall in 1905', *History of Economic Ideas* Vol. 8 No. 2 (2000), pp. 121–52.

[4] As made clear in the previous chapter, 'teaching' up to the early 1900s meant college classes, where the student was exposed on a more or less daily basis to exercises and drills. The reorientation of college teaching to personal supervision for just one hour a week seems to have been an innovation that coincided with the reorganisation of the University on a Faculty basis in the 1920s, which in turn was linked to the opening of the Mill Lane lecture rooms in 1928 as a central university institution. R. B. McCallum's account of Oxford tutorials admits ignorance of when the parallel Oxford system was inaugurated; 'The Tutorial System at Oxford', *Universities Quarterly* Vol. 2 No. 1 (1947), p. 26. The account of Cambridge in the same issue is limited to the Natural Sciences, and so not directly comparable to the humanities and social sciences. Its author simply assumes that the supervision is a 'traditional' element of Cambridge teaching: J. A. Ratcliffe, 'Supervision at Cambridge: With Special Reference to Natural Sciences', *Universities Quarterly* Vol. 2 No. 1 (November 1947)m pp. 31–35. In Oxford and Cambridge, 'teaching' has never meant 'lecturing'. This presumption mars many accounts of the Tripos: see, for example, Peter Groenewegen, 'Teaching Economics at Cambridge at the Turn of the Century: Alfred Marshall as Lecturer in Political Economy', *Scottish Journal of Political Economy* Vol. 37 (1990), pp. 40–60; and David Collard, 'Cambridge after Marshall', in John Whitaker (ed.) *Centenary Essays on Alfred Marshall*, Cambridge University Press Cambridge 1990, pp. 174ff.

supervisor and one or two supervisees; but since this replaced the college classroom, rather than supplemented it, the introduction of the weekly supervision tended to undermine Marshall's interest in systematic training. By the mid-twentieth century the organisation of Cambridge undergraduate teaching was entirely unsuited to the kind of economic training that Marshall had envisaged in the later 1890s.

This was the view of Harry Johnson, a Canadian who in his year as a Cambridge undergraduate first wore British Army battledress, like many of his ex-service colleagues.[5] Later he wore civilian clothes and was taken for an American, for whom there was rather less ready acceptance among the local population, given the wartime proximity to Cambridge of several US Army Air Forces airfields. Johnson's views on Cambridge have sometimes, and rather predictably, been dismissed as the sour grapes of an outsider,[6] but as Max Corden's *Oxford Dictionary of National Biography* entry demonstrates, Johnson always had a critical but constructive eye for the way in which economics was taught to undergraduates. In the course of this chapter it will be shown that his comments on Cambridge economics do in fact have substantial empirical support.[7] For one of the curiosities in the literature on the development of the Cambridge Economics Tripos is a narrow focus upon the new autonomy for the teaching of economics, almost entirely neglecting how this new autonomy was used by students and staff once it had been introduced. Furthermore, such accounts of twentieth-century teaching in Cambridge that we have from insiders are inevitably written by the few whose time in Cambridge marked the beginning of a successful public career. For them, it was more their personal intellectual qualities and the simple fact of being a Cambridge graduate that were decisive in the opportunities that opened up. For the broad mass of students who passed through the Tripos, a teaching system built around a weekly supervision left them less well-trained than their peers in London or Manchester.

This chapter therefore examines the arguments directly associated with the establishment of the Tripos, outlines the successive reorganisations of syllabus and lectures, and then uses a database of student records to evaluate the way in which aspirations were translated into reality over the first 50 years of its operation. During this half-century, some 4,500 individual students passed either Part I of the Tripos, or Part II, or sat for both parts. Initially Part I was examined after two years, and Part

[5] Harry G. Johnson, "Cambridge in the 1950s," in E. S. Johnson, H. G. Johnson (eds.) *The Shadow of Keynes*, Basil Blackwell, Oxford, 1978, p. 127. Johnson (1923–1977) studied at Jesus College during the academic year 1945–1946 and gained a First in Part II; he then studied for a year at Toronto for an MA; and completed a Harvard PhD in 1948 (the year during which, in the normal course of events, he would have graduated from the Economics Tripos). He was an Assistant Lecturer, then Lecturer, in Cambridge from 1948, being appointed Professor of Economic Theory at Manchester in 1955; from where he went to Chicago in 1959, later commuting between LSE and Chicago. See Max Corden's *Oxford Dictionary of National Biography* entry.

[6] See, for example, Aubrey Silberston, *Harry Johnson as a Young Man*, Imperial College of Science and Technology, London 1978, pp. 12–13.

[7] Johnson was also fortunate to have attended the university's Political Economy Club during 1945–1946 before Maynard Keynes's death in April 1946; he commented that Keynes always found something positive to say about student contributions, but was less accommodating of Faculty members; Johnson, 'Cambridge in the 1950s', p. 133. See, for similar comments on Keynes from former students, my *Economic Careers: Economics and Economists in Britain 1930–1970*, Routledge, London 1997, p. 61 (Hans Singer); p. 72 (Brian Reddaway).

II after a further year; in the early 1930s this was changed to a one-year Part I and a two-year Part II. Some students took Part I and then switched to another subject; some switched into Part II after having done a different Part I; some students took both Parts. The existence of these options means that we cannot equate a 'Cambridge student of economics' with Marshall's ideal student who had studied economics for three years. During the 1930s, in particular, students taking Part I only in the first year were in the majority. Using the examination results as printed in the *Cambridge University Reporter* for any one year—with name, college, and class of degree—it is possible to use student names to establish the pathway that each took, and whether this pathway, or the college at which they studied, might have contributed to their eventual degree result.[8] Tracking choices made in this way by students, and their relative performances, sheds further light on the way in which the Tripos was perceived, and also lends perspective to periodic complaints about a shortage of teaching staff, whether employed by University or by college. As we shall see, even very basic student statistics yield some unanticipated insights regarding the Cambridge undergraduate degree in economics.

The examination data presented here cast a new light on Johnson's critique: they provide a consistent empirical framework within which we can test the performance of the Tripos as a vehicle for the education of generations of economists. Moreover, Marshall's undergraduate training programme began to produce significant numbers of graduates who had studied for three years and gained a First or an Upper Second just at the time when attention was shifting internationally to graduate training, tending if anything to hinder the rapid acceptance of a need for graduate education in Britain. Johnson taught in Cambridge at a time that this problem would have been increasingly evident. Furthermore, the Tripos was the ostensible reason for the existence of the Faculty;[9] auditing the outcome sheds light upon the formation of student expectations and also upon the effectiveness of teaching input. This is a mode of procedure that is all too familiar today, but which is here set to work for historical, rather than bureaucratic, ends.

[8] Since the 1990s, grade inflation in British universities has altered the distribution of Firsts, 2:1s, and 2:2s, a small minority of students now being classified with a 2:2, and significant numbers achieving a First. In the century up to that point, a 'normal' distribution of graduates from any university would have been 2%–5% Firsts, 20%–25% 2:1, 50%+ 2:2, and 10%–15% Thirds. A significant number would also fail to complete, or fail at completion, as confirmed in the 1960s (Committee on Higher Education, *Higher Education. Report of the Committee appointed by the Prime Minister under the Chairmanship of Lord Robbins 1961–63*, Cmnd. 2154 Her Majesty's Stationary Office, London 1963, Appendix Two (A) Students and their Education, Table 5, p. 129). The grades achieved for the Cambridge ordinary degree noted in the previous chapter were not at that time anything unusual. The data used in this chapter were collected from the *Cambridge University Reporter*, and so do not record students who failed, or who studied economics but left Cambridge without taking a degree.

[9] The Tripos was originally administered by a Special Board for Economics and Politics; following the Oxford and Cambridge Universities Act 1923, the Special Boards were reconstituted as Faculties, with effect from 1926.

Designing the Tripos

As noted in the previous chapter, Marshall's ambitions for the teaching of economics exceeded the Cambridge institutional framework within which he initially worked. The death of Henry Sidgwick in 1900 appears to have precipitated the final move to establish a separate Economics Tripos, and so we can confine our attention here to the arguments made during the subsequent three years before the University agreed to create this new undergraduate programme.[10] Outlining these arguments and the framework to which they eventually led provides a sense of Marshall's aspirations, as he struggled to realise a vision for the future of economic science shared by few of his Cambridge contemporaries, whether teacher or student. Student performance can then be used to assess how students actually fared in passing through the Tripos, following which arguments made by Harry Johnson about his experiences in the 1940s and 1950s will be assessed in the light of this record.

Marshall would later suggest that the fragmentary manner in which political economy was taught in Cambridge hindered its proper development, but the most obvious impediment was the limited number of students who displayed any great interest in the subject. In the Part I Moral Sciences examination for 1895, for example, just 11 students gained honours; in Part II there were two firsts and two seconds.[11] These were not untypical numbers for the decade. Matters were little better in the political economy examinations for the ordinary degree: in 1893 there were a mere 21 sets of answers for political economy in the Special Examination, as against 90 in modern languages and 173 in history.[12] During the 1890s Marshall did succeed in directing a small number of students into the study of economics, among them Chapman, Clapham, and Macgregor; but from the evidence of paths followed by great majority of students, general interest in the subject was very moderate. Marshall's efforts to create an independent three-year course in economics was driven therefore not by existing student demand, but by his vision of what systematically-trained graduates might do in the world of business and administration. This was the occupational domain into which the coming generations of Cambridge students would in fact be moving; away from the traditional emphasis upon the Church and the land.[13] Marshall, seeking to bridge this gap between reality and aspiration, between the actual lack of students, on the one hand, and his vision of prospective strong labour market demand for trained economists, on the other, resorted as usual to empirical

[10] See Marshall's letter to Neville Keynes, 22 September 1900 (Letter 619; *Correspondence* Vol. 2, p. 284). Marshall had favoured Neville Keynes as the replacement for Sidgwick as Chairman of the Moral Sciences Board, but Ward, with whom Marshall was at odds over the place of economics, was appointed. He concluded the letter by stating, 'For those who are interested in economics & politics, will, I expect soon sound the University as to the establishment of a Tripos, in wh [*sic*] these subjects could have adequate space. And during that time it would be unfitting to propose any material change in the position of economics in the Mo Sc Tripos.'

[11] *Cambridge University Reporter* No. 1076 (4 June 1895), pp. 886–88. This was a good year: in 1893 the one Part II candidate gained a Third; *Cambridge University Reporter* No. 988 (6 June 1893), p. 927.

[12] *Cambridge University Reporter* No. 1020 (6 March 1894), p. 537.

[13] H. Jenkins, D. Caradog Jones, 'Social Class of Cambridge University Alumni of the 18th and 19th Centuries', *British Journal of Sociology* Vol. 1 (1950), p. 100.

evidence of dubious plausibility.[14] The entire basis for the introduction of commercial and economic studies into universities rested everywhere upon this appreciation of changes in the pattern of employment and the increasing importance of appropriate educational provision. But the problem of weak student demand for the teaching of economics was a general one, repeated in the Faculties of Commerce founded at this time in Manchester and Birmingham: educational provision for the managerial and administrative transformation that was about to occur in the British occupational structure ran far ahead of any real labour market demand.[15]

While Marshall averred in early May 1901 that 'because of Sidgwick's death, I do not want to do much just yet', it was at this time that his plans for a separate Economics Tripos were formulated, through the medium of the History Board.[16] Whitaker notes that an unsigned memorandum included with the minutes of the History Board for 21 May 1901, presumably drafted by Goldsworthy Dickinson,[17] was headed 'Scheme for a course of study designed as a preparation: (1) For business on a large scale, (2) for public life, (3) For the professional study of Economics and Politics'. Part I was to include papers from the existing Historical Tripos, while Part II would include three papers on Advanced Economics 'covering General Problems, Money and Trade including Railways, Industry and the Economic Function of Government.[18] On 8 May, Marshall wrote to Foxwell reporting on a History Board meeting of 6 May, noting that a committee had been appointed, including Marshall, Dickinson, and Ward,[19] to study

[14] Marshall had elicited letters of support from prominent businessmen, bankers, politicians, and others, on the basis of which he then claimed that a substantial unsatisfied demand for economics graduates existed. These empiricist reflexes were well-honed; he could always find a fact suitable to substantiate an otherwise implausible argument, as Michael White has shown with respect to the Giffen good: 'A Peculiar Archaeology: Searching for Mr. Giffen's Behaviour', *European Journal of the History of Economic Thought* Vol. 22 (2015), pp. 26–50. This argumentative style was a constant source of irritation to colleagues and dinner guests alike.

[15] Alon Kadish, Keith Tribe, 'Introduction: The Supply of and Demand for Economics in late Victorian Britain', in Kadish, Tribe (eds.) *The Market for Political Economy: The Advent of Economics in British University Culture, 1850–1905*, London Routledge, London 1993, pp. 3–4.

[16] Marshall to Oscar Browning, 1 May 1901, Letter 640 in Whitaker, *Correspondence* Vol. 2, p. 311. Hence the separation of political economy from its principal teaching context was achieved indirectly, embracing the historical context of the teaching of political economy rather than deliberately rejecting it. See fn. 19 below regarding the election of James Ward as Sidgwick's successor as Chairman of the Moral Sciences Board in October 1900. For an account that traces the general relationship of the teaching of economics in Cambridge to that of history, see Alon Kadish, 'University Reform and the *Principles*', *Quaderni di Storia del'Economia Politica* IX Nos. 2–3 (1991), pp. 289–309.

[17] Goldsworthy Dickinson (1862–1932) was a Fellow of King's who had gained a Classics First in 1884, but who later developed an interest in modern politics, lecturing on the subject both in Cambridge and at the LSE from 1896 to 1920. In the mid-1880s he had been inspired by the work of Henry George.

[18] Note 3, Marshall to Browning 4 May 1901, Letter 641 in Whitaker, *Correspondence* Vol. 2, p. 313.

[19] In the early 1870s, James Ward (1843–1925) was encouraged by Henry Sidgwick to study at Cambridge and in 1874 he gained a First in Moral Sciences, becoming a fellow of Trinity College the following year. He was made College Lecturer in Moral Sciences in 1881, and then appointed to a new Chair in Mental Philosophy and Logic in 1897, having played a significant role in the development of the study of physiology and psychology in Britain. See the *Oxford Dictionary of National Biography* entry written by his colleague W. R. Sorley, revised by Terrie M. Romano. Ward succeeded Sidgwick as Chairman of the Moral Sciences Board in October 1900, proposed by Marshall and seconded by Neville Keynes; but Marshall was at odds with Ward and had favoured Neville Keynes for the appointment. His differences with Ward suggest why in 1901 Marshall chose to initiate plans for an Economics Tripos from the History Board; see Whitaker's notes to Marshall to Neville Keynes, 22 September 1900, Letter 619 in Whitaker, *Correspondence* Vol. 2, pp. 284–85; and the following fragment of Marshall to James Ward, 23 September 1900 in which Marshall outlines his stance with respect to Mental Science (Letter 620, p. 285).

'how best to extend the study of modern economics & politics in the University'.[20] Marshall was clear that his 'own hobby now is an entirely separate Tripos', albeit under the general auspices of the Historical Tripos.

In this letter Marshall refers to an 'old scheme' that had been discussed with Foxwell, Sidgwick, and Neville Keynes, although Whitaker notes that that no record of any such discussion can be located.[21] Whatever the circumstances, Marshall included in his letter to Foxwell two typed carbon copies (one to be passed on to Foxwell's Cambridge neighbour Neville Keynes) of a 'Scheme for an Economic and Political Sciences Tripos'.[22] This was intended not only for 'professional students of economics and politics', but for a number of other groups, preparing for work in Parliament or local representative bodies; the Home or Indian Civil Service, diplomacy, and the consular service; the higher work of public and private firms, including railways, shipping, foreign trade, and the more technical parts of manufacturing; the list concluding with 'the duties of a country gentleman' and 'the service of the poor'.[23] The programme envisaged a two-year Part I covering modern history (since 1780), economics, and 'the English polity'; while in Part II no less than six and no more than eight papers would be taken (including essays), with a compulsory economics course covering 'contemporary economic and social conditions', divided between a survey of conditions of production and distribution in different countries, money, credit and trade, and public business and finance. Optional papers were to be selected from the history of economic doctrines, mathematico-economic and statistical methods, plus four papers in politics and two in law.[24]

We might regard this as the first draft of the Economics Tripos;[25] so what does it tell us of the way in which Marshall first conceived his project? Most striking is the limitation of the material in *Principles Vol. I* to a 'general study' of economics in Part I.[26] Besides the optional course on mathematics and statistics, there is no higher-level

[20] The committee did not survive past the meeting on 21 May, since Ward was unable to serve. Marshall to Foxwell, 8 May 1901, Letter 643 in Whitaker, *Correspondence* Vol. 2, p. 314.

[21] Letter 643, p. 315. Note that despite Goldsworthy Dickinson's involvement in the drafting of the initial outline, political science never played a significant role in the design of the Tripos; lasting provision for modern political theory in Cambridge was only realised with the appointment in 1927 of Ernest Barker (1864–1960) to a chair in political science funded by the Rockefeller Foundation. The chair was located in the History Faculty, not in Economics and Political Science. See Julia Stapleton's entry for Barker in the *Oxford Dictionary of National Biography*.

[22] Keynes and Foxwell lived in Harvey Road (Keynes from 1882 and Foxwell from 1898), not far from the railway station; from 1886 Marshall lived in Balliol Croft, Madingley Road, rather less than two miles away to the north-west. That Marshall regularly corresponded in this way with people living in the same city is further confirmation of Johnson's critique of the Cambridge archipelago: for there was at this time no institutional location at which all these individuals might regularly meet. There was no faculty building; Marshall and Foxwell could in principle have easily arranged to meet each other, since they were both fellows of St. Johns College, but Marshall favoured domestic arrangements for living and working, and Foxwell commuted to teach in London. College life does not seem to have been central to either of them. Once Balliol Croft had been built, Marshall's Cambridge correspondence bears that address, not that of his college.

[23] Letter 643, p. 315.

[24] Ibid., pp. 316–17.

[25] Underlined by the fact that in June, Marshall enclosed a copy of the scheme 'wh I drew up a few weeks ago for a Tripos here' when writing to Hewins, Director of the LSE, regarding a new London course in economics; Marshall to W. A. S. Hewins 6 June 1901, Letter 654 in Whitaker, *Correspondence* Vol. 2, p. 329.

[26] This general approach is confirmed by Raffaelli's account of Marshall's teaching of Keynes in 1905; see his 'Keynes's Apprenticeship'. I come back to this issue in the following chapter.

study of economic principles envisaged. The compulsory element of Part II would instead cover economic and financial structures, conveying to the student a working knowledge of the contemporary international economy—the kind of material that eventually found its way into Marshall's *Industry and Trade* and *Money, Credit and Commerce*, which had originally been envisaged as the substance of the abandoned *Principles of Economics Vol. II*.[27]

Marshall's *Plea*: His Final Argument

Some time in the autumn of 1901, Marshall elaborated these plans, and then arranged for an outline to be printed as a flysheet for circulation to members of Senate.[28] Here Marshall assembled all the reasons and arguments that he would use in the next two to three years in justification of his proposal, whether writing letters to *The Times* or presenting his case in Cambridge.[29] As we have seen in the previous chapter, there was in Cambridge no consistent demand for extending the study of economics; nor, as will be demonstrated at length in Chapters 9 and 10, was there any such pressure of demand, or extensive provision for such demand, elsewhere in Great Britain and Ireland, Western Europe, or the United States. Marshall was arguing for a significant and unprecedented innovation, a three-year honours course in economics; but he did so by suggesting that Cambridge was falling behind the march of progress elsewhere, that this innovation was no more than a catching-up.

He began his argument by noting that economics had been part of the Moral Sciences Tripos when it began, but that mental science and logic had not. In 1867 law and history had been detached, and since then mental science and logic had 'struck the keynote of the Moral Sciences Tripos'.[30] The path to the serious study of economics in the Tripos now led, according to Marshall, through mental science and logic, representing a 'partial blocking up of the doorway to economic studies against the

[27] Parallel to this was Marshall's ongoing argument with Foxwell about the latter's teaching, designed without consulting Marshall and which, in Marshall's view, failed to provide an adequate foundation for Marshall's lectures. Marshall eventually paid Pigou to provide adequate lectures, which further exacerbated the friction between Foxwell and Marshall; see Marshall to Foxwell 14 May 1901, Letter 645, in Whitaker, *Correspondence* Vol. 2, pp. 319–20; Marshall to Neville Keynes, Letter 648 in Whitaker, *Correspondence* Vol. 2, pp. 323–24.

[28] In January 1902, W. R. Scott, then Lecturer in Political Economy at St. Andrews, sent Marshall a scheme for higher commercial education (since lost). Thanking Scott in a letter of 27 January 1902, Marshall noted that his own 'plea for extension of economic studies here' was at the printers, and would be available in four to six weeks; Letter 672, in Whitaker, *Correspondence* Vol. 2, p. 347. During January and February, Marshall shared his draft *Plea* with Foxwell, Neville Keynes, and Robert Giffen, all of whom responded with suggestions for revision; see Letters 673, 674, 675, 767 and 677 in Whitaker, *Correspondence* Vol. 2, pp. 348–55. When finally printed, the *Plea* was dated 7 April 1902.

[29] Edwin Gay's account of 'The New Economics Tripos at Cambridge University', *Quarterly Journal of Economics* Vol. 17 (1903), pp. 492–96, published in May before the initiation of the Tripos, recapitulates the arguments of the *Plea*, while James Bonar's review of Marshall's *The New Cambridge Curriculum in Economics*, published in November of the same year, covers the same ground; *Economic Journal* Vol. 13 (1903), pp. 620–22.

[30] 'A Plea for the Creation of a Curriculum in Economics and Associated Branches of Political Science', flysheet reprinted in Alfred Marshall, *Principles of Economics Vol. II Notes*, ninth (variorum) edition with annotations by C. W. Guillebaud, Macmillan, London 1961, p. 162.

vast majority of our most promising students.' Consequently too little time was available for the study of economics within the Moral Sciences Tripos. However, revision to the Historical Tripos had made it possible to switch from Part I in History to Part II in Moral Sciences, where a 'clear field is left to political philosophy and advanced economics'.[31] He then recruited the memory of Sidgwick to his cause: but for Sidgwick's early death, the project of an honours degree in economics and political science might have been initiated a year previously.

Next Marshall pointed to developments in London and Birmingham to suggest that 'England is prepared now to follow the example of other western countries, and take the study of economics seriously.' Marshall here raises the prospect of Cambridge being a laggard, the better to make Cambridge an innovator. And he reinforces this message with the idea that, while English economists had once been at the forefront of development, English universities now so restricted the study of economics

> ... that the English economist is largely dependent on the work of foreigners for a thorough treatment of many urgent problems. In the United States, in Germany and elsewhere, great numbers of business men and Government officials have studied economics at the universities, and have thus learnt to consider particulars in relation to general principles. They are quick to see the results of their experience may be serviceable to the public, and to make clear to others what they have learnt from life. But such men are rare in England.[32]

He continued on to emphasise that economic and social considerations were everywhere becoming influential in the work of governments, a process accelerated by the falling cost of ever-faster communication; such that decisions made by any one government had to be weighed against those being made elsewhere. The cost to governments of maintaining their international position was rising; in England's case, the productivity of its workforce was falling by comparison with that of rivals. This presented problems not only of political stability, but of social welfare. Faced with these issues, it was vital that students be trained now who 'in later years ... will be qualified to go to the root of the urgent social issues of the day, and to lay bare the ultimate as well as the immediate results of plausible proposals for economic reform.'[33]

He next turned to the needs of business and the appropriate response of 'the older English universities'. He suggested that a trend had emerged in business towards greater specialisation in the work of subordinates, and a broadening in the skills required of senior executives. Other institutions could cater to the technical needs of the former; Cambridge, by contrast, was well-placed to provide for the latter. The question was, however, what kind of training was suitable for those who would occupy senior positions in private business and public administration?

[31] Ibid., p. 163. In fact it had been Marshall who proposed this possibility to the History Board in 1894; see Jean O. McLachlan, 'The Origin and Early Development of the Cambridge Historical Tripos', *Cambridge Historical Journal* Vol. 9 No. 1 (1947), p. 92.

[32] 'A Plea for the Creation of a Curriculum', p. 164.

[33] Ibid., pp. 166–67.

> I myself think that the higher study of economics gives as good a mental training, its breadth and depth being taken together, as any other study: and that, in addition, it develops the human sympathies in an exceptional degree. But even should this not be conceded, economics may yet claim a first place among university studies if account be taken of the mental activities in after-life which may result from a thorough study of it here.[34]

And so Marshall's argument is oriented not primarily to the substantive content of a training in economics, but to the intellectual habits and reflexes required of administrators and executives. He quoted approvingly a description in *The Times* of the new Cologne Commercial College, and that the Cologne Chamber of Commerce had recently declared that the 'great merchant … ought to follow industrial and commercial legislation in all countries, to know their economic history, their future, and therein forecast the progress of industry and of science.'[35] What kind of formal training is needed to promote this kind of reflex? Of course, the executive is remote from the lives of the employees whose support he needs if he is to act on his insights into the development of the international economy. Marshall suggests that 'broad modern economic studies will have prepared him to look at the problems of employment from the point of view of the employee as carefully as from that of the employer.' Where does the executive learn to approach matters in this way?

> On the river and in the football field the student learns to bear and to forbear, to obey and to command. Constant discussion sharpens his wits; it makes him ready and resourceful; it helps him to enter into the points of view of others, and to explain his own; and it trains his sense of proportion as regards things and movements and persons, and especially as regards himself.[36]

Where decisions have to be made by persons who lack direct experience of the issues involved, the larger details can be left to 'salaried officials'; but

> … it will be their part to bring to bear broad strong well-balanced judgments, insight into character, tact in managing men, and fine intuition as to when to take risks and when not.[37]

For this, 'elasticity of mind' and 'quickness of sympathy with aspirations and ideals that are not their own' were required. And he brought his argument to a close as follows:

> It is not suggested that a technical preparation for business should be given here: nor that those looking forward to public life should leave Cambridge provided with ready made opinions on controverted issues of the day. It is suggested merely that economists should be able to obtain here a three years' scientific training of the same

34 Ibid., p. 168.
35 Cited from *The Times*, 26 September 1901, in ibid., p. 169.
36 Ibid., p. 170.
37 Ibid., p. 170.

> character and on the same general lies as that given to physicists, to physiologists or engineers.[38]

The substance of this training was then outlined.

Although the Historical Tripos had provided a framework for the study of political economy, students of history were committed to studies that became progressively less intense, the closer to the modern day they came. By the third year a student would have begun to study the nineteenth century, but for want of publicly-available sources, the issues and events of the modern world were insufficiently accessible for thorough historical study. It was the opposite with the student of economics and politics: the international relations of the present day, the conditions of modern economies, were of paramount interest, while a general knowledge of former times was quite sufficient. To 'disentangle the interwoven effects of complex causes' the student of economics

> ... should learn how things, which seem alike and are called by the same name, are often really dissimilar; and how those, which seem dissimilar and are called by many different names, are often fundamentally alike. He should seek for the Many in the One, and the One in the Many: – a task in which skill is to be acquired only by long practice: unless the student has rare natural genius, or has mastered some branch of physical science.[39]

This is the central thesis of Marshall's *Plea*—that while knowledge of existing conditions and economic problems provides the material for the training of students of economics, the implicit aim is to inculcate habits of mind, a particular kind of orientation to the modern world conveyed through an 'international comparative method' that comprehends economic geography, industrial structure, financial systems, labour relations, property relations, incomes and consumption patterns, international trade, fiscal system, market regulation, and public undertakings.[40] Importantly, 'mathematical work in statistics should be united with mathematical versions of pure economic theory as an optional subject at the end of the course'.[41] Through all the preceding pages, this is the first time that Marshall directly alludes to economic theory, and from the outline provided here it is evident that Marshall believed that the reasoning he sought to inculcate was best fostered not by the adumbration of theoretical principles, but by the presentation of practical problems whose solution required systematic analysis.

Appended to the text was an outline syllabus, Part I having three papers[42] (British Empire, United States, and Continental Europe); a further three papers were organised under the heading 'Principles of Economics': methodology and the general

[38] Ibid., p. 171. Note that, as argued in the previous chapter, the Mathematical Tripos as taken by Marshall was not as such a training for mathematicians, but served as the foundation for the study of natural sciences and engineering.

[39] Ibid., p. 173.

[40] Ibid., pp. 174–75.

[41] Ibid., p. 176.

[42] A Cambridge syllabus is organised as 'papers', i.e. examination papers for which a reading list provides the description of subject matter to be examined; university lectures are more or less loosely directed to particular papers, but are not constitutive of them. Supervisors direct the reading and lecture attendance of their supervisees; examinations are set by third parties and marked by fourth parties.

doctrine of value, modern industries, and employment; a sixth paper under 'Political Science' on 'The structure of the modern State'; and a seventh essay paper. Part II was headed 'Economics', with six papers (modern industries, employment and international trade, taxation and government, a 'paper of questions', history of economic doctrine, and a 'Mathematical treatment of economics and statistics'); with two further papers, one on 'ethical aspects of economic problems' and another of 'elements of law'; plus another essay paper.[43]

The Committee Stage and Subsequent Dissent

The *Plea* quickly came before Senate for discussion, and on 26 April 1902 it was agreed that a committee, the Economic and Political Science Syndicate, should be established to examine the arguments for an independent Tripos.[44] The Syndicate held its first meeting in late May; Marshall read out a sheaf of supporting letters, including those from the Bishops of Southampton, Exeter, and Bristol, and an agenda was agreed for discussion at the following meeting.[45] This did not take place until October, with 13 members present, voting 11 to 2 in favour of a motion proposed by Marshall and seconded by Foxwell, that economics, with the allied parts of political and legal subjects, provided sufficient material for a three-year course and that this could not be supplied by another Tripos.[46] At the third meeting, on 22 October 1902, Neville Keynes proposed that economics was a proper subject for university study, which was agreed; following which a motion was agreed 8 to 1 that the course of study should be an undergraduate, and not a graduate, degree. Having got this far, a sub-committee was formed to consider the distribution of time and subjects of study within the proposed Tripos. Included with the minutes is a typewritten copy of their conclusions, which provides an insight into the relative weighting of lecturing hours:[47]

Economic and general history, chiefly recent, of UK and in a less degree the rest of the western world, geography included	Min 4 Max 6
General Principles of Economics	Min 3 max 3
Elements of method, espec. statistical	Min 1 Max 1
Special Subjects (lectures in some cases in alternate years)	
Money and banking	Min 2 Max 4
Trade, Transport & Industrial Development	Min 3 Max 6

43 *Plea*, p. 177.

44 Memorial signed by 131 members of Senate, but not by Neville Keynes, nor by Cunningham: *Cambridge University Reporter* Vol. XXXII No. 34 (29 April 1902), pp. 762–3. See Alon Kadish's account of this phase in the establishment of the Tripos in his 'Marshall and the Cambridge Economics Tripos', in Kadish, Tribe (eds.) *The Market for Political Economy: The Advent of Economics in British University Culture, 1850–1905*, Routledge, London 1993, pp. 154ff.

45 Meeting of Thursday 29 May 1902, *Minutes of the Syndicate appointed to enquire into the best means of enlarging the opportunities for the study in Cambridge of Economics and associated branches of Political Science*. Cambridge University Archives, CUL, UA Min.VI.68.

46 Meeting of Wednesday 15 October 1902, *Minutes*.

47 Note the minimal amount of time originally envisaged for 'Politics and Law'.

Conditions of Employment	Min 2 Max 4
Ethical aspects of economics	Min 1 Max 2
Taxation. Economic functions of government, Socialism	Min 2 Max 4
History of Economic Doctrine	Min 0 Max 2
Mathematico-economics and statistics	Min 0 Max 2
Politics and Law	Min 2 Max 6

As already noted in the discussion of the *Plea*, here any formal or abstract treatment of economic principles comes very far behind a largely empirical appreciation of economies.

Subjects in political science were added during the subsequent four meetings in December 1902, and then the list of subjects for study was whittled down and structured into compulsory and optional papers. Matters proceeded onwards into the new year, Marshall rarely taking the initiative in discussion, until at the fifteenth meeting in March, with the Syndicate's report completed, McTaggart[48] and Cunningham requested that a dissenting memorandum (dated 4 February 1903) be appended to it. This was defeated 4 to 2, but a copy was included in the minutes and then circulated to members of Senate as a flysheet dated 9 March 1903.

Cunningham, a member of the Syndicate, had a conception of economics very different from that of Marshall; significantly, he disputed the idea that economics could provide for the formation of mental discipline on the part of an undergraduate:

> Though the phenomena with which Economic Science deals are of very great importance, the study itself does not appear to us to supply a good mental discipline. We do not think it desirable for any undergraduate to concentrate attention upon it as his main subject of study. There is reason to fear that such concentration would be of too specialised a character to be compatible with a liberal education or to give a claim to a degree in Honours. The evils of this concentration would, we think, be increased by the exceptionally large proportion of controversial matter in Economics, as compared with the proportion of such matter in other sciences.
>
> We are of the opinion that the existing examinations of the University offer opportunities for specialising in Economics that are as large as it is desirable to afford to students who are still undergraduates. What is required in our opinion is not more examining, but more teaching. It would be important to provide fuller instruction for those preparing for existing examinations, and ampler facilities for guiding and encouraging research on the part of older students of exceptional ability.[49]

This clearly ran counter to Marshall's entire strategy for the development of economics as a separate subject of study with its own logic and system. Instead of a new

[48] John McTaggart (1866–1925) studied Moral Sciences and gained a First in 1888, becoming Trinity College Lecturer in Moral Sciences in 1897, following publication of his *Studies in the Hegelian Dialectic* (1896).

[49] Proposal by Cunningham and McTaggart, *Minutes of the Syndicate appointed* ... 15th Meeting, 4 March 1903.

discipline for increasing numbers of undergraduates, Cunningham proposed advanced economics as a research subject for a select few. If teaching were to be expanded at the undergraduate level, he suggests, then this should occur within the existing framework—the Moral Sciences and History Triposes, and of course the ordinary BA. His argument was, however, supported in exactly the same manner as Marshall's—by reference to the vocational needs of the labour market:

> While the instituting of an Economics Tripos, intended for the training of economic experts, might provide a good course for the exceptional men who are destined for high places in financial houses, it does not appear to afford a very useful scheme of academic work for men who are looking forward to commercial or industrial life. What seems to me most important for this object would be the establishment of a 'Modern Side' General Examination, to include at least one Modern Language, and such subjects as Physical Geography, and the Government of the British Empire. It might also be desirable to institute a 'Business' Special, in which Commercial Law should be a principal subject.[50]

Cunningham was therefore advocating the combined teaching of economic and commercial subjects, as was being developed in Manchester, Leeds, and London, although restricting it to the postgraduate level. Marshall had set his face against both the vocational emphasis that this implied, and the level at which it was to be provided. He must, however, have been sensitive to the contemporary tide of opinion in favour of higher commercial education, and to the activities of his former students Chapman and Clapham on behalf of commercial education in the universities of Manchester and Leeds.

This argument did not abate in 1903. In November 1905, Sydney Chapman,[51] then Professor of Political Economy at Manchester, delivered a lecture in Cardiff suggesting that the older universities were not capable of contributing to commercial education, while at the same time pointing to the moves being made in Oxford and Cambridge. This was reported in *The Times*, and then a letter was published in response to this report. Marshall then wrote to *The Times* emphasising the commercial slant of Cambridge teaching, noting that the Secretary of the Cambridge University Appointments Board had assured him that

> ... applications to him from leading business firms for men who have received a Cambridge training of one sort or another is large and increasing fast, and that the reports which he receives of their work are as a rule very satisfactory.[52]

[50] Ibid.

[51] Sydney Chapman (1871–1951) had gained a London BA from Owens College, Manchester, in 1891, then entered Trinity College, Cambridge, and having been persuaded by Marshall to study economics, gained a double First, in 1897 and 1898, in the Moral Sciences Tripos. He then returned to Manchester, where he was Jevons Research Student for a year, before being appointed Lecturer in Economics at University College, Cardiff, in 1899. In 1901 he was appointed Professor of Political Economy in Manchester, as successor to Flux, another of Marshall's students.

[52] Alfred Marshall, 'Education for Business Men', *The Times*, 23 November 1905, p. 4.

On 11 December 1905 an unsigned entry in the 'Educational Notes' section of *The Times* disputed the adequacy of a Cambridge training for a business career.

> But the scheme for the Part II. of the Economics Tripos is chiefly remarkable in connexion with the training of business men, not so much for the subjects included as for those omitted. If there is one subject a knowledge of which is indispensable to a business man, it is surely the theory and practice of accountancy, and the omission of this subject from the Cambridge scheme is certainly significant. Accountancy in some form is generally accepted by the newer Universities of this country and also by American Universities as forming an integral part of the course for business men. Even Harvard, one of the most 'academic' of American Universities, provides a course in this subject. According to the prospectus, the course is designed primarily for students who expect to enter a business career and wish to understand the processes by which the earnings and values of industrial properties are computed. 'It is not intended to afford practice in book-keeping, but to give students a grasp of principles which shall enable them to comprehend the significance of accounts.' Such subjects as the forms and accounts adapted to different classes of undertakings, balance-sheets, sinking funds and depreciation, goodwill, and the finance of machinery, which would be dealt with in a course in accountancy, may be mentioned as indicating the importance of the subject to those preparing for commercial life; and, if it is thought impossible to treat the subject in a sufficiently academic manner in the older Universities, the attempt to provide any special preparation of this kind may as well be abandoned.[53]

This was no doubt written by William Ashley, whose semi-fictional claims about the contemporary teaching of accountancy in American universities are discussed in Chapters 9 and 10.

Whether Marshall picked this authorship up is unclear, and he responded by stating, rather implausibly, that his third-year students were 'set to read the more important parts of standard treatises on factory accounts, depreciation, &c.'; but

> [i]f the University should ever decide to adapt its pass examinations in economics to the wants of those business men who do not aim at education of the same high order as is given in our honours courses, it will probably be necessary to have lectures on the common routine of accounting.... For Honours men, at all events, such work is inappropriate. The three sacred years of their University life are already fully occupied with studies which claim to help the able business man to be a leader in the world.[54]

As another correspondent pointed out, there was an inconsistency in this line of argument: that while Marshall maintained that they were not seeking to teach principles of business to pass men, but only honours men, he then went on to suggest that accountancy was inappropriate for honours men:

[53] Anon. [W. J. Ashley], 'Commercial Education', *The Times*, 11 December 1905, p. 6.
[54] Alfred Marshall, 'Education for Business Men', *The Times*, 18 December 1905, p. 13.

> As forms and accounts adapted to different classes of undertakings are ruled by the professor as beneath notice of honours men, I am bound to conclude that he considers that the time given to the acquisition of knowledge of such matters can be well spent only by second and third rate men.[55]

In response, Marshall invoked the contrast between filling the mind and enlarging it: 'And the ablest business men tell us that it is faculty rather than knowledge which the business man of to-day needs. It is a powerful and capacious mind, rather than one already crammed with dead matter, that a University should send out to the work of the world.'[56] These were arguments that had already been rehearsed in Senate, but which went to the heart of the function of teaching economics, rather than commerce, in a university setting. As we shall see, this bifurcation characterised the early existence of the London School of Economics, whose undergraduate students were largely interested in history, politics, and commerce, but who were from the 1930s confronted with teaching that emphasised formal economic principles.

When the Syndicate's Report came before Senate in May 1903, argument still turned on the suitability of the Historical Tripos as a framework for the study of economics. Marshall's criticism that, as it stood, the Historical Tripos was an English Historical Tripos, did gain the explicit support of Maitland; although Marshall's larger point, already suggested in the *Plea*, was that the study of economics had to deal with the contemporary international economy, and so on both counts the Historical Tripos was unsuitable. Foxwell also supported Marshall by arguing that significant numbers could not be attracted into the study of economics unless it led to an honours degree; also reinforcing the idea that it was the 'habits of mind' of future businessmen that needed developing, not their technical skills.[57] In June, Senate agreed to the creation of the new Tripos, the first year to begin the following October,[58] admitting students who would go on to sit their Part I in the spring of 1905, the first examination in Part II then following in 1906. It would now be possible to study economics at honours level in Cambridge over three years, so that the structural impediment to the proper training of minds about which Marshall had complained so long was removed. But did students pursue their studies of economics for three years? And did students who had done so perform better in Part II than those who, before the 1930s, had spent two years studying a different subject and then switched to economics for their final year only? These and related questions will be examined in the following, but first we need to clarify how the Tripos was structured once it began operation.

[55] J. Odell Vintner, 'University Education for Business Men' *The Times*, 26 December 1905, p. 8.

[56] Alfred Marshall, 'University Education for Business Men', *The Times*, 29 December 1905, p. 5.

[57] 'Discussion of Report of Economic and Political Science Syndicate Held 7 May', *Cambridge University Reporter* Vol. XXXIII No. 37 (14 May 1903), pp. 767–8.

[58] *Cambridge University Reporter* Vol. XXXIII No. 44 (9 June 1903), p. 963.

The Inauguration of the Tripos

In 1903 Marshall rewrote his *Plea* as *The New Cambridge Curriculum in Economics*, adding some of arguments made in Senate, and quoting letters from the great and the good who had written in support. His presentation of the curriculum in Part II was characterised by the ambiguity that would be picked up in *The Times* correspondence of 1905: that while the new Tripos was directed to those 'destined to take part in public affairs or to fill the higher and more responsible positions in industrial and commercial life',[59] it was somehow also suitable as preparation for those who would work in routine subordinate positions. Marshall reconciled this by supposing that the differences within each class of men were greater than those between the two;[60] and that because any specialisation only occurred in the third year, the fact that this could either be by subject matter or by a focus on the 'higher theoretical difficulties of Economics' permitted this to be reconciled. While Marshall did allow that students might opt into Part II from other subjects, his view was firmly fixed upon progressive study through three years:

Part I:

1. Subjects for an Essay (1 paper)
2. The existing British Constitution (1 paper)
3. Recent Economic and General History (2 papers)
4. General Principles of Economics (3 papers)

Part II:

1. Subjects for an Essay (1 paper)
2. General Economics (3 papers)
3. Advanced Economics, mainly realistic (2 papers)
4. Advanced Economics, mainly analytic (2 papers)
5. Modern Political Theories (1 paper)
7. International Law with reference to existing economic conditions (1 paper)
8. Principles of Law as applied to economic questions (2 papers)
9. Special subject or subjects (1 paper each).

In Part I, candidates had to sit all papers, and in Part II, the essay and three papers on general economics were compulsory, combined with not less than two nor more than five of the remaining papers. Economic history, politics, and law therefore played a subordinate part in the Tripos as a whole, with rather more scope to include legal subjects in Part II than political. The reading that went along with these papers determined more exactly the nature of the course of study. Section III of the first reading list begins as follows:

> Students are expected to read the general treatises by Hadley, Marshall and Pierson together with at least one of those by J. S. Mill, Nicholson and Sidgwick; Bowley,

[59] Alfred Marshall, *The New Cambridge Curriculum in Economics*, London 1903, p. 22.
[60] Ibid.

> Elements of Statistics, Part I; Keynes, Scope and method of political economy; Seignbos, La méthode historique appliqué aux science sociales; Bagehot, Lombard Street; Bastable, International Trade, Goschen, Foreign Exchanges; Clare, The Money Market . . .[61]

Thus there was little indication to the student of the analytical content of the subject that had been embarked on. Three papers were set on this material, but the remaining three papers in Part I involved comparative politics and general economic history; and this was for a two-year course of study. The accompanying lectures were similarly diffuse: Marshall lectured three times a week throughout the year, Pigou twice a week—as Professor and Girdlers' Lecturer the only members of the University whose time was exclusively dedicated to the Economics Tripos. The remaining lectures were taken from the existing History and Moral Sciences courses, although by early 1904 the Moral Sciences Board had concluded that political economy should be excluded from both Parts I and II of its Tripos.[62]

By 1910 it was evident that some changes were required, the examiners being of the opinion that candidates tended to read too much, in a superficial manner.[63] Part II was reorganised, abolishing the analytic/realistic distinction in favour of papers on industry, distribution, and money, and introducing compulsory papers on 'Principles' and 'Economic Functions of Government' in place of the three 'General Economics' papers. One paper each on 'Political Science' and 'International Law' was now included. The Board reported that the division of papers according to 'method of study' had worked badly, and that the substitution of three papers defined according to subject matter would provide an opportunity for every student to study at least one area of economics in some depth.[64] Not until 1922 was the published lecture list divided according to level of study, headed by Pigou's course of lectures on the Principles of Economics as an introduction. For Part I, Robertson, Sargant Florence, and Clapham lectured for the first year; Guillebaud, Benians, and Evans[65] lectured for the second, in every case twice a week over two terms. In Part II, there were only four courses of economics lectures: Lavington on 'Structure and Problems of Industry', Shove on 'Distribution and Labour', and Henderson on 'Money, Credit and Prices', twice a week over two terms; plus Maynard Keynes on Fridays during the first term on 'Realistic Monetary Problems. Advanced'. Alston, Thatcher, Lavington, Welbourne, Shove, and Cohen lectured to the ordinary degree students.

Reading assigned for the ordinary degree papers in the early 1900s included established works by Jevons, Bastable, Bagehot, and Marshall's own 1892 *Economics of Industry*—a collection of references that could easily have come from the early

61 'Economics Tripos. Part I. Books Recommended by the Special Board for Economics and Politics', *Cambridge University Reporter* Vol. XXXIV No. 9 (10 November 1903), p. 163.

62 'Report of the Special Board for Moral Science on the Moral Sciences Tripos', *Cambridge University Reporter* (9 February 1904), p. 454.

63 Minutes of the Special Board for Economics and Politics 1903–1911, 39th Meeting, 11 November 1910, Cambridge University Archives, UA Min.V.114, Report of Examiners appended f.149.

64 *Cambridge University Reporter* Vol. XLI No. 38 (9 May 1911), p. 949.

65 Benians lectured on the economic history of the United States and Evans on that of Europe for second-year students at the same lecture hour; they were therefore alternatives. *Cambridge University Reporter* Vol. LIII No. 5 (5 October 1922), p. 67.

1890s.[66] However, the course soon began to attract more students, and the reading list was revised, and a voluntary subject on Railway Economics was also included. There were further revisions in 1922 and 1928, when 'Economics II' was divided into four sections:

1. Evolution of Finance and Industry
2. Problems of Social Welfare
3. The Working Constitution of Britain
4. Subjects for an English essay.[67]

These changes to the ordinary degree are noted here for three reasons:

no significant changes were made to the Tripos structure between 1911 and 1930;
during the 1920s the economics papers in the ordinary degree became the most popular student choice, more students sitting its examinations than Part I of the Tripos;
when reform of the Tripos was again broached in 1930, Part I was reduced to a one-year course remarkably similar in structure to the ordinary degree syllabus.

By 1933–1934, it is striking that the lectures directed to Part I (delivered by Robertson, Fay, Austin Robinson, Dobb, and Guillebaud) now covered the ground previously dealt with in the ordinary BA lecturing—'Elementary Economic Theory', economic history, economic structure, social problems, currency, and banking. Pigou's course on Principles was now included under the Part II list, with Robertson lecturing on money, Keynes on the 'Monetary Theory of Production', Shove on 'Production, Value and Distribution', Clark on statistics; together with Kahn on the 'Short Period' in the second term, and Joan Robinson on the economics of imperfect competition.[68] Even though Part II was now taken over two years, rather than one, there are still only three or four core courses. Comparison with the lecture lists for the immediate postwar years reveals little further structural change.

As already noted, lectures did not define 'teaching', but provide a sense of the weighting of material in the Tripos as conceived by those organising it. From the 1920s 'teaching' meant college supervision, and here another problem emerges: that students studying economics in colleges that were either small, or which had few students of economics, would have had to attend supervisions in other colleges. While the college, and not the Faculty, was central to staff and students alike, for many economics students their teachers were in other colleges.

Student Performance

Cambridge colleges do vary quite significantly in size; they are also differentiated by subject and cultural reputation. We should not therefore expect students of economics

[66] *Cambridge University Reporter* Vol. XXXV No. 3 (11 October 1904), p. 60.
[67] *Cambridge University Reporter* Vol. LIX No. 7 (16 October 1928), p. 179.
[68] *Cambridge University Reporter* Vol. LXIV No. 2 (2 October 1933), p. 55.

to be evenly distributed among colleges; as can be seen from Table 5.1, overall Corpus Christi had 3.89% of Tripos students up to the mid-1950s, while Trinity had 13%, which does not directly represent their relative sizes. King's had twice as many students taking only Part II as those taking only Part I; the reverse is true for Queen's. Trinity Hall's 104 students taking only Part I is almost twice that of Sidney Sussex's 53, accounted for by the higher proportion of law students at Trinity Hall, the smaller college.

Nor did all Cambridge students sit final examinations in the early years of the twentieth century, and a large number of those who did opted for the ordinary BA degree rather than the specialised Tripos. During the period 1855–1914, of the nearly 3,000 students admitted to Trinity Hall, only 700 were classed in Tripos examinations, half of these sitting the Law Tripos. Around a quarter of those students who entered the college between October 1918 and April 1920 left without formally graduating; of those who did take examinations, 43% took the ordinary BA, and 57% honours.[69] The development of the Economics Tripos coincided therefore with general changes in the character of the University and student behaviour. During the 1930s the BA ordinary degree gave way to the Triposes, so that by the end of the decade all students who sat University examinations were sitting Tripos examinations. But, as already noted, Part I of the Economics Tripos had by this time adopted much of the material previously included in the economics paper for the ordinary degree, and so one cannot assume that the disappearance of the ordinary degree indicated a general upgrading of undergraduate teaching. These changes clearly have an impact upon student demand for the Economics Tripos, and the consequent rising demand for the Tripos is at least in part generated by changes in student behaviour that have little to do the attractiveness of economics as a subject per se.

Austin Robinson suggested that the number of Cambridge economists was small—with respect to 1930–1931, for instance, he states that '... the entire graduate staff of the Faculty of Economics and Politics in all capacities consisted of 13 persons.'[70] He then notes that Evans and Burn taught economic history; and that Alston and Thatcher were wholly engaged in pass degree teaching—survivals, he writes, of an earlier system. But as we have just seen, this 'earlier system' was about to become the Part I. In any case, by any contemporary standard the Faculty had ample lecturing resources in 1931. Even in 1922, lectures on the Tripos had been delivered by some 25 different people, and there were other college fellows supervising in economics who never figured in the lecture list or the Faculty Board meetings. This was reflected in the balance of the teaching staff in the early 1930s: one professor (Pigou); one reader (Robertson); 10 lecturers; and one assistant lecturer. The composition of the Faculty in Cambridge was determined by the constraints of a system where no-one was permitted to spend more than 40 hours a year lecturing. By 1949 the Faculty numbered 34 persons;[71] at least 20 of these can be classed as economists. There were 3 Firsts and 18 2.1's in Part II that year.

[69] C. Crawley, *Trinity Hall: The History of a Cambridge College 1350–1975*, Trinity Hall, Cambridge 1976, pp. 181, 184.

[70] E. A. G. Robinson, 'Keynes and his Cambridge Colleagues', in D. Patinkin, J. C. Leith (eds.), *Keynes, Cambridge and the General Theory*, London, Macmillan 1977, p. 25.

[71] *Cambridge University Reporter* Vol. LXXX No. 4 (3 October 1949), p. 147.

Table 5.1 Numbers of Economics Tripos Students by College, 1905–1955, Taking Only Part I, Only Part II, and Parts I and II

	Pt. I	Pt. II	I & II	Total	% of all Is	% of all IIs	% of all Is & IIs	Students as % of Total
Caius	105	36	52	193	4.26%	3.59%	5.05%	4.29%
Christ's	138	45	41	224	5.60%	4.48%	3.98%	4.98%
Clare	200	62	61	323	8.11%	6.18%	5.92%	7.18%
Corpus	114	34	27	175	4.62%	3.39%	2.62%	3.89%
Downing	63	17	29	109	2.56%	1.69%	2.82%	2.42%
Emmanuel	149	62	46	257	6.04%	6.18%	4.47%	5.71%
Fitzwilliam	55	16	16	87	2.23%	1.59%	1.55%	1.93%
Girton	40	78	64	182	1.62%	7.77%	6.21%	4.05%
Jesus	121	27	34	182	4.91%	2.69%	3.30%	4.05%
John's	228	112	72	412	9.25%	11.16%	6.99%	9.16%
King's	77	89	64	230	3.12%	8.86%	6.21%	5.11%
Magdalene	100	18	31	149	4.06%	1.79%	3.01%	3.31%
Newnham	49	62	111	222	1.99%	6.18%	10.78%	4.93%
Non-Collegiate	27	7	29	63	1.10%	0.70%	2.82%	1.40%
Pembroke	147	38	57	242	5.96%	3.78%	5.53%	5.38%
Peterhouse	77	39	28	144	3.12%	3.88%	2.72%	3.20%
Queen's	127	25	38	190	5.15%	2.49%	3.69%	4.22%
Selwyn	49	22	9	80	1.99%	2.19%	0.87%	1.78%
Sidney Sussex	53	38	34	125	2.15%	3.78%	3.30%	2.78%
St. Catherine's	97	29	44	170	3.94%	2.89%	4.27%	3.78%
Trinity	345	121	119	585	14.00%	12.05%	11.55%	13.00%
Trinity Hall	104	27	24	155	4.22%	2.69%	2.33%	3.45%
TOTALS:	2465	1004	1030	4499	100.00%	100.00%	100.00%	

Before turning to an assessment of student performance on the Tripos, perhaps the principal developments sketched earlier could be re-emphasised. The Tripos completed its first full cycle in 1906, and within a few years had undergone revisions intended to sharpen the analytical focus of the students, and limiting the space allocated to law and politics. Although the Economics Tripos did include elements of economic history, law, and politics, the subjects examined were, from the students' point of view, always primarily economic subjects. This feature consistently distinguishes the Tripos from the London BSc (Econ.) and the Oxford PPE,[72] neither of which were in mid-century devoted uniquely to the study of economics. The academic character of the Tripos is not therefore in doubt. What the following analysis does place in question is the *level* of the economics taught to the *majority* of the students. During the 1920s economics became popular in Cambridge, but chiefly among pass men, not Tripos students, tending to confirm Cunningham's rather than Marshall's position. The increase in Tripos student numbers during the 1930s had much to do with the absorption of the ordinary syllabus taught to these students into the new one-year Part I, which became something of a soft option not necessarily related to preparation for Part II.[73] The recruitment strategy followed by the Faculty deployed the resulting increase in demand for Part I to justify claims that it needed new staff, appointments then being used to lecture on special subjects in Part II, in which there was anything but a crisis of student numbers.[74] Marshall's vision of a three-year course as the basis for the training of future economists was still, at the end of the 1930s, a long way from general realisation.

Some 4,500 students passed through the Economics Tripos in its first 50 years; 3,503 were classed in Part I and 2,019 in Part II. The distribution of candidates over time can be seen in Figure 5.1.

Evident from this is that the increase in numbers for Parts I and II kept more or less in step up to the early 1930s, at which point there was a sudden increase in Part I candidates, the numbers of which by the later 1930s were running at around twice the number of Part II candidates, a situation that resumed after the war. The fact that the numbers in Part I roughly match those taking Part II up to the early 1930s might lead one to surmise that Marshall's vision of a three-year degree was quickly realised, but this fails to take account of those who gained a Part II after only one year's study.

Before turning our attention to this problem, we should note that the marked change in the early 1930s is the outcome of reducing Part I to a one-year course equivalent to the ordinary degree options, leading to an influx of students whose dedication to the subject, if we are to judge by their performance, was very moderate. In 1932, for

[72] The creation of the Oxford PPE (Philosophy, Politics, and Economics) is dealt with towards the end of Chapter 7; while for the structure of the London BSc (Econ.) see Chapter 11, p. 300. The London degree was in fact a general social sciences degree, not a specialised economics degree; and during the interwar years only a minority of students chose to sit the advanced economic papers.

[73] Quite apart from the elementary nature of the questions, the fact that in 1947 all papers for Part I required students to write five answers in three hours suggests the relative superficiality of the answers that could be expected; *Cambridge University Economics Tripos Papers 1947–1951 with the Papers Set for the Preliminary Examination*, Cambridge University Press, Cambridge 1952.

[74] An argument advanced by Johnson confirmed by the following data: H. G. Johnson, 'Cambridge as an Academic Environment in the Early 1930s: A Reconstruction from the Late 1940s', in D. Patinkin, J. C. Leith (eds.) *Keynes, Cambridge and the General Theory*, London Macmillan 1977, p. 111.

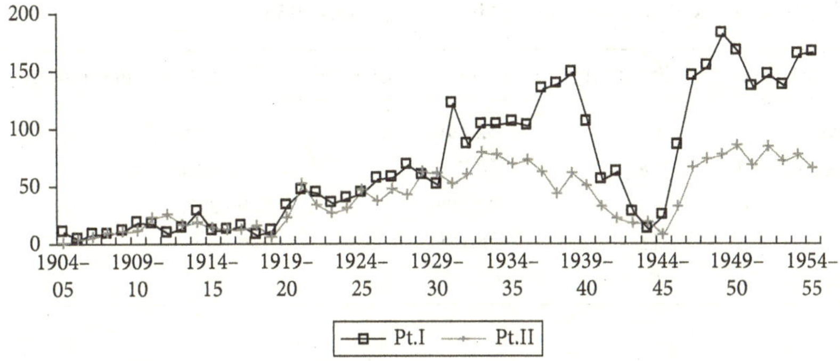

Figure 5.1 Cambridge Economics Tripos, 1905–1955.

Table 5.2 Classes of Degree Attained in Part I, 1905–1955

Degree Class	Frequency	Percentage of Total	Cumulative Percentage
Third	1750	49.96%	49.96%
Lower Second	1177	33.6%	83.56%
Upper Second	442	12.62%	96.18%
First	134	3.83%	100%
Total	3503	100%	

Note: Aggregated in the same way, we can present the Part II results as follows in Table 5.3.

example, 66% of students classed in Part I gained a Third. The best result during this decade was 46% Thirds. Looked at the other way around, treating those with Firsts and Upper Seconds as 'good students', then in 1932 13% fell into this category, generally a typical proportion for the decade when the highest proportion reached was 19%. The postwar picture was rather better: most years just under half the students gained Thirds, exactly half in 1954. The proportion that gained Firsts and Upper Seconds was less consistent, varying in the early 1950s between a high of 20% in 1951 and a low of 7% in 1953. Since there were never less than 137 students taking Part I after 1949, these low proportions do, however, translate into a reasonable number of students. Taken together, the Part I results over this 50 years can be grouped as shown in Tables 5.2 and 5.3.

Again, taking the First and Upper Seconds together, the 29.08% of candidates in Part II who gained this class contrasts sharply with the 16.45% in Part I, representing an average performance compared with which college performances do in fact vary greatly. In Part II, King's had 51.64% of its candidates gaining a First or Upper Second (from a total of 153 students), compared with 6.67% (from a total of 45 students) for Downing.[75] Johnson's story that Law students, averse to the study of Roman Law

[75] Magdalene achieved 14.58% in Part II. College results are dealt with more systematically in the following.

Table 5.3 Classes of Degree Attained in Part II, 1906–1955

Degree Class	Frequency	Percentage of Total	Cumulative Percentage
Third	650	32.19%	32.19%
Lower Second	782	38.73%	70.93%
Upper Second	450	22.29%	93.21%
First	137	6.79%	100%
Total	2019	100	

in their Law Part I, took the Economics Part I but had little interest in the subject is amply confirmed by Trinity Hall's lamentable performance, 50% of students gaining a Third and 6.25% a First or Upper Second (from a total of 128 students).[76] Magdalene here records the worst performance for Thirds at 62.59% of candidates, but pipped Trinity Hall on First and Upper Seconds at 8.64% (out of 139 students). King's by contrast scored 28.37% and 36.88%, respectively (from a total of 141 students).

The distribution of students taking the Economics Tripos by college has been shown in Table 5.1, which also gives an indication of the relative shares in those taking only Part I, those taking only Part II, and those taking both Parts I and II. Here it becomes apparent that this last group is in fact roughly equal to those taking only Part II: it transpires that less than a quarter of all students did in fact read economics for three years in the fashion that Marshall had thought desirable. Evidently, therefore, the rough equality between numbers sitting Part I and Part II up to 1930 in Figure 5.1 conceals Part I students switching out and Part II students switching in. The next question that arises therefore concerns the relative performance of those students taking only one part compared with those who studied economics for three years. Figure 5.2 compares the annual score achieved by students who moved on to other subjects after Part I of the Economics Tripos with that achieved by those who continued on to Part II.

If we bear in mind that a Norrington score[77] of 50% is a Lower Second average, the fact that for those students reading only Part I the score is well below this after 1920[78] is indicative of a less than wholehearted commitment to economic science on the part of students. It is also notable that this poor performance becomes relatively consistent from year to year in the 1930s, after the reform of the Tripos that made Part I a one-year course of study, and hence more attractive to students seeking an easy first year at Cambridge. As we might expect, the performance of students whose commitment to economics was greater, and who probably entered Cambridge with

[76] Trinity Hall students were predominantly law students; Johnson, 'Cambridge as an Academic Environment', p. 111.

[77] Student degree results were scored as follows: 4 points for a First, 3 points for a 2:1, 2 points for a 2:2, and 1 point for a Third. Fails were not recorded in the *Cambridge University Reporter* from which the data were drawn. Female students were not awarded degrees until 1948; but the examination results of female students had been reported in the *Cambridge University Reporter* since the later nineteenth century, and the fact they were not formally awarded a degree for their efforts is in this context irrelevant.

[78] The one observation above 50% after 1920 is for 1944, when there were only five students.

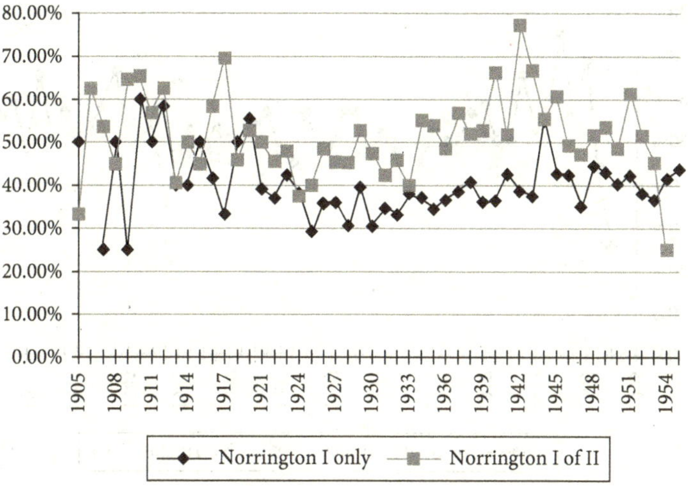

Figure 5.2 Comparative scores at Part I.

the intention of reading economics for three years, is very much better, although not brilliant.[79]

Austin Robinson was of the view that by the later 1930s it was indeed the better students who did carry on from Part I to Part II.[80] We can test this view by comparing the Part II results gained by students completing only Part II with those who had previously studied Part I, the better performers in Figure 5.3.[81]

From this it is evident that the average performance at Part II of students completing three years of economics was during the 1930s mostly inferior to that of students who switched into Part II from another subject—who had not, we can assume, originally intended to read economics. In fact, if we again take the 50% score as a reference point, for most of this period three-year students were moderate performers as a whole. Austin Robinson's view finds little confirmation at this aggregate level; and in fact, as will be shown in the following, the better classes of degree were generally gained by students who had *not* read Part I. By the 1950s no more than a quarter of the students taking Part I went on to sit Part II of the Economics Tripos: the figure for 1949, for instance, is 20%.

Thus far we have established that most students took only Part I of the Tripos, and did so because they treated it as a soft option and got generally poor results. Less than a quarter of those who took Part I proceeded to Part II, where they gained results that were not consistently better than students with Part I in other subjects, and in many years inferior. During the early 1950s this relationship is stable through the expansion in student numbers taking the Tripos, perhaps the one positive feature of the

[79] Here again the peaks occur during war years and are therefore unrepresentative.

[80] Robinson, 'L'Université de Cambridge', p. 97.

[81] A break in the series is introduced at 1933 to synchronise the cohorts after Part II has become a two-year course.

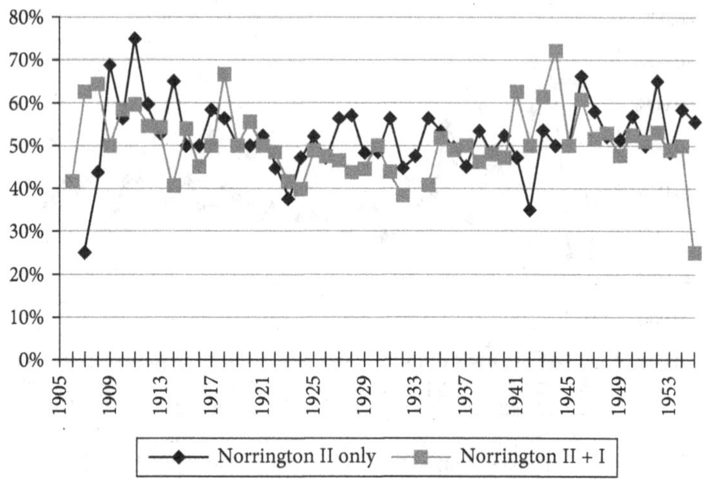

Figure 5.3 Comparative scores at Part II.

three-year group here being that year-on-year performance is less volatile than that of two-year students.

College performance can also be assessed using Norrington scores, expressing aggregate student performance in any one year as a percentage. This produces some surprising results:[82] attention has already been drawn to some of the poorer college performances, as well as to the fact that King's had consistently good results. Between these two extremes there lies, however, an interesting story that flies in the face of Marshall's obdurate belief than economics was an unsuitable subject of study for women.

As is already apparent from Table 5.1, Newnham had a disproportionate number of its students taking the Economics Tripos over three years, 111 against Trinity's 119, although Trinity is a far larger college. These women students did rather well, and in Figure 5.4 we see that in a majority of years they achieve better overall results. If performance across all colleges is taken into account, a remarkably stable relationship can be established: King's was the best performing college, Trinity represented the average, and Newnham consistently lay between King's and Trinity. This was generally true for those students who completed three years of study, those who only sat Part II, whether for the entire run, for the 1930s, and for the stabilised postwar era from 1949. This relationship is most easily appreciated through a direct comparison of the Norrington scores for each college:[83]

[82] Figure 5.4 subtracts the annual Norrington score of Trinity from that of Newnham. Where no three-year students took Part II, the overall average has been inserted to prevent non-significant deviations (Trinity averaged 50% and Newnham 59%). Comparison of Alfred and Mary's respective colleges would have been interesting, but in the case of St. John's there are several years without Part II results for these students, weakening the significance of observed differences.

[83] Table 5.4 averages Norrington scores for those years in which the college had candidates. There are significant gaps for the early years and for the wartime periods which makes year-by-year comparison a

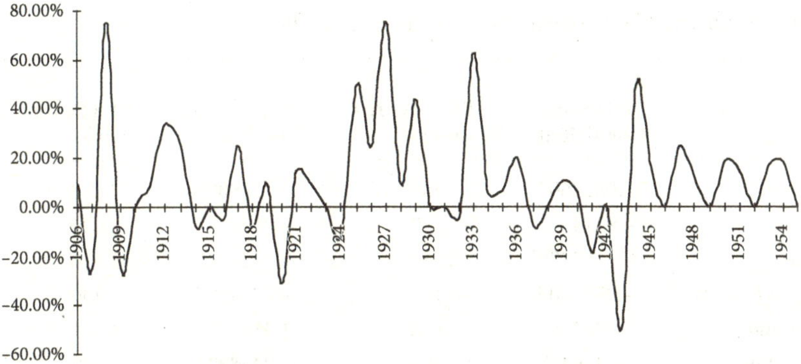

Figure 5.4 Three-year Part II differential between Newnham and Trinity.

Table 5.4 Mean College Scores, 1905–1955

	King's	Newnham	Trinity
Part I only	49%	48%	40%
Part II only	71%	51%	56%
3 yr. Part I	66%	55%	50%
3 yr. Part II	62%	58%	50%
3 yr. Part II 1948–1955	63%	53%	44%

Eighty-nine King's students sat Part II only, while 64 took it after three years of study; the former group, in the best-performing college, recorded higher average scores, which again rather puts in doubt Austin Robinson's argument that by the later 1930s the better students were studying for three, rather than two, years. Indeed, if we take the three-year Part II results for the postwar years, it is evident that there is a slight deterioration, not an improvement. Comparing the three-year Part II performance of just these three colleges captures 27.5% of all students in the group, providing a clearer focus on relative performances than is available by considering all 21 colleges involved. By contrast, the comments made earlier concerning the poor performance of Downing and Magdalene students at Part I relate to just 6.6% of the students who sat only Part I, which is clearly less representative of the whole.

It is possible to present a cross-section of college performance by ranking the performance of all students with respect to one college. Choice of this college is of course moot, since it is the ranking that interests us; here Newnham is taken so that we can view more directly the relation between male and female performance (Table 5.5). Performance at Part II is linked here to performance at Part I and college attended, and performance at Part I linked to college attended.

problem; interpolating the mean for years where no score is recorded has uneven consequences given the differing numbers of students involved.

Table 5.5 Ordered Logit of Performance in Part I and Part II

	A) Pt. II Score Coefficient	Pt. II Score t value	B) Pt. I Score Coefficient	Pt. I Score t value
Caius	.0822605	.346	-.7169005	-3.472
Christ's	-.921436	-3.767	-.8037054	-4.029
Clare	-.6185228	-2.813	-.9334145	-5.116
Corpus Christi	-.0503307	-0.182	-.7204493	-3.436
Downing	-1.195316	-3.886	-1.214503	-4.968
Emmanuel	.0466447	0.208	-.8448225	-4.300
Fitzwilliam	-1.266591	-3.381	-1.297338	-4.720
Girton	-.5215514	-2.531	-.2011383	-0.894
Jesus	-.8403086	-2.976	-1.257076	-5.944
St. John's	-.3545539	-1.845	-.9187094	-5.149
King's	.7726119	3.785	.212341	1.012
Magdalene	-1.199307	-3.825	-1.402593	-6.346
Non-collegiate	-.647005	-1.974	-.5526809	-1.916
Pembroke	-.5605897	-2.423	-1.094892	-5.614
Peterhouse	-.76449	-2.820	-1.47163	-6.013
Queen's	.1746161	0.667	-.8393786	-4.126
Selwyn	-.4966491	-1.372	-.8588224	-2.962
Sidney Sussex	-.0476245	-0.187	-.8052811	-3.307
St. Catherine's	-.1002339	-0.407	-.823259	-3.875
Trinity	-.4516839	-2.488	-1.04912	-6.305
Trinity Hall	-.7979735	-2.763	-1.033117	-4.810
Part I	-.2322969	-2.771	n/a	n/a

A) Dependent variable = Part II score (First = 4, 2.1 = 3, 2.2 = 2. 3 = 1)
Independent variables college and Part I score (Part I = 1 if student did Part I, = 0 otherwise); Newnham omitted
Number of observations = 2,019
Chi2 = 138.49
Prob. > Chi2 = 0.0000
Log likelihood-=-2453.2661
Pseudo R2 = 0.0275

B) Dependent variable = Part I score
Independent variable = college (Newnham omitted)
Number of observations = 3,503
Chi2 = 140.63
Prob. > Chi2 = 0.0000
Log likelihood = -3780.169
Pseudo R2 = 0.0183.

The figures in columns two and four provide a clear picture of the ordering of the colleges, it being evident that King's is the best-performing college, and that at Part I Peterhouse is marginally worse than Magdalene. The performance of Newnham's Part I students is bettered marginally by King's; at Part II the gap is larger, and students from three other colleges have a better performance. Also evident is that the rankings in Parts I and II do not strictly coincide, although most colleges are closer to Newnham's performance in Part II than in Part I. The figures presented in Table 5.5 confirm the generalisation made earlier concerning the relative rankings of King's, Newnham, and Trinity, but shows in finer detail the relation between the colleges outlined previously.

Some Conclusions from the Data

Oxbridge students, whatever their personal qualities, can be assumed to have enjoyed a more thorough schooling than those admitted to other universities. Hence any consideration of the effectiveness of the teaching of economics in Cambridge has to take into account that its students begin their studies with a considerable advantage. We should also note that during the period in question the inter-university system of external examination did more or less ensure that similar standards applied across similar university courses in Britain. A First or a 2:1 in economics from Cambridge, Manchester, or London meant broadly the same thing as far as substantive knowledge and ability went.[84] Hence the rather dismal story revealed in the preceding statistics cannot be attributed to the higher standards of Cambridge examinations. Things are in fact substantially worse: having admitted students selected from among the most gifted or hard-working in their year, the teaching that the majority received at Cambridge led to degree results that compare badly with those, for example, at the LSE.[85] While this does mean that Marshall's ambitions for the Tripos were met only in a very limited way, it has been argued in this and the previous chapter that Marshall sought to inculcate a particular disposition in the economics graduate. If the results of the Tripos examinations throw doubt on its success in realising this, no criticism of the quality of lectures or of lecturers and teachers is necessarily implied. Rather, we should look to the Cambridge pedagogic routine, and consider whether the organisation of Cambridge itself left it unsuited to the realisation of Marshall's vision.

This was, broadly, Harry Johnson's conclusion. He was for one year a student in Part II of the Tripos, having already graduated in 1943 from the University of Toronto with honours in economics and political science. During 1943–1944 he had then become acting professor and sole member of staff for economics at St. Francis Xavier University, Novia Scotia. Then he had joined the army, and having been assigned to clerical work in Canada House, London, on demobilisation he was able to enter Cambridge University. Subsequently he studied again at Toronto, then at Harvard; he

[84] With the addition of many different kinds of institution to the university system since 1992, this claim could not now be sustained; although as previously noted a general inflation of grades has made attainment by subject or by institution less transparent that it was.

[85] Year-by-year comparisons can be made in the results in the Appendix to this chapter.

returned to Cambridge, then moved to Manchester, following which he taught at the LSE and Chicago. A strong interest in the way in which economics might be conveyed to students at any level was fostered by this very varied experience, an experience that none of the Cambridge faculty had.

In any case, at the time that Johnson taught in Cambridge the 'Faculty' was a set of university employees, not a building. Members of the Faculty were united by lecturing and supervisory responsibilities for the Tripos, responsibilities that were shared with a number of other college fellows. Professors were not permitted to supervise; other faculty members were limited to 12 hours' supervision a week, while for College Fellows like Gerald Shove there was no statutory limit. All Faculty members were permitted a maximum of 40 lecture hours a year, which meant in effect two lectures a week in the first two terms of the year, and for the first four weeks of the final term. The lecture list was published in the *Reporter* and students went to whichever lectures they thought fit; they also attended, singly or in pairs, a weekly college supervision that was the principal source of guidance for their studies. A weekly essay was usually prepared for and discussed in each supervision, placing a premium on the rapid assimilation of material and the construction of arguments. Students would tend to associate chiefly with students of economics and other subjects from their own college, rather than with other economics students per se. This would also apply to library facilities: those colleges with significant numbers of economics students would make books and periodicals available to their students in the college library, which would be more accessible than the departmental library. This was, during the early years of the Tripos, a small collection of economics books shelved in one of the lecture rooms under the general supervision of a porter. The Marshall Library was created in the mid-1920s, located first in the Balfour Laboratory in Downing Place, moving in 1935 to the Squire Law Library in Downing Street.[86] Apart from college and Faculty Library, students could also of course use the University Library, which has a substantial collection of international economic literature and periodicals.

Johnson notes that there were few occasions on which Faculty members met each other as such. Meetings of the Faculty Board provided an opportunity for senior staff; they would also encounter each other at the various examination boards, at the weekly Political Economy Club which Keynes had founded in 1909, and possibly at a Faculty sherry party. There were no Faculty offices, and there were limited opportunities for staff to discuss their work or teaching with colleagues. Lecturing was a one-way process, and discussion with peers was restricted to conversation at High Table with non-economists. The most sustained discussion of economic matters experienced both by students and supervisors occurred in the weekly undergraduate supervisions; and most of these students were reading only Part I, such as those who would later take Part II in Law but could in this way avoid studying Roman Law. The level of discussion in the majority of these supervisions was inevitably very elementary. Johnson suggested that these circumstances fostered a style of argument on the part of Cambridge economists that favoured controversy, or was reductive, or both:

[86] Donald Ross, 'An Unusual Commitment. Alfred and Mary Marshall and the Establishment of the Marshall Library 1903–1944', Marshall Library of Economics, Cambridge 1991.

> This kind of audience for one's everyday teaching and discussion of economics necessarily forms and distorts one's concept of the audience one is addressing through one's written work – if, that is, one does not, as many Oxford and Cambridge dons do, content oneself with oral communication through lectures, supervisions and discussions with economist and non-economist academic cronies and colleagues. The most obvious example is actually a common Oxford style, related to the character of the Politics, Philosophy and Economics course and examination tradition, and best exemplified in the work of R. F. Harrod, J .R. Hicks, and many other lesser luminaries, which can best be described as a sort of conversation with oneself, a dramatic monologue performed for a somewhat dim audience of economic amateurs, in which one works one's way laboriously through a succession of false starts and red herrings, eventually winding up with the more or less obvious and correct approach and solution to the problem at hand. It is a style presumably effective for instruction of a captive audience of bashful undergraduates, whom one is committed to instruct for an hour on some basic principles that could be communicated in a few minutes to anyone with a logical mind and a distrust of the economic pronouncements of the socially powerful but economically illiterate; but it is tedious in the extreme for a professional economist to have to wade through. The Cambridge equivalent is a little less tedious but equally irritating to a professional. It posits a nameless horde of faceless orthodox nincompoops, among whom a few recognisable faces can be discerned, and proceeds to ridicule a travesty of their published, presumed, or imputed views in the process of revealing the unorthodox truth in a simple encapsulated form suitable for the average undergraduate to swallow without gagging. This is the extreme form of the modern post-Keynesian-Cambridge style, which unfortunately the *General Theory* did much to implant. It has three major elements in it, traceable directly to salient characteristics of Cambridge as an academic environment: the belief that fundamental questions of social and economic policy are ultimately determined by debate among a handful of academic economists, in Cambridge and at most two other British universities; that policy failure is the result of bad – and bad means orthodox, or more generally pedestrian, tedious and unimaginative – economics; and that the world is to be put right by instructing the undergraduate students at Cambridge and elsewhere in the complex fallacies committed by orthodox economics and the simple truth as derived by anti-orthodox theory.[87]

Johnson points up the manner in which the level and organisation of the teaching combined with the social geography of Cambridge to produce an introverted attitude on the part of Faculty staff and fellows that was damaging to the development of scholarship and teaching. Analysis of the examination results achieved by Cambridge students over the years lends general support to the charges made by Johnson, for they reveal that those who read economics in Cambridge fell into two distinct groups: a majority, dominated by students sitting only Part I, who treated the subject as a soft option; and a quite small minority who had a genuine interest in the subject. Given the

[87] Johnson, 'Cambridge as an Academic Environment', p. 111.

institutional features outlined earlier, this necessarily modifies our picture of the relative success or effectiveness of Marshall's programme.

Support for Johnson's diagnosis of Cambridge in mid-century comes from a 1939 Rockefeller Foundation report on Oxford, where the institutional features were comparable. The Foundation was engaged in a review of the prospects for investment in European social science research; and the report noted that the development of Nuffield College could in the future represent a worthwhile use of Foundation grants. But at the end of the 1930s Oxford was an institution geared to the work of lone scholars in libraries, not social science researchers. This was currently a real limitation:

> The causes do not lie merely in the character of the problems but in the character of Oxford itself. The system of highly individualized undergraduate education under the tutorial system is not only financially very expensive but makes heavy demands on the time of the teachers. Moreover, I suspect that the tutorial system puts less emphasis upon the discovery of new truth than it does upon thinking about and arguing logically about the ideas already believed.... These circumstances tend to make of instructors experts in the dialectics of economic or political theory which is likely to be removed from the facts of life. This was especially apparent in interviews with Harrod and six or eight younger men. Brilliance, cleverness, breadth of culture, splendid personalities, – you felt; but in many of them also remoteness and naivete as to the methods of modern research attack.[88]

The Foundation was much more impressed by the work of Jewkes and Campion in Manchester, who had developed a 'close laboratory relation' with their local industrial region.[89] This kind of direct connection with commerce and industry was not possible in Cambridge, and only to a limited extent in Oxford.

It is perfectly obvious that many brilliant economists began their career as students of economics in Cambridge, and a considerable number of less distinguished graduates doubtless benefited from their studies and entered careers in which this was of direct use to them. The points made previously are not intended to cast doubt on this; they instead direct attention to the generally poor performance of students on the Cambridge Tripos, relative to what one might reasonably have expected, and also to the performance of contemporary students at, for example, the LSE.[90] From the large number of students who failed to gain a Lower Second or above, it can be inferred that getting a good class of degree was not a priority for many students; and this is relatively unsurprising, since the only sure employment for economics graduates at this time was teaching economics in school, college, or university. Furthermore, the

[88] 'General S.S. Policy in Europe (written in June 1939)', Rockefeller Foundation Archives, Series 910, Box 3, Folder 16 f.3–4; partially cited also in Salma Ahmad, 'Institutions and the Growth of Knowledge: The Rockefeller Foundations' Influence on the Social Sciences between the Wars', University of Manchester PhD dissertation 1987, p. 123. The lack of interest on the part of the Foundation in the teaching of economics in Cambridge is something that Ahmad noted, but for which she found no explanation (p. 124; see also p. 135 n. 54).

[89] Ibid., f. 9.

[90] In 1953, 274 students were classed in the internal BSc (Econ.): 9 gained Firsts, 64 Upper Seconds, 145 Lower Seconds, with 56 pass degrees awarded. In 1937 the distribution was 9, 27, 48, and 27, respectively (figures taken from the *London University Gazette*, various years).

approach taken here has sought to keep in view the broad mass of students, rather than the eminent individuals of whom one has heard. This broad mass is important, for it was the sheer numbers of (unengaged) students reading Part I that provided employment for Faculty and College members alike. It is also assumed here that the large number of Thirds is indicative of unmotivated students, not bad teaching. Nonetheless, this still bears out Harry Johnson's charge: that, given the organisation of college and University, Cambridge economists spent a considerable amount of term in supervisions discussing elementary economics with uninvolved students, around half of whom went on to gain Thirds in their Part I. This is the daily reality of Cambridge economics in the first half of the twentieth century, lending general plausibility to his argument that this would have had a damaging effect on the intellectual reflexes of Cambridge economists.

It is not suggested here that Marshall's vision of a three-year undergraduate training in economics was in itself mistaken; but he was, in 1885, unfortunately about 80 years at least ahead of his time. Not until the mid-1960s in Britain did the public and private sector begin to recruit graduates in economics in preference to those with other kinds of degrees. Up until then, the prime opening for economics graduates was as teachers of economics in school, college, or university. A fashionable criticism of the 'Establishment' at this time was that the Civil Service was dominated by Oxbridge civil servants trained in classics and history—Marshall would have raised the same complaint. The programme of training that the Syndicate laid out in 1902–1903, revised in 1911, had considerable virtues. And during the 1920s the *Cambridge Economics Handbooks* became staple fare for advanced students of economics in Britain, representing a clear exposition of fundamental economic principles.

But, as we have seen, Cunningham was more prescient: the Cambridge pedagogic routine was unsuited to this project, and it seriously misjudged the market for rigorous training in economics. For most Cambridge students, some elementary acquaintance with economic principles, combined with aspects of applied and descriptive economics, was quite enough. For the limited number who found this inadequate, and who sought more: they had their weekly supervisions with some of the world's leading economists. It can be argued, of course, that the kind of graduate school favoured by Cunningham would not have made the impact upon the university that the Economics Tripos did; or that without the broad mass of undergraduates that emerged in the 1950s a graduate school would not have been financially viable.

The issue here is rather different. First, it took over 50 years before significant numbers of students came to Cambridge to study economics over the three years that Marshall considered the bare minimum. This development coincided with the rapid expansion of American graduate schools, which were still in the immediate postwar years very small. During their period of rapid growth in the 1950s, British academics resisted pressures to develop similar institutions, in part because they felt that the three-year Tripos was adequate training. Second, the gradual expansion of the Cambridge Faculty was made on the back of elementary teaching, a success story in its own terms since it enabled Cambridge to establish an international eminence in the development of economic analysis. However, the daily reality for most Cambridge economists was that their time was heavily taken up with teaching elementary economics, and Johnson's criticisms are properly directed to the misdirection of effort involved, as well as to the deleterious effects this had on styles of argument and selection of issues. When one considers the economic controversies with which Cambridge is associated from the 1950s to the 1970s, who can doubt the accuracy of this judgement?

Appendix: The Tripos Data Set

Classified examination results are published annually in the *Cambridge University Reporter*, listing students by examination (Part I and Part II), by class of degree, and giving the college of each candidate.[91] Aegrotat results are printed, but were not included in the data set; failures are by definition not listed, and cannot therefore be recorded. This is unfortunate, since the Robbins Report drew attention in the early 1960s to significant wastage rates in British universities.[92] Furthermore, as noted earlier, in the early days of the Tripos not all Cambridge students sat final honours examinations, while many studied political economy as part of an ordinary degree. The data set does not therefore include every student from 1903 onward who studied economics in Cambridge; but it does include all students who were classified in the Tripos examinations.

The results printed in the *Reporter* simply report the results gained by candidates for the current year; it is therefore not possible to determine from any one set of results whether those students sitting Part II have previously sat the Part I, or have instead switched into economics after completing a different subject at Part I. Collation of the results by student name deals with the first problem, each record in the database representing a named student, together with college attended, class, and year of examination results. In this way three student types can be distinguished: those who have sat and been classified at Part I only; those who have sat and been classified for Part II only; and those who have completed and been classified in both parts.

The database was assembled alongside a general read-through of the *Cambridge University Reporter* from 1880 to 1955. The data have passed through five separate software programmes, starting in Cardbox Plus and ending in Stata v.4.[93] In the course of transfers some anomalies have come to light, and in cleaning up the data some losses have doubtless occurred. Given the overall size of database, however, these do not appear to be significant, since unanticipated results are stable over many years by college, by class of degree, or by type of student.

It is also possible to review results by college, although comparing raw performances across colleges is problematic owing to disparities in numbers of candidates in each year. This can be compensated by use of a Norrington Score for college performance, a weighted average that expresses the examination performance of students in any one year as an index, in which 100 would indicate that all students gained a First. The Norrington Score can then be used to compare overall performance between colleges, and within the three groups of students sorted with respect to Part of Tripos sat. A limited number of variables therefore yields a large quantity of results that illuminate development of the Tripos, quality of student performance, ranking of colleges and, inferentially, the effectiveness of the teaching received by students.

91 Women's results were listed separately until 1947.

92 A 14% wastage rate was reported at this time for universities across all subjects (Committee on Higher Education, *Higher Education*, p. 20).

93 My thanks to Mike Devereux for his timely help with this.

6
What Is 'Marshallianism'?

That Marshall played a critical role in shaping modern economics has long been accepted, by his own students as much as by those whose vision of economic analysis and its purposes was very different.[1] His legacy is usually associated with *Principles of Economics*, the 1890 text that sold so well that when the plates wore out it was reset in 1949 and reissued in paperback.[2] The building blocks of modern economic analysis were here laid down in prose and diagrams that have a familiar look to them, inviting comparison with the textbook exposition of microeconomic theory from the 1940s onwards. But as we have seen in the previous chapter, the pedagogic plan of the Tripos only distantly reflected *Principles*, rather than reproduced it. Nor did *Principles*' didactic structure outlive the 1920s; as will be shown in Chapter 12, the template for the modern economic textbook owes far more to Lionel Robbins's LSE lectures during the 1930s than to Marshall's landmark text. A rather more nuanced approach to a Cambridge legacy has been offered by Nahid Aslanbeigui and Guy Oakes, who distinguish between 'a pedagogical regime of canonical texts, analyses, and unresolved problems', a 'consensual apparatus of governance designed to refine and reform the tripos, recruit faculty, and manage production of new generations of economists', and an 'ethos of civility', a kind of social switchboard that bound generations of students and economists to a perceived tradition.[3] This mix of active pedagogy, institutional dynamics, and social adhesion has been touched on in the previous two chapters; here they will be brought into focus to suggest that 'Marshallianism' hardly outlived its namesake. By the 1930s it was already superseded, as direct pedagogy, vocational aspiration, and institutional practice; relegated to a prehistory by an emergent 'economic science' divorced from substantive connection with the 'ordinary business of life' that was at the centre of Marshall's concerns.

Any detailed account of this process of displacement would call for an entire monograph at least, for want of any reliable synthesis of the international development of interwar economics.[4] Here I can only sketch out the elements of this story, directing

[1] Typically George J. Stigler, 'The Place of Marshall's Principles in the Development of Economics', in John K. Whitaker (ed.) *Centenary Essays on Alfred Marshall*, Cambridge University Press, Cambridge 1990, pp. 1–13. See also for a summary at the millennium: William J. Baumol, 'What Marshall Didn't Know: On the Twentieth Century's Contribution to Economics', *Quarterly Journal of Economics* Vol. 115 (2000), pp. 1–44. Baumol begins his account with a 'textbook test', seeking to ascertain how much the presentation of the subject in modern elementary textbooks has moved beyond Marshall's own *Principles*. While he concludes that there is a remarkable degree of continuity, he suggests that this is because developments in economic analysis have been too technical for incorporation into basic textbooks, while the force of tradition also plays a role (p. 8).

[2] Peter Groenewegen, *A Soaring Eagle: Alfred Marshall 1842–1924*, Edward Elgar, Cheltenham 1995, p. 400.

[3] Nahid Aslanbeigui, Guy Oakes, 'The 'Cambridge Tradition' Reconsidered', *History of Political Economy* Vol. 50 (2018), p. 880.

[4] G. L. S. Shackle, *The Years of High Theory. Invention and Tradition in Economic Thought 1926–1939*, Cambridge University Press, Cambridge 1967, does cover some of the relevant material, but with its focus

Constructing Economic Science. Keith Tribe, Oxford University Press. © Oxford University Press 2022.
DOI: 10.1093/oso/9780190491741.003.0006

attention towards the way in which Marshall conceived the study of economics, and away from any fabricated theoretical genealogy.[5] Rather than treat *Principles of Economics* as a key to Marshall's heritage, I will first take up the point made in the preceding chapter about Marshall's pedagogy—that his design for the Tripos gave no opening to systematic theoretical exposition, the emphasis being on what later became known as 'applied economics': more *Industry and Trade* than *Principles.* In Chapter 4, I drew on Cannan's notes of his lectures during the autumn and winter of 1891–1892 to provide a sense of how Marshall then lectured on political economy; to these we can add later, more impressionistic, reports. However, Tiziano Raffaelli's account of Marshall's tutorials with Maynard Keynes in 1905 provides a much more direct and detailed perspective on the way in which Marshall sought to communicate economics to a receptive student—foreshadowing the pedagogy of the weekly supervision, while at the same time suggesting that for this to function effectively you needed an economist like Marshall and a student like Maynard Keynes.

Secondly, I will consider how Pigou became a representative Marshallian economist in little more than two or three years after his switch for his final undergraduate year from History to Moral Sciences, being awarded a First in Part II in 1900. Commentary on Pigou's appointment in 1908 as Marshall's successor to the Cambridge chair has usually been diverted by his youth—just 30 when appointed—and by Foxwell's petulant reaction to the failure of his own candidacy. But any consideration of what Pigou had been publishing in the previous few years shows that Marshall's partisan support for Pigou[6] is no more than evidence of an understandable desire to secure his legacy, something that none of the other candidates—William Ashley, Herbert Foxwell, Edwin Cannan—would or could have done. That Pigou could at the age of 25 write the definitive rebuttal of the argument for 'Tariff Reform' demonstrates both his alignment with Marshall and his precocious talent.[7] The bibliography appended to Maynard Keynes's obituary of Foxwell indicates that he published nothing at all between 1899 (the introduction to Anton Menger's *Right to the Whole Produce of Labour*)[8] and 1907 (a short introduction of a letter from Malthus to Ricardo printed in the Notes and Memoranda section of the *Economic Journal*).[9] By contrast, from

upon Sraffa, Maynard Keynes, and Joan Robinson, is very much a retrospective (Cambridge) theoretical history that fails to register the marginal contemporary significance of 'theory' in the development of economic analysis to the mid-twentieth century.

[5] Although this Cambridge tendency to construct a theoretical lineage can be seen at work early on in Gerald Shove's centenary essay, 'The Place of Marshall's *Principles* in the Development of Economic Theory', *Economic Journal* Vol. 52 (1942), pp. 294–329, it presents an account of Marshall's relationship to Ricardo and Malthus that bears little relationship to what Ricardo and Malthus actually wrote; pp. 295–302.

[6] Older accounts of Pigou's appointment recycle contemporary speculation and gossip; for a balanced assessment, see Nahid Aslanbeigui, Guy Oakes, *Arthur Cecil Pigou*, Palgrave Macmillan, Basingstoke 2015, pp. 21–25.

[7] *The Riddle of the Tariff*, R. Brimley Johnson, London 1903. This episode is discussed further in Chapter 8.

[8] Herbert Somerton Foxwell, 'Introduction' to Anton Menger, *The Right to the Whole Produce of Labour: The Origin and Development of the Theory of Labour's Claim to the Whole Product of Industry*, Macmillan, London 1899, pp. v–cx.

[9] John Maynard Keynes, 'Herbert Somerton Foxwell' in his *Essays in Biography*, Collected Writings of John Maynard Keynes Vol. X, Macmillan, London 1972, pp. 294–95; Letter from Malthus to Ricardo,

1900 to 1906 inclusive, Pigou published some 34 book reviews, essays, pamphlets, and comments, together with various contributions to the *Economic Journal*.[10] One could object that a comparison of this kind introduces a modern academic standard, but that simply proves the point—that this is indeed a contrast between an older scholarly style that laid emphasis on conversation and correspondence, and a new ethos of publication. Along the way Pigou also invented the template for a standard journal article that endured—directed to a specific problem, employing graphical analysis to elucidate theoretical or hypothetical points, above all brief: around 10 pages, quite unlike Edgeworth's lengthy disquisitions,[11] whose theoretical work is otherwise a harbinger of future substantive developments.[12] Pigou outlived Maynard Keynes by 13 years, and both had been taught their economics by Marshall; but Keynes's relegation, in the second chapter of his *General Theory*, of Pigou's work to a superseded 'classical' tradition gives the impression that Pigou was already part of a much earlier generation.[13] To supplement this focus upon Pigou as a representative of Marshallianism, we can also consider one specific text: Sydney Chapman's *Lancashire Cotton Industry*, which provides another perspective on what Marshall conveyed to those he taught.

A thorough treatment of the composition and structure of *Principles* through its various editions, and exactly why the planned second volume materialised only in the form of two apparently very different books—*Industry and Trade* and *Money, Credit and Commerce*—lies beyond the scope of the present argument. Nonetheless, given its status, some remarks do need to be made here, if only to reorient our attention to the text, rather than the reputation that it acquired. While it can be shown that the text did not form any kind of didactic thread for Marshall's own lecturing, it was quickly assumed to be representative of Marshallian economics. Reviewing the history of the text will reveal that the canon is more complex than might be thought.

Fourthly, during the 1920s Marshall's theoretical approach to industrial organisation came under scrutiny, beginning with criticism from John Clapham and quickly moving first into a more general critique of the concept of returns to scale, and then to his concept of the representative firm. In the latter case, this introduces Lionel Robbins's criticism of Marshall, but more generally suggests that by 1930 many features of the Marshallian heritage were being discarded. Here we are not so much interested in the theoretical merits of the various lines of argument made, but in the forms of legitimation upon which they drew.

9 October 1814, 'A Letter of Malthus to Ricardo', *Economic Journal* Vol. 17 (1907), pp. 272–76. Maynard Keynes's essay was first published in the *Economic Journal* for December 1936.

[10] See Aslanbeigui, Oakes, *Arthur Cecil Pigou*, pp. 284–85.

[11] Even in the section of his *Papers* collecting together his contributions on mathematical economics each piece is usually between 20 and 40 pages; F. Y. Edgeworth, *Papers Relating to Political Economy* Vol. III, Macmillan, London 1925, Section VI.

[12] See the discussion in Aslanbeigui, Oakes, *Arthur Cecil Pigou*, pp. 35–39.

[13] Keynes cements this impression left on the reader by describing Pigou in the book's first footnote as a 'follower' of Ricardo, and hence a member of the 'classical school': *The General Theory of Employment, Interest and Money*, in The Collected Writings of John Maynard Keynes Vol. VII, Macmillan, London 1973, p. 3 fn. 1. Keynes was in many respects as much a representative of the 'Marshallianism' sketched here as was Pigou, but given the interpretive framework into which Keynes was himself soon fitted, demonstration of that thesis here would divert my argument.

Before all this, however, there is some prehistory to discuss. For before Marshall there was Jevons. Those who turned to political economy in Britain during the 1880s largely turned to the version that Stanley Jevons had put into circulation with his *Theory of Political Economy* of 1871. Francis Edgeworth learned his economics from his Hampstead neighbour, while Philip Wicksteed discovered Jevons having had his interest in political economy aroused by Henry George. Henry Sidgwick's *Principles of Political Economy* adopted a discursive framework that recalled Mill, but which made creative use of Jevons's concept of 'final utility' to develop conceptions of inequality that would be developed by Pigou in his *Economics of Welfare* (1920). Edwin Cannan's own understanding of economic principles was lent a Jevonian cast during the 1880s, and he was the vehicle for their eventual transmission to the London School of Economics in the 1920s. What then does 'Jevonian' mean?

'Jevonian Economics'

Marshall's *Principles* was published in a context where the dominant account of modern economic principles had been authored by Jevons; but Marshall already had form when it came to deprecating the significance of his rival's work. Writing in 1883 to Léon Walras, Marshall claimed (implausibly) that he had taught the doctrine of final utility in Cambridge before 1871, and that he had anticipated all the principal points of Jevons's *Theory of Political Economy*.[14] His review of that work had appeared in *The Academy* for 1 April 1872, in which he denied all novelty to Jevons's account of agents making choices between 'pleasure' and 'pain' on the basis of marginal choices expressed in the terms of differential calculus.[15] This framework had originally been starkly presented in the paper Jevons had sent to Section F of the British Association's Cambridge meeting during the summer of 1862, well before Marshall developed an interest in political economy, and before he would have returned to St. Johns after the summer vacation for his second undergraduate year.[16] Of relevance here is the way that 'Jevonian economics' was treated by Marshall, by most of his contemporaries, and indeed in its modern reputation, as a relentlessly formalistic enterprise eschewing recognition of the empirical aspects of human behaviour and the institutional contexts

[14] Marshall to Walras, 1 November 1883, Letter 133 in *The Correspondence of Alfred Marshall, Economist*, Vol. I: *Climbing, 1868–1890*, ed. J. K. Whitaker, Cambridge University Press, Cambridge 1996, p. 169. Marshall had been appointed College Lecturer in the Moral Sciences in 1868.

[15] See my discussion in 'Utilitarianism, The Moral Sciences, and Political Economy: Mill-Grote-Sidgwick', in Katia Candari, Marco Dardi, Steen G. Medema (eds.) *Marshall and the Marshallians: Essays in Honour of Tiziano Raffaelli*, Palgrave Macmillan, Cham 2021, pp. 149–84. Marshall fails to support his denial of novelty to Jevons by identifying any prior instance; Sidgwick's *Methods of Ethics* (1874), and importantly John Grote's *An Examination of the Utilitarian Philosophy* (ed. Joseph Bickersteth Mayor), Deighton Bell, Cambridge 1870, are plausibly suggestive of a related Cambridge oral culture developing in the course of the 1860s, but the roots of this culture would coincide independently with Jevons's 1862 paper, and there is no reason to think that Jevons would have been aware of it.

[16] W. S. Jevons, 'Brief Account of a General Mathematical Theory of Political Economy', *Journal of the Statistical Society of London* Vol. 29 Issue 2 (June 1866), pp. 282–90. Mike White has discussed the genesis of Jevons's own turn to political economy in 'The Moment of Richard Jennings: The Production of Jevons's Marginal Economic Agent', in Philip Mirowski (ed.) *Natural Images in Economic Thought: 'Markets Read in Tooth and Claw'*, Cambridge University Press, Cambridge 1994, pp. 197–230.

to which this behaviour was oriented. More broadly, this formal account of economic action appears to contrast with Marshall's own formulation of economics as linked to the 'ordinary business of life', and indeed the shape that *Principles* took in 1890, in which the first 100 pages formed a 'Preliminary Survey' presenting an evolutionary history of economic activity and doctrine, and a basic account of the social nature of economic motivation.

This perception of Jevons's interests is, however, a very attenuated one. In 1863 he was appointed to a tutorship in political economy at Owens College, Manchester, largely on the strength of his work on logic, publishing a primer on the subject the following year. But his breakthrough, and subsequent professorial appointment at Owens, was owed to *The Coal Question* (1865), a substantial monograph in which he argued that the reliance of economic expansion on the consumption of ever larger amounts of coal would inevitably drive the price of coal higher and so progressively choke off prospects for continued economic growth as energy costs increased. Considering in detail the improvements in efficiency of steam engines over the previous century, he concluded that this had increased perhaps by a factor of ten. But not only would there be a progressive diminution in such gains, '... every such improvement of the engine, when effected, does but accelerate anew the consumption of coal'.[17] Developing an empirical argument about population growth, technological change, and energy use, the book was discussed in Parliament and went into a second edition the following year. This very practical interest was also evident when in 1870 Jevons was President of Section F of the British Association, taking the opportunity in his Presidential Address to emphasise that statistics 'in its true meaning denotes all knowledge relating to the condition of the State or people.' This was not therefore merely numerical information, but all information pertaining to the state: 'We must not only have facts, numerical or otherwise, but those facts must be analysed, arranged and explained by inductive or deductive processes ....'[18]

So Marshall and Jevons shared an interest in the empirical materiality of economic activity. Marshall not only argued in general terms for the understanding of economic action within institutional context—which is why a 'toolbox', his *organon*, was needed, and not the rigid principles of a 'science'. While he did eventually fail to synthesise the material collected for later volumes of *Principles*, he also maintained a strong and wide-ranging empirical interest in economic organisation. His draft for a book on foreign trade, on which he worked from 1873 to 1877, indicates a synthesis between the analysis of economic activity and an empirical understanding of the forms this activity takes of the kind that he later sought, but failed, to achieve.[19] For his part, Jevons's interest in sunspots to explain the periodicity of economic cycles related to his efforts to link together weather patterns, grain prices, and pressures in capital

[17] William Stanley Jevons, *The Coal Question: An Inquiry Concerning the Progress of the Nation, and the Probable Exhaustion of our Coal-mines*, Macmillan, London 1865, p. 112.

[18] William Stanley Jevons, 'Opening Address of the President of Section F (Economic Science and Statistics) of the British Association for the Advancement of Science, at the Fortieth Meeting, at Liverpool, September, 1870', *Journal of the Statistical Society of London* Vol. 33 Issue 3 (September 1870), p. 309.

[19] Alfred Marshall, 'The Theory of Foreign Trade and Other Portions of Economic Science Bearing on the Principle of Laissez-Faire', in John K. Whitaker (ed.) *The Early Economic Writings of Alfred Marshall 1867–1890 Vol. 2*, Macmillan, London 1975, pp. 1–236.

markets, developing in the 1860s a 'Statistical Atlas' presenting data as graphs that facilitated insight into the underlying trends of commercial fluctuations. In April 1861 he described this as follows:

> The chief interest of the work will be in the light thrown upon the Commercial storms of 1793, 1815, 1826, 1839, 1847, 1858 etc. the causes of which will be rendered more or less apparent. I find that the number of acts of Parliament, the number of patents, and the number of bricks manufactured are the best indications of an approaching panic, which arises generally from a large investment of labour in works not immediately profitable, as machinery, canals, railways etc. It is truly curious how [well] the curve of *bricks produced* shows this, bricks and mortar being the most enduring form of product. Most of the statistics of course is generally known but has never been so fully combined, or exhibited *graphically*.[20]

But this shared practical and empirical interest was not a terrain upon which Jevons and Marshall ever met. It was, however, a terrain that Pigou, Marshall's pupil and successor, recognised. In closing his demolition of John Clapham's critique of Marshallian economics, Pigou remarked that Jevons was the 'towering exception' to the rule that those people

> who have the qualities required for conducting a detailed intensive study of particular industries and writing monographs about them, are not usually well versed either in the more intricate parts of economic analysis or in modern statistical technique; while the 'analytics' lack alike the capacity and inclination for these detailed studies. We must endeavour to train up more men of the calibre of Jevons, who are equally at home in both fields.[21]

And as was shown in the previous chapter, the Economics Tripos was designed as a means for providing the kind of training Pigou alludes to here.

Few, if any, shared this perspective on Jevons, even in the later nineteenth century, let alone the 1920s. While his writings on political economy were only one part of a corpus that included logic, natural sciences, and meteorology, for those interested in political economy Jevons was known mainly as the author of *Theory of Political Economy*, and possibly also his *Political Economy*, an introductory textbook whose purpose derived from his work in Manchester instructing pupil-teachers.[22] Transposed to the history of economic thought, in which Jevons also had a very strong interest—his bibliophilia got Foxwell started on collecting literature that eventually

[20] Letter from Stanley Jevons to Herbert Jevons, 7 April 1861, Letter 150 in *Papers and Correspondence of William Stanley Jevons*, Vol. II: *Correspondence 1850–1862*, ed. R. D. Collison Black, Macmillan, London 1973, p. 427. See, for an assessment of this project, Mike White, 'Riders on the Storm: W. Stanley Jevons, Meteorology and the Analysis of "Commercial Fluctuations"', paper presented at the History of Economics Annual Conference, Goldsmiths, London 2019.

[21] A. C. Pigou, 'Empty Economic Boxes: A Reply', *Economic Journal* Vol. 32 (1922), p. 465. Pigou went on to suggest that the 'next best thing' would be that those 'moderately qualified' for each sort of inquiry could work together 'and not ... waste time in quarrelling, perhaps on the basis of an imperfect understanding, with the deficiencies of one another's methods.'

[22] W. Stanley Jevons, *Political Economy*, Macmillan, London 1878, p. 5.

formed the basis of first the Goldsmiths' Library in Senate House, London, and then the Kress Collection in Harvard's Baker Library[23]—Edwin Cannan's approach to earlier economic writing was heavily marked by an understanding of Jevons based upon his reading of *Theory of Political Economy*. Cannan showed little interest in the economic history being developed in Germany, nor in contemporary English argument about Henry Maine's account of social evolution as one from status to contract, an argument that influenced both Ashley and Marshall. He was instead committed to a conception of 'modern economics' as a set of formal principles that were employed to demonstrate the errors of earlier economic principles.[24] He did show a profound knowledge of these earlier economic principles, but the errors that the 'abstract method' there revealed were employed to demonstrate that modern theory had overcome these problems. And this approach also illuminates the divergence of Cannan from Marshall. For while this 'Jevonian' approach served Cannan well as critique, for a critical assessment of past systems of economic theory, it works rather less well as an engine of practical economic analysis. The Marshallian approach had exactly the opposite problem, especially in the hands of Marshall: for while he developed a novel and flexible engine of practical economic analysis, he obstinately maintained an allegiance to a spurious theoretical heritage reaching continuously back to Ricardo. Whatever the strengths of Marshallian analysis, Alfred Marshall is entirely unreliable as a guide to the political economy on which he had built. Cannan, on the other hand, saw in Jevons the warrant for an idiosyncratic understanding that the economic theory of earlier times was a lumber room to be explored not for its own sake, but in order to advance contemporary thinking.[25]

Given that Jevons died while swimming in 1882, he was in no position to rectify a selective reading of his political economy that took from his work abstract principles, while overlooking his continuing interest in statistical and descriptive material that represented the 'modern facts' by which Alfred Marshall set such store. That Marshall himself contributed to this selective reading of Jevons is yet another indication of his contrary nature, fully on display in the short tribute he drafted in 1883:

> Mr. Jevons was an Economist of the highest order. In his '*Theory of Political Economy*' he explains the nature of economic quantities & their relation to one another. Work of this kind involves no startling discovery, but its effect is much greater than appears

[23] J. H. P. Pafford, 'Historical Introduction' to *University of London Library: Catalogue of the Goldsmiths' Library of Economic Literature Vol I*, compiled by Margaret Canney and David Knott, Cambridge University Press, London 1970, p. xii fn. 6, recording that the first book purchased by Foxwell for his collection was Lardner's *Railway Economy* (1850), bought at the suggestion of Jevons.

[24] 'Judged then, by what we may, perhaps, using the term in a sense which has very often, though not very accurately, been given to it, call the "abstract method," the theories of production and distribution arrived at in the first half of the nineteenth century must be visited with almost unqualified condemnation.' *A History of the Theories of Production and Distribution in English Political Economy from 1776 to 1848*, 3rd edition, P. S. King & Son, London 1924, p. 383.

[25] Jevons did attach importance to an understanding of past theoretical work in political economy, as demonstrated by his valuable 1879 'Preface' to the second edition of *Theory of Political Economy*. He also shared with Cannan a particular admiration for Adam Smith's *Wealth of Nations*, having in 1878–1879 begun work on a new edition—see my essay 'Adam Smith in English: From Playfair to Cannan' in Keith Tribe, with Hiroshi Mizuta (eds.) *A Critical Bibliography of Adam Smith*, Pickering and Chatto, London 2002, p. 43.

> at first sight. It makes us master our thoughts, and founds new empires in science.... Truly mathematical as was the tone of his best work, he was not at his ease when using mathematical formulae. But the great body of his work is unaffected by these blemishes; the lapse of time will but add to its lustre, and it will probably be found to have more truly constructive force than any, save that of Ricardo, that has been done during the last hundred years.
>
> His contributions to Statistics are well known. The pure honesty of his mind, combined with his special intellectual fitness for the work, have made them models for all time. But it is in his Essays on the application of Economics to the theory of governmental action that his full greatness is seen.[26]

Marshall was here still some seven years off publishing his *Principles*, until which time his reputation would necessarily be that he was the joint author of *Economics of Industry*—and Jevons's own, rather more concise, primer had appeared the year before that work had been published. Jevons had been 36 when *Theory of Political Economy* was published; Marshall would be 48 by the time *Principles* appeared. Here again, what Marshall might have sought to present as a generational gap amounted to only seven years, on top of which his predecessor was a lot speedier than he was. In 1883 Marshall was still in Bristol; his real academic career would only get going at the end of 1884, at the age of 42.

And so while the idea of 'Jevonian economics' might have some plausibility as a foil for 'Marshallianism', this simplification did, and does, considerable disservice to the work of Stanley Jevons. The arguments he advanced in *Theory of Political Economy* should today be read in the light of his broader interests, in the context of the developing sciences of the later nineteenth century.[27] This would involve not only physiology,[28] but also fluid mechanics and linguistics. Jevons would be brought closer to the Alfred Marshall that Simon Cook has revealed.[29] But this was not how Jevons was read as an economist by Edgeworth, Wicksteed, Cannan, or even Ashley. They read Jevons as the author of an economics of disembodied agents making choices in such a way that economic action could be conceived independently of context, as a series of calculations trading pleasure against pain—in a later terminology, of satisfaction against effort. Superseded by the Marshallian juggernaut of the 1890s—not so much *Principles* as *Elements of Economics of Industry*, standard reading for those being taught economics in university, college, and extension class—this 'Jevonian economics' of frictionless planes has long been discounted as a passing phase in the development of economics. But it was the foundation on which Lionel Robbins began to build his own new science of economics, stripping Marshall of all qualification

[26] Enclosed with letter to Foxwell, 22 May 1883, Letter 126 in John K. Whitaker (ed.) *The Correspondence of Alfred Marshall*, Vol. I: *Climbing 1868–1890*, Cambridge University Press, Cambridge 1996, p. 164.

[27] As does Harro Maas, *William Stanley Jevons and the Making of Modern Economics*, Cambridge University Press, Cambridge 2005.

[28] As in Mike White's 'The Moment of Richard Jennings', and outlined by Maas, *William Stanley Jevons*, p. 154.

[29] See Simon J. Cook, *The Intellectual Foundations of Alfred Marshall's Economic Science*, Cambridge University Press, Cambridge 2009, Ch. 4.

and interest in the context of economic action, and deploying his own versions of Marshall's concepts and graphs to negate the 'Cambridge legacy'.

Marshall as Teacher

I will continue this argument in Chapter 12, but for the moment the preceding discussion serves to clarify how and why 'Jevonian economics' might be distinguished from 'Marshallian economics'. In developing an account of the latter, I now turn to how Marshall taught economics to his students. In part we can draw upon accounts of his lectures, but in Cambridge lectures have never been the prime conduit of 'teaching'. Throughout the nineteenth century 'teaching' meant either college classes or the classes run by private coaches; around the 1920s this was displaced by the college supervision, a weekly one-hour meeting of supervisor and one or two students that provided them with guidance on reading and lecture attendance, and comments upon essays they had prepared. We have already seen in Chapter 4 that on his return to Cambridge, Marshall began to think of how he might add to the existing basic provision of lectures on political economy. At the same time he placed a notice in the *Reporter* inviting students to visit him at home for informal instruction and advice between 4 p.m. and 7 p.m. from Mondays to Thursdays, establishing in this way a practice that anticipated the college supervision but which, importantly, took place in his own home, not in college. Peter Groenewegen's synopsis of Marshall's lecturing style suggests that once *Principles* had been published in 1890, he was able to adopt a more spontaneous approach to lecturing, dispensing with a more systematic presentation.[30] It seems more likely, however, that he never did treat his lectures as an opportunity to establish theoretical foundations that would be subsequently illustrated and elaborated; that his style was always deliberately discursive and allusive, although this did become more marked over time.

In a letter of 1894 to his former Oxford student, E. C. K. Gonner,[31] Marshall first noted that he sought to keep out of his lecture room students 'whose minds are merely receptive' and who might wish for a lecturer to 'speak an elementary text-book at them'.[32]

> Even my more elementary teaching makes no pretence at being systematic, but aims at treating certain dominant ideas and representative problems more fully than would be possible if every side of the subject had to be discussed equally. If I think the class are merely listening and not thinking for themselves, I try to shake them out of the rut. If they are thinking for themselves, I try to lead them on until they have got

[30] Peter Groenewegen, 'Teaching Economics at Cambridge at the Turn of the Century: Alfred Marshall as Lecturer in Political Economy', *Scottish Journal of Political Economy* Vol. 37 (1990), p. 50 for the January notice; p. 40 for the argument that the publication of *Principles* altered Marshall's approach to lecturing.

[31] Gonner was preparing a survey of economic education, discussed in Chapter 3; 'Methods of Economic Training in this and other Countries', *Report of the Sixty-Fourth Meeting of the British Association for the Advancement of Science (1894)*, John Murray, London 1894, pp. 365–91.

[32] Marshall to Gonner, 5 May 1894; Letter 448 in John K. Whitaker (ed.), *The Correspondence of Alfred Marshall*, Vol. 2: *At the Summit 1890–1902*, Cambridge University Press, Cambridge 1996, p. 110.

> pretty well into the middle of a real difficulty and then help them to find their way out if it.

Marshall's assumption that he is talking to a 'class' is significant here, even though we also know that in the later 1880s his lectures drew an average attendance in the mid-forties.[33] He went on to suggest that his aim was 'to help [students] to acquire a delicate and powerful machinery for scientific investigation, without requiring them to attend long courses of lectures.'[34] In the same letter he confirmed that he set aside six hours a week for students to visit for advice, leaving the initiative to the students, and recommending reading for the particular problems that concerned them. While I have previously expressed some doubt about the reliability of Marshall's own testimony, his account here of lecture and student consultation is supported by other evidence.

Detailed notes have been published of the course of lectures that Marshall gave for women in 1873, but this was concerned with 'Some Economic Questions Directly Related to the Welfare of the Labourers', and so dealing already with a specialised topic.[35] More recently, notes for his 'Advanced' course for the Moral Sciences Tripos in the early 1870s have been published, and these confirm the approach that he later outlined to Gonner. The editors suggest that these notes 'would allow the young Marshall to 'jaw away for several hours' about definitions and methods ... departing ... from the relative safety of J. S. Mill's *Principles of Political Economy*, which had formed the text book of the 'ordinary' lectures.'[36] Marshall seems to have compiled extracts and comments on Mill, Cairnes, Roscher, Smith, Bastiat, and Ricardo and arranged them thematically, under for example 'Productive and Unproductive Labour', or 'Capital', so that he would never be short of a reference or a quote if he needed it. What the notes do not provide is any sense of the structure or sequence of the lectures. In his obituary essay, Maynard Keynes recorded that when he had attended Marshall's 1906 lectures, he was unable to make coherent notes: 'His lectures were not, like Sidgwick's, books in the making.'[37] This is therefore as much a remark about the overall structure of Marshall's lectures as about actual delivery.

Lynda Grier, who together with Eva Spielman was classified with a First in Part II in 1907, commented that Marshall complained about her because she did not 'look sufficiently attentive during his lectures'. This was because she was partially deaf, but her hearing did improve and she was able to hear his last lecture, 'of which I took copious notes, in spite of the fact that he thought poorly of any one who thought that

[33] Groenewegen, *A Soaring Eagle*, pp. 325 Table 10.1, 326 Table 10.2. Maynard Keynes wrote that at this time the general courses would have from 40 to 70 students, his special courses half that number, and that the 'less serious students' gradually fell away, 'choked off' by his methods; John Maynard Keynes, 'Alfred Marshall' in his *Essays in Biography*, Collected Writings of John Maynard Keynes Vol. X, Macmillan, London 1972, p. 215.

[34] Marshall to Gonner, 5 May 1894, p. 111.

[35] Eugenio F. Biagini, 'Marshall's 1873 "Lectures to Women"', *Quaderni di storia dell economia politica* Vol. 9 No. 2–3 (1991), pp. 335–54; see also Tiziano Raffaelli, Eugenio Biagini, Rita McWilliams Tullberg (eds.), *Alfred Marshall's Lectures to Women*, Edward Elgar, Aldershot UK 1995.

[36] Simon J. Cook, Tiziana Foresti (eds.) 'Marshall's Notes for his Advanced Course in Political Economy, c. 1871', *Marshall Studies Bulletin* Vol. 11 (2010), p. 2.

[37] Maynard Keynes, 'Alfred Marshall', p. 216.

it was possible to reproduce his lectures.'[38] Grier's painful recollection of her and two fellow Newnham students taking tea with Marshall likewise confirms that when students visited him at home he expected the student to ask the questions and respond to what he said. At the one visit that Grier made, Marshall had stated, after some initial chitchat, that 'I leave it to you to direct the conversation.' A stony silence ensued, the three students feeling overwhelmed. Only after he had twice repeated himself did Grier think of something to ask—'and then he was most interesting and helpful.'[39] While the context here is Marshall's belief that women were unsuited to the study of economics,[40] we should also note that Marshall was anything but the conventional overbearing professor—not only did he refuse to make use of the monologic lecture format to simply 'read out' his book, in his more informal meetings with students he insisted on a dialogic exchange dictated by the interests and needs of the student.

Maynard Keynes graduated from the Mathematical Tripos in the summer of 1905 and immediately began his preparation for the Civil Service examinations by immersing himself in the study of economics. In October he signed up for Marshall's lectures and in so doing listed the books he had read earlier in the summer.[41] Around the same time he began to take personal supervisions from Marshall, completing 15 papers for him up to late November, and which Keynes preserved. Raffaelli's summary of what these papers show cannot be improved upon:

> Even more interesting than the *quantity* is the *type* of economics that Keynes learned. From his lecture notes, book excerpts, comments and, above all, from the papers he wrote for Pigou and Marshall, it emerges that Keynes's apprenticeship was truly special, with much time devoted to applied economics: transport, financial and stock markets and industrial organization. Adding statistical data and monetary economics to the list, we have a glimpse of the tight interdependence between abstract theorizing and historical knowledge that characterize's Marshall's method and explains his impatience with abstract problems of no practical relevance—with 'toys', as he used to define purely academic exercises.[42]

In Keynes's papers there is a file labelled 'pure economics' whose contents correspond broadly with the reading he had done in June and July; there are also sets of notes on 'public finance' and 'taxation' that include work by Bastable and Edgeworth

[38] Cited in Rita McWilliams Tullberg, 'Marshall's Final Lecture, 21 May 1908', *History of Political Economy* Vol. 25 (1993), p. 607. The notes on the lecture are reproduced on pp. 611–15.

[39] Ibid., pp. 607, 608.

[40] Emphasised by Macgregor's observation that for his lectures Marshall '. . . would go to his desk, with the men on his right and the women on his left and, leaning on his left elbow, would address himself to those who, he thought, were capable of doing economics. This was one of his idiosyncracies.' D. H. Macgregor, 'Marshall and His Book', *Economica* New Series Vol. 9 No. 36 (1942), p. 313.

[41] These are listed in Peter Groenewegen, 'Alfred Marshall and the Establishment of the Cambridge Economics Tripos, *History of Political Economy* Vol. 20 (1988), p. 667, and also in Tiziano Raffaelli, 'Keynes's Apprenticeship with Marshall in 1905', *History of Economic Ideas* Vol. 8 No. 2 (2000), p. 124 fn. 16. Besides Marshall's *Principles*, Keynes had read Jevons, Cassel, Bagehot, Toynbee, Cournot, Ricardo, Nicholson, his father's *Scope and Method*, and some Edgeworth. These were all broadly theoretical works, and importantly not the kind of thing that Marshall directly lectured upon. He had, however, also read Bastable's *International Trade* and *Public Finance*, central texts of the time and closer to Marshall's teaching.

[42] Raffaelli, 'Keynes's Apprenticeship', p. 126.

that he had likewise read then. By contrast, there are notes on trusts and railways and on 'modern business methods'—principally American material—reading that was most probably suggested by Marshall, since besides Bastable none of this had been read earlier than the autumn. There are also notes on money and on index numbers that must date from the autumn of 1905 and early winter of 1905–1906. Raffaelli cites a remark by Hayek to the effect that Keynes's economic education was 'somewhat narrow' because it was mostly limited to works in English,[43] a misleading comment given Keynes's reading of American material and that, reciprocally, contemporary German and Austrian economic texts generally neglected non-German language sources.[44]

Marshall's detailed commentary on Keynes's work, its constructive and supportive *tone*, provides some sense of the way in which Marshall's oral encounters with students must have worked. Keynes's written answers to Marshall's questions range from one page on the distinction of income and wealth in estimating national prosperity to 11 pages on the comparative merits of national railway systems. While broadly theoretical questions predominate, what is evident from these encounters between Marshall and Maynard Keynes is that the former did not seek to teach the latter by catechising economic principles. As Raffaelli summarises, 'Teaching was not confined to showing the tools in the box: knowledge of their limited uses and proper range of action was even more important.'[45] And as we shall see in the controversies of the 1920s, this was a principle lost on a later generation of economists.

Pigou as Student of Marshall

We can extend this consideration of how Marshall taught his students to consider more directly how they used what he taught them, and here the early career of Pigou is instructive. Pigou's first publications in economics appeared in the December 1900 issue of the *Economic Journal*, six months after he had gained a First in Part II of the Moral Sciences Tripos.[46] He had just turned 23. Within another six months Marshall announced that Pigou would be giving his 'General Course';[47] this began that autumn with lectures on 'Political Economy' three times a week over two terms for those taking both the History and the Moral Sciences Tripos[48] The following year, 1902, Pigou announced a course of lectures for Moral Sciences students on 'Modern Developments

[43] Ibid., p. 129.

[44] Menger, Schmoller, Wagner, and Wieser corresponded with Marshall in German, suggesting that their knowledge of the English language was limited. By contrast, Marshall, Edgeworth, and to some extent Pigou were well read in Continental European sources, and so mediated this work for English readers.

[45] Raffaelli, 'Keynes's Apprenticeship', p. 146.

[46] Pigou was one of three Firsts in the Moral Sciences Tripos, taking the paper in 'Political Economy', three other students being classified; D. H. Macgregor gained a First in Pt. I the same year—*Cambridge University Reporter* Vol. XXX No. 40 (12 June 1900), pp. 1038–39.

[47] *Cambridge University Reporter* Vol. XXXVI No. 41 (21 May 1901), p. 892: 'A course of lectures on the same lines as his 'General Course,' of recent years, will be given on his behalf by Mr. Pigou: and his own lectures will not be suitable for students in their first or second years, unless they have already a considerable knowledge of economics.' This means that a year after he graduated, Pigou started teaching the same course on economics through which he had first learned economics.

[48] *Cambridge University Reporter* Vol. XXXII No. 3 (9 October 1901), pp. 28–29.

of Industrial Combinations', to be given in the Easter (i.e. summer) term, hence over four weeks.[49] In May 1903 he was awarded the Adam Smith Prize for his essay 'A Study in the Principles and Methods of Industrial Peace'.[50] In June 1904 he was appointed to the Girdlers' Lectureship in Economics, to run until 1907.[51] At the end of May 1908, aged 30, he was elected as Marshall's successor.[52]

As Sidney Webb then wrote to William Ashley:

> What a jump for Pigou is the Cambridge appointment! I don't at all approve, for more reasons than one. But Marshall seems to have moved heaven and earth to exclude you and Foxwell. I happen to have learned, a couple of years ago, that Marshall intended & expected Pigou to succeed him, but scarcely believed it to be possible with such more experienced and distinguished persons in the field.[53]

This sense of astonishment that Pigou should have been appointed over Ashley and Foxwell has had some resonance over the years, but a contemporary report for the Vice-Chancellor of the University of Cambridge shows that the electors were in fact unanimous in their choice.[54] As already suggested, it should be more cause for astonishment that either Ashley or Foxwell thought themselves capable of succeeding Marshall in the Cambridge chair. On the evidence of his writings, Ashley had lost interest in contemporary economic analysis around 20 years before, and he had in effect announced this to his fellow economists the previous summer in his Presidential Address to Section F of the British Association. As if to make sure that everybody got the point, the Address was published as the lead article in the December 1907 issue of the *Economic Journal*, and then republished with slight changes in the Schmoller Festschrift the following year. In the version published in the *Economic Journal* his narrative of 'modern economics' ceased with Jevons, characterising the new 'marginalists' as follows:

> They all begin, at any rate, by laying stress on the doctrine of marginal or final utility, some as the key to the whole problem of value, some as the key to the demand side of it. And what has one to say to it? Of course, in the first place, it is quite true, so far as it goes; and, in the second place, it is pedagogically of some use.

49 *Cambridge University Reporter* Vol. XXXIII No. 3 (8 October 1902), p. 29.

50 *Cambridge University Reporter* Vol. XXXIII No. 36 (12 May 1903), p. 727.

51 *Cambridge University Reporter* Vol. XXXIV No. 45 (14 June 1904), p. 994. He was reappointed in 1907 for another three years; Vol. XXXVII No. 38 (4 June 1907), p. 975.

52 *Cambridge University Reporter* Vol. XXXVIII No. 41 (2 June 1908), p. 1015; the Girdler's lectureship was simultaneously declared vacant, and H. O. Meredith appointed for three years in August; Vol. XXXVIII No. 50 (8 August 1908), p. 1350. Among the electors were Neville Keynes, A. J. Balfour (nominated by the Senate); Palgrave, Stanton, Sorley (nominated by the General Board of Studies); Edgeworth, Nicholson, Courtney (nominated by the Special Board); *Cambridge University Reporter* Vol. XXXVI No. 15 (8 January 1906), p. 368, the appointments of Palgrave and Keynes being renewed in April 1906 and January 1908, respectively.

53 Sidney Webb to W. J. Ashley, London, 16 June 1908, William J. Ashley, Assorted Correspondence, Birmingham University Library Archives, 9/iv/4–5.

54 Aslanbeigui, Oakes, *Arthur Cecil Pigou*, p. 25.

> Instead of leading us to the very heart of the problem, the doctrine of marginal value seems to me to remain entirely on the surface: it is not much more than a verbal description of the superficial facts at a particular point in time.[55]

Ashley had opened with the proposition that the classical economics of Ricardo and Mill was now definitively in the past; but his view of the 'present position' was that contemporary economics was uninteresting, and the promise of 'historical economics' had led so far only to some developments in economic history. Sceptical equivocation of this kind was hardly the platform upon which he might present himself as the new Cambridge Professor.

What was it that Marshall saw in Pigou?[56] For one thing, clearly a candidate who engaged with the propositions that he had set out in his *Principles*, as demonstrated by Pigou's first note published in the September 1902 issue of *Economic Journal*. He here took up an argument previously advanced by Edgeworth, that there would be a differential fiscal impact of duties across different kinds of grain, and that it could be that foreign producers would have to accept lower prices for some grains because of the related inelasticities of demand. Pigou does not dispute this analytical approach; rather he suggested that, while Edgeworth seeks to demonstrate analytically that the price of wheat *might not* rise by the full amount of the tax, he can demonstrate that it *probably will not do so*.[57] Pigou opposes an empirical demonstration to Edgeworth's theoretical proposition.

> Let us begin then by simplifying the problem, and, ignoring barley and oats, concentrate attention upon wheat and maize. The British demand for the former is likely to be inelastic about the point of consumption, as Professor Edgeworth suggests; and for the latter it is 'derived' from our demand for meat, which, as having to do with something that is more or less of a luxury to many classes, is likely to be fairly elastic. Further, the British demand for maize itself will, in the present case, be considerably more elastic than that for meat, because, when the price of raw maize is raised by the tax, there will be a tendency to import a quantity of it, which had hitherto come into the country in this form, as the finished product meat.[58]

This is the starting point of a line of thought which first establishes that the impact of British consumption on the price of maize in America is small, then considers the possibility that British farmers will switch from stock feeding to wheat growing, advances

[55] W. J. Ashley, 'The Present Position of Political Economy', *Economic Journal* Vol. 17 (1907), pp. 476–7. This was republished the following year with a small addition concerning Marshall's 'static analysis' and some footnotes to passages in Jevons and Marshall as 'The Present Position of Political Economy in England', in *Die Entwicklung der deutschen Volkswirtschaftslehre im neunzehnten Jahrhundert* Bd.I (Schmoller Fs.), Duncker und Humblot, Leipzig 1908, pp. XV 1–26.

[56] For a thorough survey of how Pigou has been linked with Marshall, see Karen Knight, 'A. C. Pigou, a Loyal Marshallian?', *History of Economics Review* Vol. 64 No. 1 (2016), pp. 42–63; and more generally her *A. C. Pigou and the 'Marshallian' Thought Style: A Study in the Philosophy and Mathematics Underlying Cambridge Economics*, Palgrave Macmillan, Cham 2018.

[57] 'A Point of Theory Connected with the Corn Tax', printed in the 'Notes and Memoranda' section of *Economic Journal* Vol. 12 (1902), p. 415.

[58] Ibid., pp. 415–16.

some data from the *Corn Trade Year Book* (assuming that its estimates 'are to be relied on') and distinguishes among other things between the feed for carriage horses and that for other kinds of horses. It is a classroom presentation of a textbook instance of the Marshallian approach to economic analysis, sharing Edgeworth's point of departure but displaying Marshall's interest in setting these principles to work in the examination of their particular impact upon specific economic agents and institutions.

A similar approach can be found in Pigou's *Riddle of the Tariff*, completed in the autumn of 1903. Writing here for an educated public, he dismisses as 'unsound' the arguments of Ashley regarding the beneficial impact of protection in attracting capital into the country, and for support calls on Marshall's comments to Section F in 1889 regarding the generally deleterious impact of protection on profitability, and hence general investment.[59] Here again, Pigou seeks to extend the abstract reasoning that Edgeworth exemplified into the impact of policy on patterns of actual economic behaviour, entirely in line with Marshall's own practice.

Earlier in 1903, Pigou had published his first article in the *Economic Journal*, directed to a purely theoretical issue, relating to utility and consumers' surplus. This took up comments he had already made in a 1902 review of Simon Patten's *Theory of Prosperity*, and while he had there expressed reservations about Patten's generalisations, he went on to endorse the value of the second part of the book. Here Patten outlined a conception of evolutionary human development, in which the effort necessary to procure goods diminished, and so a constant input of effort secured an increasing amount of 'utility'. In this process, demand for any one commodity diminishes, creating a 'surplus' of 'energy' that can be employed in other directions. Patten argues that this evolutionary movement selects in favour of altruistic, rather than self-seeking behaviour; in Pigou's summary:

> Otherwise, when wealth increases, the rich, looking only to their own interests, become dissipated, while the poor of the race remain underfed. On both sides, therefore, the selfish group undergoes physical degeneration, while the unselfish becomes stronger. In them, the rich when they feed the poor are thereby preserved from feeding themselves too much, and the provision of public libraries and so forth shows itself 'twice blessed; it blesses him that gives and him that takes'.[60]

Patten concludes that as countries become wealthier, the more prosperous members of these countries will demonstrate a concern for the well-being of the less advantaged. Pigou commends this idea to his readers; but then suggests that the earlier parts of the book are replete with poorly-formed definitions, noting also that

[59] A. C. Pigou, *The Riddle of the Tariff*, Brimley Johnson, London 1903, pp. 17–18. Edgeworth reviewed this in the *Economic Journal*, noting that in the previous number he had reviewed 'what seemed the best book on the Protectionist side'; Ashley's *The Tariff Problem*, *Economic Journal* Vol. 13 (1903), pp. 571–75. Pigou's book, stated Edgeworth, appeared to occupy a 'similar position on the other side'; *Economic Journal* Vol. 14 (1904), p. 65, noting in conclusion of Pigou that '[t]he power with which he wields the organon of economic theory is of the highest promise', p. 67.

[60] A. C. Pigou, review of Patten, *The Theory of Prosperity*, *Economic Journal* Vol. 12 (1902), p. 371.

> [t]he method of total utility diagrams, which is profusely employed, cannot but suggest to the careless that those difficulties connected with consumers' rent, which Professor Marshall faces with such courage, can be got over by the simple expedient of ignoring them. In certain other respects complications which can be avoided by considering groups of men seem to be unduly emphasized by concentrating attention, as Professor Patten does, upon the conditions of individual consumption (e.g., p. 101).[61]

This forms the starting point of Pigou's first *Economic Journal* article: the Marshallian problem of consumers' surplus. Here Pigou first raises the question of the measurement of utility, rejecting Edgeworth's definition in *Mathematical Psychics* as 'just perceivable increments of pleasure'[62] since we might suppose this metric to be purely formal. Instead, the 'desire for some definite object' has to be taken as the unit, and Fisher's adoption of the 'util' is deemed the most suitable.[63] From this, Pigou is able to develop the argument that any sudden increase in wealth will change the price given for any one good, but also the intensity of desire for any commodity. This leads to the substitution of one commodity for another with increasing income. But the utility of one good to the consumer is also a function of the quantity possessed by other consumers, this leading Pigou into an extended discussion of Cunynghame's alleged exposition of the relation of the desire for top hats and diamonds.[64] Quite how this dependence of total utility on the distribution of any one good might be expressed mathematically is not, however, clear, Pigou next veering off into a discussion of the utility to him of a third carriage.[65]

After some criticism of Patten, Pigou then seeks to link the individual to the market. This cannot be done by summing the individual utilities since the use of *ceteris paribus* has fixed all other consumption while considering the consumption of consumer *I*:

> . . . we commit the same fallacy when we combine individual utility curves into a market utility curve, as we do when we add together the consumers' rent from coffee, estimated upon the assumption of a given consumption of tea, and the consumers' rent from tea, estimated on a similar assumption with regard to coffee.[66]

Pigou then adds successive increments of one good in the order of utility yielded to a series of agents, noting that while there are problems with this approach, it is workable for evaluating small changes in consumption, and it is these kinds of changes which are relevant to Marshall's discussion of taxation. 'The engine which he has devised, though limited in range, can therefore often serve us.'[67]

61 Ibid., p. 373.

62 Peter Newman, *F. Y. Edgeworth's Mathematical Psychics and Further Papers on Political Economy*, Oxford University Press, Oxford 2003, p. 99.

63 A. C. Pigou, 'Some Remarks on Utility', *Economic Journal* Vol. 13 (1903), p. 59.

64 Henry Cunynghame does mention diamonds; 'Some Improvements in Simple Geometrical Methods of Treating Exchange Value, Monopoly, and Rent', *Economic Journal* Vol. 2 (1892), pp. 37–39—but not top hats.

65 Pigou, 'Some Remarks', p. 61.

66 Ibid., p. 64.

67 Ibid., p. 66.

Pigou followed this discussion up the following year, considering monopoly and price discrimination in the context of consumers' surplus, building on Edgeworth.[68] In 1905 he published a book worked up from his Adam Smith Prize essay and lectures he had given at University College London, reflecting his parallel interest in industrial welfare.[69] But in the year before his appointment as Marshall's successor, he responded to a request from Edgeworth as editor of the *Economic Journal*, and in the December issue reviewed the fifth edition of Marshall's *Principles*—not without some trepidation, he made clear, but with the advantage, as Marshall's pupil, of having a clear conception of the 'organic unity of the whole.'[70] First detailing some of the revisions to this edition, he stated that he wished to concentrate his attention on two conceptions which Marshall considered fundamental, but which Marshall considered to have been misunderstood in England and America:

> I mean the conceptions of the *rôle* played in Economics by Time, and by the National Dividend.[71]

The first of these is described as Marshall's most original contribution, since the latter idea had been present in the writings of Adam Smith; but it was the second which was of greater importance:

> There is one point only which I should like to make. *The conception of the National Dividend is not an academic toy, but a practical instrument of great power designed for service in the concrete solution of social problems.* The unavoidable but regrettable delay in the appearance of Prof. Marshall's second volume has obscured this fact.[72]

This is 'the flow of economic goods and services made available during the year' that is at the centre of Marshall's reasoning. Many areas of social policy could not be approached without reference to it—from the treatment of trade unions to that of the poor, and poor children in particular, the central question was how any policy would affect the National Dividend. Pigou likewise points out how Marshall argues that invention and innovation have historically been the province of independent workers, not governments, casting the debate over collective and private ownership in a new light. And the review ends with a peroration that recalls that of Marshall's own inaugural lecture of 1885:

> The dividend constitutes the kernel of economic theory because ... it is the centre of sound philanthropic endeavour. It is to an analysis of this that we are driven when, throwing off the moral torpor of indolent optimism, we refuse, 'with our modern

[68] A. C. Pigou, 'Monopoly and Consumers' Surplus', *Economic Journal* Vol. 14 (1904), pp. 388–94.

[69] A. C. Pigou, *Principles and Methods of Industrial Peace*, Macmillan, London 1905: this he described as an ethical work, directed to the principles that ought to be employed in the settlement of industrial differences, rather than describing those which are in fact are employed (p. 3).

[70] A. C. Pigou, review of Marshall, *The Principles of Economics Vol. I*, fifth edition, *Economic Journal* Vol. 17 (1907), p. 532.

[71] Ibid., p. 533.

[72] Ibid., pp. 533–34.

resources and knowledge, to look contentedly at the continued destruction of all that is worth having in multitudes of human lives,' and demand from social science guidance for social reform.[73]

Pigou's own inaugural lecture extended this idea, asserting that the purpose of the study of economics lay in its contribution to social improvement. Addressed to the 'ordinary business of life', the subject matter of economics was neither inspiring nor that interesting in itself. The economist needed the physiologist's impulse, '... knowledge for the healing that knowledge in some measure may help to bring'. Echoing Marshall's own peroration to his inaugural lecture, he declared that he would be

> ... glad if a man comes to Economics because he has been interested by Professor Edgeworth's *Mathematical Psychics* or Dr. Fisher's *Appreciation and Interest*: just as I shall be glad if he comes to it because he is looking forward to business and wishes to learn something of the broader aspects of his future career; but I shall be far more glad if he comes because he has walked through the slums of London and is stirred to make some effort to help his fellow-men. Wonder, Carlyle said, is the beginning of philosophy: social enthusiasm, one might add, is the beginning of economic science.[74]

This unambiguous declaration of the purpose of economic analysis is all the more valuable since Pigou's papers are lost or destroyed, and we have little in the way of reliable evidence with whose help we can chart the development of his work—other than the work itself, study of which has only recently begun.[75]

The intellectual path that led Pigou to publish *Wealth and Welfare* in 1912 is therefore unclear;[76] as also why, after a war divided between teaching in Cambridge during term-time and driving an ambulance in Flanders and Italy during the vacation, he revised this into *The Economics of Welfare* in 1920. In his review of *Wealth and Welfare*, Allyn Young identified the theoretical and practical tenor of the work as continuous with the work of Marshall (even though we know that Marshall was, in his curmudgeonly way, critical of the work):[77]

[73] Ibid., p. 535.

[74] A. C. Pigou, *Economic Science in Relation to Practice*, Macmillan, London 1908; Inaugural Lecture given in Cambridge, 30 October 1908, pp. 12–13.

[75] For example, Pigou's contribution to welfare economics is usually discussed in relation to the fourth edition of his *Economics of Welfare* (1932), ignoring the fact that this was published 20 years after *Wealth and Welfare*, the 1912 book from which *Economics of Welfare* (1920) was developed. Moreover, each successive edition of that book involved a substantial reorganisation of the text. For a lucid discussion, see Aslanbeigui, Oakes, *Arthur Cecil Pigou*, pp. 60–80.

[76] For a lucid appraisal of *Wealth and Welfare*, see Michael McLure, 'One Hundred Years from Today: A. C. Pigou's *Wealth and Welfare*', *History of Economic Review* Vol. 55 No. 1 (2012), pp. 101–16.

[77] See Krishna Bharadwaj, 'Marshall on Pigou's *Wealth and Welfare*', *Economica* Vol. 39 (1972), pp. 32–46, for a discussion of Marshall's thoughts about *Wealth and Welfare*; his own copy of the book has marginal annotations which show disagreements with Pigou's account of marginal supply price and its behaviour in industries with increasing and decreasing returns—anticipating the arguments over rates of return in competitive industries that would develop in the 1920s (p. 36).

> Nowhere do the advantages of the particular kind of economic theory in which Professor Pigou is an adept appear more clearly. Theory of this sort (if I may characterize it briefly) is not concerned with the vain attempt to formulate concepts so general and abstract that the whole economic process may be viewed as a relatively simple mechanical system. The purpose is, rather, that the fabric of theory shall be a yielding garment, fitting the varied and complex reality of economic life as closely as is demanded by the criterion that the conclusions to which the theory leads shall be both useful and general.[78]

Young suggested that Pigou did not seek to read the world with a finite set of theorems; rather, theory was to inform an approach to economic life whose aim was practical application to the betterment of that life. He endorsed Pigou as a student of Marshall.

Sydney Chapman as Student of Marshall

Sydney Chapman (1871–1951) was another of Marshall's students, whose book on the Lancashire cotton industry sheds further light on what 'Marshallianism' might mean. Living in Manchester and attending Manchester Grammar School, he took a London BA at Owens College in 1891, then became a schoolmaster. Four years later he entered Trinity College Cambridge, reading Moral Sciences and attending all of Marshall's lectures for three years, graduating with a double First in 1898.[79] His brief comments on Marshall's lecturing style confirm the reports of others: that they were not 'constructed like a work of art', and that Marshall's approach came into its own in small classes, where his method was 'thinking aloud and not uncommonly on what he had been thinking about in his own work.'[80]

In 1901 Chapman succeeded Alfred Flux as Stanley Jevons Professor in Manchester, and when the Faculty of Commerce was created in 1903–1904 he quickly built it into the most successful university venture into commercial education outside London.[81] In part this was because of the existing linkages between Owens College and the local business community, and his book *The Lancashire Cotton Industry: A Study in Economic Development* also reflected this local and practical involvement. At its most elementary level, this work represents, as Chapman describes it in his 'Preface', 'some notes for an industrial morphology'[82]—a study of economic development, not of economic history, and so aligned with the position Marshall would take in the opening pages of *Industry and Trade*. Short early chapters outline the origins of the industry, the development of factory production, the displacement of handloom weaving by

[78] Allyn Young, 'Pigou's Wealth and Welfare', *Quarterly Journal of Economics* Vol. 27 No. 4 (1913), p. 686.

[79] In Cambridge a Double First means a First in both Parts I and II. Chapman's unpublished autobiographical essay begins with his entry to Trinity College in 1895, shedding little light on why it was that he first went to Cambridge in his mid-twenties; Sydney Chapman, *Some Memories and Reflections*, unpublished quarto typescript, c. 1942, pp. 261 [BLPES Archive].

[80] Chapman, *Some Memories and Reflections*, p. 18.

[81] This is outlined in Chapter 10, and in more detail in my 'The Faculty of Commerce and Manchester Economics, 1903–44', *Manchester School* Vol. 71 (2003), pp. 680–710.

[82] Sydney J. Chapman, *The Lancashire Cotton Industry: A Study in Economic Development*, Manchester University Press, Manchester 1904, p. i.

power looms, and the technology of production up to the mid-nineteenth century. Turning then to the state regulation of working conditions, the chapters lengthen, but instead of directly pursuing this social aspect of cotton production Chapman deals next with the development of markets and the institutional arrangements this called into being, ending with appendices on the import and export of cotton goods and on the role of the markets in cotton futures—an aspect of his work to which he drew attention much later when writing his autobiography.[83] This part of the book is then concluded with a chapter entitled 'Localisation, Industrial Specialism, and Modern Problems of Organisation', prefiguring the core arguments of *Industry and Trade*. The final three chapters form one-third of the book and deal with the development of trade unions and employers' associations, ending with a consideration of structures and methods of remuneration for workers that is followed not by any conclusion, but by a select bibliography intended to provide the foundation for future research.

The Lancashire Cotton Industry can be seen as an early foray into the study of industrial organisation—considering the location and genesis of economic activity, the changing technologies involved, and the social impact of industrial labour, but also treating this industry as a business that sought markets for its raw materials and finished products and which created trading institutions that would secure costs and revenue. The focus is on explanation of the present structure of the industry; since, as Marshall emphasised, the study of a modern economy required modern facts, not the investigation of previous configurations of economic activity, production, and distribution for its own sake. The line to G. C. Allen's *British Industries and Their Organization* is plain,[84] that work carrying forward the orientation towards modern problems, and away from their genesis.

In 1899 Marshall wrote to W. A. S. Hewins, then Director of the London School of Economics, about his understanding of the relative importance of economic theory and a practical knowledge of the modern economy when teaching the subject. Dismissing Launhardt's *Mathematische Begründung der Volkswirthschaftslehre* (1885), he conceded that Launhardt's more recent work on railways might be better, but that he would only put such a work in the hands of the strongest students. Launhardt, Marshall wrote,

> ... goes to work by what I think a wrong route. He seems to ransack pure reason for general doctrines that may be of practical guidance. He talks about railways as one might about spheres & cylinders, the same now & forever, here & everywhere.... My route would be parallel to his or what I believe to be his, but turned through 180°. I would not let students look at Launhardt, till they had attained enough of railway instinct to know beforehand whether passenger rates would be high or low relative to

[83] Chapman, *Some Memories and Reflections*, p. 68.

[84] Longmans, Green and Co., London 1933. This was a study of the principal sectors of contemporary industrial production, with chapters on coal, iron and steel, engineering, shipbuilding and marine engineering, the 'motor trade', and textiles. At the time, Allen (1900–1982) was 'Professor of Economics and Commerce' at the University College of Hull; he had gained a First in the Birmingham B.Com. in 1921, then worked as a WEA lecturer before a spell teaching at Nagoya High School from 1922 to 1924. Returning to a post in Birmingham, he played an important part in reorienting the Birmingham commerce degree to the study of industrial organisation.

> goods rates in America, & in what parts of the world the quickest train speed would bear the lowest ratio to ... the average train speed & so on.[85]

And as we have seen, this dedication to the practical aspects of railway operation in order to arrive at an understanding of railway economics had been part of the training that Maynard Keynes had from Marshall. Subsequently, writing in response to Arthur Bowley's *Elements of Statistics* (1901), in which he thought there was 'too much mathematics', Marshall deprecated the use of 'mathematical toys':

> I think the economic, as distinguished from the mathematical, student is hurt by being invited to spend his time on them, before he has made a sufficiently realistic study of those statistics to know roughly, without calculation, on which side of the target the centre of the shot lies. He assumes there is no wind. I believe that a Boer marksman, who takes account of the wind, will by instinct get nearer the truth than he by mathematics.[86]

Drawing attention to this essentially practical and empirical aspect of the Marshallian pedagogic heritage reorients our appreciation of *Principles*—no longer a founding theoretical text, but a set of instruments used in the acquisition of economic knowledge. This was the organon that Marshall referred to, more popularly thought of as a toolbox from which the economist needed to know which tool to select for the task at hand. To extend the metaphor, during the 1920s a growing critical preoccupation with the design of the tools, detached from any consideration of the use they were intended to serve, undermined this Marshallian heritage, clearing the way in the 1930s for a science built around the refinement of tools, and not of their application.

The Composition of *Principles of Economics*

To appreciate how this could happen—on what Marshallianism foundered—we do, however, need some sense of the *Principles* as a text, the elements that it assembled, and how these were progressively revised until it reached a final eighth edition in 1920.[87] As John Whitaker noted, the Variorum edition published in 1961 is a good starting point, but obscures the way that textual revisions in successive versions altered the overall direction of the argument.[88] It does not help in coming to terms with

[85] Marshall to Hewins, 12 October 1899, Letter 597 Whitaker (ed.), *Correspondence Vol. 2*, p. 257.

[86] Marshall to Arthur Lyon Bowley, 21 February 1901, Letter 634 in Whitaker (ed.), *Correspondence Vol. 2*, pp. 300, 301. See further comments by Marshall on 'method' in his letter to Bowley of 3 March 1901, Letter 637, pp. 306–307.

[87] See the useful outline supplied by John K. Whitaker, '*Principles of Economics*: Genesis, Structure and Evolution', in Tiziano Raffaelli, Giacomo Becattini, Marco Dardi (eds.) *The Elgar Companion to Alfred Marshall*, Edward Elgar, Cheltenham UK 2006, pp. 66–72.

[88] Edited by Claude Guillebaud, 2 vols. Macmillan, London 1961; Guillebaud himself thought the third edition the best: 'Marshall brought out the third edition of the *Principles* in 1895, when his powers as an expositor were probably at their peak. It would seem that from then onwards the further process of polishing, revision, and compression to which the book was subjected, even though this was combined with expansion in certain directions, did a good deal to devitalize it; and robbed it of much the spontaneity and

the history of the text that Marshall was able to make revisions whenever any one edition was exhausted, so that variations were introduced into different printings of the same edition.[89] Marshall himself noted in correspondence with his German publisher that the fifth edition of 1907 moved nearly 120 pages of the main text into appendices, and that about 200 pages had been added.[90] Much of the material then consigned to an appendix was the historical and evolutionary account of economy and economics contained in Chs. II to VIII of Book I, these being replaced by three chapters on the nature and scope of economics. This underwrites Guillebaud's sense that after 1895 *Principles* lost more in scope than it gained in the precision Marshall sought to achieve through detailed revision; that by 1920 it read in many respects like a different text to the one published in 1890, rendering the Variorum edition a mixed blessing. While for subsequent readers the 1920 edition is the one that was studied and argued over, the route by which the first edition of 1890 turned into the eighth of 1920 is long and complex, and not irrelevant to an understanding of the way in which Marshall himself sought to shape understanding of his legacy.

Some sense of the career of *Principles* as a text can be gained from examining the annual sales, which serve as a proxy for the waxing and waning of a public interest in economics up until the later 1930s (Table 6.1).[91]

The first print run of 2,000 did sell out within six months, but from the early 1890s to the early 1900s sales were consistently in the low hundreds. This was also true for the United States, where the second edition sold over a thousand within a year.[92] Sales picked up in the United Kingdom in 1907, the year before Marshall retired; and then were consistently high throughout the 1920s in the United Kingdom, and also very strong in the United States. Even in the late 1930s *Principles* was selling twice as many copies every year than it had in the 1890s. Most striking here are the consistently high UK sales during the 1920s, reflecting both the rapid expansion of teaching in economics and commerce, and the continuing centrality of Marshall's work to this.[93] That

freshness of expression which characterized it in this and the two earlier editions.' Variorum edition Vol. 2 (Notes), p. 18.

[89] John K. Whitaker, 'Editing Alfred Marshall', in Donald Moggridge (ed.) *Editing Modern Economists*, AMS Press, New York 1988, pp. 62–63. The first edition is not affected by this problem; published in mid-July 1890 with a print run of 2,000, it had sold out six months later, and the revisions that Marshall was already engaged in drafting went into the next printing, which was the second edition published in June 1891. See Letter 333 in Whitaker (ed.), *Correspondence Vol. 2*, p. 1. While a digital copy of the first edition is now available in Internet Archive, hard copies of this edition have for many years been scarce.

[90] Marshall to J. G. Cotta, 12 April 1913, reprinted in Andrés Vázquez, Francisco Pérez, 'Alfred Marshall and the German Translation of His *Principles*: Some Unpublished Letters', *Marshall Studies Bulletin* Vol. 10 (2008) https://www.disei.unifi.it/cmpro-v-p-122.html.

[91] *Elements of Economics of Industry*, a condensed form of the second edition published in 1892, was more likely to be the text used for teaching before the First World War.

[92] See the discussion of the sales of *Principles* in the United States compared with American texts in Roger E. Backhouse, Bradley W. Bateman, Steven G. Medema, 'The Reception of Marshall in the United States', in Tiziano Raffaelli, Giacomo Becattini, Katia Caldari, Marco Dardi (eds.) *The Impact of Alfred Marshall's Idea: The Global Diffusion of His Work*, Edward Elgar, Cheltenham UK 2010, pp. 64–66.

[93] The sales of Cannan's *Theories of Production and Distribution* (1893) suggest the same relatively limited demand in the 1890s, and a boom in the 1920s: the 502 copies of Cannan's book that were initially printed took until the end of 1902 to be sold, the publisher writing to suggest it be allowed to go out of print given that the last 57 copies had taken four years to sell; but there was after all a second edition in 1903, then a third in 1917, which was reprinted in 1920, 1922, and 1924. See S. Rivington to Cannan, 5 December 1902, Correspondence with Publishers I 1890–1916, Cannan Collection 1018 BLPES Archive, f.43.

Table 6.1 Annual Sales of *Principles of Economics*

Year from 1 July	UK Sales	US Sales	
1890–1891	2,018		1st ed. (1890): 2,000 copies, xxviii + 754 pp.
1891–1892	734	1,042	2nd ed. (1891): 3,000 copies, xxx + 770 pp.
1892–1893	263		
1893–1894	278		
1894–1895	246	153	3rd ed. (1895): 2,000 copies, xxxi + 823 pp.
1895–1896	291	312	
1896–1897	293	254	
1897–1898	322	259	4th ed. (1898):5,000 copies, xxix + 820 pp.
1898–1899	359	344	
1899–1900	271	180	
1900–1901	298	76	
1901–1902	290	175	
1902–1903	393	169	
1903–1904	417	128	
1904–1905	349	221	
1905–1906	550	155	
1906–1907	469	107	5th ed. (1907): 5,000 copies, xxxvi + 870 pp.
1907–1908	1,034	295	
1908–1909	1,102	131	
1909–1910	1,114	170	6th ed. (1910): 5,000 copies, xxxii + 871 pp.
1910–1911	598	176	
1911–1912	574	317	
1912–1913	583	230	
1913–1914	733	62	
1914–1915	509	161	
1915–1916	511	331	7th ed. (1916): 5,000 copies
1916–1917	590	100	
1917–1918	496	210	
1918–1919	938	132	
1919–1920	1,542	476	8th ed. (1920): 500 copies, xxxiv + 871 pp.
1920–1921	1,564	506	
1921–1922	1,381	1,300	1922 (Reprint): 5,000 copies
1922–1923	1,408	999	
1923–1924	1,411	277	
1924–1925	1,196	406	1925 (Reprint): 5,000 copies
1925–1926	1,332	428	
1926–1927	1,196	1,297	1927 (Reprint): 4,930 copies

Continued

Table 6.1 *Contined*

Year from 1 July	UK Sales	US Sales	
1927–1928	1,413	1,050	
1928–1929	1,387	1,081	
1929–1930	1,263	1,096	1930 (Reprint): 10,000 copies
1930–1931	937	524	
1931–1932	969	819	
1932–1933	919	360	
1933–1934	936	535	
1934–1935	760	1,033	
1935–1936	685	878	1936 (Reprint): 5,000 copies
1936–1937	880	1,047	
1937–1938	869	1,260	1938 (Reprint): 8,190 copies
1938–1939	815	543	
1939–1940	698	794	
	40,184	21,557	

Source: Daniel Macmillan, *The* Principles of Economics: A Bibliographical Note', *Economic Journal* Vol. 52 (1942), pp. 292–93.

a work written in the 1880s could retain its force in the very different world of the 1920s is easily overlooked. A downturn came in 1930–1931; but the work would remain a point of reference into the 1950s.

The centenary of Marshall's birth came around in 1942, and to mark it, two contrasting essays were published. In the *Economic Journal*, Gerald Shove drew the line from *Principles* to 'economic theory' that this chapter has eschewed.[94] Shove had gained a First in Part II of the Economics Tripos in 1911; but at this time the Part II was a one-year course following on from a two-year Part I, and Shove had studied classics for his Part I. A Cambridge lecturer in economics from 1923, the year before Marshall died, Shove's perspective on Marshall was necessarily derivative, and not immediate. Even Maynard Keynes, connected to Marshall through several strands, was not free of this problem: his obituary essay on Marshall recycles a family mythology conveyed to him by Mary Paley Marshall that was only finally debunked by Ronald Coase in 1990.[95] Today Shove's article tells us less about the work of Alfred Marshall

[94] Shove, 'The Place of Marshall's *Principles*'.

[95] See Steven G. Medema: 'Between LSE and Cambridge: Accounting for Ronald Coase's Fascination with Alfred Marshall', in Katia Caldari, Marco Dardi, Steven G. Medema (eds.) *Marshall and the Marshallian Heritage: Essays in Honour of Tiziano Raffaelli*, Palgrave Macillan, Cham 2021, pp. 231–68, for a detailed account of Coase's decades-long engagement with Marshall's biography. Megan Stevens's detailed critique of Coase's use of sources and defence of the Marshall family alters nothing of his general point: that Alfred Marshall came from a far more humble background than Maynard Keynes was given to understand; Megan Stevens, assisted by Alun Stevens, 'The Wrong Marshall: Notes on the Marshall Family in Response to Biographies of the Economist, Alfred Marshall', *History of Political Economy* Vol. 52 (2020), pp. 239–73.

than about the construction of a Cambridge narrative around Marshall and economic analysis, a narrative that in the 1960s segued into a story centred on the work of Piero Sraffa.

The other centenary essay was by D. H. Macgregor (1877–1953), at the time Drummond Professor in Oxford; this was published in the LSE's house journal *Economica*. Macgregor had graduated from Edinburgh in 1898, then entered Trinity College Cambridge to read Moral Sciences, was taught political economy by Marshall, and graduated with a First in 1901.[96] Macgregor's essay opens on a personal note, remarking that *Principles* had been the first economics book that he had read, then moving on to discuss Marshall's tutorial and lecturing style. The subsequent presentation of *Principles* is still the most concise and informative introduction to the work. He remarks that the work is constructed 'like the development of a plot': things are wanted (Book 3), so they are produced (Book 4), they are exchanged (Book 5), and then 'the price is divided' (Book 6, on the distribution of national income). Macgregor does not mention that he is here talking about the organisation of the book only from the sixth edition onwards, and most likely of the final eighth edition—itself indicating how the reception of the book adjusted itself to Marshall's revisions and recastings. He sums the work up as follows:

> The most fundamental idea is the consumers' benefit, from its explanation in the third Book to the climax of the fifth, where the good monopolist or the public authority comes in to maximise it.[97]

This identifies the centrality of a consumer surplus to Marshall's thinking, described as '... the lynch-pin of the structure. There is no doubt that he established it, whether as a principle or a problem.'[98] Here Macgregor details why it was that Dupuit and de Quincey had not formulated the idea in a recognisable way. By contrast, the prior discussion of the concept of elasticity employed by Marshall in 1885[99] traces the idea back to Gregory King in 1696, to Whewell's inverse formulation of the problem, through Cournot and Dupuit, to its final naming by Moffatt in 1878. *Economics of Industry* (1879) does not include the concept; the *Principles* stated the concept both graphically and algebraically.[100]

Macgregor also discusses the exposition of diminishing returns and the context of competition in Book 4, drawing into his argument here the material in *Industry and Trade* bearing on the idea of a representative firm and of external economies of scale to point out the empirical nature of Marshall's treatment of issues that were, by the 1940s, dealt with primarily in graphical analysis. But he also draws attention to the manner in which the long delay in the publication of *Industry and Trade*, even

[96] Fellow of Trinity College from 1904, he followed on from John Clapham as Professor of Economics at the University of Leeds in 1908; after war service he was briefly Stanley Jevons Professor at Manchester before being appointed to the Oxford chair in 1921, which he held until 1945.

[97] D. H. Macgregor, 'Marshall and His Book', *Economica* New Series Vol. 9 No. 36 (1942), p. 315.

[98] Ibid., p. 317.

[99] Alfred Marshall, The Graphic Method of Statistics', *Journal of the Statistical Society of London* Jubilee Volume (June 1885), p. 260.

[100] Macgregor, 'Marshall and His Book', p. 316.

after the formal abandonment of a *Principles* Vol. II in 1910,[101] caused the empirical material supporting his account of business organisation and competition to become outdated. Published in the wake of the First World War, the material with which Marshall built his arguments came from a prewar world that now seemed very remote; and by elaborating his arguments about competition in this context Marshall mingled the old and the new in a way that made them easier to discount.[102] Marshall's strictures about economic history—that it presented facts about the economic organisation of the past, when what was needed were 'modern facts'—now seemed to apply to his own writing.

A less obvious feature of revisions to the 1890 edition of *Principles* is that it never had been designed as a single volume; the eventual appearance of *Industry and Trade* and *Money, Credit and Commerce* did publish material he had hoped to use in *Principles*, but this still fell short of Marshall's original plan for his work. Like the earlier *Economics of Industry*, written with Mary Paley Marshall for use in Extension classes, the 1890 edition of the *Principles* was announced on the title page as 'Vol. I'.[103] There never would be a 'Vol. II', but even in 1890 he gave no indication of what that further volume might contain. 'Vol. I' was dropped from the sixth edition of 1910 onwards, but in the preface to that edition Marshall did summarise his changing conceptions of what a multivolume *Principles* had been intended to include. He had already despaired of completing *Principles* in two volumes by the mid-1890s, and so had planned the addition of a third volume on the 'Economic Functions of Government', his description of this as a *Wirtschafts-politik* indicating that he here had in mind contemporary German textbook literature.[104] He also rearranged his material on modern industry and trade, credit, and employment, but then eventually realised that he would need a fourth volume. This decision was, however, quickly followed by another: that life is too short, that he must abandon the planned additional volume(s), and publish an independent volume, given here the title of *National Industry and Trade*, with a possible independent volume on *Money, Credit and Employment*. There could perhaps be a third (and so completing the four-part scheme) 'which will treat of the ideal and the practicable in social and economic structure, with some account of taxation and administration.'[105] He went on to elaborate on the German model that he had in mind:

> The scope of the present volume is similar in some respects, though not in all, to that of volumes on *Foundations* (*Grundlagen*), which Roscher and some other economists have put in the forefront of groups of semi-independent volumes on economics. It

[101] See, for this tortuous story, John K. Whitaker, 'What Happened to the Second Volume of the *Principles*? The Thorny Path to Marshall's Last Books', in J. K. Whitaker, *Centenary Essays on Alfred Marshall*, Cambridge University Press, Cambridge 1990, pp. 193–222.

[102] As Tiziano Raffaelli suggests in '*Industry and Trade* Reconsidered', *History of Economic Ideas* Vol. 17 No. 3 (2009), pp. 60–61.

[103] While there is no mention in the 'Preface' of the 1890 edition of *Principles* of what 'Vol. II' might contain, the equally non-existent 'Vol. II' of *Economics of Industry* was at least described in its 'Preface' as to cover 'Banking, Foreign Trade and Taxation ... a companion volume on the "Economics of Trade and Finance"'. Alfred Marshall, Mary Paley Marshall, *The Economics of Industry*, Macmillan, London 1879, p. v.

[104] Alfred Marshall, 'Preface to the Sixth Edition' in Alfred Marshall, *Principles of Economics*, 9th (Variorum) edition Vol. II ed. C. W. Guillebaud, Macmillan, London 1961, p. 55.

[105] Ibid., p. 56.

avoids such special topics as currency and the organization of markets; and in regard to such matters as the structure of industry, employment, and the problem of wages, it deals mainly with normal conditions.

He then turned to outline his view that economic evolution was gradual, and that this applied to the development of economic thinking as much as anything else. True to his definition of economics as the study of 'man's actions in the ordinary business of life',[106] he here distinguished between regularly recurring events that formed the basis of economic study, and those that were 'spasmodic, infrequent, and difficult of observation', reserved for special, later examination.

To illustrate this, he drew a contrast from the study of business organisation. The rise and decline of firms within any branch of industry was such a common occurrence as to enable the construction of a 'representative firm' 'which enjoys a fair share both of those internal economies which belong to a well organized individual business, and of those general or external economies which arise out of the collective organization of the [industrial] district as a whole.'[107] This level of study belonged, he thought, in a volume devoted to 'Foundations'. The same would be true of the way in which an established monopoly managed prices in relation to its revenue, 'but with more or less consideration for the well-being of its customers'.[108] All of this was, however, distinct to the way in which large organisations could well be diverted by financial or political considerations; this belonged in a volume dealing with 'some part of the Superstructure'.

Industry and Trade was finally published in 1919, *Money, Credit and Commerce* in 1923; the fourth projected volume, on social and economic policy, never materialised. The 'Preface' to *Industry and Trade* notes that some of the text had already been typeset in 1904;[109] in 1916 he announced that he was now engaged in writing 'an independent work, which is to extend to more than one volume, on *Industry and Trade*.'[110] When this did finally appear, Marshall's reflections on the 50 years that had elapsed since he had begun a concrete study of industrial organisation, and the way that he related his early 'tendency to socialism' to John Stuart Mill's essays in the *Fortnightly Review* for 1879,[111] together with the age of the material he included, all combined to create the sense that Marshall was by 1919 recalling a distant pre-war world; as Maynard Keynes that same year would recall, 'Europe before the War' in the second chapter of his *Economic Consequences of the Peace*.[112] In August 1922 Marshall still expressed the hope that some parts of his final, fourth volume might be completed, concluding the 'Preface' to *Money, Credit and Commerce* with the 'hope that some of the notions, which I have formed as to the possibilities of social advance, may yet be

[106] *Principles*, first edition 1890, p. 1.

[107] Marshall, 'Preface to the Sixth Edition', p. 57.

[108] Hence the approach that would by the 1930s become known as 'monopolistic competition', i.e. the theory of oligopoly.

[109] Alfred Marshall, *Industry and Trade. A Study of Industrial Technique and Business Organization; and of their Influences on the Conditions of various Classes and Nations*, Macmillan, London 1919, p. vi.

[110] Marshall, 'Preface to the Seventh Edition' in *Principles of Economics*, 9th (Variorum) edition ed. C. W. Guillebaud, Vol. 2, p. 61.

[111] Marshall *Industry and Trade*, p. vii.

[112] John Maynard Keynes, *The Economic Consequences of the Peace*, Collected Writings of John Maynard Keynes Vol. II, Macmillan, London 1971, p. 6.

published.'[113] But he died in July 1924, in his own mind the *Principles* as he had originally conceived it still unfinished.

The very delayed appearance of this later material as separate titles, the non-appearance of his thinking on governments and social policy, and the status of the 1920 edition of *Principles* as a free-standing work now shorn of 'Vol. I', in which form it would continue as a source of reference until the 1950s at least, all this contrived to convert Marshall into an economic theorist, when those he had taught—Macgregor, Pigou, Maynard Keynes—were well aware of his very substantial interest in, and knowledge of, the practicalities of economic organisation. *Principles* had in 1890 been the first part of a multi-volume work; by 1920 it had become the only part. It did not help that the way in which Marshall had gone about reorganising the content of the 1890 version of *Principles* over the years lent emphasis to its theoretical status. This would have made perfect sense to Marshall, refining his ideas while at the same time having in mind the complementary volumes in which these ideas would have been set to work. But the separation of a unitary *Principles*, as it came to be read and known, from these complementary volumes, altered perspective on what Marshall himself had sought to achieve; so much so that his legacy was already embroiled during the later 1920s in theoretical controversy over the nature of increasing returns, culminating in a critique by Lionel Robbins of Marshall's idea of the 'representative firm' that showcased the air of condescension that was unfortunately typical of the younger Robbins.[114]

Furthermore, Marshall's original decision to place all of the mathematics in an appendix, and confine the graphs to footnotes[115] and the mathematical appendix, maintained the discursive presentation of his ideas at a time when the 'geometric political economy' that Marshall had championed was becoming more common in new publications. All the same, despite the sparse use of graphs in Marshall's exposition, and his reliance on prose, Cunynghame's little book *A Geometrical Political Economy*[116] shows that Marshall's graphic conceptualisations would become standard in twentieth-century microeconomics, and be conventional both in introductory textbook and theoretical debate.

113 Alfred Marshall, *Money, Credit and Commerce*, Macmillan, London 1923, p. vi.

114 Lionel Robbins, 'The Representative Firm', *Economic Journal* Vol. 38 (1928), pp. 387–404. Robbins concluded that the notion was not only superfluous, but 'misleading' (p. 399). Nowhere in his article does he refer to Marshall's casual introduction of the term in the 1910 'Preface' to clarify his approach to the study of economics.

115 Just how sparing Marshall was with his graphical analysis is shown by a complete listing of their occurrence in the 1920 edition, all included in footnotes, not the main text: pp. 96, 99, 102, 104, 106, 110, 155, 158, 159, 464, 466, 467, 468, 469, 473, 480, 483; page references to *Principles of Economics*, 9th (Variorum) edition, ed. C. W. Guiillebaud.

116 Henry Cunynghame, *A Geometrical Political Economy. Being an Elementary Treatise on the Method of Explaining Some of the Theories of Pure Economic Science by Means of Diagrams*, Oxford University Press, Oxford 1904.

The 1920s: Moving on from Marshall

The inevitably dated feel to Marshall's material in *Industry and Trade* and *Money, Credit and Commerce* contributed in the early 1920s to a growing chorus of Marshall criticism. First came John Clapham's 'Of Empty Economic Boxes', published in September 1922, which suggested that the Marshallian analytical apparatus had little practical bearing on the workings of the contemporary economy.[117] Clapham's argument here resembles that of Ashley some 15 years previously, placing in question the general utility and validity of all recent work in economic analysis. In the December issue, Pigou published a robust, witty, and detailed response. This echoes his 1902 note on corn duties that I discussed earlier, where he distinguished between Edgeworth's suggestion about what *might* happen to prices and his own proposition about what *would probably* happen. Both involved analytical argument, but in Pigou's case he was interested in the likely practical outcome of a given policy. This is not a contrast between 'theory' and 'practice' of the kind that Clapham appears to work with; it is a contrast between two levels of analytical argument, and Pigou's position is distinctly Marshallian. Clapham appeared to be validating 'practice' and abjuring 'theory', but he was in fact making the epistemological argument that theoretical knowledge had no practical application and so was of no value. This was one of the points that Pigou identified and rebutted.

He reduced Clapham's argument to four moves. First, the conception of rates of return in industrial undertakings, especially of increasing returns, was not as clear as it should be; second, it was hard to assign actually existing industries to either increasing or decreasing returns; third, if this could be done it would be of no consequence anyway; and so fourthly, the conception itself was purposeless.[118] Pigou conceded that the first was true, but that since Clapham did not identify any new issues, there was not here anything worth discussing. Instead, he considers the different types of knowledge, suggesting that Clapham cannot decide 'how far his antipathy to the categories of increasing and decreasing returns is due to his belief that they cannot be given a concrete filling, and how far to his belief that they cannot show us the way to card wool or impose taxes.' If Clapham rejects this conception because it cannot serve as a guide to practice, then the same argument applies to the great bulk of historical knowledge. His argument is therefore in this regard self-refuting. 'On what metaphysical or other basis is he entitled to lay it down, that knowledge of the form, "If X, then Y," is inferior to the knowledge of the form, "In the year 1600, X"?'[119] Knowledge of *implications* is just as much knowledge as is knowledge of *matters of fact*; although Pigou conceded that he did not regard that the knowledge of implications of the kind that pure economics can provide was of much interest to him; what Pigou sought in economic knowledge was 'practical usefulness of some sort'.[120]

117 John Clapham, 'Of Empty Economic Boxes', *Economic Journal* Vol. 32 (1922), pp. 305–14.
118 Pigou, 'Empty Economic Boxes: A Reply', p. 458.
119 Ibid., p. 459.
120 Ibid., p. 461.

> Dr. Clapham has learnt from the *Principles of Economics* that, if we knew, as between two articles, that one was being produced under conditions of increasing and the other under conditions of diminishing returns, we could draw inferences that were relevant to the comparative effects on social welfare of putting taxes on the one or the other of them. Because there are also other considerations relevant to that problem, Dr. Clapham considers that this knowledge would be useless! What is there to say of reasoning of this quality?[121]

This was, however, a robust statement of aims and procedures made by Marshall's chosen successor, not by a product of the Economics Tripos. As we have already seen with Gerald Shove, being a graduate of the Economics Tripos did not imply automatic agreement with the principles Pigou exemplifies here. This was confirmed two years after this exchange, when Dennis Robertson (1890–1963) published his own response to Pigou's reply to Clapham. Robertson had the same academic background as Shove: he studied Classics for two years before the one-year Economics Part II, gaining a First in 1912. Robertson's mannered prose makes it difficult to grasp the point he seeks to make, but what is clear is that his interest in this discussion is theoretical, not 'practical' in the sense outlined earlier by Pigou.[122] The point was further underlined in 1926 when Piero Sraffa published his critique of Marshall's treatment of increasing and diminishing returns, stating that '[a]t present the laws of returns are of special importance owing to the part they play in the study of the problem of value.'[123] This was Sraffa's problem, not Marshall's.[124]

A degree of Marshallian pushback to this focus upon the purely theoretical aspects of returns to scale came in early September 1928 with Allyn Young's Presidential Address to Section F of the British Association, meeting that year in Glasgow. Young's chief point of reference in his appraisal of costs and returns is not any 'theory of value', nor 'alluring but highly technical questions relating to the precise way in which some sort of equilibrium of supply and demand is achieved in the market for the products of industries which can increase their output without increasing their costs proportionately'. Indeed, the apparatus constructed for this purpose 'may stand in the way of a clear view of the more general or elementary aspects of the phenomena of increasing returns.'[125] His point of reference is instead the structure of modern industry, in which innovation alters 'the conditions of economic activity and initiates responses elsewhere in the industrial structure which in turn have a further unsettling effect.'[126]

121 Ibid., p. 464.

122 D. H. Robertson, 'Those Empty Boxes', *Economic Journal* Vol. 34 (1924), pp. 16–30. Pigou wrote a terse response, noting that '[i]n his discussion of increasing returns Mr. Robertson does not seem to have understood the nature of the issues involved. My conclusions, which he considers new and revolutionary, are identical with those established thirty years ago by Dr. Marshall (cf. *Principles of Economics* Book V. ch. xiii)' (p. 30).

123 Piero Sraffa, 'The Laws of Returns under Competitive Conditions', *Economic Journal* Vol. 36 (1926), p. 536.

124 As Carlo Cristiano notes, Sraffa's critique of Marshall was only plausible if one accepted that Sraffa's priors were the appropriate starting point, while discounting Marshall's; the apparent force of Sraffa's argument is therefore an illusion; 'Marshall at Cambridge', in Tiziano Raffaelli, Giacomo Becattini, Katia Caldari, Marco Dardi (eds.) *The Impact of Alfred Marshall's Idea: The Global Diffusion of His Work*, Edward Elgar, Cheltenham UK 2010, p. 24.

125 Allyn Young, 'Increasing Returns and Economic Progress', *Economic Journal* Vol. 38 (1928), p. 527.

126 Ibid., p. 533.

Upon this phenomenon, economic analysis sheds little light. Young's focus is upon a changing industrial structure, not on the behaviour of the individual firm. As he sums up:

> First, the mechanism of increasing returns is not to be discerned adequately by observing the effects of variations in the size of an individual firm or of a particular industry, for the progressive division and specialisation of industries is an essential part of the process by which increasing returns are realised. What is required is that industrial operations be seen as an interrelated whole. Second, the securing of increasing returns depends upon the progressive division of labour, and the principal economies of the division of labour, in its modern forms, are the economies which are to be had by using labour in roundabout or indirect ways. Third, the division of labour depends upon the extent of the market, but the extent of the market also depends upon the division of labour. In this circumstance lies the possibility of economic progress....[127]

Young, at the time Professor of Economics at LSE, would be dead within the year, and his place taken by Lionel Robbins, who had in March 1928 submitted his paper 'The Representative Firm' to the *Economic Journal*.[128] When this was published it included a footnote repudiating 'a strange myth' that 'economists of the tradition in which I was trained have a secret grudge against Cambridge and all things Marshallian. In fact, of course, nothing could be more ridiculous.'[129] Whether there was at this time any such 'tradition' to which someone who had only graduated from the LSE five years before could have belonged is a moot point. The distance between the approach taken to Marshallian analysis by Young and that by Robbins was marked, and itself undermines Robbins's implication that in 1928 Cambridge and the LSE were on divergent disciplinary paths. Matters are more complex: Cambridge was already detaching itself from Marshall's legacy in the 1920s, while the polarity of London and Cambridge was fostered from London during the 1930s, and not before.

In seeking to outline what we might mean by 'Marshallianism' I have not sought here to identify a 'philosophy', some kind of method, or intellectual rationalisation. Nor have I sought to identify any analytical unity in the various economic instruments that Marshall invented, adapted, or used. Instead, I have emphasised the orientation that Marshall sought to convey to young economists: a firm grasp of the material world of commerce, manufacture, and public administration, how this world shaped the activities of those who laboured in it, and the instruments appropriate to understanding economies as vast networks of institutions and relationships. Without such a grounding, the economist would, he thought, become diverted by 'toys'. Maynard Keynes was a true disciple of his teacher. His first book, *Indian Currency and Finance* (1913), owed a great deal to the fact that his first job was in the India Office. *The Economic Consequence of the Peace* (1919) largely arose out of his work in the Treasury during the war. In the course of the 1920s he absorbed the developments

[127] Ibid., p. 539.
[128] Susan Howson, *Lionel Robbins*, Cambridge University Press, Cambridge 2011, p. 155.
[129] Lionel Robbins, 'The Representative Firm', *Economic Journal* Vol. 38 (1928), p. 387 fn. 4.

of contemporary economics through his work as editor of the *Economic Journal*, and at the same time made a name in economic journalism. The works of economic theory for which he is known—the *Treatise on Money* (1930) and the *General Theory* (1936)—developed from years of practical engagement as a civil servant, journalist, and editor. This was, however, the kind of pathway that few, if any, subsequent eminent economists would follow.

PART III
ALTERNATIVE HISTORIES

So far I have presented a dual argument. Firstly, to forge an academic discipline out of the diverse elements of later nineteenth-century economic discourse would require the fusing of a number of apparently unrelated elements—new and old economic ideas, of course, but also among other factors the politics of franchise reform, an increasingly urban population developing new forms of sociability, new technologies of communication, reforms to schooling and popular education, and very importantly, the argument that national welfare depended on a labour force schooled in modern subjects—English (not classics), modern languages, natural sciences, geography, and modern history. Secondly, and for a number of contingent reasons that would seem to run counter to the tendencies just noted, the critical move in making discourse into discipline occurred in Cambridge: an ancient, not a modern, university. This latter argument does not deviate so very greatly from existing arguments that place Marshall's Cambridge centre stage, although I do so for different reasons, together with greater and lesser differences of emphasis. However, Parts III and IV will now consider contemporary alternatives and subsequent developments that place Cambridge in a rather different light to the one with which we are familiar, making clear why the 'Cambridge moment' was just that: a passing episode, but an episode that at the time could only have occurred in Cambridge.

First I consider why it was that other possible contemporary paths for the development of a new discipline were not taken. Then in Part IV I will demonstrate why it was that disciplinary initiative quickly moved away from Cambridge: first in Britain to the London School of Economics (LSE) in the course of the 1920s, and then subsequently in the course of the 1930s and 1940s to American institutions. By mid-century both Cambridge and LSE were eclipsed by American departments, American media, and the careers they made possible. The mainstream became an American mainstream.

The first of the paths not taken was Oxford. As Alon Kadish demonstrated many years ago,[1] during the 1880s students and teachers in Oxford were placed at the centre of British political economy; many of these went on to influential careers in academia and public administration. But this brief flowering did not directly contribute to the institutional and intellectual work required to establish and perpetuate economics as a discipline. A number of factors combined to ensure that the kind of innovations that Marshall made in Cambridge could not have been made in contemporary Oxford. Chapter 7 identifies the principal reasons for this, demonstrating how features specific to the nineteenth-century development of the University of Oxford distinguished

[1] Alon Kadish, *The Oxford Economists in the Late Nineteenth Century*, Oxford University Press, Oxford 1982.

it from Cambridge, and presented impediments to the development of the kind of teaching and scholarship associated with economics in Cambridge during the first decades of the twentieth century.

To anticipate, one obvious impediment was that Francis Edgeworth was elected Drummond Professor of Political Economy in 1891, and Edgeworth had little interest in promoting the study of economics along the lines of Marshall. Instead, in 1920–1921 economics began to be taught as part of a joint degree with politics and philosophy, and so as part of a structure rather similar to that of the Moral Sciences Tripos from which Marshall had struggled to detach his subject. And rather ironically, during the second half of the twentieth century this Philosophy, Politics, and Economics (PPE) degree became the qualification of choice for those beginning careers in public administration, politics, and the media, thus largely fulfilling Marshall's original aspiration for his own Economics Tripos, but in a radically reduced form.

The second path not taken in the development of economics as a discipline was that of economic history. During the later part of the nineteenth century the international pre-eminence of German universities was also associated with the idea that German economic thought had an especially historicist cast; the majority of German academic economists did indeed self-identify as historical economists, and this identity was lent clear contours by the work of their principal organisation, the *Verein für Socialpolitik*. For many of those in Oxford with a strong interest in political economy, German historical economics represented a clear model that was buttressed both by historical studies of economic development and by the fact that, in Oxford, political economy was closely related to the curriculum for the study of history.

Interest in German historical economics was not of course confined to Britain; as outlined in Chapter 2, during the 1870s and 1880s many American students who could not find in their own country the systematic economic teaching and qualifications they sought travelled to German universities, where they attended lecture courses, took part in seminars, and completed doctorates.[2] Once back in the United States they found positions as teachers, working with the historical and institutional perspective they had absorbed in Europe. The rapid expansion in the number of well-funded American universities during the last two decades of the nineteenth century created major opportunities for the teaching of economics, with many of those appointed to new positions bringing their experience of German universities with them. However, this itself weakened the pressure on students to travel elsewhere for advanced study; from the 1890s developments in American teaching and research were oriented largely to American problems, such as the ongoing arguments about railroads, regulation, anti-trust legislation, and competition. These would all turn out to be issues of great and general importance for twentieth-century economics, but from the 1890s to the early 1920s American institutions were disengaged from the international policy context that European economists shared.

[2] The story of nineteenth-century American political economy is one in which American economists have shown little specific interest, presumably because of its clear theoretical indebtedness to Jean-Baptiste Say and its general policy commitment to protectionism. See the useful overview provided by W. J. Barber (ed.) *Breaking the Academic Mould: Economists and American Higher Learning in the Nineteenth Century*, Wesleyan University Press, Middletown Conn. 1988.

While the first flow of students to Germany and back again was for a time a very significant factor in the development of teaching in American universities, it was very much a one-way street. It had no lasting impact on the routine of German universities, where the teaching of economics was oriented to law students, some of whom would be destined for public administration. German professors continued to write and publish prolifically, but more or less entirely ignored developments in the subject taking place in France, Italy, Britain, and the United States. The theoretical and analytical developments that followed on from the publication of Marshall's *Principles* in 1890 found little resonance;[3] likewise the work of Vilfredo Pareto and Maffeo Pantaleoni, or that of Knut Wicksell, went largely unacknowledged in German textbooks and handbooks. By the second decade of the twentieth century, many in the established German professoriate were quite detached from the way economics was being taught and studied in leading universities elsewhere in the world, and this detachment was reinforced by the collapse in prestige that German universities suffered as a consequence of the First World War. By the 1920s the historical framework that had, in the 1870s, appeared to promise so much for the development of economics now seemed obsolete.[4] The initiative in Germany had passed from universities to private-sector institutes such as Wagemann's *Institut für Konjunkturforschung*, founded in 1925,[5] followed two years later by the foundation of an Austrian institute of the same name led by Ludwig von Mises and Friedrich von Hayek.

There was, however, in Germany a new generation of students, encouraged by the creation in 1923 of a pre-doctoral qualification, the *Diplom-Volkswirt*, which built upon an existing emphasis upon social and economic statistics to generate analytical thinking that could also draw upon new statistical techniques. Many in this generation then in the 1930s fled Germany and found permanent refuge in the United States, where they played a major role in the development of the new discipline of economics. Indeed, it could be said that the advance of American economics to pre-eminence in the later twentieth century was built upon two waves of migration: of Americans to Germany in the later nineteenth century, who returned to the United States with a sense of the university as a centre of specialised scholarship; and then in the 1930s, a wave of young refugees from Germany and elsewhere who had a better grounding in mathematics, statistics, and formal technique than their American peers.

Stepping back to the way things looked during the 1880s and 1890s in Britain, it did appear that economic history might play a formative role in the creation of a new discipline of economics, more or less explicitly modelling the German example. When the first edition of Alfred Marshall's *Principles of Economics Vol. I* was published in

[3] Marshall's *Principles* was translated into German and published in 1905, but the limited reception testifies to the increasing international isolation of German (not Austrian) economists; see Volker Caspari, 'Marshall in German-Speaking Countries', in Tiziano Raffaelli, Giacomo Becattini, Marco Dardi (eds.) *The Elgar Companion to Alfred Marshall*, Edward Elgar, Cheltenham UK 2006, pp. 129–34.

[4] See, for an assessment of the limitations of German historical economics, the entry that Simon Cook and I wrote on 'Historical Economics' in Gilbert Faccarello, Heinz D. Kurz (eds.) *Handbook on the History of Economic Analysis Vol. II*, Elgar, Cheltenham UK 2016, pp. 295–312.

[5] See Adam Tooze, *Statistics and the German State, 1900–1945: The Making of Modern Economic Knowledge*, Cambridge University Press, Cambridge 2001; notable for our purposes here is the irrelevance of the standard account of German historical economics to his path-breaking account of economic knowledge in interwar Germany.

1890, it had a substantial introductory historical section on the genesis of the modern economy, inspired in part by Marshall's own contact with German historical economics; and for 15 years Marshall sparred with William Cunningham's claims that the emergent discipline must be founded in economic history.[6] In Oxford, a significant advocate of economic history and historical economics was William Ashley, a student during the 1880s and contributor to the posthumous editing of Arnold Toynbee's final lecture course. Ashley went on to become the founding professor of political economy in Toronto in 1888, founding Professor of Economic History at Harvard in 1892, founding Professor of Commerce at the University of Birmingham in 1900, the author of a well-regarded work on the issue of tariff reform in 1903 and, shortly before his death, a moving spirit in the creation of the Economic History Society in 1926. Why then, given this career profile, did not the early development of economics in Britain take a more historical approach?

The standard story has for a long time been that the consolidation of economics in Britain was directly linked to the systematic exclusion of economic history from the new curriculum: that the new economics purified itself by expelling the study of economic history.[7] There are various reasons why this story became established, but there is little substantive evidence for it; rather more, in fact, for the contrary view, that representatives of economic history such as William Cunningham, William Ashley, and Richard Tawney nurtured a deep hostility to contemporary economic theory, whether British, French, German, Austrian, Italian, Swedish, or American. Part of the difficulty was that British historians seem to have consistently overlooked the fact that German historical economists were, through their work for the *Verein*, deeply enmeshed in the study of contemporary social and economic problems—this was indeed the reason for the existence of the *Verein*, and the annual publication of conference proceedings testifies to this at length. Marshall was not being disingenuous when he argued that economic history could contribute little to the development of modern economic ideas; in the British case, the texts of economic history that existed terminated in the early nineteenth century at the very latest, describing a world already quite remote from that of the later nineteenth century. Marshall was the last person to overlook 'economic facts': but, as he argued, for modern economics you needed modern facts. Here I explore the real prospects for a 'historical economics' in the later nineteenth century by following the career of William Ashley. Supplemented with a consideration of the criticisms of Marshall made by William Cunningham, we can shed some light on claim and counterclaim, and demonstrate quite why economic history was, by the 1920s, set on a separate pathway to the new discipline of economics.

[6] See my essay 'The Historicisation of Political Economy?', in B. Stuchtey, P. Wende (eds.) *British and German Historiography 1750–1950*, Oxford University Press, Oxford 2000, pp. 211–28.

[7] See in particular Gerard M. Koot, *English Historical Economics, 1870–1926: The Rise of Economic History and Neomercantilism*, Cambridge University Press, Cambridge 1987.

7
Why Not Oxford?

The drive to create a place for the systematic teaching of economics in a British university, and to establish for the first time anywhere a specialised degree in the subject, owed a great deal to the intellectual and personal ambitions of Alfred Marshall. At the time he was appointed to the Cambridge chair for political economy in December 1884, Marshall was teaching at Balliol College Oxford, positioned to succeed a 77-year-old Bonamy Price as Oxford's Drummond Professor of Political Economy. If he had in fact become the Drummond Professor in 1888, when Price died, Marshall's plans might have taken a rather different direction, given the institutional differences between Oxford and Cambridge. Indeed, we might speculate that, but for the Cambridge chair becoming vacant on the unanticipated death of Henry Fawcett at the age of 51 in late 1884, the early history of the discipline of economics would not have turned out the way that it did.

Why was this? What was it about Oxford that obstructed the development of the kind of economic education that Marshall introduced in Cambridge? The short answer to this question is: the lasting predominance of classics in the Oxford university curriculum. But it is more complicated than that, since several Oxford history graduates of the 1880s did play a major role in the development of economics in Britain and overseas. The location of the study of political economy in the Oxford history curriculum initially fostered a particular approach to contemporary economic problems, but then impeded the development of more analytical work. Then, in 1920, within the new PPE (Philosophy, Politics, and Economics) degree, economics became one element in combination with the teaching of politics and philosophy; from the 1930s onwards, Oxford became much more strongly oriented to policy than Cambridge, marked by the creation of the Institute of Statistics in 1935 and the foundation of Nuffield College in 1944–1945. By the 1950s, a distinct Oxford teaching model was formed that was both broader and more policy oriented than the Cambridge approach to economics, in which the Department of Economics was central and the Department of Applied Economics a poor relation. By this time, however, it was too late to make any international impact on the development of a discipline now dominated by American departments and graduate schools.

Oxford had been in the 1880s central to political economy in Britain in a way that Cambridge was not. Besides the teaching of Arnold Toynbee, a significant number of History graduates took an interest in political economy and embarked on careers built on this interest. Edwin Cannan went on to become founding Professor of Political Economy at the London School of Economics (LSE) in 1907, having taught at the School since its foundation in 1895. Another Oxford graduate of the time, W A. S. Hewins, was founding Director of the LSE. E. C. K. Gonner gained a first in History in 1884, and then was appointed in 1891 to the new Brunner Chair of Economic Science at Liverpool, until the appointment in 1898 of Alfred Flux as Professor of

Constructing Economic Science. Keith Tribe, Oxford University Press. © Oxford University Press 2022.
DOI: 10.1093/oso/9780190491741.003.0007

Political Economy in Manchester, the only full-time professorial appointment outside Cambridge in England.[1] In 1881 W. J. Ashley had gained a first in History; in 1888 he became Professor of Political Economy in Toronto, in 1892 the founding Professor of Economic History at Harvard, and then in 1901 the founding Professor of Commerce at the University of Birmingham. He applied, unsuccessfully, to become Marshall's successor at Cambridge in 1908. Alon Kadish has written of this 1880s cohort as the 'Oxford Economists', emphasising their shared intellectual culture. In this chapter I raise a rather different issue: what was it about the organisation of the University of Oxford that formed prominent individuals like these with an interest in economics, but obstructed the development of institutional mechanisms that could foster the systematic study of economics?

In the early nineteenth century the universities of Oxford and Cambridge were relatively moribund collegiate institutions whose main function was the training of clergy. Continental European and Scottish universities were by contrast typically organised as four faculties—of theology, law, medicine, and philosophy, hence also with a vocational purpose, but one broader than that of Oxford and Cambridge universities. English lawyers and physicians were trained in separate institutions—the Inns of Court and teaching hospitals. It was also true that well into the nineteenth century many students attended an Oxbridge college as part of their general education and left without taking a degree; while among those Oxford students who did formally graduate, in 1830 some 60% moved on to a living in the Church of England.[2] In any case, for Oxford and Cambridge students the university as an institution was remote from their immediate concerns, for they lived and studied in their colleges; the university was only of relevance to them when it came to taking university examinations. In both universities, chairs of political economy were established in the early part of the nineteenth century, but these foundations remained largely irrelevant to teaching in Cambridge until the appointment of Marshall as Professor of Political Economy in 1884; and as we shall see, not really in Oxford either, even with the appointment of Edgeworth in 1891 to the Drummond Chair. As centres for ecclesiastical training, both universities naturally excluded women; Jews, Roman Catholics, and assorted Dissenters were also excluded through the simple mechanism of requiring students to subscribe to the 39 Articles appended to the *Book of Common Prayer*. Until 1854, Oxford students were required to do this on matriculation; in Cambridge, they had to do so before having their degree conferred upon them.

There were, however, other differences between Oxford and Cambridge, and some of these differences would turn out to be significant for any explanation of why it was that Marshall succeeded in creating a specialised economics degree in Cambridge, whereas Oxford still does not have a single honours undergraduate economics degree

[1] In 1892 a Lectureship in Political Economy was created in Glasgow, an additional endowment in 1896 raising this to the status of a professorship, with William Smart as the incumbent—see P. L. Robertson, 'The Finances of the University of Glasgow before 1914', *History of Education Quarterly* Vol. 16 (1976), p. 468. The teaching remained nonetheless relatively limited, although based upon Marshall's *Principles*; see *Glasgow University Calendar for the Year 1898–99*, p. 68.

[2] M. G. Brock, 'The Oxford of Peel and Gladstone, 1800–1833', in M. G. Brock, M. C. Curthoys (eds.) *The History of the University of Oxford*, Vol. VI: *Nineteenth-Century Oxford Part I*, Oxford University Press, Oxford 1997, p. 9.

programme. In the first half of the nineteenth century it could, for example, be said that Oxford was broadly Tory (later Conservative), while Cambridge was broadly Whig (subsequently Liberal). Several nineteenth-century Tory Prime Ministers were not only Oxford graduates, but also students of one particular college: Christ Church.[3] This political divergence was itself reflected in the theological differences between the two institutions, Oxford eventually harbouring an anglo-catholic revival that left Cambridge virtually untouched. Studies in both universities did revolve around classics and mathematics, the two basic subjects of schooling for centuries. But here there was a difference of emphasis. As we have seen, in Cambridge the focus of teaching and examination was on mathematics, qualification in classics following on optionally from examination success in mathematics. In Oxford, the reverse was the case: mathematics was a minor part of a curriculum dominated by classics, examined subsequently to success in classics. This was a difference relevant to our interests here, for it was in part the *style* of analysis engendered by the Maths Tripos that Marshall sought to replicate in a new Economics Tripos. While the study of classical texts and success in an Oxford oral examination required familiarity with sources and rhetorical facility, it did not call for the analytical skill and systematic preparation of a Cambridge student working through several days of written examinations in mathematics.

Indeed, part of the story here involves a transition from oral to written examinations in the early part of the century, a transition made later in Oxford than in Cambridge, and prompted in Oxford largely by the much greater number of candidates for examination following the reforms of the early 1800s. Although teaching continued to be a college matter, university examinations came to dominate undergraduate education in Oxford, increasingly preoccupying college tutors dealing with an extending number of degree subjects as the century wore on. The complexity of the curriculum that they faced led to the publication in 1860 of Montagu Burrows's *Pass and Class*, an unofficial comprehensive overview that would soon be imitated by the Cambridge University student guide. From January 1870 the *Oxford University Gazette* provided a single current source for notices that had hitherto been circulated in college, also giving over much of its space to lists of examinees and the regulations to which they had to attend. Extensive revision of these regulations in 1872 prompted the appearance of a semi-official *Student's Handbook to the University and Colleges of Oxford* the following year.[4] The opening of the Examination Schools in 1882, designed to process more than 4,500 students a year, further underscored the way in which the university was embodied as an increasingly complex system of examination and

[3] Robert Peel (1788–1850) studied at Christ Church before moving on to Lincoln's Inn to study law in 1809; George Canning (1770–1827) attended Christ Church from 1787 to 1791; the Earl of Derby (1799–1869) studied there too, and Lord Salisbury (1830–1903) did so from 1847. And so did the Liberal William Gladstone (1809–1898), who was at Christ Church from 1828 to 1831. The only break in this pattern of Tory Prime Ministers is William Pitt (1759–1806), who studied at Pembroke College Cambridge from 1773 to 1776; and Lord Palmerston (1784–1865), who studied with Dugald Stewart in Edinburgh from 1800 to 1803, then moved on to St. John's Cambridge where he studied from 1803 to 1806. Palmerston was originally Tory, then switching to Whig; Benjamin Disraeli (1804–1881) was of course of Jewish background and so did not attend either Oxford or Cambridge.

[4] M. C. Curthoys, 'The Examination System', in Brock, Curthoys, *History Vol. VI Part I* (1997), pp. 339–40.

qualification, a system that did not, however, make regular provision for the teaching of economic subjects until 1920.

The Oxford Examination System

We can best approach the continuing domination of classical studies in the Oxford University curriculum by considering the progressive reconstruction of the system of (university) examinations, and the consequent changes to the paths of study that students could follow.[5] The dominance of the classical curriculum had encountered criticism in the later eighteenth century; but it would be another hundred years before it was seriously displaced from its central role in teaching, and even today a first- or a second-class Oxford degree in classics can be accepted as an adequate preparation for high office in Britain. Understanding this resilience requires that we begin with the first moves for reform in the early nineteenth century.

Intercollegiate rivalry and increasing external criticism promoted the introduction of a new examination statute in 1800, introducing the term 'Literae Humaniores' to designate the requirement of 'a competent proficiency, not only in the Latin and Greek languages, but also in Rhetoric and Moral Philosophy, as drawn from the Greek and Roman writers,—in Logic,—and in Latin Composition'.[6] In 1830 Greek and Roman History was added to the list of subjects, lending the course the tripartite structure that it has had ever since; while permission was also given to 'illustrate' ancient with modern authors. This meant that reference could be made to modern authorities such as Barthold Georg Niebuhr, and later George Grote and Theodor Mommsen, permitting the evolution of the study of classical philosophy into the study of philosophy for its own sake, and so forming one of the reasons for the persistence of a classical foundation to an Oxford education. Important here was that the curriculum was constituted as a set of books to be studied, and this approach carried over into the early development of the study of history. In the mid-nineteenth century, to study history in Oxford meant to study a number of classic historical works.[7] The idea that the study of history involved a study of institutions or persons in the context of particular historical periods did not properly develop until the 1870s at the earliest, most notably linked to the influence of Stubbs. The same basic pattern can be seen in the study of political economy: if when working for History Honours or a Pass Degree the Oxford student of the later 1860s or 1870s encountered the subject matter of political economy, this took the form of a book to be studied—usually Adam Smith's *Wealth of Nations*, or perhaps Johns Stuart Mill's *Principles of Political Economy*. The idea that

[5] There is of course a complex history of debates both within and between colleges regarding the qualities and purposes of study in Oxford, and notably the controversy stirred up by a number of critical articles in the *Edinburgh Review* published between 1808 and 1810; but this history is not central to the argument here, which seeks to identify significant differences between Oxford and Cambridge that help explain the prospect each offered for the systematic teaching of political economy.

[6] W. H. Walsh, 'The Zenith of Greats', in M. G. Brock, M. C. Curthoys (eds.) *The History of the University of Oxford*, Vol. VII: *Nineteenth-Century Oxford, Part 2*, Oxford University Press, Oxford 2000, p. 311, quoting the *University Calendar* for 1813.

[7] See P. H. Slee, *Learning and a Liberal Education*, Manchester University Press, Manchester 1986, pp. 40–41 for details of 1859 and 1864.

the leading writers of political economy were engaged in debates over issues or principles that for their proper understanding needed to be placed in a historical context was first introduced into Oxford by Arnold Toynbee, whose influence is discussed in the following chapter.

Another important feature of the 1800 reform was to establish a distinction between honours and pass degrees,[8] and to enable candidates to fail—from 1810 the failure rate was around 20%. However, Oxford candidates were not ranked, as they were in in Cambridge: from 1807 in Oxford the names of students awarded 'Honours' were placed in two lists, those placed in the second class making up around 80% of the honours totals; in 1809 a line was drawn through the names of those placed in the second class to create a lower division. In 1825 this lower division was redesignated third-class honours, and this in turn led marginal students to prefer the anonymity of a simple unclassified 'pass'. A fourth class was added in 1830, adding a further level of discrimination between classified and unclassified graduates. Importantly, however, Oxford students were listed in each class alphabetically, not ranked as Cambridge students were, in part because an oral examination based upon literature did not lend itself to scoring in a way that an examination based on mathematical problems did.[9] It was thought that a broad division into four parts for honours would act as a greater incentive for participation, since the largely oral examination of this period involved a direct confrontation of candidate and examiner in the presence of other candidates and examiners.[10]

As in Cambridge, up until the end of the eighteenth century, formal graduation from the University of Oxford was conditional on a successful oral defence. In Oxford this primarily took the form of one or more sessions of disputation between candidate and examiner[11] that could in some cases last more than a day, a circumstance that rendered the total amount of time devoted to examination uncertain, and implied that unexamined candidates would witness the performance of their peers.[12] From 1830 examiners were permitted to 'try several persons at the same time, at answering the same questions', opening the way for printed papers and written answers. Mathematics examiners had introduced printed questions first in 1828, following the Cambridge example; in 1831 the first printed papers in Literae Humaniores included questions on logic, rhetoric, criticism, and history, together with Greek, Latin, and English passages for translation.[13] Initially those waiting their turn for formal oral

[8] After 1830 the distinction turned on the range of books that students submitted in advance of their examination, so that they began their oral examination either as an honours candidate or a pass candidate. Students could fail, but a 'pass degree' was not in this framework awarded to a failed honours student; throughout the nineteenth century it represented a different course of study. Edwin Cannan, for example, elected to sit in 1884 for a pass degree and not honours because of poor health.

[9] In Oxford a 'double first' originally meant that a student had gained first-class honours in both classics and mathematics; in Cambridge, a 'double first' meant in the twentieth century being placed in the first class in both Parts I and II of a Tripos, whatever the subject in which this was achieved.

[10] Curthoys, 'The Examination System', p. 344.

[11] Examiners were drawn from the ranks of college tutors, not from those of university professors.

[12] In 1827 there were 404 candidates, and only six students could be examined per day; until 1849 candidates were only admitted for examination if they could produce a certificate testifying that they had witnessed examinations on two previous occasions; public oral examination remained a feature of the system until the 1880s; Curthoys, 'The Examination System', pp. 345ff.

[13] Ibid., p. 347.

examination were required to respond to questions in writing while they waited, their responses then being used in determining a final assessment. A formal five-day written examination period became established in the 1830s, with an oral religious test surviving in Oxford in which failure could still negate excellence in other subjects. Marking in Oxford was by letter of the Greek alphabet, with the addition of pluses and minuses; candidates could not therefore be assigned to numerical ranges, excluding the possibility of ranking graduates ordinally from highest to lowest.[14]

The Intercollegiate and University Lecture Systems

Once this system was established, it became difficult to persuade students to study anything that fell outside the syllabus, represented by the list of books on which they were prepared to be examined. As a consequence, student attendance at university lectures was very limited—attendance at all lectures fell following the reforms of 1800 and 1807,[15] fewer than half the auditors being students, and in the case of history lectures in 1817, only seven students being recorded as attending.[16] Since the range of subjects to be covered in university examinations also now overtaxed individual college tutors, ambitious students began to engage the services of private tutors who guided their study. In response, colleges developed the college tutorial system that replicated the personal bond between student and private coach, re-establishing the centrality of the college to study in Oxford. The 'traditional' weekly college tutorial as the central element of tuition was therefore consolidated in the later nineteenth century as a response to the employment by students of extra-collegial coaches.[17] Up until around 1870, it was usual for those graduating with first-class honours to have used private coaches; as in Cambridge, private tuition was more advanced and structured than anything available in college, and was used by stronger, rather than weaker, candidates.

Linked to the adoption of the weekly college tutorial was the emergence of an intercollegiate lecturing system, a development pioneered by college history tutors that allowed each of them to specialise more fully than they were otherwise able, organised through a History Tutors' Association founded in 1869 that met termly to organise teaching.[18] This development strengthened the position of college tutors as against university professors, in effect isolating the professoriate; but it also converted the college lecture from classroom catechism, delivered to a small number of students[19]

[14] Christopher Stray, 'From Oral to Written Examinations: Cambridge, Oxford and Dublin 1700–1914', *History of Universities* Vol. XX/2 (2005), pp. 99–100.

[15] It was quickly discovered that the 1800 statute included too many subjects; in 1807 mathematics and physics were separated out, law and Hebrew dropped, establishing the broad range of Literae Humaniores subjects—Richard Jenkyns, 'The Beginning of Greats, 1800–1872. I. Classical Studies', in Brock, Curthoys, *History Vol. VI Part I* (1997), p. 513.

[16] Brock, 'The Oxford of Peel and Gladstone', pp. 19–20.

[17] William Ashley, for example, worked as a history coach for three years until his appointment as a Fellow of Lincoln College in 1885.

[18] M. G. Brock, 'A Plastic Structure', in Brock, Curthoys, *History Vol. VII Part 2* (2000), p. 47.

[19] 'The general system of these [college] lectures may be described as that of reading through the principal books of the course (chiefly the Greek and Latin ones,) chapter by chapter, book by book, the men construing in turns, the Tutor correcting, questioning and illustrating.... The thorough knowledge of

drawn from the same college, into something more like a university lecture, in which the lecturer no longer had a personal connection with his auditors.[20] In addition, this intercollegiate system itself became an obstacle to the development of any specialisation in political economy, since it promoted diversity and weakened the role of the university; a larger, specialised role for political economy required support at the university level, together with a degree of standardisation, and the power of college tutors in the Oxford teaching system militated against this.

A university professorship had indeed been established in 1825 with the Drummond Chair in Political Economy, but this remained of marginal relevance for Oxford students throughout the nineteenth century.[21] As Burrows's handbook emphasised, 'The Professor's lectures must be considered as *supplementary* to the College Tutor's, and by no means as a substitute for them',[22] this being true until the final year for the honours candidate, after Moderations has been passed, when they could be considered 'the crowning part, the finishing polish of the University course'[23] in those subjects directly relevant to honours examination. As noted earlier, the new system of study and examination that had developed in 1800 and 1807 led students to focus strictly on material that was examined, providing little incentive for attendance at university lectures. Later, with the development of intercollegiate lectures, formal college tuition entirely bypassed professorial lectures.

The conditions originally attached to the Drummond Chair further limited any impact it might have made on the study of political economy in Oxford. Until 1868, incumbents could hold the chair for five years only; two years had to elapse before an incumbent could be re-elected, so discouraging the holder from embarking upon any independent initiative linked to the teaching of political economy. The terms of the appointment required only that a short course of annual lectures be delivered in the university, unrelated to the actual courses of study followed by Oxford students. Besides Nassau Senior, who was twice elected to the chair (1825–1830, and 1847–1852), early incumbents were drawn from the clergy (Richard Whately held the chair from 1830

certain books is still, and, we may hope, will always be, the characteristic of the Oxford system . . . '. Montagu Burrows, *Pass and Class. An Oxford Guide-Book through the Courses of Literæ Humaniores, Mathematics, Natural Science, and Law and Modern History*, J. H. and Jas. Parker, Oxford 1860, pp. 49–50.

20 A significant shift in relationship, not dissimilar to the impact of modularisation in British universities during the early 1990s. Replacing a situation in which a lecturer addressed students all of whom were progressing through the courses taught by one department, any one lecture course having a place within a progressive teaching structure established by teaching staff, the module assembled a heterogeneous group of students who might, or might not, share a common understanding of the subject matter. As a consequence, lecture courses shifted away from progressive specialisation over three years to the rehearsal of textbook-based material, a change reinforced and accelerated by rapidly-deteriorating student-staff ratios. Teaching became increasingly generic, departments could no longer design coherent courses of study, and qualification resulted from the accumulation of grades rather than the completion of a course of study designed, delivered, and monitored by teaching staff. Departments lost control of their subjects, and teaching staff became agents delivering generic courses.

21 For an account of early holders of the Drummond chair, see Richard Brent, 'God's Providence: Liberal Political Economy as Natural Theology at Oxford 1825–1862', in Michael Bentley (ed.) *Public and Private Doctrine. Essays in British History Presented to Maurice Cowling*, Cambridge University Press, Cambridge 1993, pp. 85–114.

22 Burrows, *Pass and Class*, p. 54.

23 Ibid., p. 56.

to 1831, succeeded in 1832 by William Forster Lloyd of Christ Church, Oxford, until 1837); while Herman Merivale (1837–1841) was a senior civil servant and Travers Twiss a lawyer who also held the Regius Chair of Civil Law at Oxford (1841–1846). George Rickards (1852–1857) was a practising barrister, and Charles Neate (1857–1862) was a fellow of Oriel College Oxford who had briefly practised as a barrister and who was MP for Oxford 1863 to 1868. In 1862 Thorold Rogers was elected and this marked a shift in the nature of the appointment, if not its function, since Rogers also held the Tooke Chair of Statistics and Economic Science at King's College London from 1859 and is chiefly remembered as the author of the seven-volume *History of Agriculture and Prices in England from 1259 to 1793* published from 1866 to 1902. He was succeeded in 1868 by Bonamy Price, who was re-elected under changed statutes until his death in 1888, creating for the first time continuity in the post. While some of these appointees did publish on matters relating to contemporary economic theory and policy, they were quite marginal to the development of the teaching and study of political economy in the university. While there was a similar story in Cambridge until Henry Fawcett began lecturing to pass men[24], the creation of the Moral Sciences Tripos in 1848 had there provided a framework that by the later 1860s made the systematic study of political economy possible. By contrast, the Modern History School in Oxford was not created until 1872, and given the contemporary development of intercollegiate lecturing, the prospects for any expansion in the study of political economy remained limited; any such initiative would require revision of the examination structure, and this remained closely linked to the classical curriculum into the twentieth century.

Classics and History

Before 1850 the Oxford BA had been awarded on the basis of two examinations. Responsions (the 'Little-Go') was introduced in 1808 as an elementary examination in Greek, Latin, and Logic or Euclid.[25] This was initially taken at the end of the first or second year, whereas the public examination (the 'Great-Go') was taken at the end of the third or fourth year and covered the rudiments of religion and those subjects described in 1807 as belonging to Literae Humaniores.[26] After 1850, Moderations was added to these two examinations as a second intermediate stage,[27] taken at the end of the second year and comprising a pass and honours examination in classical subjects and a voluntary examination in mathematics. This rearrangement established Greats in a form that would continue until 1968—studying literary texts for Moderations, followed by history and philosophy.[28] In 1825 a separate Board of Examiners had been

[24] See pp. 87–88.
[25] For the content of Responsions, see Burrow, *Pass and Class*, pp. 63–64.
[26] The 'Examination Statute' of 1800 stipulated that the subjects to be studied for the degree of BA were Grammar, Rhetoric, Logic, Moral Philosophy, and the Elements of Mathematics and Physics, special stress being placed on the knowledge of Greek and Latin writers. Between 1807 and 1825 candidates for honours were expected to be familiar with the works of 20 classical authors.
[27] Burrow, *Pass and Class*, pp. 65ff.
[28] Jenkyns, 'The Beginning of Greats', p. 514.

established for mathematics, candidates being able to sit for this subject three weeks after they had sat for Literae Humaniores, which itself remained compulsory for all students until 1864. This model was followed in the changes introduced in 1850, when examinations in natural science, law, or history could be sat after Literae Humaniores; but since this required up to another year of study, the new subjects had a limited appeal. Single-subject specialisation became possible after 1864: a Theology Honours School was established in 1869, and Honours Schools for Jurisprudence and Modern History in 1872. A separate Pass School for Literae Humaniores was also established in 1872 for which students studied three subjects and a language, on the lines of the London BA. This was a significant innovation since it enabled students to study modern languages, ancient and modern history, together with literary and scientific subjects; but few opted for languages or science. In fact, most students opted to study Greek philosophical works and a Greek or Latin historian, a course described as 'pass Greats'. Within this new schema it was also possible to study some elementary political economy: this proved popular, because it was easy.

The movement for any kind of specialisation in Oxford was hampered by this resilience of the classical curriculum. Moral Philosophy, Politics, and History were until the 1870s understood as subjects to be taught exclusively within the classical curriculum, using classical texts. Adam Smith's *Wealth of Nations* is noted in *Pass and Class* as a suitable book to be read for the Second Final School in Law and Modern History,[29] although Burrows considered it to be a valuable work that was nonetheless generally neglected. Indeed, even as late as 1907, specialisation was described as 'most foreign to the spirit and traditions of Oxford'.[30] Until 1887 all Oxford students had to spend at least the first year of their study working for a mainly classical examination. In 1886 a waiver was achieved for those students intending to specialise in the natural sciences; but the ambition at that time of establishing an honours Moderation examination in ancient and modern history failed, and so for another 30 years the only way that students wishing to graduate in history could avoid classical Moderations was by sitting the jurisprudence preliminary examination that the lawyers had likewise established in 1886. Limited proposals for historical papers in pass Moderations were defeated in 1897; not until 1914 did historians gain their own Previous examination.[31]

Significant also here was the way that Responsions, the first university examination sat by Oxford students, gradually became an examination of work done at school before entering Oxford, some colleges requiring their students to sit this at the end of the first term of residence, and offering no tuition for the examination. Exemption from Responsions could be gained by possessing one of an extending list of pre-university qualifications; and while there was no university entrance examination before 1914, Responsions or a prior recognised qualification became a hurdle that the student had to clear in order to proceed beyond the first year of study at Oxford. Given the continuing importance of a school curriculum centred upon classics and mathematics,

[29] Burrow, *Pass and Class*, p. 211. W. P. Emerson (ed.) *Questions and Answers in Political Economy*, James Thornton, Oxford 1879 assembled questions that had been set in Oxford, and the book was ordered in line with Henry Fawcett's *Manual of Political Economy*.

[30] Curthoys, 'The Examination System', p. 355, citing *Oxford and the Nation: by some Oxford tutors*, reprinted from articles in *The Times*.

[31] Curthoys, 'The Examination System', pp. 355–56.

the development of Responsions into a form of entrance examination further entrenched these subjects in the Oxford curriculum.

Turning to patterns in the degrees actually obtained by students, by the later part of the nineteenth century some 70% of students entering an Oxford college graduated with either an honours or a pass degree—honours rising from 40% to 50% of all students over the 20 years from 1880.[32] Among honours students, those graduating in modern history eclipsed Literae Humaniores in 1898, becoming the subject with the greatest number of graduates and accounting for some one-third of all honours graduates by 1914.[33] This numerical pre-eminence was, however, moderated by the fact that modern history was generally regarded as the easiest of the honours schools. In 1910 most of those classed in Literae Humaniores, mathematics, and natural science gained first- or second-class degrees. By contrast, about 60% of those classed in jurisprudence, modern history, and theology gained thirds and fourths. While strong in numbers, graduates in history were uneven in quality; and because of the framework in which they were taught, they did not necessarily command the kind of analytical skills that Marshall sought to inculcate in Cambridge students.

Indeed, as appointments to the higher levels of the civil service increasingly presupposed that candidates possessed an honours degree, Oxford classicists came to predominate in recruitment. Early on, Oxford graduates captured a significant share of Indian Civil Service (ICS) appointments after the ending of East India College's monopoly, accounting for one-third of appointments from 1855 to 1859.[34] In 1876 the age limit for acceptance into the ICS was reduced to 19, 'probationers' being then permitted to spend two years at Oxford in an arrangement not dissimilar to that previously typical of East India College. This change was seized upon by the Master of Balliol, Benjamin Jowett: he wrote to every candidate and appointed Arnold Toynbee as a tutor for the ICS probationers. Of 255 candidates selected for the ICS during the period 1878–1885, 51 went to Cambridge, and 161 to Oxford, of which 103 went to Balliol.[35] On Toynbee's death, Alfred Marshall succeeded him as ICS tutor; when Marshall moved to Cambridge, John Neville Keynes took his place in 1885.[36] The presence of so many ICS students during the 1880s represented an important constituency for the study of political economy.

However, as already noted in Chapter 3, the idea of making entry to the home civil service conditional on open competition through examination ran decades ahead of reality: in the twenty-four years following implementation in 1870, the Treasury offered only 232 clerkships; public sector graduate recruitment was still too limited and irregular to support courses of specialised training.[37] Before 1890 the Church had dominated the career patterns of Oxford graduates; after this date, a university education became the norm for higher appointments in the civil service, and when combined with the increasing demand for school and college teachers, the influence of the Church receded. In 1892 the age limit for entry into the ICS was raised again,

[32] Ibid., Figure 11.1, p. 360.
[33] Ibid., Figure 11.2, p. 361.
[34] M. C. Curthoys, 'The Careers of Oxford Men', in Brock, Curthoys, *History Vol. VI Part I* (1997), p. 488.
[35] John Prest, 'Balliol, for example', in Brock, Curthoys, *History Vol. VII Part 2* (2000), p. 164.
[36] Alon Kadish, *Historians, Economists, and Economic History*, Routledge, London 1989, pp. 88–89.
[37] Curthoys, 'Careers', p. 488.

to 23, reopening India Office employment to graduates; in 1895 the examinations for ICS and home civil service were merged, with about 90 appointments being made per year, Oxford and Cambridge accounting for three-quarters of all places before 1914.[38] Oxford here predominated; and the favoured degree was a first in Greats, Oxford classicists taking the majority of places in annual examinations extended to the diplomatic service and the Foreign Office. Of 243 Oxford candidates who were successful in the civil service examination from 1897 to 1901, only 29 had read modern history.

There were then many factors, major and minor, that combined to either hinder the development of any specialised study of political economy in Oxford before 1914, or to divert it away from the course Marshall pursued in Cambridge. Symbolic of this was the *Economic Review*, published by the Oxford University Branch of the Christian Social Union from 1891 to 1914 and which was launched just weeks in advance of the *Economic Journal*. At one level the existence of a dedicated economics journal linked to Oxford indicates the existence of a broad interest in economics, albeit centred upon social questions and so distinct to the *Economic Journal*. On the other hand, association with the Christian Social Union suggests a continuity in Oxford of theological concerns that were out of step with the cultural politics of Cambridge and London, and especially with new civic colleges that would soon become independent universities in their own right.

Edgeworth as Oxford Professor

Very significant, however, was the way that the position of university professors remained marginal to the conduct of teaching. After Bonamy Price died in 1888, Thorold Rogers returned to hold the chair, but he too died in 1890. Neither of them contributed anything to the teaching of political economy in the 1880s; intercollegiate arrangements predominated, and here Balliol was central. The existence of the chair was important enough for William Ashley to apply for the post in 1890;[39] but the subsequent appointment of Francis Edgeworth ensured that whatever leverage the Drummond Professor might have had went unused. Edgeworth had certainly demonstrated with the publication of *Mathematical Psychics* (1881) that he was the foremost British economic theorist; he continued to publish important work, and also in 1891 he became editor of the *Economic Journal*, continuing to play an editorial role up to his death in 1926. But he had neither the interest nor the practical ability to match Marshall's promotion of economics at Cambridge. In person unassuming and deferential, assisting individual students who were capable of appreciating his ability, he entirely lacked the institutional ambition of Marshall. Langford Price walked weekly with Edgeworth, and summed the man up as follows:

> In sheer honesty for my own part I must declare that never, or hardly ever, could I extract from my balancing friend a positive conclusion on matters that allowed room

[38] Ibid., p. 496.

[39] Letter from Ashley to Brentano, 16 October 1890, in H. W. McCready, 'Sir William Ashley: Some Unpublished Letters', *Journal of Economic History* Vol. 15 (1955), p. 35.

> for dispute, except occasionally the damnation of an outrageous fallacy, and strictly that could be labelled negative. Generally Edgeworth hedged. When pressed hard he sought refuge without delay by invoking one, or often more than one, authority, even if they might conflict sometimes, as they were employed in quick sequence. When I examined jointly with him he invariably waited for the verdicts of his colleagues before he disclosed his own, in spite of the fundamental fact that he was a discerning as well as a just judge. In his lectures, I heard, he soon outstripped the reach of understanding of the majority of his hearers, and even the more clever among them naturally dwindled in number, while in his small classes for informal discussion, admirably as he tempted the reluctant to take part, he rarely, if ever, led the way. At the meetings of the Oxford University Political Economy Club he was at his best in summing up, with his habitual extreme courtesy, the varying deliverances of others and he did not shine, it was evident, in introducing the question to be treated. I still remember the look passing slowly but inevitably from perplexed bewilderment to manifest disgust or despairing abandon, on the face of a very able and informed, but also very sensible and just, member of our body, as he listened, trying in vain to follow Edgeworth's subtly intricate if not tortuous statement of the nice refinements of the case in hand. I could not for myself, in particular, indeed truly pretend a capacity to grasp his technical mathematical expositions of economic theory or his elaborate exercises in statistical probabilities, and I must confess, perhaps from ignorance, that I remain doubtful of the utility or enlightenment of the former for most students. I may be anxious on the future but happily they can still master Economics without expert or amateur mathematics; such is my comforting belief. But Edgeworth I know, convinced that Economics as he conceived it was so intrinsically hard a study that it could not possibly be made popularly plain, by his own mode of approach, I fear, increased repellant difficulty.[40]

However talented Edgeworth was as an economist, he plainly lacked the kind of qualities that Marshall had needed to persist in his pursuit of an Economics Tripos.

In October 1891 Edgeworth gave his inaugural lecture as Drummond Professor of Political Economy, and from its opening lines the presentational style to which Price alludes above was fully on display:

> Many of those who have spoken on occasions similar to the present, have signalized their entrance on the work of a Professor by indicating the scope and method of the science professed.[41]

The overwhelming majority of his contemporaries did not speak or write in this way; but this circumlocutory style was characteristic of his writing, remaining determinedly archaic while presenting very modern ideas. It might be assumed that, given Edgeworth's command of mathematical economics, his writings would be marked by

[40] L. L. Price, *Memories and Notes on British Economists 1881–1947*, unpublished typescript, 1946, p. 32. University of Leeds Special Collections MS 107.

[41] F. Y. Edgeworth, 'An Introductory Lecture on Political Economy', *Economic Journal* Vol. 1 (1891), p. 625.

the formality and conciseness of expression that became usual in leading economic periodicals by the mid-twentieth century. But as already noted,[42] it was Pigou, writing in the pages of the *Economic Journal*, who pioneered the 10-page article in plain language with diagrams, not Edgeworth, whose articles could be lengthy and appear in several parts over a long period.

Another presumption might be that, disregarding these personal idiosyncracies, the appointment of Edgeworth would inevitably disrupt the Oxford focus upon classics and history. But Edgeworth was himself a product of Oxford, of Balliol even, gaining a First in Literae Humaniores in 1869. Arguing for economic education in his inaugural, he noted that

> ... the history of theory is particularly instructive in political economy as in philosophy. History and literature, dialectics, and all that the Greeks comprehensively call *words*, seem the best corrective of the narrow prejudices and deceptive associations which are sure to be contracted by those who have been confined to a single school or system. Words indeed in a literal sense require the attention of the economist as well as the philosopher.[43]

And while he went on to argue that economics was the study of maxima and minima, and that here differential calculus was an essential tool, he concluded by suggesting that it was 'impossible to overrate the importance of the historical method', commending the work of Ashley.[44]

Ashley had established an 'Economic Society' in October 1886, meetings to be held twice a term; at the third meeting on 1 March 1887, Cannan read a paper on 'The Economic Conception of Capital', with Cannan then succeeding Ashley as Secretary in 1888 when Ashley went to Toronto. By October 1890 the Society had its twenty-third meeting at which six members were present; in June 1891 the Society was reconstituted with Edgeworth as President and a formal programme issued; but then, after one more meeting at which Hewins presented a paper, it foundered.[45] If Edgeworth was not able to sustain a university society that had existed for several years, then the prospects of his succeeding in raising the profile of economics within the University of Oxford were slight. He did, however, fulfil his teaching obligations conscientiously, providing lectures on general theory, applied topics, and statistics, but as before, college tutors organised and provided teaching oriented to the examinations, and these tutors were for the most part historians, not economists.[46]

[42] See Chapter 6, pp. 142–43.

[43] Edgeworth, 'Introductory Lecture', p. 628.

[44] Ibid., p. 633.

[45] 'E.C. and the Oxford Economic Society 1886-91', Cannan Collection Box 905, British Library of Political and Economic Science Archives. This Economic Society must be distinguished from Oxford's Political Economy Club, which was a dining club for graduates of the university of at least three years' standing plus 'gentlemen eminent as economists or distinguished in commerce', with membership limited to 40, a maximum of 30 ordinary and 10 honorary members—'Rules of the Oxford University Political Economy Club (MDCCCXC)' p. 3. Discussion took place after dining, with members only being able to speak once on a question, lengthy written papers being 'inadmissible'. Miscellaneous Papers of the Political Economy Club, Oxford University 1879–1923 (Bodleian Library G. A. Oxon. 80 258; 40 499).

[46] Kadish, *Historians*, pp. 96–97.

The Oxford Diploma in Economics and the PPE

Change came in 1903, following on from events in Cambridge. First, Marshall had published his *Plea for the Creation of a Curriculum in Economics and associated branches of Political Science* as a pamphlet in early April, supported later that month by a Memorial presented to the Council of the Senate signed by 130 members, asking that a committee be appointed to investigate the possibilities for enlarging the study of economics in Cambridge. Then, on 12 May 1903, members of Oxford University's Convocation presented a 'Memorial as to Economics' to Hebdomadal Council, likewise arguing for an extension of economic studies in Oxford. The previous year Langford Price had sent an open letter to the Vice Chancellor arguing the case for economics teaching, but given the greater detail of Marshall's *Plea* the Council opted to consult that document. The proposals differed in that Marshall sought a new honours degree, while in Oxford there was no support for anything of this kind. Marshall's *Plea* did not involve an argument for the teaching of pure economics, and so any comparable Oxford proposal would have involved potential competition with the established teaching of classics and history, where politics was part of the former and economic history part of the latter. In Cambridge, by the time that Marshall composed his *Plea*, historians and moral scientists were so irritated by his constant complaints that they were only too glad to see economics removed from their teaching and placed in a new specialised Tripos. Here again, Edgeworth lacked the abrasiveness and determination that drove Marshall's project to success; also, unlike Marshall, who believed that it took three years to make an economist, Edgeworth thought that economics could be quickly learned by anyone with a good first degree; preferably a degree in classics, like his own.[47]

Agreement to provide for a Diploma in Economics as a two-year postgraduate course in the autumn of 1903 was helped by the parallel establishment of Diplomas in other fields—in Geography (1900), then Scientific Engineering and Mining Subjects (1904), Anthropology (1905), and Classical Archaeology (1907). The course included two compulsory papers in economic theory and one in economic history, plus two special subjects to be chosen from among topics in economic theory, economic history, and applied economics. In 1909 topics in political science were added, including the history of political ideas and constitutional history, thus moving toward what would later become the PPE.[48] The first three candidates examined in 1905 had a First and a Second from the Modern History School, while the third had a degree from the University of Paris. There were five candidates in 1906, two of whom were Rhodes Scholars. The foundation of Ruskin Hall in 1899 as a college for disadvantaged working-class students provided many candidates for the new diploma: after the first two candidates gained distinctions in 1910, the following year Ruskin students took 8 out of 13 distinctions, and 4 of 12 passes; in 1912, 6 of 12 distinctions and 6 of 13 passes; while in 1913 they took 6 of 13 distinctions and 7 of 15 passes.[49] From another

[47] Norman Chester, *Economics, Politics and Social Studies in Oxford, 1900–1985*, Macmillan, London 1986, p. 11.

[48] Ibid., pp. 13–14.

[49] Ibid., p. 21.

perspective, the number of students passing examinations was very significant: 25 in 1911, 25 in 1912, and 28 in 1913 graduating with an Oxford Diploma compares with 5, 13, and 9 students, respectively, graduating in these years from the Cambridge Part II examination. These were significant numbers by the standards of any institution offering an economic education in Britain at that time.[50]

A later prospectus outlined five different classes of student for whom the Diploma was intended—those intending to follow a career in business; those intending to enter public administration and politics; those who had a personal interest in economic and political affairs—plus foreigners seeking a knowledge of English economic thought and practice, and women 'who may belong to any of the above'.[51] As for the kind of economics to be taught, the *Prospectus* stated, 'By Economic Theory is meant the Principles of Economics as expounded in modern treatises', going on to specify Mill's *Principles of Political Economy* as the main text, supplemented by 'some recent treatises': by Alfred Marshall (1890), Arthur Hadley (1896), Shield Nicholson (1893–1901), and Henry Sidgwick (1883).[52] When these sources are set in the context of the detailed course outline, it is evident that in 1917 the Oxford Diploma was a long way from the Cambridge model that had originally provided the basis for discussion leading to its creation.

Given that the only university teaching available in 1904 was the lecturing of the Drummond Professor, teaching for the Diploma was reliant primarily upon the established intercollegiate model of lecturing, coupled with college tutorials. In other words, the way that economics was taught in Oxford was determined by the fact that the principal academic interest of those who taught it was not economics, but history or classics. In 1907 a Lectureship in Economic History was created, to which Langford Price was appointed, promoted to Reader in 1909; while in 1910 All Souls appointed N. B. Dearle to a Fellowship in Political Economy. Correspondingly, in 1909 a Lectureship in Political Theory and Institutions was established, first converted into a Readership with funding from All Souls, then in 1912 endowed as the Gladstone Chair in Political Theory and Institutions. Hence in the early 1900s appointments were made that would sustain the teaching of economics and politics in Oxford, while still relying primarily on college tutors who came primarily from a historical background. Between 1910 and 1913 an initiative aimed at establishing a Diploma in Commerce and Economics was discussed, and then rejected; and then, in May 1915, Hebdomadal Council accepted a proposal to establish a degree in 'Political Economy, Political Science and Public Law'. By the time that the committee established to examine the proposal reported, this had become a two-year postgraduate master's degree in Civil Science, but in any case, discussion stalled in the course of 1916. When discussion resumed in 1919 it was based on a new initiative: a decision by the Faculty of Literae Humaniores to entertain the prospect of teaching philosophy

[50] According to a note in the *Economic Journal*, in the years 1905–1918, 231 candidates had presented themselves for examination, 96 gaining distinctions and 99 being awarded a pass; 19 of these successful candidates were women. Ruskin students had notched up a total of 26 Distinctions, Rhodes Scholars 20. Unsigned note, *Economic Journal* Vol. 28 (1918) p. 468.

[51] *Prospectus for Oxford Diploma in Economics and Political Science* (1917), p. 3, Bodleian Library G. A. Oxon 8 900 (6).

[52] Ibid., pp. 8, 11.

without connecting it to ancient history in the established fashion. This initiative would in the following year turn into a new undergraduate degree in Philosophy, Politics, and Economics.

Novel in this proposal was the explicit restriction of the curriculum to modernity: no further back in philosophy than Descartes, no further back in economics than Smith's *Wealth of Nations* of 1776.[53] At this stage the natural sciences were also involved, but this was dropped in favour of a course that quickly became known as 'Modern Greats', the Literae Humaniores Board proposing that candidates could specialise in philosophy, politics, or economics, but would be required to take papers from all three subjects. In so doing they put forward a scheme in which six of the nine papers offered could be read in terms of philosophy, while only four were open to economists—reflecting the earlier concern on the part of philosophers that their student numbers were falling. There followed a considerable amount of discussion and dispute, and by the time the list of subjects for examination was laid down in November 1920 there were eight papers, two of which were in philosophy, one in economics, with a further two papers that could be oriented to any one of the three main subjects.[54] A student graduating with a PPE degree might therefore have sat one paper in economics and seven in the other two subjects; or, alternatively, a maximum of three papers in economics and five in the other subjects. The limitations of this Statute were amplified in the specification for Paper VI, where candidates had to offer prescribed books from two of the three subjects, those for economics being Smith's *Wealth of Nations*, Ricardo's *Works* in the McCulloch edition, Marx's *Capital Vol. I*, Jevons's *Theory of Political Economy*, and List's *National System of Political Economy*.[55] The elementary level of the economics taught is also apparent from revisions made in the 1930s; Chester reports that in 1933 Pass Moderations set Gide's *Principles* together with Shield Nicolson's *Elements of Political Economy*, a one-volume synopsis of his *Principles of Political Economy* first published in 1903.[56]

The very different approaches in Oxford and Cambridge to the teaching of economics are underscored by their juxtaposition in the summary published in the *Economic Journal* in 1921. This was occasioned by the new Oxford degree, together with recent changes to the Cambridge Economics Tripos. Evident in the former is not only the breadth, but the absence of what would become known as 'applied economics', the application of economic theory to specific problems. Also evident in the Oxford curriculum is that Jevons's *Theory of Political Economy* (1871) is the most modern text referred to. By contrast, the two-part Cambridge Tripos combines papers on theory, economic history, and applied economics (in Part I, papers on Industry and Labour, and Trade and Finance; in Part II, Public Finance, Structure and Problems of Industry).[57] The only text cited in the summary of Cambridge teaching is Marshall's *Principles of Economics*, while the listing of topics for 'Structure and Problems of Industry' quite clearly bears on the contents of Marshall's *Industry and Trade* (1919).

[53] Chester, *Economics, Politics and Social Studies in Oxford*, p. 31.
[54] Ibid., p. 38.
[55] Anon., 'The Economic Curricula at Oxford and Cambridge', *Economic Journal* Vol. 31 (1921), p. 402.
[56] Chester, *Economics, Politics and Social Studies in Oxford*, p. 39.
[57] Anon, 'Economic Curricula', p. 403.

These are plainly two very different educational strategies, and only the Cambridge curriculum provided a replicable foundation for the study and teaching of economics as an independent subject.

As such, then, Cambridge represented a foundation for disciplinary development that Oxford did not. On the other hand, we also know that the PPE degree was very far from being a failure. In the early twenty-first century it remains the premium British undergraduate qualification for those who seek a career in politics, public administration, and the media—the objective for which Marshall had designed the Economics Tripos, and which turned out to be effective as a means of disciplinary development, but ineffective in the pedagogical purpose for which it was intended. Indeed, by the later twentieth century there would be a widening gulf between what private- and public-sector employers wanted from their graduate recruits,[58] and what a graduate with a degree in economics had been trained to do. These labour market issues—the way in which a given educational structure can mismatch labour market demand, and the possibility that reform of the first will increase, rather than diminish, problems in the second—will be touched on in Part IV But since my aim in this chapter is to explain why Oxford did not—could not—provide a platform upon which a new discipline of economics took shape, I need here do no more than sketch out what eventually, by the 1950s, became a recognisable 'Oxford economics'.[59] For by the 1930s, when this 'Oxford economics' first took shape, the initiative in disciplinary development had already passed from Cambridge to the LSE, and was in the process of being consolidated in the United States.

One part of the interwar Oxford story was that, despite the limitations of the PPE degree as a means of specialised teaching in economics, several notable economists did take the course, while economists trained elsewhere moved to Oxford to teach it.[60] Among those who graduated with a PPE who were then appointed to teach in Oxford were Robert Hall (1927), R. F. Bretherton (1928), Henry Phelps Brown (1930), Evelyn Wilson (1930), and James Meade (1930). Roy Harrod was appointed Lecturer in Modern History and Economics at Christ Church in 1922, having gained a first in Literae Humaniores the same year. Other notable interwar PPE graduates were E. F. Schumacher (1911–1977),[61] Harold Wilson (1916–1995),[62] and Hugh Gaitskell (1906–1963).[63] Lionel Robbins, Maurice Allen, and Redvers Opie were appointed to

[58] A gap that accounts for the development of business education in the course of the twentieth century, where formal economics played an ever-decreasing role.

[59] Besides Norman Chester's detailed institutional history, Warren Young and Fred Lee have provided a detailed account of 'Oxford economics'—see their *Oxford Economics and Oxford Economists*, Macmillan, London 1993. If we also take account of the work of Alon Kadish, the development of economics teaching and research in Oxford is far more thoroughly and reliably covered than that in Cambridge.

[60] For an overview of developments to mid-century see Robert Currie, 'The Arts and Social Studies, 1914–1939', in Brian Harrison (ed.) *The History of the University of Oxford*, Vol. VIII: *The Twentieth Century*, Oxford University Press, Oxford 1994, pp. 109–38.

[61] Schumacher was from 1950 to 1970 Chief Economic Adviser to the National Coal Board, but is remembered chiefly as the author of *Small Is Beautiful: A Study of Economics as if People Mattered*, Blond and Briggs, London 1973.

[62] Wilson was elected to Parliament in 1945, became Leader of the Labour Party in 1963, and served two terms as Prime Minister—1964–1970 and 1974–1976.

[63] Gaitskell taught economics at University College London during the 1930s, entered Parliament in 1945, and became leader of the Labour Party in 1955.

teaching posts during the same period. As Young and Lee note, by the 1930s an emphasis was emerging in Oxford on combining theoretical and applied work,[64] belying the historical bias of teaching that had lasted into the early part of the century. This was reinforced by the creation of the Institute of Statistics in 1935, directed until 1939 by Jakob Marschak;[65] and the move in the later 1930s for the establishment of a new college specialising in the applied social sciences, which emerged in 1944–1945 as Nuffield College.[66]

Besides these institutional matters, in 1936 two young Oxford economists published the first post-Marshallian economic textbooks: James Meade's *An Introduction to Economic Analysis and Policy*, and Henry Phelps Brown's *The Framework of the Pricing System*. While Meade's book would not become as widely-used as Benham's 1938 textbook,[67] it deserves recognition as the first Keynesian, primarily macroeconomic, textbook, and so in terms of scope and theoretical sophistication also rather ahead of Cairncross's *Introduction to Economics*, which although first published in 1944 had mostly been drafted by 1939 and was based on lectures he had been giving to Glasgow accountants since 1935.[68] Phelps Brown's book was less ambitious in scope, but articulated a conception of the connection of theory to empirical inquiry that would come to characterise Oxford economics:

> It tries to present theoretical inquiry so that the student of economics, like the student of mechanics, may be conscious of learning a technique. It lays stress on the unity of the system. It devotes attention to the relation between the abstractions with which it is itself concerned, and the empirical study which must go with them hand in hand.[69]

Notable here is also the distance that has already been travelled from the older methodological framework for economic argument embodied in the design of the PPE curriculum.

The foundation of *Oxford Economic Papers* in 1938 was also indicative of a combination of theory with empirical research that had broad support among Oxford economists, and was not confined to the work of the Institute of Statistics.[70] In its

[64] Young, Lee, *Oxford Economics and Oxford Economists*, p. 21.

[65] Jacob Marschak (1898–1977) was born in Kiev and as a student became a Menshevik, also serving briefly as Commissar for Labour in the Terek Republic. He emigrated to Germany in 1919, studied in Berlin and Heidelberg, worked as a journalist, and then, in 1928, joined the Kiel Institut für Weltwirtschaft, before moving back to Heidelberg as a Privat-Dozent. Stripped of his appointment in April 1933, he moved to Britain and was appointed Lecturer at All Souls, then becoming founding Director of the Oxford Institute of Statistics. After moving to the United States in 1939, he was appointed research director of the Cowles Commission in 1943. See Harald Hagemann, 'European Émigrés and the 'Americanization' of Economics', *European Journal of the History of Economic Thought* Vol. 18 (2011), pp. 657–63.

[66] See Roy Harrod, 'Lord Nuffield's Foundation in Oxford', *Economic Journal* Vol. 47 (1937), pp. 757–61.

[67] Frederic Benham, *Economics. A General Textbook for Students*, Sir Isaac Pitman & Sons, London 1938; see Chapter 12 for an outline of this work.

[68] See Cairncross's outline of this in Tribe (ed.) *Economic Careers. Economics and Economists in Britain 1930–1970*, Routledge, London 1997, pp. 42–43.

[69] E. H. Phelps Brown, *The Framework of the Pricing System*, Chapman and Hall, London 1936, p. vi.

[70] See, for detailed discussion of work in the later 1930s, Daniele Besomi, 'Roy Harrod and the Oxford Economists' Research Group's Inquiry on Prices and Interest, 1936–39', *Oxford Economic Papers* Vol. 50 (1998), pp. 534–62.

second number, Hall and Hitch—an Australian and an American—published some results of work on pricing that had been pursued in Oxford based on a survey of business practice. Rather than speculate about markets and prices, Oxford economists had devised and administered a questionnaire to businessmen, and then conducted interviews with 38 of them based on their responses to the questionnaire. Having reviewed recent theoretical advances in the understanding of market structure and pricing policy, the research demonstrated that firms did not set their prices in the way that economic theory would presume, equating marginal cost and marginal price; or, more exactly, firms apparently behaved in a uniformly irrational manner.[71]

That Hall and Hitch were, respectively, Australian and American was also significant here in marking Oxford off from Cambridge, where both teaching staff and their interests were relatively detached from the increasingly international nature of research and publication in economics. This was not true of the LSE even in the 1920s, where an American, Allyn Young, had been recruited as successor to Edwin Cannan as Professor of Political Economy in 1926. Unlike in Oxford, however, there was a strong tendency by the 1930s for LSE economists to presume that reality ought to conform to theory. This attitude was exemplified by Lionel Robbins's *The Great Depression* (1934), which argued that governments could do nothing to mitigate unemployment and that prosperity would return only if the market were permitted to work without hindrance. This was likewise the view of Friedrich Hayek, who was recruited to the LSE in 1931, and who came to symbolise an opposition between Cambridge and the LSE around the axis of pro- and anti-Keynesianism. Oxford was different: unlike Cambridge, it was very open to emigré economists from Continental Europe; but also unlike the LSE, pursued empirically-grounded theoretical economics—as for example in *The Economics of Full Employment*, to which six economists contributed—one Hungarian, one Pole, three Germans, and David Worswick.[72] That the kind of economics done in Oxford would look like this in the mid-twentieth century was not something that could have been easily foreseen from the viewpoint of the later nineteenth, which is where the next chapter begins.

[71] R. L. Hall, C. J. Hitch, 'Pricing Policy and Business Behaviour', *Oxford Economic Papers* No. 2 (May 1939), p. 18. See, for a general discussion of this research project, Young and Lee, *Oxford Economics and Oxford Economists*, pp. 131ff.

[72] T. Balogh, F. A. Burchardt, M. Kalecki, K. Mandelbaum, E. F. Schumacher, G. D. N. Worswick, *The Economics of Full Employment. Six Studies in Applied Economics Prepared at the Oxford University Institute of Statistics*, Basil Blackwell, Oxford 1944.

8
The Unrealised Prospect of Historical Economics

The enthusiasm that greeted publication of Marshall's *Principles of Economics Vol. I* in 1890 was not unalloyed. For adepts it finally provided a ready means of positive self-identification; sceptics, however, saw it more negatively, representing a new pathway for economic knowledge, but an undesirable one. The Cambridge Moral Sciences Tripos formed the backdrop for these positive and negative associations, and the way that Marshall sought to free himself of this framework in creating a new and independent Tripos was a further source of antagonism. Whichever side one stood on this argument about the scope of economics and its proper place, these developments reinforced the association of Cambridge with advanced and specialised work in economics. The previous chapter has demonstrated why it was that the curricular and pedagogic evolution of Oxford obstructed such specialisation; and how in subsequent decades the teaching and study of economics in Oxford continued to follow a path diverging from that of Cambridge economics. All the same, before 1890 Oxford had been an important centre for the study of political economy in Britain. And when Arnold Toynbee died in 1883, Benjamin Jowett, Master of Balliol, appointed Marshall his successor as tutor to the Indian Civil Service (ICS) probationers. Marshall might have ended up trying to establish the new discipline of economics from a base in Oxford—something that would have been very difficult, as the previous chapter has suggested.

The majority of those Oxford students who took an interest in political economy during the 1880s were following courses in modern history, so that their interest in the subject arose out of an engagement with historical studies. This combination fostered two conjoint commitments: an understanding of the development of civilisation that laid emphasis on the economic forces that had shaped this process, hence an economic history; and an understanding of the development of economic ideas that laid emphasis upon the way in which these ideas were moulded by the contexts in which they emerged, hence a historical economics. Together and separately these were associated with ideas of progress and reform at home, while several of these 'Oxford economists' developed into Liberal Imperialists abroad. Very influential here was the teaching of Arnold Toynbee at Balliol College, reinforced by the fact that the audience for such teaching was drawn primarily from ICS Probationers and those studying modern history. Toynbee died in March 1883 having completed during 1881–1882 a course of lectures that were transcribed, edited, and then published in 1884 as *Lectures on the Industrial Revolution in England*, lending political economy a context in a new developmental economic narrative explicitly organised for the first time in terms of

Constructing Economic Science. Keith Tribe, Oxford University Press. © Oxford University Press 2022.
DOI: 10.1093/oso/9780190491741.003.0008

an 'industrial revolution'. The book quickly became a printed programme for the combined study of history and economics.[1]

This circumstance, that interest in political economy in the Oxford of the 1880s combined an interest in history and economy, has in the past been linked to the idea that a distinct school of English historical economists emerged at this time in Oxford among students of a new economic history. However, linked to this story is a narrative suggesting that any possible contribution to the emergent discipline of economics that might have been made by economic historians was soon cut short by the activities of adversaries who succeeded in marginalising the challenge that historical economics and economic history presented to Marshallian economics. Historical economists were thought to have been personally excluded from appointments, most notably as successors to Marshall's chair in 1908; while the study of economic history was said to have been progressively excluded from the training of economists, leading in 1926 to the formation of a separate Economic History Society alongside the Royal Economic Society. Furthermore, this bifurcation is said to have become public during the confrontation in 1903 between liberal economists opposing Joseph Chamberlain's proposals for protection and imperial preference and 'historical economists' who supported these policies. This, broadly, is the story told in Gerard Koot's book *English Historical Economics, 1870–1926*,[2] a story that has been repeated down the years and has more recently resurfaced in William Ashley's *Oxford Dictionary of National Biography* entry.[3]

In this chapter I will argue that there is little evidence for these claims. On the contrary, a distinctive and coherent English historical economics never moved beyond its initial general programmatic statements; there never was a 'school' of historical economists that represented a clear challenge to the new Marshallian synthesis; and it was the *kind* of economic history pursued by Ashley and Cunningham that led to their diminishing influence, not any denial on the part of others that the study of economic history was a valuable resource for understanding economic processes. The greater part of this position was elaborated long ago by Alon Kadish, who spent many years studying Oxford history and economics.[4] My purpose here is more limited: to demonstrate that 'Cambridge prevailed' in the establishment of a new form

[1] The publication history of *Lectures* is not straightforward and is outlined in fn. 16 below; it is, however, significant that there was a second edition in 1887, reprinted in late 1890; a new edition in 1894, reprinted in 1902 and 1906; and a new edition in 1908, reprinted in 1912, 1913, 1916, 1919, 1920, 1923, 1925, and 1927.

[2] Gerard M. Koot, *English Historical Economics, 1870–1926: The Rise of Economic History and Neomercantilism*, Cambridge University Press, Cambridge 1987. Koot builds upon an earlier study, Bernard Semmel's *Imperialism and Social Reform: English Social-Imperial Thought 1895–1914*, George Allen and Unwin, London 1960.

[3] 'Like other British historical economists, notably W. Cunningham, H. S. Foxwell, W. A. S. Hewins, and L. L. Price, Ashley argued that deductive, abstract reasoning could not provide the basis for meaningful or effective theory or practice, and that statements of economic principle were true only in relation to given historical conditions. This historical relativism was anathema to Marshallian, neo-classical economists who were keen to establish economics as a science, and in both academic debate and in the distribution of senior academic appointments the Marshallians sought to marginalize the historical school.' E. H. H. Green, 'Ashley, Sir William James', *Oxford Dictionary of National Biography* (version last revised 3 January 2008).

[4] Most specifically his *The Oxford Economists in the Late Nineteenth Century*, Oxford University Press, Oxford 1982; his biography of Toynbee, *Apostle Arnold. The Life and Death of Arnold Toynbee 1852–1883*, Duke University Press, Durham N.C. 1986; and *Historians, Economists, and Economic History*, Routledge, London 1989.

of economics because there never was a viable programmatic alternative; and I focus upon the work of William Ashley and William Cunningham so that I can trace arguments about economic history and historical economics in the contexts of both Oxford and Cambridge.

Ashley and Cunningham are important to our story here for rather different reasons. William Cunningham (1849–1919) first gained an Edinburgh MA before entering Caius College Cambridge in 1869, graduating joint Senior in the 1872 Moral Sciences Tripos with Frederic Maitland. In a career centred principally upon Cambridge, he combined work as a teacher of economic history with appointments in the Anglican Church (he was Archdeacon of Ely from 1907 until his death). For several years he worked as an extension lecturer, returning to Cambridge in 1878 and finding a niche as a teacher of economic history for the History Tripos. The absence of a suitable textbook led him to publish *The Growth of English Industry and Commerce* in 1882, the first general survey of economic history to appear in English and one that was expanded in subsequent editions. From his base in the History Tripos, and as an examiner on the Moral Sciences Tripos, Cunningham became in the 1890s a staunch critic of Marshall's economics and of his plans for a specialised Economics Tripos. His debates with Marshall are of interest not so much for the substance of his criticism as for the response that they elicited from Marshall. Historiographically his work was quickly overtaken, but it is his standing as an economic historian that is of greatest interest here.

William Ashley

The emphases in Ashley's arguments about history and economics fall differently to those of Cunningham. Born in 1860 in Bermondsey, the same deprived area of London that had been home to Alfred Marshall as a boy, William Ashley (1860–1927) entered Balliol College Oxford in 1878 and graduated with a First in Modern History in 1881.[5] A growing interest in political economy was fostered by Arnold Toynbee, and it was Ashley's notes on Toynbee's last lecture course in 1881–1882 that were used in compiling Toynbee's *Lectures on the Industrial Revolution in England*. After working as a history coach, he was elected to a fellowship at Lincoln College Oxford in 1885, working in the mid-1880s on his *Introduction to English Economic History and Theory* (2 parts, 1888 and 1893). In 1888 he was recruited to a reorganised University of Toronto, where he became Professor of Political Economy and Constitutional Law and worked on the second part of his *Introduction*, which when it appeared in 1893 concluded in the early sixteenth century. Before this was published, Ashley had been recruited by Harvard to fill a new chair of economic history, the first such dedicated chair in the world. He returned to England, however, in 1901 to take up an appointment at the new University of Birmingham, heading the Faculty of Commerce. He

[5] Unfortunately no consistent attempt seems to have been made by Ashley (or perhaps his family) to preserve his papers. For the most part such unpublished material as exists is in the archives of his correspondents or the institutions for whom he worked; the British Library, for example, has papers relating to his official activities during the First World War and after.

remained in this post until his retirement in 1925; diagnosed with cancer, he died in 1927, having played a major role in the foundation of the Economic History Society shortly before his death. Ashley's career thus spans the arc from Toynbee's manifesto for a political economy embedded within a developmental economic history to the abandonment of that ambition in the later 1920s. As we shall see, Ashley did devote a significant part of his teaching to the history of 'economic theory'; but while he did continue to publish on issues of economic history, he never systematically developed his *Introduction* into an account of early modernity that led up to contemporary times.[6] Ashley is nonetheless of more central interest to us than Cunningham, since he embodied a commitment to economic history and historical economics in a way that Cunningham did not.

Ashley would have spent his first year as a student at Balliol reading classics, so that it was only in his second and third years that he was able to focus on the study of history. The University history lectures of the time were designed for students with little knowledge of history, and Ashley's biography records that he attended few.[7] Instead, he would have attended the Balliol College lectures of his tutor, A. L. Smith,[8] presenting Stubbs's *Constitutional History* (1874–1878) and the collection of *Select Charters* (1870).[9] Having decided to focus upon medieval history, he went to Göttingen for a month in 1880 to attend Reinhold Pauli's lectures, which inflected the institutional account of English medieval history he had from Stubbs into German historical sources that dealt with the same period, but took a more systematically economic approach to institutions.[10] By the time he graduated with first class honours in 1881 he was synthesising his Oxford teaching with his German reading,[11] and this is clear from the essay with which he won the Lothian Prize in 1882. Published the following year, we can use this to assess more directly Ashley's understanding of what economic history represented at the time he was attending Toynbee's lectures.

The Prize essay ostensibly deals with two medieval Flemish brothers, James and Philip van Artevelde, and their relationship to the development of urban Flanders. He acknowledged his debt to three main published sources in French, also noting that the account of early fourteenth-century Ghent and other towns had been developed from

[6] The last three of eight lectures he gave in Hamburg in 1912 do extend the framework presented in his *Introduction to English Economic History and Theory* into a general consideration of capitalist development of the later nineteenth century; *The Economic Organisation of England: An Outline History*, Longmans, Green, & Co., London 1914.

[7] A. Ashley, *William James Ashley: A Life*, P. S. King & Son, London 1932, p. 19.

[8] Edwin Cannan commented that as a contemporary of Ashley at Balliol he learned from A. L. Smith 'the truth that all important change is gradual, and that social institutions are not created by the sudden efforts of inspired geniuses but grow "of themselves," usually slower than oak trees.' Cannan, *The Economic Outlook*, T. Fisher Unwin, London 1912, p. 11. Alon Kadish summarises Smith as focussed upon the general course of historical development in which institutions and ideas were treated in relation to the circumstances in which they were created. See Kadish, *Oxford Economists*, pp. 37–38.

[9] Reba N. Soffer, 'Modern History', in M. G. Brock, M. C. Curthoys (eds.) *The History of the University of Oxford*, Vol. VII: *Nineteenth-Century Oxford, Part 2*, Oxford University Press, Oxford 2000, pp. 365–66.

[10] Kadish, *Oxford Economists*, pp. 35–36. He visited Germany again in 1883 and 1884.

[11] Gras reports that Ashley bought a copy of Cliffe Leslie's *Essays* in 1882, read Gustav Schmoller's *Zur Geschichte der deutschen Kleingewerbe im 19. Jahrhundert: statistische und nationalökonomische Untersuchungen* (Halle 1870) in 1886, and in the same year visited Knies in Heidelberg; N. S. B. Gras, 'The Rise and Development of Economic History', *Economic History Review* Vol. 1 (1927), p. 21.

a reading of Georg Ludwig von Maurer,[12] although 'much has to be done before we can quite understand the growth of municipal life.'[13] However, the hinge of his study is the emergence of the town, drawing on Maurer's account of the *Mark* and the formation of the German town:

> The Flemish town may therefore be regarded as springing from a community or aggregation of communities each member of which, besides the farmyard attached to his house and the strips of arable land which he was bound to cultivate according to a general plan—usually the so-called 'three-field system,'—had a right to the use of the mark or common land belonging to the whole body.[14]

While the town was initially distinguished only by perimeter walls, the gradual development of markets transformed towns into centres of commerce, rights initially granted to merchants then being extended to the whole population. Political leadership emerged and, following this, a merchants' guild which became a governing body ruling over an increasingly differentiated set of artisans, the landless poor, and escaped serfs. Hence

> [t]he earlier history of Ghent illustrates with sufficient clearness the general lines of development in other towns—the growth of a burgher oligarchy from the mark community, and the gradual substitution for an hereditary and irresponsible magistracy of one elected and answerable to all the members of the guilds.[15]

From his later writing it is clear that Ashley quickly built up a good working knowledge of contemporary German historical scholarship; but the fluent synthesis that he achieved in his Prize essay was very likely also influenced by his attending Toynbee's lectures, their presentation coinciding with the period following his graduation when he was preparing for the Lothian Prize. And since the *Lectures* were based in part on Ashley's notes, the interesting possibility arises that any convergence we might see between Toynbee's *Lectures* and Ashley's own thinking is because there is a great deal of Ashley in the published form of Toynbee's lectures.

Toynbee's *Lectures*

Toynbee's *Lectures on the Industrial Revolution*[16] was prepared from student notes made by William Ashley and Bolton King, but it is likely that Ashley did most of the

[12] Georg Ludwig von Maurer, *Zur Geschichte der Mark-, Hof-, Dorf- und Stadtverfassung*, Christian Kaiser, Munich 1854. Maurer traced the emergence of public powers from the development of collective agrarian forms into urban and regional entities.

[13] William James Ashley, *James and Philip van Artevelde*, Macmillan, London 1883, p. vi.

[14] Ibid., pp. 10–11.

[15] Ibid., pp. 29–30.

[16] *Lectures on the Industrial Revolution in England, Popular Addresses, Notes and Other Fragments*, Rivingtons, London 1884 was published with a 'Memoir' by Benjamin Jowett (pp. v–xxvii) and a 'Prefatory Note' by Charlotte Toynbee (pp. xxix–xxxi). It was republished as a second edition with the same contents and running order by Rivingtons in 1887 as *Lectures on the Industrial Revolution of the 18th Century in England*. A 'Fourth Edition with Appendix' was published in 1894 by Rivingtons under the same title, the

drafting, converting two sets of student notes and Toynbee's own notes into one continuous narrative. This is mainly because Bolton King did not graduate until 1883, by which time the text was complete; while Ashley was at the time working as a history coach, and so presumably with more free time at his disposal than a student preparing for his final examinations. Alfred Milner put the final touches to the text in collaboration with Toynbee's widow, but he was during this period working as a journalist in London and so not in regular and direct contact with either Ashley or King.[17] We do not know what these original materials looked like, nor do any sources indicate exactly how Toynbee's own working notes and those of his auditors were combined into a continuous narrative. The fact that the book quickly assumed canonical status as the blueprint for a new historical economics has rather distracted attention from the mechanics of the text's composition; but Ashley played a major part in drafting the published text, and so it is possible to read it in relation to Ashley's own writings. For one thing, there are obvious passages in the book that could not have been presented in the course of a lecture, such as the detailed statistical treatment of 'England in 1760'.[18] There are, however, also stylistic and substantive elements of the lectures that strongly suggest that Ashley played a significant part in composing their finished version. Before elaborating this line of thought, however, we first need to understand how Toynbee came to deliver them.

Arnold Toynbee (1852–1883) lacked the systematic schooling of Marshall and Ashley, two youths from poor backgrounds who won university scholarships[19] and

running order being the same as that of the original edition, with the appendix being included after the index. This appendix was the text separately published in 1883 as *'Progress and Poverty', A Criticism of Mr. Henry George. Being Two Lectures Delivered in St. Andrews Hall, Newman Street, London*, Kegan Paul, Trench & Co., London, including also Alfred Milner's 'Prefatory Note' from the 1883 edition on p. 266, in which he explained that the lectures had been transcribed from shorthand notes, but that Toynbee had been too ill to review them. Milner here notes 'trifling and obvious corrections' that he had made to the transcripts of these two lectures, so carrying no implication about the editing he had done for the *Lectures* published in 1884. The work then appeared as a 'New Edition' in 1908 with the title *Lectures on the Industrial Revolution of the Eighteenth Century in England*, now published by Longmans, Green, and Co. In this edition 'Ricardo and the Old Political Economy' was moved from its original position at the front of the 14 lectures of 1881–1882 to follow them; this edition also has a revised 'Prefatory Note' by Charlotte Toynbee (pp. v–viii) and a 'Reminiscence' (pp. ix–xxx) by Alfred Milner that replaces Jowett's contribution, and which reproduces an address he had given at Toynbee Hall in 1894. The two Henry George lectures added to the 1894 edition were excluded from the 1908 edition and all future printings. The 14 lectures were also reprinted as *The Industrial Revolution*, Beacon Press, Boston 1956.

17 Bolton King (1860–1937) entered Balliol to study history in 1879, the year after Ashley, and took a First in 1883. His connection with Toynbee related more to social reform than to economic history, being closely involved in the foundation of Toynbee Hall, where he lived and taught until 1892. Alfred Milner (1854–1925) entered New College, Oxford as a classics student in 1873, and quickly formed a close friendship with Toynbee. He graduated with first class honours in 1876, then was a Fellow of New College 1876–1879, after which he moved to London and was called to the bar in 1881. In 1882 he joined the staff of the *Pall Mall Gazette*, and began his movement into national politics in 1884, when he became private secretary to G. J. Goschen, the Liberal politician. By 1886 Goschen was Chancellor of the Exchequer in Salisbury's cabinet as a Liberal Unionist, and Milner moved with Goschen to the Treasury. Milner's career as a Liberal Imperialist developed apace; in 1897 he was appointed High Commissioner for South Africa, in which post he played no small part in causing the Boer War. See Colin Newbury, 'Milner, Alfred, Viscount Milner', *Oxford Dictionary of National Biography* [4 October 2008].

18 Toynbee, *Lectures* (1884), pp. 34ff.

19 Alfred Marshall won a scholarship to St. John's College Oxford, but wishing to study mathematics, he borrowed money from his uncle and entered St. John's College Cambridge instead.

went on to graduate with outstanding first class honours. His family was also much better off—his father was a successful London physician who unfortunately died while experimenting with chloroform as an anaesthetic in 1866. As a child Arnold Toynbee had envisaged a career in the army, attending a military prep school before leaving it in 1868 and spending two years reading unsystematically, developing what Alon Kadish calls 'grandiose projects'.[20] Plans to prepare for the Civil Service examinations quickly dissolved, replaced by an ambition to read for the bar. This likewise faded. He then took himself off to remote rural places, where he would read in solitude. Perhaps the one positive feature of all this was his habit of closely reading one book at a time; although this also had the disadvantage that while he came to have great confidence in what he knew, the breadth of his reading remained quite limited. Partly as a result of this, he never wrote if he could talk, as his wife later acidly observed;[21] writing for readers demands preparation, and the process reveals gaps in knowledge and argument that flights of rhetoric can gloss over.

Influenced in his choice of college by a tutor engaged to repair his ignorance of the classics, he entered Pembroke College, Oxford, in January 1873, passed the initial examination, and during the summer made plans to prepare for the Brackenbury Scholarship that would allow a transfer to Balliol College. In November 1873 he sat the examination and failed—in part, as one of his examiners explained, because he had picked up his ideas from the clever talk of London society and written them down in the same way that one would talk about them.[22] Toynbee fled Oxford and had some kind of mental collapse following on from the strain of the examination; but possibly as a result of a misunderstanding on his part, he had previously come to a rather irregular arrangement with Benjamin Jowett, Master of Balliol, to take rooms at Balliol while still a student at Pembroke. Complications arose when Toynbee, still away from Oxford convalescing, sought to move colleges, eventually resolved by an arrangement that he would formally leave the University, visit Balliol as a guest of Jowett, then rematriculate at Balliol in the New Year of 1875. Jowett took an almost paternal interest in Toynbee, as his 'Memoir' prefacing the *Lectures* attests.

During the summer vacation of 1875, Toynbee moved to Whitechapel in London to offer his services to the Charity Organization Society, initiating a connection to social work in the East End of London that would outlive him and lead to the creation of Toynbee Hall as a fixed settlement. It was also in this new context that Toynbee discovered his powers as a charismatic lecturer,[23] addressing a meeting of the Tower Hamlets Radical Club on the topic of religion and politics.[24] He was later, in 1877, a founding member of the Tower Hamlets branch of the London Society for University Extension, recruiting in the spring of 1879 as one of its first lecturers James Bonar,

[20] Kadish, *Apostle Arnold*, p. 15.

[21] 'He never wrote if he could possibly help it or if there was any chance of talking instead.' Charlotte Toynbee to Albert Grey, 30 December 1883, quoted in Kadish, *Apostle Arnold*, p. 218.

[22] Ibid., p. 28.

[23] Milner wrote of his early acquaintance with Toynbee: 'I fell at once under his spell, and have always remained under it. No man has ever for me had the same fascination, or made me realise as he did the secret of prophetic power—the kind of influence exercised in all ages by the men of religion and moral inspiration.' 'Reminiscence', in Toynbee, *Lectures*, 1908 edition, p. xiv.

[24] Ibid., p. 47.

likewise of Balliol, to lecture on political economy.[25] In 1880 Bonar founded an 'Adam Smith Club', with him as president and Toynbee as vice-president; and from discussions about poverty and wealth conducted in this context Toynbee developed a personal commitment to social reform. As his sister later wrote, 'for the sake of religion he had become a social reformer; for the sake of social reform he became an economist.'[26] Around this time he determined to read for Greats in Oxford (which, however, offered only classics, and no political economy), and then find elsewhere a position in which he could teach political economy. This contradictory ambition was resolved by his decision, prompted by his persistent ill-health, to sit for a pass degree and not honours; and in this context he would have the opportunity to study Adam Smith's *Wealth of Nations* and John Stuart Mill's *Principles of Political Economy*. Still taking breaks away from Oxford to convalesce, he sat for his final papers in his pass degree in the summer of 1878. Jowett's confidence in him was, however, undiminished, and even before he had received his degree the College Committee on Lectures recommended that Toynbee be employed by the college as the tutor responsible for the ICS probationary students.[27]

During the winter of 1878–1879, Toynbee took up another cause, that of church reform, encouraged in part by T. H. Green of Balliol, recently elected White's Professor of Moral Philosophy and a keen supporter of the devolution of church government to local congregations as a means of reviving support for the Anglican church. Toynbee's engagement with church reform through 1879 and 1880 is detailed by Kadish,[28] and there are two points arising from this of relevance here: that the movement for church reform would provide a platform for the creation, rather more than 10 years later, of the Oxford branch of the Christian Social Union and its new journal, the *Economic Review*;[29] and that the proselytising group activity in which Toynbee now became involved lent him a platform upon which he could exercise his rhetorical gifts.

In January 1880, Toynbee delivered three lectures at the Bradford Mechanics Institute on political economy, opening with the assertion that political economy shared with morality and religion a dedication to 'the development of man's life in all its aspects'.[30] Furthermore, whereas Adam Smith had been concerned principally with the actual distribution of wealth, and John Stuart Mill with how wealth should be distributed, the tendencies they had identified had been subject to particular

[25] Bonar is not usually counted as an 'English historical economist' (see the one reference in Koot, *English Historical Economists*, p. 168), despite sharing many characteristics with the 'School'—Balliol, university extension, interest in Adam Smith and Malthus. Like Cunningham, he was Scottish, not English; he gained a First in Greats in 1877, had studied at Leipzig and Tübingen, and in 1885 published a work on Malthus. However, unlike Ashley, Bonar also used his German to read the Austrian economists, publishing an early appreciation as 'The Austrian Economists and their View of Value', *Quarterly Journal of Economics* Vol. 3 (1888), pp. 1–31. See T. A. B. Corley, 'Bonar, James (1852–1941)', *Oxford Dictionary of National Biography* [published online 23 September 2004].

[26] Gertrude Toynbee, quoted in Kadish, *Apostle Arnold*, p. 49. Milner lifts this phrasing unattributed in his 'Reminiscence', p. xxi.

[27] These students followed a two-year course of study covering Indian languages, law, and political economy that was not subject to college or university examination; Kadish, *Apostle Arnold*, p. 53.

[28] Ibid., pp. 55–71.

[29] The Oxford branch of the Christian Social Union and its journal, *Economic Review*, is discussed in Ch 3.

[30] Cited from *The Bradford Chronicle and Mail*, 6 January 1880, in Kadish, *Apostle Arnold*, p. 72.

conditions. In time, however, these tendencies had been converted into universal laws that supported the idea that 'the existing arrangements of society were inevitable and just'. Here Toynbee appears to draw upon Cliffe Leslie's recently published collection of essays.[31]

What comes next is, however, quite startling for anyone familiar with the conventional account of historical economics in Britain. The first lecture addressed 'Free Trade and Protection' and amounted to an enthusiastic defence of free trade. The system of complete economic freedom, he argued, was a great contribution to social harmony; the division of labour enforced sociability, each coming to depend upon the labour of others. Competition ensured that wants would be satisfied at the lowest possible cost. These points did not go down well with his audience; the objection was made that Britain's commitment to free trade was exploited by others who failed to reciprocate. Toynbee incautiously suggested that Britain's imports were overwhelmingly made up of raw materials, and when challenged on this (erroneous) idea had to admit that he had made up the figure of '90%' and had no real idea of the actual composition. Nonetheless, he maintained, protection was a bad thing, since it increased costs for consumers while preventing the positive force of competition doing its work on the industrial system.[32] As we shall see, English historical economists who took their inspiration from Toynbee are supposed to believe the opposite of all these things.

Two days later, Toynbee delivered a lecture on wages, later included in his *Lectures on the Industrial Revolution in England*.[33] While he here aligned himself with the rejection of the wage fund theory and name-checked John Stuart Mill's 1869 article in the *Fortnightly Review* where Mill had endorsed Thornton's *On Labour*, his presentation differs notably from a parallel passage in his 1881–1882 lecture course.[34] 'Wages and Natural Law' does emphasise the importance of labour productivity to the level of wages, and that cheap imports benefited the consumer, but his argument in Bradford is chiefly by example, rather than principle; as was made plain when responding to a local manufacturer who suggested that longer hours on the European Continent could force down English wages.[35] A final lecture in this series considered the future of England's industrial system, in which the task of the political economist was to show how it could be purged of apparently inevitable evils—'the age of criticism is past'. Instead of class antagonism, the future should be built on unity across the classes ('employers, and labourers, and students') co-operating for one common end. Kadish concludes that Toynbee's argument was here quite simple:

[31] T. E. Cliffe Leslie, *Essays in Political and Moral Philosophy*, Hodges, Foster and Figgis, Dublin 1879.

[32] Kadish, *Apostle Arnold*, p. 74. See below for later use of this same argument as stated by Pigou in his criticism of tariff reform in 1903, p. 216.

[33] Toynbee, 'Wages and Natural Law', *Lectures*, pp. 155–77.

[34] The 14 lectures of 1881–1882 were printed in 1884 together with lectures and addresses he had given previously and which he had either drafted himself, or were recorded by shorthand writers and presumably reviewed by Toynbee. This difference in the provenance of the material assembled in 1884 makes it possible to contrast the substance and style of the Oxford lecture course, shaped posthumously, with other material that can be more directly linked to Toynbee as writer or speaker.

[35] Reported in *Bradford Chronicle*, 8 January 1880, cited in Kadish, *Apostle Arnold*, p. 77.

> The old theories ignored reality and, when confused with reality, had a detrimental effect on society. The modern theories took account of reality, addressed themselves to real problems, and consequently provided a valuable aid to progress.[36]

'Modern theories', it should be noted, were the work of writers such as Cliffe Leslie, not Stanley Jevons who would during the 1880s, and especially before the publication of Marshall's *Principles* in 1890, be the leading British representative of a distinctly post-Millian political economy. More generally, while this contrast between 'old' and 'new' reflected the sentiment of the lectures he would deliver the following year in Oxford, as printed in 1884 these lectures would assume a coherence that was more than merely rhetorical.

We can judge this from the essay 'Ricardo and the Old Political Economy',[37] with which the first edition of the *Lectures* opened. Toynbee had begun drafting his appraisal of Ricardo in 1879 but had abandoned it;[38] it is therefore one of the few sources that gives us a sense of how Toynbee wrote, rather than how other people talked about what he said. Using the newspaper reports of his public lectures as written records of his presentations, this draft essay suggests that he wrote rather like he talked: in generalities, by allusion, with little direct reference to sources.[39] While he does on the second page of the Ricardo essay quote from Torrens, John Stuart Mill, and De Quincey, this is only to emphasise the high esteem in which Ricardo was held; and it is not until the fifth page that we are given some idea of the principles with which Ricardo was associated. A contrast drawn with Adam Smith to make the point that Ricardo lived 'in the midst' of an industrial revolution leads only to a conclusion that 'competition' was the central feature of Ricardo's work, making him 'appear to his contemporaries like the revealer of a new gospel.' Coupled with this was Ricardo's supposed dedication to deductivism as a method, and Toynbee maintains that this blinded Ricardo's followers to the importance of observation.[40] Although the essay had opened by asserting that intellectual criticism had led to the supersession of Ricardian political economy, he now maintained that the Corn Law reform of 1846 had ended the era of deductivism, heralding a new era of observation associated with the demise of the Wage Fund theory. This had reset political economy: 'Political Economy was transformed by the working classes.'[41]

Next, Ricardo's 'philosophical assumptions' were said to come from Adam Smith, and so Toynbee turns to an exposition of the economic philosophy of Smith. As already noted, Toynbee would have read *Wealth of Nations* while studying for the pass degree,[42] and so this reliance upon Adam Smith can be easily explained. Not so

[36] Kadish, *Apostle Arnold*, p. 92.

[37] Toynbee, *Lectures* (1884), pp. 1–26.

[38] Charlotte Toynbee, 'Prefatory Note', *Lectures* (1884), p. xxx.

[39] While it is true that the auditors of the Bradford lectures differed from those in Oxford, it is clear that Toynbee's style of presentation relied for its effect upon striking contrasts and aphorisms, not the construction of systematic argument. The Oxford lectures retain the former, but also introduce the latter; how far this can be attributed to Ashley must of course remain an open question.

[40] Toynbee, *Lectures* (1884), p. 9.

[41] Ibid., p. 10.

[42] Edwin Cannan reported that in the early 1880s his prescribed books for the pass degree were Smith's *Wealth of Nations* and Fawcett's *Manual of Political Economy*; Cannan, *The Economic Outlook*, p. 11.

easily explained is the fact that in an essay ostensibly devoted to Ricardo there is no direct citation of Ricardo, nor one footnote to his work. Instead Ricardo is presented to us through the writings of others, as for example in the opening quotations from Torrens, De Quincy, and Mill, and here in a passage taken from Malthus's *Essay on Population*.[43] The contextualisation provided by Toynbee's 'historical method' turns out to have failed to even examine very closely the object of contextualisation. Instead, we move from premises directly to conclusion, without any intervening examination. Although the essay breaks off unfinished, its claim is unmistakable:

> The historical method has revolutionised Political Economy, not by showing its laws to be false, but by proving that they are relative for the most part to a particular stage of civilisation. This destroys their character as eternal laws, and strips them of much of their force and all their sanctity. In this way the historical method has rescued us from intellectual superstitions.[44]

Toynbee abandoned the essay in part because he believed that Bagehot's *Economic Studies* covered the same ground.[45] However, as the reader passes from this first essay to the following 14 lectures, there is a marked shift of structure and argument, and this is something that repays some attention.

The lectures were dedicated to the 'industrial revolution'—Toynbee's own title for the book—and they deal with the economic transition in England from the later eighteenth to the early nineteenth century. The writings of Adam Smith, Robert Malthus, and David Ricardo are deployed as representative of three separate stages of this transition: on the eve, in the midst of the process, and postwar England. This structure is all explained in the opening paragraph, and so a radical departure from the way Toynbee usually begins. By placing 'abstract propositions' in their context, it is said that they can be rendered 'more vivid and less likely to mislead'; while studying history in connection with political economy enables many phenomena to be properly accounted for.[46] This much can be found elsewhere in Toynbee's writings; but consider the following:

> The Historical Method ... examines the actual causes of economic development and considers the influence of institutions, such as the mediæval guilds, our present land-laws, or the political constitution of any given country, in determining the distribution of wealth.[47]

[43] Ibid., p. 12.

[44] Ibid., p. 25.

[45] Walter Bagehot, *Economic Studies*, Longmans, Green & Co., London 1880; see Charlotte Toynbee, 'Prefatory Note', *Lectures* (1884), p. xxx. Bagehot's text provided the model anglocentric account of political economy, beginning with 'The Postulates of English Political Economy', the assumption that political economy began with Adam Smith's *Wealth of Nations*, and that '[t]he true founder of abstract Political Economy is Ricardo.' (p. 197). Luigi Cossa's *Guide to the Study of Political Economy* was published in the same year (originally published in Milan in 1876, a translation was published by Macmillan in 1880) and is a work of far greater scope than Bagehot.

[46] Toynbee, *Lectures* (1884), p. 28.

[47] Ibid., pp. 29–30.

This seems to be channelling Stubbs; a way of delineating the historical method that is not replicated elsewhere in his addresses.

The early lectures paint a picture of England on the eve of industrial transformation, brought about by agrarian changes that reorganised the countryside into relationships between employer and employee. A footnote at the opening of Lecture 5, 'The Decay of the Yeomanry', notes that the text here is largely based on an essay written by Toynbee. There is a reference to the French edition of Marx's *Capital*, denying Marx's claim that the yeomanry had ceased to exist by the mid-eighteenth century, and proposing instead that the process of extinction was located in the last third of the century.[48] Political power and social prestige played their part in the reconstruction of the countryside and of its working population, so that this phase follows quite closely Marx's account of 'primitive accumulation' in *Capital* Vol. I, except that this is displaced into the last few decades of the eighteenth century and so falls together with the advance of the industrial revolution.

There is an evident lurch from the end of this lecture to the one following that deals with the condition of agricultural labourers, who are said to have experienced growing relative prosperity earlier in the eighteenth century, and noting the decline that took place into the nineteenth.[49] The argument becomes once again detailed and logically structured, reconstructing rural relations, living conditions, and wages. Then with Lecture 7 there begins an exposition of the guild system and wage regulation, together with the transition 'from the Mercantile System proper to modern Protectionism.'[50] Here Smith's *Wealth of Nations* functions as a source of principles for the exposition of a developmental economic history that can, in part, qualify these principles.[51]

Lecture 8 opens by asserting that

> [t]he essence of the Industrial Revolution is the substitution of competition for the mediæval regulations which had previously controlled the production and distribution of wealth. On this account it is not only one of the most important facts of English history, but Europe owes to it the growth of two great systems of thought—Economic Science, and its antithesis, Socialism.[52]

The tripartite schema of Smith, Malthus, and Ricardo is repeated, with John Stuart Mill now forming a fourth element concerned with the issue of how wealth *ought* to be distributed, recognising that 'competition alone is not a satisfactory basis of society.'[53] In this context the decline of the rural population in number and condition is examined, as also the replacement of domestic industry by the factory. This all led into the growth of pauperism, the subject of Lecture 9. Discussion of poor law relief leads back to the manorial system, and Stubbs's *Constitutional History* is here cited and duly

[48] Ibid., p. 61. If Ashley were to have cited Marx at this time, then he would have probably done so in German.

[49] Ibid., p. 69.

[50] Ibid., p. 77.

[51] Ibid., pp. 79–84.

[52] Ibid., p. 85.

[53] Ibid. p. 86.

footnoted. A moderate and measured tone prevails as evidence is assessed and arguments tested.[54]

Lecture 9 is directed to the wage fund theory, and as noted earlier, the argument presented here contrasts with the substance as well as style of his earlier public address on the issue that is printed later in the book. The wage fund theory—that there is a sum of capital dedicated to the remuneration of labour, and that the greater the number of labourers, the less each will receive—is attributed to Malthus, since the populationist implications of the theory are evident. Nonetheless, criticism is here levelled in terms of principles: that the capital any one individual possesses for the payment of wages is fixed, and that wages are always paid out of capital. Nor is there any ground for believing that there exists at any one time a fixed quantity of capital for the payment of wages.[55] Having demonstrated the falsity of the theory, the question is raised: What is to replace it in accounting for the remuneration of labour? This is said to be something that has not yet been determined: 'no economist has yet succeeded in giving us a complete theory of wages in its place.... instead of saying that wages are paid out of stored-up capital, we now say that they are the labourer's share of the produce.'[56] Following this, a discussion of labour productivity is introduced to explain the different levels of wages in various countries, and between manufacturing and agriculture in the same country.[57]

As has happened before, in moving to Lecture 12, 'Ricardo and the Growth of Rent', there is a marked shift of style, reverting to the generalisations found in the essay on Ricardo. These stylistic transitions in the text, shifts of voice from dry exposition of a developmental history to rhetorical flourishes and back again, suggest a varying amount of editorial input in the completion of a continuous narrative. At the very least, nothing in Toynbee's other addresses and writings suggests that he would elaborate such a well-organised developmental history of the kind we find in his *Lectures*. He was certainly capable of painting the picture; but it seems hardly plausible that his Oxford lectures would adopt a structured style of argument encountered nowhere else in reports of his addresses and his other writings. And it is not difficult to account for this difference: Ashley was an honours student, not a pass student; he read German and had absorbed von Maurer's account of the *Markgenossenschaft*; and even more significantly, his *Introduction to English Economic History and Theory* reads like a prequel to Toynbee, taking the story up to the point where Toynbee starts. Then, developing some lectures he had given at the University of Birmingham, in 1912 Ashley presented an overview of the economic development of England that added to his existing economic history an account of the eighteenth and nineteenth centuries. Here we find him recommending Toynbee as '[t]he best introduction to the agrarian history of the eighteenth century', and for the following lecture emphasising that any study of the Industrial Revolution had to begin with Toynbee.[58]

[54] See, for example, the question raised in ibid., p. 100, regarding whether pauperism was increasing during the seventeenth and eighteenth centuries.

[55] Ibid., pp. 116–17.

[56] Ibid., p. 119.

[57] Ibid., p. 124.

[58] W. J. Ashley, *The Economic Organisation of England: An Outline History*, Longmans, Green & Co., London 1914, pp. 202, 203. These lectures were given at the Colonial Institute in Hamburg.

Ashley's Economic History

What are the implications of all this? As we have seen, Toynbee's *Lectures* were reprinted many times up to the later 1920s, and then republished in 1956. The general narrative of agrarian development and industrialisation that they presented provided the template upon which English economic history would be written in the twentieth century. They also proposed a linkage to the history of economic thought and policy, although this linkage was developed only in relation to Adam Smith, Robert Malthus, David Ricardo, and John Stuart Mill, terminating chronologically in 1869 with Mill's critique of the wage fund doctrine and so ignoring the work of Stanley Jevons, whose *Theory of Political Economy* (1871) was in fact widely recognised by the 1880s as the central 'modern' English text. Importantly, this truncated and resolutely anglophone version of 'political economy' that Toynbee put into circulation was one with which Ashley persisted. As we shall see in his teaching in Toronto and Harvard, Ashley long continued to associate 'political economy' exclusively with Smith, Malthus, Ricardo, and Mill, the template that Toynbee had provided. As for the economic history, Ashley's own interests were plainly in the medieval and not the early modern period. While his work on Toynbee's lectures contributed to the creation of the 'industrial revolution' as an organising historiographical concept, he never sought to develop on his own account the related historical narrative of capital and labour that Toynbee had sketched out. To anticipate: on both counts, as historical economics and as economic history, it is indeed difficult to see how in the 1890s this approach might have had any relevance for the work in which contemporary 'economists' were engaged: whether academics like Alfred Marshall, or civil servants like Robert Giffen, or essayists like J. A. Hobson. This perspective has long been hidden from us by the tendency of historians of economics to rely for their appraisal of contemporary views upon Langford Price's *Political Economy in England*, or John Kells Ingram's *History of Political Economy*,[59] neither of which is especially reliable for an assessment of what political economy had come to mean by the later 1880s.[60]

This line of argument can be developed further by taking a step back, to the sources of the history that Ashley absorbed. We have already seen how his Lothian

[59] L. L. Price, *A Short History of Political Economy in England from Adam Smith to Arnold Toynbee*, Methuen, London 1891; John Kells Ingram, *A History of Political Economy*, Adam and Charles Black, Edinburgh 1888. Both texts amplify an anglophone truncation of political economy that we find in Toynbee and Ashley, entirely ignoring the growing importance of Austrian, Italian, and American writers, while also discounting the contemporary importance of Jevons. For a sense of the context, see the discussion of the new specialist journals of the time in Chapter 3.

[60] For the discussion of economics in contemporary London, see D., 'Economics in 1889', *The National Reformer* 5 January 1890, p. 3, which deals with 'economics' in relation to Jevons, Edgeworth, and Sidgwick, concluding with a comment on Giffen; noting that the 'mathematical school of economists ... has done something to check this amorphous tendency [a "muddle of economics and ethics"] not so much by the application of mathematics to economics as by the greater precision of terminology which such a method demands.' 'D' was very likely J. H. Levy, a former lecturer in 'logic and economics' at the City of London College and Honorary Secretary of the National Liberal Club; see his 'Distribution as a Branch of Economics', paper read at the National Liberal Club Political Economy Circle, 18 June 1890, *Transactions of the National Liberal Club Political Economy Circle* Vol. 1, pp. 95–103, P. S. King & Son, London 1891. My thanks to Steven Medema for bringing the *National Reformer* piece to my attention, and to Gregory Moore for the suggested authorship.

essay explicitly acknowledged the influence of von Maurer's developmental history of the *Mark* to urban civil life. Translated into an Oxford historiography created by Stubbs's institutionalist history, this was in turn rooted in Henry Maine's developmental schema, from the dominance of status-bound kin relationships to the individualism of modernity, where relationships were contractual.[61] We find the same kind of story, inflected into a narrative of communal loss and social detachment, in Ferdinand Tönnies's *Gemeinschaft und Gesellschaft*, published in 1887 and carrying the subtitle 'Treatise on Communism and Socialism as Empirical Cultural Forms'.[62] Maine then later published *Village Communities in East and West*,[63] outlining this transition in terms of institutions, from the primitive village community to the institutions of modern commercial society, a text that itself drew on von Maurer. As Simon Cook explains,

> Maine's first innovation was to recognize von Maurer's early Germanic *Mark* community in the village community of nineteenth-century India. His second innovation was to build upon the genealogical connections established by nineteenth-century comparative philology and bring Indian, ancient Roman, and Germanic (including English) social forms together within a single account of so-called Aryan social evolution. The starting point of this account was the nomadic tribe, in which all property was held in common and individual identity entirely defined in terms of kinship relations within the tribe. The basic idea was that, when a tribe bound together by ties of kinship and holding its land in common settled down to till the soil, two changes commenced: the gradual transformation of the social bond—from ties of kinship to ties based on shared territory . . . ; and the gradual transformation of common into private property.[64]

This general story informed Cunningham's *Growth of English Industry and Commerce*; but it also quite clearly informs Ashley's Lothian Prize essay, written the same year that Cunningham's book was published. However, the following year Seebohm published his *English Village Community* which, using recent physical evidence, argued that the Anglo-Saxon settlement of Britain during the fifth to eighth centuries simply took over existing Romano-British institutions and 'turned the British population into serfs'.[65] Instead of being shaped over millennia by a process of social evolution, the institutions of medieval and early modern Britain were instead the product of much more recent coercion and cultural assimilation.

[61] Henry Sumner Maine, *Ancient Law: Its Connection with the Early History of Society, and Its Relation to Modern Ideas*, John Murray, London 1861.

[62] Ferdinand Tönnies, *Gemeinschaft und Gesellschaft. Abhandlung des Communismus und des Socialismus als empirischer Culturformen*, Fues, Leipzig 1887. During the 1880s Tönnies studied in England, locating the manuscript for Hobbes's *Behemoth* and publishing this for the first time in 1889.

[63] Henry Sumner Maine, *Village Communities in East and West: Six Lectures Delivered at Oxford*, John Murray, London 1871.

[64] Simon J. Cook, Keith Tribe, 'Historical Economics', in Gilbert Faccarello, Heinz D. Kurz (eds.) *Handbook on the History of Economic Analysis Vol. II*, Edward Elgar, Cheltenham UK 2016, p. 307.

[65] Ibid., p. 308.

Ashley responded to this historiographical revision by shunting the origin of the evolutionary history he had sketched in his Lothian Prize essay forwards into the eleventh century: Book I of his Introduction to *English Economic History and Theory* runs 'From the Eleventh to the Fourteenth Century'. This was because

> ... there can be no reasonable doubt that at that time the whole of central England was covered with manors of substantially the same character; and we cannot begin earlier because it is by no means agreed how that condition of things came about.[66]

There is the same progression in this book from 'The Manor and Village Community' (Ch. 1) to 'Merchant and Craft Gilds' (Ch. 2) as there was in his *James and Philip van Artevelde*, but it is now compressed into rather less than two hundred years. While still in Toronto, Ashley then collaborated with his wife, Margaret, on an English edition of Fustel de Coulanges's 1889 essay on the origin of property in land,[67] Margaret translating the text and William writing a lengthy introduction, 'The English Manor'. Here Ashley made very clear the need to abandon any idea that English history 'began with a population of independent freemen', that in fact the 'village community' was in Britain a modern creation, not an original state.[68] The rejection of Maurer's theory of the Germanic *Markgenossenschaft* as the original state of social organisation concluded with its point:

> The history of the mark has served Mr. George as a basis for the contention that the common ownership of land is the only natural condition of things; to Sir Henry Maine it has suggested the precisely opposite conclusion that the whole movement of civilisation has been from common ownership to private. Such arguments are alike worthless, if the mark never existed.[69]

Linked to this new evolutionary history was a history of political economy shaped by the tenets that we have seen at work in Toynbee's *Lectures*. The 'Preface' of *English Economic History and Theory* was dedicated to a six-point exposition of the historicist perspective that Toynbee had proposed. The fourth of these argued that

> As modern economists have taken for their assumptions conditions which only in modern times have begun to exist, so earlier economic theories were based, consciously or unconsciously, on conditions then present. Hence the theories of the past must be judged in relation to the facts of the past, and not in relation to those of the present.[70]

66 W. J. Ashley, *An Introduction to English Economic History and Theory. The Middle Ages*, Rivingtons, London 1888, p. 13.
67 Numa Denis Fustel de Coulanges, 'Le problème des origines de la propriété foncière', *Revue des questions historiques* N.S. t. 1 no. 1 (1889), pp. 349–439.
68 W. J. Ashley, 'Introductory Chapter. The English Manor', in Fustel de Coulanges (ed.) *The Origin of Property in Land*, Swan Sonnenschein, London 1892, pp. vii, xxiv.
69 Ibid., p. xliv.
70 Ibid., pp. x–xi.

Accordingly Ashley's third chapter deals with Canon Law, doctrines relating to usury and money, and the regulation of trade and of goods. He notes that the only English writer who had previously drawn attention to medieval economic ideas was Cunningham; but that Knies and Roscher had dealt with this during the 1850s.[71] Later, in the twentieth century, this historicising principle came to be directed against the retrospective histories that economists began to construct for the theories they employed, seeking legitimation in apparently historical precedent. This was not yet true of the later nineteenth century; Ashley was here arguing that historical arguments could be employed as evidence illuminating the medieval world in a way that provided insight into past action, into institutional processes rather than simply the institutions themselves. As a principle, this approach has much to recommend it; the problem remained, however, of relating this principle to modern theory. On this Ashley's text remained silent. While Ashley cites recent French and German commentaries (Gide, Knies, and Schmoller), there is never any acknowledgement that, by the later 1880s, new economic work is being published at an increasing rate in Europe and the United States that can be connected with the policy issues relating to labour movements, trade, and industrial combinations, issues about which Ashley would in fact teach in Toronto.

Ashley did implicitly distance himself from the more extreme historicism of Cliffe Leslie, who had cast his criticism of English political economy in terms of the fallacy of a deductive approach to historical phenomena. Ashley later suggested that Cliffe Leslie introduced English readers to German historical economics by publishing in 1875 a partial summary of Roscher's *Geschichte der National-Oekonomik in Deutschland*.[72] In his Toronto inaugural address he rather more accurately credited Cliffe Leslie, along with Ingram and Toynbee, with leading an 'onslaught on economic orthodoxy',[73] and it would be more defensible to suggest that Leslie translated Maine's comparative jurisprudence into a comparative economics. Here again, in terms of the chronology of principal publications and impact, Cliffe Leslie actually postdates Jevons, but quickly fades in influence; rather like Cairnes, by the early 1880s Cliffe Leslie looks more like part of the past than part of the future. Ashley tended to look back to this past, rather than orient himself to his present. His later work in establishing the Faculty of Commerce in Birmingham might seem to belie such an assessment; but as will be shown in Chapter 10, even here he failed to establish a successful institution capable of reproducing itself, and after his death the Faculty's teaching was reoriented to the study of industrial organisation.

[71] Ibid., p. 125.

[72] W. J. Ashley, 'The Present Position of Political Economy', *Economic Journal* Vol. 16 (1907), p. 475; Cliffe Leslie first published 'The History of German Political Economy' in the *Fortnightly Review* in 1875, then in 1879 included it in his *Essays*, pp. 167–78.

[73] W. J. Ashley, *What Is Political Science? An Inaugural Lecture Given in the Convocation Hall of the University of Toronto, 9th November, 1888*, Rowsell & Hutchison, Toronto 1888, p. 15.

Ashley in Toronto and Harvard

In Toronto, Ashley taught in the Faculty of Law:[74] a course in elementary political economy, taking as his textbooks Walker's *Political Economy* and that of John Stuart Mill; more significantly, his second-year course on 'The History and Criticism of Economic Theories' covered Smith, Malthus, List, and Ricardo, using Ingram's *History of Political Economy* as his course textbook. This was essentially the same range of material that he had heard Toynbee deliver in 1881–1882. Beyond this, he taught the 'History of Economic Development' on the basis of his own book, plus Cunningham and Toynbee; while also taking 'Modern Economic Questions', covering labour movements, taxation, railways, currency, and related policy issues. He also taught a course on the constitutional history of England and Canada; for the former, 'Students are expected to acquire a textual knowledge of the following documents: *Assize of Clarendon, Magna Charta, Parliamentary Writs of 1295, Petition of Right, Habeas Corpus Act, Bill of Rights, Act of Settlement*' all of which were to be found in Stubbs's *Select Charters*. And finally, he gave a course on the history and criticism of political theories—Aristotle, Hobbes, Rousseau, Burke, Spencer, and T. H. Green.[75] The Calendar for the following year provides more detail on the topics covered and extends the list of recommended texts, but curiously substituting for Walker and Mill in the elementary course John Symes's *Short Text-Book of Political Economy* (1888); hence not, for instance, introductory texts by two other Oxford near-contemporaries, Gonner's *Political Economy* and Cannan's *Elementary Political Economy*, both of which appeared the same year as Symes's otherwise obscure book, and with the definite advantage for an introductory course of being considerably more concise.[76]

One innovation that Ashley did make in Toronto, and continued at Harvard and Birmingham, was a seminar in which students presented papers, discussing them with Ashley and other students while one student kept a record in a minute book. We can read of a meeting on 28 February 1889 where two students presented papers on Ricardo, one on the history of rent and one on its theory, from the discussion it being recorded that '[t]he commentators of Ricardo commit a fault in turning general laws into precepts, into advice as to what should be done.'[77] In April 1889 students addressed the 'Postulates of Abstract Political Economy', using texts by Ricardo, Cliffe Leslie, and Cairnes; while a year later the seminar was devoted to topics in economic history drawn from the second part of Ashley's *Introduction*.[78]

[74] For the reorganisation of degrees and courses at Toronto, see Ian M. Drummond, *Political Economy at the University of Toronto: A History of the Department, 1888–1982*, Faculty of Arts and Science, Toronto 1983, pp. 18–22.

[75] *Calendar of the University of Toronto and University College for MDCCCLXXXIX–MDCCCLXXXC*, Toronto 1889, pp. 42–44 [University of Toronto Archives P1978–1010].

[76] E. C. K. Gonner, *Political Economy (An Elementary Text Book of the Economics of Commerce)*, R. Sutton & Co., London 1888; Edwin Cannan, *Elementary Political Economy*, Henry Frowde, London 1888. The most commonly encountered textbook around this time was the Marshalls' *Economics of Industry* (1879); that Ashley studiously ignores it is itself significant. See *Calendar of the University of Toronto and University College for MDCCCLXXXX–MDCCCLXXXCI*, Toronto 1890, pp. 135–39 [University of Toronto Archives P1978–1010].

[77] Minute Book of the Economic Seminary, University College, Toronto 1889–1892, p. 13 [University of Toronto Archives B65-0032].

[78] W. J. Ashley, *An Introduction to English Economic History and Theory. Part II The End of the Middle Ages*, Longmans & Co., London 1893.

There was a similar lack of development in his teaching after he was appointed to the new Harvard Chair in Economic History. His teaching was listed under 'Economics' together with that of Frank Taussig,[79] appointed to a full professorship the same year. In 1892–1893 he taught the introductory course to 322 students alongside Taussig, the first half year on Mill's *Principles of Political Economy*, the second on the kind of applied issues that Ashley had covered as 'Modern Economic Questions' in Toronto.[80] Ashley also gave courses on the 'Economic History of Europe and America, to 1763', and 'History of Economic Theory, down to Adam Smith'. Ashley led a small seminar chiefly devoted to economic history; by the mid-1890s he was no longer involved in the big introductory economics course, teaching the history and literature of economics to the mid-nineteenth century at the very latest, and European economic history on a pattern similar to that established in Toronto.[81] During the 1890s Ashley published a series of book reviews and short essays that primarily consolidated his earlier work on medieval agrarian and economic history,[82] rather than developing his former commitment to the historical connection of economic theory and policy.[83] He also edited for Macmillan a series of 'Economic Classics'—his translation of Turgot's *Réflexions* was published in 1898, preceded by the first six chapters of Ricardo's *Principles* in 1895, an abridged version of *Wealth of Nations* and of Malthus's *Essay on Population*, and a translation of Schmoller on the mercantile system in 1897.[84]

He had already noted in his Harvard inaugural lecture that the earlier hopes of Cliffe Leslie and Ingram for the development of a 'historical' economics had failed to materialise.[85] He now proposed that the path to follow would be the 'actual investigation of economic history itself', a path he associated with the work of Schmoller and Knapp, who had shifted attention away from individual human behaviour in given social conditions to 'the life and movement of whole industries and classes, of the creation and modification of social mechanism ...'.[86] This project, too, would founder: and neither Schmoller, nor Knapp, nor any of their German contemporaries succeeded in converting extensive historical studies into a new understanding of 'the character and sequence of the stages in economic development' that went beyond the work of Karl

[79] Taussig had graduated from Harvard in 1879, travelled in Europe for a year, returning to Harvard to complete a doctorate in 1883 on 'Protection to Young Industries as Applied to the United States'. He became an assistant professor at Harvard in 1886; see Byrd L. Jones, 'A Quest for National Leadership: Institutionalization of Economics at Harvard', in William J. Barber (ed.) *Breaking the Academic Mould: Economists and American Higher Learning in the Nineteenth Century*, Wesleyan University Press, Middletown Conn. 1988, p. 109.

[80] *Annual Report of the President and Treasurer of Harvard College 1892–1993*, p. 67.

[81] In his final year at Harvard it was noted that Ashley had added a new seminar topic 'The Mercantilists', while Taussig took a seminar on Smith and Ricardo; *Annual Report of the President and Treasurer of Harvard College 1899–1900*, p. 93.

[82] W. J. Ashley, *Surveys Historic and Economic*, Longmans, Green, & Co., London 1900.

[83] Ashley wrote to Cannan in 1896 that he was working on a translation of Turgot's *Réflexions*, that he had started out wanting to revise the 1795 translation (reputedly by McCulloch), but found it so poor that he felt a new translation was needed—Ashley to Cannan, 26 December 1896, Cannan Papers, Correspondence 1889–1899 Cannan Collection, LSE Archives Box 1020.

[84] See Edgeworth's rather bemused review of the Smith, Malthus, and Ricardo texts in the *Economic Journal* Vol. 5 (1895), pp. 257–58.

[85] W. J. Ashley, 'On the Study of Economic History', *Quarterly Journal of Economics* Vo. 7 (1893), pp. 116–17.

[86] Ibid., pp. 120, 121.

Bücher's *Entstehung der Volkswirtschaft*, which itself originated in lectures during the 1880s.[87]

The Tariff Controversy and Liberal Imperialism

Ashley left Harvard in 1901 to return to Britain and found the Faculty of Commerce at the University of Birmingham.[88] There is, however, one further episode in which Ashley was involved of relevance to the relationship between economic history and historical economics: the Tariff Controversy of 1903–1904. Joseph Chamberlain's proposals for protection and imperial preference made in May 1903 were quickly given academic support by Ashley's book *The Tariff Problem*.[89] Ashley signed off his book in September 1903; one month later, A. C. Pigou completed *The Riddle of the Tariff*,[90] a response to Chamberlain's proposals from one of the new economists whose work Ashley had largely ignored, and who was furthermore a very young 'new economist'—Ashley was in his early forties, Pigou not yet 26. Here we are not concerned with the political ramifications of the debate, nor the real policy options involved, but instead with the confrontation of two styles of economic argument.

On 15 August 1903 a letter was published in *The Times* under the title 'Professors of Economics and the Tariff Question', signed by thirteen professors and lecturers—including Edwin Cannan, E. C. K. Gonner, Shield Nicholson, and W. R. Scott, so clearly not a Marshallian caucus, as is sometimes implied.[91] The letter made points regarding the problems of protectionist policy that are today quite unremarkable, but which constantly recur in all such disputes—that in protecting one sector another, perhaps more significant, sector is unintentionally harmed, or that it was unlikely that the total burden of a tax on imported wheat would be entirely borne by the exporting country. A flurry of hostile responses followed, notably one from H. S. Foxwell on 20 August which objected to the presence among the signatories of C. P. Sanger and A. C. Pigou, both of whom gave their affiliation as University College London, where Foxwell held the chair of political economy. His objection was that they had no right to sign the letter without first asking his permission: 'Neither of the two gentlemen who have signed has been connected with the department of economics for half as many months as I have been years at the head of it. . . .'

[87] Karl Bücher, *Die Entstehung der Volkswirtschaft*, Verlag der H. Laupp'schen Buchhandlung, Tübingen 1893; see, for a thorough discussion of this, Shiro Takebayashi, *Die Entstehung der Kapitalismustheorie in der Gründungsphase der deutschen Soziologie. Von der historischen Nationalökonomie zur historischen Soziologie Werner Sombarts und Max Webers*, Duncker und Humblot, Berlin 2003.

[88] His role in shaping that institution will be examined in Chapter 10.

[89] W. J. Ashley, *The Tariff Problem*, P. S. King & Son, London 1903.

[90] A. C. Pigou, *The Riddle of the Tariff*, R. Brimley Johnson, London 1903. Ashley's 'Preface' was dated 7 September 1903, Pigou's 1 October 1903. The standard history of the controversy, detailing the political background and manoeuvring, is A. W. Coats, 'Political Economy and the Tariff Reform Campaign of 1903', *Journal of Law and Economics* Vol. 11 (1968), pp. 181–229.

[91] As in E. H. H. Green's *Oxford Dictionary of National Biography* entry on Ashley, for example. John Clapham, future Professor of Economic History at Cambridge, wrote to expressly associate himself with the 'Professors' letter of 15 August on 2 September 1903; as did Sydney Chapman, Jevons Professor at Manchester, on 7 September 1903.

Foxwell concluded his letter by remarking that '... with scarcely an exception, the historical group of English economists declined to sign the manifesto. The fact, I venture to think, goes far to justify the position they hold as to the importance of historical study in economics.' Here Foxwell identifies 'historical economists' with non-signers, so that in reverse it could then be argued that 'historical economists' supported protection, arguing from circumstance rather than from principle. As with Foxwell's outraged objection to the appointment of Pigou as Marshall's successor in 1908, his own prejudiced judgment was implicitly adopted by later historians who failed to question the reliability of Foxwell's opinions, and who built them into a story about the deliberate marginalisation of economic history by contemporary economists.

What might it mean instead to argue from principle, rather than circumstance? This is essentially what Pigou did in his *Riddle of the Tariff*, which exhibits a style of argument quite at variance with that encountered so far in this chapter. It was only the previous year that Pigou had published his first contribution to the *Economic Journal*, in the September 1902 issue taking up a point made by Edgeworth regarding the impact of a tax on corn. As already outlined in Chapter 6,[92] Pigou began from Edgeworth's analytical point but moved on to examine how principles worked in the light of particular economic agents and institutions. Pigou's *Riddle of the Tariff* follows the same expositional logic. Writing for an educated public, he dismissed as 'unsound' the arguments of Ashley regarding the beneficial impact of protection in attracting capital into the country, drawing support from the comments made by Marshall to Section F in 1889 regarding the generally deleterious impact of protection on profitability, and hence general investment. Here again, Pigou sought to extend the abstract reasoning that Edgeworth exemplified into the impact of policy on patterns of actual economic behaviour, entirely in line with Marshall's practice. Pigou's line of reasoning does not depend upon the assertion of 'abstract principles' to which 'contemporary circumstance' can be contrasted to provide historical context. The basic argument he defends in *Riddle of the Tariff* is that while changes in patterns of trade can result in the dislocation of industry and unemployment, there are many other factors that bring about the same circumstance:

> Dislocation through foreign competition is only a single species of a far larger genus. People who are prepared to welcome mechanical inventions for the sake of their ultimate contribution to national wealth, and in spite of the temporary disturbances which they almost always create, cannot logically object when the same result, accompanied by the same disadvantages, is introduced by foreign competition.[93]

Hence the real problem was not temporary changes in the trading relationships of different countries, but what the merits of free trade and protection might be in regard to the real income of the population of Great Britain.

This was not the position from which Ashley started in his defence of protection. He assumed from the first, without any supporting argument, that the British economy was under threat from foreign competition, and that the Empire was in

[92] See pp. 154–55.
[93] Pigou, *Riddle of the Tariff*, pp. 19–20.

need of consolidation. Much later, he opened a chapter devoted to Imperial interdependence as follows:

> The essential and ultimate problem for Great Britain is whether, in a more closely united Empire, she can find that basis for her economic well-being which is gradually being withdrawn from beneath her feet in the foreign market.[94]

However, the problems that Ashley identifies are those of declining staple industries, for which other exports might be substituted, and where increasing complexity in the relation of winners and losers is an issue. Throughout *The Tariff Problem* discussion of principles relies upon a narrative supplied by Adam Smith: Ashley's initial discussion of state regulation looks back to 1846, and so to Smith's own remarks on the grain trade. The second chapter likewise begins from Smith on free trade and protection, ending with remarks on the agricultural distress of 1874. Statistics of trade are presented at length, but as Pigou had observed, '... to measure general well-being by the very small part of them represented in our foreign trade returns is not only inadmissible, but is little short of ridiculous.'[95] Pigou applied the basic instruments of Marshallian economics to a contemporary policy problem, in the process asking what the problem exactly was; Ashley, by contrast, treated this contemporary problem as a given, and sought a historical explanation for its existence that both reaffirmed an unexamined problem and provided no specific guidance on what measures might alleviate the perceived problem other than those already proposed. Critics of the 'Professors' in the letters columns of *The Times* during the late summer of 1903 suggested that these academics had failed to present a detailed refutation of Chamberlain's proposals,[96] as though any problem had ever been adequately identified and detailed proposals presented capable of being refuted. Their criticism was said to be premature because the new policy had not yet been fully elaborated. It never was. Ashley's mode of defence simply compounded this problem.

In 1907 Ashley gave the Presidential Address to Section F of the British Association and, as in his Toronto and Harvard inaugural addresses, presented a survey of contemporary economic thinking. His reference points changed little in the interim—Mill, Ricardo, Cliffe Leslie, Malthus. As at Harvard, he did observe that there had not yet been a 'substantial reconstruction among English-speaking economists on *historical* lines'.[97] For the first time he added criticism of the new economics: it was all true, 'so far as it goes'; but

> [i]nstead of leading us to the very heart of the problem, the doctrine of marginal value seems to me to remain entirely on the surface: it is not much more than a verbal description of the superficial facts at a particular point in time. The intensity of demand varies inversely, more or less rapidly, with the extent to which it is satisfied; for different commodities there are different scales of intensity; under certain conditions

[94] Ashley, *The Tariff Problem*, p. 139.
[95] Pigou, *Riddle of the Tariff*, p. 3.
[96] As, for example, W. A. S. Hewins, *The Times*, 20 August 1903.
[97] W. J. Ashley, 'The Present Position of Political Economy', *Economic Journal* Vol. 17 (1907), p. 475.

> one demand will be substituted for another. True, doubtless. But *why* do people demand just those things? On what does the rapidity of satiation depend? Have their desires always been the same; or the possibilities of production in order to meet them? How are desires related to one another? What are they likely to become? What are the limits to demand set by the economic situation of the demanders? These are the things we really want to know. The problem is, in a wide sense of the term, an *historical* one; or, if you prefer the phrase, a *sociological* one, both 'static' and 'dynamic'.[98]

And so rather than the divergence of economics and economic history in the early 1900s being the consequence of a process of progressive exclusion, it is more plausible to identify the emergence of a diverging array of problems. Pigou posed questions, adduced analytical instruments and evidence, in order to arrive at a solution for a present problem (if it indeed existed). Ashley's interest in *why* people seek the satisfactions that they do is not, as he here seems to concede, an economic question; it is a historical one. To understand the implications of choices people make, we do not need to know why they make them; that is part of the (subsequent) policy process, not the (prior) analytical process. With Marshall's retirement in 1908, Ashley applied for the Cambridge chair; given the preceding statement of his own interests, he had been quite openly detached from the direction taken by teaching in Cambridge since the 1880s.

William Cunningham's Historical Economics

A more direct confrontation of historical and analytical approaches to economics than that encountered in the writings of Ashley can be found in the work of William Cunningham. His *Growth of English Industry and Commerce* was the first concise textbook of English economic history;[99] when the book appeared, no hard and fast division had yet been established between economic history and economic science. Such a division became more evident during the 1890s, as teaching at Cambridge became more specialised, and of course consequent upon the formation of the British Economic Association, together with its raison d'etre, the *Economic Journal*—both projects initiated and promoted by Marshall. Cunningham remained undeterred by the implications of these developments. He continued to pronounce confidently upon economic history and economics alike. During the 1890s he tirelessly proclaimed the limitations of economics,[100] in 1892 delivering an especially provocative address to the Royal Historical Society which rehearsed the inadequacies of Marshall as an economic historian on the evidence of the first edition of his *Principles*. As he there stated,

[98] Ibid., pp. 476–77.

[99] The first edition in 1882 was in one octavo volume; subsequent editions led to a major expansion of the text into two multipart vclumes.

[100] His Inaugural Lecture as Tooke Professor of Economic Science and Statistics, King's College, London, damned contemporary economics with faint praise: '... Economics may help us to see the extent and nature of the difficulties involved in some particular scheme of improvement.' W. Cunningham, 'The Relativity of Economic Doctrine', *Economic Journal* Vol. 2 (1892), p. 15.

> The underlying assumption against which I wish to protest is never explicitly formulated by those who rely upon it; but it may I think, be not unfairly expressed in some such terms as these. That the same motives have been at work in all ages, and have produced similar results, and that, therefore, it is possible to formulate economic laws which describe the actions of economic causes at all times and in all places.... It would seem to follow that these economic laws could be most conveniently studied in the present, under our own eyes, as it were; but that when once recognised and state, they serve to explain the past.[101]

This, Cunningham then states, is the only interpretation that he is able to put upon the work of Marshall.

As previously noted,[102] the first edition of *Principles* opened with a lengthy account of the historical evolution of economic forms, rooted in Marshall's reading of Maine, Hegel, and German historical economists during the 1870s. The slow and deliberate path that Marshall trod from his first engagement with political economy to the publication of *Principles* can lead one to forget that he had started on this route long before, in the later 1860s; and that he had as a consequence along the way shared many of the historical interests more usually attributed to Cunningham, Toynbee, and Ashley, respectively 7, 10, and 18 years his junior. The second chapter of *Principles* as published in 1890 still bears the marks of this engagement. While this opens with a direct rebuttal of Ashley's embrace of institutions and social groups—Marshall bluntly states that the 'chief events in history are due to the actions of individuals'[103]—he proceeds with an account of the development of civilisation that pays due attention to climate, migration, settlement, and custom. His survey of the European Middle Ages, characterised with regard to feudalism on the one hand and the rise of towns on the other, is followed by a third chapter on the specifically English evolution through Reformation to early modernity; and this is followed by a fourth chapter on 'The Growth of Economic Science' that culminates in a consideration of German historical economics. However, in the sixth chapter we find the historical path inflected into a brief consideration of economic motivation that amounts to a historicised account of the twin human spurs of pleasure and pain that Jevons had laid out in his *Theory of Political Economy* of 1871. In brief, Marshall embedded his exposition of economic principles within a historical framework very similar to that which Ashley and Toynbee had originally sketched out.

But this was only a foundation for what followed, the presentation of analytical tools capable of being employed in the study of economic formations, past and present. Cunningham, by contrast, saw the development of an analytical apparatus as significant merely as a means to the creation of a classification of all possible economic activity, present and future:

101 W. Cunningham, 'The Perversion of Economic History', *Economic Journal* Vol. 2 (1892), pp. 491–506: here at p. 493.

102 See the discussion in Chapter 6, pp. 166–67.

103 Alfred Marshall, *Principles of Economics Vol. I*, Macmillan, London 1890, p. 9.

> We require an exhaustive analysis of all possible forms of exchange: we might thus discriminate the different kinds of bargains that can possibly take place, so that we might at once recognise any type when we come across it.... If it were worked out as to give us a complete analysis of the process of exchange in all its various forms, it would be a boon of the greatest possible advantage to the historian. He would have at once a means of naming and discussing phenomena which are no longer actual in the present day, and which are therefore very unfamiliar, but which may have been the prevailing type in some bygone age. The complete analysis of the process of exchange in all its possible forms would furnish him with an organon of the first importance as an instrument of study and with a most convenient terminology for his investigations.[104]

Cunningham proposed that the purpose of studying economic history was to arrive at a complete classification of exchanges; Marshall, by contrast, sought analytical tools that lent insight into the economic dynamic such exchanges created or inhibited. And he by no means denied his interest in economic history, acknowledging the influence upon him of Sir Henry Maine, and acknowledging the work of Vinogradoff and of Ashley.[105]

Hence also Marshall's frustration with Cunningham's criticisms: far from subscribing to the view that the same motives have been at work through the ages, producing similar results and hence demonstrating the constancy of economic laws, Marshall described his *Principles* as follows:

> The whole volume is indeed occupied mainly in showing how similar causes acting on people under dissimilar conditions produce more or less divergent effects. The leading motive of its argument is the opposite of that which Dr. Cunningham ascribes to it.[106]

As he stated in conclusion, Cunningham assumed that Marshall held opinions that he did not hold, or express; and where he might, on occasion, have expressed directly contrary opinions.[107]

Furthermore, Cunningham's account of the process of exchange was to be developed from the standpoint of the seller, an approach which, as John Maloney has demonstrated, results in an incoherent account of price formation. By leaving the consumer's demand schedule out of the account entirely, Cunningham is forced into a series of contortions in seeking to account for the emergence of a stable level of prices, in which it is the seller alone who determines the final level of prices.[108]

This is an economic theory of sorts, however, even if an untenable one; and it had characterised the framework within which Cunningham's *Growth of English Industry*

[104] W. Cunningham, 'A Plea for Pure Theory', *Economic Review* Vol. 2 (1892), pp. 28, 29. Marshall used the term *organon* to denote the instrumentaria of the trained economist.

[105] Alfred Marshall, 'A Reply', *Economic Journal* Vol. 2 (1892), p. 509.

[106] Ibid., p. 508.

[107] Ibid., p. 517.

[108] J. Maloney, *Marshall, Orthodoxy and the Professionalisation of Economics*, Cambridge University Press, Cambridge 1985, pp. 93–94.

and Commerce is written. Book I consists of three chapters, on property, collective industry, and exchange. The economic system is introduced from the first as an organism, rather than a machine, for

> ... a machine only produces, but each part of an organism needs to be constantly nourished, and the means by which the various parts are sustained is a most important part of animal economy.... A great nation is not a mere machine for producing the greatest amount of wealth with the greatest amount of speed, it is an organism which cannot be healthy unless the conditions of distribution are satisfactory as well as those of production. Indeed, when the distribution of wealth is thoroughly unsatisfactory there can neither be really good production nor true national progress.[109]

The nature of this interdependence is then elaborated metaphorically through the following pages, but the interdependence envisaged is constantly one between production and distribution, the latter treated as a means for the continuation of production; consumption, the third pillar of the classical system as first outlined by Say, plays no part here.

As far as the history of economic systems themselves goes, the shift from 'ancient' to 'modern' is conceptualised by Cunningham in terms of the emergence of competition as the principal agent of change, a concept which has a key role in Cunningham's treatment of modernity.[110] The degree of equality and fairness inhering in the 'modern' system is related to the number of agents engaging in economic activity; although when dealing with the medieval idea of the 'just' price, Cunningham writes of the number of buyers, not of sellers, as being decisive.[111] Furthermore, by dealing with 'modern times' as ruled by the principle of competition, Cunningham is able to deny that modern economic theory has any analytical purchase upon older economic forms.[112] The history of industry and commerce, Cunningham states,

> ... is only the story of the various ways in which these human *resources* have been applied so as to satisfy constantly developing human wants.[113]

Wants, Cunningham implies, develop autonomously, they are not primarily historically given; the object of historical understanding is instead the changing character of the resources embodied in the spheres of production and distribution.

[109] W. Cunningham, *The Growth of English Industry and Commerce*, Cambridge University Press, London 1882, p. 3.

[110] Semmel notes that Cunningham underwent a conversion from free trade to protection between the second 1892 edition of *Growth of English Industry and Commerce* and the fifth in 1910, occurring about 1902; Semmel, *Imperialism and Social Reform*, pp. 191–93.

[111] Ibid., pp. 244–47. Although Cunningham does discuss the issue of consumers' utilities here in the formation of prices, he also refers to *sellers'* utilities. The treatment of exchange and the price mechanism is extremely confused, and gets no better in later work.

[112] 'Unless the free competition which they take for granted existed to some considerable extent, modern economic principles only confuse our study of the actual industrial development of any period of the past.' Cunningham, *Growth*, p. 8.

[113] Ibid., p. 12.

On this point Cunningham was perfectly consistent: in his critique of free trade he argued that

> [t]he Free Trader insists that he looks at economic life from the point of view of the consumer.... He argues that by Free Trade and the competition of nation with nation, every country will receive from the total of the world's stock an equivalent for the contribution which that nation has made to the world's stock.... This is an inadequate view of economic life. Consumption is certainly the object in view in manufacturing or transporting goods, and it is a necessary phase in utilising them at all. As we have seen, the question as to what persons shall have a claim to share in consuming is of supreme importance; but apart from this, consumption does not call for much consideration: after all, it is a form of destruction, and can be left to take care of itself.[114]

But, argues Cunningham, the future of national prosperity cannot be left to itself with such equanimity: this must be the object of constant vigilance, with the government formulating national aims based upon forecasts of future conditions:

> The maintenance of prosperity depends on calling forth the active principles of energy and enterprise which shape the materials furnished by nature, so that they may serve human purposes to better advantage.[115]

Historical economics is rendered, therefore, as supply-side economics, an account of production that neglected the way in which human activity created the needs that human industry then sought to satisfy, the interaction that lay at the heart of the 'new economics'.

Cunningham's history, in its first edition, ended its account in the late eighteenth century, as the production and distribution of wealth become part of an autonomous sphere, and thus susceptible to analysis '... as though they were almost isolated from other social phenomena'.[116] History ceases here, and modern political economy takes over—the entire nineteenth century is an undifferentiated present not susceptible to historicising interpretation.[117] Here there was indeed some complementarity with Marshall, whose new Cambridge curriculum gave an important role to economic history, where the

> ... student of economics is invited to give his main attention to recent history, that is chiefly the history of the nineteenth century, with some reference to earlier times.[118]

[114] W. Cunningham, *The Case against Free Trade*, John Murray, London 1911, pp. 42–43.
[115] Ibid., p. 43.
[116] Cunningham, *Growth*, p. 387.
[117] This was modified in later editions, but only through the extension of the period of study into the early nineteenth century. The third edition, published in three sections between 1896 and 1907, brings the account up to the 1840s in its later pages.
[118] Alfred Marshall, *The New Cambridge Curriculum in Economics*, London 1903, p. 27.

As has already been noted, the first edition of Marshall's *Principles* had begun with a lengthy treatment of the growth of both industry and commerce on the one hand, and economic science on the other. From the opening passage of the first chapter, however, there is a clarity of purpose quite absent from Cunningham's accounts of the nature and purpose of economics:

> §1. POLITICAL ECONOMY, or ECONOMICS, is a study of man's actions in the ordinary business of life; it inquires how he gets his income and how he uses it. Thus it is on the one side a study of wealth and on the other, a more important side, a part of the study of man.[119]

The history which Marshall unfolds from this starting point is one of dynamic development, formed in the conflict between human interests, with the Darwinian principle of natural selection playing a major role. Hence industry and enterprise are part of an evolutionary system; a system undergoing progressive adaptation and change.

> These were the conditions under which the modern industrial life of England was developed: the desire for material comforts tends towards a ceaseless straining to extract from every week the greatest amount of work that can be got out if it. The firm resolution to submit every action to the deliberate judgement of the reason tends to make every one constantly ask himself whether he could not improve his position by changing his business, or by changing his method if doing it. And, lastly, complete political freedom and security enables [*sic*] every one to adjust his conduct as he has decided that it is his interest to do, and fearless to commit his person and his property to new and distant undertakings.[120]

Nonetheless, Marshall did not harness this evolutionary history to an unalloyed belief in progress. Already in the first chapter of *Principles* the hope had been expressed that poverty might be eradicated, while the wretchedness of those millions living in near-poverty was also recognised.[121] Although this might be a worthy ethical aim, evolutionary change would not automatically rectify the plight of the poor. Marshall recognised that the Darwinian principle of 'natural selection' (his quotation marks) stated that those organisms tended to survive which were best fitted to benefit from the environment for their own purposes—not those which most benefited the environment.[122] In an after-dinner speech to the Royal Economic Society in 1907, he extended this thought to include the importance of urban planning for the welfare of future generations, and thence reversed the customary meaning of laissez-faire to '… Let the State be up and doing…'[123] It was of course Pigou, Marshall's successor, who developed these thoughts into a welfare economics circumscribing the role and

119 Marshall, *Principles* (1890), p. 1.
120 Ibid., pp. 36–37.
121 Ibid., pp. 3–4.
122 Ibid., p. 302.
123 Alfred Marshall, 'The Social Possibilities of Economic Chivalry', *Economic Journal* Vol. 17 (1907), p. 19.

functions of the state, in which government activity at most facilitated and directed those forces already at work in the economy.

As we have seen previously, Ashley approached economic phenomena with a different set of questions to those of Marshall and his like-minded peers. Ultimately the economic histories which Ashley and Cunningham produced were indebted to the principles of the very political economy that they are thought to have displaced. This in turn undermined their position when disputing the authority of contemporary economics. Cunningham understood its principles poorly, and his forays into economic analysis are confused and contradictory. He did nevertheless provide a substantial basis for the teaching of economic history in his *Growth of English Industry and Commerce*. Ashley understood these principles rather better, but found them uninspiring; he was, shortly before his death, instrumental in the formation of the Economic History Society, which secured the institutional place of Economic History in much the same way that the foundation of the British Economic Association had inaugurated that for economics.[124]

[124] T. C. Barker, 'The Beginnings of the Economic History Society', *Economic History Review* Second Series, Vol. 30 (1977), p. 5.

PART IV
COMMERCE AND ECONOMICS

Elements of a commercial curriculum predated the creation of an economics curriculum, and in many respects pre-empted it. In Germany, it took just over 20 years to progress from the first attempt to upgrade existing commercial teaching in 1898 to a fully-fledged higher qualification with a dedicated curriculum, textbooks, purpose-built institutions, and a constant stream of students.[1] Commercial colleges also flourished in France, the Netherlands, Italy, and Belgium. Hitotsubashi University in Tokyo began as an "Institute for Business Training" in 1875, changing its name in 1920 to the Tokyo College of Commerce and modelling itself on the German *Handelshochschulen*. The London School of Economics (LSE) was late to this development, not initiating a Bachelor of Commerce (BCom) degree until 1920, but then already by the later 1930s making plans for its merging with the existing BSc (Econ.). Accounts of this early development of commercial education have tended to treat it as a premature and unsuccessful forerunner to modern business education. Here instead I point to the way that this more vocational and technical education could have provided a framework for the teaching of economics, in a kind of reciprocal move to that of Marshall, but with the same underlying aim. While I keep in view international, and especially German, developments, my focus is on British institutions in the later nineteenth and early twentieth centuries that did combine commercial and economic education, so that the vocational alternative to Marshall's Economics Tripos is made clear. However, teaching in British provincial institutions drifted away from vocational and towards academic provision, converging with more specialised economics teaching rather than providing a framework for a more vocational variant. Chapter 10 seeks to explain why higher-level teaching of commerce converged in Britain with a more academic economics, rather than provide a basis for an economics oriented towards business and commerce.

The accounts of commercial initiatives in Birmingham, Manchester, Edinburgh, Liverpool, Leeds, and the LSE given here are in no respect full histories of departments and faculties. As already noted, in Britain archives usually lack the records that would be needed for any detailed reconstruction of the development of British university institutions after 1940. Instead, the following three chapters address one particular question: Why in Britain did the early adoption of higher commercial education outside Oxbridge eventually become a vehicle for the development of economics, and not the basis for today's business schools? Why was it that an evident student demand for vocational training in commercial subjects transmuted into the provision of the

[1] See Ch. 5 In my *Strategies of Economic Order, German Economic Discourse 1750–1950*, Cambridge University Press, Cambridge 1995/2007.

teaching of "economics" and the eventual suppression of higher commercial education? In commercial education at any level, Britain was something of a laggard, as Chapter 9 makes clear in reviewing developments in the United States, France, and Germany. Chapter 10 considers the fortunes of university commercial education in four main centres: Birmingham, Manchester, Liverpool, and Leeds. The foundation in 1901 of the Faculty of Commerce in the new University of Birmingham had very mixed results until the Faculty was lent a new sense of direction with the appointment of Sargent Florence as professor in 1929. Manchester was altogether the most successful in developing a viable Commerce degree, but this too had by the mid-1940s been eclipsed by the teaching of economics. A similar trajectory is shown to have occurred in Liverpool, a thriving commercial city in the later nineteenth century with a large number of potential students for vocational degrees. Chapter 11 then demonstrates how the LSE, founded to serve vocational ends, was from the early 1930s deliberately transformed into the leading centre for university economic education in Britain. In each of these cases, the purpose is not to simply rehearse a historical account of these institutional developments, but to demonstrate how it was that commerce had, by the 1940s, ceded its role to economics. Chapter 12 then demonstrates how the turn to economics was achieved through the elaboration of economics as a set of abstract principles, displacing the Marshallian conception of economics as a toolbox from which instruments could be selected that were suited to the analysis of current problems.

9

Models for Commercial Education

The United States, France, and Germany

As already noted, the peroration to Alfred Marshall's 1885 Inaugural Lecture foresaw the future for economics in preparing young people for the demands that the modern world of industry and administration would place upon them. This general sentiment was, however, by no means novel. All around the world—in Europe, the United States, Canada, Australia, Japan—the argument was being made that the wealth and welfare of a country ultimately depended on the skills of its people, and that educational reform was urgently needed at several levels to provide populations with the technical and vocational skills that a modern economy demanded of them. Fritz Ringer neatly summarised the argument as follows:

> Pointing to international economic competition, in which they supposed other countries to have threatening initial advantages, they urged greater attention to the need for trained manpower. Occasionally, they implied that the nation would benefit from a new kind of business leadership, perhaps one with greater scientific or technical expertise. Much more often, what they principally had in mind was a need for new skills at the intermediate and lower levels of the commercial and industrial hierarchy. They therefore recommended or supported a more 'modern', 'scientific' or 'technical' emphasis in secondary or post-primary schools; or they championed 'applied' studies at institutions of a more advanced type that later came to be ranked at university level.[1]

Ringer was writing here of France in the 1860s, but as we shall see, criticism of failures in the existing national provision for technical and commercial education was commonplace in the closing decades of the nineteenth century. What marked Marshall out was his argument that, at university level, a specialised education in economics was what was needed, and the inauguration of the Tripos in 1903 seemed to fulfil this. Why, then, as economics became a subject regularly taught in educational institutions at different levels, did it so quickly become detached from those contemporary initiatives for vocational education that had lent it vital support? Why, just 50 years after Marshall's inaugural lecture, had the teaching of economics already become its own rationale, with no special vocational imperative? And why did commercial education itself not generate a disciplinary framework for economics that might have provided an alternative to the path the new discipline did take, from vocational aspiration to

[1] Fritz Ringer, 'On Segmentation in Modern European Educational Systems: The Case of French Secondary Education, 1865–1920', in D. K. Müller, F. Ringer, B. Simon (eds.) *The Rise of the Modern Educational System*, Cambridge University Press, Cambridge 1987, p. 61.

Constructing Economic Science. Keith Tribe, Oxford University Press. © Oxford University Press 2022.
DOI: 10.1093/oso/9780190491741.003.0009

academic specialised routine? Why did commercial education eventually transmute into a business education that more or less does without any formal economic training at all?

In this and the following chapter I will examine the early history of higher commercial education from this perspective: why a vocational pedagogy directed towards management and public administration gave way in university institutions to a new discipline of economics that, *contra* Marshall, came to have very limited direct vocational application. As it happened, in Britain the first Faculty of Commerce opened in Birmingham just one year before the Cambridge Economics Tripos was inaugurated; compared with developments in the United States, France, and Germany, the development of higher commercial education in Britain ran in parallel with the initiation of systematic undergraduate teaching in economics, not in advance of it. British initiatives in commercial and economic education could draw upon existing models in making arguments and designing curricula; but at the same time they competed with the early development of university economics in Britain. In this chapter I will review what American, French, and German models offered, all of them organised by the widespread contemporary perception that changes in the contemporary labour markets of industrial economies required an educated workforce: most basically, a modern school curriculum, coupled with specialised higher technical and commercial education.[2] In the next chapter I track the early development of British higher commercial education, and show why this beginning did not turn into the kind of business education that developed in the United States, France, and Germany. And the most convenient place to start for these purposes is with the foundation of the Wharton School at the University of Pennsylvania in 1881, four years before Marshall's Inaugural.

The View from the United States

Joseph Wharton (1826–1909) made his money managing metalworks, eventually gaining a majority shareholding in Bethlehem Steel. Born into a Quaker family, together with his mother and several other Quakers he had already co-founded Swarthmore College in 1864. Having started out as a bookkeeper, he was also conscious that little in the way of systematic business education existed.[3] In 1881 he offered the University of Pennsylvania $100,000 to found a School of Finance and Economy, his formal letter to the Trustees of 24 March 1881 stating his aims in terms not that dissimilar to those of Alfred Marshall four years later:

[2] For an accessible and reliable survey that begins with eighteenth-century German and Austrian initiatives, see Fritz Redlich, 'Academic Education for Business: Its Development and the Contribution of Ignaz Jastrow (1856–1937)', *Business History Review* Vol. 31 (1957), pp. 35–91. Also useful for the general context is Robert R. Locke, *The End of Practical Man: Entrepreneurship and Higher Education in Germany, France and Great Britain 1880–1940*, JAI Press, Greenwich, Conn. 1984.

[3] An early proposal made in 1868–1869 for a School of Commerce at Washington College, Lexington (now Washington and Lee University), oriented to teaching the principles of commerce, economy, trade, and mercantile law, and not simply bookkeeping, got as far as a detailed curriculum, but no further; see C. S. Marsh, 'General Lee and a School of Commerce', *Journal of Political Economy* Vol. 34 (1926), pp. 657–59.

> To provide for young men special means of training and of correct instruction in the knowledge and in the arts of modern Finance and Economy, both public and private, in order that, being well informed and free from delusions upon these important subjects, they may either serve the community skillfully as well as faithfully in offices of trust, or, remaining in private life, may prudently manage their own affairs and aid in maintaining sound financial morality: in short, to establish means for imparting a liberal education in all matters concerning Finance and Economy.[4]

Although a number of technical and scientific colleges had recently been founded, no systematic provision was made for industry and trade, where it was expected that young recruits would acquire the skills they needed as they went along. Many would, therefore, spend much of their time doing routine work; but Wharton maintained that there were now college graduates who were too old for this kind of drudgery:

> No country can afford to have this inherited wealth and capacity wasted for want of that fundamental knowledge which would enable the possessors to employ them with advantage to themselves and to the community .... Nor can any country long afford to have its laws made and its government administered by men who lack such training as would suffice to rid the minds of fallacies and qualify them for the solution of the social problems incident to our civilization.[5]

Wharton's gift was only one, and by no means the most substantial, of many that would transform American universities in the later nineteenth century. But while his choice of beneficiary was strictly local, it was not random. The University of Pennsylvania was strongly connected to the protectionist political economy of Henry Carey, and in 1868–1869 a Careyite 'social science' course was made a requirement in the senior year elective curriculum, its teacher Robert Ellis Thompson being regarded as an apostle of Careyite political economy. Then, in 1871, Stephen Colwell, an iron manufacturer, Careyite economic writer, and friend of Wharton, died and left a library of 6,000 works on political economy to the university, on the condition that the university would expand teaching in the social sciences. In 1874 Thompson was made Professor of Social Science; and he then published his lectures in 1875 as *Social Science and National Economy*. Thompson's text and his course became the core of the new school's teaching, because for the first two years at least little was added to existing provision besides courses in commercial law. Not until the mid-1890s did commercial education at Wharton begin to cohere around courses in banking, insurance, commerce, and transportation. While Wharton School represents the inaugural foundation for higher commercial education in the United States, it did not immediately create a curriculum that could serve as a model for replication elsewhere.

Instead, arguments for the development of higher commercial education in the United States would be made by Edmund J. James (1855–1925), who in 1883 was appointed Professor of Public Finance and Administration in the Wharton School. He

[4] Cited in S. A. Sass, *The Pragmatic Imagination: A History of the Wharton School 1881–1981*, University of Pennsylvania Press, Philadelphia 1982, p. 21.
[5] Ibid., p. 22.

had studied at Northwestern and Harvard and then in 1875 went to Halle, where he completed a dissertation on the American tariff system with Johannes Conrad.[6] Sass notes that James brought German manners to Pennsylvania: on Sunday afternoons his house was open to students and faculty, his lectures were based on a German professorial style rather than recitation and drills, and in 1885 he founded a 'Seminary for Political and Economic Science'.[7] James went on in December 1889 to found the American Academy of Political and Social Science, his core support coming from Wharton faculty and students; but his chief interest for us here lies in his general advocacy of commercial education. In the autumn of 1889 the American Bankers' Association invited James to make a presentation on the need for schools of finance and economy, modelled on the Wharton School, at their annual meeting the following year. This he did with such success that the Association printed his address as 'Education of Business Men' and circulated it to banks, newspapers, universities, and colleges, seeking to encourage the foundation of more institutions on the Wharton model. There was such a positive response to this initiative that James was then commissioned to travel to Europe in the summer of 1892 to report on provision for business education.[8]

In his preliminary report of 1892, James seems to have recapitulated many of the arguments already made in founding the Wharton School, but his full report of the following year assembled a great deal of material relating to European curricula, methods of instruction, examinations, attendance, and teaching staff.[9] He included Leipzig, where the initiative for the German *Handelshochschulen* would begin six years later; he also covered the two leading institutions in Paris; and in his final chapter, after almost two hundred pages, he turned to Britain, where provision and aspiration could be quickly summed up:

> It is not far from the truth to say that there is no such instruction [higher commercial education] given in England at all, at least such thorough, systematic and advanced instruction as would justify our putting it in the same category as that of France, Austria or Germany.[10]

His principal source was the chapter on commercial education in Philip Magnus's *Industrial Education*,[11] which rehearsed the lack of vocational training in British secondary schools, and the lack of any suitable institutions of further education. James,

[6] Edmund J. James, *Studien ueber den amerikanischen Zolltarif. Seine Entwickelung und seinen Einfluss auf die Volkswirtschaft*, Verlag von Hermann Dufft, Jena 1877, 80 pp.

[7] Sass, *The Pragmatic Imagination*, p. 62.

[8] Edmund J. James, *A Plea for the Establishment of Commercial High Schools: An Address before the Convention of the American Bankers' Association at San Francisco, September 7, 1892*, American Bankers' Association, New York 1893, p. 5.

[9] He reported on the Commercial Academy in Vienna; the Commercial Academy, Prague; the Superior School of Commerce and the School of Higher Commercial Studies, Paris; the Public Commercial Institute, Leipzig; the Superior Institute of Commerce, Antwerp; and the Superior School of Commerce, Venice. Edmund J. James, *Education of Business Men in Europe: A Report to the American Bankers' Association through its Committee on Schools of Finance and Economy*, American Bankers' Association, New York 1893.

[10] Ibid., p. 194.

[11] Sir Philip Magnus, *Industrial Education*, Kegan Paul, Trench & Co., London 1888, Ch. III, 'Mercantile Training—Schools of Commerce'.

following Magnus, attributed the absence of educational provision to the commercial advantage Britain had long enjoyed; this leading to the neglect of formal educational provision, with the result that the former commercial advantage was now being eroded by superior educational provision in France, Germany, and elsewhere. James reproduced the syllabus for the London Chamber of Commerce Commercial Certificates, as well as extracts from examination papers—on letter writing, commercial geography, English history, and German—from the University of Oxford's commercial certificate.[12] Also included was a report to the Sheffield Chamber of Commerce, as well as a summary of points made by Walter G. Blackie in an address to the Glasgow Local Association of the Educational Institute of Scotland in March 1888.[13] This rehearses the same issues—the lack of provision in Britain, the superiority of the German school system, the teaching of the Leipzig Commercial Institute, noting that during 1886 80 students attended a one-year course for former Gymnasium students offered by the Vienna commercial college.

James continued as an advocate for commercial education, presenting in a survey of American commercial education for the Paris Exposition of 1900 a comprehensive account of provision at all levels in the United States at the end of the century. He began by distinguishing four levels:

independent commercial colleges;
business courses in public high schools;
private endowed schools;
college and university courses.

There had been perhaps a dozen independent commercial colleges in the mid-1850s, located in the larger cities and training young men for work as clerks and bookkeepers. Provision initially involved mainly evening classes over three months for those already in work, with for example exercises in accounting being set by local accountants. These colleges had gradually evolved into predominantly daytime institutions with practical instruction in clerical methods, at the time of writing there being 341 institutions with 77,746 students.[14] Another significant factor promoting increasingly uniform provision at this level was that the University of New York had established a set of conditions for the recognition of schools—that they have at least six qualified teachers, $5,000 worth of classroom equipment, and a one-year course of at least 500 hours.[15] Linked to these conditions was the provision of a business diploma awarded to students who had studied for one year and had passed examinations in advanced bookkeeping, commercial law, business English, arithmetic, business practice and office methods, commercial geography, and the history of commerce. However, James went on, American commercial colleges were not

[12] Ibid., pp. 201–207.
[13] W. G. Blackie, *Commercial Education*, Blackie and Son, Glasgow 1888.
[14] E. J. James, *Commercial Education*, Monographs on Education in the United States No. 13, J. B. Lyon, Albany N.Y. 1900, p. 7.
[15] Ibid., p. 13.

> ... educational institutions in any broad sense of the term at all. They are trade schools pure and simple, and that in a very narrow sense. They train for facilities. Of course all training has intellectual results, even that of a prize fighter. But the commercial college aims not to train the best bookkeepers, or stenographers, for, to such, a high degree of education is necessary, but to take the boy or man as he is, with or without education, stupid or bright, and make as good a bookkeeper or stenographer out of him as is possible, by simply superadding a brief technical training. The limitations of such a school are perfectly evident to every educationist. It trains the clerk, the routinist, the amanuensis, not the manager or director of a business enterprises.[16]

These issues of age of instruction, level of institution, and of curriculum would recur in contemporary debate on the development of commercial education.

Besides post-school vocational training, teaching in high schools was also developing. James included in his text a plan for a four-year course at the Philadelphia Central High School drawn up in 1898, moving from more conventional subjects in the first year to foreign languages, industrial and commercial history, and statistics by the fourth.[17] And, besides high school provision, James also considered that of private secondary schools, the total enrolment in these institutions being estimated at 20,000 nationwide. Here his example was the Drexel Institute of Arts, Science and Industry, Philadelphia, where students had to be 16 before being admitted to a course in commerce and finance lasting two years.[18]

Echoing Magnus, James had already noted in 1893 that, for commercial education to be conducted at anything beyond a routine level in college and university, a modern school syllabus was needed that could provide the foundation for vocational training. This was not an especial problem in the United States, but a modern school syllabus was entirely absent in Britain. All the same, the interface between school and university in the United States remained a problem. Whereas it had been difficult to introduce anything other than purely practical training in the non-university institutions considered so far, universities were by contrast reluctant to engage with the practical side of commercial education. On the one hand, commercial colleges regarded political economy, commercial geography, and similar topics as subjects too remote for their curricula; while in the universities accounting, commercial arithmetic, and the like were considered too elementary.[19] This dilemma continually resurfaced in arguments about the scope and function of university commercial education, especially where attempts were made to introduce commercial courses alongside established curricula. Indeed, as the German and French examples would demonstrate, to retain a vocational focus for higher-level commercial education, the surest solution was to found an entirely independent institution connected to the business community, bypassing the established university system altogether.

In 1900 James discussed only four American universities—the University of Pennsylvania (Wharton School), the University of Chicago's College of Commerce

[16] Ibid., pp. 17–18.
[17] Ibid., p. 26.
[18] See ibid., pp. 29–34, for an overview of courses, syllabus, organisation, and fees.
[19] Ibid., p. 36.

and Politics (first enrolments 1898), the University of California at Berkeley, and Columbia University. Of these, only Wharton could be said to be truly established;[20] James had no real information on California, Columbia was only at the planning stage, and while Chicago had been functioning since 1898, only 12 students had enrolled in its first year of operation. In any case, the four-year course at Chicago followed a conventional liberal arts programme for two years before turning, in years three and four, to focus upon commerce, politics, journalism, and diplomacy; so at the time of writing the core commercial courses in Chicago were also only in plan.[21] James placed greatest emphasis upon Columbia, since its plan represented the most comprehensive attempt to combine practical teaching with existing university courses, which is how in fact much American business education would develop in the 1920s.[22] The Columbia proposal involved 15 hours a week over four years for graduates of public or private secondary schools in which English, mathematics, history, natural science, and one modern language had been systematically studied to the level required for admission to a college department of Columbia University. This itself was an important condition, given the variability of secondary tuition and the danger that university-level institutions attracting a broader constituency would find themselves remedying the schooling of their students. James ended his survey on a downbeat note, emphasising that at the time of writing no independent college of commerce with adequate funding had been founded in the United States, nor anything that could be accurately termed a commercial high school.

A more comprehensive international survey of commercial education was published in 1904 by Cheesman Herrick, Director of the School of Commerce, Central High School, Philadelphia. Besides updating James's 1900 survey of American provision, Herrick gave a thorough account of the new German *Handelshochschule* movement, of institutions in Paris and Lyons, and of the well-established commercial college in Antwerp. He drew attention to the fact that in Belgium commercial subjects formed an option within the secondary education system for three years up to the age of 15 or 16, after which students could seek clerical employment or pursue their studies in evening classes and in higher schools of commerce.[23] The Antwerp Superior School of Commerce had been initiated in 1853, with an average attendance during the 1860s of 86, of 128 from 1870 to 1886, in 1903 having a total attendance of 208.[24] Post-school French and Belgian institutions were therefore already well-established by the time that the Wharton School was founded, while the rapid development of the German *Handelshochschulen* after 1898 would soon eclipse the quality of provision anywhere else. By contrast, Herrick's survey of British provision began from James's earlier observation that little could be said about British commercial

[20] Student numbers at Wharton were given by James as 59 in 1892–1893; 71 in 1893–1894; 113 in 1894–1895; 97 in 1895–1896; 101 in 1896–1897; and 87 in 1897–1898; ibid., p. 40.

[21] James was now Professor of Public Administration at Chicago, and noted that there were at the time no special technical courses on accounting, business law, and business practice in Chicago; ibid., p. 42.

[22] See F. Ruml, 'The Existing Curriculum and Offerings in Collegiate Education for Business', in L. C. Marshall (ed.) *The Collegiate School of Business*, University of Chicago Press, Chicago 1928, pp. 94–95.

[23] Cheesman A. Herrick, *Meaning and Practice of Commercial Education*, Macmillan, New York 1904, p. 127.

[24] Ibid., p. 129. See also William Layton, 'Commercial Education in Belgium', *Journal of the Society of Arts* Vol. 43 (7 June 1895), pp. 690–95.

education because it barely existed. He laid emphasis upon the obstacle that the lack of a modern school curriculum presented,[25] but went on to summarise the work done by the London Chamber of Commerce, the Society of Arts examinations in technical and commercial subjects, and also the Pitman Metropolitan School, which had 1,500 day students in the early 1900s. Herrick also included in his survey the London School of Economics (pp. 163–66); the Liverpool School of Commerce (pp. 166–70); as well as the new Faculty of Commerce at Birmingham (pp. 171–73).

Herrick's survey of Europe from the perspective of the United States confirmed that British provision for commercial education at any level had progressed little since James's report to the American Bankers' Association in 1893. In that report James had reproduced passages from Walter G. Blackie's 1888 Glasgow address in which the lack of training in language skills for commercial clerks was compared unfavourably with provisions made in France and Germany. Like Herrick, Blackie saw the root of the problem in the existing school system, which in Scotland prepared their pupils for university, not for work; and that when pupils left school at 15 or 16 seeking employment, their education was of little use to them. Most of Blackie's address provided an account of the German and Austrian secondary education system, an appendix outlining the teaching programme of the Institut Superieur in Antwerp.[26]

Things were, however, quickly changing in the United States—in 1900 the Amos Tuck School of Administration and Finance opened at Dartmouth College, admitting students with three complete years of college education. The two-year course therefore completed a four-year undergraduate degree, and added a graduate year. At Harvard the prospect of founding a school modelled on the Paris *École des Sciences Politiques* for potential diplomats and civil servants was first raised in 1898, then resumed in 1906 when the idea of forming a separate school was adopted. By 1907 this had transmuted from public service to business education, and in March 1908 the Graduate School of Business Administration opened, offering a two-year course and a Master of Business Administration. Twenty-four regular students joined its first intake, studying three required courses—Principles of Accounting,[27] Commercial Contracts, and the Economic Resources of the United States—plus one elective drawn from a growing array of commercial subjects. Lack of a clear rationale and distinct syllabus for a second year meant that initially most students left after one year; steady expansion around a two-year programme only became established in 1914, with the case-study method being explicitly adopted in the 1920s as a distinctive style of pedagogy.[28] Harvard Business School had by the early 1920s a distinctive approach to

[25] Herrick, *Meaning and Practice of Commercial Education*, pp. 135–36. 'England has no well-organized national system of secondary education. Her secondary schools are mainly private institutions, and they have given themselves to grounding boys in classics and mathematics preparatory to competition for university honors in these subjects. Chambers of Commerce and other bodies of practical men have felt the disability under which England suffers from failure to furnish secondary education, and they have repeatedly put themselves on record as favoring an entirely new sort of secondary education.' (p. 161). This repeats Magnus's lament, *Industrial Education*, p. 95, that British provision lagged far behind German.

[26] Blackie, *Commercial Education*, pp. 41–50.

[27] William H. Cole had begun teaching a half-course in Principles of Accounting in the Harvard undergraduate economics course in 1900; *Harvard University Catalogue 1900–1901*, p. 383. This eventually became a Business School course in 1914–1915; M. T. Copeland, *And Mark an Era: The Story of the Harvard Business School*, Little, Brown, Boston 1958, p. 22.

[28] Ibid., pp. 37f.

management education, while the fact that it was a graduate institution brought more clearly into focus the kinds of occupation its students would be headed towards, in turn helping define the level and content of its teaching. It was only during this period that plans for building were drafted; the site was dedicated in June 1927, shortly after the Weeks Bridge and the Baker Library had opened.[29]

The rapid consolidation of American business education in the course of the 1920s was reflected in an important survey of domestic provision published in 1928. Leon Marshall recorded the foundation of 12 new institutions up to 1910, 21 more in 1900–1915, and 143 more from 1915 to 1924, so that by 1925 some 183 American colleges and universities, with perhaps 50,000 students, had some formal provision for business education.[30] A survey of 38 representative institutions made in 1925–1926 confirmed the variety of level, duration, and content across the field; it was noted that the broad qualifications required of most entrants increased the amount of time devoted to general education, especially since there were no generally agreed high school standards for English, foreign languages, the sciences, and history. All 38 institutions surveyed did offer accounting, with 37 offering money and banking, and business finance; and 36 offering marketing, business law, and statistics. Provision varied considerably, and so also the value of the qualifications awarded:

> In consequence of this and in consequence of the fact that so many collegiate schools of business have grown out of colleges of liberal arts, the typical school of business feels a divided responsibility. It seeks to give, or at least to enforce, both general education and technical education.
>
> In some sense, then, the typical collegiate school of business is sprawling over two areas of education, seldom with any definite, clear-cut standards of purpose or of performance with respect to either area, and never with any adequate control of the work of the preceding units of the American educational system.[31]

While the American system of higher commercial education had been established in the early 1880s, by the 1920s it had still not evolved into a standard form with a core curriculum. Economics teaching was usually elementary, and there was no alternative system of pedagogy that might provide a framework for specialised disciplinary development. The Harvard Business School did quickly acquire a distinctive profile, but this was not one that was widely imitated. Instead, diversity of provision and level prevailed.

Hence those in Britain who favoured the development of technical and commercial education did not as a rule look towards the United States for their models. In 1897 Sidney Webb, invoking James's remarks about British provision, had joined his voice to those of many contemporaries lamenting the relative lack of commercial education in Britain, emphasising that the major problem lay in the very real limitations

[29] J. L. Cruickshank, *A Delicate Experiment. The Harvard Business School 1908–1945*, Harvard Business School Press, Boston 1987, pp. 101–28.

[30] Leon C. Marshall, 'The American Collegiate School of Business', in Marshall (ed.) *The Collegiate School of Business*, University of Chicago, Chicago 1928, p. 4; the institutions concerned are listed on pp. 4–9.

[31] F. Ruml, 'The Existing Curriculum and Offerings in Collegiate Education for Business', in L. C. Marshall (ed.) *The Collegiate School of Business*, University of Chicago Press, Chicago 1928, p. 95.

of secondary education, once again pointing to the higher commercial colleges that had been founded in France since the 1860s.[32] The German schooling system was also in the 1890s widely thought to be exemplary, together with the role of *Technische Hochschulen* in the promotion of technical education. By the early 1900s attention had, as with Herrick, shifted to the new German commercial colleges. But before considering German provision, we need first to outline the early history of French commercial education. These three national histories will then provide the models against which we can judge the course taken by English Faculties of Commerce in the early 1900s, foundations which provided the immediate context for the development of economics in Britain outside Oxford and Cambridge.

French Commercial Education

Before 1870 there were only two commercial colleges in France: the *École supérieure du commerce* in Paris and the *École supérieure* in Mulhouse.[33] The first had been a private institution originally founded in 1820,[34] and acquired in 1868 by the Paris Chamber of Commerce, which already ran a commercial school in the rue Trudaine, founded in 1863. Both the Paris and Mulhouse colleges admitted students aged 15 or 16, the second opening in 1866 as a joint undertaking between the municipality and the local chamber of commerce. At Mulhouse there was a two-year course involving 30 hours of classes a week, divided among four hours each for English and a second foreign language, four hours on 'knowledge of goods', and four for commercial geography, with 12 hours a week devoted to *bureau commercial*, or 'commercial practice'. The annexation by Germany of Alsace in 1871 put an end to this initiative, but it became the model for several new French *Écoles supérieures de commerce*: in Rouen in 1871, Le Havre in 1871, Lyon in 1872, Marseilles in 1872, Bordeaux in 1874, with Lille, Nancy, Dijon, and Nantes some years later.[35] These were all two-year institutions with a commercial curriculum for 15- to 16-year-old day students (apart from Lyon, which admitted boarders), financed by a mixture of fees, municipal funding, and local chambers of commerce.[36] Student numbers in Lyon quickly climbed to 155 by 1875, declining somewhat in the 1880s; and in Rouen, for example, numbers rose to 71 in

[32] Sidney Webb, 'The Provision of Higher Commercial Education in London', *Journal of the Society of Arts* (6 August 1897), pp. 939–40.

[33] Redlich, 'Academic Education for Business', pp. 67–71, provides an overview of early French commercial education; for a broad outline of developments in French school provision related to technical subjects, see C. R. Day, 'Education for the Industrial World: Technical and Modern Instruction in France under the Third Republic, 1870–1914', in R. Fox, G. Weisz (eds.) *The Organization of Science and Technology in France 1808–1914*, Cambridge University Press, Cambridge 1980, pp. 127–53.

[34] A. Renouard, *Histoire de l'École supérieure de commerce de Paris (1820–1898)*, Association des ancien élèves, Paris 1898.

[35] E. Léautey, *L'Enseignement commercial et les Écoles de commerce en France et dans le monde entier*, Libraire Comptable et Administrative, Paris 1886, pp. 61–177; also P. Astier, I. Cuminal, *L'Enseignement technique industriel et commercial en France et à l'étranger*, Georges Roustan, Paris 1908, pp. 154–58.

[36] See the summary of provision in Jacques Siegfried, 'De l'enseignement commercial', *Revue internationale de l'enseignement* t. 9 (1885), pp. 289–302; also summarised in his 'Rapport sur l'enseignement commercial supérieur en France', *Journal of the Society of Arts* Vol. 45 (30 July 1897), pp. 911–14.

1875 then declined to much smaller number in the mid-1880s, when it was integrated into the university.

After its acquisition by the Paris Chamber of Commerce, the *École supérieure du commerce de Paris* mirrored the student numbers in Lyon, with 140 in the mid-1870s; but it differed from the other *Écoles supérieures* in having a three-year course and admitting students up to the age of 20. The additional teaching made possible by a three-year course appears to have been partly devoted to remedial schoolteaching—writing and composition, history, geography, physics, and chemistry being taken in the first year, besides some elementary bookkeeping. Correspondingly, however, the third year seems to have been more advanced than that in the *Écoles supérieures*, including the study of foreign exchange, commercial law, and insurance. As Léautey reported,

> ... a good student graduating from the third year is able not only to understand German, English, and Italian or Spanish, but even to correspond in three of these languages. Some of the more talented students—rarely the French—are able to speak the languages and be understood.[37]

This emphasis on a capacity to read and write in foreign languages, and to understand the principles of commercial correspondence, would be one of the more significant dimensions along which vocational institutions differentiated themselves from later, more academic, foundations.

The Parisian *École supérieure* admitted both day and boarding students, so that the provision of a three-year course was the principal marker of difference with the provincial *Écoles supérieures*. Before its acquisition in 1868, however, the Parisian Chamber of Commerce had already been discussing a more elite residential institution; these discussions were resumed in 1874, and a decision made to build a new higher commercial college. Substantial funds were spent on land and buildings, and the *École des hautes études commerciales* opened its doors in November 1881 with 62 students. Entrants had to be 17 and hold a baccalauréat, as contrasted with the provincial institutions where entrants were on average 15 years and had of course not studied to the level required by a baccalauréat. Although the new institution resembled the existing Parisian *École supérieure* in that the course lasted three years with a very similar curriculum, it was argued that the greater maturity of the students enabled them to study the subjects in greater depth. More significant perhaps was the social selection involved in the new institution; the fees for the *École des hautes études* doubled the cost of secondary education, and so limited entrants to the sons of comparatively wealthy parents.[38]

There were problems with the level of courses from the beginning. Students' abilities did not match what the Chamber of Commerce had anticipated; in 1882 the history of commerce was dropped from the first year and purely practical material introduced instead, including a course on calligraphy in 1883. The part of the curriculum devoted to legislation was deliberately extended, since this was the only point

[37] Léautey, *L'Enseignement Commercial*, p. 29.

[38] M. Meuleau, *Histoire d'une grande école*, HEC, Jouy-en-Josas 1981, p. 18.

on which the College distinguished itself from the other technical institutions. The form of teaching was also typical for the time: students crammed intensively over two years—a student who was sick for six weeks in 1886 had to copy 1,200 pages to catch up.[39] There was little progression in the material, and no linkage between courses; classes took up six and a half hours per day, and more than one examination a week was held on average.[40] In all, the routine of the institution was until the early 1900s more that of a secondary school than a higher-level college. Despite complaints and reviews, changes were slow to be introduced—there were piecemeal reforms in 1904 and 1913, the general effect of which was to weaken more general teaching to the advantage of more utilitarian material, but the working week remained very full into the 1920s. In 1928 an effort was made to introduce the case-method from Harvard Business School, but this did not fit with the strongly didactic pedagogic practice, and teachers were unfamiliar with the idea.

Hence while post-school commercial education was well-established in France by the 1870s, it became trapped in a school-based model of pedagogy. Even when the Parisian *École des hautes études* was founded in 1881 as an avowedly elite institution, it adopted an intensively didactic method of instruction that provided little substantive advance on the strictly vocational approach of the two-year *Écoles supérieures*, from which students graduated between the ages of 17 and 18. Political economy was by this time taught at university level as part of a law degree; the practical and vocational teaching of the *Écoles supérieures* was for young men between the ages of 15 and 17, and so not a fertile basis for the elaboration of political economy; the aim was to provide the clerks recruited by commercial enterprises with office staff who had a grounding in the work they would be asked to do. While commercial education successfully took root outside French universities, the rigidities of the existing French higher educational system meant that the expansion of business education the growth of American higher education had facilitated was obstructed in France. The strictly vocational orientation of French commercial pedagogy was a mark of its success in providing the skills that its students would need; but this is at the same time a mark of its limitation for our interests here. In Germany, by contrast, the higher educational system proved flexible enough to absorb both technical and commercial education, in the process shaping an entirely new 'business economics'.

German Commercial Education

German developments combined elements of the American and French initiatives: technical education developed through the foundation by individual states of a number of important *Technische Hochschulen*, while higher commercial education resulted from local business and municipal interests. However, three of the early commercial colleges—Cologne, Frankfurt, and Mannheim—did end up as (state)

[39] Ibid., p. 66.

[40] A German commentator remarked in 1908 that the daily routine was one more typical of a school than a college, students having no choice in their subjects of study; A. Calmes, 'Das Handelshochschulwesen in Frankreich', *Deutsche Wirtschafts-Zeitung* Jg. 4 (1908), col. 447.

universities, and in the early 1920s colleges gained the right to award diplomas that were comparable to degree-level qualifications.[41]

Admission to *Technische Hochschulen* was restricted to students with an *Abitur*, and this equivalence with the prerequisite for university admission de facto made them university-level institutions. The *Verein Deutscher Ingenieure* (VDI)[42] advocated the standardisation of courses and its corollary: recognition by state governments of the equal standing of courses and qualifications for the purposes of recruitment. In addition, the *Verein* sought, and achieved, the transfer of responsibility for the *Technische Hochschulen* from their original patrons, the various state ministries of trade, to their respective ministries of education. Combined, these features brought the *Technische Hochschulen* even closer to the existing university institutions, a progression that was underlined in 1892 when senior staff gained equality of status with university professors. Finally, in 1899 the *Technische Hochschulen* gained the *Promotionsrecht*, the right to award their own doctoral degrees, which carried with it the ability to create an academic career path for those trained within the new institutions.[43]

In Britain some of the earlier proponents of technical education, such as Stanley Jevons's cousin H. E. Roscoe, argued that the graduates of the *Technische Hochschulen* were over-educated, that the institutions themselves were over-equipped. Coupled with this attitude was a view that the sooner students left college for the practical world of industry, the better: around 19 or 20 years of age being thought quite old enough. Nevertheless, the German model—symbolised by Berlin's showpiece *Technische Hochschule* in Charlottenburg[44]—was influential in the British municipal movement for higher technical education, establishing a standard of technical education and an organisational structure in which municipal, private, and public interests co-operated. Both Manchester's Municipal School of Technology and Imperial College, London, appealed to the example set by Charlottenburg when arguing for expansion and reorganisation. In time all of the *Technische Hochschulen* merged into the higher education sector, nonetheless retaining their separate identities either as faculties of a larger institution, or as independent technical universities.

German higher commercial education passed through an almost identical evolutionary path. Beginning with the foundation of the Leipzig *Handelshochschule* in 1898 as a joint undertaking between the University and the Municipal College of Commerce, several new foundations followed in quick succession. Two of these, at

[41] The following summary is drawn from my essay 'Business Education at the Mannheim Handelshochschule 1907–1933', *Minerva* Vol. 32 (1994), pp. 158–85. See also the overview provided by David Lindenfeld, 'The Professionalization of Applied Economics: German Counterparts to Business Administration', in Geoffrey Cocks, Konrad Jarausch (eds.) *German Professions 1800–1950*, Oxford University Press, Oxford 1990, pp. 213–31, and for a perspective from the mid-1920s, August Wilhelm Fehling, 'Collegiate Education for Business in Germany', *Journal of Political Economy* Vol. 34 (1926), pp. 545–96.

[42] Association of German Engineers: see K. Gispen, *New Profession, Old Order: Engineers and German Society, 1815–1914*, Cambridge University Press, Cambridge 1989, Ch. 6, for a detailed account of the relation of the VDI to academic engineering training.

[43] E. P. Hennock, 'Technological Education in England, 1850–1926: The Uses of a German Model', *History of Education* Vol. 19 (1990), pp. 303–4. For a general survey of the *Technische Hochschulen* around 1900, see the various essays in W. Lexis (ed.) *Das Unterrichtswesen im deutschen Reich Bd.4 T.1: Die Technischen Hochschulen im deutschen Reich*, Verlag von A. Asher & Co., Berlin 1904.

[44] The original institution from which the modern *Technische Universität*, Berlin, developed.

Cologne and Frankfurt am Main, provided the basis for the creation of their respective universities at the close of the First World War. Berlin was such a great success that in 1913 nearly 40 percent of its students were foreigners.[45] These were attracted at least in part by the provision of a commercial curriculum much wider in scope and at a substantially higher level than that available elsewhere—in Paris, for example. Hayashima has pointed out that, while the *Handelshochschulen* differed in their individual developmental paths, Mannheim provided the ideal type for the movement as a whole: initiated with public lectures, then the provision of college courses, the formal creation of a college, its legal recognition as a public institution, granting of power to confer doctorates, integration into an existing university, separation from that university, the restoration of former independence, and then finally recognition as a university institution.[46] By 1912 reforms to teaching and examination had contributed to the formation of a distinct framework for commercial education, in which the original organising role of law and economics had been displaced by an emergent discipline of business economics, called at this time *Privatwirtschaftslehre*. The war slowed this rapid pace of development, but by 1919 this new branch of economics had been renamed as *Betriebswirtschaftslehre*, reflected in the titles of textbooks and institutes alike.

The emergence of this new commercial science reacted back upon the function of the teaching of economics in universities. Lecture courses on *Volkswirtschaftslehre*, or general economics, had long been provided in universities as one of the subjects required of students preparing for the state law examinations. It was not, however, possible to gain any qualification in the subject other than a doctorate, limiting the number of students who would study economics at anything other than an elementary level to those few who aspired to academic careers as professors of economics. However, the promotion of the Cologne and Frankfurt colleges to university status after the war increased the number of students studying economics, since these institutions offered a much wider range of economics courses than that found in the older universities. In 1898 Leipzig had created a new intermediate qualification, the *Diplom-Kaufmann*, requiring a minimum of four semesters' study and which was adopted by all other *Handelshochschulen*. The solution adopted for economics was to replicate this certificate as a *Diplom-Volkswirt*, for which a minimum of six semesters' study was required, and with eight subjects listed for examination. When introduced in 1923, this qualification included the new business economics as one of its required subjects; and in 1924 the *Diplom-Kaufmann* was itself revised to require six semesters of study, so that from the mid-1920s there was formal parity between the two diplomas: the *Diplom-Kaufmann*, and the *Diplom-Volkswirt*, became equivalent qualifications for admission, after study for two further semesters, to a doctoral examination. The formation of new universities out of *Handelshochschulen* in Cologne and Frankfurt had already opened a path to a doctorate in commerce for students in

[45] To be precise, 39.8 percent, or 235 students: see Akira Hayashima, 'Die Frequenz der deutschen Handelshochschulen 1898–1920', *Kwansei Gakuin University Annual Studies* Vol. 33 (1984) Table D34, p. 136.

[46] Akira Hayashima, 'Der Mythos vom fehlenden Hinterland. Zur Gründung der Handelshochschule Mannheim 1897–1907', *Kwansei Gakuin University Social Sciences Review* Vol. 10 (2005), p. 23.

these institutions; and this academic privilege was then extended to the remaining *Handelshochschulen*: to Berlin in 1926; to Mannheim and Nuremberg in 1929; and to Leipzig and Königsberg in 1930.

The *Handelshochschulen* therefore followed a similar path to the *Technische Hochschulen*: beginning as specialist institutions with broad-based local support, expansion in the number of institutions and students was accompanied by standardisation of curricula and examinations, so that their new qualifications were soon of equivalent status. At the same time the general character of the student body converged with that in the universities, in educational and social background, and in age and the length of time spent in study. With the granting of the right to award doctorates, institutions gained formal recognition from the German states, and also provided the means for the training and recruitment of junior staff, so that the *Handelshochschulen* became capable of generating their own qualified teachers.[47]

German higher education therefore adapted over the course of several decades: first to the need for higher technical education, then to the need for higher commercial education, the new institutions eventually converging with the existing university structure. In the process, a particular kind of 'business economics' was created—a discourse, a pedagogy, with a staff of teachers and an increasing stream of graduating students. But this discourse remained almost entirely confined to Germany, and influenced business education in the United States only indirectly, via the large number of refugees from Germany and Austria during the 1930s who had been trained in its principles. We have here, then, a third variation of the relation of commerce and economics. In the United States commercial education did develop in university-level institutions, but this remained diffuse and did not generate a vocational and theoretical discourse that could provide an armature for a new discipline. In France commercial education developed on a national basis by the 1870s, but remained at the level of a vocational pedagogy even in the highest-level institution, and this had no direct impact upon the existing higher educational structure. In Germany, by contrast, a vocational and theoretical discourse did develop and also became established in university institutions, although this new discipline remained resolutely vocational. The defining character of this new discipline was a focus on the enterprise as a going concern and the analysis of the economics of the enterprise; it was a business economics whose roots lay in the *Kameralwissenschaften* of the eighteenth century, not in the Anglo-French discourse of nineteenth century political economy, centred on issues of value and distribution. This was *Betriebswirtschaftslehre*, or as it is still known today, BWL, the core of a systematic approach to business education against which we can measure British efforts to introduce commercial education directly into university institutions. To properly understand the ways in which British initiatives fell short, we need some familiarity with this German model, a model that 'failed' only insofar as it provided a solution for higher commercial education that no other system then imitated.

47 As noted in Chapter 2, the German doctorate qualifies its holder to engage in research as an assistant while working upon a thesis for the *Habilitation*. This second higher degree is a form of licence to practice, entitling its holder to teach as a *Privat-Dozent* in the institution in which the doctorate has been gained for a limited number of years. During this period a *Privat-Dozent* applies for chairs elsewhere. The professorial career therefore always begins somewhere other than the institution where an academic has completed this final stage of qualification.

The early history of commercial education in Germany began from the vocational/academic divide that we have already encountered. The *Handelshochschule zu Leipzig* was founded in 1898, based on co-operation between the local Commercial College and the University; its students attended university lectures in law and economics, together with lectures in the Commercial College on practical commercial subjects such as commercial correspondence, economic geography, and accounting. The inherent difficulty here was that university teaching in law and economics was not adapted to vocational needs,[48] while on the other hand the academic content of those vocational subjects taught in the Commercial College was below that normally required for university study. The *Handelshochschule zu Leipzig* was an administrative entity, rather than a separate institution; it simply drew on existing lecture courses and had no control over their content. It did, however, offer its own *Diplom*, and it also directed its efforts towards two distinct groups of students: young men at the beginning of their careers in business, and teachers from commercial schools. There was a clear recognition that a dual task existed for higher commercial education: the education of a new business class, and the education of the teachers of lower commercial schools. The Leipzig *Handelshochschule* was open to students with an *Abitur*, who might otherwise have attended university; and, in addition, to a range of candidates with practical experience or previous commercial education. The independence from state governments that the new commercial colleges enjoyed also meant that they were able to develop their curricula in any way that they thought fit; a freedom of course that Leipzig did not at first enjoy, because of its dependence upon teachers and lecture courses associated with other institutions.

By contrast, the Cologne *Handelshochschule*, founded in 1900 thanks to generous private endowment and support from the Cologne municipal administration, was from the first an independent institution with its own staff, although it did in its early years draw upon academics from the University of Bonn as well as upon local professionals. Eberhard Gothein, Professor of Economics at Bonn,[49] drafted the memorandum used by the City Council as the basis for its application to the Prussian government.[50] He argued that the approach adopted in Leipzig, where students attended university lectures in law, economics, and geography, was no adequate substitute for a systematic course of commercial studies. At the same time, Gothein emphasised that study in a *Handelshochschule* must be based upon the same elective principle of *Lernfreiheit* that prevailed in the universities; without this, he argued, a German institution of higher education was inconceivable.[51] He accordingly rejected

[48] Law students gained their strictly vocational training during their *Referendarzeit*; there was therefore no need for university teaching to directly orient itself towards the more practical aspects of legal training.

[49] Gothein had already played an important role in the development of commercial teaching in Mannheim, and in 1903 became Max Weber's successor in the Heidelberg Chair of Economics.

[50] Letter of Mayor Becker to Prussian Ministers of Culture and Trade, 13 July 1900, reprinted in A. Hayashima, 'Der Kölner Weg zum Promotionsrecht. Zur Geschichte einer deutschen Handelshochschule', *Kwansei Gakuin University Annual Studies* Vol. 31 (1982), pp. 27–29.

[51] E. Gothein, 'Denkschrift über Errichtung einer Handelshochschule in Köln, Mai 1900', in A. Hayashima, 'Zur Geschichte der Kölner Handelshochschule', *Kwansei Gakuin University Annual Studies* Vol. 30 (1981), p. 199. *Lernfreiheit* opened all lectures of a university to the students, who were in principle free to follow whatever lectures they wished. Although studies terminated with state examinations covering a fixed syllabus, it was not prescribed when, or where, these should be sat.

the rigidity of the fixed courses and regular examinations that he had found at the *École des hautes études commerciales* in Paris, and argued that what was needed in a higher commercial college was a two-year course, combining obligatory and optional lecture courses.

The natural basis for such a commercial course, argued Gothein, was the study of economics. This should begin with general lectures of a broadly similar character to those delivered in the university, following this with a range of applied subjects not normally covered in such depth in the university context, and taught by the college's own specialist staff. By contrast, for the courses on law—procedure, civil law, and administrative law—Gothein considered that the college would be permanently reliant on the teaching of academic and practising lawyers. Instead of augmenting the university curriculum as in the case of economics, he envisaged an abbreviation of the university law curriculum, omitting subjects of no direct relevance, such as legal history and criminal law. Alongside the teaching in law and economics, courses in commercial subjects were to extend throughout all four semesters. This teaching would centre upon an *Allgemeine Handelslehre*, a general commercial course presented over two semesters. Beginning with *Comptoirkunde*, office practice, it would proceed to cover domestic and external trade, techniques of trade, means of payment, and other related subjects. Gothein's vision of the commercial curriculum did not therefore diverge sharply from the Leipzig curriculum; it combined academic courses in law and economics with systematic preparation in commercial skills based upon the contemporary curricula of the commercial schools. Although the teaching of economics in Cologne might simply extend the existing university curriculum by the addition of applied economic subjects, the fact that the courses were to be taught by the college's own staff was an important development—this was a significant innovation. Likewise with *Allgemeine Handelslehre*: although the detail of the teaching in this area might not differ so markedly from that in Leipzig, it was conceived as part of a unitary subject, a *Lehre*, even though this might as yet be inadequately elaborated.

The Cologne curriculum followed Gothein's recommendations in placing economics at its core, repeating an introductory course every semester, so that it could be taken by all entrants at the beginning of their studies at the college. Attendance at these lectures was a condition for entry into the remaining economics courses, for which no particular sequence was prescribed, although it was evidently expected that students would attend between four and six economics lectures a week over the four semesters of study.[52] Courses on economic policy and applied economics ranged more widely than would be usual in a university—international trade, money and banking, commercial policy, social policy, and colonial policy were all the object of one or more courses. Other courses were more condensed than would normally be the case in universities, so that the lectures on finance covered only the major topics, and those on statistics only economic statistics. The law curriculum followed a similar plan, beginning with an introductory course on civil law, with special emphasis on commercial law. In addition to this, some acquaintance with legal procedure and solvency law was required as part of the introductory course. Following on from this were

[52] See the comments on p. 50 of C. Eckert, *Die städtische Handels-Hochschule in Cöln. Bericht über die zwei Studienjahre 1903 und 1904*, Julius Springer, Berlin 1905.

lectures on commercial law, in particular company law, dealt with in greater detail than customary in the university context. These and other related subjects were taught by practising lawyers and officials from Cologne, and not by academics from Bonn.

A foundation in the principles of economics and law was therefore required of all students, reflecting the association of economics with the teaching of law in German universities. There were also a number of elective subjects available, including topics in insurance, geography, 'knowledge of goods' (*Warenkunde*), natural science, and technology. However, these were distinct from the practical basis of the college's curriculum, which was assembled under the heading 'commercial technique' (*Handelstechnik*), and introduced as follows:

> Commercial Technique strives to provide a comprehensive picture of business practice. It is intended to serve the individual interests of merchants and industrialists and should be regarded, in contrast to *Volkswirtschaftslehre*, as a part of *Privatwirtschaftslehre*. Commercial Technique begins where the modern office, training virtuosi in detailed work along established lines, goes awry; it seeks to provide an overview of the entire range of business skills, and identify their nature and effects.[53]

This is the area that Gothein had referred to as *Handelslehre*, covering all the areas of practical business affairs. Given the novelty of teaching these subjects within a higher education institution, those charged with their teaching had, in addition to their regular teaching, the task of developing disparate elements into a coherent discipline. The purpose of such teaching was not the provision of routinised training in the various practical aspects of business life, as was the task of commercial schools; it was instead intended to provide a comprehensive overview of commercial administration, combined with a reliable insight into its detailed aspects. Teaching in accounting and commercial calculation was followed by instruction in the organisation of commercial enterprise, covering commercial correspondence, sales, international trade, markets and exchanges, duties, insurance, export and import. The final part of the Cologne Curriculum was modern languages, which were given a high priority in all higher commercial institutions founded at this time.

The Berlin College, which opened in 1906, was explicitly modelled upon its forerunner in Cologne, but it had a rather different genesis, and its administrative and teaching organisation also varied in important respects. The administration of the Cologne College was in the hands of a permanent academic director, appointed by the city mayor in consultation with a governing body of academics and other representatives. The director was able to organise teaching in whatever manner he deemed appropriate for the college, and his ability to recruit staff was subject only to the approval of the Prussian Ministry of Trade and Industry. The Berlin College, by contrast, was established by the Elders of the Berlin *Korporation der Kaufmannschaft* on land owned by the *Korporation* adjoining the Stock Exchange, and headed by a *Rektor*, a position filled from the existing staff on a rotating basis, overall control of the college

[53] Ibid., p. 75.

administration being retained by the Elders.[54] The formal link between the college and the business community was therefore more direct than in Cologne, although this also carried with it the danger that friction between the academic and business interests in the running of the college could arise.

The curriculum in Berlin was distinguished by the priority given to the *Handelswissenschaften*, although this was still in 1907 a fairly loose collection of practical subjects. Nevertheless, whereas Cologne placed an introductory course in economics at the beginning of its study programme, Berlin developed a general introductory course providing an overview of the work of the *Handelshochschule*. The official recommendation was to supplement this during the first semester with lectures on accounts and commercial arithmetic, and a foreign language. In addition, it was suggested that students take an introductory course either in economics, or law, or physics, or chemistry, or economic geography.[55] A similar pattern, without the introductory course and following on at a higher level from individual subjects selected in the first semester, was recommended for the second semester. The third and fourth semesters involved further specialisation along the path already established, with the addition of practical classes permitting students to develop specific areas of interest in association with individual teachers. Quite evident from this is the clear break with the core role of law and economics lectures on the university model that characterised Cologne. Not that students were unable to specialise in these areas if they so wished; in Ignaz Jastrow and Werner Sombart the college had two experienced teachers of economics, and the range of specialised topics available was great. Indeed, apart from languages, economics continued as the subject with the greatest number of lecture hours devoted to it.[56] Whereas in Leipzig business education was in practice ancillary to an academic understanding of the general subject matter of law and economics, in Berlin the curriculum and pattern of teaching facilitated the development of an autonomous business curriculum, but on an elective basis.

Developments in the Leipzig, Cologne, and Berlin *Handelshochschulen* exemplify the various stages through which German higher commercial education passed as it sought to establish a coherent advanced curriculum distinct from the practical curricula of lower schools and colleges. Together with the Frankfurt Akademie, these Colleges remained the largest and most influential foundations. We can, however, also briefly consider some aspects of the Mannheim *Handelshochschule* which, established after Leipzig, Cologne, and Berlin, does provide, as Hayashima suggests, an insight into the diffusion of established models.[57]

[54] Berlin, Mannheim, Leipzig, Frankfurt, and Nuremberg were all headed by a *Rektor* whose period of office lasted from two to three years; C. Eckert, 'Handelshochschulen', *Handwörterbuch der Kommunalwissenschaften* Bd. 2 Gustav Fischer Verlag, Jena 1922, p. 471.

[55] I. Jastrow, *Die Handelshochschule Berlin. Bericht über das erste Studienjahr Oktober 1906/7*, Georg Reimer, Berlin 1908, pp. 164–65.

[56] Out of 247 weekly hours in WS 1910/11, economics took up 41 hours, *Handelswissenschaften* 33, and law 22: A. Binz, *Bericht über das vierte und fünfte Studienjahr der Handels Hochschule Berlin. Oktober 1909/1911*, Georg Reimer, Berlin 1911, p. 25.

[57] The later phases outlined by Hayashima were the dissolution of the Mannheim *Handelshochschule* in 1933 and its integration into the University of Heidelberg as a new *Staats- und Wirtschaftswissenschaftlichen Fakultät*; then in 1946 its exclusion and return to Mannheim. By the 1930s the Mannheim college was a hotbed of National Socialism, and the move was intended to transform Heidelberg social sciences into Nazi

No specific course of lectures was prescribed for the early students of the Mannheim college: the lecture list for opening summer semester in 1908 simply groups courses by subject, beginning with economics and law, and then proceeding through insurance, geography, technology, commercial technique, and languages. A distinction was made between general lectures and more specialised courses, and with few exceptions both lectures and classes at first took place in the evenings between 6 and 10 p.m. In the early years, therefore, it was possible to combine full-time study with employment. However, by the winter semester (WS) of 1908–1909, some of the more general lectures were scheduled for the morning, and by WS 1913–1914 the majority of the lectures and classes were scheduled during working hours, carrying the clear implication that study was to be treated as an alternative to, rather than as a complement of, employment. Gothein, Levy, and Jaffé travelled from Heidelberg to provide the principal teaching in economics, while the teaching in commercial law was supported by a combination of academics from Heidelberg and local lawyers. The more practical aspects of the teaching were covered by local professionals, or teachers from the Commercial College.[58]

The Mannheim regulations, as they eventually emerged in 1913, stipulated that all students had to show adequate knowledge of law, economics, and commercial science, while introducing a higher Diploma for more specialised students after a further two semesters of study. Four subjects were formally examined in the *allgemeine kaufmännischen Diplomprüfung*: two principal subjects (selected from commercial science, economics, and finance, law, transport, and commodities); and two subsidiary subjects (selected from the preceding, plus economic geography, insurance, and a foreign language). Commercial science was an obligatory examination subject, either as a principal or as a subsidiary.[59]

What was this 'commercial science'? In the original lecture outline for the summer semester (SS) of 1908, section VI covers *Handelstechnik*, including under this heading classes in banking and exchanges, bookkeeping, commercial arithmetic, commercial correspondence, stenography, and typing—the kind of subjects routinely taught at the time in commercial schools for 15- to 18-year-olds.[60] The following semester, the same subjects are to be found under a new heading, *Handelswissenschaften*, the commercial sciences. When it opened in 1906, the Berlin *Handelshochschule* had made an introductory course in commercial science obligatory for new students, displacing the introductory role hitherto played by economics; without, however, clearly specifying the intellectual content of this 'science'. By 1910, the *Handelswissenschaften* had likewise been moved to the front of the Mannheim teaching programme, but a convincing pedagogic argument for this was still lacking: Calmes suggested, in

social sciences. This initiative was unsuccessful; see R. Bollmus, *Handelshochschule und Nationalsozialismus*, Verlag Anton Hain, Meisenheim an Glan 1973.

[58] Handelshochschule Mannheim, *Vorlesungen und Fachkurse im Sommer-Semester 1908*, pp. 14–26; *Verzeichnis der Vorlesungen und Fachkurse im Winter-Semester 1908/1909*; *Vorlesungs-Verzeichnis Winter-Semester 1913/14*.

[59] Decree of Baden Ministry of Culture, 24 January 1913, printed in *Bericht des Rektors Prof. Dr. Ch. Glauser über das Winter-Semester 1912/13 und das Sommer Semester 1913*, pp. 66–70.

[60] *Vorlesungen und Fachkurse im Sommer-Semester 1908*, pp. 21–24.

a review of the college's teaching, that this subject represented a synthesis of practical and academic teaching, but there is little evidence at this time of analytical content to the teaching.[61] By 1913, the list of lectures in the commercial sciences was headed by a course repeated every semester (and therefore intended to serve as an introductory course) on *allgemeine Privatwirtschaftslehre*, split between a general treatment of enterprise organisation, and that of commerce. The remaining subjects were similar to those noted earlier—exchange and credit, advertising, political arithmetic, commercial arithmetic, and bookkeeping. But the use made here of the term *Privatwirtschaftslehre* is significant, for this represented the axis along which a new business economics was to develop.

During 1912 the nature of *Privatwirtschaftslehre* had been vigorously debated in the specialist literature.[62] *Volkswirtschaftslehre* formed the staple of university lectures in economics, dealing with the general nature of economic phenomena and providing an overview of the general principles governing economic activity. It was this generality which had at first been considered suitable for introductory courses to clerks and businessmen—for example, Max Weber's first set of lectures in Mannheim,[63] and the teaching of Gothein. But there were serious limitations in this general appreciation of economic activity, for it provided no especial insight into the organisation of specific enterprises. Presented to the future managers of banks, offices, and factories, it lent no very clear understanding of their functioning: no framework within which they might make rational decisions concerning the management of these enterprises was so provided. *Privatwirtschaftslehre* was a response to this problem. It focused attention upon the internal organisation of economic enterprises, providing a general descriptive framework in whose terms the proper management of an insurance office or an engineering company could be evaluated. This was the core of a 'commercial science' which went beyond the practical pedagogy of the commercial school, and which formed the basis upon which *Betriebswirtschaftslehre* developed. By WS 1912–1913 in Mannheim, the number of lecture hours devoted to this area represented 25 percent of all teaching time, as against 16 percent for economics and 16 percent for law; only languages had more time devoted to them.[64]

A report by Nicklisch in 1913 on the work of the *Handelswissenschaftliche Seminare* throws some light upon the transformation of the disparate and practical matters of commercial teaching into a new, independent discipline. Students were normally admitted to the seminars in their third semester, having already completed a literature survey of general issues in enterprise organisation. They were expected to attend meetings of the seminar on a regular basis, and to take turns in presenting a report of their own independent work. The topics ranged over case studies, topics in

[61] A. Calmes, 'I . Handelswissenschaften', in 'Über "Allgemeinbildung und Fachbildung" beim Handelshochschulunterricht', *Die Handels-Hochschule in Mannheim*, Mannheim, 1910, pp. 15–16.

[62] For an overview of this debate see my essay 'The "Handelshochschulen"' in *Strategies*, pp. 122–28.

[63] Max Weber delivered a series of lectures during four evenings in November and December 1897, presenting a general survey from the agrarian foundations of the European economy, through the development of urban economies, the emergence of mercantilism, and ending with the historical situation of modern capitalism; *Jahresbericht der Handelskammer für den Kreis Mannheim für das Jahr 1897 T.1*, Mannheim 1897, p. 153.

[64] 'Bericht des Rektors über das Wintersemester 1911/12 u. Sommersemester 1912', in *I.Jahresfeier der Handels-Hochschule Mannheim am 6.Juli 1912*, Mannheim 1912, p. 19.

accounting, and general questions of factory organisation.[65] In concluding his report, Nicklisch announced his attention of altering the name to *Betriebswissenschaftliches Institut*; the name being formally adopted early in 1914. The prime academic objective of the institute was, stated Nicklisch, 'the promotion of the science of organisation'.[66]

By the end of the war, the name *Handelswissenschaften* as the generic term for commercial subjects had been replaced in the lecture list by an alternative formulation, *Kaufmännische Einzelwirtschaftslehre*, which can be roughly translated as 'Business Enterprise Economics'. At the head of this section in 1919 stood Nicklisch's two-hour weekly lecture on *Allgemeine Betriebslehre*: 'the general theory of enterprise organisation'. By the mid-1920s this section had been renamed simply *Betriebswirtschaftslehre*—and the lectures were listed as follows:

Introduction to *Betriebswirtschaftslehre*
Betriebswirtschaftslehre of Merchandise Trade
The Technique of Merchandise Trade
Theory of Industrial Enterprise
Financial Management
International Transactions
Future Contracts
Commercial Practice and Terms of Delivery
Introduction to Bookkeeping
The Theory and Technique of the Balance Sheet
Bookkeeping, Calculation, and Statistics in Banking Enterprise
The Mathematics of Banking and Capital Transactions
Introduction to Calculus
The Psychology of Work in the Enterprise
Introduction to Marketing (*kaufmännische Werbelehre*).[67]

This course of lectures was followed in the by-then usual pattern with economics, and then law; the former focused upon commerce, finance, and international trade,[68] the latter upon those elements of law related to business. These three groups of lectures accounted for the core of the teaching, which was supplemented by a smaller number of lectures on insurance, commercial geography, commodities, chemistry, technology, mathematics, and languages. In the 20 years since the foundation of the *Handelshochschule* its teaching had moved from an uneasy

[65] Among examples given by Nicklisch are 'Analysis of the Balance Sheet in a Cable Firm'; 'Enterprise Organisation of a Shoe Factory'; 'The Organisation of Relations between a Firm and Its Foreign Subsidiaries'; 'Organisation of Brush Factory'; 'Depreciation'; 'Cartels in the Iron Industry, especially the Steel Union': *Bericht des Rektors Prof. Dr. Ch. Glauser über das Winter-Semester 1912/13 und das Sommer Semester 1913*, pp. 26–27.

[66] *Bericht des Rektors Prof. Dr. Ch. Glauser über das Winter-Semester 1913/14 und das Sommer Semester 1914*, p. 32.

[67] *Vorlesungs-Verzeichnis. Sommer-Semester 1927*, pp. 8–9.

[68] The relation of the teaching of economics in the *Handelshochschule* and in the prewar University was discussed in an article by Behrend: 'Die Volkswirtschaftslehre an den Handels-Hochschulen', *Akademische Nachrichten der Handels-Hochschule* (Mannheim) Jg. 1 Nr. 3 (March 1925), pp. 39–41.

assortment of existing commercial school and university teaching, to a coherent business curriculum in which the organising role was provided by a business economics, *Betriebswirtschaftslehre.*

Parallel to this, a new form of cost accounting was developed, addressing the material flows into and out of the business enterprise. Eugen Schmalenbach had been among the first graduates of the Leipzig Handelshochschule in 1900, and in his teaching he devoted his efforts to a new area of commercial calculation, that of the analysis of balances. The result, 'dynamic accounting',[69] focused attention on the viability of the enterprise as a going concern, and this had great implications for the conduct of both research and teaching. Research was provided with a medium of discussion with the foundation of the *Zeitschrift für Handelswissenschaftliche Forschung* under Schmalenbach's editorship in 1905. His point of departure was the argument that accounting theory had hitherto treated the factory as a fixed sum of capital that, over time, produced money. If the enterprise was viewed in this manner as a *Geldfabrik*, a 'money-making factory', its sole purpose was conceived as the production of profit; but viewed as a machine for producing profit, it was not at all clear where the source of this profit was. The development of industrial techniques had increased the role of production costs in establishing the profitability of an enterprise; and, as a result of this shift in the composition of assets, the search for increased profitability had shifted away from the exploitation of the price mechanism and markets, and towards the regulation of the production process.

Schmalenbach's argument was that the entrepreneur could not do very much to influence prevailing market conditions, but he was on the other hand in a stronger position to have a direct influence upon enterprise performance. This could only be achieved, however, if the actual economic performance of the enterprise could be treated in isolation, setting to one side external contingencies. The basic principles of Schmalenbach's project can be summarised as: firstly, the isolation of enterprise performance from market conditions; and secondly, the establishment of a clear dynamic framework within which enterprise performance could be assessed. The role of the balance sheet here was therefore not the determination of asset value, but rather of profitability and the overall level of activity.

These were, and remained, essentially problems in accounting theory and practice; but when linked to the progressive detachment of commercial science from *Volkswirtschaftslehre*, it provided the means to knit together the apprehension of the enterprise as the object of economic analysis. In the Mannheim curriculum, accounting played a relatively small role in the developed curriculum, and little or no role in the transformation of an aggregate of commercial topics into a new academic subject. Nicklisch did teach bookkeeping; but the emphasis in his *Institut* was on a broad conception of enterprise organisation, not on a specific form of accounting practice. The emphasis upon the enterprise—whether it be bank, industrial concern, or retail agency—which was implicit in dynamic accounting did, however, provide a core around which the hitherto disparate elements of commercial education could be reorganised into a pedagogic programme.

[69] See the summary in my *Strategies of Economic Order*, pp. 132–35.

The importance of Schmalenbach's work here is that German accounting methods did adapt to the new industrial environment, while also providing business education with an appropriate set of principles and methods. This was once more an issue arising from the level at which commercial education was pitched. So long as teaching was directed towards future clerks, as in the French *Écoles supérieures*, then simple bookkeeping was all that was needed. If, on the other hand, teaching was directed to future managers, then elementary bookkeeping was of limited relevance, and financial accounting even less so, since it provided no real perspective on what actually happened in any given enterprise. Schmalenbach's dynamic accounting resolved this problem. In the United States, by contrast, there was a conflict between engineers who were interested in properly attributing overhead costs to the activities causing those costs, and accountants more interested in the relation of inventory costs to profits—in effect a clash between cost and financial accounting that was resolved in favour of accountants and financial accounting.[70]

In Britain the idea that teaching financial accounting might not be of much relevance to future managers never arose. As we shall see, it was simply assumed that it was important to teach 'accounting' to students of commerce, and what was taught was whatever it was that the existing accountancy profession was used to doing. Across the board, the issue in seeking to develop commercial practice into higher commercial education was this tension between existing practical skills and the kind of knowledge that future graduates would need.

While this tension was resolved in the German case—so that institutions were founded, a specialised curriculum developed and diffused, textbooks written, journals founded—the model business curriculum that emerged had no imitators. Instead, after 1933, some of those with first-hand knowledge of BWL, either as students or as teachers, fled Germany and applied their skills to the existing national pedagogical frameworks—chiefly to the American university system.[71] Nonetheless, this problem of a leader with no followers was also clearly apparent in the design of the first Faculty of Commerce in Britain, inaugurated at the University of Birmingham in 1902.

[70] H. T. Johnson, R. S. Kaplan, *Relevance Lost: The Rise and Fall of Management Accounting*, Harvard Business School Press, Boston 1987, pp. 130–132.

[71] For an overview of this movement of economists from Germany and Austria to the United States and elsewhere, see my 'German Emigré Economists and the Internationalisation of Economics', a review essay of Harald Hagemann, Claus-Dieter Krohn (eds.) *Biographisches Handbuch der deutschsprachigen wirtschaftswissenschaftlichen Emigration nach 1933*, 2 vols., K. G. Sauer, Munich 1999; *Economic Journal* Vol. 111 (2001), pp. F740–46.

10
Higher Commercial Education in Great Britain and Ireland
Late Start, Early Dissolution

The immediate context for Marshall's argument regarding the reform of the established Cambridge Moral Sciences curriculum can be found in the new British provincial colleges of the later nineteenth century—first Owens College, Manchester, then institutions in Liverpool, Sheffield, Birmingham, Newcastle, and Leeds, followed by university colleges in Nottingham, Bristol, Leicester, Cardiff, Aberystwyth, Hull, Reading, Southampton, and Exeter. These were all founded in order to broaden access to higher education, and to render the content of this educational provision more suited to the modern world than the teaching in Oxford and Cambridge. As indicated in the previous chapter, these new British institutions were themselves part of an international trend, albeit perceived to lag behind provision elsewhere, and German provision especially. Although the London School of Economics (LSE) in its early years from 1895 to the 1920s is related to the story presented in this chapter, its linkage to the University of London lends it a broader significance, not only in the United Kingdom but in the wider British Empire; and that calls for separate treatment.

The teaching of economic subjects in all British and Irish institutions shifted by the mid-twentieth century from vocational to academic provision—from commerce to economics. But this was not simply a matter of chronology: the lag in the early development of commercial education in Britain placed it in direct competition with the emergent science of economics, rather than an existing viable alternative. Indeed, outside Cambridge the teaching of economics was everywhere overshadowed by commerce. That academic economics soon enough displaced commerce as the principal vehicle for training new generations of managers, administrators, and teachers was owed to the failure of commercial education in Britain to develop the coherence that any claim to institutional hegemony for a new university discipline requires. When challenged in the 1930s by the project to entrench economics as an academic 'science', little or no support was forthcoming for the vocational importance of commercial education. As we shall see with Manchester, the LSE, and then later Dundee, outside Oxford and Cambridge the teaching of commerce was primarily the vehicle through which the teaching of economics became established, not the medium for the elaboration of an alternative vocational education. Business schools were in Britain a separate development of the later twentieth century, by which time American university institutions were defining what economics was, and what it might be.

This chapter provides an outline of higher commercial education, beginning with Birmingham because it was here that the first formal university Faculty of Commerce was founded. Birmingham was, however, far less successful than usually assumed,

Constructing Economic Science. Keith Tribe, Oxford University Press. © Oxford University Press 2022.
DOI: 10.1093/oso/9780190491741.003.0010

especially if compared with its near contemporary in Manchester; and Manchester itself had a history that for a while connected it to developments in Liverpool. The vigour with which Manchester developed is then contrasted with the failure of Liverpool to match its success, compared also with developments in Leeds, another former college of the federal Victoria University. The chapter concludes with a brief consideration of initiatives in Aberdeen and Belfast, both in fact far more successful in the business of teaching commerce and graduating students than Birmingham, but whose relative success has hitherto been overlooked.

The history of higher commercial education in Britain and Ireland is largely unknown territory, and its linkage to the emergence of academic economics not an aspect of the latter that has hitherto been systematically identified.[1] This chapter can do no more than provide an outline, but it foreshadows the arguments made in the following chapter, dedicated to the LSE and its satellite in Dundee.

The Birmingham Faculty of Commerce

As with nearly all of the new English provincial universities founded before the First World War, the University of Birmingham developed from an earlier municipal college that had provided tuition in the arts and sciences at different levels to full- and part-time students. Formally established in 1870 with an endowment from Sir Josiah Mason, with which land was purchased in the centre of Birmingham and a substantial building constructed, Mason Science College opened its doors in October 1880. The original deed of foundation specified that two courses of instruction were to be provided: 'regular systematic instruction'[2] 'of a level sufficient to qualify students either for passing the examinations necessary to obtain the degrees of B.Sc. and D.Sc. of the University of London, or for any profession or pursuit in which scientific knowledge can be usefully applied'; and 'popular instruction', evening lectures 'to artisans and others who cannot attend the classes for regular systematic instruction'.[3] Students were to have a minimum age of 16, and the college was 'open to both sexes on the same terms'. By the end of its second year, the College had 198 students in day classes and 236 in evening classes; by 1890–1891 there were 323 male and 169 female students in the day classes, with 107 students preparing for university examinations.[4] The college also engaged with Extension teaching—although a political economy evening class taken in 1895 by Langford Price of Oxford was deemed a failure, attracting only 19 students.[5] However, the appointment for 1898–1899 of J. H. Muirhead as 'Professor

[1] J. G. Smith's 'Education for Business in Great Britain', *Journal of Political Economy* Vol. 36 (1928), pp. 1–52, provides a very thorough survey of commercial education at its peak, and very usefully begins with an account of the schooling system, the deficiencies in which early initiatives in commercial education sought to compensate.

[2] At its opening there were four teachers for regular instruction in mathematics, physics, chemistry, and biology. It was intended that instruction would also include geology and mineralogy, botany, zoology, physiology, and anatomy; *Calendar of the Mason Science College 1880–1881*, pp. 19, 21. Seven further teachers, including teachers of English, French, German, and Latin and Greek, were appointed by the beginning of the second year; *Calendar* 1881–1882, p. 24.

[3] Ibid., p. 22.

[4] Mason College *Calendars* for 1882–1883, p. 135; for 1892–1893, pp. 366, 367.

[5] *Calendar* 1894–1895, p. 381.

of Mental and Moral Philosophy, and Political Economy' to teach on the London external BA degree brought with it regular elementary teaching in political economy, using as a textbook Alfred Marshall's *Elements of the Economics of Industry*.[6]

In 1897 the college had applied for the status of a university college, focussing its teaching provision on the external London BA and BSc degrees. This was granted the following year, during which the Education Committee of the Birmingham Chamber of Commerce conducted a study of the provision for commercial education, concluding that a modern school should be established locally that could serve as a stepping-stone to a Faculty of Commerce in a new university. In January and February 1899 the Chamber of Commerce and Mason University College agreed on an outline plan to found a Faculty of Commerce, their respective proposals coinciding in placing modern languages at the top of the list of subjects, with commercial geography a high priority in both. They differed with respect to economics: for the Chamber this was second only to languages, while the Mason University College version placed economics last.[7] The commentary to this plan that the Education Committee's report provides makes quite clear that the general impetus lay in a sense that Britain's international manufacturing leadership was being challenged by the United States and Continental Europe. Here again we find the argument made by Philip Magnus: that the fact of leadership had insulated Britain's firms and workers from a need to adapt: 'While other nations have shown themselves apt scholars in all that we had to teach, we now have a great deal to learn from them.'[8] At school level it was proposed that the existing teaching of geography should be supplemented with attention to commercial conditions in foreign countries. The greatest emphasis here, however, fell upon the need for modern language teaching. German practice was here said to be exemplary, the Committee appending a report on the school system in Hamburg; and it was also emphasised that the teaching of Latin should give way to modern languages, 'especially German'. To encourage this, it was suggested that Latin should not be a compulsory subject in the matriculation examination for the new Faculty of Commerce.[9]

Although these and other sources provide an indication of an interest in a Faculty of Commerce,[10] unlike Manchester or Liverpool there had previously been little in the way of local provision for commercial education; the new institution was created by fiat, without there being a demonstrable existing constituency of potential

6 *Calendar* 1898–1899, p. 74.

7 Although with the same list of topics: values, foreign exchanges; production and consumption; associations and commercial companies; distribution of wealth, wages, profits and interests; 'Proposed Faculty of Commerce in the University of Birmingham, Mason University College 17 January 1899', University of Birmingham, University Collection 7/iv/4; and *Report of the Council of the Birmingham Chamber of Commerce for the Year 1899*, pp. 20–21.

8 *Report of the Council of the Birmingham Chamber of Commerce for the Year 1899*, p. 39.

9 Ibid., p. 41.

10 Barbara Smith pieced together some background from local newspaper reports and related sources that indicate the interest during 1888–1889 in developing a modern curriculum with some commercial content (elementary economics, commercial geography, commercial law); B. M. D.Smith, 'Education for Management: Its Conception and Implementation in the Faculty of Commerce at Birmingham', Faculty of Commerce and Social Science, University of Birmingham *Occasional Paper* No. 5 (1965), pp. 1–13. A revised and expanded version was published as Barbara M. D. Smith, *A Hundred Years of Business Studies at the University of Birmingham 1902–2002*, Birmingham Business School, Birmingham 2002.

students. Conversion of this interest in the creation of a new faculty into a central component of the new university appears to have been largely due to the involvement of Joseph Chamberlain. During 1888 and 1889 Chamberlain had corresponded with Andrew Carnegie in connection with the provision of funds for the equipment of science departments in the new institution; and from their exchanges it is clear that some additional funds had been reserved for a Faculty of Commerce.[11] There was initial disagreement between Chamberlain and Carnegie about the use to which funds should be put; Chamberlain wanted to use all available funds for the appointment of staff, since financing teaching posts through the payment of fees 'would involve a scale of fees which would shut out the very class that you & I desire to bring forward & to benefit—the better class of workmens' sons who have shown special capacity, the men who are being brought up as managers, & the small manufacturers....'[12]

Late in 1900 the Principal of the new university, Oliver Lodge, drafted some 'Suggestions towards a Commercial Faculty' that began by emphasising that the objective was not the education of a clerk, but of a chief, providing an education suitable for the discharge of public duties both at home and in the wider Empire. How did he see such an education?

> ... our commercial education must centre around a great School of *Economics*, understood in its largest sense; that is to say, the subjects of Economic Science, of Commercial History and Commercial Law must be its backbone. Geography and Modern Languages must by no means be omitted; and inasmuch as we shall have to train students aiming at a great variety of work we must have a Lecturer in Accountancy, who shall be able not only to 'open a complete set of Books for a Merchant's or Manufacturer's office', but likewise so to organise accounts that profit and loss in every department of such a business can be traced and analysed.[13]

As we shall see, this set of priorities was not in fact realised in the new faculty; although the fact that its newly-appointed head could freely disregard the Principal's own ideas does rather suggest that no-one in Birmingham had a clear or fixed vision of how the new faculty would operate. And the fact that it was William Ashley who was appointed to head the new faculty only adds to this sense that insufficient thought had been given in Birmingham to the purpose and function of a Faculty of Commerce, given the absence of any recent local experience of formal commercial instruction.

We can only speculate about why it was Ashley who was selected to head the new faculty.[14] During the academic year 1898–1899 he had been in Britain on sabbatical

[11] Joseph Chamberlain to Andrew Carnegie, Birmingham, 27 May 1899, Correspondence relating to the Foundation of the University of Birmingham, University Collection 1/i/3.

[12] Chamberlain to Carnegie, 8 June 1899, University Collection 1/i/3.

[13] Oliver Lodge, 'Suggestions Towards a Commercial Faculty', December 1900 University of Birmingham, University Collection 7/iv/4.

[14] As does Barbara Smith—she writes that while the University had not decided upon the kind of person they were seeking, 'Ashley was "unanimously elected to the post" on the strength of the recommendations of Alfred Marshall and Dr. Cunningham.' This is a reference to Muirhead's statement in the biography of Ashley by his daughter (p. 63, n.); Barbara Smith includes (p. 48 n. 28) remarks attributed to J. G. Smith (appointed, however, only in 1919) that other applicants were L. L. Price and Herbert Foxwell (neither of whom had any special expertise in commerce either, but who were also Liberal Imperialists). Maynard

from his post at Harvard as Professor of Economic History. Whether he was in contact with anyone in Birmingham during this period we do not know; the biography written by his daughter sheds no light on how Ashley came to apply for, and be appointed to, the Birmingham chair, the relevant chapter having been written by J. H. Muirhead and so reflecting an institutional rather than a personal perspective on the appointment to the new faculty.[15] Formal advertisement of the position was not made until May 1901, but by the autumn Ashley had already left his post at Harvard and had returned to England to plan the new faculty. That Joseph Chamberlain played a role in this is possible. As MP for Birmingham he had gained a reputation as a municipal activist; while his government position as Colonial Secretary amplified this activism considerably. The Boer War had broken out in October 1899, and would not end until May 1902; Alfred Milner had been appointed High Commissioner for South Africa by Chamberlain in the spring of 1897; Milner had worked with Ashley on Toynbee's *Industrial Revolution*; all three were Liberal Imperialists. There is no surviving formal record of who else applied for the post, nor how Ashley was selected.

Whatever the circumstances, Ashley was appointed to head the first Faculty of Commerce in Britain. From his past teaching in Oxford, Toronto, and Harvard there is no indication that he had any particular academic interest in commercial education. Instead, it can be surmised from the arguments that he advanced in *The Tariff Problem*[16] that it was a political interest—the Liberal Imperialist vision of a world in which Britain and its Empire might continue to be the principal trading bloc—that brought about the switch from economic history and historical economics to commerce.[17] He was familiar with German institutions, and this would play a role in his thinking about higher commercial education.[18] But his design of the new faculty, and the student constituency to which it appealed, diverged not only from ideas that Chamberlain and Lodge had for the University of Birmingham, but also from the example of the *Handelshochschulen*.

The new faculty opened its doors in October 1902 to five students. Initially it had rooms over a shop next to the Mason College building; later it moved into the old Mason College building as the Bournbrook site was developed and the science departments were able to move in.[19] Earlier that year Ashley had published a pamphlet

Keynes's obituary of Foxwell confirms that he applied for the Birmingham chair, with the support of A. J. Balfour, Giffen, Marshall, Edgeworth, Nicholson, and Neville Keynes; Ashley, according to this account, had the support of Goschen and Milner only; *Economic Journal* Vol. 46 (1936), p. 598.

[15] A. Ashley, *William James Ashley: A Life*, P. S. King and Son, London 1932 Ch. 11.

[16] See Ch. 8, p. 215.

[17] Emphasis upon this political interest—Liberal Imperialism—is a more reliable guide to any developing schism in contemporary British economics than common assumptions and conjectures about the fate of 'historical economics'. Liberal Imperialists like Ashley and Hewins stood with those like Cunningham, whose sympathies were more Conservative, against other British economists who were also Liberal, but unimpressed by appeals to Empire: not only Pigou and Marshall, but also Cannan and Clapham.

[18] He provided a detailed overview of the development of German *Handelshochschulen* in *The Times*, 2 April 1903. The byline attributed the piece to 'a Birmingham correspondent', but it reproduced arguments about accounting that had become something of a hobby-horse for Ashley.

[19] Ashley to Hadow, Principal of Armstrong College, 13 January 1913: 'The work was started in two rooms in a building next door to the Mason College which belonged to the University. These were over a shop which occupied the ground floor and a way cut through. Some four years ago the number of students having grown in the Faculty of Commerce, a much more adequate set of rooms, including one large and

for prospective students identifying a managerial, rather than commercial, rationale for the Faculty, which would aim at

> ... the provision of a course of training suitable for men who look forward to business careers. Its object is the education, not of the rank and file, but of the officers of the industrial and commercial army: of those who, as principals, directors, managers, secretaries, heads of departments, etc., will ultimately guide the business activity of the country.... It is believed that a training can be devised which, while strengthening the powers of judgement, widening the sympathies, and stimulating the imagination—the ends of all really liberal education—will yet be of real value as a preparation for the practical duties of later life.[20]

When speaking the following year to Staffordshire businessmen, Ashley was rather more specific on the kinds of student that he sought. He maintained that hitherto too much attention had been paid in Britain to training clerks and mechanics, something that was not the business of a university, but which meant that technical education had languished. Birmingham, he maintained, was following America:

> We want the ambitious young men of the Midlands, who have already received up to the age of 17 or 18 a secondary education, such as our Grammar Schools or even our Higher Grade Board Schools provide, to come to us for three solid years....[21]

He envisaged therefore a route into higher commercial education in which full-time schooling was succeeded by full-time study at university level, a very restrictive condition that could at that time be met by very few young people;[22] it was not an approach that would be emulated elsewhere. This in part reflected the fact that the new faculty did not develop from any established local provision for commercial training, as would be the case in Manchester, Liverpool, Leeds, and London; nor was the local economy dominated by larger firms engaged in textiles, insurance, shipping, and railways, as in these cities, firms that might provide a destination for graduates. What evidence there is for the destinations of all BCom graduates in the early twentieth

two small lecture rooms, a Seminar room, and my private rooms, was provided for the faculty of Commerce in the Mason College building.' University of Birmingham, Dean of the Faculty of Commerce, *Letterbook*, University Archives 3/vii/4–5. Mason College was demolished in 1964 to make way for Birmingham Central Library, which was in turn demolished in 2016.

[20] W. J. Ashley, *The Faculty of Commerce in the University of Birmingham*, Birmingham 1902, p. 1 (dated 23 April 1902, 16 pages).

[21] W. J. Ashley, 'The Universities and Business', *Minutes of Proceedings of the Staffordshire Iron and Steel Institute* (4 April 1903), p. 160.

[22] Many of the young people to whom the new Faculty was addressed would have already left school at 14, 15, or 16, receiving their vocational training as an employee. The LSE and Manchester, by contrast, admitted part-time and mature students. This is mirrored by German developments: a two-year course in Commercial Sciences at Aachen established in 1898 lasted only 10 years, being aimed at students meeting the requirement for university entrance, unlike the model institutions of Berlin and Cologne; see Fritz Redlich, 'Academic Education for Business: Its Development and the Contribution of Ignaz Jastrow (1856–1937)', *Business History Review* Vol. 31 (1957), pp. 54–55.

century also suggests that they were more likely to become commerce teachers than middle managers.[23]

When it came to designing a curriculum for these students, Ashley's approach emphasised the transmission of information rather than intellectual training: he wrote that 'The place of the academic teacher is not to elaborate some *a priori* theory, but to gather, arrange, and present the lessons of practical experience.'[24] The four main headings he listed in 1902 were:

1. languages and history;
2. accounting;
3. applied science and business technique;
4. commerce.[25]

In elaborating the rationale for this choice, Ashley first drew attention to the need to teach the history of nineteenth-century Europe and America, since this would not have been taught in school. Secondly, while one modern language would be sufficient for matriculation, all graduates should be 'adequately equipped' in two of four modern languages: German, French, Spanish, and Italian, beginning with the ability to speak the languages, in the final year focussing upon commercial correspondence:

> The time ought not to be far distant when the library of every manufacturing town—and, indeed, of every really great undertaking—shall possess all the good current literature bearing on its particular interests in each of the chief languages of Europe, and when a man of business will be as much in the habit of casting his eye over the chief foreign periodicals as he is (or should be) over the *Economist* or *Engineering*.[26]

Such knowledge was, however, in the main instrumental; and so quite distinct from the central role given to 'accounting' in the teaching programme:

> Birmingham will be the first English University to realise the importance and the educational value of proper training in this subject, and to appoint a Professor to take it in charge. In giving Accounting a place in a commercial curriculum it will only be following the example recently set by several of the greater American universities, —by Harvard University and the Universities of Michigan and Wisconsin; and it proposes to use the term 'Accounting', which has come into common use in America, rather than 'Accountancy', to indicate that what it aims at is not so much the preparation of professional accountants for their future occupation (though it

[23] In the early 1950s, Prof. Gilbert Walker compiled a report on the destinations of Birmingham BCom graduates, 1905–1950 (referred to in 'The Occupation of Commerce Graduates. Results of a Survey Carried out during 1962', the *Commerce Graduates Association Newsletter* (1963, n.p.)). Unfortunately no copy of the report can now be traced (letter from Christine Penney, University Archivist, 1 February 1991). During the summer of 1990, Ian Wyatt sorted papers in the basement of Birmingham University Library and retrieved limited records of student destinations for 1920–1981; my thanks to him for his assistance.

[24] Ashley, *Faculty of Commerce*, p. 2.

[25] Ibid., p. 7.

[26] Ibid., p. 9.

> expects to do something in that direction), as to teach the ordinary business man the proper use and interpretation of accounts.[27]

But as we have already seen,[28] William Cole had only begun teaching a half-course in accounting at Harvard in 1900; and even contemporary American commentators were silent on Michigan and Wisconsin.[29] The idea that the teaching of accounting was already established in American universities has little foundation; but it was a claim that Ashley used to make the teaching of accounting the core of the Birmingham degree, taught through all three years and with a professorial appointment to support it.[30]

Ashley proposed that first-year students would be taught simple systems of book-keeping; then in the second year a higher level 'so as to enable a student to plan a set of books for a particular enterprise';[31] then in the final year a consideration of departmental accounts, together with the advantages, requirements, and difficulties of cost accounts. Ashley also emphasised the importance of intellectual training that such a course would provide:

> It must be evident that courses such as the University proposes to offer will call throughout for the exercise of judgment and reasoning power on the part of students. The amount of dead technical information to be simply committed to memory will be comparatively small: the study as a whole will be an educational one in the best sense.[32]

Clearly Ashley had never studied accounting.

More importantly, as the sole element of continuity throughout the course, accounting had also to bear the weight of providing coherence to a disparate set of subjects. Third among the leading topics identified by Ashley were various courses on commercial law, techniques of trade, money and banking, and transport—'This will be almost the first time that the problem of Transport by land and by water, and the question of railway rates and freight charges as they affect both the carrier and the merchant, have been systematically treated in an English University.'[33] Birmingham did later develop a specialism in railway operation, but as part of the Engineering School, not the Faculty of Commerce; although some insight into these early plans is conveyed by a memorandum by Ashley printed in late 1901 that summarises American

[27] Loc. Cit.

[28] See pp. 234–35 of the previous chapter. The summary of developments in Liverpool and Leeds in the following also shows that a commercial curriculum that included accounting predated the foundation of the Birmingham faculty.

[29] The School of Commerce at Wisconsin was founded in 1900. The prospectus for 1900–1901, reprinted in Marshall, *The Collegiate School of Business*, pp. 71–72, lists no courses on accounting.

[30] The Limited Liabilities Acts of 1856–1862 required all companies to keep proper accounts; the 1879 Companies Act introduced compulsory annual audit for all limited-liability banks, and the 1900 Companies Act made this obligatory for all companies registered under the Act; Michael Sanderson, *The Universities and British Industry 1850–1970*, Routledge and Kegan Paul, London 1972, p. 185. Quite possibly the emphasis on accounting arose through these developments, rather than supposed American models.

[31] Ashley, *Faculty of Commerce*, p. 10.

[32] Ibid., p. 10.

[33] Ibid., p. 11.

teaching on 'railway economics', and outlines William Acworth's course on railway administration at the LSE.[34] Railway administration would prove to be a major source of student demand during the early years of the LSE; but, as in Manchester, taught to part-time students who were mainly (clerical) employees of railway companies by specialists recruited for the purpose. These arrangements—part-time teaching to clerical staff—ran counter to the stated aims of commerce teaching in Birmingham, and in the event no specialised commercial teaching in this area was developed.

The final element in Ashley's initial prospectus was teaching on commerce, which would in the first two years be 'largely descriptive'. The courses

> ... will seek to set forth the modern development and the present structure and position of industry and trade in the leading countries of the world. This will involve a consideration of geographical position and natural resources on the one side, and on the other side, of the supply and organisation of capital and labour, and of the state of the mechanical arts; and the courses will lead up to a critical account of international commercial relations.[35]

There followed a long list of topics: location of works; capitalisation; scale of production; differentiation and consolidation of manufactures; combinations of manufacturers or merchants; limited companies; factoring and manufacturing; machinery; works management; relations of employer and employed, remuneration, hours; markets; advertising; relation of selling price to cost; fixed charges; methods of scale and purchase; credit; goodwill; trade cycles. It was noted that no textbooks as yet existed for these subjects; and so the Professor of Commerce would attempt to pull together and codify the relevant material into a form that students could use.[36]

The prospectus for the new faculty diverges from Oliver Lodge's 1900 plan in giving no role at all to the teaching of economic principles;[37] instead, it was accounting that provided a common thread to all three years. Also gone is Joseph Chamberlain's expression of hope in a letter to Andrew Carnegie that the new faculty of commerce would attract 'the better class of workmens' sons'.[38] Instead, Ashley now addressed

[34] 'From the Principal to the Faculties of Science and of Arts. A School of Railway Administration and the Economics of Manufacture' is a 14-page printed memorandum introduced by the Principal but drafted by Ashley, dated 30 November 1901—University Collection 7/iv/4.

[35] Ashley, *Faculty of Commerce*, p. 12.

[36] Ashley never did produce any texts of this kind. By contrast, A. W. Kirkaldy published a valuable text on shipping—*British Shipping. Its History, Organisation and Importance*, Kegan Paul, Trench, Trubner & Co, London 1919—which appeared in a series edited by Henry Higgs on 'National Industries' that also included H. Stanley Jevons's book *The Coal Trade*.

[37] 'Economic Analysis' was originally scheduled for examination in one paper at the end of the second year; the course was described as a '... rapid survey of the whole of the wealth-producing and wealth-distributing activity of society. It will seek to disentangle the larger forces at work, to direct attention to the complex relations of cause and effect, and to indicate the general causes and criteria of national prosperity. It will thus supplement the courses of Commerce by (1) emphasising the general considerations only incidentally touched upon therein, and (2) connecting commerce with other sides of national life.' University of Birmingham, *Calendar for the Session 1902–1903*, pp. 287–88. For the session 1906–1907 the same course was moved back into the first year, taught by A. W. Kirkaldy; *Calendar for the Session 1906–1907*, p. 354.

[38] Joseph Chamberlain to Andrew Carnegie, 8 June 1899, Correspondence relating to the Foundation of the University of Birmingham, University Collection 1/i/3. As suggested previously (p. 209), Ashley had never been that enthusiastic about contemporary developments in political economy while a student, and by the early 1900s was clearly in conflict with Marshall; see Alon Kadish, 'The Foundation of Birmingham's

himself 'in the first instance to the substantial businessmen of the country. What is offered is designed in the first place for *their* sons and relatives, most of whom are 'going into business' in any case'.[39] How Ashley arrived at this particular set of aims for the new faculty is not evident; but what is clear from all of the foregoing is that he had a free hand to shape the Faculty in any way he saw fit. He was not constrained by the existence of any established teaching in Birmingham in commerce and economics; the existence of a local demand for teaching in commerce had been expressed by the Chamber of Commerce, not directly by employers or potential students; and because there was little in the way of local teaching in commerce and economics, there were no teachers standing ready to teach the subjects that Ashley identified. The significant choices he did make, anticipating an intake composed predominately of school-leavers, and that graduates would be recruited directly into intermediate levels of management, were flawed and idiosyncratic.

Since there were so few regular students[40] it was at first possible for Ashley himself to fill in the gaps in the teaching staff. For the accounting core the University appointed in 1902 Lawrence Dicksee (1864–1932), a practising accountant with some experience of teaching in technical schools, and who in 1892 had published a book on auditing which went through 14 editions in his lifetime.[41] An American edition of this was published in 1905, edited by Robert H. Montgomery, who then used it as the basis for his own *Auditing Theory and Practice* in 1912, which initiated American accounting literature.[42] The creation of a professorial post for the teaching of accounting was largely symbolic: the salary offered was only £300 after three years,[43] and so calibrated to the very limited teaching time the post would demand. During his four-year tenure of the chair, Dicksee spent only one day a week during term-time at Birmingham, and combined his work there with teaching at the LSE, resigning his Birmingham post in 1906 to concentrate on the latter. In a move that conceded how very few Birmingham students there were, this core course was scheduled for the early evening so that articled clerks and members of the municipal administration could also participate, bringing student numbers up to a total of 28 for the first year.[44]

Faculty of Commerce as a Statement on the Nature of Economics', *Manchester School* Vol. 59 (1991), pp. 160–72.

[39] Ashley, *Faculty of Commerce*, p. 15.

[40] Totals of 11 in the second year of operation, 15 in the third, and 20 in the fourth; see the figures for enrolment and graduation 1900–1940 in the Appendix.

[41] J. Kitchen, R. H. Parker, *Accounting Thought and Education: Six English Pioneers*, Institute of Chartered Accountants of England and Wales, London 1980, p. 57.

[42] Dicksee wrote a number of textbooks on bookkeeping and accounts that went into several editions; see Kitchen, Parker, *Accounting Thought*, p. 59.

[43] Less than £6 per week; compared with around £220 per annum at the time for a secondary school headmaster.

[44] The students attending included the five regular Birmingham students; nine accountants' articled clerks preparing for the Intermediate Examination of the Institute of Chartered Accountants; five municipal officials preparing for the Examination of the Institute of Municipal Treasurers and Accountants; plus a manufacturer, a solicitor, a solicitor's articled clerk, a bank official, a lecturer from the Department of Engineering, a student in the Department of Mining, and three unspecified attendees. Report of the Dean of the Faculty of Commerce, 14 November 1902, p. 4, University Collection.

While admitting the modesty of the start that had been made in Birmingham by comparison with the United States and Germany, the Dean's Report on the first year of operation of the Faculty ended on an upbeat note:

> Nowhere as yet, in England, has a curriculum of study been provided so appropriate, I venture to say, for the purposes of the commercial classes as in Birmingham: in some respects it represents an advance on American or Continental programmes. But it can only succeed if the Midland business community takes a real interest in it.[45]

And this last qualification already registered what would become a sore point: that the local business community did not take a practical interest in the work of the Faculty, since it offered little to its existing employees; nor did local employers later seek out its graduates. Full-time student numbers reached 36 in 1914, and were around 50 in the mid-1920s; many of these, however, were not local students, nor did they seek local employment on graduation. Noting the foundation of the Manchester Faculty of Commerce in 1903, the Dean's Report explained away the immediate success of that institution by the fact that it admitted a wide range of part-time students;[46] later, in 1924, the Principal would continue to insist that the relatively small number of students of commerce in Birmingham was a reflection of Birmingham's commitment to quality, that Manchester's higher numbers reflected the fact that its academic standards were less rigorous—an entirely fallacious line of argument that he repeated two years later.[47] As we shall see, Manchester's relative success in recruiting staff and students in part built on years of previous teaching, the active involvement of the Chamber of Commerce, and the recruitment of local lawyers and bankers to teach their areas of specialism. None of these conditions applied to the Birmingham foundation.

Besides Dicksee, Adam Kirkaldy was an early appointee as a lecturer in commerce. Kirkaldy was in his mid-thirties and (another) graduate in Modern History from Oxford, but who had also been a partner in his family's shipping business before entering Wadham College in 1893. John George Smith later suggested that Ashley had invited Kirkaldy to assist him in part because Ashley was never at ease with business men, and Kirkaldy helped with this problem. He also remarked that Kirkaldy's appointment to the chair of finance in 1906[48] was not a reflection of Kirkaldy's interests,

[45] Report of the Dean of the Faculty of Commerce, 14 November 1902, p. 4, University Collection.

[46] Report of the Dean of the Faculty of Commerce, 8 December 1903, p. 4, University Collection. The 1902 Report (p. 4) had been explicit that '[i]t is not the policy of the University to carry on evening classes.'

[47] Report of the Principal to the Council, for the Twenty-Fourth Session, 1923–1924; Report of the Vice-Chancellor and Principal to the Council for the Twenty-Ninth Session, 1926–1927: 'We do not propose (as at Manchester, or Liverpool or Sheffield) to cater for those who cannot by either time or educational qualifications be full-time university students working for a degree. If we did, and offered an elaborate curriculum of evening classes to part-time students in pure technology, we could, as at Manchester, swell our Faculty in twelve months into 300 or 400 students, and give certificates and diplomas and academic passports or even allow the B.Com. degree to be won, like the kingdom of heaven, by violence accumulated between 5.30 and 9.30 p.m. But we leave this work very properly to the Municipal College of Commerce under its energetic Principal; we give at Edmund Street all the facilities that we can to its expanding activities, and we wish it every success in its determination to meet the legitimate needs of some hundreds of young men and women by the appropriate classes.' Reports of the Proceedings of the Council, University Collection.

[48] 'Within the sphere of the new Chair will fall not only what is generally known as Public Finance (the finance of public authorities), but also the operations of banking, of the stock exchange and of the money

but rather 'because Ashley's concepts of the duties to be attached to such a chair could easily be fitted into the general framework he had outlined for his Faculty when, ultimately, its permanent organisation should have to be considered.'[49] The fact that Kirkaldy regularly attended the Commerce Seminar with Ashley, and for a time had responsibility for the teaching of the 'Economic Analysis' course, also fits with Smith's view that Kirkaldy was capable of 'all the instruction in economic theory that Ashley could be persuaded to acquiesce in for students undergoing definite training for careers in business.'[50] For a short period Ashley took over (what was now) the first-year economics course, then in 1910 Kirkaldy resumed responsibility for 'Elementary Economic Analysis', with Ashley now teaching 'Advanced Economic Analysis' in the second year. The very general level of the latter course can, however, be judged from its description:

> This course will deal with the problem of Distribution as dealt with by modern economists, and will give special attention to the writings of Marx, Rodbertus, Böhm-Bawerk and Clark.[51]

Comparison of this early curricular structure with that for the session 1920–1921 shows that little changed in the basic design of a teaching programme in which the economics that was taught was extremely elementary, and was taught at first- and second-year level only. John George Smith, appointed as first Mitsui Professor of Finance in 1923,[52] also contributed a general survey of commercial education in Britain to Leon Marshall's *Collegiate School of Business*, including an outline of the teaching in Birmingham for the later 1920s together with teaching hours per week: here 'Elementary Economics' was assigned two hours in the first year, as was economic history, from a total of 12½ hours a week.[53] And that is not simply two hours a week in the first year; it is the sum total at this time of formal economic teaching in the whole three-year course.

The papers read at the commerce seminar lend further insight into the study of commerce in Birmingham. The five regular students admitted in 1902 devoted much of their first year to language study, meeting on Saturday mornings for the seminar.[54] To begin, Ashley presided while one or two students presented papers; students took turns to write up a report of the session, the surviving minute books providing insight into the substance and level of the teaching. The first meeting was on 6 November

market, together with the financial aspects of commercial undertakings in general. This is the first time that a Chair bearing that title has been created in any British University.' Report of the Dean of the Faculty of Commerce, 13 December 1906, p. 2, University Collection.

[49] John George Smith, Obituary of Adam Willis Kirkaldy, *Economic Journal* Vol. 42 (1932), p. 155.
[50] Ibid.
[51] *Calendar for the Session 1910–1911*, p. 419.
[52] The chair in Finance was re-established in 1923 with a gift of £5000 from Mitsui. Smith (1881–1968) had graduated from Trinity College Dublin in Mathematics, and had been teaching at University College, Cardiff, before being appointed Assistant Professor of Commerce at Birmingham in 1919; *Economic Journal* Vol. 33 (1923), p. 434.
[53] See Marshall, *Collegiate School of Business*, pp. 394–95.
[54] Report of the Dean of the Faculty of Commerce, 14 November 1902, p. 2, University Collection.

1902, attended by six students, and one of them read a paper on 'The Climate of England and Its Economic Effects'.[55] On 4 December 1902 a paper was read on the Corn Laws, which Ashley criticised as 'too full of detail'; then on 24 October 1903 a second-year student read 'An Economic Report of France':

> The French are, said Mr. Edge, as a nation much shorter and not nearly so well developed as the English. The men are very short, a fact which Mr. Edge ascribes to the continuous smoking of a cigarette. The women of a slightly larger stature; Dark hair and complexions are their chief characteristics, a fair haired person is seldom seen. The people are timid, thrifty, and polite, almost too polite in fact.

On this occasion both Ashley and Kirkaldy were present, but there is no indication in the minutes that they raised any objection to this line of argument. It was not until the nineteenth meeting on 18 March 1904 that a presentation on piece wages addressed an issue that was not simply descriptive.[56] Ashley, who was sometimes recorded of complaining of too much detail, did this time praise his student—'one of the best papers ever read at a meeting of the Seminar'—and by this time some 20 students were regularly attending. Also of note was a meeting on 18 February 1905 at which a student presented a well-informed survey of higher commercial education. Ashley's response was recorded as follows:

> Professor Ashley before concluding the meeting then spoke a few words.... The course, which was now influencing the courses of other countries, had been drawn up after great consideration, & had been influenced to a certain extent by the courses at American Universities.
>
> With regard to the commercial schools of France & Germany, they resemble more an English school for big boys than anything. The students are treated very much like schoolboys & the instruction is far too technical.
>
> With regard to America the drawback about the Universities is that the courses look much more impressive than they really are, owing to the difficulty in obtaining really good teachers for them.

Ashley looked to American courses while at the same time disparaging their content; and while the report may be unreliable about the relative merits of French and German commercial education given Ashley's published accounts of German developments, on this day and in this seminar he talked favourably of American, not German institutions. Furthermore, the notion that 'great consideration' had been given to the design of the Birmingham faculty seems highly questionable, given the very brief period during which the general idea had been mooted, Ashley appointed, and the faculty inaugurated. And insofar as the extensive records of the commerce seminar provide a

[55] Faculty of Commerce Commercial Seminar 1902–1905, University Collection 9/iv/21. The early minutes were unpaginated.

[56] For example, on 18 November 1905: 'Farquharson read paper on "German Toy Industry"; Kerr on "Factory Inspection as applied to Steam Laundries".'

window into the nature and effectiveness of teaching, it suggests more a cumulation of material descriptive of economies and processes than a commercial pedagogy.

Ashley retired in 1925 and was replaced by J. F. Rees, yet another Oxford historian from Lincoln College. He had been teaching economic history in Edinburgh, and in the four years he was at Birmingham, Rees made no substantive changes to the organisation of teaching. His appointment suggests that, more than 20 years after the inauguration of the faculty, little progress had been made in the development of a commercial curriculum; that there had not only been a failure to arrive at a satisfactory structure for the teaching of commerce, but that the work of the faculty had produced no younger candidates trained in commerce who might have succeeded Ashley. This last was not, however, quite true: in 1921 G. C. Allen had gained a first in his BCom; he taught for the Workers' Educational Association for a year and then went to teach in Nagoya for two years, returning to a research fellowship in the Faculty. At the time of Ashley's retirement, Allen had just turned 25; from 1926 to 1928 he held a lectureship in industrial organisation in Birmingham, leaving for the chair of commerce and economics at University College Hull.[57] Then, in 1929, Rees was succeeded as Professor of Commerce by Philip Sargant Florence, born in New Jersey in 1890 but, more importantly, having gained a first in the Cambridge Economics Tripos in 1914, then teaching at Cambridge from 1921 to 1929. Sargant Florence would extend the work that Allen had begun, creating a central role for the study of business organisation. Although accounting remained a common thread through the three years of the commerce degree, the third year was now lent focus by Sargant Florence's new course on 'The Organization of Industry and Commerce', building upon the 'theoretical, descriptive and practical aspects of industrial economics learnt in the first two years.'[58] The appointment of J. G. Smith in 1919 also had a more indirect impact; Smith remained in Birmingham and was Dean of the Faculty from 1926 to 1946, and it can be no accident[59] that from the later 1940s a number of significant mathematical economists were appointed in Birmingham. Frank Hahn was appointed in the later 1940s to an assistant lectureship, and remained in Birmingham before leaving for the Massachusetts Institute of Technology (MIT) in 1956; in 1949 Terence Gorman joined the staff;[60] and in 1952 Alan Walters was appointed a lecturer in statistics and

[57] Allen (1900–1982) was subsequently Brunner Professor of Political Economy in Liverpool (1933–1947), then Jevons Professor of Economics at University College London (1947–1967), and worked as Assistant Secretary at the Board of Trade (1941–1944). See M. Gowing, 'George Cyril Allen', *Proceedings of the British Academy* Vol. 71 (1985), pp. 473–91.

[58] University of Birmingham, Faculty of Commerce, *Regulations and Syllabus 1930–31*, p. 37. That Sargant Florence built upon the work of Allen can be judged from Allen's own *British Industries and Their Organisation* (Longmans, Green, & Co., London 1933), a work that became a standard textbook.

[59] The non-publication of the University Calendar during 1941–1948 means that there is now no university record of appointments made through the 1940s; when the calendar resumed publication it no longer carried descriptions of courses, and the university archives contain little detail on developments in the 1950s.

[60] Known as Terence, William Gorman (1923–2003) was born in Northern Ireland but studied from 1941 to 1943 at Trinity College Dublin, serving in the Royal Navy 1943–1946, then resuming his studies, graduating in economics in 1948 and mathematics in 1949. He taught at Birmingham from 1949 to 1962, then moved to Oxford and later in 1967 to LSE. The absence of departmental records for the postwar period in Birmingham and the limitations of university records make it very difficult to reconstruct this important phase in the development of economics in Britain.

econometrics, then promoted to a chair before leaving for LSE in 1969. These and other appointments set the teaching of economics in Birmingham on a path entirely unrelated to the prior existence of the Faculty of Commerce.

From the later 1920s onwards, the Faculty of Commerce did finally develop the clear profile that it had hitherto lacked, but by this time its position as the initiator of higher commercial education in Britain had been eclipsed by Manchester and by the LSE. Before the arrival of Sargant Florence in 1929, the Birmingham Faculty of Commerce had not developed a replicable curriculum capable of providing a disciplinary framework for the study of commerce and economics. Ashley had invented the Birmingham curriculum on the hoof, having had little personal contact with commercial education in the United States, nor being able to draw on existing local provision for commercial education in Birmingham even if he had wished to do so. Quite plainly his personal contacts with local business were likewise limited. Nor did the programme he devised and the appointments he made create opportunities for an opening towards the teaching of contemporary economics—it might be supposed that such an idea would hardly have occurred to Ashley. Not until the 1940s did an opening to economics begin to take shape in Birmingham, decisions being made at that time that owed little, positively or negatively, to the earlier history of the Faculty of Commerce. Nevertheless, the example of Manchester will demonstrate that there were indeed alternative options elsewhere for the teaching of commerce that did not shut out the introduction and expansion of teaching in economics. We can see in Manchester the outline of a more general story that would come to characterise the teaching of commerce and economics in Britain outside Oxford and Cambridge: that provision for the teaching of economics within a commercial framework transmuted into the displacement of commerce by economics, and the eventual suppression of commercial teaching and qualifications.

The Manchester Faculty of Commerce

The Faculty of Commerce of the Victoria University of Manchester was created in late 1903; but the teaching of commercial and economic subjects was already well-established in the city. Victoria University had originally been a federal institution granting its own degrees, founded in 1880 with Owens College Manchester as first constituent member, with University College Liverpool joining in 1884 and Yorkshire College Leeds in 1887.[61] Changes to the University of London and the transition of Mason College into the University of Birmingham created pressures, both internal and external, for the breakup of the federal structure. Liverpool received its University Charter in July 1903, and the name Victoria University was then adopted for the reorganised Manchester institution. Owens College itself had been founded in 1851, modelled on University College London: secular, open to men and women, and

[61] For a fuller account of the teaching of political economy at Owens College and the Victoria University, see my chapter 'Political Economy in the Northern Civic Universities', in Alon Kadish, Keith Tribe (eds.) *The Market for Political Economy: The Advent of Economics in British University Culture, 1850–1905*, Routledge, London 1993, pp. 199–206.

teaching a modern curriculum. Admitting 62 day students in its first year, numbers dwindled during the first decade, recovering however in the 1860s, especially with new evening classes that were especially well-attended; by 1870–1871 there were 527 students registered in the evening classes, against 264 in day classes.[62] Stanley Jevons began teaching evening classes in political economy, geometry, and logic from 1863, advancing to a Chair of Political Economy and Mental and Moral Science in 1866, the title reflecting the connection to the University of London BA, of which political economy formed a part.[63]

Jevons offered his students '... an elementary course of lectures on the nature of wealth, labour, capital, land, wages, profit, rent, exchange, money &c.', nominating Mill's *Principles* as his textbook; and while he had only three students in his day class for 1866, there were 28 in the evening class, together with 22 schoolteachers enrolled in the Cobden class for schoolmasters.[64] By 1869–1870 there were 56 evening class students for political economy, including 40 Cobden class students. The age profile of the college's students is also indicative here of the kinds of audience Jevons had: in his Report on the session 1876–1877, the Principal noted that of the 397 daytime students enrolled in the previous session, 27 were under the age of 16, 133 between 16 and 18 years old, 79 between 18 and 20, and 158 above 20.[65] This broad range and relative maturity of students at Owens indicates that the college succeeded in attracting an educationally diverse student body, unlike for example the much younger intake of the contemporary French *Écoles de commerce*. Jevons continued teaching the same basic course until he moved to University College London in 1875; the course announced for 1876–1877 by his replacement, Robert Adamson, had changed very little since 1866, besides the addition of Jevons's own *Theory of Political Economy* to the reading.[66]

Adamson overhauled the teaching that he had inherited from Jevons: by 1880–1881 he had divided the daytime course in two: the first part being 'Economics', beginning with 'Province, Method, and Divisions of Political Economy', moving on to the theory of production and the theory of distribution; and the second part 'Applied Economics', which was specified as taxation.[67] There were now two textbooks: the Marshalls'

[62] H. B. Charlton, *Portrait of a University 1851-1951*, Manchester University Press, Manchester 1951, Appendix V.

[63] Jevons assumed the chair following the retirement of Richard Copley Christie, a lawyer appointed Professor of History in 1853, but who had in 1854 been given the title 'Professor of Political Economy and Commercial Science' and an additional £50 p.a., but who only gave a few lectures in the subject; C. Lees, A. Robertson, 'Characteristics of Professional Life in the First of the Civic Universities, 1851–1918', *Bulletin of the John Rylands University Library of Manchester* Vol. 82 No. 1 (Spring 2000), p. 230, and E. Fiddes, *Chapters in the History of Owens College and of Manchester University 1851–1914*, Manchester University Press, Manchester 1937, p. 149.

[64] *The Calendar of Owens College, Manchester, Session 1867–68*, pp. 36, 60, 74. John Owens, with whose legacy Owens College was founded in 1850, was a supporter of Richard Cobden and the Anti-Corn Law League. The College leased Cobden's house in Quay Street from him in 1850, but the same year Cobden sold it to George Faulkner, who then in 1854 gifted it to the college. The name Cobden was therefore closely related to the existence of the college, and was used for the special classes established for Manchester teachers.

[65] *The Calendar of Owens College, Manchester, Session 1876–77*, p. 136. There are some small discrepancies in recorded student numbers between different sources: information from Jeff Brider, Assistant Registrar of the University of Manchester, 2 August 1993.

[66] Ibid., p. 50.

[67] *The Calendar of Owens College, Manchester, Session 1880–81*, p. 57. Adamson (1852–1902) had studied at Edinburgh 1866–1871, with the summer of 1871 spent in Heidelberg. Before his appointment to Owens

Economics of Industry, and Jevons's *Money*. For the session 1881–1882, Cossa's *Guide to the Study of Political Economy* was added to the day course.[68] This reading was already in advance of what would be on offer in Birmingham 25 years later. Then, in 1882, J. E. Crawford Munro was appointed Professor of Law and Cobden Lecturer in Political Economy, taking over responsibility for teaching political economy from Adamson. While Adamson's new two-part rubric for political economy remained unchanged until the 1890s, Munro added Henry Sidgwick's *Principles of Political Economy* to the assigned reading, another significant move. Then, for the session 1890–1891, Elijah Helm, Secretary of the Manchester Chamber of Commerce, took over the evening classes for political economy, teaching taxation and banking in relation to the Victoria University Technical and Commercial Certificates that had been introduced in the previous session.[69] With the departure of Munro in 1892, an opening was also created for the appointment of Alfred Flux as Cobden Lecturer—a Cambridge student of mathematics bracketed Senior Wrangler in 1887, then a student of Marshall who won the Marshall Prize in 1889.[70] For the session 1894–1895 he added Marshall's *Principles of Economics* to an unaltered day class syllabus.

By this point, political economy was a third-year option in the Victoria University ordinary BA degree, while honours history students had to present proof of attendance at political economy classes in their second or their third year.[71] For the session 1895–1896, Flux introduced a two-year cycle, the session 1895–1896 being devoted to 'the economics of industry' using the 1892 condensed version of Marshall's *Principles*,[72] while the session 1896–1897 was devoted to 'the economics of trade and finance'. This reflected a progression that Marshall had had in mind for the first and second volumes of his *Principles*. The net effect of this change was to increase the time devoted to the exposition of economic principles, while also extending their application to an area with which those attending the evening classes would be familiar. Progression in the teaching was therefore ensured, since students could only enter the cycle every other year. Alterations to the evening classes around this time were also significant. In 1897–1898 a new set of 20 lectures, 'Outlines of Economics', was announced, linked to the Manchester and District Institute of Bankers and held in the rooms of the Bankers'

College in 1876 he had worked as an assistant for the Edinburgh professors of Moral Philosophy & Logic and Metaphysics; from 1895 until his death he was Professor of Logic and Rhetoric at Glasgow.

68 *The Calendar of Owens College, Manchester, Session 1881–82*, p. 63.

69 *The Calendar of Owens College, Manchester, Session 1890–91*, pp. 228–29.

70 Henry Clay's original *Dictionary of National Biography* entry was revised by John Whitaker for the *Oxford Dictionary of National Biography*, adding in the process misdirection about the character of Flux's contemporary significance as an economist. Far from Flux being merely 'sound', as Whitaker suggests, Flux's *Economic Principles: An Introductory Study* (1904) stands out from contemporary publications as the first post-Marshallian textbook. See Sydney Chapman's obituary in the *Economic Journal* Vol. 52 (1942), pp. 400–3, for a more balanced assessment of his achievements. For a local assessment, see Anon., 'Mr. A. W. Flux, M.A.', *Manchester Faces and Places* Vol. 6 No. 8 (May 1895), pp. 124–26.

71 *The Calendar of Owens College, Manchester, Session 1894–95*, p. 84.

72 When *Elements of the Economics of Industry* was published in 1892, Alfred Marshall made sure that the earlier *Economics of Industry* that he had written with his wife became unavailable. Reading lists continued to refer to the earlier title, but the book was reprinted in 1894, had a second edition in 1896, and a third in 1899; it can be assumed that the familiar title was used to refer to the new book.

Institute.[73] There were also additional evening courses, including one for teachers from elementary schools entitled 'The Industrial and Commercial Arrangements of Modern Life'.[74]

Flux was made Stanley Jevons Professor of Political Economy in 1898, further consolidating his position. He continued to develop the teaching of both commerce and economics, the Bankers' Institute lectures continuing with great success, attracting 67 students in 1899–1900. At this time Flux had five daytime courses: an 'Economic Theory' course met twice a week, while the title to another course, 'The Principles of International Trade, with special reference to the alleged decline of British commercial prosperity', foreshadowed the argument over protection that would break out in 1903. In 1899 a two-year daytime course for the Certificate in Commerce was also introduced for students required to provide evidence of 'attainments of about the standard required for the Preliminary Examination of the Victoria University',[75] further pushing commercial teaching towards regular university provision. In the first year the course included modern languages, geography, law, and economics, and in the second, modern languages, commercial law, and economics or economic history.

In 1901, however, Flux left for a chair at McGill, and was replaced by Sydney Chapman, who had in 1898 gained a First in the Moral Sciences Tripos. Chapman (1871–1951) was in fact originally a Manchester graduate, having taken a London BA there in 1891 before moving on to Cambridge. He had returned to Manchester in 1899 as Jevons Research Student, conducting a study of the cotton industry for which he was awarded the Cambridge Adam Smith Prize in 1900. Marshall had approved the research topic, and the monograph is quite clearly a case study in Marshallian analysis, rather than a historical-descriptive account of the industry's development that might have been more usual for the time.[76] Chapman later suggested in his obituary of Flux[77] that his move to Montreal was made because of the apparently poor prospects for teaching economics in Manchester at the time, but by comparison with anywhere else, Flux had successfully built on an already strong foundation. Chapman continued in the same direction, first continuing with the courses that Flux had established, then planning for the Faculty of Commerce.

Like Ashley in Birmingham at this time, in his planning Chapman looked first to Germany. In the spring of 1903 he published two newspaper articles reporting on foreign provision for commercial education, referring also to Ashley's recent

[73] Twenty students attended this course in 1897–1898, and 56 the following year; *The Calendar of Owens College, Manchester, Session 1897–98*, p. 261. The Institute of Bankers had been founded in 1879, and included political economy in its subjects for examination—see the discussion in Chapter 3, p. 66.

[74] 'A plain exposition of important facts such as different forms of wage-contract, co-operation, profit-sharing, outlines of factory legislation, etc., together with explanation of the meanings of some of the more usual terms in use in trade, on the Stock Exchange, etc.'; *The Calendar of Owens College, Manchester, Session 1897–98*, p. 261. Eleven students attended this course.

[75] *The Calendar of Owens College, Manchester, Session 1899–1900*, p. 71.

[76] Chapman, *The Lancashire Cotton Industry: A Study in Economic Development*, Publications of the University of Manchester. Economic Series No. 1, Manchester University Press, Manchester 1904. See the discussion of this in Chapter 6. He had first intended to study psychology at Cambridge, but was persuaded to specialise in political economy, attending Marshall's lectures for three years and having weekly supervisions; S. Chapman, *Some Memories and Reflections*, unpublished manuscript, c. 1944, p. 19, John Rylands Library, Manchester, MSS. EH C91.

[77] *Economic Journal* Vol. 52 (1942), pp. 400–3.

(anonymous) article in *The Times*. He dealt first of all with new institutions in Leipzig, Aachen, Cologne, and Frankfurt, noting that the *Handelshochschulen* were properly staffed and supported, with adequate number of teachers to cover the syllabus. Antwerp and the French *Écoles* were dealt with briefly, noting that their curricula were less economically-oriented than those in Germany. A second article covered commercial education in the United States, including Wharton, Chicago, California, Wisconsin, and Vermont.[78] His commitment to higher commercial education was later also reflected in an address he gave in November 1905 to the Cardiff and District Educational Society, where he concluded by casting doubt on the willingness of Oxford and Cambridge to engage with the task of training students for business careers.[79] The report drew a response from Marshall, who made a clear distinction between the kind of work suited to honours economics students, and that of pass men whose degrees were comparable in status to the ordinary BCom:

> If the University should ever decide to adapt its pass examinations in economics to the wants of those business men who do not aim at education of the same high order as is given in our honours courses, it will probably be necessary to have lectures on the common routine of accounting. And, if they are given by a professional accountant, he may be asked to give a short course adapted to the needs of abler students. It is, however, not probable that the University will allow much time to be given even by passmen to absorbing prematurely technical information about those 'forms and accounts adapted to different classes of undertakings', on which your Educational Notes lay stress. For Honours men, at all events, such work is inappropriate. The three sacred years of their University life are already fully occupied with studies which claim to help the able business man to be a leader in the world.[80]

Not only then were Chapman's plans distinct from those of Ashley, they also differed sharply from those of his teacher Marshall, who regarded commercial subjects as suited only to 'pass men', not to the honours students for the whom the Tripos was constructed.

Further evidence for Chapman's own views on higher commercial education can be found in a paper that he read to the Manchester Statistical Society on 12 February 1902. He began by noting the manner in which training through pupillage and apprenticeship was everywhere being superseded by formal education and examination, and that the time had come to extend this to the world of business:

> At the present time there is a special need among those who are to elicit the greatest possible value from industry and commerce and shape their future, of a higher education including (a) instruction in economic principles, since in these the business man has instruments by which he can solve his own particular problems in detail,

[78] S. J. Chapman: '"Business" Education Abroad and at Home' I & II, *Manchester Guardian* 21 April 1903, 24 April 1903.

[79] 'Commercial Education', *The Times*, 18 November 1905, p. 17.

[80] Alfred Marshall, Letter of 14 December 1905, printed as 'Education for Business Men', *The Times*, 18 December 1905, p. 13.

> and (b) instruction in special branches of economic investigation, since in these the business man will find large parts of the solutions which he is seeking. It is certain that the complications of modern industry and commerce cannot be faced successfully by those who are innocent of all economic knowledge.[81]

Chapman made clear, however, that he was not simply concerned with business education in a commercial context, but with all forms of public administration, including local and national elected representatives:

> The people with whom we have to deal may afterwards work in the world as bankers, accountants, actuaries, brokers, jobbers, commission agents, manufacturers in many industries, shopkeepers or shippers, persons employed in gas works or on railways, tramways, or canals, members of Parliament, diplomats, town councillors, town clerks or clerks in the Civil Service, justices of the peace, or social workers of various kinds.[82]

He then proceeded to sketch out a university curriculum appropriate to the training for such employments, combining modern languages, political economy, political science, political philosophy, history and geography, law, and statistics as a general foundation, with a variety of special subjects taken in the second and third years which might include public administration and finance, accountancy, demography, banking and currency, international trade, transport insurance, and poor relief.[83] The new faculty, he suggested, should be modelled on that of law or of medicine, by which he meant that much of the specialised teaching would be covered by local professionals, three full-time teachers sufficing to cover the core academic subjects of the first group. He acknowledged in conclusion that Oxford and Cambridge lacked business communities capable of supplying such occasional teaching, lending Manchester an advantage in this respect. This was a valid enough point, but it was not one applicable to Birmingham or Liverpool, where, as in Manchester, there was a substantial pool of accountants, bankers, lawyers, and railway managers upon which a new institution might draw for its practical teaching.

The University Court had already determined in March 1900 to explore the possibility of higher commercial education, in partnership with a number of other bodies.[84] Additional funds were raised, and on 8 December 1903 the 'Faculty of Commerce and Administration' was formally inaugurated, this being the final academic year for the old Owens College.[85] Four related appointments were made at this time: a lecturer

[81] S. J. Chapman, 'On Education for Business and Public Life', *Transactions of the Manchester Statistical Society* (1902), p. 126.

[82] Ibid., p. 128.

[83] Ibid., pp. 132–33.

[84] E. Fiddes, *Chapters in the History of Owens College and of Manchester University 1851–1914*, Manchester University Press, Manchester 1937, p. 152. A brief, if in places unreliable, overview of the development of the teaching of commerce and economics in Owens College can be found in G. W. Daniels, 'Economic and Commercial Studies in the Owens College and the University', *Manchester School* Vol. 1 (1930), pp. 3–9.

[85] For a full account of the history of the Faculty until its redesignation in 1944 as the 'Faculty of Economic and Social Studies', see my 'The Faculty of Commerce and Manchester Economics, 1903–44', *Manchester School* Vol. 71 (2003), pp. 680–710.

in economic and political geography;[86] a lecturer in commerce and economics;[87] a lecturer in accounting;[88] and a lecturer in banking.[89] This pattern of appointment clearly distinguished Manchester from Birmingham; to cover the directly vocational teaching, Chapman drew upon the contacts with the Manchester business community that he had developed while studying the cotton industry, while he assumed responsibility for the economics teaching, assisted by a new generation of young economists, many of whom later went on to head economics departments of their own. This also permitted him to establish an honours degree in economics to run alongside the existing commercial courses, making the most of the limited resources available to him, but at the same time laying the foundations for a broadly-based Manchester school of studies in commerce, economics, and public administration.

Chapman's draft programme of 1902 provided the template for the new BCom syllabus outlined in the 1904–1905 university calendar. Eight courses were required to complete the degree, listed in the following order:[90]

1. Political Economy (The economics of consumption, production, exchange and distribution), 2 hours per week;
2. Geography (Definition and description of geographical conditions and their influence on economic and political development), 2 hours per week;
3. Modern History (Outlines of general history from the fall of Napoleon, with special reference to social and economic conditions), 2 hours per week;
4. A Modern Language (Interpretation of prescribed books with literary and grammatical questions; unseen translation from and into English; composition and commercial correspondence; dictation and conversation), 3 hours per week;
5. The Organisation of Industry and Commerce (A description and analysis of modern industrial and commercial conditions), 2 hours per week;
6. Accounting (The principles and practice of accounting), one hour a week for two winter terms;[91]
7. Commercial Law (The principles of law applicable to, and the more important cases bearing upon, Principal and Agent, Partnership, Limited Companies, Mercantile Securities; Guarantees; Carriage by Land; Carriage by Sea; Policies of Insurance; Sale of Goods; Bills of Exchange; Cheques and Notes; Bankruptcy), 1 hour per week for two sessions;

[86] J. Macfarlane (MA Edinburgh, BA Cantab.).

[87] William George Stewart Adams (1874–1966), a graduate of Glasgow and Oxford, had spent the year 1902–1903 as a teacher of economics in the Graduate School of the University of Chicago; in 1905 he left Manchester to become Superintendent of Statistics in the Irish Department of Agricultural and Technical Instruction, leaving this post to become Reader in Political Theory at Oxford in 1910, being promoted in 1912 to the position of Gladstone Professor of Political Theory and Institutions, a post he held until 1933, when he became Warden of All Souls.

[88] Roger N. Carter (F.C.A.) was a Manchester accountant who taught in the University part-time until 1918.

[89] D. Drummond Fraser (Fellow of the Institute of Banking).

[90] The Victoria University of Manchester, *Calendar 1904–1905*, pp. 254–56.

[91] 'Candidates who are not practising accountants will find it necessary to attend one hour a week for three terms or its equivalent, and attendances for four terms are desirable.' *Calendar 1904–1905*, p. 256.

8. Special Subject—*Either* one subject from A; *or* two subjects from B (including one modern language); *or* one subject from B (including one modern language) and two from C:
   Group A: a science
   Group B: a science; second modern language, or advanced modern language; currency and banking
   Group C: accountancy, foreign trade and foreign exchanges; railway economics and transport; the cotton industry; special period in economic history; public finance; statistics; insurance; the law of patents, designs and trade marks; international law; special subject in geography; political science.

The principal change here with respect to the 1902 draft programme was to move accountancy from the list of special subjects to become a mandatory paper on 'accounting', the downgrading of statistics to an optional special subject, the omission of political science and political philosophy from the main list, and the associated omission from the list of special subjects of public administration and demography. The immediate consequence was to sharpen the focus of the degree upon more strictly commercial subjects, while the range of special subjects includes economic topics which, if taken in combination, would represent something like an ordinary economics degree course. It was not only Chapman's staffing strategy that permitted the development of economics teaching within a commercial context, nor the fact that an honours economics degree was also offered in the Arts School; the design of the commercial curriculum kept open what would today be called an 'economics pathway'. Moreover, the subjects that were initially excluded between draft programme and its eventual form found their way back later. During the 1920s the BCom degree was divided in two, the original degree continuing as a BACom, and a new BA in Public Administration being formed alongside it. Here therefore is the origin of more specialised teaching in government and social policy, pointing up the manner in which Chapman's original design for commercial education in Manchester provided a foundation upon which the general development of teaching in the social sciences could be built.

The prime source that we have for the development of teaching in the social sciences in Manchester is the *University Calendar*, which records members of staff, teaching regulations, syllabi, recommended reading, and examination papers, but which does so in a manner which makes reconstruction of the actual distribution of teaching somewhat laborious. Individual members of staff can be attached to specific classes and lectures, but these classes were open to students from a number of different faculties: the introductory course on Political Economy, for example, might be attended by ordinary BA students, honours economics students, honours history students, as well as students of commerce. Seventeen students are recorded[92] as having attended the 'Advanced Economics' course run by Chapman and Adams through the session 1904–1905, a course for 'Honours Students';[93] but since there were only 13

[92] *Calendar 1905–1906*, p. 689.
[93] *Calendar 1904–1905*, p. 260.

honours economics graduates in total before 1914, it is anyone's guess how the class was composed. Nominally, the Faculty of Commerce possessed at its foundation only one full-time member of staff: Chapman. MacFarlane and Adams, who were among the four related appointments made at the time, were listed both under the Faculty of Arts and under Commerce; although Adams was, like the increasing number of assistant lecturers in economics who succeeded him, entirely occupied in daytime and evening teaching for the commerce degree. Other tutors listed under the entry for the various specialised courses of the Faculty of Commerce were either local professionals or other members of the University.[94]

Teaching was by lecture,[95] duplicated for day and evening students, with many of the more specialised courses being assigned exclusively to evening hours, when students in full-time employment could attend.[96] Some courses—Chapman's on railway economics,[97] Drummond Fraser's on banking, and Professor Seaton's on Commercial Law—extended over two years, while the modern language courses (French, German, Spanish, Arabic, and Chinese) included practice of translation and conversation. In October 1904, 14 students had registered for the degree, with another 14 attending lectures; and some of the individual specialised courses were very well attended, the railway companies for example paying the lecture fees for employees attending the course on railway economics.[98] The Institute of Bankers likewise established 10 scholarships covering the cost of two years' courses in currency and banking, and these lectures were also typically well-attended;[99] and since these lectures later attracted an exemption, they would have been attractive for those intending to work in banking.[100]

[94] So, for instance, the Secretary of the Chamber of Commerce lectured on the cotton industry, and A. D. Lindsay on political philosophy.

[95] Even if the number of students was small, the class followed a lecture format, with an occasional seminar in the honours economics course in the 1920s; see Sir Henry Hardman's account, in my collection of interviews, *Economic Careers: Economics and Economists in Britain 1930–1970*, Routledge London 1997, p. 16. By the later 1930s, Ordinary and Honours students were differentiated by the fact that the latter had classes additional to lectures, while the former did not. Marjorie Tivey began the Ordinary BA (Admin) degree in 1940 and it was only when she switched to Honours economics in 1941 that she received class-based tuition; Interview with Marjorie Tivey, Hall Green, Birmingham, 11 October 2000. By the time that Dennis Coppock began an Ordinary BA (Com) course in 1946, classes had been introduced for Ordinary degree students, but this must have been a new development. He then converted to Honours economics, and recalls initially being in a group of around eight with Jack Gilbert as tutor; Interview with Dennis Coppock, Stockport, 29 April 1994.

[96] The Senate had resolved on 5 November 1903 that 'qualifying courses for degrees in the Faculty of Commerce should be arranged on such lines as to make it possible for students engaged in business during the day to graduate in the Faculty' (Minute Books of the Proceedings of the Senate, 1903–51, University Archives, Manchester University Library RA/3/5 Vol. 1 Item 7). Sir Henry Hardman recalled that in the mid-1920s there might be up to a hundred for a core evening lecture, with perhaps 30 for German. In his daytime honours economics course there were, by contrast, only five students; see *Economic Careers*, p. 16.

[97] Chapman was assisted in this course by A. E. Clear, Assistant Goods Manager for the Great Central Railway, on Railway Transport; and H. Pilkington-Turner, Barrister at Law, with respect to Railway Law; *Calendar 1904–1905*, p. 62.

[98] Which clearly had an impact upon numbers, over 900 students having attended in 1903–1904 the course on the history of railway transport, and 856 the course on railway transport practice; *Calendar 1904–1905*, p. 643.

[99] 'Manchester University. The Faculty of Commerce', *Manchester Guardian*, 9 March 1905.

[100] 'The Council of the Institute of Bankers, London, has agreed to exempt from their preliminary examination in practical banking those students who attend the course on "The principles and practice of banking" and who pass the usual examination held at the end of the course.' Report of courses run by Drummond Fraser and Meredith, *Manchester Guardian*, 9 October 1908.

Generally speaking, in these early years the substantial fee-income from these occasional commercial students provided a firm basis for the recruitment of staff suitable for teaching commercial and economic subjects at an advanced level, so that the BCom students had from the very beginning a full range of courses, and there were generally at least two economists capable of teaching their subject to an advanced level for the few Honours students.

When the Faculty opened its doors it was possible for students to proceed to examination as and when they felt able.[101] This was a provisional arrangement, however, presumably adopted to accelerate the development of teaching and examination during the transition into an autonomous institution. Regulations were, however, to come into force during October 1906 which laid down a minimum period of study of three years after matriculation.[102] There is some difficulty in interpreting the statistics that the University published on age at matriculation, which was possible from 16, although the available figures indicate that before the First World War there were twice as many students aged 18–20 as 16–18, and twice as many again over 20 as those aged 18–20. Since these figures do not discriminate between day and evening enrolments, nor between medical and non-medical students, it is difficult to determine the age and employment status of students registering for degrees in commerce and economics.

As recorded in Table 10.1, some general remarks, however, can be made concerning student numbers to the mid-1920s. Firstly, very few students graduated with an Honours economics degree, and there was no change in this pattern right up to 1944. If we were to employ a rule of thumb to the effect that significant numbers of Honours economics students are necessary to justify the level and quality of appointments capable in turn of founding a major school, then on these numbers Manchester was nowhere near a critical mass of students, even after 40 years. But by the 1930s Manchester was indeed a significant centre for economic research; over the years the Honours economics students were taught by some of the leading economists of the day, and after 1945 the new Faculty of Economics and Social Studies quickly expanded into a major national centre of teaching and research in economics. This could happen because of the manner in which Chapman set up the teaching for the commerce degree and associated vocational courses. The popular evening sessions on currency and banking, noted earlier, were for example taught by Drummond Fraser, a local banker, in combination firstly with Adams, appointed in 1912 as Gladstone Professor of Political Theory in Oxford, and then with Meredith, Pigou's successor in 1908 as Girdler's Lecturer in Cambridge and then in 1910 appointed to the chair of Economics at Queen's University, Belfast, with the task of establishing a Faculty of Commerce.

Secondly, while the number of Birmingham graduates in commerce fluctuates around a small number throughout the period 1905–1926 (with a brief postwar surge), in Manchester numbers remained above 20 per year after this postwar surge, being a respectable number for the period.[103] The commerce syllabus designed by

[101] *Calendar 1904–1905*, p. 254 para. 4.

[102] Ibid., p. 100 para. 2.

[103] And the degree had a good reputation with Manchester employers, as shown by a survey of employment opportunities for graduates in January 1908: 114 replies were received, 72 of which were favourable, 24 being favourable but with few openings, and only 18 replying to the effect that they were unfavourable or

Table 10.1 Manchester and Birmingham Graduates in Commerce and Economics

	Manchester BA (Hons.) Econ	Manchester BCom	Manchester Commerce Students	Birmingham BCom
1904–1905	1		16	3
1905–1906	1		31	5
1906–1907	0	5	36	1
1907–1908	0	7	38	5
1908–1909	3	6	35	4
1909–1910	2	6	33	4
1910–1911	1	7	45	7
1911–1912	3	7	47	3
1912–1913	2	8	42	7
1913–1914	0	11	57	8
1914–1915	2	8	46	7
1915–1916	1	7	26	5
1916–1917	3	3	24	2
1917–1918	5	4	17	5
1918–1919	0	6	35	1
1919–1920	2	14	63	14
1920–1921	3	10	131	29
1921–1922	4	39	142	23
1922–1923	6	33	129	7
1923–1924	3	25	118	9
1924–1925	2	22	129	6
1925–1926	1	26	144	6

Source: *University Calendars* (various years).

Note: After 1926 the BCom became the BACom. and a new BA (Admin.) was introduced. The column 'Manchester Commerce Students' includes the number of students registered for a degree in each year, both full- and part-time; after some initial variation, presumably related to students graduating early, the pre-war figure settles to represent an average annual intake of around a dozen students, and we might presume that the outbreak of war led several students to break off their studies. The *Manchester Guardian* reported, for example, that 11 new students registered for the session 1907–1908: 'Board of the Faculty of Commerce' (27 April 1909). By the mid-1920s there is an increasing drift between numbers enrolled and numbers graduating; as noted earlier, we can establish retrospectively that those who graduated had generally studied for three years, but since we have no record of enrolments by name, it is not possible to detect dropout rates.

Chapman also had a solid core of analytical and applied economics, so that students graduating in Manchester with a commerce degree would not necessarily be any less skilled in economic principles than students elsewhere who had completed what passed for an economics degree. By the later 1930s this was no longer true, since the

that no openings of this kind occurred in their firms: 'The Faculty of Commerce' *Manchester Guardian*, 27 March 1908.

teaching of economics was becoming more specialised; and so Manchester's response was to turn the Faculty of Commerce into a Faculty of Economic and Social Studies.

Ashley's perspective upon economics and commerce was quite different to that of Chapman. In 1908 he delivered a lecture in Manchester entitled 'The Enlargement of Economics', in which he expressed the hope that the formation of new Faculties of Commerce would stimulate the study of economics, and suggested that

> Political Economy should be widened to take account of facts of commercial and industrial activity, and complemented with the creation of a '... "Business economics", which frankly took for its point of view the interest of the individual man or business concern'.[104]

'Business economics', argued Ashley,

> ... would 'drive at practice', but would not profess to be a series of recipes for success. 'It will be simply a serious and systematic grouping and weighing of the known results of actual experience. In this work the academic teacher will enjoy no advantage that may not be possessed by any man of common sense; he will pursue no subtle train of reasoning; he will make use of no peculiar 'organism'.[105] His sole advantage will result from his wider acquaintance with the field of inquiry than most men actually engaged in trade have time to acquire. His function will simply be to interpret to the business world that world's own experience.

Chapman clearly thought otherwise, as is apparent from the character of his junior appointments. In 1905 H. O. Meredith (1878–1964)[106] was made Lecturer in Economic History and Commerce, sharing with Chapman the teaching of basic principles of political economy and of 'advanced economics', while taking responsibility for courses on economic history, currency and exchange, and public finance.[107] In addition he took an introductory evening class 'Outlines of Economic Theory—on Production, Distribution and Exchange' in the Bankers' Institute, so he was clearly kept very busy. When Meredith returned to Cambridge he was replaced by Douglas Knoop (1883–1948), who was the first student to graduate from Manchester in economics, being awarded a First in 1905. The 1909–1910 edition of the *Calendar* shows that Knoop simply slotted into Meredith's place in the teaching programme before moving to Sheffield the following year, where he was subsequently Professor of Economics from 1920 to 1948. Three assistant lecturers replaced him: C. F. Bickerdike (1876–1961), H. M. Hallsworth (1876–1953), and R. B. Forrester.[108] Bickerdike had read Mathematics and Modern History at Oxford, and after two years at Manchester he

[104] W. J. Ashley, 'Business Economics', *Manchester Guardian*, 12 February 1908.

[105] Presumably here the reporter misheard an allusion by Ashley to Marshall's economic 'organon', the set of analytical principles with which the properly trained economist was equipped.

[106] Meredith had graduated from Cambridge in 1901 with a First in History, having read Classics for Part I, in which he also got a First; he was a Fellow of King's College during 1903–1905; Girdler's Lecturer in Cambridge, 1908–1911; and Professor of Economics, Queen's University, Belfast, 1911–1945.

[107] *Calendar 1905–1906*, pp. 287–88.

[108] No biographical details for Forrester can be located.

joined the Board of Trade, spending the rest of his working life in the Civil Service. Before moving to Manchester he had already published innovative papers on the theory of rents, and devised a formula for the determination of an optimal tariff, in 1906 becoming an LSE research student with Cannan as his supervisor.[109] Hallsworth, a Manchester graduate, had already completed research on local unemployment under the direction of Chapman, and the following year he was appointed to the new chair of Economics at Armstrong College, Newcastle, where a Faculty of Commerce was planned.[110] Forrester came from Edinburgh, where he would have been taught political economy by Shield Nicholson; in 1912 he became Lecturer in Economics at Aberdeen, moving in 1922 to the LSE where he was appointed Reader in Foreign Trade in 1926, finally holding the Chair of Political and Economic Science at Aberystwyth from 1931 to 1951.

Apart from the evening teaching associated with the degree courses, members of the Faculty also took tutorial classes at regional centres.[111] Hallsworth, Knoop, and Forrester together taught a three-year course on 'Industrial History' to seven different classes, Hallsworth for instance teaching in Blackburn, Bolton, Manchester, and Nelson. At Bolton, 31 students attended and 26 completed essays, and so this teaching represented a considerable addition to an already substantial teaching commitment—but, on the other hand, increased the number of assistant lecturers in economics that the Faculty could support. In the following year a change of direction was introduced, the courses becoming an introduction to economics; Forrester taught 'Economic Theory' on Thursdays at 8 p.m. in Blackburn Technical School to 32 students, while Bickerdike took a course based on the Manchester second-year 'Principles of Economics' lectures to 33 students at Manchester Grammar School.[112] This pattern continued, in 1917 Daniels being recorded as teaching the second-year economics course at a secondary school in Macclesfield.[113] Each tutorial class appears to have attracted at least 30 students, and while the tutors quickly took their material from standard Manchester courses, these classes represented a substantial continuing commitment for both individuals and faculty.

It was perhaps then not entirely coincidental that there was such a rapid turnover of assistant lecturers before the Great War. When Hallsworth left, two further assistant lecturers were appointed: Conrad Gill (1883–1962), later Professor of History at University College, Hull, and Francis Hubback, who had studied in Cambridge[114] but

[109] B. Larson, 'Bickerdike's Life and Work', *History of Political Economy* Vol. 19 (1987), pp. 1–22.

[110] *Economic Journal* Vol. 22 (1912), p. 512. See also Sydney J. Chapman, H. M. Hallsworth, *Unemployment: The Results of an Investigation Made in Lancashire and An Examination of the Report of the Poor Law Commission*, Sherratt & Hughes, Manchester 1909.

[111] Under a scheme inaugurated in April 1909 and administered by a joint committee on which Manchester University, the Co-Operative Union, the National Conference of Friendly Societies, the Northern Counties Amalgamated Associations of Weavers, the Workers' Educational Association, the Miners' Federation of Lancashire and Cheshire, and the Lancashire and Cheshire Federation of Trade and Labour Councils were represented. The students were mainly classed as 'skilled artisans and cotton operatives'; 'First Annual Report, Session 1909–10', pp. 1, 4, Manchester University Tutorial Classes, *Annual Reports 1909–22*, University of Manchester Archives UA/3/24.

[112] *Annual Reports 1909–22*, 'Second Annual Report. Session 1910–11', pp. 4, 7.

[113] *Annual Reports 1909–22*, 'Ninth Annual Report, 1917–18', mimeo.

[114] But not economics, although his wife, Eva Spielman, had taken Parts I and II of the Economics Tripos and gained a First in 1908.

who was killed on the Western Front in 1917. Bickerdike and Hubback left in 1912, to be replaced by A. F. Jack[115] and George Daniels (1878–1937),[116] both Manchester graduates. During the last year before the War there were three assistant lecturers: Jack, Daniels and A. N. Shimmin, who in 1915 left for an economics lectureship at Leeds, later in 1945 becoming Professor of Social Science. None of these junior appointees stayed very long at Manchester, apart from Daniels. They do almost all, however, share a background in, or an aptitude for, the Marshallian economics of the time, forming a generation whose conception of economics was primarily analytical, rather than historico-descriptive. Appointment in Manchester led on to a career in which they contributed to the development of commerce and economics, teaching in provincial universities. This entire phase came to an end with the Great War; Chapman was recruited in 1915 by the Board of Trade because of his knowledge of industrial structure, and he remained in the Civil Service for the rest of his career, becoming Chief Economic Advisor to the Government in 1927.[117] He was briefly succeeded as Stanley Jevons Professor by D. H. Macgregor, who quickly moved on to the Drummond Chair in Oxford and was in 1922 replaced by Henry Clay.[118] The previous year T. S. Ashton[119] had been appointed to a lectureship in economics, and Daniels promoted to the new Chair of Commerce and Administration. These two appointments would mark interwar Manchester until the arrival of Hicks in 1938 and the reconstruction of the Faculty after the war, recruiting, among others, W. Arthur Lewis, Alexander Henderson, Ely Devons in the later 1940s, and Harry Johnson in the mid-1950s. Our focus here is not, however, on the history of commerce and economics in Manchester, but on the question of the relationship between the teaching of commerce and the place given to economics within the commerce curriculum.

Table 10.1 shows that in the 1920s Manchester had on its books a significant mass of commerce students, and that it awarded commerce degrees at around three to four times the rate of Birmingham. As suggested previously, during the 1930s the study of commerce in Birmingham was lent greater coherence by a focus upon industrial organisation, but Manchester had a clear advantage in a long history of post-secondary education prior to the foundation of the Faculty of Commerce—Victoria and London BA and BSc degrees. External London degrees, adult and evening education

[115] Jack had been awarded an M.Comm. for a thesis on the history of life assurance, which he presented in Cambridge as part of an application for a degree. Clapham's comments were emollient, Pigou's not—in fact, one of the very few recorded statements that survives from Pigou apart from his published writings—see Minutes of Degree Committee, 8 May 1912, Minutes of the Special Board for Economics and Politics 1911–23, Cambridge University Archives: UA Min.V.115 f. 17.

[116] George Daniels, a former electrician, was a graduate of Ruskin College, Oxford, and had gained degrees in both economics and commerce in Manchester. He was made Reader in Administration in 1920, Professor of Commerce and Administration in 1921, and Stanley Jevons Professor of Political Economy in 1927. He died in 1937 of a heart attack, and was succeeded by John Hicks.

[117] See the outline of Chapman's career in my *Oxford Dictionary of National Biography* entry for him.

[118] Clay came from New College, Oxford. He had graduated in 1906 lit. hum., was afterwards warden of a settlement in Sheffield, an Assistant Lecturer in Social Organisation at Leeds from 1911 to 1913, and had also been an extension lecturer for many years.

[119] A Manchester graduate in history and political economy, he had been a lecturer in economics at Sheffield from 1912 to 1919, then a tutor in economics and political science at Birmingham from 1919 to 1921; from 1927 to 1944 he was Reader in Currency and Finance at Manchester before moving to a chair in economic history at the LSE.

combined with active involvement in its teaching by the local commercial community. By drawing upon the community to provide the specialised commercial teaching, Chapman was able to recruit young men trained in economics who, even when they had to teach at an elementary level, could bring to their teaching an understanding of recent developments in the subject. The small number of students who actually ended up taking honours economics does not indicate a lack of available teaching in economics; it rather indicates that an honours economics degree was not then perceived by students as having an appropriate vocational relevance. They were not wrong: even having a double First in economics from Cambridge during the 1930s did not necessarily lead directly on to any particular path. That some students could nonetheless follow this economics pathway is a reflection of Chapman's appointment strategy, recruiting young graduates familiar with contemporary economics while relying on the part-time input of local professionals for the specialised commerce teaching.

Manchester was the strongest provincial centre for commerce teaching until the 1940s, when commerce gave way to economics as part of the faculty reorganisation in 1944. Chapman's initiative in bundling the teaching of economics within a commerce degree led not to the creation of a new form of vocational economics, but simply created a vehicle within which a future department of economics would grow. Again, we are not here primarily concerned with the history of commercial education in Britain, but with a different question—why the teaching of commerce did not provide a viable alternative to the emergent discipline of economics, but instead through the 1930s and 1940s progressively ceded ground to the new academic discipline. Part of the answer has to be a shift in the public profile of economics; certainly, from the later 1940s, economics was seen as a 'modern' subject, and commerce as its poor relation. More important, however, was that the teaching of commerce everywhere remained an eclectic mix of modern languages, commercial geography, commercial law, and accounting, with no progressive core nor, importantly, any individuals who saw their future career in representing it academically. This was also the story in Liverpool, where a well-funded university college rapidly developed in the later nineteenth century; here, as in Manchester, there were employers interested in commercial education, and large numbers of young people seeking employment in trade and commerce.

The Teaching of Commerce and Economics in Liverpool

During the later nineteenth century Liverpool was England's second city and largest port,[120] with significant employment in shipping, insurance, and chemicals industries. Its population of around 500,000 in 1881 was not much smaller than that of Manchester and Leeds combined; in 1861 almost half of the population were immigrants, and about half of these from Ireland. It was wealthy: where other cities, like Bristol and Leeds, would struggle to raise relatively small amounts to endow new

[120] In 1857 Liverpool accounted for 45% of UK exports by value, and around 33% of imports. At that time 4 million tons of shipping used the port; by 1881 this had risen to 7 million. Even in 1914 Liverpool still handled 36% of all UK exports and nearly 25% of imports. T. Kelly, *For Advancement of Learning: The University of Liverpool 1881–1981*, Liverpool University Press, Liverpool 1981, p. 15.

educational initiatives, in Liverpool money was always quickly found. And there was a long history of such institutions, the Royal Institution being founded in 1814 by a group of Liverpool merchants and professional men, with its first chairman William Roscoe, from a family that would dominate intellectual life in the city. The Liverpool Royal Institution was formed for 'the Promotion of Literature, Science and the Arts'; it was to be a teaching institution for the middle classes, combining lecture courses on science and the arts, a day school, a school of design, a library, a museum, an art gallery, a laboratory, and an observatory. An issue of £50 and £100 shares quickly raised £20,000, a building was acquired, and it formally opened in November 1817. A lecture programme, strongly slanted to the needs of medical students and practitioners, continued for 20 years, but by mid-century the initiative passed to the Liverpool Borough Council, which sought to transfer the Institution's assets and activities to the city. Negotiations failed, but the Council went ahead anyway, creating the William Brown Library and Museum in 1860, the Walker Art Gallery in 1877, and the Picton Reading Room in 1879.[121]

It was the Royal Institution that had in 1825 founded the 'Mechanics' School of Arts', one of the largest and most successful of the Mechanics' Institutes providing lectures in the arts and sciences to an audience composed chiefly of clerks, shopworkers, and artisans. In 1856 it altered its name to the Liverpool Institute, and the following year founded Queen's College, offering a variety of day and evening classes in the arts and sciences. Total enrolments were between 200 and 300 students pursuing post-school studies in Latin, Greek, French, German, English, mathematics, and chemistry. While Queen's College closed in 1881, a School of Science had been established in 1861 providing technical education for artisans, and by 1878–1889 it had 1,200 students registered, and was supported by a grant from the Science and Art Department in London. Besides these institutional developments, Liverpool was significant in the development of women's education, and through this the creation of the University Extension movement. In 1866 Anne Clough[122] formed Liverpool Ladies' Educational Association, meeting in the Royal Institution; the following year this combined with similar organisations in Manchester, Leeds, and Sheffield to form the North of England Council for Promoting the Higher Education of Women, and to sponsor a series of lectures on astronomy by James Stuart.[123] These initiatives fed back into local developments, and on 20 January 1874 a public meeting in Liverpool Town Hall convened by the mayor agreed to establish a Society for the Promotion of Higher Education in Liverpool.[124]

By 1878 a draft plan for a University College had been drawn up, modelled on Owen's College; and by July 1879 nearly £90,000 had already been raised, nationally a very significant sum of money for such a foundation.[125] The new organisation

[121] Ibid., pp. 19–22. See also H. A. Ormerod, *The Liverpool Royal Institution: A Record and a Retrospect*, Liverpool University Press, Liverpool 1953.

[122] Clough (1820–1892) was invited by Henry Sidgwick in May 1871 to take charge of a house for women students in Cambridge, a venture that quickly led to the foundation of Newnham Hall in October 1875, and the foundation of Newnham College with Clough as its Principal in 1879. See Gillian Sutherland's *Oxford Dictionary of National Biography* entry for Anne Jemima Clough.

[123] See Chapter 3 for an account of the Extension movement and Stuart's role in it.

[124] Kelly, *For Advancement of Learning*, pp. 31–37.

[125] Kelly, *For Advancement of Learning*, pp. 48–49, details some individual donations and endowments: among them a Chair of Logic, Mental and Moral Philosophy, and Political Economy was endowed

was chartered in October 1881, using as its template the revised constitution of Owens College, as embodied in the Owens Extension College Act of 1870 and the Owens College Act of 1871.[126] Owens itself had already moved to create a new federal Victoria University, chartered in 1880 with Owens as its sole constituent college; University College Liverpool would become a constituent college in 1884. In January 1882, University College, Liverpool, was formally inaugurated, with the first classes meeting later that month. Students enrolled by subject and term, being certified accordingly and so adapted to the requirements of individual students and employers. This tended to militate against the development of degree-level tuition, but the association with Victoria University held open this pathway.

John MacCunn (1846–1929), who had graduated from Glasgow and in 1872 became a Snell Exhibitioner at Balliol, was a founding professor. His academic title, linking 'Logic, Mental and Moral Philosophy, and Political Economy', reflected the London BA; it was the same title that Jevons had assumed in Manchester around 20 years previously. However, most of those Liverpool students who graduated with a BA opted for the Victoria University course, where political economy was one subject of examination in the Ordinary BA history stream.[127] Initially MacCunn taught a daytime class in elementary political economy over two terms, but in 1884 he dropped both logic and political economy from the Day Course, instead giving 20 lectures in an evening course on English political economists, from Adam Smith onwards. Smith, Malthus, and Ricardo were the subjects of the first 10 lectures, with John Stuart Mill and Cairnes forming the core of the remainder. MacCunn did, however, extend his coverage beyond these writers:

> Some account will, however, also be given of the more prominent followers of Ricardo and the old Political Economy, as well as of the chief modifications and attacks to which the earlier Political Economy has been subjected by more recent writers. In this connection some attention will be given to the doctrines of Henry George, in *Progress and Poverty*.[128]

Despite the mention of Henry George, this was a survey of political economy for popular understanding that took no account of the new understanding of political economy taking hold in the 1880s, associated with the names of Jevons, Edgeworth, and of course Alfred Marshall.

with £10,000 by 41 Scottish merchants of Liverpool (John MacCunn of Balliol College was appointed in 1881); the Roscoe Chair of Art had 47 subscribers, mainly Unitarians; and 10 representatives of Liverpool shipowners contributed £6230 towards a separate chair of mathematics. A list of donors and amounts given can be found in the *University College, Liverpool Calendar 1882–83*, pp. xii ff.

[126] And so incorporating a structure of governance in which a Court of Governors was the ruling body, a mainly lay Council was in charge of college administration, and a Professorial Senate dealt with academic affairs; Kelly, *For Advancement of Learning*, p. 52.

[127] 'Principles of Political Economy; Principles of Taxation (Adam Smith's *Wealth of Nations*)'; *Victoria University Calendar 1885*, p. 61.

[128] *Calendar of University College, Liverpool 1884–85*, p. 67. The nominated texts were Smith's *Wealth of Nations*, Malthus's *Essay on Population*, J. S. Mill's *Principles of Political Economy*, J. E. Cairnes's *Leading Principles of Political Economy* and his *Logical Method of Political Economy*.

The appointment of E. C. K. Gonner in 1888 altered this. He had graduated from Oxford with a First in Modern History in 1884, worked briefly for the London Extension, then been appointed to University College Bristol in 1885. In 1888 he published a concise and coherent *modern* introductory textbook on political economy[129] that recommended Jevons's *Theory of Political Economy* for the theory of exchange, and identified Sidgwick's *Principles of Political Economy* as the current most advanced general text. He had overlapped briefly with Marshall in Oxford, and attended his lectures; but Marshall was typically churlish in his appreciation of Gonner—'He is not quite first rate', he commented to Foxwell in 1885, when forwarding a letter from Gonner proposing the foundation of a monthly economic journal.[130] Marshall's opinion could well have been linked to Gonner's ability to straddle the teaching of commerce and economics. This ability was later more positively received and valued in Liverpool, since in 1891 he was appointed, aged 29, to a new Chair in Political Economy funded with £10,000 from J. T. Brunner, joint owner of the major chemical concern Brunner Mond.[131]

The Calendar for 1888–1889 includes Gonner's teaching under a new section, 'Economic and Commercial Science', comprising three daytime courses: an introductory course, twice a week over two terms, using as its textbook the Marshalls' *Economics of Industry*; a course on commercial geography,[132] likewise twice a week over two terms; and 'Commercial History and Theory', taught one hour a week over two terms, dealing with 'the growth of our present system of Commerce, especially during the last 100 years, and its relation to the doctrines of Political Economy.'[133] All three courses were aimed in part at students taking the College Business Curriculum, introduced in 1886 as a two-year course in which students could choose between an arts and a natural sciences stream. The course of instruction was to be completed by the age of 18, political economy being one element of the arts side. The practical support given 'by the undermentioned Mercantile Bodies and Firms in Liverpool' was noted, listed individually in double columns over four pages of the Calendar.[134] The content of this curriculum catered for 'Students preparing for a business life' and was essentially made up of modern school subjects—composition, history, mathematics, languages, physics, chemistry, and biology. This was a supplementary school curriculum for young persons lacking a modern schooling, not one dedicated to commercial training.[135] That the College saw no problem in opening Gonner's courses to this

[129] E. C. K. Gonner, *Political Economy (An Elementary Text Book of the Economics of Commerce)*, R. Sutton & Co., London 1888. See my *Oxford Dictionary of National Biography* entry for Gonner (1862–1922).

[130] Alfred Marshall to Herbert Somerton Foxwell, 8 November 1885, forwarding a letter from Gonner dated 6 November 1885; printed respectively as Letters 165 and 164 in John K. Whitaker (ed.) *The Correspondence*, pp. 199, 198. Evidently Marshall later used a draft by Gonner for his own proposal for the foundation of an economic journal; Letter 297, Marshall to Foxwell, 2 June 1890 in *Correspondence Vol. I*, pp. 319–20. But see also his comment in a letter to Neville Keynes, 30 January 1902; Letter 675 in Whitaker, *Correspondence Vol. II*, p. 351, discussed in Chapter 2.

[131] MacCunn remained in Liverpool but as Professor of Philosophy, retiring in 1910.

[132] Dealing with 'The Geographical Distribution of Raw Materials; The Manufacturing Industries of Europe and the United States; Means of Communication and Locomotion'; *University College, Liverpool, Calendar 1888–89*, p. 69.

[133] Ibid.

[134] *University College, Liverpool, Calendar 1886–87*, pp. 22–23, for the syllabus; pp. 24–28 for the list.

[135] Although a note called attention to the fact that 'Some of the undermentioned firms having expressed a desire that Shorthand and the Study of Foreign Currencies should form part of this Curriculum,

younger audience as well as to regular daytime College students indicates a flexibility that would later be notably absent in Birmingham. In addition, in 1888 Gonner also offered a course of 20 evening lectures over two terms—at 8.30 p.m. on Mondays—on 'Work and Wages', 'dealing with the different kinds of work; the laws regulating wages and profits; rent; the important effect of social organization, as for instance, in the case of co-operation, trade unions', and listing the headings under which he would lecture in advance.[136]

In 1890 the possibility of forming an advanced class in economics was mooted, although the principal change in the Calendar that year is that commercial geography was given a more detailed outline, and stated to be designed for the College Business Curriculum.[137] However, the most marked pattern in Gonner's own teaching was not the progressive elaboration of daytime courses in economics, but his regular presentation of evening lecture courses on different subjects. In 1890, he announced a course on the history and theory of socialism; in 1891, 10 lectures on 'Money and its Forms'; in 1893, 10 lectures on Wednesday evenings on 'Great Economists; their Lives, Writings and Works', with another set of 10 evening lectures on Thursdays on 'The Trade and Geography of the Countries of South America'.[138] During the autumn term of 1894 he gave a course of lectures on 'Socialism and Anarchism', giving as his reading Schäffle, *Quintessence of Socialism*, Marx, *Capital*, and Rae, *Contemporary Socialism*.[139] By 1895, while the day courses remained largely unaltered, Gonner announced four separate course of lectures over two terms: in commercial geography, 'The Trade and Industrial Condition of the United Kingdom', the 'Trade and Geography of the Countries of South America' as before, and 'The Labour Question'.[140]

We do not know how well-attended Gonner's evening courses were, but since he both increased the range of topics and the number of separate courses in any one year, we can presume they were well-received. Commercial geography was clearly a popular subject; but then Gonner had also published a textbook on commercial geography in 1894. The first half of its 200 pages detailed agricultural products, textiles, coal, oil, and other minerals, the second half considered the nations and regions of the world according to their products and economic activities.[141] As such, this was a natural complement to Bastable's text on international trade, which presented principles of commerce and finance;[142] while the Tariff Controversy that was to flare up in the early 1900s demonstrated the importance of having a clear grasp of the geography

the College will be prepared to make provision for these subjects, and also for Physical and Commercial Geography, should a sufficient number of Students present themselves'; ibid., p. 23. A more detailed outline of the curriculum published in 1889 listed nine Liverpool banking and insurance firms willing to waive the first year of an apprenticeship for those with a College Certificate, while another 800 had undertaken to recognise the qualification; *University College, Liverpool, Calendar 1889–90*, pp. 26–27.

136 *University College, Liverpool, Calendar 1890–91*, p. 129. The textbook assigned was Chisholm, *Handbook of Commercial Geography*.

137 *University College, Liverpool, Calendar 1890–91*, p. 69.

138 *University College, Liverpool, Calendar 1893–94*, pp. 161–62.

139 *University College, Liverpool, Calendar 1894–95*, p. 168.

140 *University College, Liverpool, Calendar 1895–96*, p. 185.

141 E. C. K. Gonner, *Commercial Geography*, Macmillan, London 1894.

142 C. F. Bastable, *The Theory of International Trade: with Some of Its Applications to Economic Policy*, Hodges, Figgis and Co., Dublin 1887; 2nd edition Macmillan, London 1897.

of production, manufacture, and commerce across the world when arguing about the prospective development of the world economy, and Britain's place within it.[143]

The first significant change in the teaching of political economy in Liverpool came in 1898, with the daytime course being divided in two, 'Course A. Economic Theory' twice a week, and 'Course B. Descriptive Economics' once a week.[144] Since this coincided with a similar change to Flux's parallel courses in Manchester, this appears to have been linked to changes at the level of Victoria University. The more significant local development at this time was that by 1898 the daytime course in commercial geography had been specified for students following the College Business Curriculum, and the following year this Curriculum was revamped into a School of Commerce organised by a joint committee drawing upon members of the College, the City Council, and the Chamber of Commerce. Full details of the new arrangement were first published in 1900, its two-year course still being aimed at school-leavers of 16 and 17 years of age, but now with a significant admixture of commercial subjects. The day course involved 23 hours' tuition per week in commercial composition, commercial geography, bookkeeping, and commercial practice, with fully eight hours being devoted to two modern languages. The evening courses were scheduled for 7.15 to 9.30 p.m., including accountancy, commercial law, commercial arithmetic, and commercial practice, together with tuition in French, German, and Spanish.[145]

In 1903 the College became a chartered University in its own right, and the character of teaching in economics and commerce altered. Evident from the preceding details of courses, lectures, and classes is that while the appointment of Gonner in 1888 did revise the teaching of elementary political economy, this remained essentially unchanged up until 1903. The impact of Gonner's appointment was felt more in the development of commercial education, and a commitment to teaching regular evening courses on more general topics. The emphasis upon commercial geography reflected broad support for knowledge of the global economy to which Liverpool was connected, while formal provision for commercial education sought to compensate for the defects of the contemporary school curriculum. While the level of teaching might have remained elementary, it was extended to include those leaving school at 16; the evening lectures, by contrast, would have been aimed at those already in work and seeking general educational development. The shift to a University structure would lay the foundations for an emphasis upon academic over vocational education, but unlike Manchester, the structure of teaching provision remained unreformed until the 1920s. A degree-level commercial qualification (the BComSci) was introduced in 1909; there is no record of student numbers, but since it built on existing provision and was soon replaced, its impact can be assumed to have been limited. The Honours

143 Much of Ashley's *The Tariff Problem* (P. S. King and Son, London 1904) was given over to details of exports, imports, and the incidence of duties.

144 *University College, Liverpool, Calendar 1898–99*, pp. 100–1; the textbooks for Course A remained Marshall, *Economics of Industry* (presumably now the *Elements of Economics of Industry*) plus Jevons's *Money*; Course B detailed the structure of agriculture, industry, and commerce, adding in remuneration and arbitration, and the economic functions of government.

145 *University College, Liverpool, Calendar 1900–1901*, pp. 236–37. The following year the daytime course amalgamated commercial subjects into a 'Commercial Bureau', taking up eight hours per week in both years; *Calendar 1901–1902*, p. 157.

economics programme was extended: the new regulations for BA (Hons.) required those studying Honours economics to attend lectures and classes for six hours a week in the first year, and four in the second and third years.[146] As examined, the subject specified two papers in 'General Economics' in Part I and one in Part II, which also required a dissertation, an oral examination, and two papers in a 'special Economic period or subject'—leaving quite open how the subject might be taught, and with what emphases. Indeed, in 1923 the course on general economics still gave as its reading Marshall's *Economics of Industry*, Walker's *Political Economy*, and Jevons's *Money* only, entirely consistent with the 1890s.[147] However, from 1905, John Shield Nicholson was listed as the external examiner, drawing attention to an important feature of all the new college foundations: that while their graduates might be limited in number, their final examinations were audited by economists of national standing. In 1908, Shield Nicholson was replaced as external by Langford Price of Oxford;[148] in 1911, Price was replaced by Sydney Chapman;[149] and in 1914, Chapman was replaced by Bastable.[150] Hence there was an implicit network linking together new initiatives in the teaching of commerce and economics that secured some degree of uniformity in the material taught and examined in scattered and undeveloped foundations.

From 1920, the teaching of commerce was reorganised: the renamed Department of Commerce abandoned the BComSci For a new BCom, and Ernest Dewsnup (1874–1950) was appointed Chaddock Professor of Commerce, a new post. A graduate of Owens College, his first appointment had been in 1899 as the Head of Department of Higher Commercial Education at Huddersfield Technical College. Briefly returning to Manchester in 1903 to teach railway transport, in 1904 he moved to Chicago and was from 1907 to 1920 Professor of Railway Administration and Head of the Department of Transportation at the University of Illinois, returning to Britain in 1918 to the War Office's Department of Military Movements and Railways. Dewsnup was listed as Head of Department, assisted by J. Montgomery, who had been appointed to a lectureship in commercial theory and practice in 1905; Gonner was listed in the new Prospectus after Dewsnup, the remaining staff listed for geography, modern history, commercial law, mathematics, and five modern languages being drawn from elsewhere in the University.

The broad aims of the Department were clearly laid out:

> The complex nature of modern business makes its administration a matter calling for skill, precision and judgment. The man who has to deal with large business affairs should be able to analyse the interaction of many opposing forces; he must evaluate their strength and direction and accurately determine their resultant. No matter how specialised a business becomes, it is still a creature of its environment and, except by chance, success in its management cannot be obtained otherwise than

[146] *University of Liverpool, Calendar 1903–4*, p. 175. 'Certificates from a Professor or Lecturer of the University are also required from all candidates, attesting their ability to use French *or* German for the purposes of their work.'

[147] *Prospectus of Faculty of Arts Session 1923–24*, p. 127.

[148] *University of Liverpool, Calendar 1908–9*, p. 111.

[149] *University of Liverpool, Calendar 1911–12*, p. 114.

[150] *University of Liverpool, Calendar 1914–15*, p. 122.

> by careful study of that environment. Consequently, in its Courses in Commerce, the University lays emphasis upon the comprehensive study of commerce and industry in their economic, geographical and historical setting, so that the future graduate may instinctively supply to his particular business problem the broad background so absolutely necessary to its proper appreciation.[151]

The 'Courses in Commerce' fell into three broad groups: the organisation of commerce and industry, dealing both with financial markets and internal business administration; trade and industry in the British Empire and elsewhere (commercial geography); and aspects of commercial office routine, including currency transactions, customs duties, and insurance.[152] By 1926 a Special Lecturer in Accounting was listed in the Prospectus, and courses offered for each of the three years—although not included in the subjects for examination, and listed in the wide range of options available to the student of what was now styled the 'Liverpool School of Social Sciences and Administration', and which included departments of economics, commerce, geography, and social science.[153]

If we consider student numbers, the total number of commerce graduates was comparable with Birmingham, although evident here is that the option to study a more specialised (honours) course was one taken only by a small number of students (Table 10.2). This reinforces the impression for the whole of the interwar period that the teaching of commerce in Liverpool remained largely unspecialised, a factor that also precluded the emergence of teaching in economics at a level much more advanced than that typical of the prewar period.

While these numbers show that Liverpool was much less successful than Manchester in developing undergraduate commercial education, it did no worse, and in some ways better, than Birmingham. Significant here is, however, the relative lack of interest in a more specialised, Honours course; and perhaps as a corollary of this, there is no record of Liverpool students before 1940 graduating with an Honours degree in economics.

This impression of a lack of interest in the teaching of economics is supported by the fact that, after Gonner's death in 1922, the Brunner chair was left unfilled until 1930; junior staff members covered what teaching in economics there was. Nor did the appointment of J. R. Bellerby (1896–1977) to the chair in 1930 suggest any significant increase in institutional commitment, given that his Leeds BCom had been awarded shortly after he had completed war service, and that he had for most of the 1920s worked at the International Labour Office in Geneva. However, when he left after only two years, he was replaced by G. C. Allen, who would remain in Liverpool until 1947 and whose interest in industrial organisation would enable him to bridge the gap that had opened up in Liverpool between commerce and economics. Ronald Coase did join the staff in 1934 as a lecturer in commerce, but left at the end of the year for the

[151] University of Liverpool, Faculty of Arts, *Department of Commerce Prospectus of Courses Session 1920–1921*, pp. 6-7.

[152] *Prospectus of Courses Session 1920–1921*, pp. 18–19.

[153] Liverpool School of Social Sciences and Administration, Prospectus of Courses Session 1926–1927, p. 72.

Table 10.2 BCom Students and Graduates, Liverpool, 1920–1939

	All BCom	All Grads	BCom (Hons)	BCom (Ord)
1920	48			
1921	50			
1922	34			
1923	31			
1924	29	8		
1925	28	6		
1926	24	8		
1927	22	2	1	1
1928	28	7	2	5
1929	31	7	2	5
1930	34	4	1	3
1931	29	7	0	7
1932	34	5	0	5
1933	37	8	0	8
1934	26	6	1	5
1935	29	7	0	7
1936	23	8	3	5
1937	23	6	1	5
1938	22	1	1	
1939	21	5	1	4

Source: University of Liverpool, *Calendars and Prospectuses*, various years.

LSE. Records show only one student per year preparing for Honours economics in the later 1920s;[154] by 1936–1937 there were 47 students in total attending economics classes, although only six in the final year.[155] Many students were also studying part-time, nearly 30% of all arts students studying for a degree, a feature that was fostered by the fact that so many students lived locally.[156]

The strong start that Gonner had given to commercial and economic studies in Liverpool faded in the early twentieth century, despite the large pool of potential students—full-time and part-time, mixed in age and gender, attending daytime courses or evening lectures—and despite the active support of employers, and substantial financial support. The foundation of the University in 1903 provided a new

154 *Classification and General Statistics*, 'General Statistics 1929–30', p. 54, University of Liverpool Archives S.5097–5098. In the following year there were 3 economics students registered for Honours economics, compared with 51 students registered for Honours in medieval and modern history, and 22 for classics (p. 59).

155 'General Statistics 1936–37', cf. p. 143.

156 The University Grants Committee noted in the late 1930s that of 2,055 full-time students in the University, 1,412 lived within 30 miles: 'General Statistics 1938–39'.

institutional initiative that was not matched by changes in the general structure of teaching in commerce and economics, which remained largely unchanged up to the 1940s. At least some of this loss of dynamism can be attributed to the long decline of the city from early in the century: the White Star shipping line moved to Southampton in 1907, and Cunard followed in 1919, taking with it the transatlantic passenger trade. The significance of Liverpool as the principal port for Atlantic convoys during the Second World War was only a temporary check to the general decline of Merseyside as an industrial and commercial centre throughout the twentieth century. By the 1930s this decline had been clearly recognised, which was one reason why in the early 1930s the most extensive new British survey of poverty and inequality was undertaken by Liverpool's School of Social Sciences and Administration.[157]

Nor did any connection to the re-founded Victoria University in Manchester, and the strong development of its Faculty of Commerce, have any significant influence. The somewhat downbeat history of the teaching of commerce and economics in Liverpool outlined here does, however, tell us something important: that outside London there was often only a limited demand for degree-level tuition in commerce, even when in the case of Liverpool a clear focus was maintained on an unspecialised curriculum and the provision of commercial diplomas and certificates. Also clear from the foregoing is a general lack of interest among students in studying for university economics degrees. As we shall see in the following chapter, this was also the case in the LSE; for if there was very little a student could do with an honours degree in economics besides teach in a school, college, or university, there was even less call for non-degree-level qualifications in economics, unlike the case with commerce. Even in Manchester, the clear inflection to a focus on the teaching of economics came only with the appointment of Hicks to the Jevons chair in 1938; and while the Brunner chair had been created in Liverpool as far back as 1891, it would be more than 50 years before any Liverpool student was awarded an Honours degree in economics.

This general assessment can be confirmed by a brief consideration of Leeds, another institution that had been linked to Manchester and Liverpool; and can be concluded with a brief account of developments in Aberdeen and Belfast, which were in many ways more successful than most in promoting higher commercial education.

Commerce in the University of Leeds

The founders of Yorkshire College, while embracing non-sectarian and local middle-class support like Owens, did not initially seek to develop a broad spread of subjects, but concentrated their attention on scientific and technical studies. In 1869 the Joint Secretary of the Yorkshire Board of Education and Yorkshire Union of Mechanics' Institutes wrote to Frederick Cavendish, the MP for West Riding and member of the Select Committee on Scientific Instruction, proposing an institution that could provide technical instruction and teacher training. A public meeting in Leeds Town Hall

[157] D. Caradog Jones (ed.) *The Social Survey of Merseyside*, 3 vols., University of Liverpool Press, Liverpool 1934.

that same year endorsed the idea, and in 1872 the inaugural prospectus for the College stated that its object was

> ... to supply an urgent and recognised want, viz., instruction in those sciences which are applicable to the Industrial Arts, especially those which may be classed under Engineering, Manufacturing, Agriculture, Mining and Metallurgy. It is designed for the use of persons who will afterwards be engaged in these trades as foremen, managers or employers; and also for the training of teachers of technical science.[158]

The need for chairs in mathematics, physics, chemistry, geology, mining and metallurgy, and engineering was emphasised, but when the College of Science opened in 1874, the money available only stretched as far as three: chemistry; physics and maths; and geology and mining. Indeed, the Planning Committee had originally set a target of £60,000, reduced later to £20,000, of which only £15,394 had been received by 1875. Local support was generally lacking; much of the direct support came from the London Clothworkers' Company. In 1876 the principle was accepted that appointments should be made in the humanities, but no financial provision was made; in 1877 University Extension teaching was brought under college control; and in 1878 the college was renamed simply as Yorkshire College. In 1887 it became a college of Victoria University, then with the dissolution of the federal body it became a university in April 1904.

In 1887 a Business Certificate, approved by the Chamber of Commerce, was introduced, but this was intended as a two-year course for 15- and 16-year-olds, its curriculum reflecting a modern school curriculum in the same way that the Liverpool Business Certificate had done when introduced the previous year—evidence that the creation of Victoria University meant more than a progressive shift from the vocational imperatives of its constituent colleges towards academic, degree-level tuition. And the stipulation that day students of the Department of Science, Technology and Arts must have reached the age of 14 at entry further emphasises the manner in which colleges of this sort were in part compensating for deficiencies in schooling.[159] Language classes included elements of commercial correspondence, were provided for both day and evening students, and prepared their students for the examinations of the Society of Arts and the Oxford and Cambridge Commercial Examinations.[160] In 1889 a basic course on 'Book-Keeping' was announced; this moved to an evening course in 1893 when it was reported as having had 30 students the previous year.[161] One unfamiliar development here was a 'Class for Agricultural Students'—offering a course in which 'Farm and Estate Accounts [are] described. Cash Book and Ledger. Accounts of Labour, Crops, Stock etc., Balance Sheet. Profit and Loss Account', the

[158] *Report of the Committee appointed to investigate, consider and propose the best means to be adopted for the establishment of a 'Yorkshire College of Science'*, Leeds 1872, p. 1, quoted in A. J. Taylor, 'County College and Civic University: An Introductory Essay', in P. H. J. H. Gosden, A. J. Taylor (eds.) *Studies in the History of a University, 1874–1974*, E. J. Arnold, Leeds 1975, p. 1.

[159] *The Yorkshire College, Leeds, Calendar for the Fifteenth Session 1888–89*, p. 33. This provision for school-age children was revised in 1897 by raising the minimum age to 16.

[160] *The Yorkshire College, Leeds, Calendar for the Fifteenth Session 1888–89*, pp. 112–16.

[161] *The Yorkshire College, Leeds, Calendar for 1893–94*, p. 224.

textbook Woodman, *Book-keeping for Farmers*—the 1893 evening class being divided between 16 general students and 23 agricultural students.[162]

In 1902, John Clapham[163] was appointed 'Professor of Economics' in a new Department of Commerce, an appointment largely unrelated to the teaching hitherto done in the college; but the course in 'General Economics' linked to the announcement was to prepare students for the Intermediate Examination of Victoria University, and the reading—Marshall's *Economics of Industry*, Jevons's *Money*, and Walker's *Brief Political Economy*—indicates that it was a course parallel to ones taught in Manchester and Liverpool.[164] Clapham was also listed for 'English Economic History' that year, replaced in 1903 by 'The Resources and Geography (1) of the British Empire, and (2) of the Principal Foreign Countries', likewise as in Liverpool.[165] In 1904 the University was inaugurated as an independent institution, and in the following year a BCom degree was announced, comprising the elementary principles of economics, the economic history of England in the nineteenth century, the economic geography of the British Empire, French or German as a modern language, plus either a second modern language, mathematics, or European history from 1763 (which was the end of the Seven Years' War).[166] There was also a course in accountancy in each of the three years, together with one course of commercial law; but in Leeds there was none of the commercial office practice that played such an important role in Liverpool's teaching.

Daytime teaching of economics remained limited, there being 16 students recorded attending in 1903–1904, and 9 in 1904–1905. But the numbers attending evening classes rose in the same years from 68 to 152;[167] and while numbers did fluctuate, this is once again indicative of a broad interest among students already in employment in economic issues; but not an interest that could be translated into sustained academic study of the subject. It was not until 1916 that the first Honours degree in Economic and Political Science was awarded; by which time it was also clear that the teaching of economics was chiefly oriented to non-degree level work. The 1913–1915 Report for the Department of Economics begins by noting that six students had obtained a Diploma in Social Organisation and Public Service after following a course in 1913–1914. The Department had also arranged a scheme of study with the Department of Textile Industries allowing for an interchange of lectures between the

162 *The Yorkshire College, Leeds, Calendar for 1894–95*, pp. 216, 233. In 1895 the textbook for agricultural students had been changed to A. W. Thomson, *Book-keeping*; and the original recommendation in 1889 of Hamilton and Ball, *Bookkeeping*, was supplemented in 1896 by Longman's *Advanced Book-keeping*. There was clearly a substantial textbook literature for these courses.

163 John Clapham (1873–1946) had gained a First in Part II of the Cambridge History Tripos in 1895 and became a Fellow of King's College in 1898. He had assisted Marshall with some marking in 1897, who in a letter to Lord Acton suggested that Clapham would be suited to writing an account of the economic development of England that took the history up to the present day—given that all existing works of economic history brought the story up to the early nineteenth century at the latest. Marshall to Lord Acton, 13 November 1897, Letter 544 in Whitaker, *Correspondence Vol. II*, p. 206. When Clapham's three-volume history was published, it did exactly this: *An Economic History of Modern Britain*, covering *The Early Railway Age, 1820–50* (1926); *Free Trade and Steel, 1850–86* (1932); and *Machines and National Rivalries, 1887–1914, with an Epilogue, 1914–1929* (1938). See Martin Daunton's entry in the *Oxford Dictionary of National Biography*, and also the obituary by G. N. Clark, *Proceedings of the British Academy*, Vol. 32 (1946), 339–52.

164 *The Yorkshire College, Leeds, Calendar for 1902–1903*, pp. 41, 115.

165 *The Yorkshire College, Leeds, Calendar for 1903–4*, pp. 121–22.

166 *The University of Leeds Calendar, 1905–6*, p. 171.

167 *University of Leeds, Second Report 1904–5*, pp. 54, 58.

two departments. A course of lectures for commercial teachers had also been given at the request of the West Riding Education Committee, and a course of Special Lectures had been delivered in Bradford Technical College to senior students and members of the business community.[168]

Clapham had returned to King's College, Cambridge, in 1908 and was replaced by D. H. Macgregor (1877–1953), who had taken Part II of the Moral Sciences Tripos in 1901—hence continuing the Cambridge connection to Leeds. Shortly after his arrival, Macgregor had introduced a new course on 'Studies of Industrial Questions', also proposing a course on 'Social Economy'—'The influence of industrial conditions on social life; the problems of poverty, trade depression, large cities, small holdings, social betterment'.[169] When presented in 1909 as a short evening course of lectures for which no charge was made, the average attendance was over 100 students, with some members of the public attending as well.[170] By 1910 the number of students reported attending classes in economics had risen to 47; there were, however, no third-year classes. An increased interest in economic subjects the year before had been attributed to new classes in social and agricultural economics, a trend that continued after the war, students including some tuition in economics as part of a more strictly vocational pathway. And since this represented the real demand for teaching in economics, there was little impetus to go beyond elementary principles. In 1920 a new course in economics for students of the Textile Department was introduced and its sessions were well-attended, prompting a new course in applied economics for engineering students. This was recorded as attracting over 60 students, and plans were also made to offer a special course for mining students. Besides that, in 1922 it was reported that eight students were studying for Honours economics, '... all of whom intend to complete the course'.[171] Nonetheless, the student numbers in Table 10.3 show that this good intention did not translate into Honours economics graduates. Given the limited demand for an Honours commerce course, as in Liverpool, it could not be expected that there would be very much demand for Honours economics; and while the numbers of Leeds graduates with an Ordinary degree in commerce were low during the interwar period, they were no lower than those of Birmingham.

The early development of Leeds before the First World War and its subsequent development during the interwar period confirm a pattern that has already been established with Liverpool: preference among students for a broad, not a specialised degree in commerce; a strong vocational interest in diplomas and certificates following one- or two-year courses; the engagement of young people already in employment in evening classes and courses; and in the actual teaching of economics a focus more on social issues. Those appointed to teach in Manchester, Liverpool, and Leeds would certainly have been familiar with contemporary advances in economic principles; but they did not teach them.

168 *University of Leeds, Twelfth Report 1915–16*, p. 73; *Eleventh Report 1913–14–15*, p. 75.
169 *The University of Leeds Calendar, 1909–10*, pp. 195, 208–9.
170 *University of Leeds, Sixth Report 1908–9*, p. 47.
171 *University of Leeds, Seventeenth Report 1920–21*, p. 71; *Eighteenth Report 1921–22*, p. 88.

Table 10.3 Degrees in Commerce and Economics, University of Leeds, 1920–1938

	BA (Hon.) Econ	BCom (Ord.)	BCom (Hon.)
1919–1920	0	2	
1920–1921	3	1	
1921–1922	4	8	
1922–1923	2	7	
1923–1924	0	5	
1924–1925	1	3	2
1925–1926	0	0	3
1926–1927	0	2	1
1927–1928	1	6	2
1928–1929	0	3	3
1929–1930	2	2	3
1930–1931	5	6	4
1931–1932	1	1	4
1932–1933	5	7	3
1933–1934	1	6	5
1934–1935	0	6	3
1935–1936	2	9	0
1936–1937	2	8	5
1937–1938	1	7	4

Source: University Calendars.

Commerce in Scotland and Ireland

In conclusion we can, however, consider three cases that offset some of the more predictable features outlined earlier. J. G. Smith's survey of commercial education drew attention to the foundation in 1918 of an Edinburgh BCom, alongside existing general teaching in political economy linked to the Chair in Political Economy and Mercantile Law, founded in 1871. Joseph Shield Nicholson (1850–1927), who had graduated from the Cambridge Moral Sciences Tripos in 1876, was appointed to this post in 1880, and for the next 45 years contributed to Arts teaching in Edinburgh where, as in Glasgow, political economy was one of the subjects students could take for an Honours degree.[172] The BCom had been independently established in 1918 alongside this, and in the following year a Chair of Accounting and Business Method

[172] *Edinburgh University Calendar, 1900–1901*, p. 148: the rubric specified 'An advanced knowledge of Economic Theory. Special knowledge of the Economic Functions of Government and Public Finance. General Economic History of England, and special study of set subjects'. Among books recommended for 'General Theory' were Marshall's *Principles of Economics*; Keynes's *Scope and Method of Political Economy*; and his own *Principles of Political Economy*. For government and finance, students were directed to Smith's *Wealth of Nations*, Book V; J. S. Mill's *Political Economy* Book V; Sidgwick's *Political Economy* Book III; and

and a Lectureship in the Organisation of Industry and Commerce had been endowed by members of the Edinburgh Chamber of Commerce, the Merchant Company of Edinburgh, and others. Although a complete listing of courses did not appear in the Calendar until 1924, Smith noted that by the later 1920s the new course was graduating around 30 students a year.[173]

Likewise in the University of Aberdeen, a lectureship in political economy had been initiated in 1904, and in 1912 R. B. Forrester was appointed from Manchester. Then, in 1919, a new BCom degree was established, co-opting Forrester's existing course on political economy, adding to it a course by him on the 'Organisation of Industry and Commerce', plus compulsory courses on economic statistics, accounting and business, modern languages, economic geography, and mercantile law.[174] Most of those teaching on the degree came from other university departments, while the more vocational classes were timed so as to enable those already in commercial employment to attend. The course was aimed at training those who wished to pursue careers in general business and financial work; banking, insurance, and accountancy; transport services; foreign trade, agency and consular services; and journalism and teaching.[175] Alexander Gray, later Professor of Political Economy at Edinburgh, was appointed to a new Jaffrey chair in 1921, succeeded by Lindley Fraser in 1935, maintaining the principle that the teaching of commerce be headed by an appointee in economics. While the numbers graduating with a BCom were not so large as they were in Edinburgh, figures published in 1931 showed that there had been 104 BCom graduates in the 10 years to 1930, although numbers did tail off to one or two a year during the 1930s.[176]

Likewise in Queen's University, Belfast, throughout the interwar period the teaching of commerce was headed by an economist: Hugh Meredith[177] was appointed to the chair of economics in 1910, the announcement in the *Economic Journal* noting that one of his first tasks would be to organise the newly-established Faculty of Commerce.[178] By 1922 it was reported that 45 students were studying for the commerce degree; 62 in 1925, as against 49 in law; and 72 in 1930.[179] As everywhere else, numbers tended to tail off in the 1930s, although 10 graduated with a BComSci in 1938, 9 having graduated the year before.[180] Meredith seems to have taught the core of the course on his own with the aid of an assistant until his retirement in 1945, when he was replaced by a different generation: Keith Isles,[181] Duncan Black,[182] Bob

Bastable's *Public Finance*. For economic history there were Cunningham's *Growth of English Industry and Commerce* and Seebohm's *English Village Community*, chaps. i–v.

[173] Smith, 'Education for Business', p. 40.

[174] *Aberdeen University Calendar 1920–21*, p. 554.

[175] *Aberdeen University Calendar 1920–21*, p. 550.

[176] *Aberdeen University Calendar 1930–31*, pp. 570–73; *Calendar 1940–41*, p. 312.

[177] See p. 276 n.107.

[178] *Economic Journal* Vol. 20 (1910), p. 669.

[179] *Queen's University Belfast Calendar1922–23*, p. 658; *1925–26*, pp. 515–16; *1930–31*, pp. 591–92.

[180] *Queen's University Belfast Calendar1938–39*, p. 490.

[181] Keith Isles (1902–1977) had a BCom from the University of Tasmania, and graduated from the Cambridge Economics Tripos in 1929; after which he held a Rockefeller Fellowship at Cambridge for two years before becoming a lecturer at Edinburgh (1931–1937), Professor of Economics at Swansea (1937–1939), then Professor at Adelaide until 1945.

[182] Duncan Black (1908–1991) only stayed one year in Belfast before moving to a post in Glasgow.

Black,[183] and Tom Wilson.[184] While the teaching initially continued within the old structure, by the later 1940s this had been replaced by a new BSc in economics and the Faculty of Commerce was renamed in 1948 as the Faculty of Economics.

All of these less familiar institutions demonstrated that there was a broad, if shallow, demand for the teaching of commercial subjects, and that the weakness of Birmingham up to the 1920s in attracting students who completed a commerce degree was largely unrepresentative of those institutions that introduced the teaching of commerce. However, Queen's Belfast would indeed imitate Birmingham in one important respect: by the later 1940s the teaching of economics had broken away from the largely descriptive and non-analytic approach typical of the interwar years, and a more robustly modern, mathematical approach was the norm. To better understand how this transition took place, we can now turn to the case of the London School of Economics.

183 For Bob Black (1922–2008) see my interview in *Economic Careers*, pp. 98–101, in which he outlines the teaching in Belfast when he arrived.

184 Tom Wilson (1916–2001) had graduated from Queen's Belfast but only stayed for two terms in 1946 before moving to Oxford (Interview, 4 April 1995).

11
Commerce and Economics at the London School of Economics

The foundation of the London School of Economics and Political Science (LSE) was the product of the same arguments about education, commerce, and national wealth that we have encountered in the previous chapters. In 1889 the Technical Instruction Act had placed responsibility for technical education on county authorities; and in the following year, funds were provided by way of a tax on spirits of sixpence a gallon. London County Council created a Technical Education Board to oversee the disbursement of these new funds. Until 1898 this Board was chaired by Sidney Webb, who had wide-ranging plans for educational developments in London. Webb's connections would be crucial to the foundation of the LSE.

Arrangements for higher technical education were soon made by the Board through agreements with University College London and Bedford College, but there was no commercial institution with which the Board or the Chamber of Commerce could collaborate. However, Webb was also a member of the Fabian Society, and the Society had recently been left a bequest of about £10,000 for the promotion of socialism. In September 1894, Webb established the Hutchison Trust to supervise the use of these funds. He was interested in founding a centre specialising in the 'investigation of problems of municipal and national administration from a collectivist standpoint', and to realise this aim, investigators would require training. Having gained the agreement of the Hutchison Trust in February 1895 that its funds could be used for this purpose, Webb then developed a plan for advanced commercial education that he put to the Technical Education Board in May, adding municipal support to a privately-financed venture. He was also able to point to lecture courses that the Chamber of Commerce had recently initiated, linked to their system of commercial certificates, and so presenting to the Chamber of Commerce the prospect of a permanent institution able to support their own efforts in the promotion of commercial education.[1] Broad support was thereby secured for the promotion of higher commercial education in London through the foundation of a new teaching institution.

The Early History of the School

At the end of May 1895, a lease was taken out for two years on a house in John Street; fees for the new School were set at £3 per session, and a prospectus drafted. For the

[1] The preceding sketch summarises Alon Kadish's account in 'The City, the Fabians and the Foundation of the London School of Economics', in Alon Kadish, Keith Tribe (eds.) *The Market for Political Economy: The Advent of Economics in British University Culture, 1850–1905*, Routledge, London 1993, pp. 227–32.

Constructing Economic Science. Keith Tribe, Oxford University Press. © Oxford University Press 2022.
DOI: 10.1093/oso/9780190491741.003.0011

first term, 203 students enrolled; at the end of the session there were 281 students, 87 of them women.[2] The only full-time employees were the Director, W. A. S. Hewins,[3] his secretary, and the porter. Most lectures were given in the lecture hall of the Society of Arts, or at the rooms of the London Chamber of Commerce at Botolph House, Eastcheap.[4] All of this was done on a part-time basis, and this would remain characteristic of the School until the 1920s, when staff and teaching were progressively reorganised on a permanent basis.

A prospectus issued in 1895 summarised the objectives of the School as follows:

> The London School starts with the cordial co-operation of the leading economists and students of political science in the United Kingdom, and with the support of the Society of Arts and, on its commercial side, of the London Chamber of Commerce. It will be organised to meet the needs of different classes of students. In the lectures on higher commercial subjects which will be given under the auspices of the London Chamber of Commerce, and the classes in connection with them, students will be able to acquire that wider knowledge of modern commercial conditions which is every day becoming more necessary for the successful conduct of business. Those students who have already, by means of university extension lectures or otherwise gained some acquaintance with economic or political science, will be able to pursue their studies under the direction of experts, and the advanced courses will supply that scientific training which is likely in the future to become essential as a qualification for the civil service, municipal employment, journalism, or public work.
>
> While much attention will be given to the study of economic and political theory, the special aim of the school will be, from the first, the study and investigation of the concrete facts of industrial life and the actual working of economic and political relations as they exist or have existed, in the United Kingdom or in foreign countries. With this object in view the school will provide scientific training in methods of investigation and research, and will afford facilities to British and foreign students to

[2] Sidney Caine, *The History of the Foundation of the London School of Economics and Political Science*, G. Bell & Son, London 1963, pp. 44, 50. In 1896 the School's offices moved to 10 Adelphi Terrace, adding to the staff a junior clerk and a librarian; ibid., p. 53.

[3] William Albert Samuel Hewins (1865–1931) studied at Pembroke College, Oxford, and took a degree in mathematics in 1887. An active member of the Oxford Economics Society, he took up the study of history and economics, lecturing for the Oxford Extension and organising its meetings in Oxford during the summers of 1888, 1889, and 1890. Recruited by Webb for his organisational abilities, he became increasingly identified with Liberal Imperialism, resigning his Directorship in November 1903 to become Secretary to the Tariff Commission. See the obituary by L. L. Price in the *Economic Journal* Vol. 42 (1932), pp. 151–55.

[4] F. A. Hayek, 'The London School of Economics 1895–1945', *Economica* n.s. Vol. 13 (1946), p. 7. This essay is a reliable guide to the early years of the School. Hayek's comments in later interviews about events at LSE during the 1930s, based on personal recollections, however, are unreliable. Although he was on the School's staff in the 1930s, he was not central to decision-making, while those to whom he later talked assumed that he was 'always already' eminent and failed to check his remarks against relevant contemporary sources. Susan Howson makes the same point in very circumspect terms in her *Lionel Robbins*, Cambridge University Press, Cambridge 2011, p. 178; the central paragraph has to be read at least twice to grasp her point. See, for a more explicit example, R. Dahrendorf, *LSE: A History of the London School of Economics and Political Science 1895–1995*, Oxford University Press, Oxford 1995, pp. 290–292, regarding Beveridge's efforts to secure the library of the Institut für Sozialforschung for the School, which Hayek later represented as part of a political threat to the School that he made sure was averted.

undertake special studies of industrial life and original work in economics and political science.[5]

The courses announced were divided among five headings: economics; commerce, commercial geography, history; banking and currency; taxation and finance; and political science. At this stage the economics lectures were to be given by Hewins and William Cunningham;[6] Halford Mackinder[7] was to lecture on commercial geography, Hewins on the 'History of English Commerce', J. E. C. Munro,[8] formerly of Owens College Manchester, on law, and William Acworth on railway economics.[9] Edwin Cannan[10] was to lecture on local taxation. Classes were also announced in economics, statistics, and political science.

Until the creation of the BSc (Econ) in 1901, the School offered no qualification of its own, but prepared students for existing public examinations—for the Civil Service, the Institute of Bankers, the Institute of Actuaries, or the London Chamber of Commerce. Students would attend such lecture courses as took their interest, and in turn courses were introduced that reflected these interests. In his account of the early years of the school, Hayek quoted Graham Wallas's observation that students were

> . . . mainly of the type to which I had become accustomed in the University Extension movement—a few ambitious young civil servants and teachers, and a few women of leisure interested in the subject or engaged in public work. But the desire for a serious study of the social sciences began to form itself among people who would not have gone to 'extension lectures', and it was, I think, at my first course of lectures that I used to be frightened by finding Mr. (afterwards Sir Robert) Morant of the Education Office, and Mr. (afterwards Sir Charles) Stewart (the Clerk to the L.C.C. and later Public Trustee) in fairly regular attendance.[11]

[5] Three printed pages, unpaginated, bound in with Vol. 5 (1895) of the *Economic Journal*, Cambridge University Library.

[6] 'The State in Relation to Industry and Commerce' and 'Economic Effects of Alien Immigrations', respectively.

[7] Mackinder (1861–1947) was at the time Principal of University College Reading, linked to the Oxford Extension movement. A student at Christ Church, Oxford, he had studied biology and modern history, lectured for the Oxford Extension movement from 1886, was in the same year called to the Bar, and in 1887 became the first Reader in Geography at the University of Oxford. In 1900 he was the Liberal Imperialist candidate for Warwick and Leamington, and was from 1910 to 1922 a Conservative MP for Glasgow Camlachie. See his *Oxford Dictionary of National Biography* entry by Brian W. Blouet.

[8] Munro (1849–1896) was a barrister with degrees in law from Dublin and Cambridge, and who had been jointly Professor of Law and Cobden Lecturer in Political Economy at Owens College, Manchester, from 1882 to 1891. See the obituary by E. C. K. Gonner, *Economic Journal* Vol. 6 (1896), pp. 660–62, and in the *Manchester Guardian*, 12 September 1896.

[9] Acworth (1850–1925) studied modern history at Oxford, graduating in 1872, after which he was for 18 months English tutor to the future Kaiser Wilhelm II, and then an assistant master at Dulwich College 1875–1885. He was called to the Bar in 1890. Involved in Conservative politics in London, he contested Keighley three times for the party in the early 1900s. During the 1890s he became a specialist on railway operation, publishing several important books on the subject. See his *Oxford Dictionary of National Biography* entry by C. E. R. Sherrington, revised by T. A. B. Corley (last updated 23 September 2004).

[10] See, for a biographical account of Cannan, my 'Edwin Cannan (1861–1935)', in Robert A. Cord (ed.) *The Palgrave Companion to LSE Economics*, Palgrave Macmillan, London 2018, pp. 197–214.

[11] Hayek, 'The London School of Economics', p. 7, citing 'A Historical Note', *Handbook of the Students' Union* (LSE) October 1925, p. 11, and the LSE Prospectus for 1896–1897.

Table 11.1 Students Registered for Study at LSE 1895–1900

	Registered Students
1895–1896	285
1896–1897	372
1897–1898	378
1898–1899	422
1899–1900	435

Source: Sidney Caine, *The History of the Foundation of the London School of Economics and Political Science*, G. Bell & Son, London 1963, p. 12.

Table 11.2 Occupational Background of LSE Students, 1901–1902

Business and Commerce	50%
Public Administration	12%
Lecturers and Teachers	9%
Barristers and Solicitors	4%
Journalists	4%
Social and Philanthropic Work	1%
Not specified	20%

Source: London School of Economics and Political Science, *Calendar 1902–1903*, pp. 25–26.

Given the lack of structure and progression in the courses studied, the figures for registered students do not directly compare with those for Owens College, for example; but the student constituency was similar. Caine provides some indication of numbers for the first few years that do at the very least indicate that the School's teaching met with a very positive and immediate response (see Table 11.1).[12]

For 1901–1902, 542 students were registered, and the School's *Calendar* breaks down their background, as shown in Table 11.2.[13]

At this point, therefore, at least 80% of the School's students were already in employment or training; its students were in the main aged 23–28,[14] and so some years removed from their schooling. This contrasts strongly with the approach taken in Birmingham at exactly this time, where the Faculty of Commerce sought to recruit its students directly from school.

An official report compiled by the Director in 1898 divided attendances between 10-week courses in the first and second years, and 'special courses' that involved perhaps

[12] Caine, *History*, p. 55.
[13] London School of Economics and Political Science, *Calendar 1902–1903*, pp. 25–26.
[14] London School of Economics and Political Science, *Calendar 1902–1903*, pp. 25–26.

one or two lectures. Edwin Cannan's first-year course on 'The Meaning and Use of Economic Terms' met both during the day and in the evening, for example, attracting in the spring term of 1897 an average of 7 students to the former and 12 to the latter. By contrast, a first-year railway economics course during the same term attracted an average of 36 students, this high attendance reflecting the engagement of the students' employers. The second-year courses for 1896–1897 attracted on average 4 to 16 students each. In the following academic year, railway economics was also the most popular first-year course, recording an average of 59 students for six meetings in the first term.[15]

In an outline of the School published in 1897, Sidney Webb distinguished between two classes of students that had registered for courses: clerks, managers, and young business men were in the majority, while a 'student class' contained 60 or 70 postgraduates—and so again, students who were mostly in their early twenties, not late teens, some of whom had previously attended foreign universities. Most of those in the first group were in junior positions, so that their lectures and classes were scheduled for hours between 6 p.m. and 9 p.m. In conclusion he maintained that

> [h]igher commercial education in England must, like the technological instruction of artizans, be not a substitute for the training of the office and the workshop, but merely its complement. Hence it must be given to men already engaged in business, and, therefore, at hours convenient to them.[16]

Nor should courses be designed for clerks or businessmen in general—rather for definite sectors of employment. Merchants, shipowners, corn factors, and produce brokers had interests distinct from the broad class of insurance clerks, actuaries, and public accountants. Railway companies and banking likewise had specific needs, while all of these differed in the kind of training required for those employed in public administration:

> So long as we offer these groups indiscriminately 'Commercial Education' in the lump they will, quite rightly, pass by on the other side. But put before any one of these classes a definitely specialised curriculum, based on the actual needs of the calling, and experience proves that the abler, more industrious, and the more ambitious of the young men will begin to take an interest in their occupation, and desire to learn something more about it than they pick up in the office.[17]

Webb's arguments found support in the real demand that the School's teaching encountered; and were also reinforced by Hewins's own comments on the lack of any such ready demand for the teaching of economic principles. Hewins observed that in 1894 the limited knowledge of economics that the University of London BA examinations required was reflected in the low level of attendance at lectures provided at

[15] W. A. S. Hewins, 'The London School of Economics and Political Science', *Special Reports on Educational Subjects* Vol. 2, British Parliamentary Papers 1898 Vol. XXIV, pp. 96–98.

[16] Sidney Webb, 'The Provision of Higher Commercial Education in London', *Journal of the Society of Arts* (6 August 1897), p. 942. These general purposes were written into the 'Constitution and Objects of the School' published in the *Calendar 1902–1903*, p. 7.

[17] Webb, 'The Provision of Higher Commercial Education', pp. 942–43.

King's College and University College. Economics was an obligatory subject in the Institute of Bankers' examinations, and also in those run by the London Chamber of Commerce. But it is evident from the School's early provision that while there was this real demand for teaching in practical economic areas—trade, banking, public finance—there was little existing demand for systematic tuition in economic principles. This was reflected in the School's undergraduate teaching of economics, for which there was a limited and elementary offering.[18] This situation would remain more or less unchanged until the later 1920s.

The London BSc (Econ)

From the session 1900–1901 the School was admitted to the University of London, the 14 regular lecturers formally becoming teachers of the University, with Hewins and Foxwell the only professors by virtue of the chairs they already held at King's College and University College, respectively.[19] The new Faculty of Economics and Political Science coincided almost entirely with the School, and this was to prove very significant, for the teaching plan of the School became the teaching plan for both internal and external University of London examinations, and so by extension provided the curriculum for all University Colleges that entered its students for them.[20] The London BSc (Econ) was created in 1901, so that for the next two decades[21] the School had a dual focus: the existing vocationally-oriented teaching that it provided for its part-time students, and teaching oriented to the three-year sequence of the new degree, organised initially for both part- and full-time students, but by the later 1920s predominately involving full-time students. By the 1930s the London BSc (Econ) had become the template for the teaching of the social sciences in Britain, and its graduates were fanning out across the Empire to appointments in new departments of economics and of commerce.

Despite its name, the BSc (Econ) was not an economics degree of the kind that would be introduced two years later in Cambridge. It was a broad social sciences degree in which elementary economics provided a common foundation, but which was a subject few students pursued at a more advanced level. The new degree was therefore in this respect continuous with the character of the teaching with which the School had been engaged since 1895. While 'General Economics' headed a list of five subjects of study for first-year students, its subject matter mostly coincided with courses that Hewins and Cannan were already teaching. The four remaining first-year subjects were the British Constitution, European history 600–1815, economic and political geography, and mathematics.[22] By twenty-first-century standards the

[18] See Hewins, 'The London School of Economics', pp. 81–82, 88–89.

[19] Duties connected with these chairs were largely nominal; see the discussion of University College later in the chapter.

[20] Among them the colleges in Exeter, Bristol, Southampton, Reading, Leicester, Nottingham, Hull, and Newcastle.

[21] I.e., until the creation of the BCom in 1919 provided degree-level tuition in commercial subjects.

[22] '... to include simple treatment of Algebra to Expansions, Trigonometry; Elements of co-ordinate Geometry and the graphic representation of functions) *or* the Elements of Inductive and Deductive Logic'.

more demanding part of the specification was the principle that '[s]tudents will be expected to read, in the original, books on economic and historical subjects in *either* French *or* German'. First-year Honours students sat five compulsory papers, only one of which was in general economics; while in the final year students could take an optional course for which they sat four papers at the examination. The second and third years included public finance as one of the four compulsory topics, while students could also select from 10 options either 'Economic Theory (including the History of Economics)'; or 'The History, Theory, and Present Systems of Banking and Currency'; or 'The History, Theory, and Present Organisation of International Trade'—these were alternative options, not complementary elements of one course. Students seeking to focus upon economics would therefore in total sit five out of nine papers in economics or economics-related material; those who were more interested in other subjects, such as public administration or politics, would sit one economics paper out of nine, and these latter students heavily outnumbered the former. For a pass degree, students would study 'General Economics, including Modern Economic History with special reference to England, and methods and applications of statistics', together with public finance, European history, public administration, and either commercial or constitutional law; and sit one economics examination paper out of nine.[23] While the economics components did after 1929 become more demanding, new subjects and departments were also added to the School,[24] so that students specialising in economics remained a small minority within the BSc (Econ) up to the later 1920s at least (see Table 11.3). Only after the commerce degree was launched in 1920 can we be reasonably certain of the character of the courses that had been followed by an LSE graduate.[25]

The *Calendar* for 1904–1905 presents the teaching in 12 groups, including economics, commerce, accounting, and banking. These represent what would later become known as pathways: the teaching that they included was in part dedicated to the topic in question, but also drew upon a common core of lectures. Cannan's introductory economics course, held on Mondays at 6 p.m., was common to economics, politics (as 'Elements of Theory'), commerce (as 'Economic Theory—General Course'), accounting (ditto), and banking (ditto).[26] These lectures were well-attended: during the academic year 1908–1909, 78 students were registered for the 'Elements' course,

London University Gazette Vol. I No.3 (21 December 1901), p. 23; University of London Library Archives UP/1/3/1.

[23] *Calendar 1902–1903*, pp. 46–47.

[24] The Department of Social Science and Administration was added in 1912–1913, resulting from the incorporation of School of Sociology and Social Economics founded in 1903 by Sir Charles Loch, James Bonar, Bernard Bosanquet, and others for training social workers and administrators; Hayek, 'The London School of Economics', p. 17.

[25] Especially since the School did not publish in the *Calendar* any report of this distribution of pathways through the BSc (Econ), nor it appears was any real effort made to collate and disseminate such data for internal use. Hence the need to emphasise here that the BSc (Econ) was not, until the later 1950s at least, a specialised course in economics, but actually a degree awarded mainly to students *lacking* a specialised training in economics.

[26] *Calendar 1904–1905*, pp. 46ff. This course was the basis for his book *Wealth: A Brief Explanation of the Causes of Economic Welfare*, P. S. King and Son, London 1914. The book went into a second edition in August 1916, this being reprinted every year up to 1924 apart from in 1921; a third edition followed in 1928.

Table 11.3 Choice of Finals Subjects by BSc (Econ) Candidates

	1922	1923	1924	1925	1926
Economics	5	5	6	7	3
Economic History (Modern)	12	19	4	11	12
Economic History (Medieval)	0	0	1	0	1
Political Ideas	1	1	2	5	1
Public Administration	10	25	9	24	14
Banking & Currency	3	7	3	5	5
Geography	7	14	6	7	4
International Trade	2	0	0	0	1
Transport	0	1	0	0	1
Insurance	0	1	0	0	0
Accounting	0	1	4	3	4
Statistics	4	2	2	3	2
International Law	1	1	3	1	1
Industrial Law	0	0	0	0	1
Commercial Law	0	0	3	3	4
Sociology	7	8	4	1	6
Total students graduating	52	85	47	71	60

Source: Meeting of 25 November 1926, Professorial Council Subject Committee: Economics 1925–1926, LSE Archives 15/7.

and 53 for the Tuesday 'Principles'; course; the following year students numbers increased to 98 and 75, respectively.[27] Besides a seminar, this was, however, the only provision for general economics teaching in the School at this time, reflecting the initial emphasis upon a practical and descriptive approach to the economy congruent with commercial education. By 1914 an 'Advanced' course was advertised, but since this was in the same slot that the Tuesday 'Principles' course had been held we can assume that this was the same course, later written up by Cannan as *A Review of Economic Theory* (1929). For 1920, Hugh Dalton[28] had taken over the introductory course; a course on 'Economic Theory' for prospective teachers had been introduced at the

[27] Arthur L. Bowley, 'The Faculty of Economics and Political Science', 5 December 1909, Appendix K of 'Report of the Academic Council, for Transmission to the Royal Commission on University Education in London', Appendix VII of *Royal Commission on University Education in London, Appendix to Second Report of the Commissioners, Minutes of Evidence June 1910–November 1910* Cd. 5528 (1911), p. 350.

[28] Dalton (1887–1962) entered King's College Cambridge to study mathematics in 1906, but switched to Part II of the new Economics Tripos, being classes with a 2:1 in 1910. In 1911 he became a postgraduate student at LSE, supervised by Cannan on the topic of income inequality. After war service in Italy, he was appointed Reader in Economics at the LSE in 1920, publishing a revised version of his doctoral thesis in the same year as *Some Aspects of the Inequality of Incomes in Modern Communities*. His *Principles of Public Finance* (1922) became a standard textbook. In 1924 he was elected a Labour MP, and for the subsequent three decades he was at the centre of Labour Party politics.

request of the London County Council, and Cannan's advanced course now took the form of 60 lectures over two years at 12 noon on Tuesdays, repeated at 6 p.m.[29]

Up to 1914, teaching in economics and commerce at the School continued on the path established in the early 1900s, a variety of courses being wrapped into the BSc (Econ), together with a substantial commitment to occasional courses for railway company employees and others. Following the war, the character of the School altered considerably. First of all, William Beveridge was appointed Director in 1919, bringing to the institution a more vigorous, if at times troublesome, head. Second, a separate BCom degree was introduced, creating a greater degree of coherence for the teaching and in so doing re-establishing some clarity in the nature of student demand. Third, previous reliance on part-time staff gave way to full-time appointments, although Cannan as Professor of Political Economy retained his part-time status up to his retirement. Additionally, through the 1920s, many of those originally associated with the School retired from teaching—Herbert Foxwell in 1922, Graham Wallas in 1923, Halford Mackinder in 1925, Edwin Cannan in 1926, with Lilian Knowles[30] dying in 1926 and Leonard Hobhouse, first Professor of Sociology in Britain, dying in 1929.[31]

The Creation of the BCom

Although there had been discussion of introducing an undergraduate degree in commerce since the early 1900s, the first detailed proposal was drafted in 1917 by the Director, William Pember Reeves,[32] looking forward to the postwar development of the School. Before the war the School had collaborated with King's College London on a two-year Higher Commercial Certificate, which in the first year included tuition in economics, geography, and economic history, together with accounting and commercial law, to a level roughly equal to the intermediate (first-year) examination.[33] As

[29] *Calendar 1920–1921*, p. 41. Lionel Robbins entered the School in the autumn of 1920, and Susan Howson's biography reconstructs his progress through the Honours BSc (Econ) course, highlighting the structure of Hugh Dalton's first-year economics course, and the rather confusing arrangement by which Cannan's third-year course was taught as a two-year cycle covering Production and Value in one year, and Distribution the next. Robbins first attended during his second year in October 1921; that year Cannan was lecturing on Distribution, and Robbins was able to make better sense of the lectures by borrowing Frederic Benham's notes on the lectures delivered the previous year. See Susan Howson, *Lionel Robbins*, pp. 69ff., for Dalton, pp. 71–73, for Cannan, pp. 81–83.

[30] Knowles (1870–1926) had studied history at Girton College, Cambridge, being classed with a First in history in 1893, and then another First in Law the following year. She assisted William Cunningham in revising his *Growth of English Industry and Commerce in Modern Times* for its third edition, and then in 1896 registered as a research student at LSE. In 1904 she became the first full-time university teacher of economic history in Britain, promoted to reader in 1907 and professor in 1921. As Maxine Berg writes in her *Oxford Dictionary of National Biography* entry for Knowles, she was a 'country tory, patriot, and imperialist'—and so a good fit with many other early LSE teachers. See also Colin M. Lewis, 'Economic History at the London School of Economics and Political Science: A View from the Periphery', in Robert A. Cord (ed.) *The Palgrave Companion to LSE Economics*, Palgrave Macmillan, London 2018, pp. 58–59.

[31] Hayek, 'The London School of Economics', p. 20.

[32] William Pember Reeves (1857–1932) was a New Zealand politician with a background in law and journalism. In 1896 he moved to London as New Zealand's Agent-General (later High Commissioner), joined the Fabian Society, was active in policy, and in 1908 was made Director of the LSE.

[33] *Memorandum by the Director of the London School of Economics in the Development of Higher Commercial Education after the War and the Position of the London School of Economics*, [1917] British Library of Political and Economic Science (BLPES) Archives 20/11, p. 3.

with Webb's comments in 1897 cited earlier, Pember Reeves noted the divergent needs of different commercial sectors, but also envisaged topics that had not hitherto been part of the standard fare for commercial education. He suggested, for example, that there could be a general course on the principles of factory administration, including treatment of both efficiency and the 'psychological conditions of administration'. He also considered that the teaching of accountancy should include cost accounts and factory bookkeeping, while a two-year course on global commerce would include geography, transport, marketing, and tariffs.[34] He envisaged a new BCom degree that shared first-year courses with the existing teaching on the BSc (Econ); and would add to two years of full-time study the alternative option of an evening course that could extend to four years.

The constituency envisaged for the new degree was outlined in a report drafted in 1919, shortly before the new degree came into operation.[35] There were three broad groups. First there was a relatively large group of young people who had been educated in a grammar or municipal secondary school and who were currently in commercial employment; these would pursue study part-time, possibly in the evening. Secondly, there was a smaller group of school-leavers who would proceed directly to the School, where they would follow a full-time course for three years. They would not have any contact with commercial employers until they graduated, or were around 21 or 22 years of age. Third, there was a small group of the sons of employers who had attended public school, had perhaps studied at Oxford or Cambridge and were now engaged in business; it was likely that these students would study on a part-time basis. In sum, then, it was anticipated that the majority of students would study part-time, and that the orientation was typically towards more mature students with post-school experience of either employment or education.

Undergraduate Teaching during the 1920s

As already noted, in the early years of the School, teachers had been recruited on a casual or part-time basis according to the needs of particular courses, teaching in commercial subjects being supplied by recruits from business and commerce. The new degree would require the recruitment of dedicated full-time staff, and the necessary expansion in the School's teaching establishment was made possible by external benefactions. The most immediately significant of these was the decision by Sir Ernest Cassel[36] to create an educational trust for the School with a gift of £150,000 that was conditional upon matching funds from other sources. It had been decided to create a Faculty of Commerce in the University of London in July 1918, and by late 1919 most of the funds to match the Cassel benefaction had been raised.[37] These

[34] Ibid., p. 5.

[35] 'Commerce Degree. Report of Distributing Trades Sub-Committee', 10 March 1919; in Correspondence, Reports and Memoranda Concerning the Establishment of the Bureau and the Institution of Degrees in Commerce, 1920–4, University of London Archives CD8.

[36] Sir Ernest Joseph Cassel (1852–1921) was an international financier of German origin well-connected in English society; see Pat Thane's fascinating *Oxford Dictionary of National Biography* entry.

[37] S. P. Keeble, 'University Education and Business Management from the 1890s to the 1950s: A Reluctant Relationship', London School of Economics PhD diss. 1984, p. 59. Rockefeller funding contributed

funds contributed directly to the transformation of the School, since full-time employment brought with it a personal identification with the work of the School that the former part-time teaching arrangements had impeded. The first Cassel Professorships were held by Lawrence Dicksee[38] in Accounting and Business Methods, and by H. C. Gutteridge in Commercial and Industrial Law, while Hugh Dalton and Theodore Gregory[39] became the first Cassel Reader in Commerce. In the course of the next few years, Sir Ernest Cassel chairs in International Law and in Banking and Currency were created, together with a Readership in Commerce with special reference to Transport (W. Tetley Stephenson); also a lectureship in commercial geography (Rodwell Jones); a lectureship in business organisation (Drummond Smith); and lectureships in commerce (R. B. Forrester in 1922,[40] and Arthur Redford[41] and John W. F. Rowe[42] in 1925).[43] Added to this, Beveridge was able to gain funding from the Rockefeller Foundation to convert Cannan's chair into a full-time post for his successor, recruiting Allyn Young in preference to any British contemporary candidate.[44]

This ability to create new posts also assisted another important aspect of the transformation of the School in the 1920s: the appointment of former students to teach at the School. Theodor Gregory's appointment to the Cassel Chair of Banking and Currency in 1926 placed the first of the School's own students in a professorial position; Lionel Robbins, an undergraduate of the School from 1920 to 1923, was appointed to the economics chair in 1929 as successor to Allyn Young, having been a lecturer on the staff from 1925 to 1927; and Arnold Plant, who was awarded an external BCom in 1922 and an internal BSc (Econ) in 1923, came back from his chair at Cape Town in 1930 to assume the Chair of Commerce. In the same year Frederic

significantly to the School during the interwar period; allocations for teaching staff, buildings, postgraduate research, and the Library amounted to £430,000 up to 1934–1935; Hayek, 'The London School of Economics', p. 25, and more generally, Salma Ahmad, 'Institutions and the Growth of Knowledge: The Rockefeller Foundations' Influence on the Social Sciences between the Wars', PhD diss., University of Manchester, 1987.

[38] See the brief discussion of Dicksee in the preceding chapter, p. 268. His approach to contemporary accounting practice is sketched in Christopher J. Napier, 'Accounting and the Influence of Economics at LSE', in Robert A. Cord (ed.) *The Palgrave Companion to LSE Economics*, Palgrave Macmillan, London 2018, pp. 82–83.

[39] Gregory (1890–1970) was born in London and studied at the LSE, joining the teaching staff as an assistant in 1913.

[40] Forrester had taught in Manchester (1910–1912) and Aberdeen (1912–1922); he was subsequently Professor of Economics and Political Science, University College, Aberystwyth 1931–1951.

[41] Redford (1896–1961) studied history and economics in Manchester, and from 1945 was Professor of Economic History at Manchester.

[42] Rowe studied classics and economics at Cambridge from 1914, interrupted by war service 1915–1919; in 1920 he sat the examination for Part I of the Economics Tripos and then registered as a postgraduate student at LSE, becoming a teaching assistant in 1923.

[43] William Beveridge, 'Report on the Teaching of Commerce in the University of London', July 1924 BLPES Archives 20/11, p. 2.

[44] Letter of Beveridge to Beardsley Ruml, 26 April 1926, Rockefeller Archive Center LSRM SIII-6 File 593 LSE. At this time Beveridge had only one (unnamed) British candidate in view, and intended to set the full-time salary at £1,500 plus pension contributions, making it the best-paid British economics appointment. He already had a clear preference for Young, who at this stage had indicated he would wish to remain at the LSE until retirement.

Table 11.4 Registered Commerce Students 1919-1924

	Total BCom	BCom New Enrolments	BSc New Enrolments
1919–1920	132	132 (90 day, 42 evening)	74 (41 day, 33 evening)
1920–1921	238	146 (81 day, 65 evening)	180 (107 day, 73 evening)
1921–1922	263	102 (56 day, 46 evening)	99 (38 day, 61 evening)
1922–1923	276	102 (55 day, 47 evening)	99 (43 day, 56 evening)
1923–1924	243	103 (45 day, 58 evening)	98 (40 day, 58 evening)

Source: William Beveridge, 'Report on the Teaching of Commerce in the University of London', July 1924 LSE Archives 20/11.

Benham, another former student, returned from Sydney to a lectureship in economics.[45] Much of this work of consolidation was also assisted by the number of new full-time students who registered for the BCom degree. The syllabus was approved in July 1919, and in October 132 students enrolled, including 54 ex-servicemen. External students were also catered for: in March 1922 the Commerce Degree Bureau opened in Russell Square, having had £50,000 allocated for the purpose from the Cassel Educational Trust.[46] Registrations of students for the new degree were summarised in Beveridge's 'Report' as shown in Table 11.4.[47]

Evident here is the generally stronger demand for the BCom degree than that for the BSc (Econ), also highlighting that not only many commerce students but also BSc (Econ) students were in employment, hence following the evening, and not the day-time courses. Beveridge's 'Report' also summarised figures for BCom graduates from other universities, emphasising the clear predominance of the London degree after the passing of the postwar bulge in student admissions (see Table 11.5).[48]

The structure of the London BCom degree was originally similar to the arrangements for the BSc (Econ): a two-part degree divided between an Intermediate examination normally sat at the end of the first year, and a final examination at the end of the third year. The Intermediate examination had four compulsory subjects (economics; banking, currency, and finance; geography; accounting), an approved modern language, and a course chosen from among the natural sciences, mathematics, history,

[45] Benham (1900–1962) gained a First in the BSc (Econ) in 1922, and was appointed lecturer in economics at the University of Sydney in 1923. From his work there he published in 1928 *The Prosperity of Australia: An Economic Analysis*, for which he was awarded an LSE PhD. Rather like Arnold Plant in South Africa, likewise a student of Edwin Cannan, Benham approached Australian economy and policy in a vigorously free-market spirit. In 1938 he published his textbook *Economics* (discussed in the following chapter). See Neville Cain, 'Benham, Frederic Charles Courtenay (1900–1962)', *Australian Dictionary of Biography*, Vol. 7 Melbourne University Press, Melbourne 1979.

[46] Beveridge, 'Report', pp. 5–6. See later in this chapter for a discussion of the work of the Commerce Degree Bureau.

[47] Ibid., pp. 5ff. It should be remembered that only a small minority of students registering for the BSc (Econ) would proceed to specialise in economics, and so this is not a direct comparison of students of commerce and students of economics. Also, these figures relate only to students registered at LSE, and do not include London external students.

[48] These figures vary in detail from those in the Appendix based on the records of respective institutions, and should be read as broadly indicative only, and primarily in relation to Beveridge's argument.

Table 11.5 Commerce Students Graduating from British Institutions, 1922

1922	
Leeds	8
Edinburgh	26
Liverpool	15
Manchester	36
Birmingham	28
London	22
1923	
Leeds	11
Edinburgh	26
Liverpool	n.a.
Manchester	34
Birmingham	16
London	53

Source: William Beveridge, 'Report on the Teaching of Commerce in the University of London', July 1924 LSE Archives 20/11.

English, or commercial art. Timetables were given for both day and evening sessions.[49] The final examination was divided into two parts: four compulsory subjects taught in the second year ('Present Organization of Industry, Banking and Transport', 'Modern Economic Development of the Empire and the Most Important Foreign Countries', 'Elements of Commercial Law (treated from the commercial rather than the legal standpoint)', and 'Statistical Method'; and a third year in which students sat a total of six papers related to one of nine groups: Banking and Finance, Trade (colonial and general), Trade (of one particular region), Industry, General Transport, Shipping, Inland Transport, Public Utilities, and Commercial Art. Apart from the last group, all others required two papers in an approved modern foreign language. There was a clear progressive principle built into the degree course, but no attempt to make either accounting or economics a continuing thread through the three years. Hence the only economics course required was Hugh Dalton's first-year course; accounting was a compulsory subject in the first year, was not taught in the second, and formed a bespoke part of the group selected in the fourth—so that if 'Industry' was selected, students were taught cost accounting, if 'Inland Transport' then railway cost accounting, and if 'Shipping' then trading accounts. This arrangement met the principle first articulated by Sidney Webb in 1897, and then repeated by Pember Reeves in 1917: that different branches of industry and commerce required bespoke versions of

[49] *Calendar 1920–1921*, pp. 104ff.

accounting; and by extension, that the teaching of economic subjects did not require any especially sophisticated understanding of contemporary economic theory.

By 1924, the total teaching staff had grown from 34 just after the war to 52, with around 30 'special lecturers', part-time teachers drawn from commerce and academia.[50] For the session 1922–1923, the fourth year of the BCom degree, there were 276 students registered, as against 264 registered for the BSc (Econ).[51] Five years later, of the 675 students reading for First degrees, 354 were registered for the BSc (Econ) and 273 for the BCom, while the proportion of students attending in the daytime had grown to just over 70%, there also being a steady decline in the number of occasional students.[52] Despite this lack of clear growth in numbers for the BCom after its strong start, it remains true that at the end of the 1920s the numbers at LSE studying for commerce were far greater than those following the economics pathway on the BSc (Econ). Unlike the latter degree, the course followed by individual BCom students was transparently one in commerce, while the figures that we do have for specialisation on the BSc (Econ) suggest that economics students were in a distinct minority, perhaps less than 25% of the numbers of BCom students.

This conclusion is reinforced if we consider the numbers graduating from the two degrees both internally and externally, reflecting not the total number of students registered with LSE, but the relative success of the respective programmes. Both daytime and evening students were, as far as the LSE was concerned, internal students; the School's *Calendar* and internal records excluded those students registered through other institutions, or taking a degree by private study. While they followed the same course as LSE students, they were recorded in London University records, not those of the LSE. Arnold Plant had himself gained his BCom by private study, and this option, to register for a London degree without having at the same time to attend any institution of further or higher education, remained an important feature of both degrees until well after the Second World War. In 1925, for example, one student gained a First in the BSc (Econ) exclusively through private study as an external student, as did three of the six students gaining Seconds. Students following this pathway—studying for a London BCom either by private study exclusively, with the assistance of the Commerce Degree Bureau, or registered as a full- or part-time student at one of the University Colleges—were, it is true, more likely to be classed with a Second or a pass degree. And so while in 1928, for example, Monica Page gained a First in the BSc (Econ) as an external student at University College, Southampton, of all pass classifications that year nine were by private study, and six in combination with institutions. In 1931 two external students gained Firsts in the BSc (Econ), one registered with University College Bristol and one with University College Nottingham. This was the year that Ronald Coase was awarded an internal Ordinary BCom after two years' study, along with 19 external students exclusively through private study, 14 through the Commerce Degree Bureau and private study, and another through

[50] 'Director's Report on the Work of the School. October 1922–June 1924'. *Calendar 1924–1925*, p. 22.

[51] Ibid., p. 24; 60% of the total of 818 regular students were day students, with another 1,800 occasional students, 900 of these being sent to the School by railway companies.

[52] 'Director's Report on the Work of the School. July 1927–June 1928', *Calendar 1928–1929*, p. 11.

Table 11.6 Total Graduates in BCom and BSc (Econ) 1922–1930

	Internal BCom	External BCom	Internal BSc (Econ)	External BSc (Econ)
1922	35	2	48	24
1923	38	11	74	24
1924	30	16	38	19
1925	34	11	64	18
1926	35	20	50	27
1927	26	32	55	34
1928	46	35	57	26
1929	41	26	59	25
1930	37	41	58	56

Source: London University Gazette, various years.

Bournville Continuation School[53] and private study. In 1933, of the 40 external BSc (Econ) Seconds, 30 were by private study, while in the same year 22 BCom degrees were gained through private study, and 14 through the Commerce Degree Bureau. In 1935 the BCom had 28 graduates who had studied privately, and 19 who had worked through the Commerce Degree Bureau.[54] By modern standards these are small numbers; but all such numbers are small in Britain during the interwar period, and so this evidence of a broad but relatively invisible engagement with London degrees alters our perspective on the significance of the LSE, and that of individual provincial centres.

An additional factor here is that London external students were not necessarily resident in the United Kingdom. Overseas students also studied for external London degrees, extending the London curriculum across the world. Such students were heavily concentrated in particular institutions, or were studying privately, and so scattered. In 1948, for example, more than 40 students in Ceylon Technical College gained a BSc (Engineering), as did two from Accra. Most of the overseas BAs were by private study, as were those gaining the LLB. Only a few students sat for the Economics and Commerce degrees in 1948: nine passed in economics in 1948, seven of these from Ceylon/Sri Lanka; seven gained a BCom—four from Ceylon/Sri Lanka, two from Egypt, and one from Trinidad.

While there are in Table 11.6 clearly more internal BSc (Econ) graduates than internal BCom graduates, this preponderance is not so generally clear-cut for external students. Furthermore, while we can simply sum the external and internal BCom columns as 'students of commerce', those graduating with a BSc (Econ) were a far more heterogeneous group. It is reasonable to assume that, like internal LSE students, only a

[53] For some sense of the diversity of educational provision at this time, see H. W. Bull, 'Industrial Education at Cadbury in the 1930's', *The Vocational Aspect of Education* Vol. 36 (1984), pp. 59–62.

[54] *London University Gazette*, Supplements to various years, University of London Library Archives UP/1/3/1-40.

small minority of external BSc (Econ) graduates would have taken advanced courses in economics. These figures therefore confirm that, outside Cambridge, in the early 1930s commercial education was a far more significant enterprise than economic education.

We are only able to estimate the annual number of students graduating in economics in Britain, since the data are only unambiguous for Cambridge and Manchester. While the University of London recorded total numbers of graduates in its *Gazette*, there are for most of the twentieth century no archival records beyond bound annual volumes of the notices posted each year for students—the University retained no independent record of student results by paper, only their final class of degree as represented by the printed notice.[55] Nor did the School itself preserve any systematic record of the subjects that BSc (Econ) students had actually studied; and so from the School's own records we cannot determine how many of those who graduated with a BSc (Econ) during the 1930s were 'economics graduates'.

Some perspective, however, can be gained by decomposing the annual total of UK economics graduates as recorded by the University Grants Commission (UGC).[56] If we subtract from the annual total those graduating from the Cambridge Part II,[57] and also subtract the number graduating with an economics degree in Manchester[58] (the only other significant centre of honours economics teaching in Britain at this time), the residual figure will represent all those students, external and internal, graduating with a London degree in economics—those BSc (Econ) students who majored in economics.[59] While there are some inconsistencies, the general relationships are clear from Table 11.7: the number of LSE graduates who had specialised in economics only increased significantly from 1932, although numbers still remained limited; and there were in every year besides 1939[60] far more Cambridge graduates who had either two or three years' training in economics.

Nonetheless, despite the obvious fact that at the end of the 1920s the vast majority of full-time and occasional students studying at the LSE were pursuing vocational courses in commerce, public administration, and social work,[61] teaching

[55] Bernard Corry reported in conversation that when in the early 1990s he had tried to establish what mark students had received by paper, so that he could establish the existence or not of any grade inflation, he was told that the University did not retain marks by paper, only the final grade of degree; and as I later discovered, the archive record is simply a bound copy of the results notices that had been posted each year.

[56] As estimated from UGC Returns in Michael Sanderson, *The Universities and British Industry 1850–1950*, Routledge and Kegan Paul, London 1972, p. 271. There is no indication of how the UGC arrived at these figures.

[57] As recorded in the *Cambridge University Reporter*, counting both those who had studied only for Part II (from the early 1930s for two years) and those who had studied for Parts I and II; as noted on p. 131, the former generally did better than the latter. Oxford can be disregarded for our purposes because the balance of subjects meant that economics was always represented by less than half of the subjects studied.

[58] *University of Manchester Calendar*, various years.

[59] The column for BSc (Econ) students is based on the annual figures in the *University of London Gazette*, which gives the numbers graduating from University College London separately. This calculation is not foolproof, since if we subtract UCL graduates from the London total to arrive at LSE plus external students there is an anomaly in 1930–1931. Additionally, the 1926 *London University Gazette* figure for BSc (Econ) (50) differs from the internal LSE figure in Table 11.3 (60).

[60] Owing to a sudden drop in Cambridge students following Parts I & II, and also to no graduates at all being recorded for UCL.

[61] Robbins wrote to Arnold Plant in January 1930 mentioning that there were 'fifty specialists this year' in economics; Howson, *Lionel Robbins*, p. 170. Given that only 58 students graduated with an internal BSc

Table 11.7 Summary of Annual Graduates in Economics (England and Wales), 1926–1939

	UGC Total	Cambridge Total	Non-Cambridge	Manc.	BSc (Econ)	All London	UCL	LSE
1925–1926	60	48	12	1	50	11		
1926–1927	65	38	27	3	55	24		
1927–1928	60	50	10	2	57	8		
1928–1929	82	57	25	1	59	24		
1929–1930	80	63	17	3	58	14	4	10
1930–1931	85	77	8	1	85	7	8	-1
1931–1932	81	63	18	3	101	15	14	1
1932–1933	127	80	47	6	107	41	15	26
1933–1934	126	72	54	4	109	50	9	41
1934–1935	106	64	42	0	112	42	16	26
1935–1936	106	60	46	3	135	43	13	30
1936–1937	99	68	31	1	111	30	19	11
1937–1938	102	65	37	4	124	33	13	20
1938–1939	115	47	68	2	113	66	0	66

Source: UGC data taken from Sanderson; *Cambridge University Reporter* for Cambridge; Manchester *Calendars*; *London University Gazette* for UCL.

appointments were already being made predominantly from those with a background in academic economics, rather than in commerce. In September 1930 the *Economic Journal* listed seven new appointments to the staff, headed by Arnold Plant, returning from South Africa to become Professor of Commerce.[62] During the 1930s Plant would develop graduate business administration at the School, but he was not a vigorous supporter of the BCom. Rowe, who had in 1925 been appointed Cassel Lecturer in Commerce, was in 1930 promoted to Reader in Economics (with special reference to Industrial Organisation); likewise Philip Barrett Whale, appointed to a Cassel Lectureship in Commerce in 1926, was promoted to Reader in Economics (with special reference to Banking and Currency). Frederic Benham, a former student of Cannan who had got a First in his BSc (Econ) in 1922, returned from Sydney to become a Cassel Lecturer in Commerce; and then became the author of one of the most successful economics textbooks of the latter half of the twentieth century. John Hicks was promoted to Lecturer in Economics.[63]

(Econ) in 1930, this can only mean 50 students over three years, which translates to something like 20% of all current internal BSc (Econ) students.

[62] *Economic Journal* Vol. 40 (1930), p. 536.

[63] John Hicks (1904–1989) entered Balliol College Oxford in 1922 to study mathematics, but switched after his first year to the PPE course, being awarded a second-class degree in 1925. Despite this, he secured a one-year scholarship and wrote a BLitt on 'Skilled and Unskilled Wages in the Building and Engineering Trades' under the supervision of G. D. H. Cole. He was appointed an assistant lecturer at LSE in 1926. In

There is a rough pattern in these appointments and promotions, besides the movement from commerce to economics. Rowe had initially entered Trinity College Cambridge in 1914 to study Classics, but was in the army from 1915 to 1919, and then finished by taking Part I of the Economics Tripos in 1920. Whale had first studied for the BSc (Econ) as an external student at University College Cardiff, and then gained a BCom in 1924.[64] As with Benham, candidates appointed for non-specialist commerce teaching mostly had a background in economics and would later be recognised as economists; combined with regular appointments such as Hicks, this meant that the teaching staff for the School, the vast majority of whose students were pursuing vocational and not specialist economic courses, became increasingly dominated by academic economists. This turned out to be such a successful niche strategy that by the 1950s the LSE was thought of as a school of economics, not of commerce. The teaching staff reflected the former reputation, the students the latter. In time, the former reputation won out, so that (eventually) the School increasingly attracted students seeking a specialist training in economics. Manchester had prefigured this approach with the appointments made by Chapman before the First World War; but from his appointment in 1929 Robbins ruthlessly pursued it, furthering the transformation of an institution designed for vocational training into one devoted to academic subjects, although this transformation was not complete until the 1960s.

Robbins as Professor of Economics

When Cannan retired in 1926, Beveridge initially favoured appointing Ralph Hawtrey to the vacancy; but the School had received a grant from the Laura Spelman Rockefeller Fund that made it possible both to convert Cannan's part-time post into a full-time one, and look further afield for a candidate. In the spring of 1926, Beveridge offered the post to Allyn Young of Harvard, who after prolonged negotiations accepted for a term of three years in January 1927.[65] In post from October 1927, the Calendar records no changes to the teaching programme before his death from pneumonia in March 1929, aged 52.[66] He was quickly replaced by Lionel Robbins, then aged 30 and so of a different generation to Young (born 1876) and Cannan (born 1861).

Robbins had gained a First in the BSc (Econ) in 1923, then after a period as a research assistant to Beveridge been appointed for 1924–1925 as a temporary lecturer at New College Oxford, standing in for Harold Salvesen, who went to the United States on a Rockefeller grant. He returned in the autumn of 1925 to LSE as an assistant lecturer with a relatively light teaching load, and was then promoted to a full lectureship in June 1926 in response to moves to recruit him to Cambridge. During the academic

1935 he moved to Cambridge, and then in 1938 to Manchester. See Harald Hagemann, 'John R. Hicks (1904–1989)', in Robert A. Cord (ed.) *The Palgrave Companion to LSE Economics*, Palgrave Macmillan, London 2018, pp. 431–33.

[64] Whale (1898–1950) was appointed to a chair at Liverpool in 1945, then became Brunner Professor of Economic Science in 1947.

[65] Howson, *Lionel Robbins*, p. 142.

[66] See his obituary by Theodor Gregory, *Economic Journal* Vol. 39 (1929), pp. 297–301.

year 1926–1927 he took over Dalton's introductory first-year economics course, following Dalton's syllabus, and also shared with Dalton the teaching for Cannan's old two-part Principles course, Cannan having left the School but no replacement as yet having been appointed.[67] Then, in March 1927, Harold Salvesen decided to quit academia for his family business, and New College immediately thought of asking Robbins to return as a college fellow and a university lecturer in economics. And so, in October 1927, Robbins returned to teaching in Oxford, arranging also to give one course of lectures at LSE on comparative economic theory. But then Allyn Young died in March 1929, and Beveridge, seeking to plug the gap in teaching that this created, first persuaded Robbins to take over economic theory classes running up to the June examinations, and then in May decided to invite Robbins to return to a 'junior' professorship at LSE.[68]

Now returning permanently to the School, he sought to make his mark, revamping the teaching of economics as inherited from Cannan,[69] courses which he had himself followed as a student and then taught alongside Dalton three years earlier. Howson notes in her biography of Robbins that with Dalton on leave serving the government, during the academic year 1929–1930 John Hicks was his sole economic colleague, with some assistance from George Schwartz, Roy Allen, and Leonard Marsh.[70] While this significantly understates the number of economists actually teaching at the School, it does perhaps reflect Robbins's own perception. As such, it also serves as indirect support to the idea that at this time teaching in the principles of economics, as contrasted with practical and applied economic issues, was a rather minor part of the School's provision. Viewed through the prism of Robbins's interests and activities, his energy in modernising and consolidating the teaching of economics in the early 1930s looks like a timely initiative; what slips out of sight in Howson's account is that up to this point the 'London School of Economics and Political Science' had not been primarily engaged in the teaching of economics and politics. In student membership, teaching provision, and overall purpose it remained continuous with its roots in commerce and public administration. This was about to change, not because of any indication of strong student demand for a more systematic and rigorous economic education, but because Robbins wanted the School to become an international centre for the developing discipline of economics. More strictly personal and academic ambitions began to displace the vocational functions and activities of the School.

In 1929 Robbins immediately took over the introductory course, telescoping 30 lectures given once a week over the year to 20 lectures twice a week in the first term. The syllabus detailed in the *Calendar* began with 'The Nature and Significance of Economic Science', the title of the book that he would publish in 1932.[71] The main

[67] Howson, *Lionel Robbins*, p. 143. He also taught a course on currency and banking, and gave a course of 12 lectures on 'The Economic Problems of the War'. Dalton continued to teach at the School while an MP.

[68] The Advisors for the Chair of Economics (Cannan, Macgregor, Pigou, Beveridge, Bowley, Gregory, and Webb) decided to make this indirect replacement for Young on 6 June 1928; Howson, *Lionel Robbins*, p. 163.

[69] Since Allyn Young had made no significant changes to the teaching structure during his tenure.

[70] Howson, *Lionel Robbins*, p. 166. As indicated earlier, in fact there were already more staff members who could be counted as economists than Howson here suggests.

[71] *Calendar 1929–1930*, p. 103.

associated reading was, however, more conventional, including Cannan's *Wealth* (the text based upon Cannan's own introductory lectures), and Henderson's *Supply and Demand* from the Cambridge Economic handbooks series. This was reading he had used during the academic year 1926–1927 for the same course. But there were two more esoteric volumes listed: Heinrich Oswalt's *Vorträge über wirtschaftliche Grundbegriffe*[72] and Colson's *Cours d'économie politique* 'Book I. (omitting Ch. II)'.[73] Presuming that Robbins intended to direct students to the first of the six volumes in this work, his direction to omit Vol. I, Book I, Ch. II, 'Production, Property and Exchange', remains mysterious, since this was little more dated in its approach than the remainder of the work. How familiar Robbins actually was with these works is unclear. The selection of these outdated, obscure, but esoteric texts for an introductory course in economics, combined with his actual reliance on Cannan's original textbook, suggests that Robbins was here seeking to mark a change in direction, but for the time being lacked the resources to do so. In the spring and summer terms, Whale and Hicks continued the 'Elements of Economics' course: Whale giving 14n lectures on 'Money, Banking and International Exchange', naming texts by Cannan, Robertson, and Hawtrey on money, while Hicks gave 14 lectures in parallel on 'Trade and Industry', referring students to *Britain's Industrial Future; Report of the Coal Commission* (1926) and Robertson's *Control of Industry*, among other works.

Robbins also took over the advanced course in economics for second-year students, here again actually recommending Cannan's *Review of Economic Theory* as the 'best introduction to the subject', this being a text written up from Cannan's version of the same lecture course. However, Robbins also suggested that a 'more extensive treatment of certain phases of the history of theory' could be found in Schumpeter's '*Epochen der Dogmen und Methoden Geschichte*' [*sic*]—while 'Those who cannot read German should read Gide and Rist's *History of Economic Doctrines*.'[74] In fact, students would have had trouble locating Schumpeter's text, which was not then actually a book, but instead his essay contribution to the first volume of the *Grundriss der Sozialökonomik*, published in 1914 as 'Epochen der dogmen- und Methodengeschichte' and translated into English as *Economic Doctrine and Method: An Historical Sketch* in 1954.[75] A number of other courses and classes were announced that to some extent drew

[72] Gustav Fischer, Jena 1905, 1920. In the *Calendar* the author and title are misspelled as Ostwalt, *Vorträge uber Wirtschaftliche Grundbegriffe*, suggesting at best a passing acquaintance with a text that has more in common with the style of Frédéric Bastiat than of any contemporary German economist. Oswalt's text had also been recommended in 1926, alongside Adolphe Landry, *Manuel d'économique: à l'usage des facultés de droit*, V. Giard and E. Brière, Paris 1908. Landry's text (p. 889) was organised as three main books typical of nineteenth-century textbooks—production, exchange, distribution. It did, however, open with a discussion of the definition of economics that rejected the idea that it was concerned with the study of wealth; instead, the economic activity of Man was defined as 'that part of his activity directed towards the acquisition of exchangeable goods, or which is otherwise related to these goods' (p. 5).

[73] Clément Colson, *Cours d'économie politique professé à l'École nationale des ponts et chaussées t.1*, Guillamin, Paris 1901. Colson's course is presented in 6 volumes (*tomes*), and t. I is divided into 2 books (*livres*), Book I chs. I–VIII and Book II chs. I–VI.

[74] Charles Gide, Charles Rist, *A History of Economic Doctrines from the Time of the Physiocrats to the Present Day*, trans. R. Richards from the 2nd edition, George G. Harrap, London 1915.

[75] Searching for the German title in the *Bayerische Staatsbibliothek* catalogue leads only to Italian, English, and French translations of the text. The Heidelberg UB catalogue gives only the English translation of 1957 and the 1970 Japanese translation.

on lectures previously listed under other sections; the upshot being that there were now 18 distinct economics lecture courses listed for 1929–1930, instead of the three or four listed in previous *Calendars*. Robbins offered 20 lectures on the 'General Principles of Economic Analysis' in the spring term, which provided an overview of 'Value and Distribution' from Smith to Pigou and Cassel; eight lectures on 'The Nature of Economics and Its Significance in Relation to the Kindred Social Sciences' in the summer term, for which Neville Keynes's *Scope and Method of Political Economy* headed a list of works by Sidgwick, Pigou, Schumpeter, Hawtrey, Robson, Hobson, and Tugwell;[76] and a special subject course on 'The Theory of Capital and Interest'. Here we stumble upon another minor anomaly: the first text named in the list is by Böhm-Bawerk, which is logical enough—except that students are directed to '*Kapital und Kapitalzins* (4th edition)'. This is the subtitle of two related volumes originally published in 1884 and 1889, translated into English by William Smart as *Capital and Interest* in 1889 and *The Positive Theory of Capital* in 1891.[77] Why should undergraduates be directed to a German text that had long been available in English translation? These small irregularities in the programme of study that Robbins announced in 1929, combined with its significant extension, do suggest a hastily improvised attempt to raise the profile of economics in the School. It was, however, easy enough to announce new courses of lectures—there were no regular classes for any of these courses, besides some possible 'special classes at times to be arranged' for third-year students specialising in economics, for whom 'Admission will be strictly by permission of Professor Robbins.' As we shall see in the following chapter, examining Robbins's *Nature and Significance of Economic Science* (1932), Robbins was in the 1930s very much a young man in a hurry, an impression reinforced by Robbins's conduct around this time on the Economic Advisory Council's Committee of Economists, chaired by Maynard Keynes.[78]

As is evident from the foregoing, by any contemporary standard the School had a large number of members of staff who were 'economists', while relatively few LSE undergraduates were interested in pursuing the study of economics beyond an elementary level. Nonetheless, early in 1930 Robbins insisted in a Memorandum that the School was understaffed in economists; and that, for example, the Principles course was reduced to 'only twenty' lectures compared with Young's 58, although presumably he had himself altered the organisation of the Principles course.[79] The new appointments in the autumn of 1930 noted previously were a response to this Memorandum.

By the session of 1935–1936 this reorganisation has settled down, with Benham now giving the Elements of Economics introductory course in 35 lectures over the year, his syllabus prefiguring the textbook that he published in 1938; while a detailed

[76] Here there is more garbled German: Schumpeter's *Wesen und Hauptinhalt der theoretischen Nationalökonomie* (1908) becomes *Wesen und Hauptinhalt der Theoretische National Ökonomie*—three mistakes in one title.

[77] Böhm-Bawerk had died in 1913; he had updated his review of capital theory since the original publication, but this too had been translated, as Eugen von Böhm-Bawerk, *Recent Literature on Interest (1884–1899): A Supplement to 'Capital and Interest'*, Macmillan, New York 1903.

[78] See Howson, *Lionel Robbins*, pp. 179–94—in particular, Robbins's private notes on its members (p. 192), testimony to how highly he thought of himself, and how little of his more experienced contemporaries.

[79] Howson, *Lionel Robbins*, pp. 170–71.

syllabus for Robbins's second-year course 'General Principles of Economic Analysis' notes that students are assumed to have read Taussig's *Principles of Economics* and Wicksteed's *Commonsense of Political Economy* Vol. I, and that the ground to be covered corresponds with that dealt with in Knight's *Risk, Uncertainty and Profit.*[80] Besides referring first-year students to Henderson's *Supply and Demand*, Marshall's *Principles* and the Cambridge Handbooks are resolutely ignored here. New appointments were made: Abba Lerner and Ursula Webb became temporary assistant lecturers in economics, while Ronald Coase and Ronald Edwards became assistant lecturers in commerce. Batson left for a chair in Cape Town, and Hicks moved to Cambridge.[81]

While this is indicative of the way that the LSE was developing into a leading centre for the teaching of economics, it remained primarily a centre for undergraduate vocational education. The notion that it was nonetheless a centre for academic economics was, however, further bolstered by the way that its economics graduates were fanning out across the world.[82] The Calendar for 1931–1932 lists 12 graduates who had recently been appointed: W. M. Allen as Lecturer in Economics at Balliol College Oxford; G. V. Billing as a Lecturer in Economics at the University of Otago, New Zealand; W. H. Hutt to the Chair of Economics at Cape Town; F. C. James to a lectureship in commerce at Aberystwyth; and N. Skene Smith to a chair at the University of Commerce, Tokyo.[83] There was a shorter list the following year, but it included Marion Bowley to Aberystwyth, J. K. Eastham to the School of Economics and Commerce, Dundee; and W. O. Henderson to the University of Liverpool.[84] The London School of Economics established itself in the 1930s as the major source for the development of the teaching of economics in Britain via a number of media—by virtue of its syllabus being followed by all those taking external London degrees; through its publishing programme;[85] from 1921 through its journal *Economica*; through its active embrace of postgraduate study, attracting young economists from all over the world; and through the movement of its students into teaching posts in Britain and overseas. While Cambridge every year had a greater number of students passing through Part II of the Economics Tripos than studied economics to a comparable level at the LSE, the strategic advantage enjoyed by the LSE within the organisation of British higher education meant that the postwar expansion of the social sciences would extend its reach

[80] *Calendar 1935–1936*, p. 105.

[81] Howson, *Lionel Robbins*, p. 280. It should be noted that Howson provides the most detailed and reliable account of the School in the course of the 1930s, albeit from the perspective of the teaching of economics as represented in the *Calendar* and in Robbins's lecture notes. This is the best that can be done, given the lack of internal documentation of the School's teaching.

[82] Which they had to, since employment prospects for academically-trained economists in Britain were primarily limited to teaching until the 1960s at the earliest.

[83] *Calendar 1931–1932*, p. 427.

[84] *Calendar 1932–1933*, p. 437.

[85] Studies in Economics and Political Science published 'Monographs by writers connected with the London School of Economics and Political Science'; for example, Persia Crawford Campbell's *Chinese Coolie Emigration to Countries within the British Empire* (P. S. King & Son, London 1923) was No. 72 in this series; Malinowski's *Argonauts of the Western Pacific* (1922) and Dalton's *The First Principles of Public Finance* (1922) were respectively Nos. 65 and 66 in the series. Frank Knight's *Risk, Uncertainty and Profit* (1921) was No. 16 in the series Reprints of Scarce Tracts in Economic and Political Science (1933).

yet further. And of course, the 1963 landmark study of the future of higher education in Britain would be headed by its professor of economics, Lionel Robbins.

Commerce and Economics during the 1930s

A report of a visitation made in 1935 by a committee of academics appointed by the Senate noted the increase in student numbers since the previous visitation in 1924, an increase they felt was especially marked among graduate students. Permanent staff numbers had increased to 84, with 25 visiting lecturers—emphasising the interwar shift away from a heavy reliance on part-time teachers. In 1933–1934, 540 students were reading for a BSc (Econ), with 255 reading for the BCom. The committee concluded that the number of students following the BCom was relatively static, while those following the BSc (Econ) had greatly expanded, an interpretation that could tend to support the idea that the BCom had failed to develop, as against students interested in the more academic economic study that the composition of staff would seem to suggest.[86] As argued earlier, this was largely an illusion, since the great majority of students studying for the BSc (Econ) did a minimum of economics; the BCom students significantly outnumbered their contemporaries who were following an economics pathway. Nonetheless, the view that the BCom was an inferior version of an economics degree did gain ground during the 1930s, and was eventually to lead to the closure of the BCom course of study in 1949.

Robbins was hostile to the BCom degree on the grounds that it overemphasised the learning of material, with many of the papers requiring the regurgitation of facts, and with too great an emphasis on frequent examinations.[87] Howson notes that a reformed curriculum was proposed in the summer of 1931, and introduced for the academic year 1932–1933. This added elementary statistics and accounting to the first-year course, while the requirement that students sit three compulsory papers in economics and economic history for the final examination reduced the number of options they could choose from among banking and finance, trade and transport, industry and public utilities. As Robbins remarked to Beveridge in 1932, it was now merely another BSc (Econ)[88]—with the important difference, which he ignored, that BCom students now followed a syllabus denser in economic issues and material than that typically followed by BSc (Econ) students.

Robbins seems to have directed his attention solely to internal BSc (Econ) students. If the internal and external student numbers are put together for both degrees, then the rather paradoxical conclusion is that from the early 1930s the majority of undergraduates studying economics on the London degree had signed up for the BCom, not the Bsc (Econ). Comparison of the annual number of internal and external BSc (Econ) and BCom students over the years 1922 to 1939 shows that until 1931 there were usually

[86] 'London School of Economics and Political Science. Visitation under Statute 114. Report of Inspectors (1936)', f. 205, appended as Document 2 to Court of Governors and Council of Management 13 May 1937, Minutes of the Court of Governors, BLPES Archives 4/1 Vol. 9.

[87] 'Observations on the Present Position and Future Prospects of the B. Comm', undated memorandum initialled LCR in Plant Papers, BLPES Archives File 222.

[88] Howson, *Lionel Robbins*, p. 221.

Table 11.8 Internal and External London Commerce and BSc (Econ) Students 1922-1939

	Internal BSc (Econ)	Extenal Bsc (Econ)	Total BSc (Econ)	Internal BCom	External BCom	Total BCom
1922	48	24	72	35	2	37
1923	74	24	98	38	11	49
1924	38	19	57	30	16	46
1925	64	18	82	34	11	46
1926	50	27	77	35	20	55
1927	55	34	89	26	32	58
1928	57	26	83	46	35	81
1929	59	25	84	41	26	67
1930	58	56	114	37	41	78
1931	85	27	112	34	44	78
1932	101	50	151	48	45	93
1933	107	69	176	21	40	61
1934	109	41	150	62	71	133
1935	112	59	171	48	60	108
1936	135	61	196	34	67	101
1937	111	48	159	39	50	89
1938	124	65	189	37	54	91
1939	113	72	185	43	49	92

Source: *London University Gazette*, various years.

rather more than half as many BCom than there were total BSc (Econ) internal students; which, given the limited number of the latter actually majoring in economics, meant that commerce students heavily outnumbered undergraduate economics students up to the Second World War. Externally, there were generally about the same number of BCom graduates and BSc (Econ), sometimes more. Adding together all students graduating, internal and external, we get the results described in Table 11.8.

Looked at this way, the BCom does not look like a failing programme. Assessment of the programme within the broader context of the School's activities—including occasional students, and especially the significant numbers of postgraduate students—is hampered by the School's apparent failure to keep systematic records beyond what was published in the *Calendar*. In the case of graduate students, there would be the familiar problem that a proportion never completed their course of study, plus the fact that at least some of the doctorates awarded by the School were for work that had already been completed, so placing no burden on the teaching staff.[89] The argument

[89] There are some remarks on graduate students in Howson, *Lionel Robbins*, pp. 227–28.

could also be made that many of the fields to which LSE economists later contributed were closer to the applied economics of the BCom than the more esoteric areas of economic theory that were gaining in prestige.

While the public reputation of the School was becoming increasingly detached from the reality of what its students were actually studying, funds had become available in 1929 to finance the development of graduate training in commerce. However, rather than appoint Plant to lead this, the Governors opted to appoint Jules Menken, whose prime qualification seems to have been that he was an old acquaintance of Beveridge.[90] The Calendar for 1930–1931 announced the creation of a Department of Business Administration Research and Training, supported by funds from private firms who were prepared to fund over five years

> ... a Department, which, on the one hand, shall research into problems of business administration, and, on the other hand, shall give specialized training to a limited number of selected students sent by the firms concerned.[91]

Teaching was organised according to the Case Method, following the example of Harvard Business School, and the course covered two sessions totalling 30 weeks from October to June.[92] Firms who had subscribed a minimum of £50 could nominate (non-graduate) candidates, suggesting that the prime constituency was among existing employees, hence continuous with an important early student constituency of the School. Accordingly, the first year aimed to provide a general background in economics, statistics, accounting, and commercial law, while the second year focussed upon marketing, production and finance, statistics and accounting, and personnel management.[93] The adoption of the Case Method required that cases be worked up from British industry, and this, combined with the novelty of training at this level, plus the Depression, had made for a slow start—12 students had attended courses in 1931–1932, and 7 the following year, but in 1932–1933 there were 28 students, and 26 in 1934–1935.[94] It was reported that little difficulty was found in placing those students who did not already have an employer, and it could be said that this graduate institution showed signs of succeeding in its connection to employers and graduates where Birmingham had failed—a failure in Birmingham related not only to the character of the local economy, but also to the priority given to recruiting new students among school-leavers, rather than mature students. Robbins predictably enough objected strongly to the new project, arguing in a 1932 memorandum to Beveridge that Business Administration 'can never be a science', while any course should include a

[90] See Howson, *Lionel Robbins*, p. 220. No details of Mencken's background and qualifications are readily available today.

[91] *Calendar 1930–1931*, p. 13. See also 'History of the Department', *LSE Calendar 1935–1936*, pp. 261–75.

[92] Robbins was vehemently opposed to graduate commercial education, too—see extracts from his memorandum to Beveridge on the issue in Howson, *Lionel Robbins*, p. 221.

[93] *Training for Business Management: The Work of the Department of Business Administration at the London School of Economics and Political Science in the University of London*, 1932. Administrative Committee of the Court of Governors, BLPES Archives 4/8 at f. 130, pp. 7ff.

[94] Department of Business Administration, *Report on the First Five Years' Work and Proposals for the Future*, London School of Economics and Political Science, April 1935. Minutes of the Court of Governors BLPES Archives 4/9 at f. 36, pp. 3–4.

significant amount of economics. In 1935 Plant assumed control of the business administration course, and in the winter of 1936–1937 organised a series of public lectures for businessmen that was then published.[95] While this departure plainly linked to later developments in business education, it was a direction that was never pursued at the LSE.

Another related aspect of commercial education at the LSE before 1939 was the creation of the Commerce Degree Bureau to support external students, lending out books and marking assignments. As noted previously, the Bureau was created with substantial funds from the Cassel Educational Trust, providing external students with resources that put them more on a level with internal students:

> External Students studying for the Commerce Degree who are unable to obtain suitable or adequate assistance in their studies are recommended to communicate with the Bureau, which gives study advice and guidance and issues lists of recommended Books in the main subjects of the B.Com. (External) Examinations (Intermediate and Final). Full assistance, including the setting and correction of written work, is now given in the greater part of the studies covered by the Degree.[96]

By the end of February 1926, 136 students were registered for full composition courses, and 61 students had been assisted by the Bureau in sitting final and intermediate examinations. The Bureau also provided a clearing house for linking students with employers, having contacted around 180 firms and employers in that year.[97] As an institution with its own funding, the Bureau was less susceptible to the changes in the School during the 1930s, continuing through the war with some perhaps unanticipated success:

> The end of the War in Europe brought to the Bureau in person a number of repatriated prisoners of war who wished to express their thanks for the study notes supplied to them during their captivity. In many camps good libraries were available, and much useful study was undertaken. Several men whom the Bureau helped in this way entered for B.Com. Examinations while in the camps and were successful, though in some instances the papers were not received by the University, and the men were able to follow the Bureau's full course of study before making a second entry in the country. Personal contacts have also been renewed with former Bureau students who since 1942 have been prisoners of war or civilian internees in the Far East and have returned to this country with their ambition to secure a degree undiminished by their experiences.[98]

[95] Arnold Plant (ed.), *Some Modern Business Problems: A Series of Studies*, Longmans, Green and Co., London 1937.

[96] *London University Gazette* Vol. XXIV No. 263 (26 September 1924), p. 9.

[97] *London University Gazette* Vol. XXV No. 282 (4 August 1926), p. 195.

[98] Twenty-Third Annual Report (for Year ended 31st July 1945), University of London Commerce Degree Bureau. Annual Reports 1939–1960. University of London Archives CD 6. The Nineteenth Annual Report (for Year ended 31st July 1941) recorded that of 6 students receiving study-schemes, 3 were prisoners of war; the following year of 15 students receiving study schemes, 19 were prisoners of war; and in 1944, of 393 students registered in one way or another, 47% were in the armed forces.

From 1932 the first two years of the BCom were merged with the BSc (Econ), providing grounds for the objection to be raised in the University of London inspection of February 1935 that the difference between the two degrees was now insufficient to warrant their continued separate existence.[99] At the time, Beveridge objected successfully that the funds for teaching the programme had been provided specifically for that purpose, and that if the degree were abolished no resources would be available for other uses—the same argument was later raised in relation to the Commerce Degree Bureau. It seems likely that the decision to roll the first two years of the BSc (Econ) and the BCom together was part of the same drive to push the School towards the study of economics that was evident in the changes to the teaching programme Robbins introduced in 1929. The undated memorandum by Lionel Robbins in Arnold Plant's papers obviously predates this merger of 1932, disparaging the BCom examination and curriculum. When Robbins observed that many brilliant BSc (Econ) students would be incapable of passing the BCom because of the emphasis upon the retention of information rather than reasoning, Plant wrote in the margin 'or BSc Eng or LL.B.', suggesting that he did not share Robbins's view of the relative merits of the two degree courses.[100] When Robbins maintained that the subjects for study were 'not suitable', Plant wrote 'Which?' in the margin. Robbins denied that business could be taught in a classroom, and that the BSc (Econ) should serve as a more suitable model. These were not new arguments, but Plant was perhaps more interested by this time in developing graduate business education than defending undergraduate commercial education that looked increasingly 'unacademic', with correspondingly poor results.[101] Although by comparison with the poor results of students taking Part I of the Cambridge Economics Tripos during the 1930s the LSE's BCom students do not fare at all badly, Robbins and others seem to have selectively compared the best of the BSc (Econ) students with all of the BCom students, with predictable results.

As will be outlined in the following chapter, the LSE would serve as a platform for the development of an 'economic science' for which there was at the time only limited demand from British students. There was, after all, little that a student could do with a degree in economics besides teach the subject, and openings were limited. The School itself had been founded primarily as a vocational institution for those seeking future employment in commerce, industry, and social administration, or already in such employment. Student destinations from the 1950s (Table 11.9) show how strongly this original purpose persisted, despite the decision to close down the BCom degree, a decision already prefigured in the early 1930s with the partial merging of the BCom and BSc (Econ) undergraduate courses.

However, as we have seen in the previous chapter, this movement, from vocational to academic education, ran in parallel with other university institutions up and down the country. Lionel Robbins might in 1929 have looked like a young man in a hurry, but he was only slightly anticipating an institutional transformation that

[99] Referred to earlier, p. 317. University of London Senate Minute 658, 16 November 1938, cited in Keeble, 'University Education', pp. 58–66.

[100] 'Observations on the Present Position and Future Prospects of the B. Comm', p. 2—this is a quarto typescript copy, initialled L. C. R. and annotated by Plant. File 222, Arnold Plant Papers BLPES Archives.

[101] See the breakdown of degree results in the Appendix.

Table 11.9 First Destinations of LSE Graduates

	1953 Graduates	1954 Graduates
Teaching	8.6%	15.9%
University	1.1%	3.2%
Civil Service	16.6%	8.4%
Colonial Service	2.8%	0.8%
Local government	1.1%	0%
Nationalised industry	1.7%	1.5%
Management (ind. & commerce)	27.4%	26.1%
Accounting	10.3%	16.9%
Secretarial	2.8%	0.8%
Private sector econ. & stats.	7%	5%
Banking & insurance	5.7%	0%
Research	7%	8.4%
Librarian	1.1%	1.5%
Journalism & advertising	4%	9.2%
Social work	2.8%	2.3%
Total	100%	100%

Source: *LSE Calendar 1955–56*, The Director's Report on the Work of the School for the Session 1953–54, p. 37.

would by the postwar years already be taken for granted. Instead of charting in detail the course that the LSE took from the 1930s to the 1950s, we can draw upon another development that, while directly linked to the LSE, helps confirm both tendency and chronology: the story of the 'Dundee School of Economics', a municipal college dedicated to the teaching of commercial subjects founded in 1931 whose staff and curriculum drew upon the LSE, but which in 1955 was incorporated into the Faculty of Social Science of the University of St. Andrews, where there had long been resistance to commercial education.[102] Offering teaching in commerce some 30 years after Birmingham and Manchester had first introduced their own BCom degrees, the rapidity with which the Dundee School followed the same track from commerce to economics lends emphasis to the dynamics of this process.

The Dundee School of Economics

The new foundation originated with an offer made to the Dundee Education Authority of £40,000 to provide the youth of Dundee with facilities for 'higher education in

[102] For an overview, see J. K. Eastham, S. G. E. Lythe, 'The Dundee School of Economics, 1931–1955', *Scottish Educational Review* Vol. 10 (May 1978), pp. 19–26.

Economics and in commercial subjects'.[103] The sum offered was to be used primarily in the construction of a commercial college, creating a focus for teaching already provided in the Technical College and elsewhere; the principal course of study was to be the equivalent of a university commerce degree, but leading to a diploma issued by the Scottish Education Office. The gift was accepted, and in 1931 the 'Dundee and East of Scotland Commercial College' was inaugurated with a ceremony addressed by Sir Josiah Stamp. This original designation was never used; it became formally known as the 'School of Economics and Commerce'; but its first Director, James Bowie, always referred to it as the 'Dundee School of Economics', a clear allusion to its model, the London School of Economics.

The School was very much an English outpost among the four ancient Scottish universities: Aberdeen, St. Andrews, Glasgow, and Edinburgh. Economic and commercial education was not, however, alien to these institutions: Bowie himself had an Aberdeen MA and DLitt; a BCom degree had been introduced in Edinburgh in the early 1920s; and Alec Cairncross's popular economics textbook was developed from lectures he gave to Glasgow accountants in the later 1930s.[104] But the Dundee curriculum was firmly linked to the LSE through the simple fact that it offered London's external degrees in economics and commerce, and that many of its teachers were recent graduates of the LSE. For Dundee, this connection with London was no novelty: when University College Dundee (UCD) opened in 1883, it had offered London University degrees until it was incorporated as a college of the University of St. Andrews in 1897.[105]

The offer of £40,000 to the municipal education authority had been made by George Bonar, a former President of the Dundee Chamber of Commerce. In 1918 the Chamber had endorsed the introduction of Junior and Senior Certificates in Commercial Education linked to courses at the Technical College. Bonar had at the same time offered an endowment of £25,000 to University College Dundee for higher commercial education, and discussion followed in St. Andrews concerning the possible recognition of the Senior Certificate as equivalent to the Preliminary Examination, the usual entry qualification.[106] A draft ordinance for a BCom was also prepared, but shortly afterwards an objection to the planned scheme was received from the University of Edinburgh, just planning its own BCom.[107] Although

[103] Minutes of Monthly Meeting of Dundee Education Authority, 10 January 1928, in Papers Relating to Modifications to George Bonar's Deed of Gift, MS 33/1 f. 204, University of Dundee Library Archives.

[104] See Alexander Dow, Sheila Dow, Alan Hutton, 'Applied Economics in a Political Economy Tradition: The Case of Scotland from the 1890s to the 1950s', *History of Political Economy* Vol. 32 Supplement (2000), pp. 183–85, for a summary of the teaching of political economy in the Scottish universities. The Edinburgh chair of 'Commercial and Political Economy and Mercantile Law' was endowed in 1870; the Adam Smith chair in Glasgow in 1896; a chair in political economy was founded in Aberdeen in 1921, and a lectureship at St. Andrews in 1921. The Glasgow economics class for accountants was introduced in 1933, and a separate Department of Commerce established in Edinburgh in 1920.

[105] D. Southgate, *University Education in Dundee*, Edinburgh University Press, Edinburgh 1982, p. 111.

[106] Entrance Board Minute, 22 November 1919, Correspondence referring to the foundation, finance and status of the Dundee School of Economics, 1930–1934 MS /33/9/1 f. 42, University of Dundee Library Archives. St. Andrews is a few miles down the coast from Dundee, 12 minutes on the train to Leuchars, the local station.

[107] Entrance Board Minute, 17 January 1920, MS /33/9/1 f. 55. See Appendix III for an outline of this degree.

the Principals of both St. Andrews and Dundee appear to have favoured the new scheme—they accepted the proposed revised entrance qualification—discussion was postponed and the plan for a Dundee BCom stalled.

Nonetheless, some commercial teaching did continue: from January 1924 lectures were given on Railway Law by a UCD lecturer; the following year there were lectures on railway geography, followed by railway operating, linked to an agreement between the Scottish Universities and the London and North Eastern Railway that they provide courses for managerial and clerical staff. In 1930 a request was made to the Principal of St. Andrews that trainee accountants be taught economics, rather than elementary political economy, for their final professional examination. This proposal was immediately rejected on the grounds that such non-graduate-level work had no place in the university. Hence there was during the 1920s a ready demand for formal commercial training in Dundee, but St. Andrews was reluctant to become too closely involved in vocational initiatives that did not involve degree-level activity.

It was this gap in the market that the Dundee School sought to fill. Bonar's Deed of Gift stipulated that a new commercial college should provide evening classes for those in full-time employment, and that the Senior Certificate of the Dundee Chamber of Commerce, or its equivalent, should be a requirement of entrance. Bonar now sought to fund the construction of a building for an entirely new institution rather than endow a university chair, and plans for this new departure were developed by Dundee's Education Committee. The new school was to be administered by a Committee of Management appointed by the Dundee Education Committee, and a Principal selected in consultation with the Chamber of Commerce. The Statement of Duties finalised in December 1930 required the Principal to develop a diploma course of university standard, open to both day and evening students; he was generally obliged to confer with the Education Committee and its officials, and his remuneration was to be £1000 per annum.[108] At the end of January 1930 the Town Clerk wrote to James Bowie and confirmed his appointment, to commence on 15 June 1931.[109] It is not recorded whether there were other candidates, nor is there evidence in the School's files of any other circumstances surrounding the appointment. Bowie was, however, an obvious choice: not only was he Scottish, he was also head of a broadly similar institution, the Department of Industrial Administration at Manchester's College of Technology.

Bowie, born in 1888, had entered Aberdeen University in 1909, the same year that he went into partnership with his father in the building trade.[110] Before joining the army in 1915, he prepared monthly reports on building and allied trades in the Aberdeen area, making regular visits to some 73 local firms. While being demobilised he applied, by telegram, on 24 February 1919, for a temporary post in the

[108] Statement of Duties to be Performed by Principal, and Conditions of Appointment, 13 December 1930, MS /33/9/1

[109] David Latts to Bowie, 30 January 1930, MS /33/9/1.

[110] The following details are taken from Bowie's application for the post of Head of the Department of Industrial Administration, Manchester Municipal College of Technology, September 1926. Filed on 7 October 1926. I would like to thank Joe Marsh, formerly of the Centre for the History of Science and Technology, University of Manchester Institute of Science and technology (UMIST), for his help in locating the remaining records of the Department of Industrial Administration, UMIST. UMIST was merged with the University of Manchester in October 2004 and these records are now the responsibility of the John Rylands University Library, University of Manchester.

new Department of Industrial Administration, Manchester Municipal College of Technology—the first such department to be established in Britain. It appears that he had been advised to apply for the post by R. B. Forrester, then Professor of Commerce in Aberdeen.[111] He was offered a six-month temporary appointment by return telegram, and in late May the appointment was made permanent.[112] By July, Bowie is recorded as giving evening lectures on topics such as Whitley Councils and Works Committees, Management, and Welfare; and he quickly developed as a specialist in industrial relations. In 1919 he applied, unsuccessfully, for a lectureship in commerce at the Technical College, Cardiff, and was one of two candidates interviewed for the new post of lecturer in commerce at Edinburgh.[113] He had in the meantime made a good impression in Manchester:

> ... he is possibly the most useful person in the Dept. He is not brilliant, but he has heaps of common sense, he works like a horse, he knows how to run things, & he is absolutely reliable. Without him the Lord knows what would happen—there'd be no non-scientific man in the whole staff.[114]

This suggests that Bowie was more practical than academic—his file testifies to his regular work training for local companies, and he also gave advice to a number of businesses on remuneration issues. In 1926 he was appointed Director of the Department. But Bowie was also an early contributor to the new genre of management literature, suggesting that his horizons lay beyond the immediate and practical orbit of department and local business.

This is apparent in the new preface for the 'Prospectus of Courses in Industrial Administration' that he drafted the following year, and which turns on a contrast of technical knowledge and administrative ability. More than half of technical graduates, he noted, move on to administrative positions where the prospects for promotion are better. Larger firms were able to provide appropriate managerial training for such employees, but the

> ... average firm can make no such provision. Moreover, the enormous amount of research and experiment, while illuminating the problems of management, has also revealed the common principles on which something approaching a science of management can be constructed.[115]

[111] J. A. Bowie, Personnel File, Manchester College of Technology.

[112] Meeting of 30 May 1919, Minutes of the Committee on Industrial Administration, Manchester College of Technology, 1918–1926.

[113] Note from Bowie to Principal, 25 February 1920, J. A. Bowie, Personnel File. This would have been for the post in Organisation of Industry and Commerce which was endowed in 1919 by subscription on the part of members of the Edinburgh Chamber of Commerce and the Merchant Company of Edinburgh; see *Edinburgh University Calendar 1919–1920*, p. 6. William Oliver was appointed; *Calendar 1924–25*, p. vi.

[114] Murray Wrong to Garnett, 1 July 1920, in Bowie's personnel file.

[115] Manchester Municipal College of Technology, Prospectus of Courses in Industrial Administration, Session 1927–1928 (Manchester 1927), pp. 3–4. These remarks elaborated a brief paragraph in earlier versions describing the two-year full-time course; see Prospectus of Courses in Industrial Administration, Session 1921–1922, p. 6.

This general line of argument is elaborated in Bowie's *Education for Business Management*, demonstrating the distance commercial and business education had already travelled from the dilemmas outlined earlier. The book opened with a survey of business problems, and the contribution that business education might make in resolving them. He noted that there was an increasing need to have a detailed knowledge of markets, requiring in turn an efficient utilisation of capacity if this knowledge were to be effectively exploited. Market growth was accompanied by the growth of business units, which was in turn linked to an increasing separation of ownership from control. This sharpened the function of management, but he laid most emphasis upon the consequences of rationalisation for business organisation. In the later 1920s this was a new concept; Bowie summarised its significance as follows:

> The predominant feature of rationalization seems to be an attempt to replace the kind of competition that leads to destructive price-cutting by mutual agreement on a common production and sales policy. Its central aim seems to be to avoid those price wars which always develop between unco-ordinated producers when the requirements of the market are less than the total productive capacity of the industry. This means either complete amalgamation, or the closest co-operation between the units. Trusts and cartels are no new things. The difference lies in this, that the older combines tended to rely on their fighting power to maintain high prices through restricting output, while the newer rely ostensibly on their power to effect economies and increase efficiency so as to enable prices to be reduced and markets extended accordingly. The problem is one purely of organization and administration. It implies a deliberate concentration on low costs of production, by sectionalizing out and allocating it to the most efficient works, by closing down unremunerative or redundant works, or departments, with due regard to maintenance or reserve plant to meet any sudden extension of demand, by the installation of the best cost-saving machinery, by the prevention of waste of effort, materials or mechanical energy, and by the centralized control of both purchasing and selling.[116]

There are two important features of this analysis—it anticipates later discussion of overcapacity and imperfect competition, and it links market developments to internal business reorganisation in which management plays a central role. The unit of control is no longer the department, but the business as a whole, implying a shift from departmental to functional management—labour, production, planning, process, equipment, purchasing, and sales management. The state now played a mediating role, protecting the interests of employers, consumers, employees, and investors.[117] The scope of management has been extended, and specialised training was now required for the effective conduct of the modern business enterprise.

The ideal curriculum that Bowie put forward in his book was divided into three, corresponding to the three years of an undergraduate degree. The first year would be spent on general subjects—history of industry, social sciences and economics, and

[116] James A. Bowie, *Education for Business Management*, Oxford University Press, London 1930, pp. 12–13.

[117] Ibid., pp. 13, 17.

industrial psychology. This would be followed by 'tool subjects': general accounting, cost accounting, business statistics, factory and commercial law, précis, reports, and correspondence. The third element covered 'operative subjects' which were common to all businesses: industrial fatigue and efficiency, industrial relations, works organisation and management, office administration, marketing, and transportation.[118] Several pages are given over to the case study method recently pioneered at the Harvard Business School, while the importance of works visits is also lent emphasis.

As a blueprint for an undergraduate training in business administration, this outline has much to commend it; but it remained a blueprint. Bowie moved to Dundee, where his chance at executing his vision was fatally undermined by the rather different vision of the staff recruited to teach there, and the fact that its teaching was determined by the LSE BCom.

It is evident from the inaugural address of Sir Josiah Stamp that Bowie wrote the prospectus for the Dundee School, since Stamp's summary of it recapitulates the view of business education contained in the 1927 Manchester Prospectus and in Bowie's own book.[119] Stamp also outlined the aims of the School:

> A broad economic outlook and social perspective.
>
> A knowledge of the basic principles of modern industry, and of the directions in which it is tending to develop.
>
> A specialised knowledge of one area of industry, with specific reference to the student's future career.
>
> Contact with actual industry as it is conducted by some of the most progressive firms today.
>
> A training in the methods of investigation and research, which will enable them to keep abreast of the changing conditions of the times.[120]

The link to the LSE was made clear by the attendance at the opening ceremony of William Beveridge, Director of the London School of Economics, and the ubiquitous Jessy Mair, the School Secretary, who it turns out had attended Dundee High School and so had a personal interest in the development of the institution.

The first staff appointments were made in early summer 1931. Garnet Wilson, Chairman of the Dundee Education Committee, not Bowie, Director of the School, travelled to London to consult with Lionel Robbins, Arnold Plant, and Josiah Stamp about suitable candidates. Wilson wrote to Bowie that Robbins and Plant were especially keen that he consider one particular candidate, 'a most promising lad, with all the Elements within him'.[121] Jack Gilbert, the candidate in question, later attributed

[118] Ibid., pp. 82–83. The same structure and listing are elaborated in Ch. 7 on the industrial administration curriculum, pp. 144–52. The inclusion of fatigue and efficiency, industrial relations, and office administration marks this ideal curriculum off from all other courses of study in British universities at the time, which generally gave more emphasis to languages, law, and accounting.

[119] Sir Josiah Stamp, 'Education and Economics', *Inaugural Address*, School of Economics and Commerce, Dundee 1931, p. 7: MS 33/9/1(3) University of Dundee Library Archives.

[120] Stamp, 'Education and Economics', p. 8.

[121] Wilson to Bowie, Waldorf Hotel, London, 18 June 1931; MS/33/9/1 University of Dundee Library Archives.

his appointment at Dundee to Jessy Mair's intervention, since she was aware of his financial straits as a young assistant at LSE.[122] Gilbert had read for a BCom at the LSE, but in his second-year course on money and banking he had been taught by Gregory. Consequently he was familiar with the writings of Robertson and Keynes, and capable of presenting monetary analysis in the context of either economics or of commerce. This was not true of the other appointment made at this time—Jack Eastham (1901–1993) had graduated in economics from the LSE in 1930 and found work as Secretary of the London and Cambridge Economics Service before moving to Dundee to cover basic teaching in economics. He was to succeed Bowie as Acting Principal in 1949 and oversee the final development of the School as a full-time centre for the study of the London BSc (Econ). The two appointments made the following year brought the actual course upon which the School had embarked into even starker relief: Ronald Coase, having completed a London BCom in two years had had to wait until 1932 to graduate, upon which he was appointed to a lectureship in Dundee. The fourth permanent member of staff was not from the LSE; but in 1932 the School appointed Duncan Black, who had studied mathematics and economics in Glasgow. Black and Coase stayed for the two years in which daytime and evening diploma teaching became established as the core of the School's programme.

A summary of the teaching from mid-1933 clarifies the distribution of responsibilities.[123] The two-year diploma, in this second year of the School's existence, was dominated by evening students.[124] Gilbert covered banking and finance, applied economics, international trade, industrial relations, and industrial fluctuations; Eastham taught economics, statistical method, marketing, problems of modern industry, and problems of business policy; Black covered economic history,[125] raw materials of industry, and commerce; and Coase taught structure of industry, business administration, and organisation of the business unit.[126] Besides this, there was teaching in commercial law and accounting by local part-time staff.

Quite obviously this structure of teaching is based almost entirely on the LSE BCom curriculum; its core could be described as a kind of applied economics. Bowie himself had no regular teaching commitment at Dundee; he mainly concerned himself with attracting students, raising funds, and establishing links with Scottish business.[127]

[122] Interview with Jack Gilbert, Sheffield, 17 June 1994. Gilbert stayed at Dundee until 1941, moved to a lectureship in economics at Manchester in 1945, and was then appointed Senior Lecturer at Sheffield, where he was Professor of Economics 1957–1973.

[123] Letter from James Bowie to Sir James Irvine, Principal of the University of St. Andrews, 9 June 1933, MS/33/9/1 University of Dundee Library Archives.

[124] Whose average age at entrance was 22, compared to the day students' average of 19—the latter being a couple of years older than the usual age upon entrance to a Scottish university. See Appendix for details of attendances by year and course of study.

[125] When Black left in 1934 he was replaced by an economic historian, T. S. Willan, who in turn was replaced in 1936 by Edgar Lythe, who had studied history and geography at Cambridge, but while working at University College, Hull had begun teaching on their external London BCom course. Interview with Edgar Lythe, Broughty Ferry, 5 July 1994.

[126] It was in the context of this course that Coase developed the ideas for his article 'The Nature of the Firm', *Economica* n.s. Vol. 4, pp. 386–405. See, for an account of his teaching in Dundee, Oliver E. Williamson, Sidney G. Winter (eds.) *The Nature of the Firm: Origins, Evolution, and Development*, Oxford University Press, New York 1991, p. 35.

[127] Interview with S. G. E. Lythe. See also his 'Introduction' to C. Blake, S. G. E. Lythe (eds.) *A Maverick Institution*, Gee & Co., London 1981, pp. iii–xiii.

Hence the programme of study that Bowie had developed in Manchester and outlined in his book on business education was never realised in Dundee. He did attract a number of good students to a one-year postgraduate diploma in which he sought to develop some teaching in business studies, but this never became a central part of the School's work. The principal effect of this was to make the existing undergraduate BCom look more like an ordinary (as opposed to honours), and hence inferior, economics degree. Even the chartered accountants in Dundee were taught a conventional economics course by Eastham, recognised by the Institute of Chartered Accountants and Actuaries as equivalent to the Glasgow University class.[128]

Bowie sought to reforge the connection to St. Andrews, with a view to making the School a college of the university offering a St. Andrews BCom, as had been mooted shortly after the end of the Great War. It was clearly recognised that the expansion of the School rested on the existence of daytime courses leading to a university degree; but here he once again encountered difficulties related to entry requirements, since the Dundee School admitted students with certificates issued by the Chamber of Commerce, and St. Andrews did not consider that these fulfilled their own entry requirements.[129]

During the war the School closed entirely, reopening in 1946 with a strong demand for courses leading to the BCom and BSc (Econ). The underlying evolution here was towards economics degrees, the LSE finally merging the BCom into the BSc (Econ) during the 1948–1949 session; from the autumn of 1949 new students had to register for the one degree. There had also been revived local discussion of the prospects for a University of Dundee, rendering University College Dundee independent of St. Andrews, and offering the prospect of merging the School into the new institution as a Faculty of Social Science. The first official report on this proposal noted that:

> 44. It is plain that the future of the School is complicated by three factors which make its incorporation into a University a matter of some difficulty. (a) By concentrating on specialised courses within narrow fields it has diverged from the Scottish University tradition; (b) the provision of evening tuition to students who are engaged by day in ordinary avocations is incompatible with Scottish University educational methods; (c) some of the tuition offered by the School would appear to be on a sub-University level.
>
> 45. Upon a long view it seems most undesirable that the School should aim at preserving a separate existence as a tributary of a distant English University, and engaging, so far as regards subsidiary subjects, in a good deal of duplication of effort with existing agencies.[130]

128 Which, as noted earlier, was taught by Alec Cairncross from 1935—see his account of this in Keith Tribe (ed.) *Economic Careers: Economics and Economic Careers in Britain 1930–1970*, Routledge, London 1997, pp. 42–43.

129 See 'Memorandum on Proposed Scheme of Affiliation, 7 July 1932 (draft)' in MS/33/9/1, University of Dundee Library Archives.

130 Scottish Office, *Report of the Inquiry appointed in February 1949 to review and report on the organisation of university education in Dundee and its relationship with St Andrews University*, HMSO Edinburgh 1949 (Cooper Report). The allegation that some of the teaching of the School was of 'sub-University' standard was rebutted with the observation that every regular course of lectures 'is required for a degree

This Report was dated 24 June 1949. On 1 September 1949 Bowie suddenly died, and Eastham became Acting Principal. The School was now headed by an economist who sought incorporation of the School in a new university institution in Dundee, with himself as Professor of Economics. He was also pressured from the municipal side, since the new local Director of Education had no interest in the current work of the School, seeking to use the building for purely practical tuition in shorthand, typing, and bookkeeping for 15- and 16-year-old girls. Although this could be forestalled by reference to the original Deed of Gift, the new focus on economics would require additional staff, and the resources for that would not be forthcoming from the local authority.[131]

Eastham's position at this time was expressed in his response to the Carr Saunders report on commercial education:[132]

> Within the terms of the definitions of vocational education and vocational training in the report our work at the School lies very definitely on the side of vocational education. Originally there was some vocational training in the curriculum but when Bowie gave me control of academic matters about 1932 I gradually eliminated it. Unfortunately he always talked outside as if we were mainly concerned with vocational training. There is of course no very clear line between the two....

There are only two BCom degrees in this country which are worthy of being called university degrees. One of them, in London, disappears in 1955 because it is undistinguishable from an economics degree, and the other at Birmingham is an economics degree in all but name.

> ... I think the technical and commercial colleges will have the greatest difficulty in tackling the new external London B.Sc. (Econ.) Degree. They appear to herd a small number of degree students into large general purpose classes where if the teaching is intelligible to the majority it will be useless for degree students. The introduction of new compulsory subjects will make this method impossible and they will either have to set up specialised courses for their small numbers of degree students or drop the degree work altogether. As an examiner for London degrees I know what an appalling waste of human effort is involved in the present procedure of many technical colleges.[133]

or diploma examination of London University. It is true that the School admits students who are not qualified for entry to a university but the lectures they attend and the examinations they sit are nevertheless of university standard.' 'The Cooper Report and the School of Economics', Appendix I, Draft Agenda of the Meeting of Further Education Sub Committee, School of Economics, 22 September 1949, MS 33/10/1(2) University of Dundee Library Archives.

[131] Eastham to Wimberley, 4 January 1950, and to Herbert Bonar, 17 March 1950, in Correspondence—Eastham, MS 33/10/2 University of Dundee Library Archives.

[132] A. M. Carr-Saunders, *Report of a Special Committee on Education for Commerce*, HMSO, London 1949—a major review of the history and development of commercial education in Britain at all levels. It has not been discussed in the foregoing since university-level commercial education was by this time being folded into the teaching of economics. It remains a valuable and thorough survey of relevance to the history of postwar educational initiatives.

[133] Eastham to Wimberley, 26 January 1950, in Correspondence—Eastham, MS 33/10/2 University of Dundee Library Archives.

The situation in Dundee was resolved by a Royal Commission, rejecting the idea of the School as the core of an independent university in Dundee. In 1953 an Act of Parliament dissolved the School and transferred its assets to St. Andrews, members of the teaching staff of the School becoming members of Queen's College, Dundee. This process was not completed until 1955, and Eastham's hopes of a professorial position in the new institution were dashed:[134] Archie Campbell, Senior Lecturer in Political Economy at Glasgow, was appointed Professor of Economics over his head.

Eastham's forte was as a teacher of undergraduate economics; he published two textbooks based on his teaching in Dundee, *An Introduction to Economic Analysis* in 1950, and *Graphical Economics* in 1960, published in Pennycuick's 'Management Science Series', presenting the principles of his first book in such a way that they might appeal to business executives. The 1950 work can best be summarised as a judicious update of Frederic Benham's *Economics*, first published in 1938.[135] Nonetheless, the way in which Eastham's text points south to the LSE provides yet further evidence of the influence exerted by the LSE in the teaching of economics and commerce in Britain, eventually imposing the teaching of economics upon students who had previously elected to study commerce.

The very limited demand from students for the teaching of economics in interwar Britain has been shown earlier in the figures that Michael Sanderson derived from Universities Grants Committee data, estimating the total output of honours economics graduates. As outlined in this chapter, the LSE began operation in 1895 as an institution whose teaching was directed primarily to those with vocationally-related demands. Before 1914 the School developed as the prime national exemplar of commercial education—part-time students taught by professional part-time teachers, responding to a large and growing demand for such tuition. The fact that most students were in their twenties further underlines this vocational commitment. Hayek's account of the School up to the mid-1940s makes very clear that after 1920 this altered into a full-time model for both staff and students, with school-leavers coming to predominate among the student intake. Although evening students were still a significant group into the 1930s, the reliance on teaching short courses gave way to teaching for degree qualifications. The LSE came late to the BCom, coincidentally at the same time that Oxford introduced its PPE degree. The new commerce degree was, however, an immediate success, attracting numbers of students both internally and externally, and was a major source of direct and indirect funding for the School. The number of honours economics students remained a minority in the BSc (Econ) up to 1939, but the presence of a number of graduate students, new appointments in economics, and the way in which the School sought to distinguish itself from Cambridge gave credence to a reputation that the School was a centre for undergraduate training in economics equal to Cambridge. This was not true, but all the same it was a public reputation that raised the national profile of the School. By the later 1940s economics was at last becoming a popular subject to study, and the LSE was perceived as central to such study.

134 See his application for the Chair of Applied Economics in Queen's College, Dundee, University of St. Andrews—MS 33/10/1 (18) University of Dundee Library Archives.

135 Eastham's work is placed in the context of contemporary teaching texts in the following chapter, p. 361.

All the same, it was too late, and too small. The courses taught at the LSE did shape the teaching of economics, politics, and sociology in Britain during the second half of the twentieth century, but the small size of the university system meant that it could not compete with the American system, where teaching at the graduate level became important. The shift towards student entry at age 18 limited the pool of potential students since in Britain few students completed schooling to the age of 18; taught postgraduate education in economics did not become established until the 1960s, and careers based on possession of an economics PhD occurred even later. Lionel Robbins's ambitions for the teaching of economics in Britain, dragging it away from vocational courses to a respectably rigorous and systematic academic framework, met with some success, but by the time that the LSE was firmly established as the centre for the teaching of economics in Britain the country itself had ceded leadership in the discipline to the United States. This general course of development will be outlined in the following chapter.

12

The Scientisation of Economics

When Allyn Young[1] arrived at the LSE in the autumn of 1927, he made no immediate changes to teaching for the BSc (Econ). While this restraint might well demonstrate the prudence, judgement, and modesty on which others remarked after his death in 1929, his appointment had initially been for only three years, at his own request. We also know that before his death he had recently received offers from Harvard and Chicago.[2] His appointment as a replacement for Cannan was nonetheless a significant departure, using Rockefeller money to signal the international standing of the School in the developing field of economics. Although his death was widely lamented, he had yet to make any direct impact on the work of the School, besides lending it his reputation.

Lionel Robbins, his successor in 1929, lacked Young's breadth of experience, his facility in economic analysis, understanding of statistical methods, and empirical knowledge; the School was more or less all he knew, besides two spells in Oxford tutoring PPE students.[3] After his appointment to the LSE, Robbins showed little or no interest in any other academic position, temporary or otherwise, remaining at the School for over four decades until he stepped down as chair of the governors in 1973.[4] However, the natural association of Robbins and the LSE that we might make today was not then inevitable. By chance, at the age of 30, he had found himself back where he felt he belonged, and in a position to actively make this place his own. His success in so doing created our sense of inevitability. That he had then no intention of moving on is obscured by our knowledge that he would not do so. The new appointment gave him a platform and an opportunity, and he immediately turned to making changes that Young had not. In so doing, he not only made the changes that Young had not; he made changes that Young would not have made, forging a very different understanding of what economics was, and what it was for.

[1] Allyn Young was born in Ohio in 1876 and died in London during March 1929, of pneumonia following a bout of influenza. He had graduated from college in 1892, then worked in the printing trade before enrolling in the graduate programme at Wisconsin in 1898. In 1900 he worked for one year as an assistant in the US Bureau of the Census, then returned to Wisconsin, where he gained his doctorate in 1902. He taught in various universities up to 1914, when he was a founding member of the American Statistical Association; was Director of the Bureau of Statistical Research for the War Trade Board 1917–1918; and then led the economic team associated with planning for the Paris Peace Conference. From 1920 he was Professor of Economics at Harvard. A good account of his personality and academic career can be found in Ramesh Chandra, *Allyn Abbott Young*, Palgrave Macmillan, Cham 2020, pp. 7–16. Chandra also emphasises Young's style of teaching (pp. 235–59), which bears comparison with that of Marshall.

[2] See T. E. Gregory's obituary, *Economic Journal* Vol. 39 (1929), p. 298.

[3] See Susan Howson, *Lionel Robbins*, Cambridge University Press, Cambridge 2011, pp. 130f, for his duties in 1924–1925; his appointment as a New College Lecturer during 1927–1928 primarily involved tutorial work for the college, although he did also give some intercollegiate lectures (pp. 151–52).

[4] As Susan Howson notes, his retirement was a process starting in 1961 and ending only in 1973; *Lionel Robbins*, p. 1022.

Constructing Economic Science. Keith Tribe, Oxford University Press. © Oxford University Press 2022.
DOI: 10.1093/oso/9780190491741.003.0012

Unlike at Oxford and Cambridge, 'teaching' at the LSE meant lecturing.[5] Rather paradoxically, those following the BSc (Econ) course externally, like Ronnie Tress at Southampton, might benefit from personal tuition,[6] whereas all early student accounts of Robbins at the LSE comment only on his polished lecturing style. Neither Sam Goldman nor Bernard Corry, internal LSE students from the early 1930s and late 1940s, respectively,[7] suggested in their interviews that classes had been an important medium of teaching, or that they had experienced regular personal contact with members of staff. By contrast, Dennis Coppock's account of his undergraduate education implied that classes were central to teaching in postwar Manchester; supported by Marjorie Tivey's contrast of studying first for an ordinary degree and then switching to honours at Manchester during the early 1940s.[8] The six years intervening between Robbins's graduation from the LSE in 1923 and his appointment to a chair in 1929 had been divided between Oxford and the LSE; between the personal familiarity of New College tutorials and small lectures, and the remoteness of lecturing to assorted groups of day and evening students at the LSE. The role of lectures as the prime form of teaching at the LSE is lent emphasis by the absence from the archives of any systematic internal record of courses followed by individual students.[9] The allocation of students and staff to classes naturally generates a student record; attendance at lectures is not usually so recorded. Susan Howson's account of undergraduate teaching at the LSE during the 1930s relies on the *Calendar* and Robbins's own lecture notes because this is more or less all there is.

When Robbins took charge of the teaching of undergraduate economics at the LSE in 1929, he did not seek to modify this reliance on the formal lecture as the prime medium of teaching. There was no specific shortage of persons capable of teaching classes, nor of money to hire part-time teachers. But such a reorganisation would have required a great deal of time and negotiation, and there is no indication that Robbins ever contemplated such a path. Instead, he expanded the number of lecture courses. Some of this was cosmetic. Student demand for such an apparently wide-ranging programme did not yet exist; in some cases he relied on the same basic teaching sources

[5] That is, a prepared monologic presentation to any number of auditors, as opposed to a class organised around group discussion or a set of problems, and so in the British context no more than 10 to 15 students. As emphasised previously, in Oxford and Cambridge from the 1920s 'teaching' was primarily done through weekly 'tutorials' or 'supervisions' in which one, or perhaps two, students presented an essay to a tutor/supervisor. Lectures were and are optional; in Cambridge today a course of study in the humanities and social sciences is represented by a reading list, not by any one set of lectures. By the 1950s it was usual outside Oxbridge for principal courses to be a weekly lecture linked to a weekly class for about a dozen students.

[6] See the interview with Tress in Keith Tribe, *Economic Careers*, Routledge, London 1997, p. 110.

[7] Sam Goldman graduated from the LSE with a BSc (Econ) in 1932, Bernard Corry in 1951. Ronnie Tress graduated with an external degree in 1936.

[8] Marjorie Tivey studied initially for an ordinary BA in Social Administration in Manchester, beginning in 1940. She followed John Hicks's lecture course, the substance of which became *The Social Framework*. This lecture course was attended by about one hundred students drawn from geography, law, commerce, economics, and administration. There were no related classes, but in her second year she switched to honours economics, for which there were classes. By her third year the men had all been called up and the only other woman on the course had failed her Part I, so Marjorie was taught one-to-one by John Hicks and Hans Singer. Interview with Marjorie Tivey, Hall Green, Birmingham, 11 October 2000.

[9] An annotated alphabetical list of graduates 1895–1932 exists (216 pages of student records, around 12 to 18 per page) from which it would be possible to compile a list of students specialising in economics in their final year; *Register 1895–1932*, London School of Economics and Political Science 1934.

that had been in use at the LSE for some years, repackaging existing courses; and added to this, there are inconsistencies in his recommendations of foreign-language texts that suggest Robbins was not himself that familiar with them—and certainly not as familiar with the German language as he wished to appear. Taken together, these factors are suggestive of hasty improvisation, more of a concern to make a point than to make a change. The Memorandum that he drafted early in 1930 did indicate his wish to focus on what he described as 'maintrack' economics—a more uniform mainstream economics that had not hitherto existed. Robbins's early years at the LSE are certainly marked by ambition, and a self-confidence bordering on arrogance. There are clear signs that he knew less than he thought he did, and that the 'new course' that he set for the teaching of economics was hastily assembled from existing, familiar, or even dated elements. My purpose in pointing to this is not, however, to denigrate Robbins. Self-belief and ignorance are important assets for those set on bringing about rapid institutional change; self-conscious reformers often begin by rearranging and relabelling what already exists, adding a gloss of novelty where possible. The path that Robbins chose, extending and revising courses of lectures, and presenting this revision in the name of a 'science', would in time prove very significant in reshaping a disciplinary pedagogy. To see how he achieved this, we need to understand the means that he used to do so.

'Science' was the initial gloss that Robbins employed: an epistemological claim, that economics was a science and so by definition beyond public knowledge; and a demarcation device, distinguishing his own version of economics as one superior to all the others, and so the sole legitimate form of economic knowledge. This is the origin of what became recognised as 'neoclassical economics'; although as noted earlier,[10] if this is a usage common enough today, it took a long time to become first a neutral self-description, and then a pejorative designation. It was the same with Robbins's definition of economics as 'the science which studies human behaviour as a relationship between ends and scarce means which have alternative uses'—this familiar formulation took many years to become familiar.[11]

As Robbins made clear in his January 1930 Inaugural Lecture, and then in 1932 with his *Nature and Significance of Economic Science*, his deliberate rupture with the Marshallian heritage turned on the promotion of economics as a formal, abstract science. However, while arguing in his Inaugural Lecture from the position that economics should be regarded as a special kind of arcane knowledge, the examples of 'theoretical work' that he then advanced were broad-brush and general. He spoke in the name of a science; but talked as a methodologist, not in terms of economic theory. He referred not to the public purpose of economic analysis, nor to the way in which students might be trained to develop their knowledge for the public good, but to the esoteric nature of a 'science' inaccessible to common understanding. This was new. Frank Knight's *Risk, Uncertainty and Profit* had opened with a chapter devoted to the nature of economic science;[12] but this was not an aspect of the book that

[10] See Chapter 1, fn. 39.

[11] As demonstrated by Roger E. Backhouse, Steven G. Medema, 'Defining Economics: The Long Road to Acceptance of the Robbins Definition', *Economica* Vol. 76 (2009), pp. 805–20.

[12] Frank H. Knight, *Risk, Uncertainty and Profit*, Houghton Mifflin Company, Boston 1921. Ch. 1, 'The Place of Uncertainty in Economic Theory', is in fact a methodological appraisal of contemporary economics.

attracted much attention, nor was Knight's purpose then to emphasise that economic knowledge was esoteric knowledge. A review of the contents of the leading American and British journals through the 1920s reveals no special interest in the idea that methodological debate represented a productive way forward for the emerging discipline. The third-year course of lectures Robbins announced for the 1930 summer term on 'The Nature of Economics and Its Significance in Relation to the Kindred Social Sciences' does not mention Knight. Instead, among the books recommended Neville Keynes's *Scope and Method of Political Economy* (1891) is the most obviously 'methodological' reference, but the list also includes Sidgwick's *Principles of Political Economy* (1883) and Pigou's *Economics of Welfare* (1920).[13] Neville Keynes did define political economy 'as the science which treats of the phenomena arising out of the economic activities of mankind in society',[14] but this statement was not intended to associate political economy with a unitary 'science', rather to demarcate the moral from the physical sciences, and the social from the moral sciences.[15] Neither Sidgwick, nor Pigou, nor any of the other sources listed, displayed any great interest in arguing that the legitimacy of economic arguments derived from their being 'scientific'; nor did they imply that 'science' was an especially arcane, restricted form of knowledge.

Allyn Young's Inaugural Lecture

To see more clearly what Robbins understood 'maintrack' economics to be, and how his Inaugural Lecture presented this idea, we can first examine the views expressed in his predecessor's Inaugural, less than three years earlier. Young had also begun with a reference to 'economic science', but attached no great weight to the term, noting only two thoughts that would strike a contemporary economist seeking a 'general view of the present state of economic science'. The first was the inadequacy of present knowledge, and that the economist was in general little better prepared to deal with new questions than a layman would be. The second was that, despite this, there was much in recent experience on which an economist could draw, but that these recent events for the most part recapitulated old problems, on which economists had been proved right.[16] 'Nineteenth-century English political economy' was here a body of knowledge that was, despite current differences, generally acknowledged to be an important common heritage. And so he addressed his remarks to an exploration of what it was about this heritage that provided a common resource for contemporary economists. He sought to establish what modern economics was by considering what economists had done.

It was not as though English political economy had been immune to criticism from positivists, romanticists, mathematical economists, and historical economists. The

[13] *LSE Calendar 1929–30*, pp. 106–107.

[14] John Neville Keynes, *The Scope and Method of Political Economy*, Macmillan, London 1891, p. 97.

[15] Neville Keynes's statement came at the close of Ch. III, 'On the Character and Definition of Political Economy Regarded as a Positive Science', and was immediately followed by the qualification, 'It is not pretended that this or any other definition can by itself suffice unambiguously to express the nature of economics.'

[16] Allyn A. Young, 'English Political Economy', *Economica* No. 22 (1928), pp. 1–2.

point was that, despite such criticism, its methods, categories, and procedures had found their way into the 'working apparatus of competent economists'.[17] What was it that lent English political economy this flexibility and vitality? Firstly, that it was an 'eminently practical subject':

> It did not come into being because men decided that here was a gap which the existing sciences left uncovered. It was not created *in vacuo*, but grew out of men's attempts to deal intelligently with large questions of national concern.... The periods when political economy has ceased its frontal attacks upon the communal problems of economic life and has turned inward upon itself to contemplate its own perfections or imperfections, or has occupied itself with questions of its proper 'method' or of its standing as a 'science' have been sterile periods. Economic theory, divorced from its functional relations to economic problems, or with those relations obscured, is no better than an interesting intellectual game.[18]

Nor was there a meaningful distinction between 'pure' and 'applied' economics; the future development of 'economic theory' would not come from 'theorists', but instead from those seeking to forge instruments 'that will help towards a better knowledge of how to deal with the communal problems of organised economic life.'[19]

The English political economists

> ... did not proceed by drawing inferences from assumptions about the nature of man or of the universe. Instead they inquired into the common place facts of the world about them and into such others as they could conveniently lay hold of.[20]

In making such inquiries, the economist 'had need of insight, imagination, breadth of view, and complete intellectual honesty'.

> It is worth remembering that one great English economist, especially distinguished for his achievements in mathematical economics, quoted approvingly the observation of another great English economist that much economic work 'has less need of elaborate analytical methods than of a shrewd mother-wit, of a sound sense of proportion, and of a large experience of life.'[21]

And so Young recruits Edgeworth to endorse Marshall's description of the qualities required of the economist, and in so doing associates himself with Marshall's conception of economics as dealing with the 'ordinary business of life', reinforced later by the assertion that

[17] Ibid., p. 3.
[18] Ibid., pp. 4–5.
[19] Ibid., p. 5.
[20] Ibid., p. 6.
[21] Ibid. p. 7, citing Edgeworth, review of the third edition of *Principles of Economics*, p. 102, reprinted in *Papers Relating to Political Economy* Vol. III, Macmillan, London 1925, p. 64 [and not p. 67 as given by Young].

> [t]he most important thing a student of political economy gets from his training is not the possession of a body of 'economic truth' but command of an intellectual technique. Confronted by a new problem he knows how to find his bearings and how to work his way through to some sort of reasoned conclusion.[22]

The general position that Young outlines here is entirely compatible with that embraced by Marshall, Pigou, and also Maynard Keynes, whose introduction to the Cambridge Economics Handbook began by stating that

> [t]he Theory of Economics does not furnish a body of settled conclusions immediately applicable to policy. It is a method rather than a doctrine, an apparatus of the mind, a technique of thinking, which helps its possessor to draw correct conclusions.

The brief introduction was concluded by noting a lack of complete unity of opinion among 'professional students of the subject'. Nonetheless, eventually research 'should clear up controversy. But, for the moment, controversy and doubt are increased.'[23] Keynes clearly considered the latter to be a quite normal state, to be overcome by research and debate, not by the imposition of a unitary methodology.

And this stance was shared by Allyn Young, who after noting some of the limitations of English political economy, proposed that part of the legacy of Jevons was the 'most promising recent line of development'. This was, he added, not really the Jevons of *Theory of Political Economy*; instead, it was his 'path-making statistical inquiries' that would assist in broadening 'the empirical outlook of economists.' 'New facts' 'challenge the accuracy of our observations and the adequacy of our systems; they put new problems before us ....' The manipulation of averages, aggregates, and their relationships was an important new tool, but one that was apt to be misunderstood, or even exaggerated. Inferences could be drawn, but the capacity to make predictions on this basis was limited, suggesting tendencies but hardly ever defining them.[24] Young presents statistical work as essentially idiographic, while theoretical work is nomothetic, a distinction that also allows for an attention to history, which 'leads to new appraisals of our economic order, and to a realisation of the variety and mutability of the institutional patterns which direct our energies into one path rather than another, and which thus establish the general framework within which, at any given time, the economic life of a society proceeds.'[25] He made clear that he sought in English political economy only those features that had contributed positively to contemporary knowledge; he was not engaged in evaluation or critique. As he pragmatically noted in conclusion, 'economic science will be made into a more perfect instrument only by continually renewing and extending its contacts with life.'[26]

[22] Young, 'English Political Economy', p. 14.

[23] John Maynard Keynes, 'Introduction to the Series', in Maurice Dobb, *Wages*, Nisbet and Co., London 1928, pp. v, vi.

[24] Young, 'English Political Economy', pp. 8, 9. 10.

[25] Ibid., p. 12.

[26] Ibid., p. 15.

Lionel Robbins's Inaugural Lecture

I have outlined in some detail the stance taken by Young in his 1927 Inaugural so that the novelty of the position taken by Robbins in 1930 stands out more clearly. Robbins's point of departure in 1930 appears at first to be similar to that of Young. Posing the question: 'What is the present position of Economic Science?' he considers first the heritage: Ricardo, Marshall, John Stuart Mill, and Jevons, all of them authors also directly or indirectly included in Young's 'English Political Economy'.[27] He then summons two illustrations of current debate—the quantity theory of money and the general theory of price. The approach is more discursive than that of Young, but at the same time presumes that Robbins has a more particular knowledge of the subject-matter of economics than his audience. In examining current deficiencies, he asks: 'May I try, without being too technical, to indicate very briefly some of the main deficiencies of which we are becoming conscious?'[28] He implies that his own technical knowledge is beyond the capacity of his audience (which included Maynard Keynes, directly addressed on the previous page); but in fact he talks only in the vaguest way about technical issues, name-checking Knut Wicksell and D. H. Robertson but saying little of what these names stand for, and against.[29]

Next he discusses deficiencies in the logical structure of existing theory. He alludes to the cost controversies of the 1920s briefly discussed in Chapter 6, concluding that today 'only the writers of cram textbooks and the examiners in certain elementary examinations ... assume that the laws of cost are simple.'[30] These kinds of problem, suggests Robbins, are very difficult, although he does not say why this might be. Then he asks for the indulgence of his audience: if he 'might become very technical for a moment', he explains that the 'old plan of analysing "one thing at a time" has definitely broken down'—an awkward allusion to partial equilibrium that does not even make use of the term *ceteris paribus*. This problem had been resolved by the 'theoretical prescience of the School of Lausanne' who recommended the adoption of methods 'which would have prevented its occurrence'.[31] He does not explain what these methods were.

The third deficiency of contemporary economics concerns the over-simplicity of 'assumptions'—that these are either too simple or do not connect to 'the facts'. He first refers to the way that the short-run equalisation of rates of pay depends upon the assumption that the population is increasing; but all Robbins does here is advance a different assumption, that population growth was slowing; he advances no 'facts'. In this instance it would have been quite possible to dispense with assumptions altogether and consider some demographic evidence, as Robbins had himself done during 1928 in his first talk in Oxford to the Political Economy Club. As Howson notes, at the time the issue of a falling birth rate was recognised, and it continued to be discussed

[27] Lionel Robbins, 'The Present Position of Economic Science', *Economica* No. 28 (March 1930), p. 15.

[28] Ibid., p. 17.

[29] '... no one, I think, can examine the path-breaking work of Mr. D. H. Robertson in this connection, without the conviction that perhaps here, in the future, are to be forged some of the most powerful instruments of policy.' Ibid., p. 17.

[30] Ibid., p. 18.

[31] Ibid., p. 18.

throughout the 1930s.[32] The other example he takes is that of international trade, much of which involves arguments about differential wage rates, where again the availability of evidence might seem to make assumptions superfluous.

The final main section of the Inaugural Lecture is devoted to a discussion of method—whether economics is too deductive or too inductive, countering the work of 'the theorist' to that of 'the statistician' in a polarisation that leads only to an equivocal resolution. Robbins is, however, unequivocal about the general conclusion that he draws from his presentation: that 'the science that which will emerge from the developments I have been indicating will not be a body of knowledge accessible to everyone ... the hope that Economics will ever become something which the layman can comprehend without training is doomed for ever to frustration.'[33] Efforts at popularisation would 'be doing our science a disservice'.

> Surely it is better to push ahead with our analysis, embrace technicality with open arms if technicality will help us, and come to be so frequently right that we acquire the respect now given without question to the practitioners of the natural sciences.[34]

This kind of aspiration became common enough in the second half of the twentieth century, but more significant here is the paradoxical stance adopted by Robbins throughout his lecture. He gave a public lecture, addressed to a predominantly lay audience, that ended with the argument that laypeople would not be able to understand economics, an echo perhaps of Marshall's belief that women were not equipped to understand economics. Why economics was worth studying, how it was best studied, what kind of consequences would follow from an increasing number of those in public and private sectors having some kind of training in economics—on all these factors Robbins was silent. He does not advocate the study of economics because it is a developing field of knowledge of vital practical importance; he defends instead the idea that it is arcane knowledge, remote from the everyday world, developed by the efforts of academic economists talking among themselves.

The last paragraph of his Inaugural prefigured Robbins's most significant publication, *The Nature and Significance of Economic Science* (1932), suggesting that the purpose of economics was to render 'our choosing more rational. Economics cannot tell you whether you ought to do a certain thing. But it should be able to tell you what will happen if you do it.'[35] This reorganisation of the definition of economics appears to be novel, but as I will show in the following, it is more a reversion to the 'Jevonian' position of the 1880s discussed in Chapter 6. To make this argument, I will first discuss the sources on which Robbins drew for his teaching, before then considering some of the propositions put forward in *Nature and Significance*. Rather than move from methodological prescription to consequences for teaching and research, I reverse this

[32] See Howson, *Lionel Robbins*, p. 157. For a review of the evidence for a secular decline in the post–World War I UK population, see Enid Charles, 'The Effect of Present Trends in Fertility and Mortality upon the Future Population of Great Britain and upon its Age Composition', Ch. II in Lancelot Hogbin (ed.) *Political Arithmetic: A Symposium of Population Studies*, George Allen and Unwin, London 1938, pp. 73–105.

[33] Robbins, 'Present Position', p. 23.

[34] Ibid., p. 24.

[35] Robbins, 'Present Position', p. 24. Hence 'rational' here implies action with knowledge of consequences.

convention: I deal first of all with the kind of economics Robbins actually taught in the early 1930s, using his practice to gain perspective on how the argument of the book was constructed.

The Sources for and Structure of Robbins's Teaching

As already emphasised, undergraduate teaching at the LSE in the 1930s was lecture-based. Sam Goldman, who took the 'Principles' course in 1931, recalled that he only ever wrote one essay for Robbins,[36] and that the bulk of his studies involved private reading. Lectures were therefore very important, given the lack of any alternative structure. When in the course of the interview Goldman reflected on his teachers—T. E. Gregory, Harold Laski, Eileen Power, George Schwartz, W. M. Allen, John Hicks, Arthur Bowley—he evaluated them all in terms of the lectures they gave. Bowley was the 'worst lecturer in the world', mumbling away at the front; Allen's lectures on the theory of costs were 'difficult'; Schwartz was an 'interesting lecturer'; Laski was a brilliant lecturer who spoke without notes. It was Hayek's four lectures on prices and production in January 1931 that made an impression on him, not anything Hayek had written, or any more personal contact. Goldman remembered Robbins as a 'good lecturer', a view confirmed by others. They were polished performances: Robbins later recorded that he wrote out his lectures in full, spent some time reading them over, then delivered his lecture freely without reading his notes out.[37] It is for this reason that we have a good record of the substance and sequence of his lectures. Goldman attended Robbins's third-year 'General Principles of Economics' course in spring term 1931, and commented that Wicksteed was central to the exposition of the demand side, utility, and preferences; that Robbins did not really refer to Knight's *Risk, Uncertainty and Profit* at this time; and that he was 'brought up on Taussig'.[38] We can ask: Why Wicksteed? Why Taussig? 'Wicksteed' was *The Common Sense of Political Economy*, published in 1910; 'Taussig' was his *Principles of Economics*, first published in 1911, with a third edition in 1921. Neither of these was commonly used for teaching in Britain at the time, and so by considering how these texts represent economics, we may gain some insight into what Robbins sought to convey.

Philip Wicksteed (1844–1927) was a Unitarian Minister (at Little Portland Street 1874–1897) and between 1887 and 1918 a very active London University Extension lecturer. Educated in classics, his Extension classes were mainly directed to the work of Dante, Appendix I of his biography listing around 300 classes for the Oxford,

[36] In his 1930 'Memorandum', Robbins stated that second-year (economics) students wrote only three papers a year; he proposed supplementing this by adding one additional essay a term, to be read out to Robbins. That this would only add two hours a week to Robbins's teaching load indicates how limited the number of students pursuing the economics stream was at this time; see Howson, *Lionel Robbins*, p. 171.

[37] Susan Howson, 'Editor's Introduction' in *Lionel Robbins on the Principles of Economic Analysis: The 1930s Lectures*, Routledge, Abingdon 2018, p. xii.

[38] Interview, 22 July 1997. Nicholas Kaldor attended the same series of lectures, but his account appears to have been coloured by hindsight—he attributes to Robbins at that time a significant Austrian connection, and suggests that the lectures followed the 'method of presentation of Wicksell and of Knight'; both statements are questionable at best. See his remarks quoted in Howson (ed.) *Lionel Robbins on the Principles of Economic Analysis*, p. xiv.

Cambridge, London, Liverpool, and Manchester Extension programmes.[39] He began lecturing on political economy for the London Extension in the early 1890s, developing his early engagement with the work of Auguste Comte, having reviewed the first volume of the English translation of *Politique positive* in 1875.[40] Comtean positivism can be summarised by the idea that, rather than seek the causes of phenomena in theological or metaphysical belief, positivism involved the mobilisation of science to identify the laws that govern them. In turn, the core sciences developed in a set sequence: first mathematics, then astronomy, physics, chemistry, biology, and finally sociology, each succeeding science presupposing the existence of the former. Hence while 'science' was uniform, it was diverse in its objects; and sociology, coming last in the series, had the task of co-ordinating the whole.[41] Primed with these ideas, Wicksteed's attention was attracted first by the explanation of economic growth and impoverishment advanced in Henry George's *Progress and Poverty* (1879), until his Hampstead neighbour Frances Edgeworth redirected him to the work of Stanley Jevons. Wicksteed's engagement with Jevons was developed through his participation in the 'Economic Circle', a London discussion group that met from 1884 to 1888 and to which Wicksteed read the drafts of his *Alphabet of Economic Science* (1888).[42] This was subtitled 'Part I Elements of the Theory of Value or Worth',[43] dedicated to explaining and demonstrating

> . . . the truth of the proposition, that the value in use and the value in exchange of any commodity are two distinct, but connected functions of the quantity of the commodity possessed by the persons or the community to who it is valuable. . . .[44]

As Wicksteed conceded in his Preface, '. . . forty pages of almost unbroken mathematics may seem to many readers a most unnecessary introduction to Economics . . .'. Nonetheless, his object was 'to bring Economics down from the clouds and make the study throw light on our daily doings and experiences, as well as on the great commercial and industrial machinery of the world.'[45] The way in which Wicksteed expounded the marginal principle via the mathematics of physical relationships (balls thrown in the air, iron bars cooling in a stream) represents a rather indirect approach to this worthy objective, but one that has clear Comtean roots: that the mathematical laws of heat and dynamics underpinned the laws of a social physics.

But the 'Wicksteed' that Robbins invoked in his lectures was the Wicksteed of *Common Sense of Political Economy*. Robbins had contributed a section on Wicksteed's economic writings to Herford's biography,[46] and in 1933 he edited and introduced a

[39] C. H. Herford, *Philip Henry Wicksteed: His Life and Work*, J. M. Dent & Sons, London 1931, pp. 347–55.

[40] Ibid., p. 185.

[41] For an outline of Comte's work and influence, see Michel Bourdeau, 'Auguste Comte', *The Stanford Encyclopedia of Philosophy* (Summer 2018 edition) https://plato.stanford.edu/archives/sum2018/entries/comte.

[42] See Herford, *Wicksteed*, pp. 206–11. The group included Bernard Shaw, Edgeworth, Foxwell, Graham Wallas, and Sidney Webb.

[43] No further parts were published.

[44] Philip H. Wicksteed, *The Alphabet of Economic Science*, Macmillan, London 1888, p. 1.

[45] Ibid., pp. ix, x.

[46] Ibid., pp. 228–47.

new edition of *Common Sense*. This work avowedly followed Jevons, but mostly proceeds in a much more narrative manner than *Alphabet*. The reader is now confronted in Book I ('Systemic and Constructive') with endless little stories. On just one page, for example, we can read, 'A girl is conscious of choosing between a number of hats in a shop, but she may hardly be conscious of choosing between a hat and something else. She never gets a hat, she will tell you, unless "she has to" . . .'. Shortly after, we encounter a man wondering whether he can afford a new greatcoat, and then a lady who liked to get up every morning feeling that everything was an open question.[47] It goes on like this for almost four hundred pages. Whereas in *Alphabet* the economic principles were overwhelmed by mathematics, here in Volume I they are lost among stories. In expounding the work of economising, he focusses on the household and the work of women because the home is a domain whose administration is in female hands, and therefore more broadly familiar to everybody than the working of a bank or a factory.[48] The hope is expressed that by this route

> . . . a careful examination of what we ourselves or those with whom we are most intimately associated are consciously doing may throw light upon the great movements, institutions, and combinations which seem to be the result of the unconscious, or half-conscious, aggregate of doings that we vaguely conceive of as due to the 'community'.[49]

As with *Alphabet*, Wicksteed's debt to Jevons went as far as the microeconomics of subjects maximising their satisfaction, but no further. This was all economics was and ever would be, according to Wicksteed.[50] And while his initial focus on the household emphasised the mundane choices that went to make up economic action, this was far from the 'ordinary business of life' as Marshall or Young envisaged it. The 'everyday examples' of which Wicksteed so freely made use were his own narrative inventions. Book II ('Excursive and Critical', pp. 401–623) is different, as we shall see; but Book III ('Analytical and Practical', pp. 627–702) reverts to the same hypothetical examples and generalisations.

In his introduction Robbins summarised *Common Sense* as 'the most exhaustive non-mathematical exposition of the technical and philosophical complications of the so-called *marginal* theory of pure Economics',[51] bearing comparison perhaps only with Wieser's *Social Economics*.[52] He located Wicksteed 'beside the place occupied

[47] Philip H. Wicksteed, *The Common Sense of Political Economy and Selected Papers and Reviews on Economic Theory* Vol. 1, George Routledge & Sons, London 1933, p. 35.

[48] Ibid., p. 18.

[49] Ibid., p. 19.

[50] 'It will easily be shown that the principle [that economic thought is based on the broad experiences of daily life and psychology of choice between alternatives, p. 2] laid down by Jevons is not exclusively applicable to industrial or commercial affairs, but runs as a universal and vital force through the administration of all our resources.' Ibid., p. 3.

[51] Ibid., p. xii.

[52] Robbins cites the title in German, although this was not a book but the third part of the first volume of the *Grundriss der Sozialökonomik* I. Abt. A. III, pp. 125–444 (1914). It was at the time available in English as Friedrich von Wieser, *Social Economics*, trans. A. Ford Hinrichs, preface by Wesley C. Mitchell, Adelphi Press, New York 1927 [London 1928].

by Jevons and the Austrians',[53] suggesting in the same paragraph that Marshall, by contrast, was more connected to the 'classics'. Marshall's intention is said to have been to revise the classics; Jevons, and by extension Wicksteed, wished to break free of them: 'He [Wicksteed] was not a revisionist, but a revolutionary.'[54] Marshall and the Marshallians, Robbins continued, made little use of the principle of marginal utility—'an embellishment to the theory of the market'—'the main substance of Marshall's theory of value and distribution relates to costs—in the first instance to money costs, but in the last analysis to a conception of real costs coming directly from Smith and Ricardo.' Robbins treats the entire edifice of Marshallianism as a (flawed) theory of costs that ignored the revolution of analytical economics effected by Menger and Jevons in 1871. 'From 1871 to the present day, the whole development of Economics in these quarters has been a steady process of refinement and extension of the application of this concept.'[55] In this perspective, Marshall is a deviation, at best a cul de sac. The following year, in his introduction to the English translation of Wicksell's *Lectures on Political Economy*, Robbins once again asserted the irrelevance of Marshall, while apparently doing the opposite. Regretting that some might seek to dispense with 'the most thorough study of Marshall's *Principles*' in undergraduate teaching (which Robbins demonstrably had already done), he went on to write that

> [i]t would be a sad thing if the uncritical acceptance of this great work, which has so long tended to stifle the development of other lines of thought in this country, were to be succeeded by an equally uncritical rejection of all the wisdom and the path-breaking intuitions that it contains.[56]

This latter path could with some justice be read as the one actively adopted by Robbins, and contrasts strongly with that taken by Pigou and Maynard Keynes.

This stance with regard to contemporary Cambridge primes us to understand rather better why Robbins would select Taussig as his central text: because it was not Marshall's *Principles*. By the third edition in 1921, each of the two volumes of Taussig's *Principles* was over 500 pages. Both the eighth edition of Marshall's *Principles* (1920) and Taussig's *Principles* move from introductory matter to utility, demand, and supply, although Taussig includes in his Book II a coverage of costs, increasing and diminishing returns, monopolies, joint cost, and joint demand that appears in later sections of Marshall's book. Perhaps the one clear advantage of Taussig over Marshall could be that, for all the book's bulk, the hundred pages of Volume 1, Book II, was all that a British undergraduate need read to absorb the basic principles; although some

[53] Robbins, 'Introduction' to Wicksteed, *Common Sense*, p. xv.

[54] Ibid., p. xvi.

[55] Ibid., p. xvii.

[56] Lionel Robbins, 'Introduction' to Knut Wicksell, *Lectures on Political Economy*, Vol. I: *General Theory*, George Routledge and Sons, London 1934, p. xi fn. 2. See also his comments on the previous page: 'He [Marshall] was so anxious to explain the reality that he knew, to make his theory appear *plausible*, that he was apt to be impatient with refinements which, though useless for this purpose, might be fruitful in other connections.' While in presenting a paper to an AUTE conference in 1934 Robbins concluded by describing *Principles* as the 'incomparably best general introduction to all problems' (Howson, *Lionel Robbins*, p. 249), this was not a view that matched his more specific recommendations of Wicksteed and Wicksell, nor his actual teaching practice.

of this material is further elaborated in Volume 2—in Chapter 39 'Interest continued. The Equilibrium of Supply and Demand' and Chapter 45, 'Monopoly Gains'.

The remainder of Taussig's Volume I is divided between Book III, 'Money and the Mechanism of Exchange' (pp. 223–443) and Book IV, International Trade' (pp. 447–545). The former covers not only the quantity theory of money and bimetallism, but also banking, credit, and financial crises; the latter not only the theory of international trade (Chs. 34 and 35) but also foreign exchanges, the balance of payments, concluding with two chapters on free trade and protection, a particularly American preoccupation but also reflecting Taussig's book on the tariff history of the United States.[57] Volume 2, Book V, 'The Distribution of Wealth' (pp. 3–278), deals primarily with investment, interest, profit, and rent; Book VI with 'Problems of Labor' (pp. 281–385); the final book dealing with railways, public ownership, trusts, and socialism. Diagrams are mostly confined to Volume 1, Book II, and Volume 2, Book V. Clearly large amounts of material—on finance, industry, labour, and trade—are oriented to American sources; and there is rather less formal exposition of costs, consumption, supply, and demand than can be found in Marshall.

As we shall see, Robbins's lectures on the principles of economics came to be organised around the basic graphical representation of demand and supply, costs, revenue, and equilibrium familiar from the introductory textbooks of the later twentieth century, for which his lectures provided the template.[58] We would look in vain to Taussig for any such graphic exposition, and Marshall's own *Principles* is not especially marked in this way, despite his interest in the graphical representation of economic relationships. A. W. Flux's *Economic Principles*[59] was a more concise, advanced, and technically sophisticated work than Taussig that covered similar ground—combining elementary principles with chapters on money, banking, and international trade and drawing on more international, less American, examples. In addition to this, Flux abolished all his graphs to a technical appendix, easing the exposition but also bringing together in one place current graphical representation of economic relationships. But Robbins made no use of this work.

In fact, the pedagogic style of Robbins's lectures is something that again derives from Wicksteed[60]—for in Volume II of *Common Sense* Wicksteed switches from stories to graphics. The chapter headings summarise this: Chapter 1, 'Margins and the Diagrammatic Representation'; Chapter 2, 'On the Diagrammatic Method of Representing Areas of Satisfaction and Marginal Significances'; Chapter 3, 'On the Nature of Curves of Total Satisfaction'; Chapter 4, 'Buyer and Seller. Demand and Supply'; Chapter 5, 'The Theory of "Increasing and Diminishing Returns"'; and Chapter 6, 'The Diagrammatic Exposition of the Law of Rent and Its Implications'. This was not in itself novel—Henry Cunynghame's *Geometrical Political Economy* was, as the subtitle explained, *An Elementary Treatise on the Method of Explaining Some of the Theories of Pure Economic Science by Means of Diagrams*, while Cunynghame makes

[57] F. W. Taussig, *The Tariff History of the United States*, G. P. Putnam's Sons, New York 1892.

[58] Although this essentially microeconomic introduction was not a model followed by Samuelson, whose textbook was originally almost entirely macroeconomic in orientation.

[59] A. W. Flux, *Economic Principles: An Introductory Study*, Methuen, London 1904. There was a revised second edition in 1923.

[60] Developing what he had taken from Jevons's *Theory of Political Economy*.

clear that it had been Marshall who had in the mid-1870s introduced him to 'the geometrical method of studying Economics'.[61] Nonetheless, until Robbins's lectures of the early 1930s the way in which students were introduced to economic principles had been essentially discursive, as *Nature and Significance* indirectly testifies.[62]

This was, moreover, an approach that Robbins also endorsed: concluding the introduction to his edition of Wicksell's *Lectures on Political Economy*, he conceded that the work was not suitable as an introduction for very young students; for them, 'some such work as Volume I of Wicksteed's *Common Sense of Political Economy* is to be preferred.'[63] What was it about Wicksell's text that rendered it unsuitable as an introduction to economics? Why, indeed, had Robbins arranged for this work to be translated into English? Robbins explicitly recommended the work of Wicksteed and Wicksell, and not that of Marshall, as an approach to the kind of economics he wanted to teach. Some comments have already been made on Volume I of Wicksteed's *Common Sense*; consideration of the first volume of Wicksell's *Lectures* might yield additional insight into Robbins's economic pedagogy. And to understand why Wicksell might have appealed, we need to know something of when he wrote the text, and how he formed his understanding of economics.

Knut Wicksell (1851–1926) entered Uppsala University in 1869 to study mathematics, eventually completing his doctoral dissertation in 1885, at the age of 34. In the mid-1880s he received a scholarship to travel in Europe, enabling him to visit Vienna, where he attended lectures by Carl Menger. Interested in social questions, with an allegiance to a neoMalthusian appraisal of population and poverty,[64] his first exposure to contemporary political economy came about in his late thirties; he subsequently read widely in contemporary German, French, and English economic writings, working up a synthesis turning on marginalism and equilibrium conditions. His first publication was a short book on value, capital ,and rent in 1893 that Flux reviewed in the *Economic Journal*, and Flux deftly sketched its bases: that it was a synthesis of 'the Austrian school' (chiefly Böhm-Bawerk), Jevons, and Walras. He went on to emphasise that Wicksell's book had mostly been written before 1890, since besides two references to Marshall's *Principles* and one to Edgeworth on the contract curve, 'he appears to regard English work on economic theory as at a standstill since the publication of Jevons' *Theory*.' Flux also remarked that '[t]he translation of these views [Böhm-Bawerk's theories relating to interest] into symbolic language is the real point of the author's treatise.'[65] This initial book was then followed by the works that made his reputation, *Finanztheoretische Untersuchungen nebst Darstellung und Kritik des Steuerwesens Schwedens* (1896) and then *Geldzins und Güterpreise: eine Studie über den Tauschwert des Geldes bestimmenden Ursachen* (1898). At the time, however, he

[61] Henry Cunynghame, *A Geometrical Political Economy*, Oxford University Press, Oxford 1904, p. 1.

[62] We have no record of Pigou's introductory lectures of the 1920s, unfortunately. Austin Robinson (1897–1993) taught during this period, but as noted in Chapter 5, he was not that reliable a witness for interwar teaching in Cambridge. Michael Kaser has a complete set of notes for Pigou's last course during 1943–1944.

[63] Robbins, 'Introduction' to Wicksell, *Lectures*, pp. xviii–xix.

[64] See the account given in E. Sommarin, 'Das Lebenswerk von Knut Wicksell', *Zeitschrift für Nationalökonomie* Bd. 2 H. 2 (1930), pp. 222–28.

[65] A. W. Flux, Review of Wicksell, *Über Wert, Kapital und Rente* and Wicksteed, *Essay on the Co-ordination of the Laws of Distribution*, *Economic Journal* Vol. 4 (1894), pp. 305, 307.

lacked a law degree and so was not able to teach political economy; a situation he remedied by gaining a law degree at Uppsala and being appointed to a teaching position there in 1899, moving to Lund in 1900.

He quickly published his first, theoretical, volume of lectures.[66] There were two main parts: 'The Theory of Value'; and 'The Theory of Production and Distribution'. The greater part of the latter was an exposition of Böhm-Bawerk's theory of capital and interest; the former presented the idea of marginal utility, elaborating exchange and price formation. Unlike Walras's *Éléments d'économie politique pure*, which is strictly organised by lecture and which Walras did in fact use as the textbook for his teaching, Wicksell's *Lectures* takes the form of a mainly discursive text; although, it has to be said, an increasingly dense and arcane one that constantly triangulates Walras, Menger/Böhm-Bawerk, and Jevons. He had only been teaching the subject for just over a year, so it is unsurprising that it is not a more didactically-structured text; it is a synthesis by a mathematician who had been enthused by economic theory as it stood during the early 1880s, and remained rooted in this early enthusiasm, in the same way that Wicksteed's writing was. Like Wicksteed, his Jevons was the theorist of *Theory of Political Economy*, not the Jevons of the *Coal Question*, sunspots, or meteorology. Wicksell comes at the standard problems of exchange and consumption from the perspective of a competent mathematician; the argument develops relentlessly from elementary principles to ever-more elaborate ramifications, illustrated with a few diagrams that bear no resemblance to contemporary graphical representations of economic relationships, nor were they later adopted as such. Whereas Edgeworth's *Mathematical Psychics* (1881) is a difficult formal text with unfamiliar diagrams, these were undoubtedly new and interesting ideas, although the difficulty of the writing hindered ready recognition of quite how important these ideas were, and no one would ever think it a suitable introduction to economic theory. Even Robbins conceded that Wicksell 'added little that was completely original' to the theory of value as it stood in the 1880s.[67] By contrast, Wicksteed's formal presentation of demand and supply does bear comparison with what had by the early part of the twentieth century become the conventional graphical representation.[68] And it is for this reason that we should look first to Wicksteed, not Wicksell, as the inspiration for Robbins's lectures on the principles of economics.

Susan Howson's edition of Robbins's lecture notes for 1929–1931 shows how central to his thinking the concept of equilibrium is—in Lecture 1 he stated that

> [i]nstead of regarding the economic system as a machine for producing and distributing and inquiring concerning its potentialities and tendencies in these respects, it is considered simply as a system of quantities of goods of

[66] Knut Wicksell, *Föreläsningar i nationalekonomi D I.1 Teoretisk nationalekonomi*, Berlingska boktryckeriet, Lund 1901. This was translated into German and published as *Vorlesungen über Nationalökonomie auf Grundlage des Marginalprinzipes I. Theoretischer Teil*, trans. Margarethe Langfeldt, Gustav Fischer, Jena 1913.

[67] Robbins, 'Introduction' to Wicksell, *Lectures*, p. xii. See the exposition of 'free exchange and market value', pp. 35–67, for a sense of how inaccessible, as an introductory text, Wicksell's account of elementary economic relationships is.

[68] See Wicksteed, *Common Sense*, Vol. II, pp. 493ff., for example.

> different descriptions—quantities of productive services—and analysis is directed to discovering under what conditions this system exhibits equilibrium—under what conditions there is no tendency for the quantities to alter or under what conditions they exhibit characteristics of orderly or periodic growth.[69]

In the following paragraph, Robbins emphasises that while this change is a recent one, the idea of equilibrium as a central concept went back to the Physiocrats—'The moderns simply make explicit the methodological assumptions of these earlier theories and generalize them.'[70] What might need pointing out here, however, is that the 'quantities' he refers to are hypothetical, not real; there is no suggestion that at any point 'real quantities' might intervene in the elaboration of theoretical principles; that indeed, economics was any more than these principles.

Robbins's second lecture then moves directly to equilibrium, marking the distinction from Marshall by noting that he had analysed one price at a time, e.g. the price of fish from day to day. Equilibrium analysis by contrast 'deals with all prices at once';[71] which means that while Marshall had the operations of a particular market in mind, for Robbins there is just one large market moving in and out of general equilibrium. This demonstrates that the integration of Walrasian general equilibrium into mainstream economic theory already involved a misreading of Walras, who was very clear that a national economy remained segmented and that his conception of general equilibrium applied to particular markets, not to the economy as a whole.[72] Following on from this exposition of equilibrium, Robbins deals first with two-commodity exchange before moving to several goods, introducing some simple graphics; then introducing production, first with fixed factors, then with flexible factors, then turning to the supply of labour, where for the first time a series of graphics illustrates the issues relating to the elasticity of labour supply arising from the equilibrium between income and effort. As with Wicksteed, these graphics are neither derived from, nor elaborated in terms of, equations; nor of course do they invoke any actual data, as was already made clear in the second lecture.[73] These are in fact merely images that enable the organisation of a prose narrative—like Wicksteed, but not like Wicksell. The entire apparatus involves the increasingly complex manipulation of hypothetical states unchecked by mathematical logic or empirical evidence. As Cunynghame wrote,

> . . . in pure Political Economy the curves employed are usually and principally of an abstract character. The truth of a theory is made to depend on reasoning, rather than on experiment; it deals with proofs rather than with results. Hence the curves will in general be abstract, instead of being concrete like those I have given above.[74]

[69] Howson, *Lionel Robbins on the Principles of Economic Analysis*, pp. 6–7.
[70] Ibid, p. 7.
[71] Ibid., pp. 12, 13.
[72] See my *Economy of the Word, Language, History, and Economics*, Oxford University Press, New York 2015, pp. 282ff.
[73] Unlike the presentation of W. E. Johnson, 'The Pure Theory of Utility Curves', *Economic Journal* Vol. 23 (1913), pp. 483–513, which links graphical with algebraic analysis.
[74] Cunynghame, *Geometrical Political Economy*, p. 34.

It is this property that makes economic analysis such a hard sell to engineers, physicists, chemists, and biologists; and it is a pedagogical style that is for the first time fully elaborated in these lectures.

The Nature and Significance of Economic Science

To support this programme, Robbins wrote up his lectures on economic method during the winter of 1931–1932, consolidating an interest in methodological issues that went back to the early 1920s.[75] He sent the manuscript to Macmillan on 19 February 1932, and Henry Higgs's very positive report was submitted just a week later, noting that it 'went beyond the standard works on economic methodology by John Neville Keynes and Henry Sidgwick'—hence confirming the point made earlier that methodological discussion was at this time very limited. By early March the publisher was pressing Robbins to sign a contract so that the manuscript could be sent to the printer.[76] A revised second edition was published in 1935, which was then reprinted in 1937, 1940, 1945, 1946, 1948, 1949, 1952, and 1962. The work initiated modern English-language discussion of the philosophy and method of economics, while at the same time representing a benchmark statement for neoclassical economics.

Robbins presented *Nature and Significance* as a definition of the subject-matter of 'Economic Science' and its generalisations, while indicating the 'limitations and significance of these generalisations' in the interpretation of reality and in political practice. There was, he went on, now 'no longer any ground for serious differences of opinion on these matters'—this was, therefore, his account of what he had called 'maintrack' economics[77] as the sole legitimate form of theoretical economic discourse.[78] His maintained that his aim had merely been 'to state, as simply as I could, propositions which are the common property of most modern economists.'[79] In closing the preface, he acknowledged his indebtedness only to Ludwig von Mises, and to Philip Wicksteed's *Common Sense of Political Economy*. At this time he had possibly not met Mises in person,[80] but he had been familiar with the second edition of his *Theorie des Geldes und der Umlaufsmittel* since the mid-1920s, when he had used it in his teaching; while also having drafted a partial translation of Mises's *Die Gemeinwirtschaft*, a lengthy critique of economic collectivism.[81] Nonetheless, the direct Austrian influence on the work can be overestimated, since this influence

[75] As noted by Susan Howson, 'The Origins of Lionel Robbins's Essay on the Nature and Significance of Economic Science', *History of Political Economy* Vol. 36 (2004), p. 418.

[76] Howson, *Lionel Robbins*, p. 216.

[77] See pp. 334–35, 337.

[78] Lionel Robbins, *An Essay on the Nature and Significance of Economic Science*, Macmillan, London 1932, p. vii.

[79] Ibid., p. viii.

[80] Robbins seems to have first met Mises in September 1931, hence after he had first met Hayek in January 1931; Howson, *Lionel Robbins*, p. 210. Howson speculates that Robbins and Mises may have met in London in 1924 and/or 1926 when Mises visited London (p. 135) but has no direct evidence for this.

[81] Ludwig von Mises, *Theorie des Geldes und der Umlaufsmittel*, Duncker und Humblot, Munich 1912, second edition 1924; and *Die Gemeinwirtschaft*, Gustav Fischer, Jena 1922. For the draft translation, see Howson, 'Origins', p. 422.

mostly came via Wicksteed and Wicksell; for what Robbins might have taken from Mises in *Nature and Significance* can already be found in Menger and Böhm-Bawerk.

The book has six chapters. Opening with a survey of the subject matter of economics, the second chapter elaborates his account of ends and means, moving on in the following chapter to distinguish economic goods from the material world in general by virtue of their scarcity. The fourth and fifth chapters deal with various economic generalisations, while the final chapter defines 'economic science' in terms of marginal utility and equilibrium. Here I am not so concerned to present in any detail the work as a whole, rather with the question of how he supports and legitimates his argument, and thereby creates a sense that he is merely restating accepted positions in a rather clearer and more systematic fashion.

And there is a basic ambiguity in the position that Robbins adopts here. While he maintains in the preface that he is simply restating a common understanding, he does not demonstrate the existence of this common understanding. Instead, the first chapter explicitly *dismisses* the existing 'common understanding'—the definition of economics 'which would probably command most adherents, at any rate in Anglo-Saxon countries'—that of Alfred Marshall, or John Bates Clark, adding an extended critique of his former teacher Edwin Cannan.[82] Furthermore, while it might appear from a casual examination of his footnotes that he is instead advancing a contemporary 'Austrian' position—already in the third footnote of Chapter 1 he is quoting Max Weber in German—Susan Howson has established that he arrived at his basic orientation in 1928 on the basis of his reading of Wicksteed, surmising that most of the Austrian references in the first edition were late additions, presumably suggested by Hayek during the winter of 1931–1932.[83] Given Robbins's failure to demonstrate that the view of economics he is advancing is widely shared among his immediate readership, the book has a more prescriptive cast than it pretends. Ironically, the version of the 'Economic Science' that he puts forward is more normative than positive; he is arguing for the adoption of a new position while also maintaining that he is simply summarising existing practice. In part, this ambiguity is part and parcel of the 'philosophy and methodology of economics', and so is a property of the genre. The historian asks: how, and with what materials, is this particular argument constructed? The methodologist tells you: a good argument should be constructed like this.

Robbins places his own definition of economics in the first chapter, following his critique of Cannan:

[82] Robbins, *Essay*, p. 4; pp. 8–12 for Cannan.

[83] Howson, 'Origins', pp. 426, 414. It could be added that, given he read the German translation of Wicksell's lectures in the mid-1920s (Howson, *Lionel Robbins on the Principles of Economic Analysis*, p. xiv), he would there have found there a formulation rather similar to his own, lacking only the explicit idea that means had alternative uses and so choice involved opportunity costs: 'By an *economic* phenomenon or *economic* activity is meant every planful endeavour to satisfy material needs, or more precisely, the endeavour to achieve the greatest possible result with the means available to us, or the endeavour to achieve a given outcome with the least possible means (the familiar expression "to achieve the greatest outcome with as little means as possible" is illogical, and so should be avoided).' Knut Wicksell, *Vorlesungen über Nationalökonomie auf Grundlage des Marginalprinzipes I. Theoretischer Teil*, trans. Margarethe Langfeldt, Gustav Fischer, Jena 1913, p. 2 (my translation). Likewise Max Weber, *Economy and Society: A New Translation*, Harvard University Press, Cambridge Mass. 2019, pp. 144–47; here the point is made that means have alternative uses and so choices involve the weighing of costs (this had been originally been published in 1921, the text dates from 1920).

> The economist studies the disposal of scarce means. He is interested in the way different degrees of scarcity of different goods give rise to different ratios of valuation between them, and he is interested in the way in which changes in conditions of scarcity, whether coming from changes in ends or changes in means—from the demand or the supply side—affect these ratios. Economics is the science which studies human behaviour as a relationship between ends and scarce means which have alternative uses.[84]

The footnote attached to this statement cites several sources. First is Carl Menger, to the entire section of *Grundsätze* on 'The Origin of Human Economy and Economic Goods', which includes an extensive discussion of the treatment of 'economic goods' going back to Smith and Say.[85] The second is to some pages in Mises, *Die Gemeinwirtschaft*. Here Mises begins[86] from the point that material goods are scarce in relation to need, and that the more urgent needs have priority—a basic point already elaborated in 1871 by Menger in perhaps the best-known element of the book, the (sole) diagram ranking the order in which a human subject maximises satisfaction across 10 goods for which a subject has differing degrees of need.[87] In the following pages Mises elaborates at length on this basic principle without adding very much to the points already made by Menger 50 years previously. The third reference is to the first chapter of Fetter's *Economic Principles*, 'Purpose and Nature of Economics', which is primarily devoted to the idea that economics is a 'science' and defines it as 'the science that seeks to arrive at such general rules and principles as will lead to the best results in the use of the resources and services of individuals, families, and nations.'[88] Fetter makes no reference here to means and ends in the manner of Menger, Mises, or for that matter Max Weber; and it could well be that Robbins had in mind Part I rather than Chapter 1, since the subsequent chapters of Part I ('Choice and Value', 'Goods and Psychic Income', 'Principles of Evaluation', and 'Trade by Barter') relate more directly to Robbins's arguments, besides looking much more like the substantive source for his Principles lectures than either Wicksteed or Wicksell.[89] Then comes a non-specific reference to Strigl's *Die ökonomischen Kategorien und die Organisation der Wirtschaft*, a work that takes an explicitly methodological approach to Menger and Böhm-Bawerk, drawing attention to the way that Böhm-Bawerk emphasised the

[84] Robbins, *Essay*, p. 15.

[85] Carl Menger, *Grundsätze der Volkswirthschaftslehre*, Wilhelm Braumüller, Vienna 1871, fn. pp. 53–55.

[86] Mises, *Gemeinwirtschaft*, p. 98, and the apodictic statement: 'The domain of rational action and that of the economy coincide; all rational action is economic action, and economic action is rational action' (pp. 98–99).

[87] Ibid., p. 93. See Roger E. Backhouse, Keith Tribe, *The History of Economics: A Course for Students and Teachers*, Agenda, Newcastle 2018, p. 173, for the diagram and an explanation.

[88] Frank A. Fetter, *Economic Principles*, The Century Co., New York 1915, pp. 3–11, quote at p. 8. Fetter (1863–1949) had completed his doctorate at Halle with Johannes Conrad in 1894, and subsequently met Menger, Böhm-Bawerk, and Wieser during a visit to Vienna in 1910. He formed an especially close relationship with Böhm-Bawerk, cut short by the latter's death in 1914. For the personal connection between Fetter and Böhm-Bawerk, Schumpeter, and Hans Mayer, see Matthew McCaffrey, 'Pure Theory and Progressive Liberalism: Frank Fetter and the Austrian Economists', *Journal of Institutional Economics* Vol. 15 (2019), pp. 471–74.

[89] The same is true of the early pages of Fetter's *Principles of Economics with Application to Practical Problems*, The Century Co., New York 1904.

ranking of needs and the availability of goods, while the nature of scarcity is linked to Gottl.[90] Finally, there is a non-specific reference to Hans Mayer, and we can again find in the second part of Mayer's article, published in 1922, a summary of 'economising action' that is rather similar to that of Robbins. Here Mayer first establishes four initial conditions: a given number of ends, a quantitative shortfall of means to meet given ends, the organisation of ends into a hierarchy, and the use of the same means in reaching different ends. The substance of economic action thus involves the distribution of all available means to the realisation of individual ends, disposing over 'goods' in an unambiguous and specific manner:

> Economic action is thus a constant process of problem solving, a constant process of decision: how do I distribute the totality of means available to me for the realisation of individual ends in such a way that my overall end is realised as completely as possible by the given means?[91]

The inclusion of these references in a footnote to his signature definition, while being vague about the arguments being referred to, reveals several things. First of all, it should by now be obvious that the definition of economics in *Nature and Significance* was indeed 'widely accepted', but really only by German and Austrian economists whose work was at the time largely unread outside Germany and Austria. By the early 1920s not only had German-language economics been technically eclipsed in the international context; there was a heavy cultural backlash against 'German science' following the First World War, reinforced by the rising global standing of the American academy and American technology. 'Austria' was also now a rump state much of whose former territory is today in Poland, Hungary, Romania, Ukraine, Slovakia, and the Czech Republic, besides there having been a connection to the Balkan states that had triggered the First World War. This makes more intelligible the way in which Robbins only indirectly absorbed the general framework of Austrian work, a style of economics devoted to detailed definition and categorisation and not to economic analysis; an approach that had so deeply shaped the work of a Briton and a Swede, both of whom had synthesised the Austrian economic theory of the early 1880s.

Secondly, the fact that some of these references come with page numbers while others are purely gestural is open to the interpretation that at least those lacking exact page references were supplied by Hayek after he had seen the draft. As already noted, Robbins had been familiar with Mises's *Gemeinwirtschaft* from the mid-1920s, when he had begun to translate some of it; but the section that he references adds nothing to what could already be found in Menger's *Grundsätze*. By contrast, the citation here of 'Mayer, *op. cit.*' refers back to a footnote in which the title of the article in question is

[90] Richard Strigl, *Die ökonomischen Kategorien und die Organisation der Wirtschaft*, Gustav Fischer, Jena 1923, pp. 11, 14.

[91] Hans Mayer, 'Untersuchung zu dem Grundgesetz der wirtschaftlichen Wertrechnung', *Zeitschrift für Volkswirtschaft und Sozialpolitik* Bd. 2 (1922), cited as reprinted in *Zeitschrift für Nationalökonomie* Bd. 15 Heft 3 (1956), p. 290. This is in fact the second part of the article; the first, published in 1921, dealt with Wieser and Böhm-Bawerk on the valuation of disposable goods.

misspelled, and a non-existent page reference is given (he refers to 'p. 123' for an article whose pagination is pp. 1–23).[92]

And so while the Austrian influence on Robbins should by now be evident, he was not a scholar in the mould of Cannan. To start with, there was in the 1920s no reason why one should have had to read Wicksteed in English or Wicksell in German to gain an understanding of what 'Austrian' theory was. Nor was it necessary to garnish *Nature and Significance* with references to obscure German-language sources. Large amounts of Austrian work had been published in English before 1900; James Bonar for one was very familiar with it,[93] and William Smart (1853–1915), teaching in the University of Glasgow from 1892, Professor of Political Economy from 1896, was an energetic proselytizer. Smart had quickly translated and edited Böhm-Bawerk's two-part work on capital theory.[94] He had also written a summary of the Austrian theory of value[95] and provided a substantial 'Editor's Preface' to the translation of Wieser's *Der natürliche Wert* (1889) that won a ringing endorsement from Edgeworth:

> Mrs. Malloch by an easy and elegant translation saves the English reader from the trouble of penetrating the original German. Dr. Smart saves him from the trouble of perusing even the translation. For there is hardly an important point in the book which is not adequately set forth in the editor's preface.[96]

Wieser had himself written a contribution for the first volume of the *Economic Journal*,[97] as had also Smart.[98] Besides which, by the early 1890s Böhm-Bawerk was very actively spreading the word in American journals.[99] If it were objected that this

92 This error was not corrected in later editions. The journal in question was founded by Böhm-Bawerk in 1892 as *Zeitschrift für Volkswirtschaft, Socialpolitik und Verwaltung*; it was refounded in 1921 as *Zeitschrift für Volkswirtschaft und Sozialpolitik*; and after editorial differences with Othmar Spann it was relaunched as *Zeitschrift für Nationalökonomie* in 1929, today known as the *Journal of Economics*.

93 James Bonar, 'The Austrian Economists and Their View of Value', *Quarterly Journal of Economics* Vol. 3 (1888), pp. 1–31.

94 Eugen von Böhm-Bawerk, *Capital and Interest: A Critical History of Economical Theory*, Macmillan, London 1890; *The Positive Theory of Capital*, Macmillan, London 1891 (see Edgeworth's enthusiastic review in *Economic Journal* Vol. 2 (1892), pp. 328–36); see also Böhm-Bawerk, *Recent Literature on Interest (1884 1899): A Supplement to 'Capital and Interest'*, trans. William A. Scott and Siegmund Feilbogen, Macmillan, London 1903; and his *Karl Marx and the Close of His System: A Criticism*, trans. Alice M. Macdonald with a Preface by James Bonar, T. F. Unwin, London 1898.

95 William Smart, *An Introduction to the Theory of Value on the Lines of Menger, Wieser and Böhm-Bawerk*, Macmillan, London 1891, reviewed by Edgeworth in *Economic Journal* Vol. 2 (1892), pp. 336–37. There was a new edition of the *Introduction* in 1910.

96 Friedrich von Wieser, *Natural Value*, trans. Christian A, Malloch, Macmillan, London 1893, reviewed by Edgeworth, *Economic Journal* Vol. 4 (1894), pp. 279–85, here at p. 279.

97 Friedrich von Wieser, 'The Austrian School and the Theory of Value', *Economic Journal* Vol. 1 (1891), pp. 108–21.

98 William Smart, 'The New Theory of Interest', *Economic Journal* Vol. 1 (1891), pp. 675–81.

99 For example, Eugen von Böhm-Bawerk, 'The Historical vs. the Deductive Method in Political Economy', *Annals of the American Academy of Political and Social Science* Vol. 1 (1890), pp. 244–71; 'Macvane's Political Economy', *Quarterly Journal of Economics* Vol. 4 (1890), pp. 331–39; 'Professor Gidding's on the Theory of Capital', *Quarterly Journal of Economics* Vol. 4 (1890), pp. 347–49; 'The Austrian Economists', *Annals of the American Academy of Political and Social Science* Vol. 1 Pt. 3 (1891), pp. 361–84; 'One More Word on the Ultimate Standard of Value', *Economic Journal* Vol. 4 (1894), 719–24; and 'The Ultimate Standard of Value', *Annals of the American Academy of Political and Social Science* Vol. 5 Pt. 1 (1894), pp. 149–208.

was, by the 1920s, rather dated material, it can be countered that there is still no better account in English of Austrian work than these various texts; and that in any case, as Flux so accurately divined, the views of Wicksteed and Wicksell were rooted in the 1880s, so actually predating this literature of dissemination. Robbins's Austrian inspiration came second-hand, when he might just as easily have read Wieser and Böhm-Bawerk in English. Strigl, Amonn, and Mayer added little of substance to what already existed, in English. But to refer back to English-language literature published some 40 years previously would have drawn attention to the rather dated character of the arguments he was advancing. Better to rely upon Wicksteed's 1910 *Common Sense*, and refresh Wicksell by publishing his 1901 Swedish lectures in English in 1934.

The Instrumentalisation of 'Austrian Theory' and Its Legacy

Robbins had first visited Vienna in 1922, attending a summer school as an undergraduate and learning some elementary German.[100] Besides his honeymoon in France and Italy in July 1924, there is no evidence from his biography that he made any further trips abroad until May 1932, when he attended a conference in Berlin.[101] He had read some of Mises and been impressed by his work, but there is no evidence in his biography that he met Mises in person until the summer of 1932. In 1930 he had met Wilhelm Röpke in London and Gottfried Haberler in Cambridge; but he did not meet Hayek until January 1931, when Hayek came to the LSE to give his four lectures on prices and production. And it had been Hayek who had first contacted Robbins, not the other way around; Hayek had been interested in organising a conference in London during 1931.[102] It was the success of Hayek's lectures that led Beveridge to invite him to fill a revived Tooke chair in April 1931.[103] Machlup invited Robbins to Vienna for a lecture in May 1932, but Robbins declined, having already accepted the invitation to the Berlin meeting. He returned to Vienna for the first time since 1922 during the Easter vacation of 1933; then had a six-week holiday in Austria that summer. Here, at last, he was able to converse at leisure with Haberler and Machlup, whose comments influenced the second edition of *Nature and Significance*. He also returned to Austria for a summer holiday in 1935.

The point made here is not simply that the 'Austrian' connection shaping *Nature and Significance* was detached from systematic engagement with the available literature; it relied on syntheses that were already about 30 years old, which themselves reflected work published 20 years before that. The connection between Robbins and Hayek was formed *after* Robbins had drafted and delivered the lectures on the scope and method of economics from which *Nature and Significance* was worked up; but

[100] Howson, *Lionel Robbins*, pp. 87ff.

[101] And it is worth noting that travelling to Vienna or Berlin by train from London in the 1930s would usually have involved an overnight North Sea ferry and the best part of the next day on a train—and so the sort of thing that would have required planning and correspondence.

[102] Howson, *Lionel Robbins*, pp. 178, 199–200. And so the fact that Hayek and Robbins first met in January 1931 would tend to confirm that Robbins had not attended seminars in Vienna in the later 1920s.

[103] Ibid., p. 200.

this subsequent connection was then retrofitted onto the text by virtue of Hayek's later reputation, facilitated by the Austrian cast lent to the text through footnotes added to it while it was being written, but which were mostly not sources for what was written. There is no evidence, for example, that Robbins was aware of Felix Kaufmann's 1923 essay on basic economic concepts,[104] even though this focussed on the essays by Strigl and Mayer that Robbins later cited, and if he had known of the essay it would have provided a useful shortcut, for him and for his readers.

Notwithstanding Robbins's patchy knowledge of Austrian literature, he was able to instrumentalise this formalised and limited approach to economics to disrupt and displace the dominant prevailing 'Marshallian' approach. As emphasised in Chapter 6, Marshall, Pigou, and Maynard Keynes viewed 'theory' as a means for the analysis of circumstances and the formulation of policies. By contrast, the hallmark of 'Austrian' theory was not merely that it was non-mathematical; it proceeded entirely without reference to any empirical world. While its attention to definition and demarcation could be of great value in clarifying the nature and scope of economic argument, it lacked engagement with practical questions. This broadly methodological function was generally an asset when it was but one source of economic thinking, not a disadvantage. But converted into the core of a new mainstream economics, this formalism could be mobilised as a 'new science' to confront the empiricist pragmatism of a Young or a Marshall. 'Theory' became the core of a mainstream, rather than a resource for the construction of analysis and argument in particular circumstances using available data. The formalism and universalism of the resulting principles could be condensed and adumbrated at length in lecture and textbook, increasingly elaborated in journal articles, and, by virtue of this, academic careers could be embarked upon and built. The academic institutional framework in which economic discourse was now developing provided a new medium through which formal and abstract argument could propagate unchecked by the need to serve any purpose other than the furtherance of formalised economic argument and the development of the careers of those doing the arguing.

But to follow the path of 'economic science' as it blossomed in the 1930s and 1940s is quite beyond the scope of this study. Rather than briefly and very inadequately sketching out the theoretical development of economic discourse in this period—oligopoly theory, econometrics, welfare economics, the beginnings of game theory, and, of course, the manifold ramifications of Maynard Keynes's *General Theory*—I will restrict myself here to sketching the emergent *representation* of economic science that *Nature and Causes* fostered. First of all, we can briefly consider the reception of that work; then turn to the newer textbook literature that, in presenting the basic principles of economics to new generations of economists, followed the path that Robbins had laid in his own teaching, reflected in the doctrines advanced in *Nature and Causes.*

A few months after *Nature and Causes* was published, the *Economic Journal* published a review by Edwin Cannan, Robbins's former teacher. He took aim at Robbins's professed 'value neutrality' over ends, his insistence that there were no

[104] Felix Kaufmann, 'Die ökonomischen Grundbegriffe. Eine Studie über die Theorie der Wirtschaftswissenschaft', *Zeitschrift für Volkswirtschaft und Sozialpolitik* Bd. 3 (1923), pp. 31–47 [reprinted in *Zeitschrift für Nationalökonomie* Bd. 15 Heft 3 (1956), pp. 304–16].

'economic ends' as such, and certainly no 'good' or 'bad' ends, and made the entirely reasonable point that

> [w]hen people ask the professor whether such and such a change will be good or bad, they will only find him tiresome if he pretends that he knows nothing of good and bad ends in economic matters and can only talk about the cheapness or dearness of different ways of attaining a given end. They will say, 'You know perfectly well that what we want from you is to be told whether this proposed change will make us and our children better off. For goodness sake give us a reasoned reply without beating about the bush and quoting dozens of foreign economists whom we shall never read.'[105]

This takes us back to Robbins's Inaugural Lecture, where he made a virtue of doing exactly what Cannan is describing here. Robbins was an early adopter of the idea, sometimes attributed to Max Weber, that since the conduct of scientific inquiry is 'value free', the scientist has to abstain from all judgement concerning ends. But as Weber pointed out, whether something is 'worth knowing' is not something that can be demonstrated scientifically, it is a judgement.[106] And Cannan's objection is that the entire practice of economics was driven by such judgements: this was why individuals opted to study it, it shaped what they hoped for from it, and what others hoped from them. This is the basic paradox of scientific knowledge: while it is a practice developed using set procedures independent of valuations, its practitioners are valuing persons—that they are pursuing scientific knowledge, that science is their 'vocation', itself involves a valuation. In turn, who gets the opportunity to pursue such a vocation in the first place is the consequence of valuations beyond those of the individual concerned. In upholding the status of economics as a 'science', Robbins implied that the economist had no views on the subject matter of economics, other than to observe ends being selected and means chosen.

This point was taken up in the next issue by Lindley Fraser, who developed Cannan's argument and pointed out that Robbins's procedure in seeking first a definition of economics, so that this definition might delimit the subject matter of economics, involved the systematic exclusion of fields upon which any reasonable economist might draw: not psychology, considering why people choose the things they do; not technology, the economist must refrain from studying industrial or agricultural production; not economic history, since the economist is not concerned with the development of social or economic institutions; not ethics, thus excluding issues of welfare and inequality and unemployment. In this way the work of an economist was whittled down to the observation of ends selected and means chosen. 'The system of generalisations which the analysis of this problem yields are all deductions from self-evident first principles, and can claim to represent a body of scientific truth.'[107]

[105] Edwin Cannan in the September 1932 issue: Review of Robbins, *Nature and Significance of Economic Science*, *Economic Journal* Vol. 42 (1932), pp. 425–26.

[106] See my 'Max Weber's 'Science as a Vocation': Context, Genesis, Structure', *Sociologica* Vol. 12 No 1 (2018), p. 131.

[107] Lindley M. Fraser, 'How Do We Want Economists to Behave?', *Economic Journal* Vol. 42 (1932), p. 560.

Reaction in the United States was also swift. A lengthy rebuttal of Robbins appeared in the May 1933 issue of the *Quarterly Journal of Economics*. This opened with the observation that *Nature and Significance* not only presented an account of the 'Austrian School', but was symptomatic of a 'general theoretical trend' on both sides of the Atlantic 'towards static formalism with an alleged increase in "logical precision"'.[108] It is important to note here what has happened: Robbins's book has initiated a new methodological debate within English-language journals, and as it happens Souter has actually read Hans Mayer. In the preface to the second edition of *Nature and Significance*, Robbins batted away Souter's criticisms, first by suggesting that he had simply repeated arguments advanced by Max Weber, then stating his agreement with Frank Knight's detailed response to Souter that identified his vigorous defence of what Souter conceived to be the Marshallian programme.[109] More explicitly methodological articles and reviews began appearing in *Economica*,[110] and especially in the pages of the *Zeitschrift für Nationalökonomie*,[111] where Terence Hutchison first published sections of what became his own contribution to the genre, *The Significance and Basic Postulates of Economic Theory*.[112] Even Talcott Parsons joined in.[113] Hutchison supplied an interesting late retrospective on these developments, noting among other things that the distinction of micro- from macroeconomics first truly emerged in the 1930s, and that methodological controversy turned almost exclusively on microeconomic issues, where policy issues were increasingly remote.[114]

The British Textbook Literature

And the British textbook literature that developed from the 1930s to the 1960s was chiefly microeconomic in orientation. As already seen, Taussig's *Principles of*

108 R. W. Souter, '"The Nature and Significance of Economic Science" in Recent Discussion', *Quarterly Journal of Economics* Vol. 47 (1933), pp. 377, 378.

109 Lionel Robbins, 'Preface to the Second Edition', *The Nature and Significance of Economic Science*, Macmillan, London 1935, pp. xi–xii; Frank H. Knight, 'Economic Science in Some Recent Discussion', *American Economic Review* Vol. 24 (1934), pp. 225–38.

110 Felix Kaufmann, 'On the Subject-Matter and Method of Economic Science', *Economica* No. 42 (November 1933), pp. 381–401; Fritz Machlup, 'Why Bother with Methodology?', *Economica* New Series Vol. 3 No. 9 (1936), pp. 39–45.

111 Gunnar Myrdal, 'Das Zweck-Mittel-Denken in der Nationalökonomie', *Zeitschrift für Nationalökonomie* Bd. 4 H. 3 (1933), pp. 305–29; Umberto Ricci, 'Die Methode der nationalökonomischen Wissenschaft', *Zeitschrift für Nationalökonomie* Bd. 4 H. 5 (1933), pp. 577–603; Alfred W. Stonier, Review of Robbins, *An Essay on the Nature and Significance of Economic Science*, *Zeitschrift für Nationalökonomie* Bd. 5 H. 3 (1934), pp. 417–24; Alfred Amonn, 'Wesen und Bedeutung der Wirtschaftswissenschaft', *Zeitschrift für Nationalökonomie* Bd. 7 H. 3 (1936), pp. 306–325.

112 Terence W. Hutchison, 'Theoretische Ökonomie als Sprachsystem', *Zeitschrift für Nationalökonomie* Bd. 8 H. 1 (1937), pp. 78–90; 'Expectation and Rational Conduct', *Zeitschrift für Nationalökonomie* Bd. 8 H. 5 (1937), pp. 636–53; *The Significance and Basic Postulates of Economic Theory*, Macmillan, London 1938.

113 Talcott Parsons, 'Some Reflections on 'The Nature and Significance of Economics'', *Quarterly Journal of Economics* Vol. 48 (1934), pp. 511–45.

114 Terence W. Hutchison, 'A Formative Decade: Methodological Controversy in the 1930', *Journal of Economic Methodology* Vol. 16 (2009), p. 298. See also, for an overview, A. W. Coats, 'Half a Century of Methodological Controversy in Economics: As Reflected in the Writings of T. W. Hutchison', in Coats (ed.) *Methodological Controversy in Economics: Historical Essays in Honor of T. W. Hutchison*, JAI Press, Greenwich Conn., pp. 1–42.

Economics combined a formal presentation of exchange, marginal utility, and price formation with material on banking and international trade, as had Flux's *Economic Principles*. For more elementary purposes, Cannan's *Wealth* presented a general and discursive account of economic organisation and development that was more an orientation to economic issues than a presentation of principles.[115] For this, the undergraduate could turn to the volumes in the Cambridge Economic Handbooks series—the first volume appeared in 1921, dealing with the basic framework of supply and demand, the only two diagrams in the book first establishing the symmetry of demand, supply, and the consequent unique equilibrium price from changes to that equilibrium price involving shifts of either curve.[116] Next in the series was Dennis Robertson on money, then in 1928 Maurice Dobb published *Wages* as the sixth text in the series. Like Cannan's *Wealth*, these were all in a duodecimo format, rather smaller than a modern paperback, but of about 150 pages each, rather than the 274 pages of Cannan. These modest dimensions emphasised their accessibility; decades later, the eighth edition of Honor Croome's *Approach to Economics* followed the same pattern.[117] Henry Clay's very popular *Economics* was also in this format, albeit much longer at nearly 500 pages because it was intended to inform general readers, not introduce students to the subject.[118]

During the early years of the twentieth century there was a marked upturn in the publication of popular introductions to the subject: the Home University Library series published Hobson's *Science of Wealth* (1911) as well as Sydney Chapman's *Political Economy* (1912), the former more descriptive, the latter more academic, but both aimed at general readers. This distinction is marked by the way that Chapman had also recently published a much more substantial *Outlines of Political Economy* that was designed as a student introduction to the subject, but was also in a smaller format.[119] These and similar works provided a stock of material that was regularly reprinted through the interwar years;[120] as we shall see, one of the features of this introductory economic literature was its longevity, indicating both the relatively unchanging foundation of economic discourse and the constant renewal of a demand for its elaboration among an increasingly stratified readership.

However, the continuing lack of a single synthetic overview suitable for use at intermediate undergraduate level is highlighted by the reading that Robbins recommended in conjunction with his Principles courses from 1932 to 1935. Here we find once again Wicksteed's *Common Sense* heading the list, followed by Wicksell's *Lectures*;[121] then

[115] Edwin Cannan, *Wealth: A Brief Explanation of the Causes of Economic Welfare*, P. S. King & Son, London 1914.

[116] Hubert D. Henderson, *Supply and Demand*, Nisbet and Co., London 1921, pp. 22, 25.

[117] Honor Croome, *The Approach to Economics*, 8th edition, Chatto and Windus, London 1964; and this format was also the one adopted by Allen Lane in 1935 when he created Penguin paperbacks.

[118] Henry Clay, *Economics: An Introduction for the General Reader*, Macmillan, London 1916.

[119] Sydney Chapman, *Political Economy*, Williams and Norgate, London 1912, p. 255; *Outlines of Political Economy*, Longmans, Green and Co., London 1911, p. 406. Shield Nicholson had also published two different accounts of political economy: his three volume *Principles of Political Economy* (1893–1901), and a one-volume *Elements of Political Economy* (1903).

[120] Clay's 1916 text was, for example, reprinted in 1917, 1918, 1919 (twice), 1921 (US edition), 1922, 1924, 1926, 1927, 1928, 1929, 1930, 1934, 1934 (US edition), 1938; second edition 1942, 1945, 1946, 1948, 1951.

[121] The 1913 German translation of this text also heads the list for 'Those who can read German'; Howson, *Lionel Robbins on the Principles of Economic Analysis*, p. 181.

Frank Knight's *Risk, Uncertainty and Profit*, Taussig's *Wages and Capital*, Marshall's *Principles*,[122] Hicks's *Theory of Wages*, and Mises's *Theory of Money and Credit*. There was, however, now an introductory text: Honor Scott's *Approach to Economics*.

This was the most successful of these brief introductions. Honor Scott (1908–1960) had been a student at the LSE from 1927 to 1931—her *Approach to Economics*[123] is based on the teaching at the LSE and she acknowledges her debt to Lionel Robbins for advice and criticism. Aimed at students who have never before studied the subject, her introductory chapter moves quickly through three distinct points: that economics is the study of scarcity, that value depends upon scarcity, and that capital is a stock and income a flow. The second chapter deals with markets, price being a co-ordinating mechanism; and in the third chapter on demand, diminishing marginal utility and the elasticity of demand are introduced. The fifth chapter, on factors of production, dismisses the pertinence of 'Land, Labour and Capital', and provides a distinctly Austrian account of capital and time, Böhm-Bawerk being mentioned by name in connection with the idea of 'roundabout production'. Later sections of the book deal with the organisation of industry, money and credit, economic geography, the national income, public finance, trade cycles, unemployment, protection, and free trade, rounded off with a two-page structured reading list. There was a note included in the final 1964 edition stating that her book had originally been written for use by grammar school pupils, aiming at an examination of roughly matriculation standard, but that in practice first-year university students also found it useful, as did candidates for professional examinations, advanced students doing revision, and general readers. This was therefore an introductory text of a new sort, angled at those entering the study of economics at university, and based upon the teaching of economics at the LSE.

In 1938 this text of Honor Scott, now Honor Croome, would be joined by another LSE product, Frederic Benham's *Economics*, consolidating the newly emerging microeconomics as the dominant pathway for undergraduate teaching. This is confirmed by the relative lack of success of James Meade's *Introduction to Economic Analysis and Policy*.[124] In some respects Meade's work is the first post-Keynesian textbook, Part I dealing with unemployment, Part II with 'competition and monopoly', Part III with the distribution of income, Part IV with the supply of factors of production—primarily labour and capital, with a substantial closing Part V dealing with 'international problems'—balance of payments, the gold standard, exchange rates, trade, and the international mobility of capital and labour. While Dalton and Bowley are acknowledged in the Preface, Maynard Keynes, Kahn, and Pigou are prominently featured, and thanks are given to Joan Robinson for having read most of the manuscript; indicative that the leading contemporary source for what would later be thought of as macroeconomic thinking was Cambridge, not the LSE. Unlike the approach taken by Robbins in his lectures and Honor Croome in her introduction, issues of equilibrium

[122] Robbins recommends 'Chapters I–VI', although it must be presumed he meant Book III of *Principles*, in the eighth edition the sole Book with six chapters only; in each of the six Books the chapters were numbered from 1; ibid.

[123] Honor Scott, *Approach to Economics*, Christophers, London 1931, p. xi; she married in 1932 and became Honor Croome.

[124] This went into a second edition the following year, but there do not appear to have been any subsequent editions or printings in the United Kingdom.

and exchange and the price system are not treated within an initial formal framework of choice and scarcity, but rather in the context of market structures in Part II: perfect competition, imperfect competition, and monopoly. We arrive at this *after* the treatment of banking policy, wages, and unemployment, hence in the context of policy, not of economic methodology.[125]

It was, however, Frederic Benham's *Economics* that cemented the teaching of economics at the LSE as the basis for the British undergraduate economics textbook for the second half of the twentieth century. Originally published in 1938 and reaching a ninth edition in 1973, its clear purpose was to serve as a textbook for first-year students of economics—providing a single key text to read alongside their introductory lectures. Benham announced the scope of his book as follows:

> The last few years have seen important changes both in economic doctrine and in economic practice. It seemed to me that there was a need for a new textbook which gave some account of those changes.
>
> Among the developments in doctrine incorporated in this volume we may name: the greater stress laid on the notion of choice between alternatives, and of scales of preference, the concept of 'utility' as something absolute and measurable being discarded and 'opportunity-cost' being emphasized rather than 'real-cost'; improvements in the theory of Diminishing Returns and of the economies of large-scale production; the analysis of monopoly, or imperfect competition, in terms of marginal cost and marginal revenue; and the treatment of money as a liquid asset, the demand to hold money varying with 'liquidity preference' and with the rate of interest. Considerable concessions have been made to the views of Mr. Keynes but I can hardly be regarded as one of his followers.[126]

Following a brief general survey and a discussion of national and international markets, the first section of the text deals with demand, introducing the downward-sloping demand curve and the conception of elasticity, the supply curve, equilibrium, and shifts in the equilibrium. The following section deals with production, clearly a hangover from the Millian approach to the exposition of economic principles; here we find discussion of factors of production, capital, division of labour. Then in Book II, dealing with the price system, there is consumer sovereignty, firm size, monopoly, wages, interest, rent, taxation, and the public sector,[127] and some remarks on the trade cycle. Book IV deals with money and banking, Book V with international trade, the final three chapters being on the gold standard, exchange control, and import duties and quotas. This combination of material recalls most strongly Taussig; a

[125] A comparable approach is followed by Alec Cairncross, *Introduction to Economics*, Butterworth & Co., London 1944; this was based on Glasgow University lectures to accountants in the later 1930s and had been almost ready for publication in 1939. 'In 1937 there was no adequate textbook. Nothing worth reading in 1937. You were told to read Marshall, but it was unreadable. Henry Clay was the nearest.' Interview with Cairncross in my *Economic Careers*, p. 43.

[126] Frederic Benham, *Economics: A General Textbook for Students*, Sir Isaac Pitman & Sons, London 1938, p. v.

[127] Ch. 19 on 'The State' was excluded from later editions.

prose narrative dominates, with a few diagrams to illustrate principles of exchange and equilibrium.

In a review, John Hicks pointed out that the lack of a single reliable text for first-year students had recently become very obvious, and that this new work appeared to fill the gap. Nonetheless, he did have criticisms:

> Benham has overdone his determination to be sound and traditional on theoretical questions. There have been a number of recent fads, but there has also been a profound change of outlook, which ought not to be neglected.... On the whole, Dr. Benham fails to achieve that sense of the economic system as something liable to great variations in *activity*, which ought to inform the whole of a really modern work on economics, and not to make its appearance only in special sections or chapters, devoted to unemployment or the trade cycle.[128]

The text was also very long—nearly 500 pages. Subsequent editions became longer, and more opaque. In the first edition we get to the principles of demand analysis by Chapter 3 (pp. 43ff.); in the 1955 edition we have to wait until Chapter 13 (pp. 174ff.) to be presented with the same material.

Jack Eastham, who had begun his study of economics with Allyn Young at the LSE, then been recruited to teach at Dundee in 1931, sought to update Benham's work with his own *Introduction to Economic Analysis* (1950). Developed from his teaching to first-year Dundee students on the London University external degrees in commerce and in economics (following therefore the LSE syllabus), this text cemented the technical priority of microeconomics over macroeconomics for the novice student. The book is in 25 chapters, and not divided into parts; but microeconomics comes first, with the third chapter on 'supply and demand' starting at p. 23, followed by a chapter on 'The Theory of Choice', and then a fifth chapter on indifference curves. This more direct approach is linked to a liberal use for the time of graphs, and some elementary algebra. By contrast the macroeconomic material, beginning at Chapter 15, makes only very occasional use of graphs and algebra.[129] However, although Eastham's text was reprinted in 1953, it was in that year eclipsed by yet another, if indirect, product of the LSE syllabus: Stonier and Hague's *Textbook of Economic Theory*.

When Douglas Hague had studied commerce at Birmingham from 1943 to 1946, his main textbook had been Benham, which he found unsatisfactory. Moving to a post at University College London in 1947 he became a colleague of Alfred Stonier, who had during the 1930s reviewed Robbins's *Nature and Significance*. In late 1948 they began collaborating on an economics textbook for Longmans, and in the process Hague went back to the problems he had experienced in learning his economics from Benham. He set about trying to explain the things that he had found hard to understand in Benham, while Stonier made extensive use of indifference curve analysis that

[128] J. R. Hicks, Review of F. Benham, *Economics. A General Text-Book for Students*, *Manchester School* Vol. 9 (1938), p. 185.

[129] J. K. Eastham, *An Introduction to Economic Analysis*, English University Press, London 1950. His *Graphical Economics*, English Universities Press, London 1960 developed on this, with for example a developed account of Cournot and Chamberlin.

was also obscured in Benham because it was not integrated into the text as a whole.[130] By 1950 they had completed a new economics textbook that was in two parts: the first part covering what we would now call microeconomics, the second macroeconomics. For the first time a British textbook made extensive use of diagrams throughout and clearly separated the micro from the macro.

> This book is designed for students with no previous knowledge of economic theory who wish to study the elements of the subject systematically. It is hoped that some parts of the book will also be useful to more advanced students. The method of exposition is similar to that used in lectures on General Economic Theory to first-year students at University College, London, who are reading for Part One of the B.Sc. (Economics) degree of London University. The book provides a general introduction to economic theory, but does not deal with special problems of international trade, public finance and welfare economics.

The text can be seen as a simple replacement for Benham, representing a shift from the 1930s to the 1950s. If we compare the running order of the chapters between the first edition of Benham and that of Stonier and Hague, Benham prefaces his Chapter 3 on demand with two general chapters on economics and markets, but once this is arrived at, the broad sequence of topics covered is similar, so that in both books the first 90 pages are devoted to demand and supply and consumers' equilibrium. The move in both texts is then to production, but here there is a clear difference, for Stonier and Hague present a standard neoclassical theory of the firm, marginal revenue, marginal costs, long-run average cost, perfect competition, external economies and diseconomies, monopoly, monopolistic competition, marginal productivity, moving on to wages, rent, interest and profits, concluding with Chapter 16 on the nature of demand for factors of production. Benham, on the other hand, is much more discursive, considering factors affecting the volume of production, the effects of the division of labour, economies of scale, and capital; the more formalised presentation of the firm is held over to Book III on the price system, but even here there is no formal presentation of perfect competition, with a chapter devoted to monopoly and then followed by costs, wages, interest, and rent, concluding with a chapter on development and the trade cycle. Benham then concludes with a book on money and banking and one on international trade. Stonier and Hague, on the other hand, at this point introduce Part II, 'Employment Theory', setting out from general equilibrium and then dealing in turn with money, employment, consumption and investment, and the rate of interest, with two concluding chapters on Keynesian economics. The book is divided fairly equally into 'micro and macro', except that these are described as 'price theory'[131] and 'employment theory'.

[130] Interview with Douglas Hague, Oxford, 15 May 1995. In Benham the treatment of indifference curves is at the end of Book I, in the Appendix to Ch. VI. See A. W. Stonier, D. C. Hague, *A Textbook of Economic Theory*, Longmans, Green & Co., London 1953, Ch. 3.

[131] And this reference to 'price theory' was given lapidary form by Louden Ryan, whose 1958 book was reprinted in 1960, 1961, 1962, twice in 1964, and in 1965; W. J. L. Ryan, *Price Theory*, Macmillan, London 1958. Ryan had taught at the LSE 1949–1953.

We can see in this way how a line is here concluded that had begun with Robbins's lectures 20 years previously: the macroeconomic framework that was initiated by Maynard Keynes's *General Theory* is *added on to* the basic microeconomic framework that Robbins had first developed using 'Austrian' theory. But in noting this familiar division, we might well ask: when was it first referred to as such? Searching JSTOR for 'microeconomics' reveals a first use of the term by Martin Bronfenbrenner in 1943, near the end of the article in a heading: 'Return to Microeconomics'.[132] Significantly, he uses the term as if the reader is already familiar with it, although there appears to be no previous printed use. The first use of 'macroeconomics' comes three years later, in the same journal, juxtaposed to 'microeconomics'.[133] This is only two years before Samuelson published *Economics*, the textbook that became the flagship of an increasingly Americanised international understanding of economics, a text that from the first was principally macroeconomic. This near-simultaneity—Samuelson had been writing *Economics* since 1945[134]—suggests something else: that the reason Bronfenbrenner and Klein use these new terms as if everyone is already familiar with them is because many people were. This first use in print was preceded by the development of teaching and the organisation of textbooks in this framework, without, however, explicitly employing the term. The textbooks that James Meade and Henry Phelps Brown had published in the later 1930s foreshadowed the emergence of a macroeconomic introduction to economics that, in the British context, had little impact. Here the principal textbook literature, from Benham through Stonier and Hague, Louden Ryan, and Lipsey, remained primarily micro, reflecting the direction that Robbins had first given to undergraduate teaching at the LSE.[135] This argument is also buttressed by the Chicago alternative to Samuelson: George Stigler's *Theory of Competitive Price* (1942) is a pared-back microeconomic introduction to economics, as the title suggests.[136] In the United States this approach encountered resistance; the first use of 'microeconomics' in the *American Economic Review* is in a review of Stackelberg's Madrid textbook, *Grundlagen der theoretischen Volkswirtschaftslehre* (1948), which according to the reviewer 'appeared at a time when many American economists have ceased to believe in the practical relevance of microeconomics.'[137]

[132] Martin Bronfenbrenner, 'The Role of Money in Equilibrium Capital Theory', *Econometrica* Vol. 11 (1943), pp. 58.

[133] Lawrence R. Klein, 'Macroeconomics and the Role of Rational Behaviour', *Econometrica* Vol. 14 (1946), p. 94.

[134] See Roger E. Backhouse, *Founder of Modern Economics: Paul A. Samuelson*, Vol. I: *Becoming Samuelson, 1915–1948*, Oxford University Press, New York 2017 Ch. 25.

[135] I owe this point about courses and textbooks to Roger Backhouse, who suggested it when I told him about the results of my JSTOR search.

[136] Although Stigler did not join the Chicago department until 1958, he graduated from Chicago with a PhD in 1938. This text represents the resolute refusal of Chicago economists to countenance the idea that oligopolistic competition had any relevance to analysis or policy; and indicates the extensive backstory to the eventual triumph of this stance as the bedrock of competition policy in the 1980s. The teaching of the theory of the firm to law students at Fordham in the 1980s, for example, focussed exclusively on the contrast of perfect competition to monopoly as the appropriate basis for an understanding of competition policy, as foreshadowed by Stigler in 1943 (interview with Valentine Korah, UCL, 1993).

[137] Arthur Schweitzer, Review of Heinrich von Stackelberg, *Grundlagen der theoretischen Volkswirtschaftslehre*, *American Economic Review* Vol. 39 (1949), p. 760. The first use of 'macroeconomics' in the AER was the previous year in an article by Kenneth Boulding, 'Professor Tarshis and the State of Economics' Vol. 38 (1948), p. 92, in quotation marks.

Nonetheless, at the end of the first chapter of Stonier and Hague, on demand and supply, there are two references: the first to Marshall's *Principles*, Book III, Chapter 4, and Book V, Chapters 1–3; the second to Wicksteed's *Common Sense*, Volume II, Chapter 4: 'Buyer and Seller. Demand and Supply.' It might be doubted whether this text from 1910 would have been on their radar at all if it had not been for Robbins's new edition of 1933, and the part it played in undergraduate teaching at the LSE. Furthermore, we might also note that in 1952 the American Economic Association had published a reader on 'price theory': the first selection was Wicksteed's 1913 Presidential Address to Section F of the British Association, held that year in Birmingham.[138] Here Wicksteed had presented his argument that in the standard presentation of supply and demand curves, the supply curve was in effect an inverted demand curve, arguing that 'what is usually called the supply curve is in reality the demand curve of those who possess the commodity'; and that '[t]he customary representation of cross curves confounds the process by which the price is discovered with the ultimate facts that determine it.'[139] Part II of Stigler and Boulding's reader was devoted to 'Costs and Returns', reprinting Clapham, Pigou, Robertson, Knight, and Sraffa from the 'Cost Controversy' of the 1920s. This American reader on 'price theory', collecting key sources in what would soon be generally recognised as microeconomic theory, was therefore rooted in the same sources that had (actually) shaped Robbins's presentation of economic theory during the 1930s. This linkage is further reinforced by the status of Stigler's own *Theory of Competitive Price*, which besides only dealing with perfectly competitive markets was one of the very first introductory textbooks written specifically for American graduate students.[140]

Graduate and Undergraduate Education: The United States and Britain

And this raises the principal emergent difference between the teaching of economics in Britain and the United States at this time: that by the 1940s, taught graduate courses in economics were offered at several major universities, while in Britain the number of postgraduate students of economics would remain generally very limited, and where they existed they mainly pursued courses of independent study, not taught programmes. We have already seen that the numbers of undergraduate economics students outside Cambridge were limited, even at the LSE; although the personal nature of teaching in Cambridge did create a need for a large number of persons capable of teaching economics, one of the conditions for the development of any subject. But, as Harry Johnson suggested,[141] other features of Cambridge, in both university and in college, subverted any positive impact this might have had.

[138] P. H. Wicksteed, 'The Scope and Method of Political Economy in the Light of the "Marginal" Theory of Value and Distribution', *Economic Journal* Vol. 24 (1914), pp. 1–16.

[139] Wicksteed, 'The Scope and Method of Political Economy', in George J. Stigler, Kenneth E. Boulding (eds.) *Readings in Price Theory*, Richard D. Irwin, Chicago 1952, pp. 15–16.

[140] David R. Kamerschen, Deepa J. Sridhar, '*The Theory of [Competitive] Price* according to George J. Stigler', *Journal of the History of Economic Thought* Vol. 31 (2009), pp. 181, 183.

[141] See Chapter 5, p. 136.

We can assess this divergence of British and American institutional developments by considering the early career of Paul Samuelson. He entered the University of Chicago in January 1932, aged 16; it was his local university, and he could live at home.[142] He arrived in the middle of the first year of a new, multidisciplinary undergraduate programme which, among other things, meant that in his second year he received a thorough grounding in biology, physics, and chemistry, while in his third year he audited Jacob Viner's graduate course, noting that there were about 35 students in the class.[143] This was in 1934–1935, the year in which only 42 students outside Cambridge graduated in economics in the whole of England and Wales, according to the University Grants Committee data.[144] Then, as a graduate student at Harvard, Samuelson took Schumpeter's economic theory course during 1935–1936, noting the main reading as 'Marshall, Wicksell, Pigou, Böhm-Bawerk, Knight and Wicksteed'[145]—echoing the reading assigned for the 'Principles of Economics' course at the LSE at that time. This does suggest that the LSE was then roughly aligned with the best of contemporary teaching in economics, except that its work was aimed at a more elementary level in which the mathematical input was very limited. At the LSE the constraint was not simply the educational background of the students, but the capacities of their teachers. Also clear from the account of teaching in Chicago and Harvard, which Roger Backhouse assembles from scratch, is that the leading American universities were already engaged in teaching economics to more students, at a higher technical level, and across a broader curricular range than anywhere else. The gap that would open up after 1945 was all the greater for the failure of British universities, outsides the sciences, medicine, and engineering, to move far beyond the level of undergraduate teaching after 1945. As we can see with Samuelson's undergraduate education at Chicago, this was a broad education of a kind not available anywhere in Britain, not in school, college, or university. While the American undergraduate programme of study was and is at a lower general level than a three-year degree in Britain, an American undergraduate studies for four years and then specialises in graduate school, where teaching is at a higher level, and more intensive, than that typical in the British university. The opportunity to develop both research and teaching was in postwar Britain much more restricted than it was in the United States, independent of any differences in scale.

This situation was not, however, so much a failure of academic vision or institutional resources as it was an outcome of resistance encountered in the labour market, and the symbiotic relationship between education and employment. From 1947 to 1972 the school-leaving age in Britain was 15, and most pupils did leave school at 15, the great majority of them uncertified. Conversely, the reason relatively few

[142] Like Donald Winch, who lived in South London and could commute to the LSE in the 1950s. Gary, Indiana, where Samuelson lived until 1926, was about 30 miles from the centre of Chicago, and so not then commutable; from 1928 he was able to attend Hyde Park School; Backhouse, *Founder*, p. 12.

[143] Ibid., p. 86. Backhouse's account of Samuelson's undergraduate education at Chicago takes up pp. 36–99, using both Samuelson's own recollections, course information, and textbook material to demonstrate exactly what the foundations of Samuelson-the-economist were; and in the process drawing attention to the advantages of a Chicago undergraduate education.

[144] See pp. 310–11, Table 11.7.

[145] Backhouse, *Founder*, p. 137.

18-year-olds went on to study at university was that most of the cohort had already left school at 15 or 16, while the small number who did stay on for another two years mostly did pass on to higher education.[146] The small minority of 15- and 16-year-olds who sat the 'ordinary' level examinations—in the early 1960s, 73% of school pupils were leaving school without any accreditation at all[147]—generally required five passes, including English and Mathematics, to progress to teacher training college, nursing training, or employment in banking, insurance, or public administration. Hence a university graduate on entering public or commercial employment would have missed five years of vocational and in-service training, not three; or, from the other point of view, five years' income. It is mainly for reasons such as these that, outside the natural and life sciences, medicine and engineering, the motivation for attending university in postwar Britain was primarily cultural and personal, not vocational. This general structure of incentives persisted well into the 1960s, which also helps explain why university education was disproportionately enjoyed by the middle classes in a labour market still dominated by unskilled (or at least uncertified) labour.

Another perspective on educational background and selection is supplied by the system of National Service, introduced from 1947 to conscript young men into the armed forces for a period from 18 months to two years. The system lasted until 1963, when the last of the 2 million National Servicemen were demobilised. The entire programme amounted to a huge natural experiment with masses of social data, and in fact the government's own report on secondary education, the Crowther Report of 1959, made good use of it. Richard Vinen shows through his analysis of allocation of conscripts to officer training that a strict hierarchy prevailed in the 1940s and 1950s by which public schoolboys were quickly selected for officer training; that the elite public schools supplied the elite regiments; that grammar school boys in smaller numbers went to other arms; and that the army itself had a category of 'weak middle class' that was considered poor material for officer class, lacking qualities of initiative and responsibility consequent on being 'provincial'. Vinen also notes that the working-class recruits did not really notice class distinctions; it was the middle-class recruits who were most sensitive to this.[148]

In Britain it was primarily the postwar schooling system that was socially selective, not the universities; hardly anyone stayed at school long enough to qualify for university entrance. In the second half of 1952, 1% of those National Servicemen actually admitted to basic training were illiterate, 18.5% were below the level of uncertified school-leavers, and 41.3% were uncertified school-leavers who had engaged in no further education or training—totalling 60.8% of those who had passed a medical test.[149]

[146] In 1954, 4.3% of the 18-year-old cohort qualified for university entrance, their peers no longer being in full-time education. Of this group, 73% did actually enter higher education. The latter proportion actually fell, towards the end of the decade, to 62% in 1960; Table 2: 'Percentage of Age Group Obtaining Minimum University Entrance Qualifications, and Entering University, Great Britain 1954–1962', in Committee on Higher Education, *Higher Education. Report of the Committee appointed by the Prime Minister under the Chairmanship of Lord Robbins 1961–63*, Cmnd. 2154, Her Majesty's Stationary Office, London 1963, p. 12.

[147] D. H. Aldcroft, *Education, Training and Performance 1944 to 1990*, Manchester University Press, Manchester 1992, p. 36.

[148] Richard Vinen, *National Service: A Generation in Uniform 1945–1963*, Penguin Books, London 2015.

[149] Ibid., Appendix VIII.

Vinen's findings suggest that entry to the professions was drawn primarily from public (i.e. private) schools, with university education only intervening as a qualification for recruitment in the 1960s, consequent upon which university education remained limited in scale until then. Given this limit on the role of university education outside technical subjects, it would be more important to study classics in Oxford to gain entry into public administration in the 1950s, just as it was in the early 1900s.[150]

Persistence to the present day in Britain of a three-year undergraduate education as the generally highest level of educational qualification in turn promoted over-specialisation in the teaching of economics in both Cambridge and Queens Belfast.[151] As it has turned out, the Oxford PPE is more suited to the ecology of the British educational system and labour market, with early over-specialisation in schools being compensated in this instance by a more general university-level education. The reality is, however, that the Oxford PPE is inferior to the better American liberal arts degrees, lacking their typical curricular breadth—as already evident in Samuelson's education at Chicago—while in the United States the idea that three years at university is an adequate preparation for public life or business would be treated with due scepticism.[152] Given also that economics is taught in the PPE alongside politics and philosophy, not only is the time available for the subject constrained, the technical level at which it can be taught is also very limited.

As already observed in Chapter 1, the history of education—more broadly, the historical study of schooling, training, and employment—is relatively undeveloped in Britain, and extending the remarks made here can form no substitute. At most they serve one simple end: to indicate why it was that the importance of Cambridge and London to the early emergence of economics as a university discipline was by the 1940s eclipsed by American developments. The scale and scope of American institutions brought together teachers of economics whose careers depended both upon their ability to teach and their facility in writing contributions that could be published in academic periodicals. Since its first 1911 volume, the *American Economic Review* has published the proceedings of the annual conference of the American Economic Association (AEA) in a separate number. As shown in Chapter 3, the British Economic Association/Royal Economic Society was founded to support the publication of a journal and editions of the writings of eminent economists, not to promote direct discussion among its members. When in the 1920s British economists initiated annual meetings at which papers were presented and discussed, this was an informal, even casual, arrangement, separate from the activities of the Royal Economic Society and which appears to have left no records. We only know of this

150 See A. E. Booth, A. W. Coats, 'The Market for Economists in Britain 1945–75: A Preliminary Survey', *Economic Journal* Vol. 88 (1978), pp. 436–54; P. D. Henderson, The Use of Economists in British Administration', *Oxford Economic Papers* n.s. Vol. 13 (1961), pp. 5–26.

151 See Bob Black's remarks on this in his interview in Tribe (ed.) *Economic Careers: Economists and Economics in Britain 1930–1970*, Routledge, London 1997, pp. 100–2.

152 In the early 1950s Dick Lipsey had a Frank Knight Scholarship for Chicago, but chose the LSE instead because there was no language requirement at the LSE. For graduate entry to Chicago he would had to have passed an entrance examination in French; see his interview in *Economic Careers*, p. 209.

today because of notices published at the time in the *Economic Journal*. The academic networks and media that were well-established by the 1920s in the United States still did not exist in Britain during the 1950s and 1960s. And as suggested in Chapter 2, it is these networks and media that are critical to the transformation of 'ideas' into the precepts and principles of a discipline.

13
Concluding Remarks

The story told here turns on the biographies of two men familiar to historians of economics: Alfred Marshall and Lionel Robbins. Their aspirations and ambitions did play a major part in forming the new discipline of economics; but as I also demonstrate, the making of this discipline cannot be understood on the basis of personal aspirations and ambitions alone.[1] The institutions in which they worked, the time at which they were employed by these institutions, what and how they were able to teach in these institutions—these all transformed personal qualities into opportunities for disciplinary development. Studying institutions as an independent variable has produced a major revision to our received picture: Cambridge and Marshall need to be moved aside to make room for London and Robbins as the key figures in the story of British economics. Oxford becomes an unfamiliar counterpoint to both Cambridge and London: for if both Alfred Marshall and Lionel Robbins had remained in Oxford, where in 1884 and 1929 they respectively were, neither would have been able to forge the reputations that they subsequently did. Personal biography is a genre familiar to historians; the organisation of institutional structures, processes, and constraints much less so. There is consequently a major emphasis in the foregoing on the routines of curriculum, finance, student numbers, and careers—matters with which academics are certainly familiar from their daily lives, but which they seem to consider too banal a concern for their research and writing.

If all of this has been persuasive, then it suggests that we need to rethink the meaning of 'context', or to at least start to notice that the coin has two sides. Historians of economics have long cleaved to a presentist bias, using the concepts, axioms, and intellectual preoccupations of modern economics as a grid through which sense can be made of past economic argument. This is not a new criticism,[2] and it is now more or less axiomatic in intellectual and cultural history that 'ideas' cannot be understood independently of their 'context'. However, for the most part, this 'context' turns out to be 'other ideas', the discursive framework that lends any one statement or argument its particular meaning for those using it. The point being made here is rather different; that such arguments have a material context that goes beyond 'thought' or 'ideas', although this context might seem so mundane or routine that it barely seems worth noting. When academic economists gather for coffee, they talk of little else but recent appointments and research funding, the developing careers of their colleagues at other national and international institutions. They do not discuss recent papers appearing in the *Economic Journal* or the *American Economic Review*. Gossip about

[1] Chris Stray makes a similar point in his review of approaches to writing the history of classics: 'Disciplinary Histories of Classics', *History of Universities* Vol. 29 No. 1 (2016), pp. 119–20.

[2] See, for example, my discussion of Samuel Hollander's presentation of David Ricardo as an early theorist of general equilibrium, 'Ricardian Histories', *Economy and Society* Vol. 10 (1981), pp. 451–66.

Constructing Economic Science. Keith Tribe, Oxford University Press. © Oxford University Press 2022.
DOI: 10.1093/oso/9780190491741.003.0013

careers, who is up and who is down, the interconnection of institutional and personal life cycles, reflects an awareness of the possibilities of career success, and of career failure. Those seeking success must pay attention to this interconnection, and adapt to its demands, however petty or mundane such demands might seem. These imperatives are a disciplinary constant; to understand the formation and development of any discipline, we need to identify and evaluate their force.

Foxwell did not adapt well to these new imperatives, presuming at almost 60 that he was the natural successor to Marshall for the Cambridge chair, but competing with a sharper economist half his age and with many more publications to his name.[3] It did not help either that he had in 1904 written a letter to *The Times* in which he berated his junior colleague for expressing an opinion contrary to his own.[4] Stated in this way, any modern academic would regard the outcome of his application for the Cambridge chair as a foregone conclusion. But Foxwell's petulant incomprehension of his failure, and the idea that the appointment was made thanks to illicit pressure from Marshall, has shaped historical perception for more than a century, echoing Foxwell instead of applying existing institutional knowledge to his case. Conversely, quite why was Ashley appointed founding Professor of Commerce at the University of Birmingham, when nothing he had taught and written up to that point seems of particular relevance in this instance? To point to his Liberal Imperialist politics[5] might seem purely reductionist; but the appointment of Ashley to the Birmingham chair calls for explanation, and none has ever been sought. As noted in Chapter 1, disciplinary knowledge is knowledge that is embedded within a career structure. We might say that as an economist Robbins was less skilled, less knowledgeable, than Marshall; but the former was able to prevail over the latter in building a new discipline because the LSE determined the economics curriculum of the University of London, and the London curriculum became the national and imperial model. This was what gave his teaching scope and force.

And the teaching styles of Marshall and Robbins differed. This introduces another institutional feature, usually regarded as of secondary importance in establishing the intellectual eminence of any one individual. After all, while some senior academics are brilliant and interesting lecturers, many are not; but this has little impact on their reputation. Reports of, and notes from, Marshall's lectures all testify to his indirect approach to economic education; that he drew on his extensive knowledge of contemporary economic organisation to develop the intellectual reflexes of his students. He did not, for example, use his *Principles of Economics* as a template for his lectures. As Lynda Grier testifies,[6] he welcomed students into his study at home, but expected them to ask the questions. His lectures were sometimes described as rambling, but no one seems to have found them uninteresting. His authority derived in part from the range of knowledge that he demonstrated, and his ability to relate this knowledge to more formal principles that he was equally capable of elaborating graphically or mathematically. Trained as a Cambridge mathematician, he was an assiduous collector of

[3] See p. 142.
[4] See p. 215.
[5] See pp. 254–55, 255n.17.
[6] See Chapter 6, pp. 150–51.

economic facts, whether in person, as in his extended visit to the United States in 1875,[7] or in the descriptive literature that he collected.[8]

The teaching style of Lionel Robbins was very different. He wrote out his lectures beforehand, but did not read them out; he studied them in advance and then spoke freely without them, his apparent command of the material lending authority to what he said. All reports of his lectures praise the coherence of their delivery. This pedagogical style was suited to the adumbration of principles, and sidestepped Robbins's own theoretical and empirical limitations. Edwin Cannan was robust in his criticism of the way Robbins quoted 'dozens of foreign economists whom we shall never read';[9] as I suggest, whether Robbins himself had read them can in some cases be questioned, and his command of the German language was certainly much more limited than he implied. In his teaching from 1929 onwards, Robbins strove to achieve authority through the clarity of his lectures and the arcane nature of the sources to which he referred his students; not responding to questions, like Marshall, but telling his students what they should know.

It turned out that the Robbins approach to the teaching of economics was what prevailed, not that of Marshall. This was mostly owed not to any personal qualities, but to the institutions in which they worked and the media that they had at their disposal. To understand the emergence of an economics discipline in Britain, we need to start from London, not Cambridge. The international prominence of Oxford and Cambridge today has too often been projected back into historical understanding of British educational structures; but Cambridge was for much of the nineteenth century very much a laggard as compared with any Scottish or German university, and later more a follower than an innovator in the modernisation of university organisation. And while the Economics Tripos was the first systematic course of undergraduate economic instruction, in England outside Cambridge and Oxford economics was at the time everywhere taught in the context of commerce. When in the 1930s the teaching of economics began to take root in British universities and colleges, it was the LSE, founded for strictly vocational purposes, that provided the model, the curriculum, and the examination structure.

The reputation of Cambridge as a centre for the development of university economics in Britain is largely owed to the efforts of Alfred Marshall. The publication of *Principles of Economics* in 1890, the creation of the British Economic Association and publication from 1891 of its *Economic Journal*, the founding of the Economics Tripos in 1903—together this created a foundation myth around which Cambridge economists could gather. But systematic analysis of the Tripos results moderates the early success of its creation, and when linked to the new system of college supervision conspired to undermine practical institutional cohesion. After his resignation from a University Lectureship in 1920, Maynard Keynes maintained his connection with Cambridge through his college activities; later, Joan Robinson and Piero Sraffa came

[7] Alfred Marshall, 'Some Features of American Industry', in John K. Whitaker (ed.) *The Early Economic Writings of Alfred Marshall 1867–1890*, Vol. 2, Macmillan, London 1975, pp. 352–77.

[8] In the later 1990s this material was ranged on a shelf across the entire back wall of the Marshall Library.

[9] See Chapter 12, p. 356.

to represent particular versions of Cambridge economics. This had, however, very little impact on national developments.

One significant feature of these developments, given the general absence of demand for economics graduates outside education until the 1960s, was the successive waves of expansion from around 1900, with the creation of the LSE and of several faculties of commerce in newly-chartered universities. As emphasised, everywhere outside Cambridge and Oxford, economics was taught in the context of commercial education, for which there was some demand from both students and employers. In many places the specialised teaching required was supplied part-time by those working in banking, accountancy, railways, and law. The new provincial universities provided employment for young graduates in commerce and economics, and professorial chairs for those who were slightly older. Arnold Plant and Lionel Robbins at the LSE were latecomers to this, both graduating after the First World War, and ordinarily both would have had to wait 20 years or more for a senior post, which by then were all filled with academics in mid-career. Chance lent them openings around 1930, and they then retained their chairs for over 30 years. By 1946 many of this first wave of appointees had retired, opening up a number of established university posts, together with the creation of new ones; this postwar surge focussed upon economics rather than commerce, and modern undergraduate economics textbooks were now available. A similar process of retirement, promotions, and new appointments occurred with the major expansion of the teaching of economics in universities and polytechnics in the 1960s and very early 1970s.

But, as is suggested towards the end of Chapter 12, outside the sciences and engineering there was little appetite in Britain for anything much beyond a first degree. During the 1950s and 1960s, for many university staff in the humanities and social sciences this was more or less all they had themselves.[10] Any demand beyond university or college employment was very limited, and the premature specialisation typical of the British schooling system created the illusion that, for example, a degree in economics might be the rough equivalent of a *Diplom Volkswirt*, the lowest level of (West) German qualification. The problem identified by Harry Johnson with teaching in Cambridge—that its economists spent a great deal of their time in dialogue with undergraduates, and not with graduate students or with their fellow economists—was broadly true of all British institutions.

Richard Lipsey, another Canadian, wrote the most successful, and long-lived, British textbook of the later twentieth century: *An Introduction to Positive Economics*, first published in 1963. While this did replicate the priority of microeconomics over macroeconomics in introducing the novice student (hence the inverse of the by-then dominant American text, Samuelson's *Economics*),[11] in other respects the text broke with the approach that Robbins had taken from the early 1930s, when he had

[10] The Cambridge or Oxford MA was and still is an honorary title awarded to those already holding a BA; schoolteachers and academics in the past might use the title, but it was never an additional qualification.

[11] And when Alan Peacock became Professor of Political Economy at Edinburgh in 1956, he completely recast the honours teaching, placing Samuelson's *Economics* at its head; *Edinburgh University Calendar 1957–58*, pp. 379–85. In the context, Samuelson symbolised a radical break with the former programme of teaching—and Peacock came from the LSE, too, where he had taught from 1948. See my *Economic Careers*, Routledge, London 1997, pp. 202–3.

presented theoretical principles bereft of mathematical elucidation or empirical reference. This austere approach had been the hallmark of a new 'science of economics' whose sourcebook was *Nature and Significance of Economic Science*, which, as I have suggested, prompted renewed interest in questions of method.

But Lipsey had during the 1950s at LSE been involved in the 'Methodology, Measurement and Testing in Economics' (M^2T) staff seminar; and he had a very different idea of scientific method, of theory, and empirical testing. He lays this out in a preliminary statement to *Positive Economics*, 'The Use of This Book':

> One of the most unfortunate tendencies in the teaching of economics, particularly in Britain, is that of making a clear split between economic theory and applied economics. All too often economic theory is taught merely as logical analysis, and is, at best, only vaguely related to the world, while applied economics becomes description unenlightened by any theoretical framework. Economic theory is meant to be about the real world. We seek, by the use of theory, to explain, understand and predict phenomena in the real world, and our theory must therefore be related to, and tested by, empirical observation of the world around us. The student of economic theory needs to ask at every stage what are the relevant magnitudes and quantities in the real world.[12]

It was with this reforming impulse that Lipsey became the founding Professor of Economics at the University of Essex, given a free hand to shape teaching and research when it opened in 1964. Taught Master's programmes were central to teaching across the university—at the time, MA students were eligible for the same local authority maintenance grants as undergraduates, fees were very limited and, in any case, paid by local authorities. As he describes in his 1994 interview, his textbook was intended to provide a means of moving on from the established framework.[13] Albert Sloman, founding Vice-Chancellor of Essex, makes clear in his own interview[14] that the aim of propelling the university quickly forward into a world-class research-led university encountered early and vigorous opposition from the Universities Grants Commission (UGC), whose members insisted that the purpose of the new universities was to innovate in teaching undergraduates, and not to pursue research. It turned out that the members of the UGC did not themselves understand what a university now was. In any case, within 10 years of the inauguration of Essex, the ongoing expansion of British higher education as a whole, in both universities and polytechnics, was reeled back, and talk now was of university closures. Lipsey abandoned the experiment at Essex and returned to Canada in 1970.

As already pointed out in Chapter 12, American graduate education had been gathering pace since the 1930s; but a graduate qualification in economics was still more hindrance than help in finding employment outside academia in the Britain of the 1970s. The future upon which Alfred Marshall had set his eyes in 1885—where

[12] Richard G. Lipsey, *An Introduction to Positive Economics*, Weidenfeld and Nicolson, London 1963, p. xii.

[13] Interview with Richard Lipsey in my *Economic Careers*, pp. 212–13.

[14] Interview with Sir Albert Sloman in my *Economic Careers*, pp. 225–37.

numbers of young men with 'cool heads and warm hearts' might go forth into public and private employment to make good use of their knowledge—had still not arrived. In the meantime, attendance at American universities had been boosted by a series of veterans' programmes—following demobilisation after the Second World War, after the Korean War, and of course the Vietnam War. In the second half of the twentieth century, the diverse landscape of US higher education provided a very much larger, and more flexible, foundation for the developing discipline of economics than existed in Britain. Today the basic LSE textbooks for teaching micro- and macroeconomics are all American.

Appendix

Cambridge

Cambridge Economics Tripos, 1905–1955 (Source: *Cambridge University Reporter*)

All Part I Candidates								
	1	2.1	2.2	3	Pt. I total	% 1 & 2.1	% Thirds	Cum. total I
1904–1905	0	2	4	4	10	20	40	10
1905–1906	1	0	3	0	4	25	0	14
1906–1907	0	3	2	3	8	38	38	22
1907–1908	0	2	2	4	8	25	50	30
1908–1909	0	8	3	0	11	73	0	41
1909–1910	2	8	6	2	18	56	11	59
1910–1911	3	4	3	7	17	41	41	76
1911–1912	1	3	4	1	9	44	11	85
1912–1913	0	1	6	6	13	8	46	98
1913–1914	1	5	9	13	28	21	46	126
1914–1915	0	3	4	4	11	27	36	137
1915–1916	2	1	6	3	12	25	25	149
1916–1917	2	4	4	5	15	40	33	164
1917–1918	0	3	1	3	7	43	43	171
1918–1919	0	2	5	4	11	18	36	182
1919–1920	3	9	12	9	33	36	27	215
1920–1921	3	3	18	22	46	13	48	261
1921–1922	3	1	16	24	44	9	55	305
1922–1923	1	6	12	16	35	20	46	340
1923–1924	0	6	8	25	39	15	64	379
1924–1925	0	3	10	31	44	7	70	423
1925–1926	3	8	12	33	56	20	59	479
1926–1927	0	10	16	31	57	18	54	536
1927–1928	2	5	17	44	68	10	65	604
1928–1929	5	5	24	25	59	17	42	663
1929–1930	1	3	18	29	51	8	57	714
1930–1931	5	10	34	72	121	12	60	835
1931–1932	4	6	19	57	86	12	66	921
1932–1933	3	10	27	63	103	13	61	1,024
1933–1934	7	13	24	59	103	19	57	1,127
1934–1935	4	9	29	63	105	12	60	1,232
1935–1936	2	12	26	62	102	14	61	1,334
1936–1937	5	13	55	61	134	13	46	1,468
1937–1938	7	12	54	65	138	14	47	1,606
1938–1939	3	11	46	88	148	9	59	1,754
1939–1940	5	12	33	55	105	16	52	1,859
1940–1941	3	7	20	25	55	18	45	1,914
1941–1942	6	7	19	30	62	21	48	1,976
1942–1943	1	5	11	10	27	22	37	2,003
1943–1944	2	1	4	5	12	25	42	2,015
1944–1945	1	7	7	9	24	33	38	2,039
1945–1946	4	13	29	39	85	20	46	2,124
1946–1947	5	21	45	74	145	18	51	2,269
1947–1948	6	31	53	64	154	24	42	2,423
1948–1949	4	30	80	68	182	19	37	2,605
1949–1950	4	20	68	75	167	14	45	2,772
1950–1951	7	20	60	49	136	20	36	2,908
1951–1952	4	18	58	66	146	15	45	3,054
1952–1953	1	9	54	73	137	7	53	3,191
1953–1954	5	15	62	82	164	12	50	3,355
1954–1955	4	19	75	68	166	14	41	3,521
TOTALS	135	439	1,217	1,730	3,521			

All Part II Candidates								
	1	2.1	2.2	3	Pt. II total	% 1 & 2.1	% Thirds	Cum Total II
1904–1905					0			
1905–1906	0	0	2	1	3	0	33	3
1906–1907	1	1	1	2	5	40	40	8
1907–1908	2	2	1	4	9	44	44	17
1908–1909	2	2	5	1	10	40	10	27
1909–1910	1	4	4	2	11	45	18	38
1910–1911	4	9	4	5	22	59	23	60
1911–1912	4	6	7	8	25	40	32	85
1912–1913	2	4	6	4	16	38	25	101
1913–1914	1	6	6	5	18	39	28	119
1914–1915	2	1	6	4	13	23	31	132
1915–1916	0	3	5	4	12	25	33	144
1916–1917	0	5	5	2	12	42	17	156
1917–1918	2	5	4	4	15	47	27	171
1918–1919	1	0	2	2	5	20	40	176
1919–1920	2	7	4	9	22	41	41	198
1920–1921	3	15	20	14	52	35	27	250
1921–1922	3	3	14	13	33	18	39	283
1922–1923	2	2	10	12	26	15	46	309
1923–1924	1	4	13	12	30	17	40	339
1924–1925	2	10	13	21	46	26	46	385
1925–1926	2	6	15	14	37	22	38	422
1926–1927	5	10	15	17	47	32	36	469
1927–1928	5	8	12	17	42	31	40	511
1928–1929	5	9	19	29	62	23	47	573
1929–1930	3	10	23	25	61	21	41	634
1930–1931	4	11	26	11	52	29	21	686
1931–1932	0	13	19	28	60	22	47	746
1932–1933	3	15	32	29	79	23	37	825
1933–1934	7	13	25	32	77	26	42	902
1934–1935	5	12	24	28	69	25	41	971
1935–1936	6	13	28	25	72	26	35	1,043
1936–1937	4	8	25	25	62	19	40	1,105
1937–1938	3	11	16	13	43	33	30	1,148
1938–1939	1	14	22	24	61	25	39	1,209
1939–1940	5	6	24	15	50	22	30	1,259
1940–1941	2	6	16	8	32	25	25	1,291
1941–1942	1	4	9	7	21	24	33	1,312
1942–1943	1	5	6	5	17	35	29	1,329
1943–1944	2	4	7	5	18	33	28	1,347
1944–1945	0	3	2	2	7	43	29	1,354
1945–1946	6	7	14	5	32	41	16	1,386
1946–1947	6	24	24	12	66	45	18	1,452
1947–1948	3	20	32	18	73	32	25	1,525
1948–1949	3	18	36	20	77	27	26	1,602
1949–1950	5	22	38	20	85	32	24	1,687
1950–1951	2	13	37	16	68	22	24	1,755
1951–1952	6	20	35	23	84	31	27	1,839
1952–1953	2	17	35	17	71	27	24	1,910
1953–1954	4	17	37	19	77	27	25	1,987
1954–1955	3	17	27	18	65	31	28	2,052
TOTALS	139	445	812	656	2,052			

Note: Many Part I candidates did not proceed to Part II; and some Part II candidates had not done Part I. These tables show the totals of annual results and grades awarded.

London

University of London Graduates, 1903–1955 (Source: *London University Gazette*)

	Internal BSc (Econ)						
	1st	2nd	2.1	2.2	Third	Pass	Total
1903							0
1904							0
1905	1	1			2	0	4
1906	1	1			1	0	3
1907	1	2			0	1	4
1908	0	0			2	1	3
1909	1	3			2	1	7
1910	3	3			4	1	11
1911	2	4			3	1	10
1912	3	6			7	5	21
1913	5	5			7	9	26
1914	1	2			6	2	11
1915	1	8			4	1	14
1916	1	3			3	1	8
1917	0	6			4	2	12
1918	0	4			4	2	10
1919	2	6			1	4	13
1920	3	4			10	1	18
1921	3	10			12	4	29
1922	6	20			17	5	48
1923	6	28			28	12	74
1924	4	18				16	38
1925	7	19				38	64
1926	5	21				24	50
1927	6	23				26	55
1928	4	30				23	57
1929	9	30				20	59
1930	12	27				19	58
1931	5	52				28	85
1932	11	55				35	101
1933	9	70				28	107
1934	10	78				21	109
1935	11		18	55		28	112
1936	19		23	66		27	135
1937	9		27	48		27	111
1938	13		33	49		29	124
1939	14		28	37		34	113
1940	11		24	35		15	85
1941	7		25	30		0	62
1942	0		3	3		1	7
1943	6		9	22		10	47
1944	0		0	7		2	9
1945	8		16	25		8	57
1946	13		26	57		26	122
1947	17		56	84		37	194

Internal BSc (Econ)							
	1st	2nd	2.1	2.2	Third	Pass	Total
1948	15		55	101		58	229
1949	24		71	184		68	347
1950	6		64	155		71	296
1951	16		43	142		72	273
1952	13		73	166		69	321
1953	9		64	145		56	274
1954	7		70	137		46	260
1955	9		61	126		68	264

Internal BCom					
	1st (Hons)	2nd (Hons)	Hons	Pass	Total
1921					0
1922				35	35
1923				38	38
1924				30	30
1925				34	34
1926			3	32	35
1927			3	23	26
1928			3	43	46
1929			3	38	41
1930			1	36	37
1931			1	33	34
1932			2	42	44
1933			2	19	21
1934	2	20	2	38	62
1935	2	26	0	20	48
1936	1	20		13	34
1937	4	16		19	39
1938	2	20		15	37
1939	4	26		13	43
1940	3	17		16	36
1941	2	5		0	7
1942	2	0		2	4
1943	1	3		0	4
1944	0	1		0	1
1945					0
1946	1	11		7	19
1947	3	15		11	29
1948	3	31		15	49
1949	1	29		21	51
1950	1	19		6	26
1951	2	21		13	36
1952	0	7		3	10
1953					0
1954					0
1955					0

	External BSc (Econ)							
	1st	2nd	2.1	2.2	Third	Pass	Total	Private Study
1903							0	
1904						4	4	
1905						3	3	
1906	1	1				4	6	
1907		2			3	3	8	
1908		1			2	2	5	
1909		2			1	6	9	5
1910		2			4	7	13	1
1911	1	2			2	7	12	1
1912	1	3			5	7	16	6
1913		3			2	2	7	
1914		5			7	5	17	
1915		1			4	9	14	
1916		4			2	4	10	7
1917		1			1	3	5	3
1918					2	4	6	6
1919		2			2	7	11	
1920		6			3	5	14	3
1921	1	5			12	10	28	5
1922	1	6			5	12	24	
1923	1	5			6	12	24	
1924		3				16	19	13
1925	1	6				11	18	11
1926	1	14				12	27	21
1927	3	16				15	34	22
1928	1	11				14	26	16
1929	0	14				11	25	13
1930	7	11				38	56	38
1931	2	9				16	27	17
1932	2	24				24	50	30
1933	0	40				29	69	49
1934	2	27				12	41	26
1935	3	37				19	59	45
1936	2		10	30		19	61	36
1937	4		6	22		16	48	32
1938	1		14	32		18	65	40
1939	1		10	36		25	72	50
1940	0		4	23		7	34	19
1941	1		4	30		0	35	21
1942							0	
1943	2		6	29		17	54	38
1944							0	
1945	2		22	40		37	101	74
1946	3		19	72		36	130	77
1947	2		18	60		42	122	85
1948	5		20	80		73	178	93
1949	1		14	86		84	185	88
1950	1		14	107		110	232	82

External BSc (Econ)								
	1st	2nd	2.1	2.2	Third	Pass	Total	Private Study
1951	5		23	110		117	255	95
1952	4		24	135		157	320	148
1953	4		20	156		125	305	125
1954	4		19	122		142	287	130
1955	2		21	54		80	157	61

External BCom							
	1st (Hons)	2nd (Hons)	Honours	Pass	Total	CDB	Private Study
1920					0		
1921					0		
1922				2	2		
1923				11	11		
1924				16	16	1	2
1925				11	11	6	3
1926				20	20	8	6
1927			1	31	32	13	9
1928			1	34	35	13	11
1929			1	25	26	10	9
1930			1	40	41	14	17
1931			0	44	44	14	19
1932			0	45	45	11	28
1933			0	40	40	14	22
1934	2	9	1	59	71		
1935	1	20	0	39	60	19	28
1936	1	28		38	67	24	30
1937	0	19		31	50	19	24
1938	2	23		29	54	8	26
1939	0	22		27	49	15	20
1940	0	16		29	45	10	13
1941	2	5		0	7	4	1
1942					0		
1943		8		7	15	4	3
1944					0		
1945					0		
1946	1	23		20	44	13	15
1947	1	12		32	45	19	8
1948	0	23		35	58	28	12
1949	1	32		40	73	13	16
1950	0	37		54	91	15	14
1951	0	33		71	104	10	19
1952	1	27		61	89		
1953					0		
1954					0		
1955					0		

Non-LSE BSc (Econ)

University of London BSc (Econ) 1905–1955 (*London University Gazette*)

	UCL	Hull	Leicester	Nottingham	Southampton	Total Non-London
1905	0		0	0	0	0
1906	0		0	0	0	0
1907	0		0	0	0	0
1908	0		0	0	2	2
1909	0		0	0	0	0
1910	0		0	0	0	0
1911	0		0	0	0	0
1912	0		0	0	0	0
1913	0		0	0	0	0
1914	0		0	1	0	1
1915	0		0	0	0	0
1916	0		0	0	0	0
1917	0		0	0	0	0
1918	0		0	0	0	0
1919	0		0	1	0	1
1920	0		0	0	0	0
1921	0		0	0	0	0
1922	0		0	4	1	5
1923	0		0	0	0	0
1924	0		0	1	1	2
1925	0		0	1	0	1
1926	0		0	1	1	2
1927	0		0	1	3	4
1928	0		0	1	0	1
1929	0	0	0	2	1	3
1930	4	0	0	1	1	2
1931	8	0	0	1	3	4
1932	14	0	0	1	0	1
1933	15	4	0	3	1	8
1934	9	1	0	4	1	6
1935	16	3	0	6	4	13
1936	13	0	1	8	5	14
1937	19	0	1	2	5	8
1938	13	2	0	1	6	9
1939	0	2	0	5	2	9
1940	11	2	0	3	1	6
1941	2	0	1	2	2	5
1942	0	0	0	0	0	0
1943	0	0	0	6	0	6
1944	0	0	0	0	0	0
1945	0	0	0	5	1	6
1946	2	0	0	0	0	0
1947	12	2	0	4	4	10
1948	21	7	0	33	14	54
1949	41	6	0	25	21	52

	UCL	Hull	Leicester	Nottingham	Southampton	Total Non-London
1950	34	6	13	10	14	43
1951	35	12	11	1	21	45
1952	25	11	15	0	17	43
1953	39	6	22	0	28	56
1954	26	7	17	0	10	34
1955	36	6	15	0	2	23

Note: These results are a subset of all external BSc (Econ) degrees.

Dundee

Attendances at the Dundee School of Economics (Day and Evening)
[Attached to 'Memorandum of Evidence for the Committee of Enquiry into University Education in Dundee, 7 March 1949'; MS 33/10/1(1) University of Dundee Library Archives]

	DAYTIME				EVENING					
Year	Degree	Diploma	Postgrad	Special	Degree	Diploma	DPA	CA	Special	Postgrad
1931–1932		2	8	7		28		28	3	3
1932–1933		6	5	3		24		24	21	3
1933–1934		18	15	8		19		23	8	
1934–1935		20	3	11	1	25		32	9	
1935–1936	1	19	9	11	2	30		19	8	1
1936–1937	4	25	7	6	1	23		16	11	
1937–1938	12	22	4	7	2	34		18	9	
1938–1939	13	13	5	3	3	10		14	5	1
1939–1940	12	3	2	4		9			2	
1940–1941	15	4		3	2	23		2	1	
1941–1942	20	5								
1942–1943	14	3		1				1		
1943–1944										
1944–1945										
1945–1946										
1946–1947	36	24	2	1	4	11	12	57	2	
1947–1948	50	24	1	1	9	10	14	54	10	
1948–1949	56	20	5		8	12	8	34	7	

Manchester Owens

Student Numbers, Owens/Manchester 1851–1950 (Source: Charlton 1951, App. V + University Calendars)

TOTAL STUDENTS REGISTERED						
	DAY (not Med & Tech)		EVENING	PolEcon Day	PolEcon Evening	Comm. Students
	MEN	WOMEN		DAY	EVENING	
1851–1852	62					
1852–1853	71					
1853–1854	71					
1854–1855	58					
1855–1856	52					
1856–1857	33					
1857–1858	34					
1858–1859	40					
1859–1860	57					
1860–1861	69		92			
1861–1862	88		235	0		
1862–1863	108		287	2	8	
1863–1864	110		312	0	11	
1864–1865	128					
1865–1866	113		282	6	26	
1866–1867	113		280	3	50	
1867–1868	173		324	7	48	
1868–1869	210		473	6	40	
1869–1870	209		434	10	56	
1870–1871	264		527	4	38	
1871–1872	327		513	10	34	
1872–1873	337		557	8	47	
1873–1874	356		889	19	58	
1874–1875	375		863	24	42	
1875–1876	395		819	10	54	
1876–1877	415		900	10	51	
1877–1878	418		826	15	30	
1878–1879	443		748	13	33	
1879–1880	392		731	17	31	
1880–1881	417		717	5	30	
1881–1882	390		692	16	53	
1882–1883	373		693	8	37	
1883–1884	400	60	623	14	33	
1884–1885	393	50	565	3	29	
1885–1886	380	66	541	12	37	
1886–1887	364	67	542	8	48	
1887–1888	389	74	521	6	43	
1888–1889	405	68	515	4	36	
1889–1890	410	72	439	12	36	

(continued)

TOTAL STUDENTS REGISTERED

	DAY (not Med & Tech)		EVENING	PolEcon Day	PolEcon Evening	Comm. Students
	MEN	WOMEN		DAY	EVENING	
1890–1891	429	61	425	15	18	
1891–1892	505	81	395	13	23	
1892–1893	507	93	320	5	23	
1893–1894	527	108	362	18	26	
1894–1895	484	108	329	11	27	
1895–1896	566	104	344	16	25	
1896–1897	524	102	224	11	26	
1897–1898	546	99	160	12	43	
1898–1899	528	111	167	29	93	
1899–1900	507	126	146	31	88	
1900–1901	506	166	163	22	76	
1901–1902	534	172	176	31	26	
1902–1903	652	201	179	55	29	
1903–1904	643	235	185	34	16	
1904–1905	680	253	199	37	7	16
1905–1906	711	263	297	50	2	31
1906–1907	704	262	226	72	14	36
1907–1908	746	302	234	77	0	38
1908–1909	798	325	199	125	0	35
1909–1910	807	328	202	113	0	33
1910–1911	808	312	162	90	11	45
1911–1912	821	330	199	119	3	47
1912–1913	770	320	201	107	10	42
1913–1914	787	328	215	118	1	57
1914–1915	608	329	153	127	10	46
1915–1916	390	325	122	67	1	26
1916–1917	301	333	216	90	1	24
1917–1918	265	345	180	87	0	17
1918–1919	553	373	229	122	0	35
1919–1920	1144	457	394	160	0	63
1920–1921	1135	508	287			131
1921–1922	1120	558	316			142
1922–1923	1021	581	360			129
1923–1924	937	626	361			118
1924–1925	907	619	296			129
1925–1926	940	604	300			144
1926–1927	1,032	586	417			147
1927–1928	1,086	600	432			137
1928–1929	1,110	611	388			125
1929–1930	1,140	596	502			108
1930–1931	1,183	604	437			133
1931–1932	1,236	582	369			136
1932–1933	1,268	595	350			132
1933–1934	1,326	605	308			137
1934–1935	1,340	553	320			116
1935–1936	1,299	511	364			97

TOTAL STUDENTS REGISTERED

	DAY (not Med & Tech)		EVENING	PolEcon Day	PolEcon Evening	Comm. Students
	MEN	WOMEN		DAY	EVENING	
1936–1937	1,183	434	368			79
1937–1938	1,211	426	359			79
1938–1939	1,208	452	418			78
1939–1940	1,095	460				61
1940–1941	965	464				
1941–1942	1,040	512				
1942–1943	977	571				
1943–1944	863	623				
1944–1945	920	719				
1945–1946	1,345	934				
1946–1947	2,122	1,081				
1947–1948	2,643	1,097				
1948–1949	3,036	1,023				
1949–1950	3,073	995				
TOTALS	67554	26539	29895	2116	1638	2949

Faculty of Commerce, University of Manchester

Faculty of Commerce, University of Manchester (Source: *University Calendars*)

	GRADUATES												
	BA(Hons.) Econ	BCom	BA (Com)	MA (Com)	BA (Admin)	Higher Comm. Cert.	CommEcon Total	BA (Hons.)	BA (Ord.)	BA (total)	BSc Hons.)	BSc (Ord.)	BSc (total)
1902–1903						3	0						
1903–1904						1	0						0
1904–1905	1					1	1			0			0
1905–1906	1					1	1			0			0
1906–1907	0	5				0	5			0			0
1907–1908	0	7				1	7			0			0
1908–1909	3	6				0	9			0			0
1909–1910	2	6				0	8			0			0
1910–1911	1	7				0	8	40	139	179	67	23	90
1911–1912	3	7				0	10	34	135	169	55	39	94
1912–1913	2	8				0	10	52	127	179	65	28	93
1913–1914	0	11				0	11	39	39	78	59	27	86
1914–1915	2	8				1	10	43	31	74	51	26	77
1915–1916	1	7				0	8	40	29	69	33	18	51
1916–1917	3	3				0	6	40	28	68	16	14	30
1917–1918	5	4				0	9	32	21	53	20	19	39
1918–1919	0	6				0	6	31	28	59	24	30	54
1919–1920	2	14				3	16	41	27	68	58	15	73
1920–1921	3	10				2	13	64	37	101	109	47	156
1921–1922	4	39				1	43	119	60	179	159	72	231
1922–1923	6	33				1	39	76	23	99	116	54	170
1923–1924	3	25				0	28	85	41	126	110	42	152
1924–1925	2	22				0	24	84	27	111	98	59	157
1925–1926	1	26				3	27	91	47	138	91	51	142

1926–1927	3		28	1		0	32	84	45	129	69	52	121
1927–1928	2		36	4		0	42	100	42	142	71	54	125
1928–1929	1		39	3	6	0	49	87	53	140	74	41	115
1929–1930	3		15	1	10	1	29	126	35	161	74	49	123
1930–1931	1		27	3	15	0	46	116	41	157	96	50	146
1931–1932	3		28	3	13	0	47	106	56	162	91	47	138
1932–1933	6		29	2	12	1	49	111	35	146	90	27	117
1933–1934	4		37	2	14	0	57	99	60	159	87	42	129
1934–1935	0		31	2	17	2	50	128	41	169	90	44	134
1935–1936	3		26	1	21	3	51	123	62	185	96	46	142
1936–1937	1		19	3	20	2	43	103	39	142	92	46	138
1937–1938	4		20	1	28	0	53	97	26	123	84	43	127
1938–1939	2		16	1	24	1	43	86	26	112	81	33	114
1939–1940	5		15	2	34	0	56	106	16	122	69	47	116
1940–1941	1		18	1	24	2	44	62	50	112	76	40	116
1941–1942	2		3	1	23	0	29	68	21	89	98	33	131
1942–1943	1		3	0	27	1	31	65	27	92	73	20	93
1943–1944	3		10	1	25	0	39	58	26	84	95	40	135
1944–1945	0		7	2	24	0	33	74	33	107	103	32	135
1945–1946	7		17	1	32	1	57	86	66	152	113	42	155
1946–1947	9		29	1	50	0	89	132	60	192	141	58	199
1947–1948	21		34	1	68	0	124	148	64	212	160	49	209
1948–1949	29		44	1	47	0	121	250	112	362	246	76	322
1949–1950	17		54	0	30	0	101	248	108	356	221	117	338
1950–1951	20		51	1	59	0	131	244	101	345	226	131	357
1951–1952	20		27	1	43	0	91	210	125	335	210	132	342
1952–1953	19		38	0	43	0	100	195	100	295	199	129	328
1953–1954	11		43	0	40	0	94	201	84	285	197	113	310
1954–1955	13		27	1	36	0	77	241	26	267	177	131	308
TOTALS	**256**	**254**	**771**	**41**	**785**	**32**	**2,107**	**4,665**	**2,419**	**7,084**	**4,630**	**2,328**	**6,958**

Birmingham

Commerce Students and Graduates of University of Birmingham, 1900–1940 (Source: *University of Birmingham Calendars*)

	Commerce Attend.	Accounting Attend.	BCom	MCom	BA (Hons) Econ
1901–1902			0	1	
1902–1903	11	57	0	1	
1903–1904	20	57	0	0	
1904–1905	23	40	3	0	
1905–1906	32	38	5	0	
1906–1907	25		1	1	
1907–1908	32		5	3	
1908–1909	32		4	0	
1909–1910	40		4	1	
1910–1911	41		7	2	
1911–1912	46		3	2	
1912–1913	47		7	1	
1913–1914	49		8	3	
1914–1915	27		7	0	
1915–1916	22		5	0	
1916–1917	19		2	0	
1917–1918	66		5	1	
1918–1919	86		1	0	
1919–1920	194		14	1	
1920–1921	183		29	1	
1921–1922	98		23	3	
1922–1923	67		7	4	0
1923–1924	58		9	3	0
1924–1925	48		6	3	0
1925–1926	54		6	4	0
1926–1927	51		6	3	0
1927–1928	61		9	2	0
1928–1929	60		7	1	0
1929–1930	70		12	2	0
1930–1931	70		17	2	0
1931–1932	70		11	0	0
1932–1933	81		10	4	0
1933–1934	93		11	5	1
1934–1935	88		6	1	0
1935–1936	83		13	4	0
1936–1937	78		17	1	0
1937–1938	67		12	2	0
1938–1939	74		9	7	0
1939–1940	67		5	1	0
	[no records for 1941–1948]				
TOTALS	2,333	192	306	70	1

Bibliography

The *Oxford Dictionary of National Bibliography* is an important online resource frequently cited in the foregoing. For the sake of simplicity I have not included urls with each citation, since it can only be accessed via an institutional site, where it is then searchable by name or subject.

Ahmad, Salma, 'Institutions and the Growth of Knowledge: The Rockefeller Foundation's Influence on the Social Sciences between the Wars', PhD dissertation, University of Manchester 1987.

Aldcroft, D. H., *Education, Training and Performance 1944 to 1990*, Manchester University Press, Manchester 1992.

Allen, G. C., *British Industries and Their Organisation*, Longmans, Green, & Co., London 1933.

Amonn, Alfred, 'Wesen und Bedeutung der Wirtschaftswissenschaft', *Zeitschrift für Nationalökonomie* Bd. 7 H. 3 (1936), pp. 306–25.

Anderson, R. D., *European Universities from the Enlightenment to 1914*, Oxford University Press, Oxford 2004.

Annan, Noel, *Leslie Stephen: His Thought and Character in Relation to His Time*, MacGibbon and Kee, London 1951.

Anon., 'Proceedings of Statistical Societies', *Journal of the Statistical Society of London* Vol. 1 No. 9 (January 1839), pp. 546–54.

Anon., *The Student's Guide to the University of Cambridge. Part VIII Moral Sciences Tripos*, Fourth edition, revised, Deighton Bell and Co., Cambridge 1881.

Anon., 'Mr. A. W. Flux, M.A.', *Manchester Faces and Places* Vol. 6 No. 8 (May 1895), pp. 124–26.

Anon., 'The Economic Curricula at Oxford and Cambridge', *Economic Journal* Vol. 31 (1921), pp. 400–6.

Anon. [LSE Registrar], *Register 1895–1932*, London School of Economics and Political Science, London 1934.

Arnold, Matthew, *Schools and Universities on the Continent*, Complete Prose Works of Matthew Arnold Vol. 4, University of Michigan Press, Ann Arbor 1964.

Ashley, A., *William James Ashley. A Life*, P. S. King & Son, London 1932.

Ashley, William J., *James and Philip van Artevelde*, Macmillan, London 1883.

Ashley, William J., *An Introduction to English Economic History and Theory: The Middle Ages*, Rivingtons, London 1888.

Ashley, William J., *What Is Political Science? An Inaugural Lecture Given in the Convocation Hall of the University of Toronto, 9th November, 1888*, Rowsell & Hutchison, Toronto 1888.

Ashley, William J., 'Introductory Chapter: The English Manor', in Fustel de Coulanges, *The Origin of Property in Land*, Swan Sonnenschein, London 1892, pp. vii–xlviii.

Ashley, William J., *An Introduction to English Economic History and Theory. Part II: The End of the Middle Ages*, Longmans & Co., London 1893.

Ashley, William J., 'On the Study of Economic History', *Quarterly Journal of Economics* Vol. 7 (1893), pp. 115–36.

Ashley, William J., *Surveys Historic and Economic*, Longmans, Green, & Co., London 1900.

Ashley, William J., [A Birmingham Correspondent], 'German Educational Experiments', *The Times*, 2 April 1903, p. 10.

Ashley, William J., 'The Universities and Business', *Minutes of Proceedings of the Staffordshire Iron and Steel Institute*, 4 April 1903, pp. 157–75.

Ashley, William J., *The Tariff Problem*, P. S. King & Son, London 1903.

Ashley, William J., 'The Present Position of Political Economy', *Economic Journal* Vol. 17 (1907), pp. 467–89.

Ashley, W. J., 'The Present Position of Political Economy in England', in *Die Entwicklung der deutschen Volkswirtschaftslehre im neunzehnten Jahrhundert* Bd. I (Schmoller Fs.), Duncker und Humblot, Leipzig 1908, pp. XV 1–26.

Ashley, William J., *The Economic Organisation of England: An Outline History*, Longmans, Green, & Co., London 1914.

Aslanbeigui, Nahid, Guy Oakes, 'The "Cambridge Tradition" Reconsidered', *History of Political Economy* Vol. 50 (2018), pp. 777–88.

Aslanbeigui, Nahid, Guy Oakes, *Arthur Cecil Pigou*, Palgrave Macmillan, Basingstoke UK 2015.

Astier, P., I. Cuminal, *L'Enseignement technique industriel et commercial en France et à l'étranger*, Georges Roustan, Paris 1908.

Augello, Massimo, Marco Bianchini, Gabriela Gioli, Piero Roggi (eds.), *La cattedre politica in Italia. La diffusione di una disciplina <sospetta> (1750–1900)*, Franco Angeli, Milan 1988.

Augello, Massimo, Marco Guidi, *Economisti e scienza economica nell'Italia liberale (1848–1922)*, 2 vols., Franco Angeli, Milan 2019.

Backhouse, Roger E., 'The Changing Character of British Economics', in A. W. Coats (ed.), *The Post-1945 Internationalization of Economics*, Duke University Press, Durham N.C. 1996, pp. 33–60.

Backhouse, Roger E., *Founder of Modern Economics: Paul A. Samuelson. Vol. I Becoming Samuelson, 1915–1948*, Oxford University Press, New York 2017.

Backhouse, Roger E., Bradley W. Bateman, Steven G. Medema, 'The Reception of Marshall in the United States', in Tiziano Raffaelli, Giacomo Becattini, Katia Caldari, Marco Dardi (eds.). *The Impact of Alfred Marshall's Idea: The Global Diffusion of His Work*, Edward Elgar, Cheltenham UK 2010, pp. 59–80.

Backhouse, R. E., Bruce Caldwell, Craufurd Goodwin, Malcolm Rutherford, 'A. W. (Bob) Coats, 1924–2007', *History of Political Economy* Vol. 40 (2008), pp. 421–46.

Backhouse, Roger E., Philippe Fontaine, 'Contested Identities: The History of Economics since 1945', in Backhouse and Fontaine (eds.), *A Historiography of the Modern Social Sciences*, Cambridge University Press, Cambridge 2014, pp. 183–210.

Backhouse, Roger E., Steven G. Medema, 'Defining Economics: The Long Road to Acceptance of the Robbins Definition', *Economica* Vol. 76 (2009), pp. 805–20.

Backhouse, Roger E., Keith Tribe, *The History of Economics: A Course for Students and Teachers*, Agenda, Newcastle upon Tyne UK 2018.

Bagehot, Walter, *Economic Studies*, Longmans, Green & Co., London 1880.

Balogh, T., F. A. Burchardt, M. Kalecki, K. Mandelbaum, E. F. Schumacher, G. D. N. Worswick, *The Economics of Full Employment: Six Studies in Applied Economics Prepared at the Oxford University Institute of Statistics*, Basil Blackwell, Oxford 1944.

Barber, William J. (ed.), *Breaking the Academic Mould: Economists and American Higher Learning in the Nineteenth Century*, Wesleyan University Press, Middletown Conn. 1988.

Barber, William J., 'Postwar Changes in American Graduate Education in Economics', in A. W. Coats (ed.), *The Post-1945 Internationalization of Economics*, Duke University Press, Durham N.C. 1996, pp. 12–30.

Barker, T. C., 'The Beginnings of the Economic History Society', *Economic History Review* 2nd Series, Vol. 30 (1977), pp. 1–19.

Barnes, Thomas, *Discourse Delivered at the Commencement of the Manchester Academy September XIV MDCCLXXXVI*, Warrington 1786.

Bastable, C. F., *The Theory of International Trade: With Some of Its Applications to Economic Policy*, Hodges, Figgis and Co., Dublin 1887.

Bastable, C. F., *The Theory of International Trade with Some of Its Applications to Economic Policy*, 2nd edition, Macmillan, London 1897.

Baumol, William J., 'What Marshall Didn't Know: On the Twentieth Century's Contribution to Economics', *Quarterly Journal of Economics* Vol. 115 (2000), pp. 1–44.

Bellot, H. H., *University College London 1826–1926*, University of London Press, London 1929.

Benham, Frederic, *Economics: A General Textbook for Students*, Sir Isaac Pitman & Sons, London 1938.

Berg, Richard van den (ed.), *Richard Cantillon's Essay on the Nature of Trade in General: A Variorum Edition*, Routledge, Abingdon UK 2015.

Bernadelli, Harro, 'What Has Philosophy to Contribute to the Social Sciences, and to Economics in Particular?', *Economica* New Series Vol. 3 No. 12 (1936), pp. 443–54.

Besomi, Daniele, 'Roy Harrod and the Oxford Economists' Research Group's Inquiry on Prices and Interest, 1936–39', *Oxford Economic Papers* Vol. 50 (1998), pp. 534–62.

Bharadwaj, Krishna, 'Marshall on Pigou's *Wealth and Welfare*', *Economica* Vol. 39 (1972), pp. 32–46.

Biagini, Eugenio F., 'Marshall's 1873 "Lectures to Women"', *Quaderni di storia d'ell economia politica* Vol. 9 No. 2–3 (1991), pp. 335–54.

Bingham, C., *The History of Royal Holloway College 1886–1986*, Constable, London 1987.

Binz, A., *Bericht über das vierte und fünfte Studienjahr der Handels Hochschule Berlin. Oktober 1909/1911*, Georg Reimer, Berlin 1911.

Blackie, Walter G., *Commercial Education*, Blackie and Son, Glasgow 1888.

Blake, C., S. G. E. Lythe (eds.), *A Maverick Institution*, Gee & Co., London 1981.

Böhm-Bawerk, Eugen von, *Capital and Interest: A Critical History of Economical Theory*, Macmillan, London 1890.

Böhm-Bawerk, Eugen von, 'The Historical vs. the Deductive Method in Political Economy', *Annals of the American Academy of Political and Social Science* Vol. 1 (1890), pp 244–71.

Böhm-Bawerk, Eugen von, 'Macvane's Political Economy', *Quarterly Journal of Economics* Vol. 4 (1890), pp. 331–39.

Böhm-Bawerk, Eugen von, 'Professor Gidding's on the Theory of Capital', *Quarterly Journal of Economics* Vol. 4 (1890), pp. 347–49.

Böhm-Bawerk, Eugen von, *The Positive Theory of Capital*, Macmillan, London 1891.

Böhm-Bawerk, Eugen von, 'The Austrian Economists', *Annals of the American Academy of Political and Social Science* Vol. 1 Pt. 3 (1891), pp. 361–84.

Böhm-Bawerk, Eugen von, 'Unsere Aufgaben', *Zeitschrift für Volkswirtschaft, Socialpolitik und Verwaltung* Bd. 1 (1892), pp. 1–10.

Böhm-Bawerk, Eugen von, 'One More Word on the Ultimate Standard of Value', *Economic Journal* Vol. 4 (1894), pp. 719–24.

Böhm-Bawerk, Eugen von, 'The Ultimate Standard of Value', *Annals of the American Academy of Political and Social Science* Vol. 5 Pt. 1 (1894), pp. 149–208.

Böhm-Bawerk, Eugen von, *Karl Marx and the Close of His System: A Criticism*, trans. Alice M. Macdonald with a Preface by James Bonar, T. F. Unwin, London 1898.

Böhm-Bawerk, Eugen von, *Recent Literature on Interest (1884–1899): A Supplement to 'Capital and Interest'*, trans. William A. Scott and Siegmund Feilbogen, Macmillan, London 1903.

Bollmus, R., *Handelshochschule und Nationalsozialismus*, Verlag Anton Hain, Meisenheim an Glan 1973.

Bonar, James, 'The Austrian Economists and Their View of Value', *Quarterly Journal of Economics* Vol. 3 (1888), pp. 1–31.

Bonar, James, 'Review of Marshall, *The New Cambridge Curriculum in Economics*', *Economic Journal* Vol. 13 (1903), pp. 620–22.

Bonneyman, Brian, 'Agrarian Patriotism and the Landed Interest: The Scottish 'Society of Improvers in the Knowledge of Agriculture', 1723–1746', in Koen Stapelbroek and Jani Marjanan (eds.), *The Rise of Economic Societies in the Eighteenth Century. Patriotic Reform in Europe and North America*, Palgrave, Houndmills UK 2012, pp. 26–51.

Booth, A. E., Coats, A. W. 'The Market for Economists in Britain 1945–75: A Preliminary Survey', *Economic Journal* Vol. 88 (1978), pp. 436–54.

Boulding, Kenneth, 'Professor Tarshis and the State of Economics', *American Economic Review* Vol. 38 (1948), pp. 92–102.

Bourdeau, Michel, 'Auguste Comte', *The Stanford Encyclopedia of Philosophy* (Summer 2018 edition) https://plato.stanford.edu/archives/sum2018/entries/comte.

Bowie, James A., *Education for Business Management*, Oxford University Press, London 1930.

Bowley, Arthur L., 'The Faculty of Economics and Political Science', 5 December 1909, Appendix K of "Report of the Academic Council, for Transmission to the Royal Commission on University Education in London," Appendix VII of *Royal Commission on University Education in London, Appendix to Second Report of the Commissioners, Minutes of Evidence June 1910–November 1910* Cd. 5528 (1911), pp. 347–53.

Boylan, T. A., T. P. Foley, *Political Economy and Colonial Ireland*, Routledge, London 1992.

Bradley, Simon, *The Railways: Nation, Network and People*, Profile Books, London 2015.

Branford, V., 'The Organisation of Economic and Political Studies in American Universities', *Economic Journal* Vol. 12 (1902), pp. 535–47.

Brent, Richard, 'God's Providence: Liberal Political Economy as Natural Theology at Oxford 1825–1862', in Michael Bentley (ed.), *Public and Private Doctrine: Essays in British History Presented to Maurice Cowling*, Cambridge University Press, Cambridge 1993, pp. 85–114.

Brock, M. G., 'The Oxford of Peel and Gladstone, 1800–1833', in M. G. Brock, M. C. Curthoys (eds.), *The History of the University of Oxford*, Vol. VI: *Nineteenth-Century Oxford Part I*, Oxford University Press, Oxford 1997, pp. 7–71.

Bronfenbrenner, Martin, 'The Role of Money in Equilibrium Capital Theory', *Econometrica* Vol. 11 (1943), pp. 35–60.

Brougham, Henry, 'Inaugural Address by the Right Honourable Lord Brougham and Vaux, President of the Association', *Transactions of the National Association for the Promotion of Social Science. 1857*, W. Parker and Sons, 1858, pp. 10–27.

Bücher, Karl, *Die Entstehung der Volkswirtschaft*, Verlag der H. Laupp'schen Buchhandlung, Tübingen 1893.

Bull, H. W., 'Industrial Education at Cadbury in the 1930's', *The Vocational Aspect of Education* (1984) Vol. 36, pp. 59–62.

Burrows, Montagu, *Pass and Class: An Oxford Guide-Book through the Courses of Literæ Humaniores, Mathematics, Natural Science, and Law and Modern History*, J. H. and Jas. Parker, Oxford 1860.

Caine, Sidney, *The History of the Foundation of the London School of Economics and Political Science*, G. Bell & Son, London 1963.

Cairncross, A. K., *Introduction to Economics*, Butterworth & Co., London 1944.

Cairnes, J. E., 'New Theories in Political Economy', *Fortnightly Review* Vol. XI (New Series) (1872), pp. 71–76.

Calmes, A., 'Das Handelshochschulwesen in Frankreich', *Deutsche Wirtschafts-Zeitung* Jg. 4 (1908), cols. 399–404, 446–49.

Campbell, Persia Crawford, *Chinese Coolie Emigration to Countries within the British Empire*, P. S. King & Son, London 1923.

Cannan, Edwin, *Elementary Political Economy*, Henry Frowde, London 1888.

Cannan, Edwin, *A History of the Theories of Production and Distribution in English Political Economy from 1776 to 1848*, Rivington, Percival & Co., London 1894.

Cannan, Edwin, *The Economic Outlook*, T. Fisher Unwin, London 1912.

Cannan, Edwin, *Wealth: A Brief Explanation of the Causes of Economic Welfare*, P. S. King and Son, London 1914.

Cannan, Edwin, *A History of the Theories of Production and Distribution in English Political Economy from 1776 to 1848*, 3rd edition, P. S. King & Son, London 1924.

Cannan, Edwin, 'Review of Robbins, *Nature and Significance of Economic Science*', *Economic Journal* Vol. 42 (1932), pp. 424–27.

Caradog Jones, D. (ed.) *The Social Survey of Merseyside*, 3 vols., University of Liverpool Press, Liverpool 1934.

Caspari, Volker, 'Marshall in German-Speaking Countries', in Tiziano Raffaelli, Giacomo Becattini, Marco Dardi (eds.), *The Elgar Companion to Alfred Marshall*, Edward Elgar, Cheltenham UK 2006, pp. 129–34.

Chapman, Sydney J., 'On Education for Business and Public Life', *Transactions of the Manchester Statistical Society* (1902), pp. 123–38.

Chapman, Sydney J., '"Business" Education Abroad and at Home' I & II, *Manchester Guardian* 21 April 1903, 24 April 1903.

Chapman, Sydney J., *The Lancashire Cotton Industry: A Study in Economic Development*, Publications of the University of Manchester. Economic Series No. 1, Manchester University Press, Manchester 1904.

Chapman, Sydney J., *Outlines of Political Economy*, Longmans, Green and Co., London 1911.

Chapman, Sydney J., *Political Economy*, Williams and Norgate, London 1912.

Chapman, Sydney J., H. M. Hallsworth, *Unemployment: The Results of an Investigation Made in Lancashire and an Examination of the Report of the Poor Law Commission*, Sherratt & Hughes, Manchester 1909.

Charles, Enid, 'The Effect of Present Trends in Fertility and Mortality upon the Future Population of Great Britain and upon Its Age Composition', Ch. II in Lancelot Hogbin (ed.), *Political Arithmetic: A Symposium of Population Studies*, George Allen and Unwin, London 1938, pp. 73–105.

Charlton, H. B., *Portrait of a University 1851–1951*, Manchester University Press, Manchester 1951.

Checkland, S. G., 'The Birmingham Economists, 1815–1850', *Economic History Review* 2nd series Vol. I (1948), pp. 1–19.

Checkland, S. G., The Propagation of Ricardian Economics in England', *Economica* New Series Vol. 16 (1949), pp. 40–52.

Checkland, S. G. 'The Advent of Academic Economics in England', *Manchester School* Vol. 19 (1951), pp. 43–70.

Chester, Norman, *Economics, Politics and Social Studies in Oxford, 1900–1985*, Macmillan, London 1986.

Claeys, Gregory, Istvan Hont, Alon Kadish, Keith Tribe, 'Editorial Preface: The Institutionalization of Political Economy in Europe, the United States and Japan' in Alon Kadish, Keith Tribe (eds.), *The Market for Political Economy: The Advent of Economics in British University Culture, 1850–1905*, Routledge, London 1995, pp. viii–xi.

Clapham, John, 'Of Empty Economic Boxes', *Economic Journal* Vol. 32 (1922), pp. 305–14.

Clay, Henry, *Economics: An Introduction for the General Reader*, Macmillan, London 1916.

Cliffe Leslie, T. E., *Essays in Political and Moral Philosophy*, Hodges, Foster and Figgis, Dublin 1879.

Coats, A. W., 'The First Two Decades of the American Economic Association', *American Economic Review* Vol. 50 (1960), pp. 555–74.

Coats, A. W., 'Political Economy and the Tariff Reform Campaign of 1903', *Journal of Law and Economics* Vol. 11 (1968), pp. 181–229.

Coats, A. W., 'The Origins and Early Development of the Royal Economic Society', *Economic Journal* Vol. 68 (1968), pp. 349–71.

Coats, A. W. (ed.), *Economists in Government: An International Comparative Study*, Duke University Press, Durham N.C. 1981.

Coats, A. W., 'Half a Century of Methodological Controversy in Economics: As Reflected in the Writings of T. W. Hutchison', in Coats (ed.), *Methodological Controversy in Economics: Historical Essays in Honor of T. W. Hutchison*, JAI Press, Greenwich Conn. 1983, pp. 1–42.

Coats, A. W., 'The American Economic Association and the Economics Profession', *Journal of Economic Literature* Vol. 23 (1985), pp. 1697–727.

Coats, A. W. (ed.), *Economists in International Agencies: An Exploratory Study*, Praeger Scientific, New York 1986.

Coats, A. W., 'Introduction' in A. W. Coats (ed.), *The Post-1945 Internationalization of Economics*, Duke University Press, Durham N.C. 1996, pp. 4–11.

Coats, A. W. (ed.) *The Development of Economics in Western Europe since 1945*, Routledge, London 2000.

Coats, A. W., S. E. Coats, 'The Social Composition of the Royal Economic Society and the Beginnings of the British Economics "Profession," 1890–1915', *British Journal of Sociology* Vol. 21 (1970), pp. 75–85.

Collard, David, 'Cambridge after Marshall', in John Whitaker (ed.), *Centenary Essays on Alfred Marshall*, Cambridge University Press Cambridge 1990, pp. 164–92.

Collini, Stefan, *Speaking of Universities*, Verso, London 2017.

Colson, Clément, *Cours d'économie politique professé à l'École nationale des ponts et chaussées t.1*, Guillamin, Paris 1901.

Committee on Higher Education, *Higher Education. Report of the Committee appointed by the Prime Minister under the Chairmanship of Lord Robbins 1961–63*, Cmnd. 2154, London, HMSO, London 1963.

Conrad, J., *The German Universities for the last Fifty Years*, David Bryce, Glasgow 1885.

Cook, Simon J., 'A Wrangling Machine', *History of Political Economy* Vol. 37 (2005), pp. 689–709.

Cook, Simon J., *The Intellectual Foundations of Alfred Marshall's Economic Science*, Cambridge University Press, Cambridge 2009.

Cook, Simon J., Tiziana Foresti (eds.), 'Marshall's Notes for His Advanced Course in Political Economy, c. 1871', *Marshall Studies Bulletin* Vol. 11 (2010), pp. 1–47.

Cook, Simon J., Keith Tribe, 'Historical Economics', in Gilbert Faccarello, Heinz D. Kurz (eds.), *Handbook on the History of Economic Analysis, Vol. II*, Elgar, Cheltenham UK 2016, pp. 295–312.

Copeland, M. T., *And Mark an Era: The Story of the Harvard Business School*, Little, Brown and Company, Boston 1958.

Cossa, Luigi, *Guide to the Study of Political Economy*, Macmillan, London 1880.

Crafts, Nicholas, 'The Golden Age of Growth in Western Europe, 1950–1973', *Economic History Review* Vol. 48 (1995), pp. 429–47.

Craik, Alex D. D., *Mr Hopkins' Men: Cambridge Reform and British Mathematics in the 19th Century*, Springer, London 2008.

Crawley, C., *Trinity Hall. The History of a Cambridge College 1350–1975*, Trinity Hall, Cambridge 1976.

Cristiano, Carlo, 'Marshall at Cambridge', in Tiziano Raffaelli, Giacomo Becattini, Katia Caldari, Marco Dardi (eds.), *The Impact of Alfred Marshall's Idea: The Global Diffusion of his Work*, Edward Elgar, Cheltenham UK 2010, pp. 17–39.

Cristiano, Carlo, *The Political and Economic Thought of the Young Keynes: Liberalism, Markets and Empire*, Routledge, London 2014.

Cruickshank, J. L., *A Delicate Experiment. The Harvard Business School 1908–1945*, Harvard Business School Press, Boston 1987.

Cunningham, William, *The Growth of English Industry and Commerce*, Cambridge University Press, London 1882.

Cunningham, William, 'A Plea for Pure Theory', *Economic Review* Vol. 2 (1892), pp. 25–41.

Cunningham, William, 'The Relativity of Economic Doctrine', *Economic Journal* Vol. 2 (1892), pp. 1–16.

Cunningham, William, 'The Perversion of Economic History', *Economic Journal* Vol. 2 (1892), pp. 491–506.

Cunningham, William, *The Case against Free Trade*, John Murray, London 1911.

Cunynghame, Henry, 'Some Improvements in Simple Geometrical Methods of Treating Exchange Value, Monopoly, and Rent', *Economic Journal* Vol. 2 (1892), pp. 35–52.

Cunynghame, Henry, *A Geometrical Political Economy*, Oxford University Press, Oxford 1904.

Currie, Robert, 'The Arts and Social Studies, 1914–1939', in Brian Harrison (ed.), *The History of the University of Oxford*, Vol. VIII: *The Twentieth Century*, Oxford University Press, Oxford 1994, pp. 109–38.

Curthoys, M. C. 'The Examination System', in M. G. Brock, M. C. Curthoys (eds.), *The History of the University of Oxford*, Vol. VI: *Nineteenth-Century Oxford Part I*, Oxford University Press, Oxford 1997, pp. 339–74.

Curthoys, M. C. 'The Careers of Oxford Men', in M. G. Brock, M. C. Curthoys (eds.), *The History of the University of Oxford*, Vol. VI: *Nineteenth-Century Oxford Part I*, Oxford University Press, Oxford 1997, pp. 477–510.

Curti, M., R. Nash, *Philanthropy in the Shaping of American Higher Education*, Rutgers University Press, New Brunswick N.J. 1965.

Dahrendorf, Ralf, *LSE: A History of the London School of Economics and Political Science 1895–1995*, Oxford University Press, Oxford 1995.

Daly, M. E., *The Spirit of Earnest Inquiry: The Statistical and Social Inquiry Society of Ireland 1847–1997*, The Statistical and Social Inquiry Society of Ireland, Dublin 1997.

Daniels, G. W., 'Economic and Commercial Studies in the Owens College and the University', *Manchester School* Vol. 1 (1930), pp. 3–9.

Daston, Lorraine, 'How Probabilities Came to Be Objective and Subjective', *Historia Mathematica* Vol. 21 (1994), pp. 330–44.

Davenport, H. J., 'Review of Flux, *Economic Principles*', *Journal of Political Economy* Vol. 13 (1904), pp. 114–15.

Day, C. R., 'Education for the Industrial World: Technical and Modern Instruction in France under the Third Republic, 1870–1914', in R. Fox, G. Weisz (eds.), *The Organization of Science and Technology in France 1808–1914*, Cambridge University Press, Cambridge 1980, pp. 127–53.

Deane, Phyllis, 'Henry Fawcett: The Plain Man's Political Economist', in Lawrence Goldman (ed.), *The Blind Victorian. Henry Fawcett and British Liberalism*, Cambridge University Press, Cambridge 1989, pp. 93–119.

Deane, Phyllis, *The Life and Times of J. Neville Keynes: A Beacon in the Tempest*, Edward Elgar, Cheltenham UK 2001.

DeVane, W. C., *Higher Education in Twentieth-Century America*, Harvard University Press, Cambridge Mass. 1965.

Donajgrodski, A. P., 'New Roles for Old: The Northcote-Trevelyan Report and the Clerks of the Home Office 1822–48', in Gillian Sutherland (ed.), *Studies in the Growth of Nineteenth-Century Government*, Routledge and Kegan Paul, London 1972, pp. 82–109.

Dow, Alexander, Sheila Dow, Alan Hutton, 'Applied Economics in a Political Economy Tradition: The case of Scotland from the 1890s to the 1950s', *History of Political Economy* Vol. 32 Supplement (2000), pp. 177–198.

Drummond, Ian M., *Political Economy at the University of Toronto: A History of the Department, 1888–1982*, Faculty of Arts and Science, Toronto 1983.

Dunbar, Charles F., 'The Academic Study of Political Economy', *Quarterly Journal of Economics* Vol. 5 No. 4 (1891), pp. 397–416.

Eastham, J. K., *An Introduction to Economic Analysis*, English Universities Press, London 1950.

Eastham, J. K., *Graphical Economics*, English Universities Press, London 1960.

Eastham, J. K., S. G. E. Lythe, 'The Dundee School of Economics, 1931–1955', *Scottish Educational Review* Vol. 10 (May 1978), pp. 19–26.

Eckert, C., *Die städtische Handels-Hochschule in Cöln. Bericht über die zwei Studienjahre 1903 und 1904*, Julius Springer, Berlin 1905.

Eckert, C., 'Handelshochschulen', *Handwörterbuch der Kommunalwissenschaften* Bd. 2, Gustav Fischer Verlag, Jena 1922, pp. 469–77.

Edgerton, David, *Warfare State. Britain 1920–1970*, Cambridge University Press, Cambridge 2006.

Edgeworth, Francis Y., 'An Introductory Lecture on Political Economy', *Economic Journal* Vol. 1 (1891), pp. 625–34.

Edgeworth, Francis Y., 'Review of Böhm-Bawerk, *The Positive Theory of Capital*', *Economic Journal* Vol. 2 (1892), pp. 328–36.

Edgeworth, Francis Y., 'Review of William Smart, *An Introduction to the Theory of Value on the Lines of Menger, Wieser and Böhm-Bawerk*', *Economic Journal* Vol. 2 (1892), pp. 336–37.

Edgeworth, Francis Y., 'Review of Friedrich von Wieser, *Natural Value*', *Economic Journal* Vol. 4 (1894), pp. 279–85.

Edgeworth, Francis Y., 'Review of W. J. Ashley, *Economics Classics (Smith, Malthus and Ricardo)*', *Economic Journal* Vol. 5 (1895), pp. 257–58.

Edgeworth, Francis Y., 'Review of Ashley, *The Tariff Problem*', *Economic Journal* Vol. 13 (1903), pp. 571–75.

Edgeworth, F. Y., 'Review of A. C. Pigou, *The Riddle of the Tariff*', *Economic Journal* Vol. 14 (1904), pp. 65–67.

Edgeworth, Francis Y., 'Contributions to the Theory of Railway Rates', *Economic Journal* Vol. 11 (1911), pp. 346–70, 551–71; Vol. 22 (1912), pp. 198–218; Vol. 23 (1913), pp. 206–26.

Edgeworth, Francis Y., *Papers Relating to Political Economy*, 3 vols., Macmillan, London 1925.

Edwards, Ruth D., *The Pursuit of Reason: The Economist 1843–1993*, Hamish Hamilton, London 1993.

Ely, R. T., 'American Colleges and German Universities', *Harpers' New Monthly Magazine* Vol. 61 (1880), pp. 253–60.

Embree, A. T., *Charles Grant and British Rule in India*, George Allen and Unwin, London 1962.

Emerson, W. P. (ed.), *Questions and Answers in Political Economy*, James Thornton, Oxford 1879.

F. R. S., 'The Proposed Discontinuance of Section F, Economic Science and Statistics, at the British Association', Letter reprinted from *The Economist*, 20 October 1877, *Journal of the Statistical Society of London* Vol. 40 (December 1877), pp. 631–33.

Farrington, A. (ed.), *The Records of the East India College Haileybury and Other Institutions*, HMSO, London 1976.

Fawcett, Henry, *Manual of Political Economy*, Macmillan, London 1863.

Fawcett, Millicent Garrett, *Political Economy for Beginners*, Macmillan, London 1870.

Fawcett, T., 'Eighteenth-Century Debating Societies', *British Journal of Eighteenth Century Studies* Vol. 3 (1986), pp. 216–29.

Fehling, August Wilhelm, 'Collegiate Education for Business in Germany', *Journal of Political Economy* Vol. 34 (1926), pp. 545–96.

Ferguson, Adam, *Principles of Moral and Political Science* Vol. I, A. Strahan & T. Cadell, London 1792.

Fetter, Frank A., *The Principles of Economics with Application to Practical Problems*, The Century Co., New York 1904.

Fetter, Frank A., *Economic Principles*, The Century Co., New York 1915.

Fiddes, E. *Chapters in the History of Owens College and of Manchester University 1851–1914*, Manchester University Press, Manchester 1937.

Flexner, A., *Universities: American, English, German*, Oxford University Press, New York 1930.

Flux, A. W., 'Review of Wicksell, *Über Wert, Kapital und Rente* and Wicksteed, *Essay on the Co-ordination of the Laws of Distribution*', *Economic Journal* Vol. 4 (1894), pp. 305–13.

Flux, A. W., *Economic Principles: An Introductory Study*, Methuen, London 1904.

Fourcade, Marion, *Economists and Societies: Discipline and Profession in the United States, Britain, and France, 1890s to 1990s*, Princeton University Press, Princeton N.J. 2009.

Foxwell, Herbert Somerton, 'Introduction' to Anton Menger, *The Right to the Whole Produce of Labour: The Origin and Development of the Theory of Labour's Claim to the Whole Product of Industry*, Macmillan, London 1899, pp. v–cx.

Foxwell, Herbert Somerton, 'A Letter of Malthus to Ricardo', *Economic Journal* Vol. 17 (1907), pp. 272–76.

Fraser, Lindley M., 'How Do We Want Economists to Behave?', *Economic Journal* Vol. 42 (1932), pp. 555–70.

French, J. C., *A History of the University founded by Johns Hopkins*, Johns Hopkins University Press, Baltimore Md. 1946.

Furner, Mary O., *Advocacy and Objectivity: A Crisis in the Professionalisation of American Social Science 1865–1905*, University Press of Kentucky, Lexington 1975.

Fustel de Coulanges, Numa Denis, 'Le problème des origines de la propriété foncière', *Revue des questions historiques* n.s. t. 1 no. 1 (1889), pp. 349–439.

Galton, Francis, Letter of June 1877 in 'Economic Science and the British Association', *Journal of the Statistical Society of London* Vol. 40 No. 3 (September 1877), pp. 468–73.

Gay, Edwin, 'The New Economics Tripos at Cambridge University', *Quarterly Journal of Economics* Vol. 17 (1903), pp. 492–96.

Geiger, Roger L., *To Advance Knowledge: The Growth of American Research Universities, 1900–1940*, Oxford University Press, New York 1986.

Geiger, Roger L., *The History of American Higher Education: Learning and Culture from the Founding to World War II*, Princeton University Press, Princeton N.J. 2015.

Gibbins, John R., *John Grote, Cambridge University and the Development of Victorian Thought*, Imprint Academic, Exeter 2007.

Gide, Charles, 'The Economic Schools and the Teaching of Political Economy in France', *Political Science Quarterly* Vol. 5 Issue 4 (1890), pp. 603–35.

Gide, Charles, 'Comment est née la Revue d'Économie Politique', *Revue d'Économie Politique* t. 45 (1931), pp. 134–57.

Gide, Charles, Charles Rist, *A History of Economic Doctrines from the Time of the Physiocrats to the Present Day*, trans. R. Richards from the 2nd edition, George G. Harrap, London 1915.

Giffen, Robert, Hammond Chubb, Letter of 13 July 1877 included in 'Considerations, in the form of a Draft Report, submitted to Committee, favourable to the maintenance of Section F. By Dr. W. Farr', in *Journal of the Statistical Society of London* Vol. 40 No. 3 (September 1877), pp. 474–75.

Gispen, K., *New Profession, Old Order. Engineers and German Society, 1815–1914*, Cambridge University Press, Cambridge 1989.

Godwin, William, *Enquiry Concerning Political Justice*, Penguin Books, Harmondsworth UK 1976.

Goldman, Lawrence, 'The Social Sciences Association, 1857–1886: A Context for Mid-Victorian Liberalism', *English Historical Review* Vol. 101 (1986), pp. 95–134.

Goldman, Lawrence, 'A Peculiarity of the English? The Social Science Association and the Absence of Sociology in Nineteenth-Century Britain', *Past and Present* No. 114 (1987), pp. 133–71.

Gonner, E. C. K., *Political Economy (An Elementary Text Book of the Economics of Commerce)*, R. Sutton & Co., London 1888.

Gonner, E. C. K., *Commercial Geography*, Macmillan, London 1894.

Gonner, E. C. K., 'The Methods of Economic Training Adopted in This and Other Countries', *Report of the Sixty-Third Meeting of the British Association for the Advancement of Science (September 1893)*, John Murray, London 1894, pp. 571–72.

Gonner, E. C. K., 'Methods of Economic Training in This and Other Countries', *Report of the Sixty-Fourth Meeting of the British Association for the Advancement of Science (1894)*, John Murray, London 1894, pp. 365–91.

Gowing, Margaret, 'George Cyril Allen', *Proceedings of the British Academy* Vol. 71 (1985), 473–91.

Gras, N. S. B. 'The Rise and Development of Economic History', *Economic History Review* Vol. 1 (1927), pp. 12–34.

Groenewegen, Peter, 'Alfred Marshall and the Establishment of the Cambridge Economics Tripos', *History of Political Economy* Vol. 20 (1988), pp. 627–67.

Groenewegen, Peter, 'Teaching Economics at Cambridge at the Turn of the Century: Alfred Marshall as Lecturer in Political Economy', *Scottish Journal of Political Economy* Vol. 37 (1990), pp. 40–60.

Groenewegen, Peter, *A Soaring Eagle: Alfred Marshall 1842–1924*, Edward Elgar, Cheltenham UK 1995.

Grote, John, 'To Members of the Senate', printed flysheet, Cambridge, 22 February 1860.

Grote, John, *An Examination of the Utilitarian Philosophy* (ed. Joseph Bickersteth Mayor), Deighton Bell, Cambridge 1870.

Guy, W. A., 'On the Original and Acquired Meaning of the Term 'Statistics', and on the Proper Functions of a Statistical Society: also on the Question Whether There Be a Science of Statistics; and if so, What Are Its Nature and Objects, and What Is Its Relation to Political Economy and "Social Science"', *Journal of the Statistical Society of London* Vol. 28 (December 1865), pp. 478–93.

Habermas, Jürgen, *Strukturwandel der Öffentlichkeit. Untersuchungen zu einer Kategorie der bürgerlichen Gesellschaft*, Suhrkamp, Frankfurt am Main 1990.

Hagemann, Harald, 'European Émigrés and the "Americanization" of Economics', *European Journal of the History of Economic Thought* Vol. 18 (2011), pp. 643–71.

Hagemann, Harald, 'John R. Hicks (1904–1989)' in Robert A. Cord, *The Palgrave Companion to LSE Economics*, Palgrave Macmillan, London 2018, pp. 431–61.

Hagemann, Harald, Claus-Dieter Krohn (eds.), *Biographisches Handbuch der deutschsprachigen wirtschaftswissenschaftlichen Emigration nach 1933*, 2 vols., K. G. Sauer, Munich 1999.

Haig, A. G. L., 'The Church, the Universities and Learning in Later Victorian England', *Historical Journal* Vol. 29 (1986), pp. 187–201.

Hall, R. L., C. J. Hitch, 'Pricing Policy and Business Behaviour', *Oxford Economic Papers* No. 2 (May 1939), pp. 12–45.

Halsey, A. H., *The Decline of Donnish Dominion: The British Academic Professions in the Twentieth Century*, Oxford University Press, Oxford 1992.

Hare, S., 'Abstract of Outline of Subjects for Statistical Enquiries', *Journal of the Statistical Society of London* Vol. 1 (November 1838), pp. 427–27.

Harrod, Roy, 'Lord Nuffield's Foundation in Oxford', *Economic Journal* Vol. 47 (1937), pp. 757–61.

Harte, Negley, *The University of London 1836–1986*, Athlone Press, London 1986.

Hayashima, Akira, 'Zur Geschichte der Kölner Handelshochschule', *Kwansei Gakuin University Annual Studies* Vol. 30 (1981), pp. 181–218.

Hayashima, Akira, 'Der Kölner Weg zum Promotionsrecht. Zur Geschichte einer deutschen Handelshochschule', *Kwansei Gakuin University Annual Studies* Vol. 31 (1982), pp. 21–88.

Hayashima, Akira, 'Die Frequenz der deutschen Handelshochschulen 1898–1920', *Kwansei Gakuin University Annual Studies* Vol. 33 (1984), pp. 121–51.

Hayashima, Akira, 'Der Mythos vom fehlenden Hinterland. Zur Gründung der Handelshochschule Mannheim 1897–1907', *Kwansei Gakuin University Social Sciences Review* Vol. 10 (2005), pp. 21–130.

Hayek, F. A., 'The London School of Economics 1895–1945', *Economica* n.s. Vol. 13 (1946), pp. 1–31.

Hearnshaw, F. J. C., *The Centenary History of King's College London 1828–1928*, George C. Harrap, London 1929.

Henderson, Hubert D., *Supply and Demand*, Nisbet and Co., London 1921.

Henderson, P. D., 'The Use of Economists in British Administration', *Oxford Economic Papers* n.s. Vol. 13 (1961), pp. 5–26.

Henderson, Willie, 'Millicent Garrett Fawcett's *Political Economy for Beginners*: An Evaluation', *Paedagogica Historica* Vol. 40 (2004), pp. 435–53.

Hennock, E. P., 'Technological Education in England, 1850–1926: The Uses of a German Model', *History of Education* Vol. 19 (1990), pp. 303–4.

Herford, C. H., *Philip Henry Wicksteed: His Life and Work*, J. M. Dent & Sons, London 1931.

Herrick, Cheesman A., *Meaning and Practice of Commercial Education*, Macmillan, New York 1904.

Hesse, Jan-Otmar, *Wirtschaft als Wissenschaft: Die Volkswirtschaftlehre in der frühen Bundesrepublik*, Campus Verlag, Frankfurt am Main 2010.

Hewins, W. A. S., 'The London School of Economics and Political Science', *Special Reports on Educational Subjects* Vol. 2, British Parliamentary Papers 1898 Vol. XXIV, pp. 76–98.

Hicks, J. R., 'Review of F. Benham, *Economics: A General Text-Book for Students*', *Manchester School* Vol. 9 (1938), pp. 184–86.

Higgs, Henry, 'Introduction' to Political Economy Club, *Minutes of Proceedings, 1899–1920*, Macmillan, London 1921, pp. vii–xxvi.

Higgs, Henry, *Bibliography of Economics 1751–1775*, Cambridge University Press, London 1935.

Higham, J., 'The Matrix of Specialization', in A. Oleson, J. Voss, *The Organization of Knowledge in Modern America, 1860–1920*, Johns Hopkins University Press, Baltimore Md. 1979, pp. 3–18.

Hodgson, W. B., 'The Instruction of the Community, Especially the Wage-receiving Classes, in Economic Science', *Transactions of the National Association for the Promotion of Social Science. Aberdeen Meeting, 1877*, Longmans, Green and Co., London 1878, pp. 468–83.

Howson, Susan, 'The Origins of Lionel Robbins's Essay on the Nature and Significance of Economic Science', *History of Political Economy* Vol. 36 (2004), pp. 413–43.

Howson, Susan, *Lionel Robbins*, Cambridge University Press, Cambridge 2011.

Howson, Susan (ed.), *Lionel Robbins on the Principles of Economic Analysis: The 1930s Lectures*, Routledge, Abingdon 2018.

Hudson, D., K. W. Luckhurst, *The Royal Society of Arts 1754–1954*, John Murray, London 1954.

Hudson, K., *Patriotism with Profit: British Agricultural Societies in the Eighteenth and Nineteenth Centuries*, Hugh Evelyn, London 1972.

Hughes, E., 'Civil Service Reform 1853–5', *History* Vol. 27 (1942), pp. 51–83.

Hughes, E., 'Sir Charles Trevelyan and Civil Service Reform, 1853–5', *English Historical Review* Vol. 64 (1949), pp. 53–88, 206–34.

Hutchison, Terence W., 'Expectation and Rational Conduct', *Zeitschrift für Nationalökonomie* Bd. 8 H. 5 (1937), pp. 636–53.

Hutchison, Terence W., 'Theoretische Ökonomie als Sprachsystem', *Zeitschrift für Nationalökonomie* Bd. 8 H. 1 (1937), pp. 78–90.

Hutchison, Terence W., *The Significance and Basic Postulates of Economic Theory*, Macmillan, London 1938.

Hutchison, Terence W., 'A Formative Decade: Methodological Controversy in the 1930', *Journal of Economic Methodology* Vol. 16 (2009), pp. 297–314.

Ingram, John Kells, *A History of Political Economy*, Adam and Charles Black, Edinburgh 1888.

Inkster, Ian, 'The Public Lecture as an Instrument of Science Education for Adults: The Case of Great Britain, c. 1750–1850', *Paedogogica Historica* Vol. 20 (1981), pp. 80–107.

J. B. Mayor, 'Moral Sciences Tripos' in *The Student's Guide to the University of Cambridge*, Cambridge 1862, pp. 140–52.

James, Edmund J., *Studien ueber den amerikanischen Zolltarif. Seine Entwickelung und seinen Einfluss auf die Volkswirtschaft*, Verlag von Hermann Dufft, Jena 1877.

James, Edmund J., *Commercial Education*, Monographs on Education in the United States No. 13, J. B. Lyon, Albany N.Y. 1900.

James, Edmund J., *A Plea for the Establishment of Commercial High Schools: An Address before the Convention of the American Bankers' Association at San Francisco, September 7, 1892*, American Bankers' Association, New York 1893.

James, Edmund J., *Education of Business Men in Europe: A Report to the American Bankers' Association through Its Committee on Schools of Finance and Economy*, American Bankers' Association, New York 1893.

Jastrow, I., *Die Handelshochschule Berlin: Bericht über das erste Studienjahr Oktober 1906/7*, Georg Reimer, Berlin 1908.

Jenkins, Hester, D. Caradog Jones, 'Social Class of Cambridge University Alumni of the 18th and 19th Centuries', *British Journal of Sociology*, Vol. 1 (1950), pp. 93–116.

Jenkyns, Richard, 'The Beginning of Greats, 1800–1872. I. Classical Studies', in M. G. Brock, M. C. Curthoys (eds.), *The History of the University of Oxford*, Vol. VI: *Nineteenth-Century Oxford Part I*, Oxford University Press, Oxford 1997, pp. 513–20.

Jevons, William Stanley, *The Coal Question: An Inquiry Concerning the Progress of the Nation, and the Probable Exhaustion of our Coal-mines*, Macmillan, London 1865.

Jevons, William Stanley, 'Brief Account of a General Mathematical Theory of Political Economy', *Journal of the Statistical Society of London* Vol. 29 Issue 2 (June 1866), pp. 282–90.

Jevons, William Stanley, 'Opening Address of the President of Section F (Economic Science and Statistics) of the British Association for the Advancement of Science, at the Fortieth Meeting, at Liverpool, September, 1870', *Journal of the Statistical Society of London* Vol. 33 Issue 3 (September 1870), pp. 309–26.

Jevons, W. Stanley, *Political Economy*, Macmillan, London 1878.

Jevons, William Stanley, 'Preface to the English Translation', in Luigi Cossa, *Guide to the Study of Political Economy*, Macmillan, London 1880, pp. vii–xii.

Jevons, W. Stanley, *Papers and Correspondence of William Stanley Jevons*, Vol. II: *Correspondence 1850–1862*, ed. R. D. Collison Black, Macmillan, London 1973.

Johnson, E. S., Johnson, H. G., *The Shadow of Keynes: Understanding Keynes, Cambridge and Keynesian Economics*, Oxford, Basil Blackwell 1978.

Johnson, H. G. 'Cambridge as an Academic Environment in the Early 1930s: A Reconstruction from the Late 1940s', in D. Patinkin, J. C. Leith (eds.), *Keynes, Cambridge and the General Theory*, London, Macmillan 1977, pp. 81–114.

Johnson, H. T., R. S. Kaplan, *Relevance Lost: The Rise and Fall of Management Accounting*, Harvard Business School Press, Boston 1987.

Johnson, W. E., 'The Pure Theory of Utility Curves', *Economic Journal* Vol. 23 (1913), pp. 483–513.

Jones, Byrd L., 'A Quest for National Leadership: Institutionalization of Economics at Harvard', in William J. Barber (ed.), *Breaking the Academic Mould: Economists and American Higher Learning in the Nineteenth Century*, Wesleyan University Press, Middletown Conn. 1988, pp. 95–131.

Kadish, Alon, *The Oxford Economists in the Late Nineteenth Century*, Oxford University Press, Oxford 1982.

Kadish, Alon, *Apostle Arnold. The Life and Death of Arnold Toynbee 1852–1883*, Duke University Press, Durham N.C. 1986.

Kadish, Alon, *Historians, Economists, and Economic History*, Routledge, London 1989.

Kadish, Alon, 'The Foundation of Birmingham's Faculty of Commerce as a Statement on the Nature of Economics', *Manchester School* Vol. 59 (1991), pp. 160–72.

Kadish, Alon, 'University Reform and the *Principles*', *Quaderni di Storia del'Economia Politica* IX Nos. 2–3 (1991), pp. 289–309.

Kadish, Alon, 'The Teaching of Political Economy in the Extension Movement: Cambridge, London and Oxford', in Kadish, Tribe (eds.), *The Market for Political Economy: The Advent of Economics in British University Culture, 1850–1905*, Routledge, London 1993, pp. 78–110.

Kadish, Alon, 'Marshall and the Cambridge Economics Tripos', in Kadish, Tribe (eds.), *The Market for Political Economy: The Advent of Economics in British University Culture, 1850–1905*, Routledge, London 1993, pp. 137–61.

Kadish, Alon, 'The City, the Fabians and the Foundation of the London School of Economics', in Alon Kadish, Keith Tribe (eds.), *The Market for Political Economy: The Advent of Economics in British University Culture, 1850–1905*, Routledge, London 1993, pp. 227–50.

Kadish, Alon, Keith Tribe, 'Introduction: The Supply of and Demand for Economics in late Victorian Britain', in Kadish, Tribe (eds.), *The Market for Political Economy: The Advent of Economics in British University Culture, 1850–1905*, Routledge, London 1993, pp. 1–19.

Kamerschen, David R., Deepa J. Sridhar, '*The Theory of [Competitive] Price* according to George J. Stigler', *Journal of the History of Economic Thought* Vol. 31 (2009), pp. 181–200.

Kaufmann, Felix, 'Die ökonomischen Grundbegriffe. Eine Studie über die Theorie der Wirtschaftswissenschaft', *Zeitschrift für Volkswirtschaft und Sozialpolitik* Bd. 3 (1923) pp. 31–47 [reprinted in *Zeitschrift für Nationalökonomie* Bd. 15 Heft 3 (1956), pp. 304–16].

Kaufmann, Felix, 'On the Subject-Matter and Method of Economic Science', *Economica* No. 42 (November 1933), pp. 381–401.

Keeble, S. P., 'University Education and Business Management from the 1890s to the 1950s: A Reluctant Relationship', London School of Economics PhD diss. 1984.

Kelley, B. M., *Yale: A History*, Yale University Press, New Haven Conn. 1974.

Kelly, T., *A History of Adult Education in Britain*, 2nd ed., Liverpool University Press, Liverpool 1970.

Kelly, T., *For Advancement of Learning: The University of Liverpool 1881–1981*, Liverpool University Press, Liverpool 1981.

Keynes, John Maynard, *The Economic Consequences of the Peace*, Collected Writings of John Maynard Keynes Vol. II, Macmillan, London 1971.

Keynes, John Maynard, 'Alfred Marshall' in his *Essays in Biography*, Collected Writings of John Maynard Keynes Vol. X, Macmillan, London 1972, pp. 161–231.

Keynes, John Maynard, 'Herbert Somerton Foxwell', in his *Essays in Biography*, Collected Writings of John Maynard Keynes Vol. X, Macmillan, London 1972, pp. 267–96.

Keynes, John Maynard, *The General Theory of Employment, Interest and Money*, in Collected Writings of John Maynard Keynes Vol. VII, Macmillan, London 1973.

Keynes, John Neville, *The Scope and Method of Political Economy*, Macmillan, London 1891.

Kirkaldy, Adam W., *British Shipping: Its History, Organisation and Importance*, Kegan Paul, Trench, Trubner & Co., London 1919.

Klein, Lawrence R., 'Macroeconomics and the Role of Rational Behaviour', *Econometrica* Vol. 14 (1946), pp. 93–108.

Knight, Frank H., *Risk, Uncertainty and Profit*, Houghton Mifflin Company, Boston 1921.

Knight, Frank, 'Review of Paul T. Homan, *Contemporary Economic Thought*', *Quarterly Journal of Economics* Vol. 43 (1928), p. 139.

Knight, Frank H., 'Economic Science in Some Recent Discussion', *American Economic Review* Vol. 24 (1934), pp. 225–38.

Knight, Karen, 'A. C. Pigou, a Loyal Marshallian?', *History of Economics Review* Vol. 64 No. 1 (2016), pp. 42–63.

Knight, Karen, *A. C. Pigou and the 'Marshallian' Thought Style: A Study in the Philosophy and Mathematics Underlying Cambridge Economics*, Palgrave Macmillan, Cham 2018.

Kohler, Robert E., 'A Policy for the Advancement of Science: The Rockefeller Foundation, 1924–29', *Minerva* Vol. 16 (1978), pp. 480–515.

Kohler, Robert E., 'The Ph.D. Machine. Building on the Collegiate Base', *Isis* Vol. 81 (1990), pp. 638–62.

Koot, Gerard M., *English Historical Economics, 1870–1926: The Rise of Economic History and Neomercantilism*, Cambridge University Press, Cambridge 1987.

Kubo, Shin, 'George Pryme, Dugald Stewart and Political Economy at Cambridge', *History of Political Economy* Vol. 45 (2013), pp. 61–97.

Larson, B., 'Bickerdike's Life and Work', *History of Political Economy* Vol. 19 (1987), pp. 1–22.

Laughlin, J. Laurence, 'The Study of Political Economy in the United States', *Journal of Political Economy* Vol. 1 No. 1 (1891), pp. 1–19.

Layton, William, 'Commercial Education in Belgium', *Journal of the Society of Arts* Vol. 43 (7 June 1895), pp. 690–95.

Le Van-Lemesle, Lucette, *Les problèmes de l'institutionnalisation de l'économie politique en France au XIXe siècle*, Oeconomia, Paris 1986.

Le Van-Lemesle, Lucette, *Le juste et la riche: L'enseignement de l'économie politique 1815–1950*, Comité pour l'histoire économique et financière de la France, Paris 2004.

Léautey, E., *L'Enseignement commercial et les Écoles de commerce en France et dans le monde entier*, Libraire Comptable et Administrative, Paris 1886.

Lees, C., A. Robertson, 'Characteristics of Professional Life in the First of the Civic Universities, 1851–1918', *Bulletin of the John Rylands University Library of Manchester* Vol. 82 No. 1 (Spring 2000), pp. 225–50.

Levy, J. H. [D.], 'Economics in 1889', *The National Reformer*, 5 January 1890, p. 3.

Levy, J. H., 'Distribution as a Branch of Economics', paper read at the National Liberal Club Political Economy Circle, 18 June 1890, *Transactions of the National Liberal Club Political Economy Circle* Vol. 1, pp. 95–103, P. S. King & Son, London 1891.

Lewis, Colin M., 'Economic History at the London School of Economics and Political Science: A View from the Periphery', in Robert A. Cord (ed.), *The Palgrave Companion to LSE Economics*, Palgrave Macmillan, London 2018, pp. 35–78.

Lexis, Wilhelm (ed.), *Das Unterrichtswesen im deutschen Reich Bd.4 T.1: Die Technischen Hochschulen im deutschen Reich*, Verlag von A. Asher & Co., Berlin 1904.

Lindenfeld, David, 'The Professionalization of Applied Economics: Germany Counterparts to Business Administration, in Geoffrey Cocks, Konrad Jarausch (eds.), *German Professions 1800–1950*, Oxford University Press, Oxford 1990, pp. 213–31.

Lipsey, Richard G., *An Introduction to Positive Economics*, Weidenfeld and Nicolson, London 1963.

Locke, Robert R., *The End of Practical Man: Entrepreneurship and Higher Education in Germany, France and Great Britain 1880–1940*, JAI Press, Greenwich, Conn. 1984.

Loria, Achille, 'Political Economy in Italy', *Economic Journal* Vol. 7 (1897), pp. 450–59.

Lottes, Günther, *Politische Aufklärung und plebijisches Publikum. Zur Theorie und Praxis des englischen Radikalismus im späten 18.Jahrhundert*, Oldenbourg, Munich 1979.

Maas, Harro, *William Stanley Jevons and the Making of Modern Economics*, Cambridge University Press, Cambridge 2005.

Macgregor, D. H., 'Marshall and His Book', *Economica* New Series Vol. 9 No. 36 (1942), pp. 313–24.

Machlup, Fritz, 'Why Bother with Methodology?', *Economica* New Series Vol. 3 No. 9 (1936), pp. 39–45.

Macmillan, Daniel, 'The *Principles of Economics*: A Bibliographical Note', *Economic Journal* Vol. 52 (1942), pp. 290–93.

Magnus, Sir Philip, *Industrial Education*, Kegan Paul, Trench & Co., London 1888.

Mahaim, Ernest, 'Economic and Social Science in Belgium', *Economic Journal* Vol. 5 (1895), pp. 462–71.

Maine, Henry Sumner, *Ancient Law: Its Connection with the Early History of Society, and Its Relation to Modern Ideas*, John Murray, London 1861.

Maine, Henry Sumner, *Village Communities in East and West: Six Lectures Delivered at Oxford*, John Murray, London 1871.

Maloney, John, *Marshall, Orthodoxy and the Professionalisation of Economics*, Cambridge University Press, Cambridge 1985.

Maloney, John, 'The Teaching of Political Economy in the University of London', in Alon Kadish, Keith Tribe (eds.), *The Market for Political Economy: The Advent of Economics in British University Culture, 1850–1905*, Routledge, London 1993, pp. 20–41.

Mandler, Peter, 'Educating the Nation I: Schools', *Transactions of the Royal Historical Society* Vol. 24 (2014), pp. 5–28.

Mann, H., 'On the Best Mode of Practically Working the Plan of Competition for Civil Appointments', *Transactions of the National Association for the Promotion of Social Science 1858*, John W. Parker and Son, London 1859, pp. 200–11.

Marsh, C. S., 'General Lee and a School of Commerce', *Journal of Political Economy* Vol. 34 (1926), pp. 657–59.

Marshall, Alfred, *The Present Position of Economics: An Inaugural Lecture*, Macmillan, London 1885.

Marshall, Alfred, 'The Graphic Method of Statistics', *Journal of the Statistical Society of London* Jubilee Volume (June 1885), pp. 251–60.

Marshall, Alfred, *Principles of Economics* Vol. I, Macmillan, London 1890^1, 1892^2, 1895^3, 1898^4, 1907^5; as single volume 1910^6, 1916^7, 1920^8.

Marshall, Alfred, *Elements of Economics of Industry: Being the First Volume of Elements of Economics*, Macmillan, London 1892.

Marshall, Alfred, 'A Reply', *Economic Journal* Vol. 2 (1892), pp. 507–19.

Marshall, Alfred, *The New Cambridge Curriculum in Economics*, London 1903.

Marshall, Alfred, 'The Social Possibilities of Economic Chivalry', *Economic Journal* Vol. 17 (1907), pp. 7–29.

Marshall, Alfred, 'A Plea for the Creation of a Curriculum in Economics and Associated Branches of Political Science', flysheet reprinted in *Principles of Economics Vol. II Notes*,

9th (variorum) edition with annotations by C. W. Guillebaud, Macmillan, London 1961, pp. 161–78.

Marshall, Alfred, *Principles of Economics*, 9th (Variorum) edition in 2 vols. ed. C. W. Guillebaud, Macmillan, London 1961.

Marshall, Alfred, 'The Theory of Foreign Trade and Other Portions of Economic Science Bearing on the Principle of Laissez-Faire', in John K. Whitaker (ed.), *The Early Economic Writings of Alfred Marshall 1867–1890* Vol. 2, Macmillan, London 1975, pp. 1–236.

Marshall, Alfred, 'Notes Taken during Discussions at the Grote Club Meetings, February–November 1867', introduced and edited by Tiziano Raffaelli, *Marshall Studies Bulletin* 6 (1996), pp. 49–64.

Marshall, Alfred, Mary Paley Marshall, *The Economics of Industry*, Macmillan, London 1879.

Marshall, Leon C., 'The Collegiate School of Business at Erewhon', *Journal of Political Economy* Vol. 34 (1926), pp. 289–326.

Marshall, Leon C., 'The American Collegiate School of Business' in Marshall (ed.), *The Collegiate School of Business*, University of Chicago, Chicago 1928, pp. 3–44.

Marshall, Mary Paley, *What I Remember*, Cambridge University Press, London 1947.

Maurer, Georg Ludwig von *Zur Geschichte der Mark-, Hof-, Dorf- und Stadtverfassung*, Christian Kaiser, Munich 1854.

Mayer, Hans, 'Untersuchung zu dem Grundgesetz der wirtschaftlichen Wertrechnung', *Zeitschrift für Volkswirtschaft und Sozialpolitik* Bd. 1 (1921), pp. 431–58; Bd. 2 (1922), pp. 1–23 [reprinted in *Zeitschrift für Nationalökonomie* Bd. 15 Heft 3 (1956), pp. 265–86; 287–303].

Mayor, Joseph B., 'Remarks on the Proposal to Grant the Degree of BA to Persons Who Have Obtained Honours in the Moral Sciences Course', flysheet, Cambridge 1860.

McCaffrey, Matthew, 'Pure Theory and Progressive Liberalism: Frank Fetter and the Austrian Economists', *Journal of Institutional Economics* Vol. 15 (2019), pp. 469–86.

McCallum, R. B., 'The Tutorial System at Oxford', *Universities Quarterly* Vol. 2 No. 1 (November 1947), pp. 26–30.

McCready, H. W. 'Sir William Ashley: Some Unpublished Letters', *Journal of Economic History* Vol. 15 (1955), pp. 34–43.

McLachlan, Jean O., 'The Origin and Early Development of the Cambridge Historical Tripos', *Cambridge Historical Journal* Vol. 9 No. 1 (1947), pp. 78–105.

McLure, Michael, 'One Hundred Years from Today: A. C. Pigou's *Wealth and Welfare*', *History of Economic Review* Vol. 55 No. 1 (2012), pp. 101–16.

Meade, James E., *An Introduction to Economic Analysis and Policy*, Oxford University Press, London 1936.

Medema, Steven G., 'Between LSE and Cambridge: Accounting for Ronald Coase's Fascination with Alfred Marshall', in Katia Caldari, Marco Dardi, Steven G. Medema (eds.), *Marshall and the Marshallian Heritage: Essays in Honour of Tiziano Raffaelli*, Palgrave Macillan, Cham 2021, pp. 231–68.

Melon, Jean-François, *Essai politique sur la commerce*, Presses universitaires de Caen, Caen 2014.

Menger, Carl, *Grundsätze der Volkswirthschaftslehre*, Wilhelm Braumüller, Vienna 1871.

Meuleau, M., *Histoire d'une Grande Ecole*, HEC, Jouy-en-Josas 1981.

Middleton, Roger, *Charlatans or Saviours? Economists and the British Economy from Marshall to Meade*, Edward Elgar, Cheltenham 1998.

Mill, John Stuart, *Essays on Some Unsettled Questions of Political Economy*, Parker, London 1844.

Mill, John Stuart, *Principles of Political Economy with Some of the Application to Social Philosophy*, ed. W. J. Ashley, Longmans, Green, and Co., London 1909.

Mill, John Stuart, *A System of Logic Ratiocinative and Inductive*, Collected Works of John Stuart Mill Vol. 7 in 2 pts., Routledge and Kegan Paul, London 1973.

Mises, Ludwig von, *Theorie des Geldes und der Umlaufsmittel*, Duncker und Humblot, Munich 1912, 2nd edition 1924.

Mises, Ludwig von, *Die Gemeinwirtschaft*, Gustav Fischer, Jena 1922.

Mitchell, B. R., *British Historical Statistics*, Cambridge University Press, Cambridge 1988.

Moore, Gregory C. G., '*Masters of Theory* and Its Relevance to the History of Economic Thought', *History of Economics Review* Vol. 42 (Summer 2005), pp. 77–99.

Moore, Gregory C. G., *Leslie Stephen and the Clubbable Men of Radical London: An Essay in Honour of John King's Retirement*, Rounded Globe 2017 [online].

Morrell, J., A. Thackray, *Gentlemen of Science: Early Years of the British Association for the Advancement of Science*, Oxford University Press, Oxford 1981.

Moulton, R. G., *The University Extension Movement*, Bemrose and Sons, London 1887.

Myrdal, Gunnar, 'Das Zweck-Mittel-Denken in der Nationalökonomie', *Zeitschrift für Nationalökonomie* Bd. 4 H. 3 (1933), pp. 305–29.

Napier, Christopher J., 'Accounting and the Influence of Economics at LSE', in Robert A. Cord (ed.), *The Palgrave Companion to LSE Economics*, Palgrave Macmillan, London 2018, pp. 79–111.

Newman, J. H., *The Idea of a University Defined and Illustrated* (1873 ed.), Routledge, London 1994.

Newman, Peter (ed.), *F. Y. Edgeworth's Mathematical Psychics and Further Papers on Political Economy*, Oxford University Press, Oxford 2003.

Newmarch, William, 'Address by William Newmarch, Esq., F. R. S., as President of the Economy and Trade Department, Social Science Association, at Leeds, 10th October, 1871', *Journal of the Statistical Society of London* Vol. 34 No. 4 (December 1871), pp. 476–98.

Nicholson, J. Shield, *Principles of Political Economy*, 3 vols. A & C. Black, London 1893–1901.

Nicholson, J. Shield, *Elements of Political Economy*, A. & C. Black, London 1903.

Northcote, Sir Stafford, 'On Competitive Examinations for the Civil Service', *Transactions of the National Association for the Promotion of Social Science 1859*, John W. Parker and Son, London 1860, pp. 279–86.

Oncken, August, 'Political Economy in Switzerland', *Economic Journal* Vol. 5 (1895), pp. 133–37.

Ormerod, H. A., *The Liverpool Royal Institution: A Record and a Retrospect*, Liverpool University Press, Liverpool 1953.

Oswalt, Heinrich, *Vorträge über wirtschaftliche Grundbegriffe*, Gustav Fischer, Jena 1905.

Pafford, J. H. P., 'Historical Introduction' to *University of London Library: Catalogue of the Goldsmiths' Library of Economic Literature*, Vol. I: *Printed Books to 1800*, compiled by Margaret Canney and David Knott, Cambridge University Press, London 1970.

Palfrey, David, 'The Moral Sciences Tripos at Cambridge University, 1848–1860', PhD dissertation, University of Cambridge 2002.

Parsons, Talcott, 'Some Reflections on "The Nature and Significance of Economics"', *Quarterly Journal of Economics* Vol. 48 (1934), pp. 511–45.

Patten, Simon N., *The Educational Value of Political Economy*, Publications of the American Economic Association Vol. V No. 6, November 1890.

Pattison, Mark, 'Address on Education', *Transactions of the National Association for the Promotion of Social Science. Liverpool Meeting 1876*, Longmans, Green and Co., London 1877, pp. 44–68.

Perkin, Harold, *Key Profession: History of the Association of University Teachers*, Routledge & Kegan Paul, London 1969.

Phelps Brown, E. H. *The Framework of the Pricing System*, Chapman and Hall, London 1936.

Pigou, A. C. 'A Point of Theory Connected with the Corn Tax', *Economic Journal* Vol. 12 (1902), pp. 415–20.

Pigou, A. C., 'Review of Patten, *The Theory of Prosperity*', *Economic Journal* Vol. 12 (1902), pp. 370–73.

Pigou, A. C., 'Some Remarks on Utility', *Economic Journal* Vol. 13 (1903), pp. 58–68.

Pigou, A. C., *The Riddle of the Tariff*, R. Brimley Johnson, London 1903.

Pigou, A. C., 'Empty Economic Boxes: A Reply', *Economic Journal* Vol. 32 (1922), pp. 458–65.

Price, Bonamy, 'Address on Economy and Trade', *Transactions of the National Association for the Promotion of Social Science. Nottingham Meeting, 1882*, Longmans, Green and Co., London 1883, pp. 90–110.

Price, L. L., *A Short History of Political Economy in England from Adam Smith to Arnold Toynbee*, Methuen, London 1891.

Price, L. L., 'William Albert Samuel Hewins', *Economic Journal* Vol. 42 (1932), pp. 151–55.

Price, L. L. *Memories and Notes on British Economists 1881–1947*, unpublished typescript, 1946, University of Leeds Special Collections MS 107.

Priestley, Joseph, *An Essay on a Course of Liberal Education for Civil and Active Life*, London 1765.

Raffaelli, Tiziano, 'Keynes's Apprenticeship with Marshall in 1905', *History of Economic Ideas* Vol. 8 No. 2 (2000), pp. 121–152.

Raffaelli, Tiziano, '*Industry and Trade* Reconsidered', *History of Economic Ideas* Vol. 17 No. 3 (2009), pp. 59–74.

Raffaelli, Tiziano, Eugenio Biagini, Rita McWilliams Tullberg (eds.), *Alfred Marshall's Lectures to Women*, Edward Elgar, Aldershot UK 1995.

Raphael, Lutz, 'Die Verwissenschaftlichung des Sozialen als methodische und konzeptionelle Herausforderung für eine Sozialgeschichte des 20. Jahrhunderts', *Geschichte und Gesellschaft* Jg. 22 H. 2 (1996), pp. 165–93.

Ratcliffe, J. A., 'Supervision at Cambridge: With Special Reference to Natural Sciences', *Universities Quarterly* Vol. 2 No. 1 (November 1947), pp. 31–35.

Reader, W. J., *Professional Men: The Rise of the Professional Classes in Nineteenth-Century England*, Weidenfeld and Nicolson, London 1966.

Redlich, Fritz, 'Academic Education for Business: Its Development and the Contribution of Ignaz Jastrow (1856–1937)', *Business History Review* Vol. 31 (1957), pp. 35–91.

Renouard, A., *Histoire de l'École supérieure de Commerce de Paris (1820–1898)*, Association des ancien élèves, Paris 1898.

Ricci, Umberto, 'Die Methode der nationalökonomischen Wissenschaft', *Zeitschrift für Nationalökonomie* Bd. 4 H. 5 (1933), pp. 577–603.

Richards, Joan L., 'The Art and the Science of British Algebra: A Study in the Perception of Mathematical Truth', *Historia Mathematica* Vol. 7 (1980), pp. 343–65.

Richards, Joan L., 'Augustus De Morgan, the History of Mathematics, and the Foundations of Algebra,' *Isis* Vol. 78 (1987), pp. 6–30.

Richards, Joan L., *Mathematical Visions: The Pursuit of Geometry in Victorian England*, Academic Press, Boston 1988.

Ringer, Fritz, *Education and Society in Modern Europe*, Indiana University Press, Bloomington 1979.

Ringer, Fritz, 'Introduction' in Detlef K. Müller, Fritz. Ringer, Brian Simon (eds.), *The Rise of the Modern Educational System: Structural Change and Social Reproduction 1870–1920*, Cambridge University Press, Cambridge 1987, pp. 1–12.

Ringer, Fritz, 'On Segmentation in Modern European Educational Systems: The case of French Secondary Education, 1865–1920', in D. K. Müller, F. Ringer, B. Simon (eds.), *The Rise of the Modern Educational System*, Cambridge University Press, Cambridge 1987, pp. 53–87.

Roach, John, *Public Examinations in England 1850–1900*, Cambridge University Press, London 1971.

Robbins, Lionel, 'The Representative Firm', *Economic Journal* Vol. 38 (1928), pp. 387–404.

Robbins, Lionel, 'The Present Position of Economic Science', *Economica* No. 28 (March 1930), pp. 14–24.

Robbins, Lionel, *An Essay on the Nature and Significance of Economic Science*, Macmillan, London 1932; 2nd revised edition 1935.

Robertson, D. H., 'Those Empty Boxes', *Economic Journal* Vol. 34 (1924), pp. 16–30.

Robertson, P. L., 'The Finances of the University of Glasgow before 1914', *History of Education Quarterly* Vol. 16 (1976), pp. 449–78.

Robinson, E. A. G., 'L'Université de Cambridge', in *L'Enseignement Économique en France et à l'étranger*, Special 50th Anniversary Issue of *Revue d'Économie Politique* (1937), pp. 91–101.

Robinson, E. A. G., 'Keynes and His Cambridge Colleagues', in D. Patinkin, J. C. Leith (eds.), *Keynes, Cambridge and the General Theory*, London, Macmillan 1977, pp. 25–38.

Ross, Donald, 'An Unusual Commitment. Alfred and Mary Marshall and the Establishment of the Marshall Library 1903–1944', Marshall Library of Economics, Cambridge 1991.

Rowe, L. S., 'Instruction in Public Law and Political Economy in German Universities', *Annals of the American Academy of Political and Social Science* Vol. I (1890), pp. 78–102.

Ruml, F., 'The Existing Curriculum and Offerings in Collegiate Education for Business', in L. C. Marshall (ed.), *The Collegiate School of Business*, University of Chicago Press, Chicago 1928, pp. 75–95.

Sanderson, Michael, *The Universities and British Industry 1850–1970*, Routledge and Kegan Paul, London 1972.

Sass, S. A., *The Pragmatic Imagination: A History of the Wharton School 1881–1981*, University of Pennsylvania Press, Philadelphia 1982.

Schranz, Andrew, 'Modern German Accountancy', *Accounting Review* Vol. 5 (1930), pp. 162–67.

Schumacher, E. F., *Small Is Beautiful: A Study of Economics as if People Mattered*, Blond and Briggs, London 1973.

Schweitzer, Arthur, 'Review of Heinrich von Stackelberg, *Grundlagen der theoretischen Volkswirtschaftslehre*', *American Economic Review* Vol. 39 (1949), pp. 756–60.

Scottish Office, *Report of the Inquiry appointed in February 1949 to review and report on the organisation of university education in Dundee and its relationship with St Andrews University*, HMSO Edinburgh 1949 (Cooper Report).

Seager, H. R., 'Economics at Berlin and Vienna', *Journal of Political Economy* Vol. 1 (1893), pp. 236–62.

Semmel, Bernard, *Imperialism and Social Reform: English Social-Imperial Thought 1895–1914*, George Allen and Unwin, London 1960.

Shackle, G. L. S., *The Years of High Theory: Invention and Tradition in Economic Thought 1926–1939*, Cambridge University Press, Cambridge 1967.

Shove, Gerald, 'The Place of Marshall's *Principles* in the Development of Economic Theory', *Economic Journal* Vol. 52 (1942), pp. 294–329.

Shovlin, John, 'The Society of Brittany and the Irish Economic Model: International Competition and the Politics of Provincial Development', in Koen Stapelbroek, Jani Marjanan (eds.), *The Rise of Economic Societies in the Eighteenth Century: Patriotic Reform in Europe and North America*, Palgrave, Houndmills UK 2012, pp. 73–95.

Sidgwick, Henry, *Principles of Political Economy*, Macmillan, London 1883.

Siegfried, Jacques, 'De l'enseignement commercial', *Revue international de l'enseignement* t. 9 (1885), pp. 289–302.

Siegfried, Jacques, 'Rapport sur l'enseignement commercial supérieur en France', *Journal of the Society of Arts* Vol. 45 (30 July 1897), pp. 911–14.

Silberston, Aubrey, *Harry Johnson as a Young Man*, Imperial College of Science and Technology, London 1978.

Slee, Peter H. *Learning and a Liberal Education*, Manchester University Press, Manchester 1986.

Smart, William, *An Introduction to the Theory of Value on the Lines of Menger, Wieser and Böhm-Bawerk*, Macmillan, London 1891.

Smart, William, 'The New Theory of Interest', *Economic Journal* Vol. 1 (1891), pp. 675–81.

Smith, Barbara M. D., *A Hundred Years of Business Studies at the University of Birmingham 1902–2002*, Birmingham Business School, Birmingham UK 2002.

Smith, John George, 'Education for Business in Great Britain', *Journal of Political Economy* Vol. 36 (1928), pp. 1–52.

Smith, John George, 'Obituary of Adam Willis Kirkaldy', *Economic Journal* Vol. 42 (1932), pp. 155–57.

Soffer, Reba N., *Ethics and Society in England: The Revolution in the Social Sciences 1870–1914*, University of California Press, Berkeley 1978.

Sommarin, E., 'Das Lebenswerk von Knut Wicksell', *Zeitschrift für Nationalökonomie* Bd. 2 H. 2 (1930), pp. 221–67.

Souter, R. W., ''The Nature and Significance of Economic Science' in Recent Discussion', *Quarterly Journal of Economics* Vol. 47 (1933), pp. 377–413.

Southgate, D., *University Education in Dundee*, Edinburgh University Press, Edinburgh 1982.

Soyeda, Jiuchi, 'The Study of Political Economy in Japan', *Economic Journal* Vol. 3 (1893), pp. 335–39.

Spufford, Francis, *Red Plenty*, Faber and Faber, London 2010.

Sraffa, Piero, 'The Laws of Returns under Competitive Conditions', *Economic Journal* Vol. 36 (1926), pp. 535–50.

Stapelbroek, Koen, Jani Marjanen, 'Political Economy, Patriotism and the Rise of Societies', in Stapelbroek, Marjanan (eds.), *The Rise of Economic Societies in the Eighteenth Century: Patriotic Reform in Europe and North America*, Palgrave, Houndmills UK 2012, pp. 1–25.

Stephen, Leslie, *Life of Henry Fawcett*, Smith, Elder & Co., London 1885.

Stevens, Megan, assisted by Alun Stevens, 'The Wrong Marshall: Notes on the Marshall Family in Response to Biographies of the Economist, Alfred Marshall', *History of Political Economy* Vol. 52 (2020), pp. 239–73.

Stigler, George J., Kenneth E. Boulding (eds.), *Readings in Price Theory*, Richard D. Irwin, Chicago 1952.

Stigler, George J., 'The Place of Marshall's Principles in the Development of Economics', in John K. Whitaker (ed.), *Centenary Essays on Alfred Marshall*, Cambridge University Press, Cambridge 1990, pp. 1–13.

Stigler, Stephen M. *The History of Statistics: The Measurement of Uncertainty before 1900*, Harvard University Press, Cambridge Mass. 1986.

Stonier, Alfred W., 'Review of Robbins, *An Essay on the Nature and Significance of Economic Science*', *Zeitschrift für Nationalökonomie* Bd. 5 H. 3 (1934), pp. 417–24.

Stonier, A. W., D. C. Hague, *A Textbook of Economic Theory*, Longmans, Green & Co., London 1953.

Stray, Christopher, 'From Oral to Written Examinations: Cambridge, Oxford and Dublin 1700–1914', *History of Universities* Vol. XX/2 (2005), pp. 76–130.

Stray, Christopher, 'The Wooden Spoon.=: Rank (Dis)order in Cambridge 1753–1909', *History of Universities* Vol. XXVI No. 1 (2012), pp. 163–94.

Stray, Christopher, 'Disciplinary Histories of Classics', *History of Universities* Vol. XXIX No. 1 (2016), pp. 112–34.

Stray, Christopher, 'The Slaughter of 1841: Mathematics and Classics in Early Victorian Cambridge', *History of Universities* Vo. XXXV No. 2 (2022), forthcoming).

Strigl, Richard, *Die ökonomischen Kategorien und die Organisation der Wirtschaft*, Gustav Fischer, Jena 1923.

Strutt, Robert John, *John William Strutt Third Baron Rayleigh O.M., F.R.S.*, Edward Arnold, London 1924.

Stuart, James, *Reminiscences*, Cassell, London 1912.

Sugiyama, C., H. Mizuta (eds.) *Enlightenment and Beyond: Political Economy Comes to Japan*, University of Tokyo Press, Tokyo 1988.

Takebayashi, Shiro, *Die Entstehung der Kapitalismustheorie in der Gründungsphase der deutschen Soziologie. Von der historischen Nationalökonomie zur historischen Soziologie Werner Sombarts und Max Webers*, Duncker und Humblot, Berlin 2003.

Taussig, Frank W., *The Tariff History of the United States*, G. P. Putnam's Sons, New York 1892.

Taussig, Frank W., *Principles of Economics*, 2 vols. 3rd edition, Macmillan, New York 1921.

Taylor, A. J., 'County College and Civic University: An Introductory Essay', in P. H. J. H. Gosden, A. J. Taylor (eds.), *Studies in the History of a University, 1874–1974*, E. J. Arnold, Leeds 1975, pp. 1–41.

Thornton, W. T., 'What Determines the Price of Labour or Rate of Wages?', *Fortnightly Review* Vol. I (New Series) (1867), pp. 551–66.

Tomlinson, Jim, *Managing the Economy, Managing the People: Narratives of Economic Life in Britain from Beveridge to Brexit*, Oxford University Press, Oxford 2017.

Tönnies, Ferdinand, *Gemeinschaft und Gesellschaft: Abhandlung des Communismus und des Socialismus als empirischer Culturformen*, Fues, Leipzig 1887.

Tooze, Adam, *Statistics and the German State, 1900–1945: The Making of Modern Economic Knowledge*, Cambridge University Press, Cambridge 2001.

Toynbee, Arnold, *'Progress and Poverty,' A Criticism of Mr. Henry George: Being Two Lectures Delivered in St. Andrews Hall, Newman Street, London*, Kegan Paul, Trench & Co., London 1883.

Toynbee, Arnold *Lectures on the Industrial Revolution in England, Popular Addresses, Notes and Other Fragments*, Rivingtons, London 1884.

Tribe, Keith, 'Ricardian Histories', *Economy and Society* Vol. 10 (1981), pp. 451–66.

Tribe, Keith, 'The 'US Model' for Higher Education: Structure and Finance', in Peter W. G. Wright (ed.), *Industry and Higher Education: Collaboration to Improve Students' Learning and Training*, Society for Research into Higher Education & Open University Press, Buckingham 1990, pp. 43–58.

Tribe, Keith, 'The *Economic Journal* and British Economics, 1891–1940', *History of the Human Sciences* Vol. 5 (1992), pp. 33–58.

Tribe, Keith, 'Political Economy in the Northern Civic Universities', in Alon Kadish, Keith Tribe (eds.), *The Market for Political Economy: The Advent of Economics in British University Culture, 1850–1905*, Routledge, London 1993, pp. 184–226.

Tribe, Keith, 'Professors Malthus and Jones: Political Economy at the East India College 1806–1858', *European Journal of the History of Economic Thought* Vol. 2 (1995), pp. 327–54.

Tribe, Keith, *Strategies of Economic Order, German Economic Discourse 1750–1950*, Cambridge University Press, Cambridge 1995/2007.

Tribe, Keith (ed.), *Economic Careers: Economics and Economists in Britain 1930–1970*, Routledge, London 1997.

Tribe, Keith, 'The Historicisation of Political Economy?', in B. Stuchtey, P. Wende (eds.), *British and German Historiography 1750–1950*, Oxford University Press, Oxford 2000, pp. 211–28.

Tribe, Keith, 'German Emigré Economists and the Internationalisation of Economics', *Economic Journal* Vol. 111 (2001), pp. F740–46.

Tribe, Keith, 'Adam Smith in English: From Playfair to Cannan', in Keith Tribe, with Hiroshi Mizuta (eds.), *A Critical Bibliography of Adam Smith*, Pickering and Chatto, London 2002, pp. 27–49.

Tribe, Keith, 'The Faculty of Commerce and Manchester Economics, 1903–44', *Manchester School* Vol. 71 (2003), pp. 680–710.

Tribe, Keith, 'Economic Manuals and Textbooks in Great Britain and the British Empire 1797–1938', in Massimo Augello, Marco Guidi (eds.), *The Economic Reader*, Routledge, London 2012, pp. 43–75.

Tribe, Keith, 'Review of Jan-Otmar Hesse, *Wirtschaft als Wissenschaft*', *German History* Vol. 31 (2013), pp. 443–44.

Tribe, Keith, *Governing Economy: The Reformation of German Economic Discourse, 1750–1850*, 2nd edition, Threshold Press, Newbury 2017.

Tribe, Keith, 'Henry Sidgwick, Moral Order, and Utilitarianism', *European Journal of the History of Economic Thought* Vol. 24 (2017), pp. 907–30.

Tribe, Keith, 'Edwin Cannan (1861–1935)' in Robert A. Cord (ed.), *The Palgrave Companion to LSE Economics*, Palgrave Macmillan, London 2018, pp. 197–214.

Tribe, Keith, 'Max Weber's "Science as a Vocation": Context, Genesis, Structure', *Sociologica* Vol. 12 No 1 (2018), pp. 125–36.

Tribe, Keith, 'Utilitarianism, the Moral Sciences, and Political Economy: Mill-Grote-Sidgwick', in Katia Caldari, Marco Dardi, Steven G. Medema (eds.), *Marshall and the Marshallian Heritage: Essays in Honour of Tiziano Raffaelli*, Palgrave, Cham 2021, pp. 149–84.

Tullberg, Rita McWilliams, 'Marshall's Contribution to the Women's Higher Education Movement', in Tiziano Raffaelli, Eugenio Biagini, Rita McWlliams Tullberg (eds.), *Alfred Marshall's Lectures to Women*, Edward Elgar, Aldershot UK 1995, pp. 47–75.

Tullberg, Rita McWilliams, 'Marshall's Final Lecture, 21 May 1908', *History of Political Economy* Vol. 25 (1993), pp. 605–16.

Vázquez, Andrés, Francisco Pérez, 'Alfred Marshall and the German Translation of his *Principles*: Some Unpublished Letters', *Marshall Studies Bulletin* Vol. 10 (2008), https://www.disei.unifi.it/cmpro-v-p-122.html.

Veblen, Thorstein, 'The Preconceptions of Economic Science III', *Quarterly Journal of Economics* Vol. 14 (1900), pp. 240–69.

Veblen, Thorstein, *The Higher Learning in America: A Memorandum on the Conduct of Universities by Business Men*, [orig. 1918] ed. Richard F. Teichgraeber III, Johns Hopkins University Press, Baltimore Md. 2015.

Vincent, E. W., P. Hinton, *The University of Birmingham: Its History and Significance*, Cornish Bros., Birmingham 1947.

Vinen, Richard, *National Service: A Generation in Uniform 1945–1963*, Penguin Books, London 2015.

Viner, Jacob, 'The Present Status and Future Prospects of Quantitative Economics', *American Economic Review* (Papers and Proceedings of the Fortieth Annual Meeting of the American Economic Association) Vol. 28 No. 1 (1928), pp. 30–36.

Voss, A., J. Oleson (eds.), *The Organization of Knowledge in Modern America, 1860–1920*, Johns Hopkins University Press, Baltimore Md. 1979.

Walsh, W. H. 'The Zenith of Greats', in M. G. Brock, M. C. Curthoys (eds.), *The History of the University of Oxford*, Vol. VII: *Nineteenth-Century Oxford, Part 2*, Oxford University Press, Oxford 2000, pp. 311–26.

Warwick, Andrew, 'Cambridge Mathematics and Cambridge Physics: Cunningham, Campbell and Einstein's Relativity 1905–1911. Part II: Comparing Traditions in Cambridge Physics', *Studies in the History and Philosophy of Science* Vol. 24 (1993), pp. 1–25.

Warwick, Andrew, *Masters of Theory: Cambridge and the Rise of Mathematical Physics*, Chicago University Press, Chicago 2003.

Waszek, Norbert (ed.), *Die Institutionalisierung der Nationalökonomie an den deutschen Universitäten*, Scripta Mercurae Verlag, St.Katherinen 1988.

Webb, Sidney, 'The Provision of Higher Commercial Education in London', *Journal of the Society of Arts* (6 August 1897), pp. 938–43.

Webb, Sidney, 'London University: A Policy and a Forecast', *The Nineteenth Century and After* Vol. 51 (June 1902), pp. 914–31.

Webb, Sidney, 'The Nature of the University Problem in the Metropolis', Royal Commission on University Education in London, *Appendix to First Report of the Commissioners. Minutes of Evidence, July 1909–April 1910*, Cd. 5166 HMSO, London 1910.

Weber, Max, *Gesammelte Aufsätze zur Religionsoziologie I*, J. C. B. Mohr (Paul Siebeck), Tübingen 1920.

Weber, Max, *Economy and Society: A New Translation*, trans. Keith Tribe, Harvard University Press, Cambridge Mass. 2019.

Weintraub, E. Roy, *How Economics Became a Mathematical Science*, Duke University Press, Durham N.C. 2002.

Weisz, G., *The Emergence of Modern Universities in France, 1863–1914*, Princeton University Press, Princeton N.J. 1983.

Welch, E., *The Peripatetic University*, Cambridge University Press, London 1973.

Whatmore, Richard, *Republicanism and the French Revolution: An Intellectual History of Jean-Baptiste Say's Political Economy*, Oxford University Press, Oxford 2000.

Whewell, William, *Lectures on the History of Moral Philosophy in England*, John W. Parker, London 1852.

Whitaker, John K., 'Editing Alfred Marshall', in Donald Moggridge (ed.), *Editing Modern Economists*, AMS Press, New York 1988, pp. 43–66.

Whitaker, John K., 'What Happened to the Second Volume of the *Principles*? The Thorny Path to Marshall's Last Books', in J. K. Whitaker, *Centenary Essays on Alfred Marshall*, Cambridge University Press, Cambridge 1990, pp. 193–222.

Whitaker, John K. (ed.), *The Correspondence of Alfred Marshall Vols. I–III*, Cambridge University Press, Cambridge 1996.

Whitaker, John K., '*Principles of Economics*: Genesis, Structure and Evolution', in Tiziano Raffaelli, Giacomo Becattini, Marco Dardi (eds.), *The Elgar Companion to Alfred Marshall*, Edward Elgar, Cheltenham UK 2006, pp. 66–72.

White, Michael V., 'The Moment of Richard Jennings: The Production of Jevons's Marginal Economic Agent', in Philip Mirowski (ed.), *Natural Images in Economic Thought: 'Markets Read in Tooth and Claw'*, Cambridge University Press, Cambridge 1994, pp. 197–230.

White, Michael V., 'Thirsting for the Fray: The Cambridge Dunning of Mr. Macleod', *Journal of the History of Economic Thought* Vol. 12 (2010), pp. 305–28.

White, Michael V., 'A Peculiar Archaeology: Searching for Mr. Giffen's Behaviour', *European Journal of the History of Economic Thought* Vol. 22 (2015), pp. 26–50.

Wickett, S. M., 'Political Economy at German Universities', *Economic Journal* Vol. 8 (1898), pp. 146–51.

Wicksell, Knut, *Über Wert, Kapital und Rente nach den neuren nationalökonomischen Theorien*, Gustav Fischer, Jena 1893.

Wicksell, Knut, *Finanztheoretische Untersuchungen nebst Darstellung und Kritik des Steuerwesens Schwedens*, Gustav Fischer, Jena 1896.

Wicksell, Knut, *Geldzins und Güterpreise: eine Studie über die den Tauschwert des Geldes bestimmenden Ursachen*, Gustav Fischer, Jena 1898.

Wicksell, Knut, *Föreläsningar i nationalekonomi D I.1 Teoretisk nationalekonomi*, Berlingska boktryckeriet, Lund 1901.

Wicksell, Knut, *Vorlesungen über Nationalökonomie auf Grundlage des Marginalprinzipes I. Theoretischer Teil*, trans. Margarethe Langfeldt, Gustav Fischer, Jena 1913.

Wicksell, Knut, *Lectures on Political Economy Vol. I*, ed. Lionel Robbins, trans. from Swedish by E. Classen, George Routledge and Sons, London 1934.

Wicksteed, Philip H., *The Alphabet of Economic Science*, Macmillan, London 1888.

Wicksteed, Philip H., 'The Scope and Method of Political Economy in the Light of the "Marginal" Theory of Value and Distribution', *Economic Journal* Vol. 24 (1914), pp. 1–16.

Wicksteed, Philip H., *The Common Sense of Political Economy and Selected Papers and Reviews on Economic Theory*, 2 vols., George Routledge & Sons, London 1933.

Wieser, Friedrich von, 'The Austrian School and the Theory of Value', *Economic Journal* Vol. 1 (1891), pp. 108–21.

Wieser, Friedrich von, *Natural Value*, trans. Christian A. Malloch, Macmillan, London 1893.

Wieser, Friedrich von, *Social Economics*, George Allen and Unwin, London 1928.

Wilson, David Gordon, *Bicycling Science*, 3rd edition, MIT Press, Cambridge Mass. 2004.

Winstanley, D. A., *Early Victorian Cambridge*, Cambridge University Press, London 1940.

Wolf, Alison, *Does Education Matter? Myths about Education and Economic Growth*, Penguin Books, London 2002.

Wren, D. A., 'American Business Philanthropy and Higher Education in the Nineteenth Century', *Business History Review* Vol. 57 (1983), pp. 321–46.

Young, Allyn, 'Pigou's Wealth and Welfare', *Quarterly Journal of Economics* Vol. 27 No. 4 (1913), pp. 672–86.

Young, Allyn A., 'English Political Economy', *Economica* No. 22 (1928), pp. 1–15.

Young, Allyn A., 'Increasing Returns and Economic Progress', *Economic Journal* Vol. 38 (1928), pp. 527–42.

Young, Warren, Frederic S. Lee, *Oxford Economics and Oxford Economists*, Macmillan, London 1993.

Index

For the benefit of digital users, indexed terms that span two pages (e.g., 52–53) may, on occasion, appear on only one of those pages.

Tables are indicated by *t* following the page number